COLUMBIA RISING

This book won the

DIXON RYAN FOX

MANUSCRIPT PRIZE

of the New York State

Historical Association.

John L. Brooke

Columbia Rising

Civil Life
on the
Upper Hudson
from the
Revolution
to the
Age of Jackson

Published for the

OMOHUNDRO INSTITUTE OF

EARLY AMERICAN HISTORY AND CULTURE

Williamsburg, Virginia,

by the

UNIVERSITY OF NORTH CAROLINA PRESS

Chapel Hill

*The Omohundro Institute of Early American History and Culture
is sponsored jointly by the College of William and Mary and the
Colonial Williamsburg Foundation. On November 15, 1996, the Institute
adopted the present name in honor of a bequest from
Malvern H. Omohundro, Jr.*

Designed by Richard Hendel
Set in Garamond Premier Pro and Castellar by Tseng Informations Systems, Inc.
Manufactured in the United States of America

Library of Congress Cataloging-in-Publication Data
Brooke, John L.
Columbia rising : civil life on the upper Hudson from the
Revolution to the age of Jackson / John L. Brooke.
p. cm.
Includes bibliographical references and index.
ISBN 978-0-8078-3323-0 (cloth : alk. paper)
1. Columbia County (N.Y.) — Politics and government — 18th century.
2. Columbia County (N.Y.) — Politics and government — 19th century. 3. Political rights —
New York (State) — Columbia County — History. 4. Citizenship — New York (State) —
Columbia County — History. 5. Civil society — New York (State) — Columbia
County — History. 6. Van Buren, Martin, 1782–1862 — Political and social views.
I. Omohundro Institute of Early American History & Culture. II. Title.
F127.C8B76 2010
974.7′39 — dc22
2010031535

The paper in this book meets the guidelines for permanence
and durability of the Committee on Production Guidelines for
Book Longevity of the Council on Library Resources.

The University of North Carolina Press has been a
member of the Green Press Initiative since 2003.

14 13 12 11 10   5 4 3 2 1

*Publication of this book has been assisted by the
College of Arts and Humanities, the Ohio State University,
and by a grant from Furthermore: a program
of the J. M. Kaplan Fund.*

For Jack & Louisa, & Fred & Judy

ACKNOWLEDGMENTS

The origins of this book lie in encounters with Columbia as place in my younger days, bus rides through the Oblong country, Copake, Hillsdale, and into Egremont; driving west from Hancock down Mount Lebanon, through the New Lebanon Valley and along Kinderhook Creek over to Albany. They lie also with formal questions about my problem, the delicacy and endurance of the fabric of civil life that has been so apparent around the world in recent decades. It has been a long but very rewarding adventure.

The research and writing of this book have been supported variously by a John Simon Guggenheim Foundation Fellowship, a National Endowment for the Humanities Fellowship, a sabbatical at Tufts University, and the generous quarter system schedule at Ohio State University. The College of Arts and Humanities at Ohio State University also provided important assistance in the publication of this book. I am extremely grateful to all of these institutions for their very generous support.

I owe many debts to many people whose assistance has shaped my efforts in many ways. First and foremost, I owe an enormous debt of gratitude to Ruth Piwonka, one of the great authorities on the history and culture of Columbia County and the surrounding region. I knew that we were on the same page from our first phone conversation. I let it be known that I was interested in the question of a revolutionary settlement in Columbia County. There was a long pause, and then she replied, "I don't think that there has ever been one." From that moment through to my final inquiries Ruth has been an amazing resource and a great friend. I also owe a great debt to Helen McLallen, Peter Stott, Phil Lampi, Donald Lampson, and Thomas Humphrey. As curator of the Columbia County Historical Society, Helen answered a host of questions and sent me innumerable bundles of Xeroxes. Peter Stott suddenly popped up one day at Tufts and lent me his massive files of research on the rise of manufacturing in Columbia County, the basis of his book, *Looking for Work: Industrial Archaeology in Columbia County, New York* (Kinderhook, N.Y., 2007). I first was in touch with Phil Lampi many years ago, and since then he has been sending me county and town election returns from what is now the American Antiquarian Society / Tufts University New Nation Votes Project, and I have been able to reciprocate in a very small way. The late Donald Lampson was a specialist in the history of the Revolution in Columbia County, especially Livingston Manor, and he was kind enough to share with me his massive collection of transcribed materials. Tom Humphrey shared with me research notes from the early stages of his dissertation and impressed upon me the importance of the various collections of papers left behind by the William Wilson family, a lesson for which I am extremely grateful.

Tom Humphrey is the author of one of a group of dissertations that have guided me in the many complexities of the history of New York in the era of the Revolution and the early Republic. Tom's dissertation is now *Land and Liberty: Hudson Valley Riots in the Age of Revolution* (DeKalb, Ill., 2004). Other fine dissertations-become-books are Martin Bruegel, *Farm, Shop, Landing: The Rise of a Market Society in the Hudson Valley, 1780–1860* (Durham, N.C., 2002); and David N. Gellman, *Emancipating New York: The Politics of Slavery and Freedom, 1777–1827* (Baton Rouge, La., 2006). I would like also to salute these exceptionally useful but as yet unpublished dissertations: Peter Van Ness Denman, "From Deference to Democracy: The Van Ness Family and Their Times, 1759 to 1844" (Ph.D. diss., University of Michigan, 1977); John Robert Finnegan, Jr., "Defamation, Politics, and the Social Process of the Law in New York State, 1776–1860" (Ph.D. diss., University of Minnesota, 1985); Michael Edward Groth, "Forging Freedom in the Mid-Hudson Valley: The End of Slavery and the Formation of a Free African-American Community in Dutchess, County, New York" (Ph.D. diss., SUNY Binghamton, 1994); Diane Helen Lobody, "Lost in the Ocean of Love: The Mystical Writings of Catherine Livingston Garrettson" (Ph.D. diss., Drew University, 1990); Robert E. Wright, "Banking and Politics in New York, 1784–1829" (Ph.D. diss., SUNY Buffalo, 1996).

A host of scholars have answered my requests for help with evidence and interpretation over the years. I want to thank Stephanie Aeder, Catherine Allgor, Bliss and Brigitte Carnochan, Thomas Donnelly, Sally Fox, Jim Folts, Christian Goodwillie, Bill Gorman, Jerry Grant, Graham Hodges, Nancy Isenberg, Sharon Koomler, Leonard A. Mancini, Will Moore, Dale Patterson, Judy Roe, Diane Shewchuk, David Stocks, Peter Watson, Patricia West, Richard Wiles, Barbara Willey, and Daniel Wright. The staffs at a wide array of institutions and libraries have been enormously helpful, including the Columbia County Clerk's Office, the New York State Archives, the New-York Historical Society, the New York Public Library, the Clemens Library at the University of Michigan, the Albany Institute of History and Art, the Livingston Masonic Library at the New York Grand Lodge, the American Antiquarian Society, the Library of Congress, the Butler Library at Columbia University, the Houghton Library at Harvard University, Bard College, the Hudson Chapter of the Daughters of the American Revolution, the National Park Service at Lindenwald, Stephentown Historical Society, Hancock Shaker Village, Old Chatham Shaker Museum, the Sabbathday Lake Shaker Village Library, the Emma Willard School, the Troy Public Library, the Rensselaer County Historical Society, the Rochester Historical Society, the Tisch Library at Tufts University, and the hard-working interlibrary loan department at Ohio State University.

Beating the results of this research into a moderately intelligible form took a lot of work, and I could not do it all. In particular, I want to thank Hilary Moss, who read reels of microfilm for booksellers' advertisements and other details and then typed up virtually the entire 1800 county assessment list, a project upon which much of this interpretation hangs. Jieun Kang has provided expert assistance in the final preparation of the manuscript.

This project has been tested in some measure in public, and I want to thank the participants at a number of seminars for their comments over the years: a panel at the Organization of American Historians, the American Antiquarian Society–Clark Seminar, the Davis Center Seminar, the Omohundro Institute of Early American History and Culture Conference on Microhistory at the University of Connecticut, the Friends of Lindenwald Meeting, the McNeil Center for Early American Studies, the Zuckerman Seminar, the University of Southern California–Huntington Seminar, the Ohio State University Political Science Seminar, and the seminars at Northwestern University and the Johns Hopkins University. It has also been read in whole and part by a number of extremely patient scholars, who have been so kind as to write me detailed comments: Paula Baker, Ronald Formisano, David Gellman, Catherine Kaplan, Don Lampson, Gerry Leonard, Michael Meranze, John Murrin, Michael Neblo, Ruth Piwonka, Andy Robertson, and Brother Alfred at the Sabbathday Lake Shaker Village. Peter Onuf and an anonymous historian read a version of the manuscript for the Institute; they were probably far too kind in their comments. I fear that I have not done justice to all of their excellent recommendations and critiques, but I am eternally grateful.

Ron Hoffman and Fredrika J. Teute long ago decided that this was a book for the Institute, and I salute their vision. Fredrika worked over the manuscript with her celebrated attention to detail, structure, and voice. During Fredrika's leave, Mendy Gladden fielded my inquiries with grand aplomb. In the final months of editing and production Gil Kelly and I held a virtual seminar on editing and the early Republic; we have learned a lot from each other as we engaged in a mutual passion, transforming a pile of manuscript into a coherent volume. One phase of this was a four-way project. As Jim DeGrand of the Department of Geography at Ohio State drew up a beautiful set of maps,

Ruth Piwonka provided local guidance, and Gil Kelly aesthetic control. It has been an amicable and fruitful experience.

As for the most important people in my life, Sara, Matt, and Benjy seem to get along just fine — strange to say — with nary a thought about the history of Columbia County. They are, however, in their own ways deeply interested in the ideals, the realities, and the entertaining vagaries of the modern public sphere. They continue to make life fun.

CONTENTS

ILLUSTRATIONS & TABLES

TABLES

COLUMBIA RISING

PROLOGUE
Consent and Civil Society in the Age of Revolution

The American revolution may prove the most important step in the progressive course of human improvement. It is an event which may produce a general diffusion of the principles of humanity, and become the means of setting free mankind from the shackles of superstition and tyranny, by leading them to see that "nothing is *fundamental* but impartial inquiry, an honest mind, and virtuous practice. . . . That the members of a civil community are *confederates,* not *subjects;* and their rulers, *servants,* not *masters.* — And that all legitimate government, consists in the dominion of equal laws made with common consent; that is, the dominion of men over *themselves;* and not the dominion of communities over communities, or of any men over other men."

   — Richard Price, *Observations on the Importance of the American Revolution*
     (1784), in the *Hudson Weekly Gazette,* I, no. 1, Apr. 7, 1785.

Aristocratic countries abound in wealthy and influential persons who are competent to provide for themselves and who cannot be easily or secretly oppressed; such persons restrain a government within general habits of moderation and reserve. I am well aware that democratic countries contain no such persons naturally, but something analogous to them may be created by artificial means. I firmly believe that an aristocracy cannot again be founded in the world, but I think that private citizens, by combining together, may constitute bodies of greater wealth, influence, and strength, corresponding to the persons of an aristocracy.

   — Alexis de Tocqueville, *Democracy in America* (1835; 1838)

On April 7, 1785, printers Charles Webster and Ashbel Stoddard, newly arrived from Hartford at Claverack Landing, a small new settlement on the east bank of the Hudson River south of Albany, published the first issue of the *Hudson Weekly Gazette.* Two weeks later the Landing would be incorporated as the city of Hudson, and, in the year following, the hinterland to the east would be incorporated as the county of Columbia. As one of two papers published north of New York City, the *Gazette* would serve as the public print for city, county, and a wide circuit in the mid-Hudson region. Thus Stoddard and Webster took some care in choosing the essay with which to open their new paper. They settled on an excerpt from Richard Price's introduction to his *Observations on the Importance of the American Revolution,* published the year before in London and being reprinted throughout the new states. Price's essay—with its paraphrasing of Montesquieu on inquiry, legitimacy, and consent—made a grand statement for these two young printers. The Revolution had forged a new basis for political legitimacy; governments were to be grounded in informed consent and equal participation among the wide body of the citizenry. Editor-printers such as Webster and Stoddard looked forward to a very special position in this new polity. They placed Price's *Observations* at the center of their front page, following both their promise "to the public" of "this flourishing CITY" that they would conduct their paper "on truly republican principles" and a short advertisement for scythes, hoes, and axes.[1]

Forty-six years later, in May 1831, Alexis de Tocqueville arrived in New York with his associate, Gustave de Beaumont, ostensibly to study prisons but in fact to examine the wider civil society forged in this Revolution. After several weeks in the city, they began their tour of the American interior by taking first a sloop up the Hudson River to Albany, racing past the city of Hudson on the night of July 1. On July 2 they met with leaders of New York's Jacksonian Democrats, known as the Albany Regency, and with a noted temperance reformer; the next day they toured the Shaker community just north of Albany at Watervliet. Early the following morning they were swept into Albany's Independence Day parade. In the midst of such festivities and in the company of men of note, Tocqueville was beginning to sketch his ambiguous portrait of equality and hierarchy in American civil life.[2]

The decades between Stoddard and Webster's first *Gazette* in 1785 and Tocqueville's upriver passage in 1831 marked the opening cycle of the evolving American revolutionary settlement, when both the ideals of Price's political consent and the institutions of Tocqueville's civil society became contested grounds in American public life. This study explores this story and its powerful contradictions from the Revolution to the age of Jackson in one American county, a county aptly named for Columbia, the mythic figure representing the past and the promise of this New World republic. The launching of the new *Gazette* and Tocqueville's passage upriver were benchmarks in this county's history, bracketing the rise of a notable American politician who formatively influenced an American understanding of consent and civil society. The story of the rise of Martin Van Buren, the first theoretician of American party politics, the eighth president of the United States, and a son of Columbia, runs through this work, linking locality with the narrative of national history.

Born in Kinderhook in 1782, three years before Webster and Stoddard issued their first *Gazette,* Martin Van Buren was shaped in his early life and political thinking by the intense civil strife that wracked his county during the American Revolution and far into the early Republic. By chance, Tocqueville and Beaumont just missed meeting Van Buren in the summer of 1831. They left Albany for Auburn on the evening of the Fourth of July just as he was returning from a trip to Utica; perhaps their stages passed in the night on the Schenectady Turnpike. Recently resigned as Andrew Jackson's secretary of state, Van Buren was attending to political affairs at home before taking ship for London as the ambassador to the Court of Saint James's. His rise to political preeminence perfectly expressed Tocqueville's "equality of condition": from his father's tavern in Kinderhook, he followed a lawyer's career to county surrogate, state senator, attorney general, governor, United States senator, cabinet secretary, vice president, and, finally, president of the Republic. As he rose in the ranks of the Democratic Party, he was increasingly worried about the reconsolidation of the functions of "aristocracy" that Tocqueville hoped would emerge from the combinations of "private citizens."[3]

Tocqueville did not meet Martin Van Buren, but he did give considerable thought to Van Buren's enduring contribution to political theory, the American system of party politics, which stood beside the steamboat as the civil machinery of the new age. If Van Buren helped to shape the machinery of politics in antebellum America, the intense struggle over legitimacy and consent among the peoples of Columbia shaped Van Buren's experience of politics in post-Revolutionary society. This contest over the terms of a Revolutionary settlement and the definitions of citizenship smoldered and flared far into the antebellum Republic. Not only was this settlement far from complete by modern standards, but contradictions that chafed between Price's equality of consent and Tocqueville's less-than-equal structures in civil society seemed to threaten its dissolution.[4]

This study thus is a simultaneous exploration of political theory and the history of a particular locality. It is about a problem and a place. The place is the county of Columbia and its surrounding region, the world of Martin Van Buren's emergence. The problem is the forging of citizenship in a revolutionary settlement, a question that lies at the core of the American experience. Typically, we think of such a settlement as a matter of constitutions and nations, of high-flying affairs of "great men" on a national stage. My meaning certainly encompasses such canonical understandings but is both more humble and more important. For my purposes here, the American revolutionary settlement is the variable and uneven fabric of consent, legitimacy, and institutions woven in thousands of localities across the new Republic. In many places, a settlement was quickly and easily arrived at, in others it required sharp but relatively short struggles to resolve, and in still others it had to be held together by raw force for decades, until a second revolution. In this settlement the nation was abstract and sentimental while the colony-become-state loomed large, an arena that fundamentally shaped the political dialogue and contest of peoples in localities. At its center lay the question of who was a citizen: the law-protected, consenting individual free to participate in civil life. The boundaries defining those who would be included within and excluded from the status of citizen were the flashpoints of post-Revolutionary politics. Would their consent indeed be freely offered; would they have equal access to the civil institutions? In great measure the history of the entire nation has revolved around these issues of extending the political and social rights that embody the promise of the age of Enlightenment.

Richard Price and Alexis de Tocqueville offered different versions of this political promise of the Atlantic Enlightenment. Price saw the Revolution as sweeping away ancient forms of hierarchy and tyranny and establishing legitimate government on the consent of the people. Tocqueville was more wary of this "equality of condition" and saw in new forms of association the basis of reconstructed hierarchy and stability. Where Price was a British radical, Tocqueville was a French conservative; each was reacting against the central tendencies of his own nation's political culture. Price voiced the certainties of popular empowerment that would reach their archetypal form in the French Revolution; Tocqueville expressed an understanding that informed the British counterrevolutionary response, arguing that consent was best bounded and channeled by existing civil structures.[5]

This book addresses questions grounded in a body of political theory informed by both sides of this Enlightenment dichotomy. The German philosopher Jürgen Habermas has devoted a lifetime to a consideration of the "Enlightenment Project." His central premise is that the legitimacy of modern governments arises, not from immutable sacred texts, but out of common and equal deliberation in the public sphere. The participation of rational individuals in a public and transparent domain of information, association, and conversation confers legitimacy to public authority. The public sphere is thus fundamental to the history and functioning of liberal democracy as shaped by the Enlightenment and the Age of Revolution. Legitimate outcomes — political decisions worthy of consent — must be debated in both the informal public sphere of the press and associated life, where opinions are formed, and in the formal arena of legislature and the court, where laws are made and confirmed. In the wake of a revolution that swept away monarchy and the last vestiges of an established church, a rough approximation of Habermas's understanding of the deliberative process emerged as the ideal for procedural legitimacy in the new United States.[6]

More an experience than a space, the public sphere mediates between private life in all its forms and the governing polity. As such, the concept has provided historians with a useful means to dissolve the tension between constitutional and socioeconomic approaches to the study of political life, since both are simultaneously negotiated and contested in this public arena. It also dissolves the boundary between formal and informal politics, because opinion is a complicated thing, coalescing around both the framing of law and the shaping of culture, providing historians with a powerful tool to explore the subtle interconnections that make societies work. If the public sphere was an arena of deliberation on matters of law, it was also an arena of informal persuasion, where the content and boundaries of common culture were negotiated and enforced.[7]

A paradoxical tension thus lies at the center of the Habermasian understanding of the public sphere. It is both an Enlightenment ideal and a social and economic reality lived in real time. If the ideal of the public sphere is one of equality, transparency, and rationality, the hard structures of social and economic power typically distort the shape of the public sphere, granting cultural authority to privileged gatekeepers. When Habermas calls it the "public sphere of civil society," he recognizes this dissonance between ideal and real. Thus Habermas's political deliberation takes place in an imperfect world: Price's equal *consent* is enacted in the context of Tocqueville's stratified *civil society*.

The paradoxical tension between equality of civil consent and a hierarchy of civil institutions comprises one foundational axis of the story that this study explores. Routine life in a liberal polity requires balancing equality of consent with inequality; it is a public compromise, more and less consciously recognized. The acceptance of this compromise is thus the unspoken ground of the revolutionary settlement. Force as a means to political and social change will yield to constitutional means, and a politics of crisis should give way to a politics of routine. Here there is the potential for change through reform, but organized violence must be set aside.

The outcome of the revolutionary settlement comprises a second foundational axis of this story. Despite all hopes and expectations, an enduring peaceable *outcome* was particularly difficult to achieve in Van Buren's Columbia County because — I shall argue — the *terms* of a revolutionary settlement were particularly unstable and contested. The failure to arrive at an acceptable balance between equal consent and stratified institutions repeatedly undermined the legitimacy of political routines and brought recourse to armed struggle perhaps unique in the early American republic. Coming of age in this fraught political environment, Martin Van Buren would formulate a particularly rigid understanding of the constitutional relationships between party, people, and nation.[8]

The failure of a revolutionary settlement in Columbia County derived not from any lack of effort. As of 1783 Americans were desperate to establish peaceable routines, and their means lay in the forms of public sphere and civil society. What is striking is how quickly the social forms that Tocqueville saw in 1831 — and that Habermas has more recently theorized — were forged in the new American states in the wake of the Revolution. Men like Ashbel Stoddard and Charles Webster were agents in a wide, almost utopian, founding of newspapers, lodges, and societies of all kinds whose early members saw themselves as fulfilling the promise of the Revolution, bringing improvement and uplift to the American people in a complex partnership with government. Rather than stand in opposition to government, these new social institutions in the 1780s and 1790s were the vehicles of participation in the deliberative process of self-governance.

My perspective flies in the face of some contemporary understandings that see "civil society" as an oppositional force, monitoring and limiting the reach of government. Although this role for civil society had certainly played an important part in the Revolutionary crisis and certainly would reemerge in the early Republic, for many decades after the Revolution governments, particularly state governments, were places where people asserted the legacy of democratic revolution: the rights and practices of self-government. Deliberation in public would determine political outcomes, and the new institutions in civil society orchestrating this deliberation comprised the *flywheel* between people and their government. Those involved would have fully understood Habermas's Enlightenment Project, as they shuttled between household, tavern, church, lodge, and society meetings, jury rooms, and legislature, setting the terms and reaping the benefits of the wider revolutionary settlement. Those men privileged by the Constitution, circulating freely in the institutions of civil society, could express their consent directly in elections, legislatures, and courts. They comprise roughly half of our story here.[9]

The other half considers those closed out from such participation. Exclusions from a role in formal deliberation were written into state constitutions, with suffrage restricted to men of various classes of property, and officeholding still more narrowly defined. Habermas's construct of equal deliberation has come under attack from a host of scholars, who rightly see the barriers and boundaries to equality imposed by the strictures of civil life and civil law. This study attempts to balance constitutionally privileged politics with a wider, more informal politics. At the core of this more informal politics lies the problem of consent and citizenship in this society, articulated along a gradient of inclusion and exclusion. White men of little or no property, women, most free people of color, and slaves all fell outside the sacred circle of the deliberative public sphere. Indeed, the universality of the founding language of the Revolution made their situation increasingly ambiguous. Certainly they were promised definite minimal protections under the law, but they were to have no role in making that law. They were ruled by but excluded from the revolutionary settlement. As nowhere else in the late-eighteenth-century world, the tension between ideals and realities was sharp and obvious in the early American republic.[10]

However, with the exception of slaves, whose consent was directly coerced by force and who stood under a condition of civil death, those excluded from *formal deliberation* were not excluded from the wider compass of an implied consent. Although such consent was expected as a matter of course, it was actively reinforced through a *cultural persuasion* shaped by expectations that the survival of the Republic lay in the virtue of its people — in ideals of order, improvement, refinement, respectability. Civil gatekeepers like the publishers of the *Gazette* increasingly conveyed and enforced the values of a broadly uniform middling culture. The persuasive reach of print in the public sphere — with its power to enforce an almost unconscious, implied consent through its definition of respectability, citizenship, and even nationhood — was a powerful force in the early Republic.[11]

But there were at least two potential loopholes in a public culture of respectability and in assumptions of a hegemonic cultural persuasion. First, the advance of a culture of respectability and sensibility through the institutions of the public sphere offered individual purchase on collective nationhood: if excluded individuals could meet the mandates of respectability, the grounds for their civil exclusion might be undermined. Thus participation in the public sphere, in its dimensions of association or print, began to establish a claim to inclusion, made possible, and possibly subversive, by the simple skills of literacy. Those excluded from deliberation could not be excluded so easily from persuasion, and at the core of eighteenth-century persuasive culture lay a second potential loophole. The ideals of sensibility and sympathy, forged in the wider orbit of the Enlightenment, required an expansive vision of the human condition that quietly militated against arbitrary and unreasonable boundaries in civil society. Sensibility slowly built sympathy and empathy and thus underwrote a slow-moving politics of reform, which in New York and other northern states led to post-Revolutionary slave emancipations and eventually — fused with evangelical immediatism — to the explosion of efforts to reduce the consumption of alcohol, to abolish slavery throughout the nation, and to expand voting rights across gender and racial boundaries. Reform, in which the informal persuasive influenced the formal deliberative, was a means to altering wider parameters of the revolutionary settlement. When this drive for reform through sympathetic persuasion and political deliberation foundered on uncompromisable difference, however, settled routines reverted to crisis and civil violence.[12]

Such is a central if contested thrust of the long-term history of the nation, interrupted by the collapse of the national settlement in a resort to arms with the Civil War. In the county of Columbia between the Revolution and the age of Jackson, the reach of the persuasive culture of sensibility and the logic of reform were all hedged in by contrary forces. Some were strategies of self-preservation: people faced with enduring civil constraints offered only minimal and the most fragile grants of consent. Of these, some withdrew by choice into communal isolates; others resisted the coercive realities of civil death with individual acts of insurgency. Still others, their expectations denied, rose in more concerted rebellions against the terms of their exclusion.[13]

The boundaries of slavery, gender, and ethnicity might be found across the breadth of the early Republic. But another civil boundary made public life in Columbia County uniquely volatile, compromising the emergence of a routine politics and undermining any possible progress toward a reformist expansion of the revolutionary settlement. What distinguished Columbia from much of the nation was an intense struggle over the inclusion of white men inside the boundaries of civility and political participation.

That contest was not apparent to a pair of French visitors, still puzzling over the collapse of the ancien régime. After spending a pleasant afternoon with one of the Livingston families in the summer of 1831, Tocqueville's companion, Gustave de Beaumont, was certain that the Hudson Valley was a tranquil place, which for "a long time past has not known civil and political dissensions." Another of their informants, who had spent his childhood in Stoddard's Hudson, ratified this understanding of the recent American past. Lawyer John C. Spencer met Tocqueville and Beaumont in Utica the day after they left Albany in July 1831, and spent many hours in conversation with them at his summer home by Canandaigua Lake. Writing the introduction to Tocqueville's *Democracy in America* in 1838, Spencer endorsed Tocqueville's understanding that Americans had been "gradually prepared by a long course of peculiar circumstances and by their local position, for self-government." Perhaps that was the case in America at large, perhaps not; but its gradualist interpretation certainly did not tell the story of Spencer's home county of Columbia's passage through the American Revolution.[14]

Five decades before, in April 1785, Colonel Henry Livingston had written in very different terms from his manor house to his brother Walter in New York City regarding the spring assembly election: "This County never had such a hard tryal since the Revolution, between Demo and Aristo, as it will have this election." In the years during and following the American Revolution Columbia County was deeply divided by a politics of land and power that reached back into the colonial era and that would endure into the 1840s. This division between Demo and Aristo, rooted in decades of oligarchic landlord rule challenged by colonial insurgencies and eight years of Revolutionary mobilization, made the county a precocious hothouse of political partisanship. The result was an enduring bitter contest that stalled the settling of the Revolution and the emergence of post-Revolutionary routines.[15]

Conflict over land and tenancy, shaping politics in Columbia County for almost a century, thus involved civil rights as much as property rights. Here partisans of oligarchic gentry rule and champions of Revolutionary popular action waged a political war that was perhaps the most intense of the confederated states. Columbia's tenant insurgents threatened—their opponents charged—to "tear up the settled establishments of society." If the public sphere established a brittle veneer of middling respectability, these forms and surfaces barely masked deep-running tensions between Demo and Aristo that periodically exploded into violence over land tenure. These ancient politics of land and dependency continually threatened the revolutionary settlement—and the transition from a crisis politics of violence, force, and "first principles" to a routine politics of interest governed by accepted channels of communication and constitutional procedures.[16]

Squatter and tenant insurgencies also contributed indirectly to a bitterly corrupt partisan politics. Threatened by violent insurgency (and an inevitable diminution of their rentier incomes), the landlord aristocrats took hold of the new institutions of the public sphere—newspapers, banks, parties—and turned them to their own devices, pursuing every avenue possible, including outright corruption, to extend and modernize their economic power. These "projects," stirring an already uniquely volatile county politics that had its roots in the land struggles, suggested to increasingly doctrinaire Old Republican ideologues that there was something inherently corrupt about the new civil institutions when they were not limited to a simple function of popular monitoring and oversight. Eventually, they were convinced that privileged associations and the wider culture of respectability and improvement threatened the legacy of the Revolution.

This, then, is the story that informed Van Buren's elaboration of the Jacksonian attack on the "money power." For decades the more militant of his

Jeffersonian associates had been suspicious of the claim to improvement through civil society in alliance with state power and had settled on a minimal, monitorial role for civil associations. By the mid-1830s Martin Van Buren had long since decided that the flywheel of civil society and indeed the public sphere itself had been corrupted by an aristocracy of wealth. In language strikingly similar to that of Tocqueville on the aristocratic functions of association, but reversing its meaning, Van Buren saw most of the institutions of civil society as aligned against the rights of the people. Shaped in great measure by the history and experience of Columbia's epic and bitter struggle between Demo and Aristo, Martin Van Buren developed a theory of the people's government threatened by corrupting forces, meaning that each election would revisit the constitutional crisis of the Revolution.[17]

Elsewhere in the North, the decisive advance of models of middling respectability, sensibility, and reform offered the prospect of a limited and gradual opening of the revolutionary settlement to women and Americans of color.[18] But fears of both armed insurgency and the corruption of electoral and legislative process immobilized public culture in antebellum Columbia. The result undermined the first promise of the Revolution: a routine politics in which government functioned as an extension of the people's interest. The mobilization of civil institutions for improvement, rather than for simple monitoring, came to be an object of suspicion. Instead of proliferating and empowering the people, forging new social capital, the evolution and elaboration of civil life slowed and stagnated in nineteenth-century Columbia County. With the rights and citizenship of white men in doubt, there was no room to consider their extension to anyone else. Violent and corrupt struggles for power undermined the possibilities for a peaceable extension of the settlement to excluded groups, compromising any movement toward a politics of sympathy and reform in Columbia.

When printers Stoddard and Webster ventured their fortunes at Claverack Landing in 1785, they were stepping into a political and cultural battleground whose exaggerated qualities make it an especially dramatic field for the historical study of civil life. In an important sense, in broad outline, this was a story unfolding everywhere in the new United States. Van Buren himself made it part of the national story. But it had a local specificity and internal dynamic here in Columbia County. The sharpness of the boundaries, the intensity of the struggles, and the pervasive sense of the irresolution make it a story that exposes the critical fault lines in post-Revolutionary society. This was not, I should warn, a happy or satisfying story. All did not go smoothly in the county of Columbia in the age of the Revolution and the early Republic.

The establishment of a liberal-democratic order was a complex, halting process, filled with struggle, contest, and unfulfilled ambitions.

This study thus presents a set of interlocking analytical narratives. Each chapter is framed in some measure by the history of the Van Buren family and the biography of Martin Van Buren. But this is not a biography; it is an ethnography. Van Buren was a son of Columbia and was shaped and molded by the patterns and struggles of its unique post-Revolutionary civil life and carried the imprint of that local experience onto the national stage. If Van Buren's life provides one integrating thread, the public sphere comprises another. Perhaps not unlike the manner in which one can treat a Martin Van Buren as a historical character, I treat the public sphere as a historical character, articulated by local circumstance, and in its evolution comprising the structure of the revolutionary settlement.

As a comment on contemporary historical practice, I give the ethnography of diverse groups of American people the same careful attention that biographers devote to the lives of particular American individuals. Well-situated ethnography of significant places and their peoples is as important as well-chosen biography or the endless stream of so-called national studies. It also fulfills a generational understanding that historians should demonstrate how ordinary peoples make national history and histories. It — and the arduous but rewarding task of record linkage that underwrites it — comprises one of the best tools we have at hand if we seek to uncover the connections that make life so complex. In this effort to find connections in this small space I roam widely and rudely across interests and specialties that occupy American historians. If my central problem is defining the shape of civil society and the public sphere in post-Revolutionary America, I perforce venture into the histories of party politics, print culture, race and slavery, women and gender, and even armed violence.

The history of a place and its particularities thus presents challenges for exposition within a broader national narrative. Such particularities deserve some comment, since they diverge from the national story. I would suggest that we need to remember that the national narrative is *lived* in the host of localities where Americans embody and enact their collective society. We need not explore the revolutionary settlement in every possible eighteenth-century American locality; we do need to know how such events played out in different *representative* contexts and how they shaped and were acted upon by ordinary lives. We examine some local stories because of their *illustrative* drama. And, occasionally, some local stories are of strategic and contingent *consequence* to the fabric of the national narrative. While I doubt the absolute representativeness of Columbia's story, its drama is certainly evident. And I am so bold as to claim that Columbia's story was of consequence to American history on the grander scale. If the conflicts and failures of the revolutionary settlement in the county of Columbia illuminate the wider problem on the national stage, they were also—through the agency of Van Buren's national reach—of national significance. They made a difference in determining the course of American history writ large.

1

The Revolutionary Crisis of Consent
1775–1783

The Declaration of Independency proceeded upon a Supposition that the Constitution under which we before lived was actually dissolved and the British Governmt here as such totally annihilated. Upon this Principle we must have been reduced to a State of Nature, in which the Power of Government reverted to as they Originated from the People who had undoubtedly a Right to establish any new Form they thought proper. . . . The Question whether a Govt. is dissolved and the People released from their Allegiance is in my Opinion a question of Morality as well as of Religion in which every man must judge. . . . In Such a Case no Majority however respectable can decide for him. . . . I hold it that *every Individual* has still a Right to choose the State of which he will become a Member, for before he surrenders any part of his natural Liberty . . . the Subjection of any one to the political Power of a State can arise only from his own *Express* consent! I speak of the Formation of Society and of a Man's initiating himself into it, so as to make himself a *Member* of it, for I admit that once the Society is formed the Majority undoubtedly conclude the Rest.

— Peter Van Schaack, Kinderhook, New York, Jan. 25, 1777,
to the New York Convention

On December 23, 1780, after a long day of "nothing but snow, hail, and frost," the marquis de Chastellux stopped for the night in the "first hamlet" in Kinderhook. Among several nondescript taverns, he chose "the best," "a very small house, kept by two young people of a Dutch family; they are very civil and attentive, and you are not badly off with them, provided you are not difficult to please." These two young people were Abraham Van Buren, a captain in the local militia, and his wife, Maria Van Alen. Their third child, born two years later, would one day become the president of the United States. Martin's future wife, Hannah Goes, was born into a local family the next March. A

PLATE 1. *Abraham Van Buren and Maria Van Alen's Tavern.*
South of Kinderhook Center, Late 1830s. Courtesy of the National Park Service

quarter century later, in the winter of 1807, Martin and Hannah would elope across the Hudson River to Catskill, to be married by Hannah's sister's husband, Judge Moses Cantine. The Van Buren and Goes families had lived and farmed in Kinderhook since the 1680s, and a deep web of kinship entangled them and their neighbors; Martin's mother, Maria, was Hannah's great-aunt, and his sister had recently married her brother. These families all shared a long history in the struggle to establish freeholds along Kinderhook and Kline Kill creeks, stretches of fertile land lying in the midst of the great holdings of the Van Rensselaer family on the east side of the Hudson.[1]

Martin and Hannah were born as the war of the Revolution was ending and peace and Independence stood on the horizon for the American people. But their families had been sharply divided for some years by the Revolutionary struggle. Hannah's father, John Dirck Goes, had sided with a group of leading men in Kinderhook who resisted the Revolution; Martin's father Abraham had risen to local prominence as a patriot whig. Both had close kin in the opposite camp: John's cousin Isaac Goes was one of Kinderhook's leading whigs, and Abraham's younger brother, Martin, namesake of the future president of the United States, had been banished for loyalism in 1778. When Hannah was born in early March 1783, John Goes was at home but still listed as a fugitive, marked by his loyalist affiliation; when Martin was six years old, he would have witnessed the sale of tory estates at his father's tavern, including land that he himself would buy for his Lindenwald estate a half century later. Even then, in the winter of 1839–1840, Martin Van Buren could not think of party politics outside the framework of the struggles of his father's time, between the whigs and tories of the Revolution. The passions of the Revolutionary struggle thus left a powerful mark and must have simmered as an undercurrent in their marriage, and in the wider Kinderhook community.[2]

The American Revolution sliced through colonial societies, imposing the stark necessity of declaring allegiance to king and empire or to a new republican state in continental confederation. In posing this choice the Revolution opened an enduring struggle over the relationship between consent and civil society. At the simplest level, the contest of whigs, tories, and the British Empire required a military encounter to settle future sovereignties and allegiances. In the long run, the most problematic settlement would not be that between the parties to the Revolutionary contest, but that involving the ensuing struggles over the nature of American life, struggles about consent and inclusion in American civil life launched but not resolved in the Revolutionary years.

BURGOYNE'S HESSIANS IN ALBANY COUNTY

Five years before Martin Van Buren and Hannah Goes were born, Kinderhook was the scene of one of the great dramas of the Revolutionary war. For months the people of Kinderhook had watched regiments and detachments of the Continental Line and New York militia marching through the village and district, heading toward battles raging on the lakes to the north. On September 19, 1777, cannon fire had been heard as far south as Claverack and Livingston Manor; on October 7 the Kinderhook people heard "the Report of cannon" upriver until nightfall. These thunderings marked the two battles at Freeman's Farm upriver in Saratoga and were followed by the surrender of British general John Burgoyne's entire army. On October 22, captured Hessian soldiers were marched into Kinderhook village. They stayed for a day to rest and reprovision before being moved south and east toward internment camps in Massachusetts. The countryside turned out to see the sight.[3]

These captured soldiers had been on the march from Montreal since June. After their Atlantic sea voyage and months of garrison duty in Canada, they had been told they would sweep aside the rebels and take Albany by the end of the summer, linking up with British armies converging from the west and south. Burgoyne's advance down the lakes, shattering Vermont's Green Mountain Boys at the battle of Hubbardton, Vermont, easily recapturing Fort

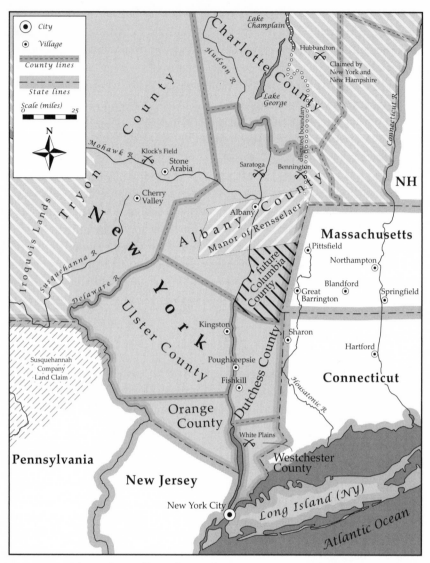

MAP 1. *The Hudson Valley in the Revolutionary Era.* Drawn by Jim DeGrand

Ticonderoga, and bearing down on the county of Albany, had been watched with rising apprehension by the people of the Hudson and western New England and impelled a massive popular mobilization. The tide began to turn in mid-August with the defeat of a large Hessian foraging party up the Hoosic River, thirty-five miles north of Kinderhook, at the battle of Bennington. Then on September 19 Burgoyne's main force was stopped by General Horatio Gates's army at Freeman's Farm and driven back in disorder in a second battle on October 7. Ten days later, surrounded by thousands of militiamen and twenty-three regiments of the Continental Line, Burgoyne surrendered at Saratoga meetinghouse.[4]

Ferried east across the river on October 19, the captured Hessian brigade was marched south down the post road running along the east bank of the Hudson. Their route toward internment in Massachusetts took them through the eastern half of Albany County. These fertile lowlands were the northern reaches of traditional Dutch-German New York, running along their line of march from Schaghticoke and Greenbush to Schodack to Kinderhook and beyond to Claverack, the two Livingston Manors, and south into Dutchess and Ulster counties. Part of this region, running from Kinderhook south to the Livingston Manor, would be set off in 1786 as Columbia County, in a patriotic tribute to the classical representation of the new Republic.

On October 22 the prisoners' column arrived in Kinderhook, described by Colonel Johann Friedrich Specht of the Hessian Brigade as "a kind of market town with widely separated houses," "wooden as well as some made of stone, 2 or 3 stories high, and built according to Dutch and English tastes." Impressed with the prosperity of these people, Specht seems not to have noticed that more than one in ten of the inhabitants were African-American slaves. Many of the people of Kinderhook village were "Tories and bemoaned our fate," he wrote in his diary, but even here the common soldiers had to sleep in the woods, though a few officers were taken into village households. The arrival of the prisoners offered a great spectacle and a source of potential profit for the neighborhood; on October 23 the village was flooded with farm wagons filled with sightseeing families and with goods for sale to feed the prisoners on their impending march east over the Taconics and the Berkshires. These country people left with an indelible image of the results of victory, a victory to which their neighbors in the district militia, the Seventh Albany County Regiment, had made a certain small contribution. They also left with gold for their provisions and the occasional Hessian deserter (and stolen horse) to work the farms along Kinderhook Creek.[5]

Kinderhook was a district of freeholders, but virtually all of the rest of Albany County lay under the reality or the threat of various systems of tenancy. The vast holdings of the Van Rensselaer family, held under century-old Dutch and English colonial grants, were divided into Upper Rensselaerwyck, spanning the Hudson at Albany, and Lower Rensselaerwyck, centered on the inland village of Claverack. Where the Van Rensselaers achieved a certain peace on much of their domain by renting their land in perpetual leases that conveyed some security of tenure, to the south on the Upper and Lower

Livingston Manors leasehold terms were not so generous. Driving a hard bargain with their Palatine German tenants, the Livingston families rented land on the life-lease system, which required a costly renewal on the death of the last of the two or three persons named in the original lease. The Livingston lands had seen intermittent violent protests since the 1750s, which would flare up again and again down into the 1840s. If they had been marched through these southern districts, the Hessian internees would not have found the manifestations of prosperity that they saw at Kinderhook village. Their route lay to the east, away from the great valley of the Hudson, and into an even poorer region (see Map 1).[6]

Rather than taking the post road south into Claverack, the Hessians were marched southeast up one of the stream valleys leading up from the Hudson lowlands into the eastern hill country. This eastern road took them out of the domain of Dutch and German settlement into a rough border country occupied by New England squatters, holding land under titles sold by the native Mahicans and challenging the claims of New York landlords. With the establishment of the King's District in 1772, some of these squatter-settlers had achieved self-government and civil identity, but the region just to the south would nominally be part of the Van Rensselaers' Claverack until 1782, when it was set off as the district of Hillsdale. On October 24 the prisoners and their militia escort climbed seventeen miles into these uplands, first through the settlement at Spencertown and then up over "hilly and stony roads" to spend a cold night in Nobletown, a tiny squatter settlement perched high on the Massachusetts border. Here they did get some shelter, but the houses and barns "were so small," Colonel Johann Friedrich Specht complained, "that they could not shelter ⅓th of the men."[7]

On the following day the prisoners continued on over the Taconic range into Egremont and Great Barrington, Massachusetts, and toward internment camps near Boston. The passage of the Hessians through southeastern Albany County, from Kinderhook to Nobletown, marked the end of serious military threats to the security of upper Hudson Valley. But the "Americans" who crowded to see them had no way of knowing that their national future had just been sealed. Indeed, recent events made the situation still seem critical. That August, one hundred miles to the west in the Mohawk Valley, a force of tories and Iroquois commanded by Colonel Barry St. Leger had ambushed and badly mauled the local militia at Oriskany. St. Leger was forced to retreat, but for years to come tory-Iroquois forces would bring devastation to the western valleys. From the south, threats were immediate. A flotilla of British vessels was on the Hudson; on October 15 and 16 they had burned the towns of Esopus and Kingston, where the Provincial Congress had lately been meeting. On October 19 they landed at Lower Livingston Manor, twenty-five miles south of Kinderhook, burning Clermont, the estate of Robert R. Livingston, who sixteen months before had been among the five drafters of the Declaration of Independence and now was the chancellor of New York's courts of equity. The British expedition encamped at Clermont for another two days, hoping to raise local tories to their standard. Hearing of Burgoyne's surrender, they turned back down the Hudson on October 21.[8]

To the men of Gates's army receiving Burgoyne's surrender on October 19, the threat of invasion was still palpable, and regiments of Continentals and militia were already heading south to face a certain British advance. If the British strategy failed, it had come terrifyingly close to success: the country people gawking and hawking in Kinderhook on October 23 could not know that the struggle for national independence had been determined at Saratoga. Their defense of their new sovereignty was deeply entangled with an internal struggle over authority, legitimacy, and consent that would shape Columbia's politics for decades to come.[9]

The experience of revolution in New York was among the most stressful and conflicted of any of the thirteen new American states. The events of 1777 saw British forces come close to crushing the Revolution on the banks of the Hudson in Albany County. Even though this strategy failed in that summer and fall, the British occupation of New York City and the southern counties, with continuing threats from the north and the west, hedged in the Revolutionary government of New York through the autumn of 1783. The breakaway state of Vermont compounded the challenge to New York, carving off an independent republic from the Hampshire Grants, disputed since the 1760s between New York and New Hampshire. The authority and sovereignty of the state of New York was thus hotly contested for many years.[10]

The British had not casually chosen New York to pursue so aggressively their claim to dominion over their American empire. New York was politically vulnerable. The British were certain that a high proportion of the population would support the crown, and they had some reason in their judgment. Recent waves of immigration, ethnic diversity, inequitable land distribution, and a century of oligarchic, even predatory government all worked to undermine the solidarity of the whig cause. Thus the Revolution in New York was an extremely complex affair, in which the new state faced both external military threats to its sovereignty on three fronts and internal threats from numbers of the disaffected: outright loyalists, neutrals, and the simply exhausted. The ultimate success of the whig cause in New York was thus not foreordained.[11]

The American Revolution in its opening phases was a struggle to defend traditional rights and institutions from royal encroachment. On the upper reaches of the Hudson River, however, these encroachments were not always easily detected. There had indeed been a demonstration against the Stamp Act in Albany City late in 1765, in which a crowd of county gentry had threatened several men who had applied for the post of stamp duty collector. More dramatic events had unfolded the next summer in the hills of east Claverack, where the Van Rensselaers had enlisted two companies of British regular troops to evict New England squatters at Nobletown, burning the settlement and driving the Nobletown people east to refuge in Massachusetts. But, if the hill people were radicalized by this encounter, most of the Dutch and German farming households along the river saw the encroachment of British imperial authority as a distant problem. The imperial interest was upheld throughout Albany County by Sir William Johnson, the squire of vast estates in the Mohawk Valley. Thus for most people along the upper Hudson the Revolution came as an intrusion into local affairs, suddenly requiring new civil allegiances and institutions. Questions of sovereignty, legitimacy, consent, and civil inclusion all flowed from this Revolutionary intrusion.[12]

Albany was one of only three New York counties to respond to Continental calls for local organization in the fall of 1774. The county gentry might well have been emboldened by the recent death of William Johnson, but it did not move with undue haste. In November and December 1774 the Albany City and County Committee of Correspondence voted to accept the Articles of Association drafted by the First Continental Congress and to gather contributions for the suffering town of Boston, printing their resolves in a pamphlet for distribution to "the remote districts" of the county. Late in the following February a General Association was signed by gentlemen from throughout the county, nervously "alarmed at the avowed design of the ministry" yet concerned for "the preservation of peace and good order." In March two gentlemen from the southeast districts—Walter Livingston from the Manor and Peter Van Ness from Claverack—attended the Albany meeting. But not until almost a month after the battles at Lexington and Concord did a large meeting of committee representatives from throughout the county gather in Albany to elect deputies to the "General Congress" in New York and to begin to consider the county's contribution to the defense of the colony. Perhaps this meeting was reminiscent of sessions of the county courts or of the board of county supervisors. But, gathering sixty-five members on its second day, it marked the beginning of an accelerating democratization of public proceedings — and establishment of new civil and military institutions — in Albany County.[13]

The Revolutionary movement, soon to open hundreds of positions for political participation on committees and in the militia, posed a powerful challenge to the conservative, oligarchic structure of public life on the upper Hudson Valley. At all levels of colonial government the landlord class had ruled through direct and indirect means. The colonial assembly in New York was a notoriously closed group, elected by counties and privileged manors and serving in sessions that could last more than five years. Albany County's representation, with representation granted by special privilege to the Manor of Livingston, was a tightly held prerogative of the Albany City merchants, the Van Rensselaers, and the Livingston family. The electorate had to have been quite small, even though a 1701 statute had enfranchised all tenants holding life leases; it might have comprised about 45 percent of the total white male population. If manor courts had long since disappeared, the county court of general sessions was typically controlled by the landlords, sitting under appointments from the governor. Only recently, in 1772, had local district bounds and governments in Albany County been regularized by province law, giving uniformity to the governance of various manors, "Villages, Neighbourhoods, and Christian Plantations." By contrast to the careful regulation of New York's incorporated cities and towns, district affairs in Albany County had been run by varying combinations of supervisors, assessors, collectors, and constables, who often resisted election and neglected their offices. Civil traditions were only weakly developed along the colonial Hudson.[14]

Religious traditions filled some of the public space where civil traditions were weak. Here the power of the landlords was also evident, in ways that hinted at certain limitations and resistance. For the great majority of people in lower Albany County, religious meetings comprised their most significant public experience before the Revolution. This was an experience fundamentally shaped by the Protestant Reformation, channeled into particular streams of Atlantic migration onto colonial frontiers. A Dutch Reformed church had been founded at Kinderhook in 1712, followed in the 1720s by churches founded by the Van Rensselaers at Claverack center and the Livingstons at Linlithgo on the Manor. In an ethnic syncretism that underwrote colonial power in early-eighteenth-century New York, the Livingstons comfortably transferred their paternal Scots Presbyterian allegiances to the church of their Dutch wives. While a popular Pietism had swept many Dutch churches around New York City, these conservative congregations, which shared a minister down to the Revolution, preserved a rigorous Calvinism and ties to the church in Holland.[15]

Ironically, ethnicity also undermined any hopes the landlords had of ruling their domains in matters religious. Palatine Germans, settled in 1711 to develop naval stores on the Manor, had established two German Reformed and two German Lutheran churches by 1730, one just over the line in Claverack. These ethnic German churches comprised a subtle barrier dividing landlords and tenants far into the nineteenth century; their affiliation with Henry Melchior Mühlenberg's Pennsylvania Lutheran Synod provided a continuing relationship with an alternative public authority. Religion also functioned as a barrier against oligarchy in the hill regions. Connecticut Yankee squatters established Congregational churches on the time-honored principles of New England settlement tradition. In Nobletown, Spencertown, and the King's District, Congregational churches were formed in concert with key claims to land or formation into a district, as happened in King's in 1772. And, as all across New England, Separate meetings splintered off from the Congregationalists, in a path carrying most to the Baptists and some further along the sectarian continuum to the Shakers, who would emerge during the turmoil of the Revolution. The landed oligarchs had no hope of controlling these people, though they would make the attempt.[16]

The Revolution, by suddenly making participation in civil affairs not just possible but mandatory, forced it out of the exclusive control of the oligarchic families. Inclusion in and consent to the Revolutionary project was not optional, but mandated in the committee's injunction of May 1775 that the General Association be distributed for signing by the first of June. Those who refused to sign would suffer at the hands of the Revolutionary committees. Over the next three years at least ninety-nine men were elected to such committees in the four southeastern districts of Albany County, attending the county committee meetings and enforcing the Revolutionary mandate in their neighborhoods. The committees typically worked with rather than against district governments and the county courts, but until the signing of the state constitution in April 1777 they formed an extralegal layer of civil power, grounded only in the agreement of the people. These were the first grounds for a popular politics along the Hudson, and many of these committee members would carry this experience forward into the political struggles of coming decades, comprising what Henry Livingston would nervously describe as the Demo.[17]

So too would the dozens of officers and hundreds of common soldiers who served in the military arms of the Revolution. Committee service comprised only a fraction, if an important one, of the wider Revolutionary political mobilization. In common with their colleagues downriver, the Albany Committee of Correspondence did not move precipitously to raise armed forces against the crown. On May 4, 1775, the day after they were informed by

"Persons from New England in the Character of Gentlemen" of the coming attack on the fort at Ticonderoga, the committee voted to ask the city of Albany to raise a militia. On May 10 the committee voted to recommend that the county's several districts form militia companies, but on May 11 they refused to send supplies to support the Yankee effort against Ticonderoga. While the county leaders hung back, the men in the border districts were the most militant, in association with neighbors in Massachusetts. Asa Douglass of the King's District led a band of men in a Berkshire contingent against Ticonderoga; John McKinstry of Nobletown raised a company that marched for Boston on May 5, serving for three months under Massachusetts orders and pay. On Livingston Manor a small club established twelve days after the battles at Lexington and Concord might have been a manifestation of ambitions to challenge the landed oligarchy's monopoly over political power. The eight young men signing the articles were by no means tenant insurgents: they were members of notable freeholding families in Claverack and Livingston Manor, but not the Van Rensselaers or the Livingstons. But, while their "regulations" laid out rules for nights of drinking and cardplaying, most of them would be Revolutionary committeemen or officers in the Continental Line, local militia, and the ranger companies. One, Leonard Ten Broeck, would be a Jeffersonian stalwart in years to come.[18]

In July the New York provisional government began raising regiments for the Continental Line, but Albany County began serious efforts to reform its militia only in August 1775, reporting seventeen regiments organized by late October. Of these, five were from the districts in the southeast corner of the county: Kinderhook formed the Seventh Albany County Regiment, Claverack the Eighth and Ninth, Livingston Manor the Tenth, and the King's District the Seventeenth. These militia regiments, with the district committees, would expand the opportunity for men to exert public authority in a world long dominated by county oligarchs—these opportunities may explain the seeming delay by the old county elite in forming these regiments. The militia regiments would form a powerful base for popular politics in the coming decades, reinforcing and even establishing the political identity of the districts and lower end of the county as a whole. In particular, the Ninth Regiment was raised in the hill section of Claverack encompassing the squatter neighborhoods of Nobletown and Spencertown where, one conservative wrote nervously in May 1775, "Levelling principles are held up." Regimental organization gave this region a local political structure before its civil organization as the district of Hillsdale in 1782. The officers of the Ninth Regiment declared their allegiance to Revolutionary institutions in November 1775, promising "under all the ties of religion, honor, and regard to our Country" to uphold the state and continental congresses. The chartering of Columbia County itself in 1786 was anticipated in the forming of a Second Brigade of Albany County Militia from these five regiments in the summer of 1780.[19]

This civil identity was forged in crisis and on the battlefield. In the raising of military forces New York and Albany County took up their role in asserting American sovereignty. Organized violence for political ends brought a militarization of society, bearing potential implications for the closure of the Revolution in the years to come. The Revolutionary service of Albany County men in the Continental Line and in the militia was often arduous if not always distinguished; it would be a formative experience. The New York regiments of the Continental Line raised in summer of 1775 would be sent that fall into the ill-fated Canadian expedition and then, reorganized, fight at Manhattan, White Plains, Monmouth Court House, and Saratoga, survive Valley Forge, defend garrisons on the Mohawk frontier and the forts at the Hudson Highlands, raze the Iroquois towns around the Finger Lakes, and eventually march south to invest Yorktown. The militia would not go beyond the bounds of the state, but, given the perpetual state of war in Revolutionary New York, these terms of service required an almost constant mustering of minute companies and other detachments for scouting, construction and transportation, and battle reserves. In January 1776 militia from Kinderhook and the King's District were mobilized to disarm loyalists up the Mohawk Valley. That summer, as the British forces landed and began their occupation of New York City, other militia companies were called south to build barracks at Fishkill; one of the Manor minute companies fought at the battle of White Plains that October.[20]

The year 1777 was one of crisis. Beginning in April, with news of the advance of Burgoyne from the north and St. Leger from the west, detachments of county militia were sent north into the Lake country; men from the King's District were said to have fought at Bennington in August. That August and September, as part of the full-scale mobilization to stop Burgoyne, detachments from the five regiments in the southeast section of the county were called up and organized into a composite regiment under Colonel William B. Whiting of the King's District. Some served with John Glover's Brigade of Continentals, and the others formed part of Abraham Ten Broeck's Albany militia brigade. On the march or held in reserve during the first battle of Saratoga, they played a more active role in the second. On October 7 the King's District men supported artillery batteries along the river, and the eighteen hundred men of Ten Broeck's brigade, among them perhaps five hundred from Kinderhook, Claverack, Hillsdale, and Livingston Manor, were ordered into battle on the left flank just as Simon Fraser was killed and the British line collapsed. With Burgoyne's surrender some of these men were sent south to reinforce the American lines south of Fishkill; some might have fought to defend the forts at the Hudson Highlands that October.[21]

Over the next four years they were continually in service against more irregular opponents. Men from Columbia County would tell stories into the next century of their struggles with tory and Iroquois foes. The Revolution in New York had qualities of a race war, a war shaped by perceptions of savagery and civilization, as Mohawk and Seneca warriors serving with British forces terrorized the people along the Hudson. At Schaghticoke opposite Albany a militia major was killed harvesting his fields that September. Others survived capture at Indian hands: John McKinstry and the men of his company, taken at the Battle of the Cedars in 1776, several of Hezekiah Baldwin's King's District Rangers, taken while scouting the upper lakes in March 1777, and Dr. Moses Younglove, also of the King's District. Captured at the rout at Oriskany in May 1777, Younglove would live to cast an elector's ballot for Andrew Jackson. Militiamen continually served for periods of weeks and months in small detachments, marching north and west to defend outlying settlements, where they saw their share of frontier warfare. In July 1778 Major Jacob Ford, commanding a detachment of the Hillsdale militia at Cherry Valley, reported to Governor Clinton in language that captures the precariousness of the situation. The township of Springfield had been destroyed by Indian raiders: "The Settlement was all in a light flame." Though the militia with him "appeared with undaunted Courage," he felt that the post should be abandoned. "The People here are in the greatest Distress," he wrote, and the "Post is all open to the Enemy and nothing to hinder their Coming."[22]

Jacob Ford would survive the frontier struggle to play a central role in the politics of the new county in the coming decades, as would the officers who led the militia into a chaotic skirmish up the Mohawk River two years later. In October 1780, when Sir John Johnson (William's son) and the Mohawk Joseph Brant led a raiding party of tories and Iroquois through Schoharie and into the Mohawk Valley, companies from the regiments of Robert Van Rensselaer's brigade marched to oppose him. Failing to link up with Colonel John Brown's garrison at Stone Arabia, which was massacred by Johnson's raiders, the advancing militia fought a sharp if chaotic engagement with the enemy at Klock's Field. Outraged by Van Rensselaer's failure to rescue the Stone Arabia garrison and to pursue the tories after Klock's Field, an allied Oneida branded him a tory, and the junior officers present forced his court martial. Although Van Rensselaer was acquitted, this was a lasting humiliation for this heir to Claverack Manor. The humiliation of a landlord oligarch such as Robert Van Rensselaer and the rise of hundreds of new men in the mobilization of Revolutionary committees and militias had laid the ground for a bitterly contested politics of Demo and Aristo in the postwar years.[23]

CIVIL AUTHORITY, CIVIL VIOLENCE

Much of the work of the militia was civil, a bulwark against internal dissent as much as external foes. The external crisis of enemy armies and raiders, challenging Revolutionary sovereignty and threatening retribution for rebellion, was matched by an internal crisis of legitimacy and consent. The Revolutionary struggle was based on an explicit, horizontal consent to a new social and political contract among the people at large, manifested in signatures to the Articles of Association. But not all agreed that British measures constituted tyranny; many refused to sign the Articles, and some actively opposed the Revolution. For many in Albany County — a majority at different times, some said — the legitimacy of the new regime was questionable, only minimally improved by the promulgation of the state constitution in April 1777 and the election of George Clinton in June. This withholding of consent gave the Revolution in New York the quality of a civil war. Here the militia was a vital arm in this civil struggle, carrying out the will of the county committee, the state convention, and the Commission for Detecting and Defeating Conspiracies established in 1778. Since allegiance could not be assumed, consent, or at least submission, had to be enforced. The Revolutionary struggle itself thus initiated an enduring question: What were the constitutional terms of inclusion in American civil society?[24]

The role of the militia in this coerced civil inclusion was complicated, as many saw the delinquents among the militia as part of the problem. Specially raised ranger companies became the military arm of the committees, tasked with suppressing the disaffected and motivating the laggardly. But the evidence of militia delinquency may simply reflect the routine difficulties of combining military service with maintaining productive farms. As many as eighty of the Livingston tenants, many of whom were sick or the sole male in a household, paid fines for failing to serve in the militia between the summer of 1776 and February 1777. But in November and December alone, about 250 militiamen from the Manor were serving in five different companies at the siege lines near West Point, and the refusal of men to serve might simply have reflected undue burdens on this militia pool.[25]

As serious as any disgruntlement in the militia, the unrelenting stress of the wartime economy engendered dissent, sometimes violent. People struggled with scarcity, currency collapse, price inflation, and the steady pressure of taxation and military provisioning. In the summer of 1776 a riot broke open a supply of salt in a store on the Manor; in the King's District in June 1779 there was "a great Cry for Bread and talk of Gathering a Mobb to search for wheat." That August a convention of delegates from Albany, Dutchess, and Westchester counties met in Claverack to propose means to protect the value of the state-issued bills of credit. It also demanded the confiscation and sale of loyalist property. September and December 1781 saw a series of riots against the collection of taxes on Livingston Manor, immediately followed by a mass meeting on the Manor protesting taxes, the impressment of crops, and various fines. This meeting was sanctioned by the Livingstons, whose sharp trading and attention to family financial interest had long since alienated the state leadership.[26]

There were more threatening groups than militia delinquents or tax evaders. Starting in the summer of 1777 and running to beyond 1783, the war in the Hudson Valley spawned gangs of bandits, who became a threat to all householders. Some were groups of loyalists; others were deserters from both armies; still others were desperate men who would have lived outside the law in times of peace. William Smith, a loyalist interned on the Manor between 1776 and 1778, wrote uneasily following a robbery of a patriot household in Kinderhook in August 1777: "This gives a general Terror — no Law." This attack might well have had a political dimension, as did the burning of the Wyncoop house and the robbery and murder of Abraham Van Ness in Kinderhook that same August. According to local lore Van Ness's murderers, neighbors heading north to join Burgoyne, were hunted down and hanged on the river bank opposite Albany. The following spring a robber band of deserters struck in Claverack and at several houses in the Manor; in most of these raids householders were threatened or tortured to reveal hidden cash. The rising tide of bandits in 1777 and 1778 brought demands that new ranger companies be raised to hunt them down.[27]

LOYALISTS AND PATRIOTS ON THE MANOR AND IN THE HILLS: CIVIL DISCONNECTION

Among these robber bands were loyalists of various stripes and even British soldiers escaped from the defeat at Saratoga. Men who acted on loyalist sentiment in this section of Albany County fell into two quite specific groups, the Dutch freeholder elite of Kinderhook, who will be considered in due course, and a broad spectrum of men newly settled in the upland sections along the Massachusetts border, especially in parts of King's District and Livingston Manor. Here it is fair to say that a conspiracy was at work. Just as the whigs enlisted men for the patriot militia, a cadre of loyalists, led by a former British officer across the Hudson in Coxsackie District, began in the summer of 1776 to recruit men in King's, Kinderhook, Claverack, Livingston Manor, and various parts of Rensselaerwyck for a loyalist regiment that was to wait secretly for the opportunity to join the advancing British forces. In May and then in October 1776, men were arrested in King's District for recruiting for this regiment, and early in May 1777 a detachment of Claverack militia attacked a group of assembled loyalists in the eastern end of the Livingston Manor, in the Copake neighborhood. Two were killed, and at least 140 prisoners were rounded up, and Nobletown militia occupied the neighborhood for the next ten days. Some of those captured at Copake admitted to taking "oaths of secrecy and allegiance to the King"; the men who killed Van Ness in east Kinderhook the following August and 45 others who marched from Claverack to actually fight in Burgoyne's army at Saratoga must have taken this same oath. Others, lurking in the King's District in September, burned Colonel William B. Whiting's mill and the state provisions assembled there while Whiting and most of the Seventeenth Albany were serving in the patriot lines at Saratoga.[28]

Why did these men choose to throw their allegiance to the king as loyalists, signing—as William Smith put it—"Pro Rege"? This question has long centered on the motivations of the Livingston tenants. The Livingstons themselves were afraid that many of their tenants would oppose the Revolution in hopes of overturning the Manor title; as early as July 1775 Robert R. Livingston wrote to John Jay that some tenants were "resolved to stand by the King as they called it, in hopes that if he succeeded they should have their Lands." There were indeed great animosities on the Manor. The local committee of safety heard dramatic testimony in the fall of 1776. One man wanted to "shoot the Whigs"; another "would as leaf shoot a Committee Man [as a] Black Duck, and damn's the Committee . . . to Hell." He had a string of horses "which he would all give if the King Conquer'd." Land did figure into the rewards offered for loyalism; in the summer of 1776, men in the King's District were enticed to sign loyalist recruiting papers with promises of "a suit of claoths and Ninepence per day" and that "after Britain had Conquered America each Regiment was to have a piece of land six miles square of the Conquered Country." And the land of Livingston Manor had been the subject of intense conflict for more than twenty years. Between 1751 and 1757 the Livingstons had struggled with New England squatters and dissident tenants for control of the Copake and Ancram lands along the Massachusetts border, and in the mid-1760s this contest had flared up again as squatters in Nobletown defended themselves against the Van Rensselaers' Claverack title. As recently as 1774 some of the claimants to a 1757 Indian deed were challenging a small section of the Livingston title. Some lines of continuity ran from these earlier events to those of the Revolutionary years, particularly among

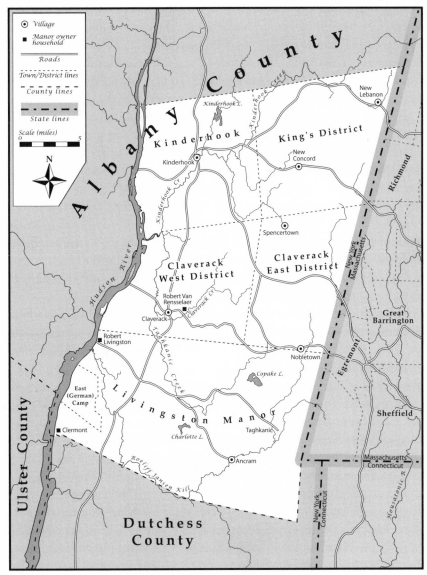

MAP 2. *Southeast Albany County, circa 1777.* Drawn by Jim DeGrand

the Spoor and Brasee families, who played central roles in tenant resistance in the 1750s and loyalist agitation in the 1770s.[29]

But most of the accused tories on the Manor did not have deep connections to the previous struggles. Many, indeed, were not even leaseholders, or had taken up land very recently. Much of the reported dissent on the Manor might have been a projection of the fears of the Manor lords. Arnout Viele, hanged at Albany in the summer of 1777 for acting as a lieutenant in the loyalist organization on the Manor, spoke in his confession of his fears of the advancing British forces: he was told that the oath was "sant True [sent through] the Country to Save our Lives and familys[,] that the Rigolars was Rathy to Com True the Contry and that there should be No Marsey Showin." Nowhere did he express hopes of gaining Livingston land, perhaps not surprisingly, given that the Livingstons themselves were pleading for his life. Viele's family was able to appeal to the local gentry, assembling a massive petition signed by many of the committeemen in Livingston and Claverack, and even by Cornelia Livingston, wife of Walter, one of the heirs to the Manor. Viele's fear of the advancing regulars was amplified in the confessions of loyalists from Schodack, just north of Kinderhook, who swore that "the Reason of our swearing was to prevent our being destroyed by the Indians, who were coming down in Great Numbers . . . [and] would destroy all that had not a certificate of their being true to the King . . . or that they would be sent to New Spain." Both sides of the Revolutionary struggle deployed threats of coercion to enforce consent.[30]

The conditions of tenancy on the Manor, compounded by the stress of the patriot impressments, certainly played a role in an undercurrent of disaffection there, and echoes of this discontent would underlie the renewed struggle against the Livingston's title in 1795. But there were other forces at work. On the Manor and elsewhere in the hill districts many, perhaps most of the signing loyalists were recently settled in the region and were often not American-born and lacked a certain purchase in local public life. Half-pay British officers, standing by their oaths to the crown, played a key role in recruiting the loyalists. They were notable among the conspirators in the King's District, where in the 1760s groups of regular officers had petitioned the province for bounty land grants among the patchwork of Van Rensselaer and New England squatter claims. A few, here and there, were Anglicans. Allegiance to the king was grounded in some measure in alienation from the dominant local culture. Allegiance, the voluntary granting of consent to sovereignty, was shaped by situation and by a calculus of the civil and personal advantage that might accrue from a British or an American victory.[31]

The peoples of the disputed hill districts north of Livingston Manor and east of Claverack were staunchly whig, and in their story lay a great lesson in the Revolutionary balance of consent and civil society. The inhabitants of Nobletown and Spencertown were still in contest with the Van Rensselaer family over the title to their land, and, since the Van Rensselaers supported the patriot cause, this struggle could well have drawn the hill people to tory allegiances. But the people of the east Claverack hills were the least touched by loyalism in the region and the most militant and united supporters of American Independence. In the summer of 1766 the settlers at Nobletown had lost everything at the hands of British troops called in by the now-patriot Van Rensselaers. Most of these "refugees" had not resettled Nobletown, though there were many living just over the border in Massachusetts in 1775: their accounts of the violence in 1766 must have underlain the militancy of the new hill town settlers against both the British and the claims of the Van Rensselaers to regional authority. The Nobletown-area militia regiment, the Ninth Albany, was clearly one of the most dependable in the county and was called up time and again to march to Kinderhook, to the Manor, across the river to the Helderberg hills, and up the Mohawk Valley to overawe suspected tories and to defend the state's western frontier.[32]

Behind this militance lay a political struggle that unfolded in August and September 1775. The organization and command of militias was already a highly charged issue, and its Revolutionary reorganization would shape the civil history of the region for decades to come. On August 15, the Albany County Committee approved a plan of county regiments that assigned three to the southeast: one for Livingston Manor, one for Claverack, and one for Kinderhook and King's District, reproducing the table of organization established between 1767 and 1772 by Governor Henry Moore and Sir William Johnson. This replication of the colonial militia structure was immediately rejected by the people in the hills. That September the county committee received a barrage of petitions from Claverack, sponsored by Peter Van Ness, complaining about the organization of the militia and demanding the election of new committeemen to represent the eastern settlements. The resulting enlargement of the district committee and division of the Claverack regiment into eastern and western battalions brought a proliferation of civil and military positions for the eastern men. The new regimental command brought a de facto emergence of a political community in the hill communities of east Claverack (in what would become the district of Hillsdale in 1782). At the same time, the King's District, which formerly had done militia duty with either Kinderhook or Claverack, was given its own regiment, the Seventeenth. The two new hill town regiments would be the most dependable in the region, their men continually serving arduous duty.[33]

The political power of this border region was manifested in May 1776, when Matthew Adgate of the Canaan neighborhood in the King's District was elected to replace Peter Silvester of Kinderhook, who was suspected of loyalism, as a deputy to the Provincial Congress. The following month, the King's District and the Spencertown settlement in future Hillsdale each voted resolutions of independence, the only such resolutions voted in all of the state. In the King's District William B. Whiting, colonel of the Seventeenth Albany Regiment, chaired a committee to instruct deputy Adgate to support independence and a new constitution. With these votes, Whiting and Adgate were established as powerful fixtures in the politics of the new state: for virtually the next two decades one or the other would sit in the state assembly or senate. With Jacob Ford, both took positions opposed to the old landlord oligarchs: in the mid-1780s Alexander Hamilton would curse Ford and Adgate as "a couple of New England adventurers" "of the *levelling kind*." In early August 1776, as the British forces were settling into their long occupation of New York City, the need for a legitimate structure for government became paramount. When the provincial convention began to consider such a constitution, Matthew Adgate, representing Albany County on the strength of the votes of the King's District, demanded that the drafting committee "prepare and report a bill of rights; ascertaining the essential rights and privileges of the good people of this State." Six months later, in January 1777, a loyalist kidnapping plot powerfully signaled the political triangulation between loyalists and conservative and radical patriots. Ignoring the oligarchic Livingstons and Van Rensselaers as irrelevant to the patriot cause, the tory conspirators had targeted Adgate, Whiting, and Peter Van Ness, respectively the provincial representative and the colonels of the King's District and east Claverack (Hillsdale) militias.[34]

If the men of the hill districts thus rose to political authority with the Revolution, no such extension of civil life occurred on the Livingston Manor or even in Claverack proper. The Manor committee was carefully controlled by the Livingstons, to the point that one election saw only a single voter turn out. So were the Manor and Claverack regiments, where Colonels Peter R. Livingston and Robert Van Rensselaer retained the landlord's traditional command while they sat—glowering at Matthew Adgate—in the provincial convention. The struggles of the 1750s and the 1760s, combined with an expectation of deference and oligarchical authority, meant that the tenants would be given no autonomous public institutions. They would have no purchase on a civil space that was not controlled and orchestrated by their landlord. This exclusion would have powerful consequences in the decades to come.[35]

LOYALISTS AND PATRIOTS IN KINDERHOOK:
PETER VAN SCHAACK'S PROBLEM OF CONSENT

Thus in some parts of future Columbia County the Revolution was a moment of emergence into the public political arena, and in others it saw the persistence of old patterns of oligarchic control. In one place, Martin Van

Buren's Kinderhook, resistance to the Revolution was grounded in deeply rooted traditions of local autonomy and authority. The story of the Revolutionary struggle in Kinderhook would echo well into the following century, as Van Buren elided the struggle between the Democrats and Whigs of the age of Jackson and that between patriots and loyalists of his father's day.

In the closing months of 1777 a notable group of loyalists in the district of Kinderhook made trouble for the patriot leadership of Albany County and the new state as a whole. The Hessians who marched through Kinderhook in October 1777 were well aware of local tensions. Among the tories "who bemoaned their fate" to Hessian officers was a "man named Van Schaaken" who "showed us many little attentions, and was a kind friend to us." This was David Van Schaack, one in a wider connection of loyalists in Kinderhook. His brother Peter Van Schaack was the leading figure among the wealthy Dutch freeholders in Kinderhook, a group that, displaced from local authority, for more than a year had refused to sign oaths of allegiance to the Revolutionary state. A year later many of these Kinderhook loyalists would be banished, and Peter Van Schaack would spend the next six years in exile in London. Others, among them John D. Goes, would evade the banishment orders and remain in hiding with their families; well before his banishment was lifted, Goes's wife Maria gave birth to their daughter Hannah. Hannah's future husband, Martin Van Buren, had been born in an ardently patriot household a few months before. Their marriage in 1807 would be only one point in a long healing of the wounds inflicted in Revolutionary Kinderhook, a healing completed only in July 1832, when Martin Van Buren sat down to make his peace with a bedridden and dying Peter Van Schaack.[36]

Kinderhook loyalism was quite distinct from that of the other tories in Albany County, and in that difference they illustrate the complex calculus of consent and civil society in determining Revolutionary allegiance. In January 1777 Peter Van Schaack had debated the finer points of the Lockean principle of consent with New York's provisional convention. If the colonies had fallen into a state of nature, Van Schaack argued, it required the explicit, voluntary consent of each individual to establish a new social compact: *"Every individual has still a Right to choose the State of which he will become a Member; for before he surrenders any part of his natural Liberty . . . the Subjection of any one to the political Power of a State can arise only from his own Express consent!"* Here Van Schaack was not positing a model of perpetual allegiance, in which birth in a given civil society required automatic consent. As did many other loyalists, he worked within the rubric of the whig paradigm, in which general Lockean ideals of the social "compact between rulers and the people" was the "only foundation of all legitimate governments." Tyranny would constitute grounds for breaking the compact, but tyranny was not proven. Rather than ministerial tyranny, Van Schaack saw a Revolutionary tyranny. The combination of legislative, judicial, and executive functions in the provisional convention and committees of safety was a "union of powers" that "puts an *end to liberty,*" he argued, invoking the "immortal Montesquieu." In the meantime the government had not yet proposed a constitution, and Van Schaack "conceive[d] it is premature, to tender an oath of allegiance." Among the patriot whigs, the oaths of the General Association were the vehicle of achieving consent and consensus in the face of a tyrannical empire; in Van Schaack's eyes, the oaths were a vehicle of involuntary, forced allegiance, a coercive civil structure to be resisted by a moral man.[37]

In January 1776, driven by "times of civil commotion," Van Schaack had set down his thoughts on the Revolutionary crisis, the rights of men, and the "nature of government." Here he posed the loyalists' conundrum: "As a man is bound by the sacred ties of conscience, to yield obedience to every act of the legislature so long as government exists, so, on the other hand, he owes it to the cause of liberty, to resist the invasion of those rights, which, being inherent and unalienable, could not be surrendered at the institution of the civil society of which he was a member."[38]

But did government still exist? And in what civil society was Van Schaack a member? Here lay the paradox of the Revolutionary situation. By the winter of 1776 there were two governments, two civil societies, competing for the allegiance of colonial Americans. In Peter Van Schaack's mind, only one was legitimate. In August 1777, as Burgoyne bore down from the north, a Kinderhook conversation inspired Van Schaack to craft some thoughts on the nature of civil war in a "political community" and the "distinction between the rights of the government which is resisted, and of those in power making the resistance." Where the "old government . . . has a right to consider all its former subjects still as such," the rebels could "only be considered *a voluntary association,* having right to command the active personal services of such alone *as have joined them.*" Clearly, Van Schaack saw legitimacy only in the "old government," the British Empire.[39]

For all his concerns as he was being pressed by the Albany County Committee to make a choice of allegiance, the issue of consent might have only recently emerged as a priority in Van Schaack's thinking. Between May 1774 and May 1775 he had engaged in the Revolutionary movement as a member of committees in New York City, with hopes of obtaining a redress of grievances within the whig definition of the imperial relation. But, following the deaths of several children, he and his family returned to Kinderhook, and there he found the limits to his opposition to the empire. By January 1776 he was sure of two things. First, the acts of Parliament, however objectionable, did not "manifest a system of slavery." Without a demonstrable tyranny there was no ground for revolution within the doctrine of consent, and he could not "think the government *dissolved;* and as long as the society lasts, the power that every individual gave the society when he entered into it, can never revert to the individuals again, but will always remain in the community." Second, and perhaps more important, membership in the "controlling common empire" was a positive good. The colonists' due subjection to Parliament was grounded in "the same compact which entitles us to the benefits of the British constitution, and its laws." They would "derive advantage even from some kind of subordination," since independence would "be introductive of anarchy and confusion."[40]

If he could have remained under the "old government," Van Schaack would have left power in the hands of the "community"; now subject to the Revolutionary *"voluntary association,"* he invoked his individual natural rights. In the end, if he was driven to think about rights and consent by the Revolutionary crisis, he would have been far happier to remain within the "benefits" and "advantage" of the British Empire. The Van Schaacks and the leading families in Kinderhook clearly had reason to prefer these benefits and advantages of the imperial connection. Following service as a militia officer in the Seven Years' War, Peter's brother Henry had suffered at the hands of the Albany City gentlemen who refused to allow his solicited appointment as a stamp tax collector in 1765. Appointed in 1770 to administer oaths of office in Albany County, Henry Van Schaack grounded his refusal to support the patriot cause in the sanctity of sworn oaths and removed himself across the Massachusetts border to Richmond and then to Pittsfield. Peter Van Schaack had followed a path to King's College and then to the law as his way toward provincial eminence. Married into a rich New York merchant family before graduating from King's in 1766, Van Schaack read law in Albany with his brother-in-law Peter Silvester, lawyer to Sir William Johnson, the Mohawk Valley baron, before joining the office of William Smith, one of New York's leading lawyers and also a future loyalist. Van Schaack rose rapidly, helping to form an elite "Moot" association of New York lawyers before being chosen to edit a complete revision of New York's colonial laws enacted since 1691. This project, completed in 1773, "a work which, in its nature, and as the basis of its usefulness," his son wrote decades later, "contemplated the stability and permanency of existing institutions."[41]

Peter Van Schaack's rise to prominence in English law suited the needs and traditions of the Dutch freeholders of Kinderhook, and others, including Martin Van Buren, would follow his path. Fiercely loyal to the Dutch

Reformed religion and its household traditions, the Kinderhook freeholders were perhaps particularly isolated and embattled. The world of the New York Dutch farming household was a bounded one, in which public affairs outside of the domains of locality and the market were viewed with suspicion and kept at a distance. On the other hand, they had carved out their freeholds through a close attention to deeds and law, and into the nineteenth century lawyers like Van Schaack and Van Buren would build their legal careers on a close reading of the boundaries inscribed in the colonial patents underwriting the district's property and prosperity. Their conservative Dutch traditionalism encouraged the emergence of the Van Schaacks as effective cultural and legal mediators between Kinderhook and the centers of power in colonial New York and Albany.[42]

In the end it was not precisely ethnicity that explains loyalism in Kinderhook. Kinderhook's loyalists were Dutch, but their adherence was situational, not ethnic: at least two-thirds of their local patriot opponents were also Dutch. Sandwiched between the great manor of Rensselaerwyck to the north and the lesser Van Rensselaer manor of Claverack to the south, the leading Kinderhook families jealously guarded their claim to freehand land tenure and local authority, apparently "the weighty reasons" that Van Schaack found "of too delicate a nature to be put upon paper."[43]

Land meant everything in colonial New York, and the leading Kinderhook freeholders had acquired theirs through arduous struggle and aspired to more. In their path stood the magnates of Albany County. In 1762, the year that Van Schaack entered King's College, some of the Livingstons had claimed the De Bruyn patent, an important tract at the center of the district. Their conflict with the Livingstons extended to a challenge to their claim to the vast Westenhook patent, an indeterminate claim to lands east of Kinderhook proper dating back to 1705. Here Van Schaack probably had some particularly "delicate" motives, since his father, Cornelius, a merchant fur trader, shared in a 1743 claim to part of this eastern wilderness region, a claim that would be settled only in 1800.[44]

Interwoven with these affairs was another extremely delicate matter, the advancing claims of the Van Rensselaers. In 1769 John Van Rensselaer, the landlord at Claverack, had been commissioned to command a militia regiment encompassing Kinderhook. In this appointment Peter's older brother, Henry Van Schaack, had seen a great threat to Kinderhook's interests, as Van Rensselaer's powers of appointment over the Kinderhook militia would support his ceaseless efforts to expand the boundaries of Claverack north into Kinderhook. Similarly, the Van Schaacks were very concerned about Van Rensselaer influence in the appointment of justices of the peace. Succeeding in getting judicial appointments to their liking, they encouraged similar resistance to the Van Rensselaer interests and influence in the hill districts. Inside Kinderhook, this struggle between the district and the Van Rensselaers translated directly into the loyalist-patriot division. Henry Van Schaack condemned Isaac Goes and Peter Van Ness in 1770 as unfit for office by virtue of their "attachment to a Family [the Van Rensselaers] who aim at the Ruin of the Township"; the two would be stalwarts in the Revolutionary cause. Conversely, of the twenty-two Kinderhook men who petitioned against the scope of Van Rensselaer's regimental command in 1771, seven would be charged with loyalism in 1776 and 1777, and only one would be among the patriots.[45]

Thus in 1775 many in Kinderhook saw the necessity of an imperial counterbalance to the power of regional oligarchs, a structural relationship anchored by Peter Van Schaack's eminent profile as a lawyer in New York City. The empire and the law would protect them from the encroachment of the manors. By February 1775, the district had become notorious as a center of loyalist sentiment. That March a shrewd observer, the Reverend Thomas Allen, the Congregational minister across the state line in Pittsfield, wrote, "The poor Tories at Kinderhook are mortified and grieved and are wheeling about and beginning to take a quickstep." In May Peter Van Schaack moved his family from New York City to Kinderhook while his brothers continued to play roles in public affairs, Henry on the Albany committee, and Cornelius as a major in the Kinderhook regiment. But by September and October a patriot cadre was emerging in Kinderhook; led by Harmen Van Buren and his brothers, Peter and Francis, patriot dissidents began to complain to the Albany committee about the loyalist tinge of recent militia elections and the conduct of Dirck Gardinier, one of the local captains. Then in November, at the mandated election of the district committee of correspondence, the Kinderhook authorities led by Henry Van Schaack attempted to restrict voting to the "old freeholders." Claiming that all taxpayers, including tenants, had the right to vote, the emerging patriots led by Isaac Goes held a competing election at Tobias Van Buren's.[46]

Internal dissent brought outside intervention. Late in 1776 Peter Van Schaack complained that "Bodies of armed Men from Claverack and Kings District and from Massachusetts Bay had invaded the District [Kinderhook] and . . . had disarmed, dragooned, and ill treated the inhabitants," and the Albany County Committee had mandated that the new election be managed by a committee of outsiders. The situation festered through the winter and spring, with the traditionalist Kinderhook committeemen publishing "scurrilous" broadsides against the county committee and the county sending committees to investigate the district committee and militia officers. In the end,

Peter Van Schaack with two others precipitated the old elite's fall from power by refusing to take the oath of allegiance. Coming just as concerns about loyalist organization were surfacing, the county committee acted swiftly, sending militia to arrest Van Schaack and fifteen others, all taken into confinement at Albany.[47]

The district's Revolutionary affairs were supervised until January 1778 by the Albany County Committee, by patriot field officers of the Seventh Regiment, and by men from neighboring districts, and much of this supervision was punitive. The King's District committee was authorized to sell the property of accused loyalists to cover the costs of their arrests; subsequent investigations were usually given over to Captain Israel Spencer, of Spencertown in east Claverack. Spencer and his neighbor Jacob Ford would lead a body of militia and a committee of field officers that occupied Kinderhook during the great fear of tory insurrection that swept the county in the spring of 1777. But new, dependable officers were appointed to lead the Seventh Regiment; Harmen Van Buren and Isaac Goes, now majors, commanded Kinderhook contingents that marched to the north during the Saratoga campaign.[48]

By contrast with the loyalists, and even the small group of officers and committeemen serving since 1775 who were whigs, these new officers were decidedly poor. Among the more prosperous was Abraham Van Buren, father of the future president, whose own land put him at the top of the second wealth decile. Abraham's wealth derived from a strategic marriage. In 1776 he had married Maria Goes Van Alen, recently widowed: their combined property put their household solidly in the wealthiest tenth of the district. These were the "two young people" whom the marquis de Chastellux found "civil and attentive," albeit the proprietors of a "very small" public house, when he came out of the snow and sleet on his ride north in December 1780. The Van Buren tavern was indeed small, a story-and-a-half structure on his farm at the southern edge of the village. At the age of forty-three Abraham was not that young, and he had made his mark in Kinderhook's Revolutionary politics. Following his cousins into the political arena, he was in correspondence with the Albany committee by March 1776 and by April 1778 was appointed captain of the Kinderhook regiment's fourth company, in place of one of the "disaffected." This Revolutionary beginning would lead, more than a half century later, to the presidency of the new Republic.[49]

As this band of patriots rose to power, the Kinderhook loyalists endured trial after trial. Those arrested in June 1776 were soon released, and many took the oath the following spring. But in the summer of 1778, with the passage of a Banishing Act, many of them were recalled to swear again before the new Commission for Detecting and Defeating Conspiracies. Peter Van Schaack was summoned on July 16, John D. Goes on July 27, and even Abraham Van Buren's younger brother Martin (who became disaffected after six months' service as a lieutenant in the militia rangers) on July 29. All refused to swear and were ordered to be sent south to British-occupied New York City. Van Schaack eventually would go south and then take ship for London, seeking treatment for a diseased eye; Martin Van Buren (the future president's uncle and namesake) would survive the war in New York City. John Goes's departure was forestalled by his role as a witness in an impending capital case, and he began five years of internal banishment. In May 1779, confined to house arrest in the Schodack neighborhood of Rensselaerwyck, just north of Kinderhook, he petitioned to visit his family, as one of his children was desperately ill. In August 1780 he was finally listed to be sent through the British lines on a prisoner exchange, but Goes escaped to Great Barrington over the Massachusetts line, where he swore an oath and settled temporarily. In February 1783, a month before his daughter Hannah was born, he was described as having "secreted" himself and now being at home.[50]

THE CHALLENGE OF PEACE: FROM CRISIS TO ROUTINE

The passions of revolution and war would eventually fade. In the late summer of 1777, with Burgoyne's forces approaching from the north, Peter Van Schaack had sat down to write about the current crisis. He had no doubt that he was living through a civil war, arising "from a difference of opinion between members of the same political community." He would have smiled to have heard Gustave de Beaumont, Tocqueville's traveling companion in 1831, argue that the Hudson Valley for "a long time past has not known civil and political dissensions." Fifty-four years had certainly eased many of the passions of the Revolutionary era. Perhaps they were almost amusing by the turn of the century. Early in 1803, writing from New York with news of Kinderhook to John P. Van Ness in Washington, the young Martin Van Buren could describe echoes of Revolutionary hostilities with a certain bemused detachment:

> Esquire [Dirck] Gardinier and Captn Harmen V[osburgh have] been so near fighting that they had to hold them both, the dispute came about the cutting down of the Liberty Tree, the Captain feeling yet (tho old) the spirit of 76 could not feel pleased that a branch from that great Tree of Liberty, being planted on his soil, should be destroyed by the invading hands of federalists.[51]

Clearly, the twenty-one years since Martin had been born in the Van Buren tavern had not erased the passions of the Revolution. But now they seemed to be those of an older generation, almost amusing, and were now conflated with the contemporary passions of party, a continuity that would weigh on Van Buren in later years. In great measure, the central issues of allegiance and sovereignty ostensibly dividing patriots and tories would be moot once the Peace of Paris was signed. But for the next three decades echoes of the Revolutionary struggle in Kinderhook, a small-scale struggle between a rising Demo and entrenched Aristo, would shape Democrat Martin Van Buren's relations with the aging and imperious Peter Van Schaack and increasingly color his understanding of party in the new nation.

At the center of Martin's world would lie the populist movement that had driven the Revolution in this section of Albany County. His father, Abraham, and others of the patriot cadre maintained their ranks in the militia through the 1780s and into the 1790s, and these positions provided a platform for politics. Abraham Van Buren's company might well have met at his tavern, which was already emerging as a focus of Antifederalist and then Jeffersonian politics in Kinderhook. Both the militia and the public house must have played a part in his election to town clerk in 1787, a position that he would hold until 1796. And in 1788 the county sale of forfeited tory lands was held at the Van Buren tavern, just as Major Isaac Goes might have held similar sales at his tavern in 1777–1778, reputedly selling much of the family pewter of the local loyalists.[52]

As Martin and Hannah were born, and well before the signing of the peace and the evacuation of New York City, new vectors of civil life were already emerging. Some of the more radical—indeed Lockean—new directions unfolding in this region lay on or just over the cultural boundary separating New York from New England. A "New Light Stir" had been moving a spirit of revival among the Baptists of the border region since 1779. In this excitement missionaries from a small English sect, settled near Albany since 1774 and widely suspected of loyalist sympathies, started drawing followers in the New Lebanon neighborhood of King's District and neighboring Hancock, Richmond, and Pittsfield in Massachusetts. Despite violent mobbing of their missionaries, like that of an "Indian Club" in the neighborhood between King's and Kinderhook, these Shaker Believers were growing in numbers. In September 1787, on a high ridge looking west over the valley, they would gather as a society separate from the world and pose a powerful critique of the civil relation of men and women in that world. In the same year, racial slavery was being directly challenged over the border in Berkshire. An African American woman named Elizabeth, or Mum Bet, born a slave at Claverack Landing about 1740, had been taken to Massachusetts about 1758 to serve in Colonel John Ashley's household in Sheffield. In 1781, after suffering a reign of abuse at the hands of the Ashleys, Elizabeth took refuge in Theodore Sedgwick's household and successfully sued for her freedom, taking the surname of Free-man. Legend, certainly apocryphal, has it that she married Tom Burghardt, enslaved to Conradt Burghardt—who had moved from Kinderhook up to the new Berkshire settlements in the 1730s—and freed following military service in the Revolution.[53]

These Lockean challenges to patriarchy and slavery presented fundamental challenges to the social order of lower Albany County. Such changes were brewing in other important arenas as Henry Livingston's Aristo families began to feel the heat of Revolutionary transformation. In May 1782 John Van Rensselaer of Claverack, deeply in debt, tried to hold a large portion of his lands together by willing them "in tail"—and thus blocking their sale outside the family—to his grandson John Jeremiah. Less than two months later the government of New York abolished the legal doctrines of entail and primo-geniture, dealing a powerful blow to the sociology of the leasehold system that controlled vast stretches of land in the new state. That spring and summer the legislature had passed acts that began to address the land questions in the hill regions to the east. One of these statutes established the district of Hillsdale out of the eastern part of Claverack, a process that had begun seven years before with the expansion of the Claverack committee and the establishment of the Ninth Regiment. The oligarchic grip of the manor lords was being loosened by a logic of civil freedom flowing from the Revolution.[54]

The next year brought both old and new trajectories to the region. John Van Rensselaer died in February 1783, and that April his son-in-law General Philip Schuyler began a campaign to assert control of lands in the hill country that would soon bring the region back to the edge of civil war. But 1783 also brought new people and a new social form to Claverack: a group of Nantucket Quakers decided to establish a port for shipping and whaling at the old merchant privilege at Claverack Landing. By that fall families had begun to arrive; in May 1784 the first proprietors' meeting was held in what would soon be the city of Hudson. While the hill regions echoed with wild Shaker chants and a popular politics of resistance to neofeudalism, the new city on the Hudson would bring a new middling and urban refinement, a world of commerce, newspapers, societies, and eventually the steamboat.[55]

These years also saw the restoration of many former loyalists to civil life. Opinion was divided in Kinderhook and the King's District, where resolves and petitions for and against loyalist civil rights were voted and circulated in the spring of 1783. But that spring the assembly passed legislation that terminated the work of the Conspiracy Commission, and the following year a bill was passed that established a process to restore rights to loyalists like the Van Schaacks. By May 1786, ten months after his return from England, Peter Van

Schaack was restored to civil privileges in the state of New York. Martin Van Buren the elder resettled in Schodack, and John D. Goes, once quartermaster of the old Kinderhook regiment, was reappointed a lieutenant in the militia reorganization in 1786, in Captain Abraham Van Buren's company. John Goes was dead by 1795, when his widow Maria had seats in the north gallery of the Dutch Reformed church in Kinderhook village, across from the Van Buren bench on the main floor. Such would be the foundations of the marriage of Martin and Hannah. The details of their relationship are lost, but the experiences of the competing factions in Revolutionary Kinderhook — and their settlement — must have run as a subtle undercurrent through their twelve-year marriage.[56]

Peter Van Schaack, Martin Van Buren the elder, and John D. Goes all refused to take oaths of allegiance in 1777 because they would not be coerced into granting their consent to a new social compact. Rather than real loyalists, they were touchy neutrals and anxious to maintain a hard-won status in an oligarchic society. But the winter of Martin's and Hannah's births saw the first initiatives leading to the settlement of this problem of a founding consent to a new sovereignty. The war was over, and an independent sovereignty had been established. The victors could afford to be magnanimous, especially to those who were suitably contrite.

Before them lay a new order of things. First, Revolutionary violence would have to be set aside. For eight years significant political differences had been settled by the mobilization of militias on the authority of committees and the state government, upheld by electoral majorities. Until the Peace of Paris, sovereignty and civil inclusion were determined by the sword. New York and the other new states in the Confederation were militarized societies and polities, but with peace authorized force could no longer stand behind the arbitration of fundamental political disputes. This new order required voluntary consent to constituted procedure. Affairs of governance would have to adhere to precise limitations established by constitution and statute. The Revolutionary contest over sovereignty would have to give way to the routine enactment of sovereignty. When these routines had been established and proved enduring, a true settlement of the Revolution, in the widest sense, had been achieved.

This revolutionary settlement would take place in an evolving space that was already called civil society. But the shape of that space was going to evolve extremely rapidly in the coming years. Most contemporaries in the early 1780s would have been comfortable with a definition of civil society as political society, in the ancient republican formulation. Indeed, the militarization of politics and the identification of consent as allegiance during the Revolution had intensified this republican model: public affairs were absolutes requiring a rigid attention to the common good. But the end of the armed struggle meant the end of coerced unanimity and the pursuit of private interest. Initiatives in public would be pursued by combinations of men in association, combinations with various agendas and motives. If not fully recognized by contemporaries, civil society would rapidly move toward its modern Tocquevillean form, as an arena of association, persuasion, and deliberation mediating between constituted state and private society.

But who would participate, and on what terms, in this revolutionary settlement, this enactment of sovereignty in civil society? Who would be included in that civil society, and on what terms would they convey their political consent? The constitution of the new state, written and promulgated in 1777 after considerable debate, set these terms in clear language. Political participation, at elections, on juries, and in office, would be restricted to men arranged along a gradient of property; women had no place in governmental affairs, and slavery would maintain a barrier of civil death at the bottom of society.

The constituted inequalities of the 1777 constitution were plain to the King's District meeting: the attending voters "express[ed] their contempt for the constitution by their refusal to officer it, or to act under its provisions." If the voters of King's soon had to act within the terms of this constitution, they and others would not forget their objections. With the coming of peace the fundamental problem of civil inclusion had shifted from allegiance to the layers of property and dependency that were so particularly deeply entrenched — and so ardently contested — in this slice of the new American republic on the east bank of the Hudson. The establishment of a public sphere of deliberation and persuasion in what was soon to be Columbia County would be immensely complicated by the enduring "hard tryal . . . between Demo and Aristo." And in turn the intensity of that inherited and refigured conflict would make expanding the civil settlement of the Revolution beyond free white men all the more difficult.[57]

I

The Revolutionary Settlement

2

Conflict and Civil Establishments
1783–1793

TO BE SOLD, *By Ashbel Stoddard,* At his Printing Office in Hudson . . .

The TEN POUND ACT. With the Supplementary Act, passed by the Legislature in April last. Price one Pistareen.

An Act for Regulating the FEES of the several OFFICERS and MINISTERS of the COURTS of JUSTICE within this STATE. Price one Pistareen.

The Hermit. A Poem. By Dr. Parnelle.

The Way to Wealth. Written Dr. B. Franklin.

A CHARTER, incorporating the Inhabitants with the City and Liberties of HUDSON. Price 2s. . . .

N.B. Two coppers per pound given for any quantity of clean linen or cotton RAGS; or one copper per pound for old sail cloth, etc.

—*Hudson Weekly Gazette,* May 18, 1786

New-Canaan, Dec. 29, 1786

Last Wednesday being the anniversary of St. John the Evangelist, a number of Brethren of the Ancient and Honourable Society of Free and Accepted Masons, met at the house of Elihu Phinney, innholder, to celebrate the feast. A learned and well adapted discourse was delivered, in the Meeting-House, on the occasion, by Rev. Mr. John Camp, to a respectable audience. The day was spent in innocent mirth and festivity, and much to the satisfaction of the Brethren and Spectators.

—*Hudson Weekly Gazette,* Jan. 4, 1787

As Martin Van Buren and Hannah Goes entered early childhood in the mid-1780s, the public face of their upper Hudson world was changing in fundamental ways, literally leading the state into Alexis de Tocqueville's America. A new civil landscape was taking shape, layered onto and competing with previous civil landscapes, and in that uneasy competition forging a synthesis of privileged centers that would command consent in the new age. Where the Revolution had raised up a militant popular politics against the old oligarchic order, both of these would have to establish a relationship with a new culture of bourgeois improvement. From the end of the war into the 1790s these three civil paradigms would spar and chaff with one another before a clear new synthesis of civil authority, a revolutionary settlement, emerged.

A NEW PUBLIC LANDSCAPE

First came commerce, followed by print and new civil institutions. In the spring of 1783, six months before the British evacuated New York City, a proprietary association of Quakers from Nantucket and Providence purchased land at Claverack Landing to establish a center for trade and whaling on these northern reaches of navigable water on the Hudson. Within two years they had successfully moved a charter for their new city of Hudson, the first in the state's post-Revolutionary history, through the legislature to enactment. In that same spring of 1785 Ashbel Stoddard and Charles Webster, until recently apprentices at the office of the Hartford *Connecticut Courant and Weekly Advertiser,* established their *Hudson Weekly Gazette,* the first of a series of newspapers that began publishing in the river towns between Albany and New York in the latter half of the 1780s. The new city begat a new county. In April 1786 this southeastern region of Albany County was set off as the county of Columbia, the first new county to be formed in New York after the Revolution. The granting of the county's charter coincided almost to the day with the opening of post offices, under private contract with the Confederation government, in Kinderhook, Claverack, and Livingston, along the north-south stage route established in June 1785 connecting Albany with New York City.[1]

Commerce, print, polity, and communication were matched by private institutions of sociability and politeness. At the close of the war the Grand Lodge of Free and Accepted Masons was reorganized in the city of New York, and by the fall of 1788 three new lodges had been formed in Hudson and outlying districts. December 1786 saw the first Masonic celebration of Saint John's Day in the limits of the new Columbia County, at the meetinghouse in New Canaan in the old King's District. When these Masons received their warrant for the Unity Lodge in September 1788, they followed the Hudson Lodge, warranted in March 1787 as the fifth new lodge in the state. The Hudson Lodge in turn had followed the establishment of the Temple Lodge, located just south of Livingston Manor in Dutchess County, warranted in September 1785, the first warrant issued by the new Grand Lodge. The Masons of the Hudson Lodge contributed to an enduring associational sociability in the new city on the river, but they were second to the young men of the city who had already formed the first of many debating groups in Hudson, a "sociably speaking society." These young men and the young women they were courting might well have attended dancing classes held that summer in Hudson and in neighboring Claverack by an itinerant French dancing master or borrowed books from a small circulating library offered that year by a city merchant. Six years later plans were afoot for a bank in Hudson; proprietors of the city, officers of the county, and members of the Hudson Lodge would all be among the first board of directors of the Bank of Columbia, the third bank chartered in the state, proudly announced in the *Gazette*.[2]

By 1793, a decade after the signing of the Peace of Paris, the new county could boast of great improvements, for an entirely new civil landscape was taking shape on the east bank of this stretch of the Hudson. Indeed, Columbia County led the entire state in its transition into the institutional infrastructure that would define the nineteenth century: a new commercial brick city, a thriving county newspaper and printing office, a string of post offices and Masonic lodges, and a bank. This new civil landscape differed in fundamental ways with that upon which it was imposed. Revolutionary civil and military institutions had, compared to the oligarchic authority of late colonial society, worked as vehicles of popular empowerment. In contrast to the multifunctional and inclusive structures of Revolutionary institutions, the elements of the new post-Revolutionary civil landscape were socially bounded and functionally specific. If the Revolutionary institutions had used coercion to enforce the common good, the new institutions were grounded in an ethos of sensible improvement. Men would voluntarily associate for mutual betterment, partaking of institutions in which the common good was advanced by deliberation and persuasion. Where critical authority had once been vested in publicly elected company officers and committeemen, now printers, privately elected society presidents, merchants, and the taverners hosting the mails and the stage would serve as cultural gatekeepers in this public sphere. Free association and communication would be the vehicles of this new order of things, an order of things that historians are increasingly calling the public sphere.

COLONIAL OLIGARCHY, REVOLUTION, AND
THE BEGINNINGS OF THE PUBLIC SPHERE

Of course, the founding of a newspaper, a few lodges and societies, and bank did not change the region's civil order overnight. Traditional public institutions did not disappear. The new county courts established in 1786, and duly noticed in the *Gazette,* operated essentially on terms established under colonial law, as did the local districts, even when reorganized as towns in a sweeping law passed in 1788. The militia, now organized into a county brigade headquartered at Claverack, met for yearly musters, though it was not the same popular institution that had acted as the arm of the committees and the Revolutionary state. Churches, old and new, Reformed and Dissenting, English, Dutch, and German, continued to provide a pervasive public experience for the people of the new county.

To further blur the picture, some of the new institutions had begun to appear in the last decade of the colonial epoch. The colonies, and the United States itself, occupied the outer edge of an eighteenth-century British cultural domain, an expanding vortex of newspapers, clubs, and lodges. These institutions of the public sphere had just begun to arrive on the upper Hudson by the 1760s, and they would have expanded, with or without the Revolution. But the Revolution did make a difference. If they were beginning to emerge, institutions of the public sphere barely impinged upon even the middling people of the pre-Revolutionary upper Hudson. Down to the Revolution the secular print and voluntary association of the public sphere remained a privilege of urban places or of the landlord oligarchy, who assiduously continued to practice a politics of courtly and personal representation. Indeed, it can be argued that there was little or no formal public sphere in this region before 1775, and during the Revolution itself public association and communication fell under the direct and coercive authority of the Revolutionary state. The Revolution both delayed the spread of these new institutions and profoundly altered the terms upon which they suddenly developed in the 1780s.[3]

There had been a few societies, lodges, and even a newspaper and printing office in the upper Hudson region in the years just before the Revolution, a thin but recognizable manifestation of a wider thickening of print and association in the colonies. If they comprised a public sphere, it was distant and almost invisible to the people of the districts on the east bank, totally inadequate to the task of mediating between society and the state. Three pre-Revolutionary lodges were founded in nearby riverfront towns, two in the 1760s in Albany and one in 1771 to the south in Poughkeepsie. In Albany the Union Lodge derived its warrant from a British regimental lodge; among the few from Columbia who seem to have been initiated before 1775 were two Kinderhook loyalists, John D. Goes and Dirck Gardinier. The leading brethren of this and Master's, the second lodge in Albany, also met between 1767 and 1774 in a secret, high-degree Lodge of Perfection; their number included Sir William Johnson, the lord of the Mohawk Valley, as well as men of Albany's established merchant families. Robert R. Livingston, Jr., the scion of the Lower Livingston Manor, was initiated into a New York City lodge sometime in the late 1760s, and in 1771, on the authority of the Grand Lodge, he constituted Solomon's Lodge in the village of Poughkeepsie, where his family had a considerable interest. By contrast, when the Hudson Lodge began to form in 1787, it was led by men who had risen with the war. The lodge met at the tavern kept by John McKinstry, the Scots-Irish soldier from Nobletown who was now seeking his fortune in Hudson. Thomas Frothingham had been a gunner in the Massachusetts artillery; the first master, Seth Jenkins, operated a sail manufactory. Samuel Edmonds, master in 1797, a soldier at Monmouth and Yorktown, arrived in Hudson in 1784 with little more than his name and the clothes on his back. John C. and Peter B. Ten Broeck, Continental officers in the New York Line, did come from an old Claverack family, but they were in a distinct minority, and not of the landlord class.[4]

Livingston, with the other great landlords, actually did most of his socializing downriver in the city, where the assembly met and where the great families of the province gathered for much of the winter season for dinners, dances, and exclusive sociability. Robert R. Livingston, his Upper Manor cousins Robert, John, and Henry as well as rising Kinderhook lawyer Peter Van Schaack were all members of the Social Club, which met in Fraunces Tavern on winter Saturdays and at a private clubhouse on Kip's Bay in the summer; he was also a member of the young lawyer's "Moot" society (as was Van Schaack) and a manager of the city's Dancing Assembly.[5]

In these private circles these leading families practiced a sociability that wove together women and men. The Livingstons and Van Rensselaers and their Beekman and Schuyler relations were entangled in a web of kinship that made wives as important as husbands to the collective life of the oligarchy. Thus men and women of the great families practiced a polite salon culture in the drawing rooms and gardens of their manor houses that would have been as congenial to the earl of Shaftesbury as it would have been alien and disconcerting to the middling and yeoman households of the surrounding districts. In this refined world men and women would exchange manuscript poetry, play the latest French music, converse upon public affairs, and write private family histories. These exclusive circles of belles lettres and witty manuscript exchange would survive into the nineteenth century, blending into the more formal literary efforts of a later generation.[6]

The colonial culture of manuscript witticism reached a somewhat wider audience in the form of manuscript and printed broadsides, of which far too few have survived. These satires sometimes might be aimed at the oligarchs, but a manuscript broadside dating from the 1769 electoral struggle in Dutchess County also suggests that the power of print lay in the hands of the landlord families, who had easy contacts with city printers:

Judge Livingston's party contriving a scheme
To set up great papers and give some great bounty
For to be assemblymen in Dutchess County.

So pull down your papers, talk no more of bounty,
You can't be assemblymen in Dutchess County.
Your printed relation
Wants confirmation
Tho' signed by Judge Thomas Hand
Your writings are discreet
But in them there's deceit
Not a vote would you get if it wasn't for your land.[7]

In the early months of the Revolution the publication of satirical broadsides bedeviled the Albany Committee of Safety. In July 1775, Peter W. Yates, member of the Albany committee but also a past master of Albany's Union Lodge and a member of the secret Lodge of Perfection, had ridiculed the parade honoring General Philip Schuyler's entry into the city. The officials, his piece mocked, were in the line of march simply "Pro Tempore" or "thro' a mistake"; the "Troop of Horse" was a mixed lot, "most beautiful and Grand, Some Horses long taild, some bob Tailed, and some without any Tails, and attended with the Melodious Sound of an incomparably fine Trumpet." Yates's ejection from the county committee was "published in Hand Bills." Six months later another Union Lodge Mason, Dirck Gardinier of Kinderhook, was similarly hauled before the committee for publishing another anonymous paper, which "contain[ed] s[c]urrelous Reflections" against the committee.[8]

These printings were apparently struck off by James and Alexander Robertson, Scottish printers who settled in Albany and started printing the *Albany Gazette* in December 1771. In this first paper published north of New York City, the Robertsons had attempted to set a tone of polite refinement, promising "a pleasing variety of recent occurences, instructive Pieces, and curious Anecdotes, properly arranged." Their paper had a decidedly Tory tone, publishing a complaint that, since "the public prints" recently had devoted so much attention to John Wilkes's challenge to Parliament, "Party dissensions have laid the ax to the very root of literature," and printing a fawning letter from the Grand Lodge in New York City on Sir John Johnson's "Accession to the Chair as Provincial Grand Master." The Robertsons gave up their *Gazette* in November 1772, departing for Norwich, Connecticut, where from 1773 to the summer of 1775 they printed the *Norwich Packet* with John Trumbull. By September 1775 they were back in Albany; regularly paid for printing handbills for the county committee, they apparently also struck off "s[c]urrelous" broadsides for Yates and Gardinier as well. Early in 1776 they fled, burying their press somewhere outside the city; their final port of call was British-occupied New York City, where they printed a *Royal American Gazette* from January 1777 until evacuating for Nova Scotia in 1783.[9]

Despite the *Albany Gazette*'s being offered by merchant-agents along the river, including in Claverack and Kinderhook, where Peter Van Schaack's father, Cornelius, managed subscriptions, the Robertsons had failed to find sufficient readership for their paper in pre-Revolutionary Albany County. If their loyalist inclinations contributed to this failure, no corresponding whig paper sprang up to serve the county either. It seems that the news was supplied sufficiently by city papers, carried in small numbers by sloops up from New York and distributed at the landings, taverns, and great houses along the river. A smaller trickle of trade brought papers from Boston and Hartford to the east. But the public sphere, as a print domain of deliberation and persuasion grounded in political information and cultural creation, was not widely apparent in pre-Revolutionary Albany County. The institutions of publicity were limited and distant, inaccessible to the majority in print as well as in association.[10]

The Revolution brought only the beginnings of change, and then subject to the exigencies of war. Information was a closely guarded secret, and rumor was rife in the wartime valley. In March 1781 the state imposed a draconian censorship, mandating a death sentence for anyone "preaching, teaching, speaking, writing, or printing" against the new government. Just as the loyalist Robertsons moved south into New York City, patriot printers moved north. In 1777 Samuel Loudon moved his New York *Packet* to the village of Fishkill, a Continental garrison at the lower end of Dutchess County; John Holt recommenced his New York *Journal* in Kingston briefly, before being burned out in the October 1777 British raid, following which he relocated in Poughkeepsie for the rest of the war. Holt had a contract with the state government and printed a considerable volume of state material, including the journals of the house and senate and the annual laws, during his term at Poughkeepsie. These were city printers in exile, and the British evacuation in 1783 allowed their return to New York.[11]

No local printers stood quite ready to fill their places: printing in Fishkill, Kingston, and Poughkeepsie had been a wartime expedient. Fishkill would not see another paper until the 1840s, Kingston not until 1792. In Poughkeepsie there was a semblance of continuity. Holt had suspended printing his *New-York Journal, and the General Advertiser* in January 1782 to print the state laws; his former journeyman Nicholas Power started a *Country Journal, and Poughkeepsie Advertiser* in August 1785, the first of a long dynasty of Poughkeepsie newspapers. But in the summer of 1785 Power was joining a new generation of young printers already publishing in the upper Hudson Valley. A new paper in Albany, the *New-York Gazetteer, or, Northern Intelligencer,* had been in print since June 1782, using the old Robertson press, resurrected from its grave outside the city. In May 1784 the junior partner of this venture, Charles R. Webster, converted the paper into the *Albany Gazette;* exactly a year later he joined Ashbel Stoddard in establishing the *Hudson Weekly Gazette.*[12]

In 1785 these were indeed young men. Power was twenty-five; Webster and Stoddard were twenty-three and twenty-two, respectively. But, from their printshops and bookstores in Poughkeepsie, Albany, and Hudson, these young men would dominate the culture of print in the region for the next thirty years. They would be key players in the building of a new civil landscape; the foundings of their presses were signal events in the construction of new civil spaces along the Hudson River.

The initiatives of the mid-1780s, bearers of a culture of bourgeois improvement, marked a fundamental reconfiguration of regional civil society. Their antecedents, the oligarchic and popular modes of the colonial decades and Revolutionary years, had each foreshortened the field of public life in critical ways. Colonial publics had been made up of isolated ethnoreligious communities linked to government through deference to the mediation of powerful landlord families. Secular public authority was encapsulated within the familial relationships and private understandings of the landlord families: politics was a closed, indeed privatized affair.[13]

The Revolutionary committees and militias radically reversed this pattern: bringing state power directly into society, straining if not shattering traditional lines of deference, and truncating the private in the name of the common good. In neither mode was there much space for a critical monitoring of the government and for deliberation by an informed public. Each might be seen as a variant of classical politics, in which civil society occupied a continuous field with the legislative, judicial, and military authority of the state, all devoted to the support of law and property. The new institutions of bourgeois respectability and improvement ventured in the mid-1780s violated this ancient configuration of civil society. They were private institutions with public purposes; they had carefully limited memberships; they had no statutory relationship with the state. They provided the associative and communicative means by which some of the people along the upper Hudson might begin to build a new space of public deliberation and persuasion. But the new post-Revolutionary institutions would fulfill some of the functions that Montesquieu had ascribed to feudal "secondary powers," now translated into the middle-class voluntary structures to which Tocqueville would attribute the stability of democratic America.[14]

In this insertion between state and private life, the institutions — and the projectors — of the new civil society were also mediating between two embattled political forces, the old landed oligarchs and the rising popular men of the Revolution. It was in this context, in April 1785, that Henry Livingston had written to his brother, Walter, in New York that Albany County "never had such a hard tryal since the Revolution, between Demo and Aristo, as it will have this election." A month later the *Gazette* was established in Hudson, beginning the process of moderating and transforming the struggle between oligarchic and popular forces in the county. What had been a two-sided contest suddenly became triangulated. The press and the new societies would challenge both oligarchs and popular men, establishing a vehicle of common local political information, deliberation, and monitorial oversight and erect new standards for personal and group conduct. In so doing it undermined oligarchic monopolies and opaque procedures and offered a route to a model of middling respectability independent of their traditional authority. On the other hand, the voluntary institutions, private societies with public purposes, also challenged the ethos of the committee-based politics of the popular men, which enforced refined standards of manners and sensibility that challenged the rough manners of men recently propelled by revolution to public prominence.[15]

In the short term, the new civil institutions would be arrayed decisively against the popular forces, their members siding with the landlord interest in supporting the ratification of the new Federal Constitution that emerged in September 1787. But the longer term, running down to the first years of the nineteenth century, would see a series of uneasy and shifting alliances and tensions among oligarchic, bourgeois, and popular politics. Groups of men, clusters of practices, and modes of publicity would combine and recombine in a complex transition. One outcome would be the first incipient political parties, Federalists and Republicans, that precociously developed in Van Buren's Columbia County. Each would include the legacy of the new civil initiatives of the mid-1780s. If Van Buren and his Republican associates tempered the Revolutionary popular tradition with bourgeois associationalism and print, so too did bourgeois forms temper the oligarchic imperatives behind Columbia's Federalist Junto.[16]

These complementary fusions were only one dimension of a wider civil development. Colonial oligarchy and Revolutionary action had provided only limited and problematic terms for the practice of consent by the people. Very rapidly, the new civil institutions forged in the 1780s would establish new and enduring terms for the practice of consent on the upper Hudson. These encompassed both active deliberation leading to an express consent and a more subtle persuasion intended to elicit tacit consent. In the deliberative arena (the central topic for the rest of this chapter and the next) the emerging relationships among associative civil spaces, a print-based imagined community, and the complex pursuit of interest and justice in state politics would establish the basis of a new legitimacy, eventually stabilized into the routine liberal political order. In a wider and more fluid arena of persuasion, the conventions of bourgeois respectability would become the terms of inclusion in this sacred circle of consent. Conformity to these conventions and construction by these conventions would determine the new and enduring shape of civil boundaries in this society (see Chapter 4).

DEMO AND ARISTO AND GEORGE CLINTON'S POLITICS OF REVOLUTIONARY SETTLEMENT

The close of the Revolutionary war found the people of the state of New York in a distressed condition. The upper Hudson counties north and south of Albany, free of British occupation, had been bled dry by the war effort; the southern counties and New York City itself had suffered the direct effects of military operations and British occupation. The restoration of prosperity would require physical and institutional rebuilding, which would unfold as patriots tried to settle scores with loyalists and neutrals, often their neighbors. Simultaneously, the question of a national government superior to the states — under debate since the opening of the Revolution — took on new life. The politics of the 1780s were thus an extended and complex process of settlement, a settlement that was required to complete the transition from the crisis politics of the Revolution to the routine politics of the coming century. Thus the sudden emergence of new institutions of civil society on the upper Hudson came at a particularly pivotal moment. Certainly a part of a tide of change washing across the wider Anglo-Atlantic world, the proliferation of societies and print in the 1780s also must be seen in the context of the politics of a revolutionary settlement; the new civil institutions played an essential role in that settlement and in the routines that followed in the years to come.[17]

New York's politics of the 1780s pitted the popular men united behind Governor George Clinton against more conservative forces, a coalition of commercial and landlord interests. This division had a geopolitical dimension, as Clinton's strength lay in the upper Hudson counties that had been the nucleus of the Revolutionary state, whereas the conservatives were stronger in the lower counties, once bastions of commercial wealth, now struggling to recover from the direct effects of the war, including the reintegration of large numbers of families that had either supported or not opposed the British. Led by Philip Schuyler and his son-in-law, Alexander Hamilton, these conservatives espoused the cause of strengthening the Confederation, leading ultimately to the Federal Constitution, ratified by New York in Poughkeepsie in July 1788.

The popular forces made their most conspicuous mark in the politics of a revolutionary settlement by opposing the conservatives on both state and protonational fronts. From the first sitting of the legislature in 1777 they worked to harass the loyalists, enacting statutes confiscating their property, limiting their right to collect debts, and after 1783 attempting to restrict their rights of citizenship. State taxes and commercial tariffs weighing on the lower counties were part and parcel of this politics of revenge. On the wider national stage, George Clinton and his faction stood for the primacy of the states, projecting New York as "the Empire State" in the postwar Confederation. During the war the Clintonian-controlled legislature had supported the Continental Congress, but in 1784 it began to resist the authority of Congress, culminating in votes in 1786 and 1787 that effectively denied the 5 percent impost duties that would have funded the Confederation and, by only a narrow margin, approved delegates for the convention that sat in Philadelphia in the summer of 1787 to write a new Federal Constitution.[18]

But the politics of revenge and antinationalism were only one part of the Clintonian agenda. Equally important, the Clintonians worked to address the material and institutional needs of a state and a people worn down by war and mired in a postwar depression. The resistance offered by the conservatives points to the often misinterpreted activism of the state legislatures in the 1780s. While the Clintonians were suspicious of a powerful and activist national government, they believed in a powerful and activist state government, closely responsive and attentive to the needs of the people at large. To the end of a distributive improvement, the Clintonians in 1784 moved comprehensive legislation to rebuild roads and bridges, in 1786, after years of struggle over paper money, to establish a series of county loan offices that would make public loans on the model of colonial land banks, and in 1788 to pass a comprehensive restructuring of county and town governments. In Columbia County, besides a reorganization of local government, this legislation renamed the old King's District as Canaan, a name that expressed the evangelical vision of these squatter communities, settled by Connecticut families caught up in the New Light fervor of the Great Awakening of the 1740s. Throughout, the legislature attended to a rising tide of petitions from constituents asking for tax abatements, compensation for military service, grants of land, and establishment of new towns and counties, of bridges and academies—indeed, a full spectrum of issues bearing on the improvement and "good police" of this post-Revolutionary society.[19]

The legislature's responsiveness to these petitions made it the fundamental arena of a revolutionary settlement for the people of New York, by which their popular sovereignty was translated into statute law. Here the consequences of New York's revolution were manifested in many ways, as were political traditions running from the colonial past. New York's government had long attended to distributive interests; vast fortunes in landed wealth had been built in the colonial assembly and the governor's council, and this politics of acquisition would not disappear. But in the post-Revolutionary decades the numbers of people looking to government for distribution, for improvement, and for police were hugely multiplied, to the extent that they might reasonably see a public good in their collective private interests. The republican structure of Clintonian governance worked to emphasize the collective over the private, turning the state's tradition of distributive politics to the purposes of a revolutionary settlement. These settlement politics go a long way toward explaining why New York avoided Massachusetts's plunge into rebellion in 1786.

The Revolution had brought a new stratum of men into public leadership, more directly representing the needs and interests of constituent voters than had the old oligarchic gentry. Legislators circulated in taverns as much as in drawing rooms; they attended county committee meetings, which often coincided with the sitting of grand juries, assembling elective majorities as they accepted legislative goals, carrying petitions from their constituents, and attending to their progress through the legislature. Under the Clintonians, the post-Revolutionary legislature became an engine of an activist, distributive politics. The war years had seen an almost seamless web of civil institutions—the committees—linking localities with the legislature, and this structure informed the postwar Clintonian program: public expenditure and improvement were monitored by public oversight. Legislation established public committees to oversee the construction of roads and bridges, public loan officers managed the county loan offices, and the municipal legislation confirmed and enhanced the traditional roles of elected town and county officers. Clintonian policy thus perpetuated the interpenetration of state and civil society that had been so apparent during the war years.[20]

Conservatives, soon to be Federalists, opposed the Clintonian initiatives for reasons that went far beyond the question of a new national government. They complained of undue taxes on commercial interests and of the harassment of the former loyalists, who were emerging as their natural allies. They opposed the emission of paper through the loan offices and complained about the growing expenditures on roads, bridges, and especially local government. In the 1790s Federalists would privatize some of these functions, incorporating banks, canal companies, and turnpikes; if authorized by the state, these private organizations would be shielded from public civil intervention. Their emergence would mark the transition of New York's post-Revolutionary politics of distributive improvement from postrevolutionary settlement toward nineteenth-century routine. But in the short term the Clintonian model of public distributive improvement prevailed, with important consequences. To the east, the failure of the Massachusetts legislature to respond effectively to popular discontent led in these same years to civil war. But in New York the distributive public improvements sponsored by the Clintonians directly linked the people to the powers of their government, which in turn was reinforced by the stabilization and widening of participatory public life. Expectations of successful legislative response were thus already fundamental in a state where politics would be a way of life for centuries to come.[21]

The southeastern districts of Albany County, soon to be set off as Columbia, were an epicenter of this struggle, Henry Livingston's "hard tryal . . . between Demo and Aristo." Ever since the beginning of the Revolution the Demo men had been on the rise, led by the Connecticut squatters in the King's District and east Claverack. Matthew Adgate, who replaced conservative Peter Silvester of Kinderhook in the provisional convention in 1776, emerged as a democratic ideologue when he moved for the drafting of a Bill of Rights in the state constitution, though he would not abandon property-based suffrage. In the first assembly, sitting in Poughkeepsie in the spring of 1778, his neighbor William B. Whiting voted to support the radical policy of an embargo on the export of wheat, meal, and flour, and — in opposition to the landlord at Claverack, Robert Van Rensselaer — voted to tax the unimproved lands that made up such a large proportion of the oligarchs' wealth. Adgate took up Whiting's seat in 1780–1781, and Whiting in turn was elected the next year to a four-year term in the senate. With Jacob Ford from the hill settlements in east Claverack and their neighbor Philip Frisbie, Adgate and Whiting dominated the region's representation in the legislature into the mid-1780s. Between 1777 and 1785 these four popular men from the eastern districts sat in seventeen of the thirty terms served in the house or senate from the towns soon to comprise Columbia County.[22]

These were all new men to the region, thus their at-large election in Albany County was all the more remarkable, though it certainly must have been grounded in a high turnout in the squatter settlements along the Massachusetts border. They all shared roots in the Connecticut diaspora: Adgate and Whiting had come of age in Norwich, Ford just to the west in Hebron, and

Frisbie's family had followed a twisting trail of migration from Branford. Each was a New Light: Whiting was a Congregational deacon at the Four Corners church from 1785, and Ford late in life moved from the Congregationalists to the Baptists and would serve as the messenger to the Shaftsbury Baptist Association from the church in his Macedonia neighborhood in Hillsdale. Adgate would affiliate with the Canaan Congregationalists, but only after he published a personal interpretation of the Bible called *The Northern Light*. Frisbie would be a leader of the Canaan Democratic Society in 1794 and 1795 and by 1800 would be among the leading Methodists meeting in Chatham. During the war Whiting, Frisbie, and Ford, colonel and majors, respectively, had put in hard service leading militia contingents to Saratoga and to the Mohawk Valley against the British, and locally to Kinderhook and to the Helderberg region west of Albany against tories. Apparently lame and thus excused from militia service, Adgate was one of only three men elected to the legislature in these years who did not hold a staff-rank commission in the militia; he and all the Revolutionary legislators were members of the county committees.[23]

These four men, like so many rural New Englanders of their generation, carried this experience into the legislature, where their priorities mirrored those of the New Light and "Country" parties of eastern New England. In 1782, Adgate and Frisbie voted together to punish the loyalists, to restrict legal proceedings for debts, and to lower the governor's salary. Although Ford supported the loyalists in 1782, he voted with Adgate on virtually every other roll call in their years in the assembly, especially in 1784 and 1785, supporting protections for debtors, the emission of paper money and establishment of the loan office, and the passage of a state import tariff, on which Ford reported the committee's progress to the house in 1784. They voted consistently to investigate the lands held by the Anglican Trinity Church of New York, to defend state law against the terms of the peace treaty in the Rutgers-Waddington case, and to incorporate a Society of Mechanics in New York City, opposing the conservative Schuyler-Hamilton faction on all of these votes. In the senate William Whiting matched their votes, most notably in 1785 when he with Peter Van Ness of Kinderhook voted in decisive roll calls that killed both the grant of the 5 percent impost (an import tariff) to the Confederation and the petition for the incorporation of Alexander Hamilton's Bank of New York.[24]

Long before the spring of 1785 the radicals of the King's District had attracted the hostility of conservatives in their locality, in Albany, and in New York City. Robert R. Livingston's brother-in-law wrote darkly to him in Philadelphia of the "strong Democratic spirit" that threatened men of property: "The first stroke would be at the Tenanted estates, which the people on

PLATE 2. *Robert Livingston, Jr. (1708–1790). Third Lord of Livingston Manor.*
Courtesy, Collections of the New-York Historical Society

the borders of New England have already in contemplation, *entre nous*." In March 1782 an Albany city committee was unhappy with the "unequal representation" that King's had enjoyed "for these two years last" and planned to "promote" more conservative candidates, and the Livingstons of the Upper Manor tried and failed to impose one of their clan on the electorate. The effort backfired, and the representation from the radical King's District increased. The next year John Wigram, the Livingstons' manager, reported that efforts to impose a conservative slate had again failed and that an "alteration" to the list "will here be made among the people." In great measure the oligarchs' failure to push aside the popular men lay in their factional division into hostile and jealous centers of traditional power. The various great families of Livingston Manor and Van Rensselaer Claverack feuded among themselves and were challenged by the Dutch freeholders in Kinderhook. Each of these local aristocratic clans was also overshadowed by a united interest in Albany and New York, linking the Rensselaerwyck Van Rensselaers, the Schuylers, and their rising young relation Alexander Hamilton. In these divided circumstances the Yankee squatters of the eastern districts easily had overwhelmed the gentry of the old river districts.[25]

Circumstances changed in 1785. The King's District men had attracted the ire of Alexander Hamilton. Writing to Robert Livingston to agree to help to settle an old boundary dispute with his Livingston cousins at Clermont, Hamilton argued that "the state is now governed by a couple of New England adventurers — Ford and Adgate" and that "those who are concerned for the *security of property* or the prosperity of government . . . [should] endeavour to put men in the Legislature whose principles are not of the *levelling kind*." The solution lay in a reunification of oligarchic interests that would structure the politics of the region for decades to come. In June Robert Livingston replied to Hamilton that they had prevailed in the "hard tryal" of the April election. The lord of the Upper Manor wrote to New York that by "uniting the interests of the Rensselaer, Schuyler, and our family, with other Gentm. of property in the County in one interest . . . we Carryed this last Election to a man." Livingston was confident: "We shall always have the like Success provided we Stick Close to Each other."[26]

A NEW CITY: ESTABLISHING HUDSON, 1785

The new political alliance of the oligarch families produced an entirely new representation from the southeast Albany districts for the 1786 session: the April 1785 assembly election replaced Adgate and Ford, the hill district radicals, with John Livingston, Colonel Abraham Van Alstyne of Kinderhook, and Lawrence Hogeboom from Claverack, all men of conservative persuasion. But the legislature sitting in the winter and spring of 1785 had enacted a wide-ranging plan for civil improvement that made the gentry extremely nervous. The proprietors of the settlement of Quaker whaling families from Nantucket and Providence established at Claverack Landing since the summer of 1783 decided in February 1785 to submit a petition for incorporation as the city of Hudson. On March 9 they introduced three petitions to the legislature, meeting in New York City. In less than two months, on April 22, the Hudson bill, empowering the mayor and other officers of the new "Body corporate and politic" to make bylaws "relative to any Thing whatsoever which may concern the good Government and Police of the said City," had passed through the senate and the house and was enacted into law. Two weeks later, when he sailed up from New York with the new charter in hand, the city's lawyer, Ezekiel Gilbert, was celebrated with a thirteen-gun salute and a joyful display of flags by the ships docked on the Hudson wharf.[27]

Unfolding as the "hard tryal" of the 1785 election was under way, the movement for Hudson's incorporation had been ardently opposed by the people of Claverack and generated anxieties and strategic divisions among the local gentry. Many in the Van Rensselaer orbit in Claverack opposed the incorporation of the new city, more than two hundred inhabitants signing four petitions opposed to the city charter introduced into the legislature on March 10. But the Hudson petitions had the recommendation of another petition sent by "most of the respectable persons of the city of Albany," and the Livingstons were nervously supportive. Robert Livingston had written to his son Walter on March 1 that they deserved "all reasonable encouragement from the state." Henry Livingston wrote nervously the next day to his brother, Walter, about the Hudson initiative; he was having the Hudson delegation for breakfast before their departure and urged his brother, "It would be good to be civil to those persons . . . a dinner or two would be well for to give them." Despite the opposition of many Claverack people, a cluster of Van Rensselaers seemed to approve of the Hudson project. General Van Rensselaer was escorting the Hudson petitioners, and Henry Livingston urged his brother to sound him out but had no hopes of useful information. The lead signatures on the pro-Hudson petitions were Robert's brother James Van Rensselaer and their nephew John Jeremiah.[28]

Factional and local animosities almost derailed the bill. It had been moving easily toward passage in the senate when Colonel Peter Van Ness of Kinderhook, an old foe of the Van Rensselaers, suddenly arrived in New York on March 30 to take a senate seat won in a by-election in the Western District. Van Ness was clearly at work two days later when a petition from Cornelius

Hogeboom was introduced into the assembly asking for a ferry privilege at Kinderhook Landing, eight miles to the north of the new city, which was also asking for a ferry right; then the Hudson bill ran into a snarl of floor challenges, producing five recorded roll calls in the senate. The senate was suddenly concerned about the size of the new city and the protections that its inhabitants seemed to have from county jurisdiction, and Van Ness opposed the city on this and each of three subsequent roll calls.[29]

Despite its support from the Upper Manor Livingstons and the Van Rensselaers, the Hudson bill was part of a wider complex of Clintonian initiatives. It might have developed support during the previous year, when proposals were made in the debates over the state import tariff for collectorships to be established in northern river ports; in 1785, debates over the state collectorship produced arguments that a customs house be established at the "port of Claverack." The Hudson bill did not fare so well in the Council of Revision, a body made up of the governor and selected judiciary empowered by the 1777 constitution to review all legislation before final passage. Concerned about the autonomous powers of municipal corporations and incorporated societies in a republic, particularly the grant of judicial powers to elected city executives, the council cast a strongly worded veto. Among the council's members were two men with local interests, Robert R. Livingston of the Lower Manor, the chancellor of the state, and Richard Morris, the chief justice, the author of the veto of the Hudson bill, and a close friend of some of the Claverack gentry (having lived in the village as a refugee during the war). If they were attempting to assert an oligarchic concern that the city of Hudson might become a new and autonomous base of power, the judges' veto was overturned by the young city's allies in the senate and the house.[30]

Some of Hudson's political allies were firmly grounded in radical Clintonian politics, but others were more conservative. The new city had the support of the powerful Federalist Schuyler-Hamilton connection, which was enough to worry the Livingstons, but it also clearly affected their calculus of place and power in an evolving local civil geography. Writing to his brother, Walter, Henry Livingston set the Hudson petition into a wider regional struggle, most particularly about the future electoral composition of the upper Hudson counties. Before the Revolution, the Upper Livingston Manor had an independent representation in the assembly, though it also voted in the Albany elections, and the Lower Manor Clermont Livingstons had a powerful interest in Dutchess County. The Revolutionary committee structure and the 1777 constitution had put both Upper and Lower Livingston into Albany County, setting the stage for this struggle. In March 1785 Henry Livingston warned Walter that there were three petitions "going about in Dutchess County" that might affect their status. One would incorporate the entire Manor with northern Dutchess precincts into a new county, another was asking for funding to rebuild the jail at Poughkeepsie, and a third was proposing that only the Lower Manor of Clermont be incorporated into a new county in northern Dutchess. Henry's panicked exhortations of civility toward the Hudson petitioners were grounded in this calculus of county political geography. "How far all these Manouvers will tend to our Political weight in the county I am not Politician enough to determine," he wrote on March 2. The Hudson voters would "in a few years, have a great weight in our [county?] Elections and we will be in their county let what division take place. For heavens sake take these matters into consideration, and determine for us all." Henry was certain that the third petition was "the child of the Chancellor's"; convinced that "it will sale thro of itself," he urged his apparently sick brother, Walter (also serving in the Confederation Congress), to "crawl to the house to oppose." But the radicals in the assembly and senate had similar concerns, although based in contrary calculations of interest. Matthew Adgate led the house committee that gave short shrift to the petitions to divide Dutchess while his longtime Dutchess allies in the senate, Ephraim Paine and Jacobus Swartout, seem to have been the protectors of the Hudson legislation. Paine sat on the committee that wrote the Hudson legislation, and he and Swartout were two of the three senators who voted for the new city on all five senate roll calls.[31]

Thus in the wake of the Revolutionary war, the civil geography of the upper Hudson Valley was the subject of a complex political game of chess, with outcomes that would reach far into the future. New centers and boundaries being drawn on the civil landscape added new fears of marginalization to the growing worries of the old Aristo oligarchy, once unassailable, but now reeling from the impact of the Revolution. The rise of the Demo in the Revolutionary committees had severely challenged former habits and expectations of deference, and then the oligarchs' own behavior and performance had further undermined them in the eyes of the new state government and the public at large.

The Upper Manor Livingstons, enraged when, under the new 1777 constitution, they lost their "manor privilege" of a guaranteed seat in the assembly, were particularly suspect. During the war Robert Livingston and his sons Walter and Henry had been assailed for their speculative trade in wheat, iron, and other commodities, and Walter was removed from his position as a commissary in 1776. Robert's eldest son, Peter R., was considered utterly unfit to lead troops and eased out of his command during the western campaign in the summer of 1778. Robert Van Rensselaer of Claverack, though he survived to lead the local militia brigade for years to come, was court-martialed for failing to save the garrison of Stone Arabia in the Mohawk Valley in October 1780; Philip Schuyler himself was similarly court-martialed for losing the forts north of Albany to General John Burgoyne in the summer of 1777.[32]

If these proud men of the Aristo survived these ordeals, the trials were permanent scars on their public personas. More immediately, the 1781–1782 legislature had shattered one of the bedrock principles of the property basis of enduring aristocracy: it outlawed entail, the legal status by which land may not be alienated from a given family line, and primogeniture, which had guaranteed that the bulk of an estate might be willed to a primary heir. The Van Rensselaers in particular had attempted to circumvent the passage of this law by executing John Van Rensselaer's will in May 1782, nine months before his death in February 1783, entailing part of Claverack to John Jeremiah Van Rensselaer. This effort was blocked by the language of the July 1782 law, and, with the death of John Van Rensselaer in 1783 and then Robert Livingston in 1790, the new inheritance laws began a half-century process of partible division of manor lands. Landed estates burdened by debt and challenged by increasingly unruly tenants and squatters would now by law be divided among numerous heirs rather than be passed down to a single manor lord. The underpinnings of the old order were beginning to unravel.[33]

Hints of this transformation were apparent by the close of the Revolution. In the winter of 1781 Walter Livingston had been worried about the unwillingness of men among the great families to lead in local politics. Writing to a relative in 1781, he articulated the fears of his entire generation. A failure to act was leading to the abyss:

> If your son will not step forth (who is a man of independent fortune) who can he expect will and if every man says let others do it, our misfortunes are only beginning and must end in the subversion of the constitution in the place of which anarchy will rise and distinction between men will cease.[34]

"Distinction between men will cease." Here was the terror that lay deep below the gentry's response to the rise of the city of Hudson. Rioting tenants they knew how to deal with, and had done so for a half century; hard-driven men of commerce, building and sailing sloops and whalers to foreign ports and distant waters, trading with countrymen and the world alike, were a different matter. If they had to be treated with civility, given breakfasts and dinners, they threatened to turn the world upside down and to advance principles as leveling as any of their Demo allies among the radical Yankees of the eastern hills. But the commerce — and the pocket of urban culture — that they were building on the east bank of the Hudson might yet be turned to advantage.

Thus in the middle years of the 1780s these gentry families were desperately casting about for strategies to recover preeminence and preserve wealth. In the long term, the antebellum landlord generation that met Tocqueville and Beaumont would have withdrawn from politics into a grand isolation of mansions with Catskill views, into a belletristic literary culture epitomized by Washington Irving's satirical flights on a lost provincial world and by the patronage of the nation's formative grand landscape painting tradition. In the middle term, between 1798 and 1821, a corps of young Federalist lawyers would energetically and creatively construct institutions and culture in the public sphere in the interests of the landlord class. But in the short term, in the mid-1780s, the great families would work to contain the power of the rising new city while they encapsulated it in their own center of power, the courts and militia of the new Columbia County.

Just as Hudson was the state's first new city, Columbia was the state's first new county to be formed after the Revolution. Columbia's civil geography had its origins in August 1780, in the forming of a second militia brigade in Albany County from the towns that would in 1786 be incorporated into the new county. The brigade's commander, General Robert Van Rensselaer, had led an early effort to form a county from his combined militia beats, petitioning the assembly on March 30, 1784, that the east bank districts "be erected into a separate County," with a courthouse to be built "in or near Claverack." An undated list of "Propositions" apparently captures the county petition effort in the spring of 1783, specifying that the county petition "shall be tendered to the Electors to be signed before, or at the day of election" and that the subscribers pledged to "use their Interest for such nomination of candidates and promote the election of such candidates only, as shall be firmly attached to the plan of attaining a new county." The list of candidates included Philip Schuyler for governor, Peter R. Livingston for senate, and, among others, Abraham Van Alstyne, Peter Van Ness, and Henry Livingston for the assembly. The subscribers included Robert Van Rensselaer and Cornelius Hogeboom, the aspiring ferry operator at Kinderhook Landing. Though he was on this list of subscribers, Peter Van Ness had been outraged by Van Rensselaer's promotion to brigade command in 1780 and had threatened to resign his regimental command; in 1784 he might still have been unhappy when he presented his committee's report on the county petition, recommending that it be resubmitted the following year, where it died for lack of a sponsor in the radical 1785 house.[35]

The final effort to form the new county came in the spring of 1786, with

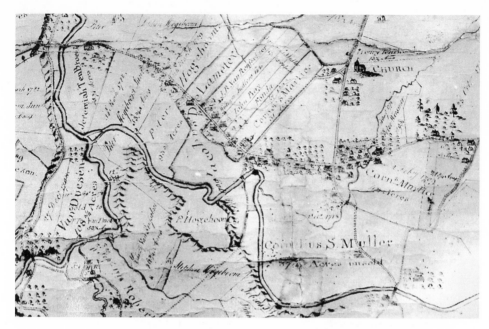

PLATE 3. *Claverack Center in 1799. Detail from the Penfield Map of Claverack Manor.*
Courtesy of the Columbia County Historical Society

new conservative representation in place. Peter Weismer of Claverack (who had attended the 1783 meeting and opposed the Hudson petition in 1785) headed one county petition, and Robert Livingston of the Upper Manor the other; the two petitions together drew as many as seven hundred signatures. They were introduced into the senate on March 2, and then on March 8 Philip Schuyler, newly elected to the senate, proposed the bill "to divide Albany County." Under Schuyler's oversight the bill passed the senate without a roll call ten days later and passed in the assembly by a large margin. The only possible hitch came in the assembly at the end of the month, when Seth Jenkins of Hudson hurriedly sent down a petition to be introduced by Schuyler, asking that the courthouse be built in the new city, not at *"Old Claverack."* Only eight assemblymen supported this petition, and a similar effort by five other groups of petitioners was equally quickly set aside in the senate.[36]

The local gentry had been defeated in their efforts to contain the 1785 Hudson petition and had then won a "hard tryal" in the 1785 election; they savored sweet victory in the 1786 legislature. Their three new assemblymen all voted to oppose the state loan office and to support the federal impost, overturning the radical votes of the previous years, if not prevailing. They did, however, achieve at least one significant outcome for the conservative cause. On April 4 the legislation incorporating the county was made law, stipulating that the courthouse be located at or near the old Dutch Reformed church in Claverack village. The day after the county's legislation was voted in New York City, three post offices were authorized by the Confederation to operate in the new county, under private contract along the new stage monopoly, in Claverack, Livingston Manor, and Kinderhook. Here Walter Livingston's influence might have been at work. The city of Hudson and the hill towns would have to wait until the 1790s for their own post offices and postal routes. Claverack, with a Confederation post office added to the new county courts, could now claim an honored place in the civil geography of the new Republic. The new county, the first in the post-Revolutionary state, was given the title of Columbia, the female emblem of the new Republic, evoking Christopher Columbus and the name recently bestowed on what had been King's College in New York City.[37]

With the other old river districts, Claverack also claimed the best part of the patronage that came with the county. Robert Van Rensselaer became the county clerk, serving until 1801; his cousin Killian was appointed the surrogate, with wide powers in matters of probate. Lawrence Hogeboom, one of the conservative assemblymen in the 1786 session, was appointed sheriff, and Dr. Walter V. Wemple (settled in the village since the late 1770s but with many connections in Albany, where he had once been a member of the secret Lodge of Perfection) served as county treasurer until his death in 1798. Hudson was represented only by Robert's brother, Henry I. Van Rensselaer, as a judge of the court of common pleas. Kinderhook got two appointments: Peter Van Ness would now sit as first judge of common pleas, and Peter Silvester, sidelined since 1776 for his loyalist inclinations, as an associate. Peter R. Livingston represented the Manor on the bench; the entire hill region of King's District and Hillsdale, comprising 40 percent of the county population, was represented only by William B. Whiting on common pleas.[38]

Claverack thus stood at the civil center of the new county, with its courthouse and its post office and the benefits of the enhanced trade that came with this position. The village was noted for its taverns, and by 1800 there would be the Columbia Hotel, a large white structure at the village crossroads. The county meetings began that June, with the first session of the county supervisors at Gabriel Esselstyne's tavern; the supervisors rated the towns for taxes and purchased a lot from Esselstyne to build a courthouse for the sum of twenty pounds. That September the offices of the county clerk and the surrogate were open for business, followed by the first meeting of the county court of common pleas and general sessions in January 1787, the surrogate's court in April, and the circuit state court of oyer and terminer in March 1788, which that May made its power known by hanging three men for horse theft.[39]

The courthouse was finished by November 1787, and it would make a physical symbolic statement about the law in this locality. Built on a row of great houses being constructed by some of the Claverack gentry on the Hudson Road, the county courthouse was designed as a five-bay Georgian mansion. In its high-style domesticity, situated in a wealthy and open neighborhood, the courthouse architecture restated the oligarchic conflation of family and authority, of private and public, that had been so challenged during the Revolution. Within a decade the Columbia County bar, crossing wits and argument in this domestic-styled courthouse, would develop a reputation for the intellectual and rhetorical power of its legal contests. Cases heard at the Claverack courthouse were events of great moment, and the lawyers trained and practicing there would be renowned across the state: Elisha Williams, Jacob R. Van Rensselaer, William W. Van Ness, Ambrose Spencer and his son John C., and Martin Van Buren.[40]

Throughout the new nation, county courts such as these would replace the militia as the primary site of masculine political presentation, but in the mid-1780s this transition was at least a decade away. In 1786 Claverack's pride of civil place also rested in the militia, as Robert Van Rensselaer maintained his position as general commanding the new Columbia County brigade, surrounded by his neighbors and kin. That November Captain Peter B. Ten Broeck published an invitation to "the young gentlemen" of the county to join the brigade's troop of light horse, and the following March the entire brigade was mobilized against Shaysite rebels from Massachusetts. In February 1787 bands of Massachusetts Regulators encamped in the Kings' District and, aided by some of the locals, conducted raids into neighboring Berkshire County. Governor George Clinton himself took to the field with Van Rensselaer's brigade and elements of the Dutchess militia, meeting in Canaan with General Benjamin Lincoln, commander of the Massachusetts forces, and pacifying the border region. Into the spring the Shaysites were still a threat to good order: early in April General Lincoln was unceremoniously routed from the Springs at New Lebanon, recently advertised as newly and "properly fitted up" for "ladies and gentlemen," where he had been taking the waters. Through the summer there were accounts circulating of Shaysite raids on the border.[41]

The martial excursion of the Columbia brigade against the Regulators surely must have reminded Robert Van Rensselaer of his youthful forays two decades previously against the Nobletown squatters in 1766. It also seems to have coincided with a swelling nationalist political culture among the gentry.

When printers Hudson and Godwin of Hartford put out subscription lists for the first edition of Joel Barlow's epic poem *Vision of Columbus,* five men from Claverack subscribed, including General Robert and his brothers, Henry and James, as well as Captain Ten Broeck of the light horse. Among the very few others subscribing from Columbia County was Robert R. Livingston of the Lower Manor. Livingston's service in the Continental Congress and briefly as the Confederation's foreign secretary had earned him an honorary membership in the Society of the Cincinnati, the fraternity of Continental officers. He was one of only a sprinkling of county gentry admitted to the Cincinnati, including his cousin, Henry, of the Upper Manor, also an honorary member, and two of the Ten Broecks, formerly of the New York Line, currently officers in the Claverack militia. Claverack society also watched the courtship of a local girl, Kitty Hogeboom, by General Samuel B. Webb, a founder of the Cincinnati who had been deeply involved in establishing its rituals and who would hold the Bible at George Washington's inauguration.[42]

Antedating all of these post-Revolutionary claims to preeminence lay an institution established in Claverack at the height of the war. In 1777 the Reverend John Gabriel Gebhard led an effort to form a private academy, the Washington Seminary, which would serve the local gentry for the next forty years. This would always be a small school, with a maximum of about a hundred students at one point, and would be eclipsed by the later establishment of academies in Hudson and Kinderhook. But the founders had high aspirations and a high sense of themselves. Since Richard Morris, appointed chief justice in 1777 (and an honorary Cincinnati in 1786), was living in the village as a refugee from war-ravaged Westchester County, he was asked to serve as a trustee with, among others, Henry I. Van Rensselaer, Peter Weismer, Dr. Walter Wemple, and Kitty Hogeboom's father, Stephen. In a grandiose flourish, the trustees decided that their number should always include the state governor and chief justice as well as the Claverack Dutch Reformed minister and the senior member of the local Van Rensselaer clan. The school opened in a new building in 1779, with a Latin class and an "A.B.C. class" drawn from the gentry families of Claverack and Livingston Manor, including Robert Van Rensselaer's sons and Walter Livingston's son, Henry.[43]

In 1780 the seminary trustees recruited a new master, Andrew Mayfield Carshore. Impressed into the British army while walking on the Dublin docks, Carshore had slipped out of Burgoyne's ranks after the battle of Saratoga and had found work as a teacher in Kinderhook. Moving to Claverack, he petitioned for naturalization in 1785 and was appointed as an artillery officer in the militia in 1786. Carshore was renowned as a teacher of the classics and of higher mathematics, and he must have brought a certain British polish to this rural academy that was appreciated by the gentry who left their children in his care. He was skilled enough at the drafting table to offer a plan for the 1792 competition for the design of the United States Capitol, drawn in classical Palladian style. Given the typical curriculum of academies of this period, it is likely that Carshore also devoted some attention to inculcating social graces in children who were already a part of a small circle of polite sociability. They would move on a far wider stage than would their peers from local farming and artisan households. In the early 1790s Henry W. Livingston would serve as the personal secretary to Gouverneur Morris during his mission in Paris, others would go to Congress, and all to Albany and New York. The great houses of these gentry were the setting of the formal rituals of sociability—dinners, assemblies, informal visits, and salons—that set their lives aside from the ordinary. In these settings informal understandings about state and county politics, the building of interest, could unfold in private, away from the harsh accents and querulous argument of the tavern-based public meeting. These were the settings also of a culture of sensibility and belles lettres and of scientific improvement.[44]

This was a world that could not be taken for granted. It was a world that evokes and evoked county culture in contemporary England, the world of Jane Austen. But in the Hudson Valley this world had to be maintained in the face of relentless contrary public forces, most recently manifested in the committee politics of the Revolution and the radical Clintonian politics of the Confederation. It required raw political and economic power for its perpetuation, since it rested on the same resources as its English counterpart: a rentier income raised from a rural tenantry. Thus these landlord families set aside their differences early in 1785 to win the spring elections, and in the next legislature they won another victory in the contest for civil authority in the formation of their own center of civil power. They would now have to keep it, in the face of challenges old and new.

AN URBAN PUBLIC SPHERE: HUDSON'S EARLY YEARS

It might well have been quite disconcerting for the gentry at Claverack in the spring and summer of 1786 to learn that they were sharing the services of James Robardet, an itinerant French dancing master, with the new city of Hudson. It might have been equally disconcerting that this information was advertised in the *Hudson Weekly Gazette,* where the Washington Seminary never stooped to announce its schedule. Hudson City brought an avenue of prosperity to the east bank of the river, but in constructing the formal and informal structures of a local public sphere it also brought fundamental challenges to the vertical dependencies underlying oligarchic hegemony. Hudson

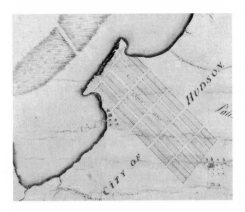

PLATE 4. *The City of Hudson in 1799. Detail from the Penfield Map of Claverack Manor.* Courtesy of the Columbia County Historical Society

would be of neither the Demo nor the Aristo, but of an as yet unknown third civil arena, the city.[45]

Resistance to Hudson's incorporation in the spring of 1785 focused on its size and its juridical powers, and the Hudsonians had to fight off continuing challenges in the spring legislative sessions of 1787, 1788, and 1789. Their charter gave the city council the authority to enact bylaws and to raise taxes for "good government and police," powers that were indeed far more extensive than for either the county or the new townships legislated in 1788. Outliers resented having to pay for the services and infrastructure required for the high density of population in the new compact city, despite the fact that the city's markets brought their farms a new prosperity. In a struggle that would reverberate far into the next century, the requirements of urban life set off a struggle over the definition of "good government and police," in which traditions of household privatism struggled with the imperative of public improvement.[46]

The new city council wasted no time in enacting improvements to its newly legislated authority. The charter delivered by the city's attorney, Ezekiel Gilbert, on May 4 appointed Seth Jenkins as the city's first mayor, and he immediately called for a city election. Over the next six months the new council passed ordinances establishing a city jail and setting up a whipping post and stocks, regulating the ferry across the Hudson to Athens, and forbidding the galloping of horses within the city limits, the disposal of broken glass into the streets, chopping wood in Main Street, the running of unyoked hogs or geese, and swimming too near the ferry dock. The council that June also established a committee to survey a formal street plan for the city, as stipulated in the charter. Completed by that December, Hudson's first street grid ran in a narrow corridor southeast from the riverfront, about a quarter of a mile wide and three-quarters of a mile long, with four major streets (Union, Main [Warren],

Diamond, and State) running up from the river, intersecting five numbered cross streets. The city hall was begun the following year, a two-story brick building at Fourth and Main taking many years to complete, funded by a combination of taxes and subscriptions. The Parade that the council set off in 1795, taking in a hill on the river, would be similarly unattended to for many years but celebrated as a secret meeting place for the young lovers of the city.[47]

In the original proprietors' settlement at Claverack Landing, construction had hugged the river bank, but by 1786 Hudson's population had reached fifteen hundred, and the city was beginning to build up the newly platted streets. In January 1789 Thomas Jenkins wrote a promotional letter to Robert R. Livingston of the Lower Manor, listing one hundred "good houses" and sixty that were "small but indifferent," besides another one hundred shops, barns, and warehouses. The city's ropeyard, distillery, tanyards, chandleries, and assorted mechanics were focused on the shipping on the river wharf: five river sloops, three whalers, eleven vessels in "the West India business," and four "in the European trade." These ships imported molasses, salt, sugar, rum, coffee, cocoa, and cotton. Hudson in 1790 was granted a federal customhouse, first proposed six years before. Equally important, these ships exported vast quantities of country goods from a hinterland including the entire county and stretching at least twenty-five miles east into Massachusetts and perhaps forty miles into Connecticut. In the winter months the country people flocked into Hudson by sleigh over frozen roads and tracks. In February 1786 it was reported that for several days twelve hundred sleighs daily came down into Hudson. The record would be marked in early March 1802, when twenty-eight hundred freighted sleighs arrived on a single day. Waiting to unload at the merchant warehouses on the dockside, their teams lining up along Front Street and up Main Street, the country people had ample time to spend in the city taverns, of which there were eighteen licensed in 1786. Here in the 1790s they would have received change in the small denomination scrip authorized by the city council and printed at Ashbel Stoddard's shop.[48]

Packed into an area that was perhaps a quarter of a mile square in the winter of 1789, the people of Hudson needed urban improvements for their health and safety. All of the state's cities were concerned about lighting dark city streets, and a 1787 state law established penalties for breaking or stealing "the Glass Lamps hung out or fixed before the Dwelling-Houses of many inhabitants"; the city waited until 1798 to put up public lights. In 1788 an existing volunteer night watch was recognized by the council, extending the system of fire inspection established in July 1785; in 1791 the first fire company was formed and then supported by state law in 1794. In 1792 the council began to attend to widening and grading the streets and in 1793 to pave the sidewalks on Main Street, efforts supported by state legislation passed that spring and in the two following sittings of the assembly. Public improvements were critical in the area of water supply. Since March 1785 a private association of subscribers had supplied the city with water in wooden pipes running from springs about a mile and half away; further improvement required state legislation introduced in 1789 and passed the next year, establishing a water corporation reporting to the council and regulating the water supply in the city. Two years later the council began to construct sewers, presumably sending the sewage into the river.[49]

Darkness, fire, water, disease: a host of natural threats attended upon close living, to say nothing of the pounding of the traffic on foot, hoof, wheel, and sled runner, which brought commerce to the merchants, mechanics, and laborers of the city of Hudson. Efficient commerce required close living; a compact settlement required a host of expensive public improvements, both possible and required within the confined bounds of the city. Improvement in turn required both political authority and political consent. Public investments in infrastructure had to be enacted by government, but governmental action depended on the agreement of the public at large.

This was not the same sort of public that prevailed only four miles to the east at Claverack village and courthouse. In Claverack, on Livingston Manor, and to some extent in Kinderhook, the ancient doctrine of public authority interwoven with inherited private position was finding a new lease on life in the late 1780s. If familial connection was lacking, then the polished performance of polite sociability might provide an opening to higher station. And, with inheritance, polite sociability was performed in private exclusive spaces, quietly building connection and interest behind closed doors.

Certainly many of the families in Hudson were interested in the forms of polite and proper sociability, and the young might well have flocked to the dancing lessons held by Mr. Robardet. Of course, at least a third of the Hudson people were Quakers, for whom dancing and the more ostentatious forms of polite sociability conflicted with the plain style. But the forms of polite respectability would certainly have been useful in a city of immigrants. None of the Hudson merchants and mechanics had been at Claverack Landing before the summer of 1783; they were self-made men, utterly lacking in local connection, and they would have to forge relations by artificial, civil means. Among the new merchants there was Samuel Edmonds, a Continental veteran of the Rhode Island Line who had had fought at Monmouth and Yorktown, arriving in Hudson in 1784 with a horse, saddle and bridle, two blankets, and a little Continental currency. By 1800 he would be one of wealthier men in Hudson: he would hold city office, be elected to the assembly and appointed sheriff and judge, serve as a director of a bank and a turnpike. He would also, in the 1790s, be a trustee of the Hudson Library Society and a master of the Hudson Lodge of Freemasons. In the building of a new privileged civil center in the corporation of Hudson, mutual and public association for purposes of public improvement fundamentally shaped the forms and purposes of sociability. In the early compact city of Hudson, then, as the outlines of Samuel Edmonds's life may suggest, we can begin to see the emergent forms of civil society and the public sphere.[50]

Classically, civil society had been seen as identical with political society, defined by the direct participation of propertied heads of household in the crafting and administration of law and justice. It was in places like Hudson that civil society began to assume the liberal nineteenth-century form. The sudden eruption of societies, lodges, and newspapers in the wake of the Revolution marked the emergence of an arena of civil society distinct from both the state and the domain of household life. Its associative and deliberative dimensions have been labeled the "public sphere." Limited as they were, these qualities of open deliberation and association were suddenly apparent in the public life, the town life, of the new city of Hudson in the mid-1780s.

The exchange of ideas and information lay at the center of this new public life. From 1786 Hudson would be known for decades for its debating societies. The first, the Union Debating Society, was formed in 1786 and might also have been known as the Socially Speaking Club. One of the society's first questions for debate was of some considerable salience. The abolition of slavery had been debated in the state assembly for months in the spring of 1785, without resolution. Agriculture in the old towns along the Hudson River in Columbia County was deeply dependent on slave labor: the more than thirteen hundred slaves in Kinderhook, Claverack, and on the Manor comprised just less than 10 percent of the total population, and in Hudson itself, concentrated on the farms outside the city proper, slaves comprised as much as 7 percent. After discussing whether "the establishment of the Union Debating Society will prove a benefit to Hudson," the members took up the key question: "Is the Slave trade consistent with the principles of humanity?" There is no record of the outcome. But the society had initiated a tradition of opinion formation in open debate that endured for decades in this city.[51]

The next group for which records survive was a Law Society, which met in 1802 and 1803, its record book reused for decades following by a Private Law Debating Society, a Forensick Club, and a Hudson Debating Society. And in the years to come a Hudson Forum would met regularly to debate the issues of the day. Debate and deliberation also took place in other associational settings. A Mechanics Society had been formed in Hudson by March

1792, when it published a powerful address on the conditions of labor by a "friend." The various library societies formed, beginning in 1786, would have provided a venue for discussion and debate as well as for the information, diversion, and improvement that reading offered. A small circulating library of several hundred volumes was opened in 1786 and replaced in December 1793 by a subscription-based Columbia Library; this in turn gave way to the Hudson Library Society, incorporated in March 1797 under the terms of a general act of legislature to encourage the establishment of libraries. By the end of the decade yet another source of books in Hudson and the other towns along the river was a huge General and Increasing Circulating Library operated on Broadway in New York City by Hocquet Caritat, advertising delivery in the upcountry papers. Delivery of books from Caritat's most likely was in packages by river sloop rather than by the expensive but vital postal service established in Hudson in 1792.[52]

In Hudson, one man stood at the center of this emerging public sphere: Ashbel Stoddard. Just twenty-two, he was unmarried when he arrived in Hudson after an apprenticeship at the Hartford *Connecticut Courant*. He operated both of the early subscription libraries, probably as an adjunct to the books and pamphlets, some already coming from his own press, that he offered for sale in his printshop along with legal forms required by the city and county courts. Stoddard was a member of both the Mechanics Society and the Library Society, for which he probably ordered books in New York, Philadelphia, and Boston. These affiliations would have been mobilized in the wake of the fire that burned his shop in 1793, leading the city to establish a second fire company, itself yet another context of association and conversation. Such connections were typical of printers in the new and growing towns along the river: Charles and George Webster were among the incorporators of the Albany Library in 1792; Robert Moffitt and Jesse Buel of the *Northern Budget* were founding members of the Troy Library in 1800.[53]

Many of these new printers were part of an actual and virtual extended family, centering on the printing office of the *Courant* in Hartford. This family equaled families of the gentry in complexity even if it lacked status and prestige, besmirched as it was with artisanal printer's ink. Stoddard and Charles Webster had apprenticed in Hartford during the war years, and, where Stoddard worked briefly with his brother and subsequently established his son, William, in the business, Webster and his brother brought their three nephews, the Skinners, into the *Albany Gazette*. Other Hartford-area printing families would send printers to Hudson. The Steeles, intermarried with the Websters, set up in both Albany and Hudson as printers and booksellers. Mackay Croswell apprenticed with Webster and Stoddard before establishing the *Catskill Packet* in 1792 with his two brothers. One of these, Harry Croswell, would buy out Stoddard's *Gazette* in 1803, consolidating the position of his *Balance, and Columbia Repository,* established in Hudson in the late spring of 1801.[54]

These tangled connections shaped a common culture of print along the Hudson. In the late 1780s these printers were recently settled in new and growing towns and were the agents of local improvement. Their futures lay in solidifying a place in the coalescing new civil geography being shaped by the Clintonian legislature. When Stoddard and Webster introduced their *Gazette* to Hudson, they stood as advocates of the "advantages in this city": their paper would be a "watchful centinel" over the "Liberties" of the public, it would provide entertainment, and "will bring Chaps to the Merchants, — Customers to the Mechanic, and it will shew the Husbandman where he best can dispose of the Produce of his Farm, — to the poor Man, who has but a penny, it tells where he can lay it out to the greatest Advantage." Advertising for scythes and red oak barrel staves, watches, and legal forms and announcements of sloop sailings and the Albany stage were all new and novel vehicles of improvement in a society heretofore completely dependent on word of mouth, private letters, and the occasional broadside printed in a distant city.[55]

The *Gazette* and the other new papers along the river made themselves a more formal source of civil and deliberative information in their publication of laws of general importance, which covered their front page from late spring far into the summer, every year. In Hudson, Stoddard made the connection with local political authority palpable in November 1786, when he began printing the common council's "assize of bread" under his masthead every week, as signed by Thomas Frothingham for the council. Council elections and meetings were noticed and reported, such as the July 10, 1793, meeting acting to pave Main Street's sidewalks; later city ordinances were simply listed. A stream of editor's comments and formal notices quickly moved from the almost casual to a focused boosterism. The notices of petitioners for underwater lands in the south bay and for a "well-regulated" bank in Hudson were duly published. In early 1788 "a correspondent" was greatly pleased "to see a Watch established; it will, if properly attended to, be a means of ensuring safety and respectability . . . [in] a city, only a few years extant, that has filled a paragraph in most of the European papers, much to the credit of the enterprising spirit of its mercantile interest." Such correspondence might well be fabricated by the editor, just as Elkanah Watson in 1792 wrote both sides of a letter exchange in the *Albany Register* between A Freeman and Polly Tenderfoot as part of his effort to advance legislation for paving in Albany and Hudson.[56]

Liberal civil society and an embedded public sphere of association and deliberation were quickly taking shape in the compact city of Hudson. Though self-conscious civil spirit did play a role and the post-Revolutionary political climate was a vital condition, the problems of close living drove the transformation. Civil society in the form of private associations and public print began to mediate between ordinary households and the wider world of marketplace and the state in ways that the old churches and district governments never had functioned before. Information, if spotty and incomplete, was assembled in the *Gazette* and read by an "imagined community" of city and country readers. Discussions based on that information, unfolding in the tangled milieu of Hudson's societies and associations, settled into "public opinion." Opinion, in turn, was being realized in law in a thickening stream of communication between the city and the lawmaking public sphere: the assembly, senate, and Council of Revision, still meeting in New York City for the winter legislative session. The papers and the printed assembly and senate journals reported the formal, indeed ritualized, process of petition, assignment to legislative committee, three readings, roll calls, amendments, bicameral concurrence, and council approval. Certainly the actual sequence from muddy feet to legislative enactment had plenty of room for backroom compromise and sleight of hand, but, even given that slippage, the record for Hudson was impressive: between 1785 and 1800 at least ten acts of the state legislature (to say nothing of dozens of city ordinances) were passed bearing on the "good government and police" of the city. These enactments comprised a "distributive outcome," improvements of a responsive activist government that shaped Hudson's place in the wider regional revolutionary settlement. Here civil society was not, as it was being viewed in absolutist Europe, an enemy of the state, jealously monitoring and protecting the liberties of the people. Here liberties were limitless and to be improved upon through the people's government. The forms of civil society here were an enabling flywheel, bringing the consent of the people into legal embodiment for public improvement.[57]

Whose consent and whose improvement, what people, are questions that will be explored more fully. Suffice it to say, this was minimally the consent of the propertied and independent voter. But among many of the propertied and independent this intrusion of new civil institutions was not necessarily welcome. In establishing newspapers in these new river towns, Stoddard and his brother printers were not establishing themselves on a raw frontier, but in a long-settled society. Each of the new papers claimed or hoped "for suitable Encouragement" from "Gentlemen," by which they meant the old Anglo-Dutch gentry as much as the new Yankee merchants. But Stoddard in particular was notably unsuccessful getting this "Encouragement" from the older river districts in Columbia County. He would have agreed with Seth Jenkins,

The Hudſon Weekly Gazette.

[VOL. II.]   THURSDAY, November 9, 1786.   [NUMB. 84]

Printed by ASHBEL STODDARD.

††† ASSIZE of BREAD, eſtabliſhed by the Council, for the month of November, 1786. viz. A Wheaten Loaf of fine flour, to weigh four pounds two ounces, for one ſhilling. A Loaf of the like flour, to weigh two pounds two ounces, for 6d. A Loaf of the like fine flour, to weigh one pound two ounces, for 4 coppers. Hudſon, November 1, 1786.   THOMAS FROTHINGHAM, Committee.

An Addreſs from the In-
habitants of Wyoming and others, contigu-
uſly ſituated on the Waters of the River
Suſquehannah; to the People at large of
the Commonwealth of Pennſylvania.
  Gentlemen, Friends and Neighbours,

PROVIDENCE having drawn the limits of our

and diſturbers of the peace, "who have not the fear of Law before their eyes." Theſe lands would better grace the "Pennſylvania Farmer," and his junto of counſellors, and ſage judges, attorneys, and depend-ants, who adore the law, "and make it honourable, and roll it as a ſweet morſel under their tongues," thereby to twiſt us out of our lands.
  Gentlemen,

You, are, undoubtedly, more or leſs acquainted with our title to the hoſtile ground, yet it may not be

ſoon after, were, by the laws of the ſtate and actual agency of the ſheriff, repoſſeſſed of the premiſes, and ſince that time, have greatly increaſed our ſettlements and numbers.

Finally, the United States in Congreſs aſſembled, by accepting the ceſſion of the claim of Connecticut to that large tract of land, contained in their charter, to the weſtward of the Suſquehannah Company's pur-chaſe, and alſo to the weſtward of a tract of land which the ſtate of Connecticut have reſerved to them-

---

Numb. 1.   Page 1.

The Balance,
COLUMBIAN AND REPOSITORY.

" HAIL SACRED POLITY, BY FREEDOM REAR'D! HAIL SACRED FREEDOM, WHEN BY LAW RESTRAIN'D!" ——BEATTIE.

HUDSON, (New-York) PUBLISHED BY SAMPSON, CHITTENDEN & CROSWELL.   Thursday, May 21, 1801.

To the Public.

THE ancient fable, that mountains were in travail and brought forth a *mouſe*, has been often uſed to ridicule undertaking, in which much was promiſed, and but little per-formed. The *Paper* that we are now com-mencing, *if good*, will commend itſelf; if

tolerance that is no leſs abſurd; inſomuch that a mere difference in opinion is often ſeen to provoke moſt virulent attacks upon cha-racter.

Now as to ourſelves, in defiance of cenſure, we mean to purſue the line of *moderation*. Whatever arrows of *invective* there may be in our quiver, they are grown ruſty for want

Miſcellany.

FOR THE BALANCE.

" Know they——
To give ſociety its higheſt taſte;
Well order'd home man's beſt delight to make;
And by ſubmiſſive wiſdom, modeſt ſkill,
With every gentle care-eluding art,
To raiſe the virtues, animate the bliſs,

the end of June, ſome of the moſt leiſure days were improved, when the neceſſary work on the farm would permit, in collecting materials for the Compoſt, and carting them to the gener-al receptacle, until at leaſt two hundred tons were collected.

The Compoſt heap was made of the follow-ing materials, viz. about ſixty tons of the top of the earth, taken chiefly from the ſides of the ſtreet, where it has had ſome benefit from

---

[SECOND EDITION.]

THE  WASP.

By Robert Ruſticoat, Eſquire.

Vol. I.]   *" To laſh the Raſcals naked through the world."*   [No. 1.

HUDSON, July 7, 1802.

If there, perchance, ſhould come a Bee,
A Waſp will come as ſoon as he.
    Myſelf.

follow—over the ſame fields, and on the ſame flowers.——Without attempting to pleaſe his *friends*, the WASP will only ſtrive to diſpleaſe, vex and torment his en-emies.—With his ſting always ſharpened for war, he will never accept of peace.—He will never accede to the philoſophical

P R O P O S A L S

PLATE 5. *Mastheads of Hudson Newspapers, 1786–1809.*
Courtesy of the American Antiquarian Society

the first mayor of Hudson, when he complained about "the Junto from without who have never ceased their opposition since we came among them" and that the inhabitants of "this Infant City . . . have in some measure to lament our Misfortune in being encompassed too much by the inhospitable spirit and illiberal prejudices of the adjacent neighborhoods." These prejudices translated into a virtual boycott of the *Gazette* by the people of the old districts of Claverack and Kinderhook for most of the first two years of its publication. Advertisements well into 1786 were overwhelmingly placed by Hudson and Albany concerns or from the Yankee hill towns to the east, extending into Massachusetts and northwest Connecticut. It might well have been that the paper was not taken in the older Dutch and German communities. When riders working on contract with Stoddard published their routes and issued notices for quarterly payment in 1786 and 1787, their circuits made no mention of stops in these river districts, yet carefully listed the tavern stands in the King's District, Hillsdale, and Berkshire County where they dropped papers and expected payment. The first notices from the old lowland districts were official in nature: on September 28, 1786, Killian Van Rensselaer announced

Conflict and Civil Establishments (81

the opening of the county clerk's office in Claverack village, followed a week later and then in early November by the first lists of letters received at the new post offices at Livingston Manor and Kinderhook and by notices of the forming of the Columbia County brigade of militia. Only after these official notices broke the ice did other paid notices begin to appear from these old communities, for stolen horses, lost account books, farms for sale, or the settling of estates.[58]

Though they would eventually become deeply involved in the publication of newspapers, the gentry of the new county provided no early "encouragement" for Stoddard's new Yankee venture. In the spring of 1785, when Stoddard commenced printing in Hudson, their opinion might well have been summarized by Robert Livingston in his postelection letter to Alexander Hamilton. In closing his account of a conservative electoral victory grounded in "the necessary Junction" of the great families, Livingston articulated the oligarchic credo: not only should they "Stick Close to Each Other," but they "Should be Cautious of letting our Enemyes know anything while that may be dangerous: these Sir, are our Sentiments on the Politcks of the times and our firm resolutions to abide by." Livingston lived in a world where information was valuable and private; it was not to be broadcast publicly, as it was by the young Stoddard, printing six miles upriver from the Manor at Hudson. One of the bulwarks of oligarchy and dependency was a tight control of information, even such limited information as Stoddard was mixing in his paper. Livingston and the county gentry were trying to maintain old relations of deference and authority, in which information was conveyed selectively in face-to-face situations as tokens of benevolence. The newspaper and its imagined community were indeed replacements for those relationships and in subtle ways would forge a new hegemonic fabric of polite sociability. A new generation of county gentry would learn and master the language and forms of this new intrusive media. But in the mid-1780s an older generation was threatened by the way in which local print challenged their notion of the "public."[59]

THE ENLIGHTENMENT IN COLUMBIA: FREEMASONRY

If the implantation of newspapers in the new commercial towns along the river threatened to undermine the oligarchic definition of the public, so too did the rapid spread of Masonic lodges in the 1780s and 1790s. But here the effect was more complex and ambiguous, since the lodges reproduced key elements of polite sociability in their exclusive membership, face-to-face relations, and even their elaborate ritual. What is more, one of the great magnates of the upper Hudson was the sponsor for the entire institution of Freemasonry in post-Revolutionary New York. In accepting the grand mastership in 1784, Robert R. Livingston of the Lower Manor probably visualized his effort as extending and elaborating circuits and habits of political and cultural deference while self-consciously building intermediate bodies in civil society between the people and the state. If so, his efforts were only partially successful. Freemasonry would build a stronghold of the Enlightenment along the upper Hudson, but it also proved remarkably pliable to local purposes. If Livingston hoped to construct a hierarchical deferential Enlightenment, the Masons of Columbia forged a popular Enlightenment, mediating between the extremes of Demo and Aristo.

If anyone had conceptualized a sociological model of civil society in Columbia County, it would have been Chancellor Livingston, who had all of the intellectual resources at hand in his house at Clermont. Livingston saw himself in the guise of the benevolent aristocrat, bringing reason and science to the improvement of his nation and its people, an intellectual, improving benevolence cultivated in part to set himself off from his grasping cousins on the Upper Manor or the Claverack Van Rensselaer clan. The only man in Columbia County to have played a major role in the Continental government, he was a member of the American Philosophical Society, the founding president of the New York Society for the Promotion of Agriculture, Arts, and Manufactures in 1791 as well as of its successor, the Society for the Promotion of Useful Arts. He would win renown for his importation of merino sheep, prized for their wool, and for his sponsorship of Robert Fulton's steamboat. His library at his mansion house at the Lower Manor held copies of Bolingbroke, Locke, and Montesquieu; he had Adam Ferguson's *Essay on the History of Civil Society,* the earl of Shaftesbury's *Characteristics,* and Edmund Burke's essay *On the Sublime and the Beautiful.* Burke and Shaftesbury undoubtedly informed his understanding of the eighteenth-century civil aesthetic, calming faction and passion with order and reason. He might have had an affinity for Ferguson as a fellow Scot, and certainly he read Ferguson as an exemplar of the Atlantic Enlightenment. Ferguson's analysis of civil society was formative, consonant with the pessimistic view of human nature that characterized eighteenth-century classical republican thought. Humanity was caught between the barbarism of primitive agrarian societies and the fatal corrupting influences of luxury that accompanied the growing refinement of the commercial societies of the eighteenth century. The problem lay in maintaining virtue in society, both the private virtues of order, politeness, and manners and the public virtues of charity, disinterestedness, and self-denial that would allow a people to defend itself against tyranny in the state.[60]

Livingston reproduced Ferguson's account of the origins of society in an 1806 *Essay on Sheep;* his estate manager, William Wilson, anticipated it in

PLATE 6. *Robert R. Livingston (1746–1813), Clermont.*
Collections of the New-York Historical Society

a series of Masonic orations delivered in the 1790s. Wilson, a Scottish immigrant physician who maintained a considerable library of his own, helped to manage Livingston lands and eventually founded the Columbia County Agricultural Society; in the 1790s he was a member of the Washington Lodge in the town of Livingston. As did many throughout the new Republic, Wilson saw Freemasonry as an institutional means to the goal of associated virtue. Masonic fraternity would temper selfish excess and discipline customary disorder; its rituals would drill its members in the precepts of order and regularity that were the Enlightenment's contribution to the emerging bourgeois order of national citizenship. "Various have been the institutions of civilized society," Wilson told the Washington Lodge, designed "to lessen the Evils necessarily attendant on Human nature." But Masonry's supposed antiquity made it the critical bulwark against human error.

> The sacred forms of rel[igio]n have been constantly changed. The Laws of Solon and Lycurgus are no more. The most valued constitutions of Civil Society are all da[i]ly alter[in]g their form. . . . But Masonry and its Forms are still the same — all the changes that take place in Rel[igio]n, in Gov[ernmen]t in Man[ne]rs effect not us — We are the same this day, yesterday and forever.[61]

Robert R. Livingston might well have had in mind this Masonic solution to Ferguson's dilemma of barbarism and luxury when he agreed in February 1784 to preside as grand master over the Grand Lodge of the State of New York, the position held before the Revolution by Sir John Johnson. Another possible framework might well have been Montesquieu's conception, developed in the *Spirit of the Laws,* of graded and intermediate centers of power and authority in a society, situated between the people and the government, and moderating extremes at either end. Montesquieu's ideas must have informed Livingston's proposition at the 1777 constitutional convention for the Council of Revision. Livingston probably was not aware that while in London in 1730 Montesquieu, in his enthusiasm for the virtues of English society and its balanced constitution, had joined not only the Royal Society but also a Masonic lodge in Westminster, and then four years later helped to found an aristocratic lodge in Paris. But Montesquieu's understanding of the positive effects of civil institutions outside the aegis of the state certainly informed Livingston's tenure as grand master, which lasted until 1800. He would be followed in the grand mastership by De Witt Clinton, Daniel Tompkins, and Stephen Van Rensselaer, men who held great political station in New York. Like Livingston, Clinton and Van Rensselaer would be architects of grand societies for civil improvement. Masonry was one way among many by which they might demonstrate a patrician devotion to charity, benevolence, and improvement and earn influence by attending to the greater public good.[62]

It was also a vehicle by which enlightenment, order, and classical virtue might reach a popular audience, which might be subtly drawn into a political interest and understanding at critical moments. Thus for these men Freemasonry, with its cloak of political neutrality, was a means of extending New York's traditional familial and personal politics into a dimension of postwar civil society, but without the risks attendant upon a full-scale embrace of political party. And, in the context of Columbia County, Freemasonry's bounds and obligations might also mediate and moderate the chasm between Demo and Aristo.[63]

Assuming authority over the Grand Lodge, Robert R. Livingston brought institution building in civil society to bear against the threats of popular politics in the 1780s. Early in his tenure, a division between lodges following competing Modern and Ancient rituals had to be negotiated, and, in total, he would preside over the warranting of eighty-three new lodges across the growing state of New York before resigning in 1801 to become Jefferson's ambassador to France. Washington's inauguration in 1789 provided him the opportunity to seal the dignity of the Grand Lodge (and that of the Cincinnati) when as chancellor he administered the presidential oath over a Bible and Masonic pillow borrowed from Saint John's Lodge. He did not, however, attend the local lodges in Columbia County, nor did his brothers, nor a cousin or two among the Upper Manor clan, who were members of the elite Holland Lodge in New York or Master's Lodge in Albany. His direct involvement in the Grand Lodge was actually very limited. He rarely if ever attended Grand Lodge meetings or intervened in its affairs. But all of the petitions to the Grand Lodge were addressed to him, and the petitioners might well have had hopes of connections in high places, establishing "terms of intimacy," as one local writer in Hillsdale put it in the 1860s, between local men and the great men of the state.[64]

Eight new lodges were warranted by Robert R. Livingston's Grand Lodge by the end of 1790; one was New York City's exclusive Holland Lodge, and the other seven were located in the rapidly growing upper Hudson Valley east of Albany, from Fishkill in Dutchess County north to Fort Edward, in what was soon to be organized as Washington County. The first to be warranted under Livingston's authority was Temple Lodge in the town of Northeast, recently known as the Little Nine Partners. Livingston must have had a hand in this warrant, since it perfectly repeated his sponsorship of Solomon's Lodge in Poughkeepsie in 1771 (four years after his family's defeat in the Dutchess County elections of 1767), where he had delivered the Grand Lodge warrant and opened the lodge with a "brotherly Charge." Now, in the spring of 1785, as the legislature was debating new county jurisdictions along the east Hudson region, Masonic patronage was extended first into neighborhoods immediately south and east of the Manor, neighborhoods that his family long had considered part of their sphere of influence. Livingston's hidden hand also seems to have been at work in the Hudson Lodge warrant, granted in March 1787. Granting a lodge at Hudson certainly furthered Livingston's unbending efforts to thwart the Claverack Van Rensselaers.[65]

But there were other centers in New York's Masonic politics. Unity Lodge, founded in Canaan (formerly the King's District) in September 1788, was warranted on the recommendation of Peter W. Yates, of Albany's Union Lodge, where some of the Canaan Masons had been members for some years. Once they received their warrants, these lodges were not always particularly deferential to the Grand Lodge. Albany's Union Lodge briefly had struggled to retain its Modern ritual when the Grand Lodge was reformed under the Ancient, or York Rite, ritual in New York City in 1784 and would continue to stir up trouble. In June 1789 the Hudson Masons, when asked to make their contribution to the Grand Lodge, pointed to "the Infancy of the Lodge here" and "the Expences our Lodge has inevitably, incurred, exclusive of Benevolences afforded distressed Brethren, in cloathing and Furniture." Canaan's Unity Lodge sent similar letters in 1789 and in 1793, when it wrote of its "many members living at a considerable distance" from the lodge: "The country that they live in is new, their Resources small, and their situation remote from Commerce and Oppulence." In 1812 Unity Lodge wrote another humble letter; though it had continued admitting members, "the distance being so great, representation [at the Grand Lodge meetings in New York City] so expensive and other conveyances so uncertain, that for a long time our dues have not been paid." In 1800 the Hudson Masons sent a long letter to New York vehemently rejecting a proposed new constitution for the Grand Lodge; in the ensuing years a group of upriver lodges led by Yates's Union Lodge in Albany (and including the Unity Lodge) attempted a secession from the Grand Lodge.[66]

Warrants in hand, the lodges thus became centers of civil privilege, essentially independent of the nominally governing Grand Lodge, meeting in New York City. Their authority to create circles of secret and exclusive sociability, with the recent history of military Freemasonry, brought an interesting cross section of men to their meetings, some attending from distant neighborhoods. Temple Lodge in Northeast, Dutchess County, attracted men from adjacent Livingston Manor and from Hillsdale; Hudson Lodge had several members from Claverack and one from Kinderhook; the Unity Lodge in

PLATE 7. *Unity Lodge Meeting Room, New Lebanon.*
Built by Elisha Gilbert, Sr., circa 1795–1800. Private Collection

Canaan drew members from Stephentown and Schodack, in the Van Rensselaer lands to the north. These scattered memberships became the ground for
further Masonic patronage, as the older lodges endorsed lodge petitions from
surrounding towns. Thus the Unity Lodge spawned daughter lodges in New
Concord in 1796, Nassau in 1799, and Stephentown in 1802; the New Concord lodge later coendorsed a lodge in Spencertown. Temple Lodge endorsed
Washington Lodge on the Manor in 1790, sending its master, Peter Bishop, to
make the installation, and joined with the Hudson Lodge to endorse the Vernon Lodge in Hillsdale in 1803, the year that Hudson sponsored the Columbia Lodge in Claverack village.[67]

These new Masonic networks symbolically linked local Masons to Grand
Master Livingston and the men of note who would follow him, among them
De Witt Clinton and Stephen Van Rensselaer, the landlord patroon of Rensselaerwyck. But otherwise they were completely new, building circuits of patronage, authority, and sociability utterly detached from those of the local
oligarchic families.[68]

Thus, ironically, Freemasonry provided a ground for the construction of polite respectability that had nothing to do with ancient family connection. If membership was exclusive, it was also always expanding and circulating. It had a different meaning for the founding members, who were self-consciously building a new base of cultural authority, and the young men who cycled through these lodges, gaining through initiation the certificates that would give them entry to distant lodges as they migrated west or, in the case of Hudson, shipped out to sea. But, for the enduring core membership, the lodge was an instrument of local improvement, both collective and individual. Enjoying Masonic privilege brought them into connections with a national institution and, indeed, the Atlantic Enlightenment. Appropriate observance required physical setting. In Canaan Master Elisha Gilbert in 1794 built a large mansion house with a long attic lodge room. For more than half a century the Unity Lodge brethren would climb a grand stair to meet in this room, surrounded by Masonic emblems of order, reason, diligence, and sociability. The Hudson Masons had more ambitious plans and even asked for a loan from the Grand Lodge, though they were in arrears in their dues. With a lot donated from the city, they built a two-story brick lodge hall "upon a liberal plan"; finished in 1796, it was dedicated in an elaborate public festival that December on Saint John's Day, complete with procession, Masonic prayer, and oration, followed by dinner at Gordon's tavern. These new accommodations led to further ventures in Masonic institution building. By March 1797 Hudson had established a chapter of the Royal Arch, and in 1798 their brethren were sitting with De Witt Clinton as officers of Grand Royal Arch Chapter; the Unity Masons in Canaan soon followed with their own Royal Arch connection.[69]

Though secret, exclusive, and ritualistic, the lodges held a key place in the wider, more deliberative public sphere. In Hudson, their membership overlapped considerably with both the Library Society and the Mechanics. Printer Ashbel Stoddard was not a Mason, but his brother Simeon, who rode post for the *Gazette* in the summer and fall of 1787, was a charter member of the Hudson Lodge, appointed junior deacon in 1787. Ashbel, as had printers for decades, paid close attention to Masonic affairs: in 1786 and 1787 he published notices for the funeral of a Mason in nearby Connecticut, of the Saint John's Day celebrations in the King's District and Hudson, and for his own imprints of Masonic sermons. The tavernkeepers who served as agents for the *Gazette* in King's District–Canaan and Hillsdale were often Masons: Elihu Phinney and Eleazer Grant of the King's District were both among the founders of Unity Lodge; in Nobletown, Charles McKinstry was a member of Temple in Dutchess County, and William Tanner, the agent at Green River, would join the Hudson Lodge by 1796. Elihu Phinney of Canaan Center would attempt to emulate Stoddard by starting a press of his own in 1794, publishing a few pamphlets and books and his own Canaan *Columbian Mercury,* before giving up and going west to Otsego County. Phinney's attempt was matched by the efforts of Eleazer Grant and others in Canaan to establish an academy in 1791. Canaan was given a post office in 1794, and Grant was appointed postmaster the next year, one of a number of Masons to serve as postmasters across the county. If, in founding presses and academies these hill town Masons were perhaps overly ambitious, they clearly saw themselves as agents in the public sphere.[70]

FREEMASONS, COMMITTEEMEN, AND ELECTORAL POLITICS IN COLUMBIA COUNTY, 1786–1801

This Masonic agency in the public sphere translated into political power in the state. Freemasons for years occupied positions of great importance in Columbia County. In Hudson and Canaan, they were a significant presence in city and town governance. In Hudson, three of the four men on the petitioning committee would be in the lodge by 1789; among them the first mayor, Seth Jenkins, was also the master of the lodge until his death in 1794. For almost two decades from 1787 the position of city clerk would be occupied by a Hudson Lodge Mason, most prominently by Ambrose Spencer, who was to become a power on the state supreme court. From 1785 to 1800 only two years passed in which there was not a Mason among the eight aldermen and assistants on the common council; every year from 1786 to 1794 there would be at least two, and usually three. In the old King's District–Canaan, Masons of the Unity Lodge dominated town government between 1784 and 1799, serving for eleven of fifteen terms as supervisor and five as town clerk; among them were Eleazer Grant and Elihu Phinney.[71]

Across the county, Masons were well represented among the assemblymen, state senators, and United States representatives elected to office from Columbia County between 1774 and 1801 (see Tables 1, 2). But here a critical distinction emerges. The local Masons were not men from the Aristo families, but neither were they men of Demo popular politics. Men who had served on the Revolutionary committees were more than twice as likely to be elected to state and federal legislatures during the last quarter of the century, serving ninety-nine terms as against the Masons' forty-four terms. Equally important, these were *almost entirely* different groups. The Revolutionary committeemen serving in the legislature almost never joined the new Masonic lodges, nor did the committeemen who did not go on to higher office. Notably, judges appointed to the Columbia County bench from the 1780s were also very rarely

TABLE 1. *Public Service, Revolutionary Service, and Masonic Membership,*
Columbia County, 1774–1816

	Total Terms of Service	Terms Served by Freemasons
1774–1801		
All Revolutionary committeemen	99	4
All not Revolutionary		
committeemen	[64	40]
Revolutionary militia officers	11	8
1786 militia officers only	8	2
All others[a]	45	30
Total terms served	163	44
1774–1788		
Revolutionary committeemen	55	0
All others[a]	2	2
Total terms served	57	2
1789–1801		
Revolutionary committeemen	44	4
All others[a]	62	38
Total terms served	106	42
1802–1816		
Total terms served	91	11
1774–1816		
Grand total terms served	254	55

Note: Public service includes the assembly, the senate, the ratifying convention, and the House of Representatives. Table includes no appointed members of the Continental and Confederation congresses.

[a]Includes two terms served by William Powers of Canaan.

members of lodges. Freemasons were thus new men of the post-Revolutionary age, literally men of the new politics that reshaped county, state, and nation between 1785 and 1788. Mutually exclusive political cadres, the old Revolutionary committeemen and the rising Freemasons would play opposing roles in the struggle to redefine the public sphere.

From 1774 through 1785 Revolutionary committee service was an absolute prerequisite for election to the legislature: every single legislator elected

TABLE 2. *Party Membership, Public Service, Revolutionary Service, and Masonic Membership, Columbia County, 1789–1816*

Total No. of Terms / No. of Terms Served by Freemasons

	1789–1792	1793–1797	1798–1801	1802–1808	1809–1816
Revolutionary committeemen					
Federalists	5/0	6/0	6/1	5/0	2/0
Republicans	11/0	11/1	5/2	2/0	0/0
Total	16/0	17/1	11/3	7/0	2/0
All others					
Federalists	2/2	14/13	12/5	21/3	35/5
Republicans	4/1	14/7	16/10	18/3	8/0
Total	6/3	28/20	28/15	39/6	43/5
Overall					
Federalists	7/2	20/13	18/7	26/3	37/5
Republicans	15/1	25/8	21/12	20/3	8/0
Grand total	22/3	45/21	39/19	46/6	45/5

in these years had served on a Revolutionary committee. With the notable exception of the apparently lame Matthew Adgate, virtually all of them had carried commissions of field grade — major and colonel — in the Revolutionary militia. The grip of Revolutionary service in the legislature was broken in the 1785 election, when the conservative forces engineered their victory, but even anti-Clintonians Lawrence Hogeboom and John Livingston had served on committees, though not as militia officers: Livingston had declined his committee election in 1776.[72]

Then, in the April 1786 election, William Powers, the wealthiest man in the King's District, was elected to the assembly with John Livingston. Powers had no record of Revolutionary service, and his brother-in-law, James Savage, had been arrested in 1777 on suspicion of loyalism. But Powers was among the emerging group of Albany-oriented Masons in the King's District; he would be among the petitioners for the Unity Lodge in the summer of 1788 and most certainly was at the Saint John's Day festival at Canaan Four Corners on December 27, 1786, just two weeks before he took his seat in the assembly.

TABLE 3. *Party and Masonic Membership and Public Service, Columbia County,*
1789–1816

	Total Terms / Terms Served by Freemasons		
	1789–1796	1797–1801	1802–1816
Federalists	18/10	26/11	63/8
Republicans	32/4	30/17	28/3
Total	50/14	56/28	91/11

Note: Public service includes the assembly, state senate, and House of Representatives.

Elected to the senate in 1792 and from there to the Council of Appointment, he would be a powerful Federalist figure until his death in 1796. The Reverend John Camp's funeral oration for Powers was printed by the lodge's request at Stoddard's office.[73]

Powers was the first of many Masons who would be elected to the assembly and the state senate from Columbia County over the next decade. Only a very few of these had been active on the committees in the 1770s; many indeed were too young to have held leading positions during the Revolution. Freemasonry thus provided a cadre of men with an important connection to a wider arena of politics and culture, an alternative to that provided to others by command experience in Revolutionary politics. But these Freemasons also embraced a common political frame of reference. At least through the mid-1790s Freemasonry was overwhelmingly Federalist in its political connection, and during these years the former Revolutionary committeemen maintained a strong allegiance to the popular politics of George Clinton, reformulated in 1788 as Antifederalism.[74]

At its peak in the 1790s the link between Freemasonry and Federalism among this post-Revolutionary cadre of legislators was overwhelming, driven by William Powers's election to the state senate and that of five other Federalist Masons from Hudson to the assembly, senate, and the United States House of Representatives. This Masonic connection with Federalism would blur in the late 1790s as a new generation of emerging Republicans also used the lodge as a stepping-stone into public life, and then almost disappeared after 1801, when formal political organizations took shape in New York. Freemasonry was the seat of the popular Enlightenment, an institutional vehicle of refinement and sensibility. However, it seems reasonable to suggest that

Freemasonry also provided a transitional context for political understandings between the radical committee-based politics of the Revolution and the structured state party politics of the Jeffersonian era.[75]

As a secret society that in principle banned political discussion from the lodge, Freemasonry was not a direct vehicle of deliberation, but it provided a set of common — perhaps persuasive — understandings for men in public in the 1790s. During this decade it superseded old Revolutionary committees as the essential flywheel in civil society between locality and the state. But Freemasonry, as did the other postwar civil institutions of the public sphere, also intervened as a new social-cultural formation in Columbia's particular struggle between Demo and Aristo and then established a political accommodation with the Aristo elements. The conditions, trajectory, and durability of that wider alliance would fundamentally shape the relationship between political action and civil society in the decades to come.

3

Deliberation and Civil Procedure
1787–1795

It is an incontrovertible principle in the science of politics that whenever the constitution or government of a state is fixed and established, nothing short of the most pressing necessity should induce a recurrence to the origin of civil and political rights. This is loosening the bands which connect society and ties the arm of the strong from oppressing the weak and the virtuous. It is inviting the usurpations of ambition, and holding out the strongest temptations to the passions of human nature.

— Columbianus in the *Hudson Weekly Gazette,* Sept. 13, 1792

For the *Columbian Mercury*.

Citizen Phinney,

The Democratic Society of Canaan far from claiming any unequal and exclusive precedence of censorship and the like: claim only the natural and constructional right of discussion, speaking, writing, etc. which we expressly assert belongs *to the people in general and to each in particular equally*[. T]o the exercise of this we applied ourselves and invited others, and should be highly gratified if all our fellow citizens would freely and attentively exercise it. Our society admits none but Democrats and cannot invite all of that description, for more than a house-full cannot deliberate[. B]ut we would fondly have others of like sentiment form other Democratic Societies, Aristocrats Aristocratical Societies, and Monarchists Tory Societies etc. And all freely discuss and publish as we do or as they might choose, that the views of each might be made manifest and bear their proper weight with an enlightened and orderly people. . . .

— *Columbian Mercury, and Canaan Repository of Rural Knowledge,* Oct. 1, 1794

It was a damp day in June 1792 when three companies of the Kinderhook militia mustered at a tavern in the Pomponick neighborhood, going through a few drills before the rain began to pelt down. As the men and spectators from Kinderhook and Canaan took shelter, an officer from another company arrived at the muster field and "read off in a loud voice" a series of toasts to the state and to Governor George Clinton, newly reelected in a close and hotly contested race. He then focused on this controverted election, toasting the "independent electors," "unawed by the menaces of aristocrats" and the bold verdict of the election canvassers against the legality of votes sent from Otsego County, not "intimidated by the threats of disappointed faction." His toasts were marked with cannon fire and cheers and huzzahs from the crowds sheltering from the rain.[1]

This officer was Lieutenant John A. Van Buren, who had begun his public life with his appointment as an ensign in Abraham Van Buren's militia company in 1790; he would rise to the command of this company in 1796 and would be a stalwart of the Clintonian-Jeffersonian cause for the next decade. Certainly his sentiments on the Otsego crisis were shared by Abraham and his wider Van Buren relations. The Otsego election crisis of 1792 was a profound test of the evolving civil fabric of the state of New York, as procedures of deliberation, election, and lawmaking settled into a stable post-Revolutionary routine. Between the chartering of the county in April 1786 and the ratification of the constitution of a new federal national government in late July 1788, citizenship was redefined in relationship to both local structures and a new national identity. This redefinition developed in a series of struggles culminating with the contest over the 1792 election. At stake were the procedures by which consent was manifested in public life, by which the opinion and interest of members of a public were translated into binding constitutional and statute law. As the routines of a new national revolutionary settlement began to emerge along the upper Hudson in the early 1790s, the new privileged centers of a liberal civil society — city, press, associations — had to reach accommodation with and redefine the operating principles of popular and oligarchic politics, Henry Livingston's Demo and Aristo.[2]

FACTION AND LEGITIMATE PROCEDURE
IN THE NEW COUNTY

The oligarchic forces in Columbia County had high hopes for the cause of state retrenchment and continental consolidation in 1786 and 1787, following their victories in the April 1785 election. They gained little in the short term. The 1786 legislature established an emission of paper money through the state's new loan office, and even Alexander Hamilton's election to the winter 1787 house failed to achieve the approval of an impost for the Confederation. The nationalists prevailed in the appointment of Hamilton and Chancellor Robert R. Livingston to attend the convention meeting in September 1786 at Annapolis to discuss trade, where Hamilton would play a key role in crafting a report calling for a constitutional convention. But in the spring of

1787 he was again outflanked in the legislature and had to attend the Phila-delphia convention as a minority Federalist, outvoted by two Clintonian stal-warts from Albany County, John Lansing, Jr., and Robert Yates.[3]

In these maneuvers, Hamilton was linked in a tenuous alliance with Chan-cellor Livingston, whose "pastoral Federalism" contrasted with the colonel's more heroic and energetic mode. On this grander stage, Livingston could not be stirred from his comfortable circumstances to attend the Annapolis convention, but, on the smaller stage of the new Columbia County, he and Hamilton began to coordinate their efforts to build a wider conservative alli-ance, especially as it might encompass the "infant city" of Hudson. They were in correspondence that spring, as Hamilton agreed to settle a long-standing dispute between the Upper and Lower Manors, and in January he drafted and introduced a bill that would incorporate the chancellor's Lower Manor as the township of Clermont. The Clermont bill passed on March 12, five days after the Chancellor's Grand Lodge granted a warrant for the Hudson Lodge. On March 5 Hamilton had made a futile but well-publicized effort on Hudson's behalf. Since mid-February three waves of petitions had been submitted to the assembly, asking variously that the new county courthouse be kept in Claver-ack or moved to Hudson. Hamilton challenged the interests of his Van Rens-selaer relations in Claverack to support the Hudson petitioners. In his mind "the people of Hudson came into this state with very great property," and their new city was "a valuable acquisition to the state" and to the county itself. "It was bad policy not to give every encouragement to its citizens." Building the courthouse in Hudson would "do away with the inconvenience of having two jurisdictions within a very small circle." Though it "had been a great party matter," Hamilton announced that his "vote should be for Hudson."[4]

Published in the New York *Daily Advertiser,* Hamilton's intervention in this "very small circle" was part of an effort to consolidate a relationship with the leading men in Hudson and to bring them into an emerging alliance, led by the Hamilton-Schuyler interests in New York and Albany. Peter Van Schaack, recently restored to citizenship and living again in Kinderhook, lay at the center of this connection, which reached east to William Powers's Masonic Federalist associates in the King's District and now south to Hud-son and Clermont. Among these now numbered Hamilton's former nemesis, the old radical Jacob Ford, who had carried Van Schaack's civil reinstatement through the assembly, then petitioned on Hudson's behalf, and was soon to appear in Federalist lists. At stake was the outcome of Columbia's first elec-tion of assemblymen as an independent county, and the result was messy.[5]

In the previous year's election in greater Albany County, apparently in a custom of some standing, the county board of supervisors had nominated a slate of candidates for the assembly. Such a nomination was regularly challenged by local meetings, and the custom does not appear to have carried over to the new county, where a flurry of meetings immediately produced competing slates of candidates. Sometime in early March 1787 "a meeting of a number of gentlemen from a majority" of the new county's districts had decided upon an assembly slate including lawyer Peter Silvester of Kinderhook, William Powers of the King's District, and Thomas Jenkins of Hudson, brother of Seth, the mayor and lodgemaster in the new city. This slate was published on March 29 in Stoddard's *Hudson Weekly Gazette,* above a second slate chosen by "a number of the principal gentlemen from the several districts" at Claverack on March 12, which had chosen John Bay of Claverack, John Livingston of the Upper Manor, and William Powers. A week later a letter from an anonymous Honestus blasted the first slate as the product of "a private and partial meeting." The Claverack nominations, Honestus complained, had resulted from "a general invitation of gentlemen from all the districts of the county." The competing "Hudson" slate was the result of a "partial invitation ... to serve the interests of party." He was not *disposed to take ... a shadow for the substance; nor to ascribe to an imaginary meeting the qualities due to a real one,* nor to a *partial meeting, that weight and authority which can only belong to a general one."* When a Freeholder replied to defend the "Hudson" meeting, the dispute both continued in the pages of the *Gazette* and spilled into the streets. Violence almost broke out in Claverack after a conversation on the street about the Freeholder letter led to the comment that "electioneering was a rascally business." The result was a very public confrontation between Peter B. Ten Broeck, captain of the county troop of horse, and Killian K. Van Rensselaer, county surrogate, and a demand for satisfaction, spilling into the pages of the *Gazette* for weeks following. The county's first election was thus a botched affair, leaving a threat of violence hanging in the air.[6]

As important, the drama in this first election involved legitimate political procedure and the critical role of print. Publication in the *Gazette* gave authority and publicity to a slate selected by a questionable procedure; publication was thus required to issue a challenge and attempt a resolution. And publication of the squabble between Ten Broeck and Van Rensselaer might well have provided a means of resolving an affair of honor short of the dueling field. Discourse in print was intervening in public life in new and complex ways.

How should elections be conducted? What were the legitimate grounds for meetings of gentlemen to propose slates of candidates for public office? Whose interests were being served? These questions were fundamental to the routinization of politics, and the answer would come with the acceptance of party as essential to those routines. In 1787 the vehemence of the struggle might have rested in its nonideological nature: these were squabbles within a potential conservative coalition. A year later these same petty divisions still prevailed, contributing to a stunning victory by the old radical Clintonian forces, now resurgent as Antifederalists.

RATIFICATION AND THE PUBLIC SPHERE

In the spring of 1788, with the ratification of the Constitution the critical public issue, the Federalists in Columbia County were hopelessly divided along ancient lines of territorial preeminence. Philip Schuyler attempted to intervene when Judge Isaac Goes of Kinderhook was insulted by General Robert Van Rensselaer's failure to invite him to the Federalist nomination meeting at Claverack. Open conflict had emerged between Hudson and the Upper Manor Livingstons; opposed to the nomination of Thomas Jenkins of Hudson, John Livingston forswore cooperation with "every person unfriendly to his family," despite Schuyler's efforts. Three different Federalist meetings were held in various parts of the county. While they agreed upon a slate of convention delegates led by Peter Van Schaack, these three meetings produced three different assembly slates reflecting the "discordant ingredients" in Columbia Federalism. The Antifederalists met once, in Claverack on March 18. Mocking the Federalist Claverack meeting's claim of "a number of very respectable citizens, and some of the first characters of the county," the Antifederalists described themselves as "respectable citizens," "though perhaps not the *first characters* in point of property, yet as such in point of attachment to the liberty, independence, and happiness of America." The Antifederalist slates overlapped: Peter Van Ness was nominated to the convention and to the senate, Matthew Adgate and John Bay to the convention and the assembly, and John Kortz of Germantown balanced the assembly ticket. All three of the leading Antifederalist candidates had long experience in the Revolutionary committees and militias; none was a Mason. Among the nine candidates advanced by the Federalists, only two (Henry Livingston and Jacob Ford) had Revolutionary experience, and two were Masons. The Antifederalists won decisively.[7]

The Antifederalist victory in Columbia and in its parent county of Albany was grounded in a fertile and effective fusion of the old committee networks with the power of print. This fusion has to be seen as formative in the wider history of the development of American political parties, and it shaped the particular regional politics that Martin Van Buren, now only six years old, would inherit twelve to fifteen years hence.

It was not a fusion in which the Antifederalists had any necessary advantage or particular claim. If Stoddard's press had vital original connections to the radical strongholds in the hill towns, they were grounded in a common New England culture rather than in ideology. In the fall and winter of 1786–1787 the *Gazette* established its inevitable relationship with the prevailing powers in the county. This accommodation between county and press began with Killian Van Rensselaer's notice of the opening of the county offices in September and Peter Ten Broeck's notice regarding the county troop in November. It seems to have culminated in the March 29 issue of the *Gazette,* when Robert Van Rensselaer ostentatiously placed an ad offering the sale of "improvements of several valuable farms" carrying perpetual leases and Peter Silvester placed the first of the thousands of court notices that would fill the Hudson papers for decades to come. With these symbolic declarations, the county gentry would begin to be comfortable with a local paper, if not yet particularly innovative.[8]

In March 1787 the gentry were not particularly unified: Peter Silvester of Kinderhook was elected to the assembly over the Claverack slate that Van Rensselaer would have supported, and there would be nomination quarrels in the following years. But, if Ashbel Stoddard could not overcome the familial and territorial feuds of his new neighborhood, he could give the Federalists ideological cohesion. With the other papers along the upper Hudson, in Poughkeepsie, Lansingburgh, and Albany, Stoddard made the *Gazette* a bastion of support for the Constitution proposed at Philadelphia that September. On September 20, 1787, noting that the Philadelphia convention was about to adjourn, Stoddard published a front-page essay by Aristides from the New York *Daily Advertiser,* describing the country's "two distinct and strongly marked political classes," of which the Federalists comprised the clergy, the merchants, and "the intelligent, independent Country Gentlemen." Over the next two weeks he prominently printed the proposed Constitution and then launched into a series of Federalist essays from the Philadelphia *Independent Gazetteer,* followed by Publius's "Federalist," which ran through No. 11 in January 1788. He closely followed the progress of ratification in all of the states, especially Massachusetts, as well as reporting the steps being taken for New York's own ratification. In April, since "the present important period" made it "necessary for every man of abilities to declare his sentiments," he put up a special letter box at his shop door in order that "his literary friends," ensured "a certain secrecy," would "at all times have access." He also published the address of the county grand jury, led by its foreman, Henry Livingston, announcing its unequivocal support for the Constitution. In the grand jury's address the Federalists demonstrated their command of traditional forms of politics, and before the April elections they had held meetings in each district "for the purpose of discussing and explaining the constitution."[9]

But Federalist efforts were more than matched by the Antifederalists. While the editors favored the Federalists, they felt an obligation to print both sides. Nicholas Power in Poughkeepsie printed a complete version of Melancton Smith's "Federal Farmer," perhaps the most influential Antifederalist series. In Hudson Stoddard printed at least three other important Antifederalist essays, the *Dissent of the Minority* from Pennsylvania (published as a four-page broadside in late 1787), Edmund Randolph's letter to the Virginia House of Burgesses, and Robert Yates and John Lansing's report to Governor Clinton. Stoddard's former partner, Charles R. Webster, a staunch Federalist too, also felt required to print the broadsides and pamphlets of the very active Albany County Anti-Federal Committee. By April Stoddard was getting a bit testy, cutting off "An Anti-Federalist" for producing an "inadmissible" essay full of "private invective"; in June he was getting particularly worried about the effect of an influential Albany publication's listing "35 objections" to the Constitution. Nervously suggesting, "Might not it be well to republish them for the edification of the southern delegates?" he did not follow his own advice.[10]

Stoddard was worried about the "35 objections," but there were many other publications available. A Federalist in Albany complained that "The Centinel, the farmer's letters, and every other publication against the Constitution are scattered all over the County." Conversely, General Samuel B. Webb in New York City was impressed by the "most astonishing influence" of John Jay's address in building Federalist opinion. By July Stoddard was expressing a sneaking, mocking admiration for his Antifederalist opponents. If the Constitution were to be adopted: "What a fund of eloquence will have been exhausted in vain! How many pamphlets circulated to no purpose, how many fears and alarms excited without a cause, how many disappointed orators and broken winded horses — in a word, how much labor and industry lost to the public!" He also saw some positive outcomes.

> One excellent effect produced by the constitution is, that almost every man now is a politician, and can judge for himself upon the great and important question, and when the debates in convention are published the people at large will be able to determine for themselves, as to the weight of argument for and against, without the aid of itinerant teachers, true or false.[11]

This intensified political education meant the voters of Columbia turned out on election day in record numbers. Turnout in Columbia's assembly election was second only to Albany County, followed by New York City, and was the highest in the state in the voting for delegates to the ratifying convention, followed by Albany and New York City. Where assembly turnout in some counties was less than 25 percent, it was 46 percent in Columbia; turnout for convention delegates was typically a third of potential voters, but in Columbia it was 60 percent. Stoddard hoped that Columbia's delegates, elected "upon Anti-Federal principles" but "unfettered by instructions," would "have a latitude to act upon their judgments" and eventually vote for the Constitution. Here he would be sorely disappointed. Confronted by Hamilton, John Jay, Justice Richard Morris, and Robert R. Livingston all representing New York City, Antifederalists Van Ness, Adgate, and Bay remained true to their Columbia constituents and on July 26 cast nearly decisive votes against the Federal Constitution, which prevailed by the narrowest of margins.[12]

That July Fourth the Hudson Federalists had met to celebrate "the glorious anniversary of American independence," complete with a salute by the militia artillery and "an elegant entertainment" at Gordon's tavern. All was not peaceful; Captain Thomas Frothingham of the artillery had to lead his men in a defense against the assault of "a few ignorant antis." In the same paper reporting this incident, Stoddard wrote hopefully that a "spirit of amity and conciliation" was "prevalent among the people at large, and all parties shew a return to good humor and a desire of once more becoming a united people." He did not mention an all-out riot that had swept the streets of Albany on the Fourth. Perhaps sentiments of "amity and conciliation" were in evidence in mid-July, but certainly Stoddard and his brother printers along the Hudson made every effort to make it appear so in the weeks and months following. On August 5 he printed accounts of the final votes in Poughkeepsie; on August 12, the proposed amendments and call for a second convention that had brokered the final vote. He published the "Federal Ode" printed on a float in New York City's grand constitutional parade and devoted a full page and a half to the August 8 Federal parade in Albany in which he himself had marched with Charles R. Webster and John Babcock, publisher of the Lansingburgh *Federal Herald*. That August and September, Babcock devoted full pages in four issues of the *Herald* to the parade in New York.[13]

PRINT, DELIBERATION, AND GOVERNANCE

Antifederalist feeling certainly did not ebb away completely in the fall of 1788, but the printers worked hard to craft that impression. Few from Columbia had actually witnessed the Federal parades of the late summer, but they experienced them vicariously through their printed accounts. Without competing local papers to provide alternative views, readers along the Hudson saw the world as constructed by proudly self-conscious Federal printers. Reports from eyewitness observers, accounts of the progress of ratification throughout the states, details of parades, fragments of poetry, notices of militia musters and Masonic festivals, arranged under the printer's careful hand, all worked to shape a certain picture of public reality. American citizens were now members of a consolidated nation, ranked under a concentric pyramid of constituted civil governments running from town and county to state and nation. The alternative to the ordered safety of the new national arrangement had been not so subtly suggested in Stoddard's inclusion of alarming accounts of continuing disorder and riot by Shaysites in neighboring Massachusetts throughout 1787, reinforced by his advertisement, running in February and March 1788, for his own printing of Stephen West's execution sermon for John Bly and Charles Rose, hanged at Lenox for burglary at the end of the Massachusetts rebellion.[14]

The printers also worked hard the following spring to depict the new federal authority, with the convening of the new government in New York City. On March 10 Stoddard carefully juxtaposed an account of the assembling of the United States Senate and House of Representatives in New York's refurbished Federal Hall with a letter claiming that Governor George Clinton had encountered Daniel Shays himself in a western tavern and "saluted him with all possible *politeness*." While Stoddard had New York's Antifederalist governor saluting the Massachusetts rebel, he also had to report that the new Congress lacked a quorum without representation from New York. A quorum was finally achieved, and on April 14 Stoddard was able to begin regular accounts of congressional proceedings and presumably printed an account of George Washington's inauguration in early May. By August he was printing the first "Laws of the United States," regarding import duties, followed by the list of federal revenue appointments, including that of John C. Ten Broeck, former Continental officer, member of the Cincinnati, and Hudson Lodge Mason, to the post of surveyor of customs at the port of Hudson.[15]

Stoddard's congressional reports might well have come from John Fenno's *Gazette of the United States,* established in New York in mid-April 1789. Establishing the print analogue to the new national government, Fenno's *Gazette* completed the pyramid of newspapers that would prevail into the antebellum decades: papers of record at the national seat, leading state and city papers, well established in New York and developing in Albany, and county papers like Stoddard's *Gazette* or Babcock's *Federal Herald.* Already linked laterally by the long-established practice of clipping and reprinting, a vertical set of print relations would emerge in the 1790s, elaborating and bifurcating as party ideologies and patronage began to become a force after 1798. Down this pyramid Fenno's *Gazette* and other urban papers had an aesthetic influence on the upriver printers. Stoddard moved his notice of the Hudson common council assize (regulated price) of bread off his masthead in February 1789; early in 1792 he dropped "Weekly" from his title and moved from a three- to a four-column layout. John Babcock's Lansingburgh *Federal Herald* already sported this sleek, hard, new aesthetic; Nicholas Power made the change in July 1789, changing his title from the *Country Journal, and Poughkeepsie Advertiser* to the *Poughkeepsie Journal* and dropping a bucolic woodcut of plow, scythe, and sheaf and a verse against "Party! whose murdering Spirit I abhore."[16]

All of these papers created a new federal reality in their pages in the months following the ratification. But, if consent in the constitutional settlement was being shaped by cultural practice, it was also being won by political procedure. Political action required basic information about the activities of government, and, in publishing the minutes of assemblies and copies of enacted law, the newspapers indeed were fulfilling a fundamental political purpose. Consent was being granted from a general sense of legitimacy, but also in a very specific and day-to-day engagement with the making and administration of law.

These papers could not quite achieve the political reflexivity that a fictional character from Massachusetts hoped for in Stoddard's *Gazette* in the summer of 1786, when he described them as "nervous fluids" of "the body politic," informing the "political head" "what was going on in the tail of the community." Where once the Romans had conducted "public debates," this "Doctor Pull" hoped that "by *instructing* our representatives, and by publishing our thoughts on public matters in a great newspaper . . . we might do almost as well as the Romans." The papers produced by the printers of the upper Hudson did not so much inform the political head of what the tail was thinking, as inform the tail of what the head was thinking. In so doing, however, they provided a series of key functions in an established and now elaborating cycle of representative governance spinning annually between state and civil society.[17]

Doctor Pull articulated a key dimension of this cycle, the formation of opinion in the public sphere. Jürgen Habermas visualizes the process of liberal governance as divided between two public spheres, one comprising the open and free formation of opinion in discourse and publication in civil society, the other the translation of opinion into law in the rule-bound settings of legislatures and courts of law. In each of these public spheres sequences of debate arrive at key moments of decision, in the election of new representatives and the enactment of legislation or in the appointment of judiciary and their interpretative actions. The newspapers conducted by these Federalist printers were certainly efforts at cultural construction, shaping possibilities and limits in an endless series of editorial decisions. But these printers were also the servants of a public that demanded information for political decisions in this cycle of governance, whose consent was grounded in its sense of the legitimacy of the procedures operating in civil society and in the branches of government, procedures particularly governing the outcomes of election and legislation. Adequate information and legitimate procedures determined the grant of consent and a routine politics; their absence might lead to a withdrawal of consent and a renewed politics of crisis.[18]

In printing the daily proceedings of Congress and the ensuing body of federal law, these printers were drawing on long-established precedent. The assembly had been printing a journal of its votes since at least 1702 and a journal of "votes and proceedings" since the 1720s. Colonial laws also were published annually and in compendiums, the last before the Revolution edited by Peter Van Schaack of Kinderhook. By the 1730s, when John Peter Zenger's *New-York Weekly Journal* was sued for libel in the Morris-Crosby controversy, the *New-York Gazette* was already routinely publishing notices of the assembly and court sessions as well as the colony and city laws. With the Revolution, the 1777 constitution mandated an "open door": the doors of the senate and the assembly were to "at all times be kept open to all persons," and "journals of all their proceedings" (with certain wartime reservations) published, and these immediately began to appear in newspapers.[19]

The routine was thus long established when it can first be followed in Ashbel Stoddard's *Hudson Weekly Gazette* in 1786–1787. The ninth session of the legislature had recessed on May 5, 1786, and on May 18 Stoddard printed a notice of its last action, appointing the Annapolis delegates. On May 25 he published a list of acts passed that session and then began the routine publication of selected acts, which filled the front page of each *Gazette* until the end of the summer and continued occasionally into the fall and early winter, interspersed with reports from the Confederation congress. On January 25, 1787, he reported the opening of the new political season, the tenth session of the legislature, with the forming of quorums in the assembly and senate and messages exchanged between the legislature and the governor. Surviving papers capture moments in the assembly routine: on February 22 it was the assembly's debate on the "bill for regulating elections"; on March 29 it was the senate debate on the bill to relieve New York merchants of British debts. The same issue brought the first publication of slates for the assembly, one of which was challenged by Honestus, in an issue containing the full text of the act regarding the time and place of county court sessions, a matter of considerable controversy in Hudson and Claverack that spring. The results of the assembly election would have been noted in mid-April, and by May 10 Stoddard had completed the cycle, listing the titles of the acts passed in the tenth session.[20]

This basic relationship of print and politics was elaborated with the addition of the federal cycle of governance in 1789 but otherwise essentially maintained for decades into the nineteenth century. If we review the entire electoral-legislative cycle, it is apparent that the service that the press provided to deliberation and lawmaking was of variable quality. The post-Revolutionary newspapers were more notable as a source of raw political information than as the site of political deliberative exchange. Printing proceedings of the legislature, and then the text of the ensuing laws themselves, provided the ground for caucusing and debate in face-to-face situations, both in taverns and drawing rooms, by which constituents might assess the performance of their legislators and the progress of their interests. They might provide the basis for the solicitation of votes and for challenges to that solicitation. Thus in the spring of 1799 An Old Spectator wrote to the *Gazette* that "an honourable gentleman of Claverack," apparently Killian Hogeboom, was "riding to and fro in the county of Columbia, electioneering for himself with the Journals of the Assembly to evince his patriotism in favor of the seditious resolutions of the legislatures of Virginia and Kentucky." But turn to his votes of January 15 and 16 and March 30, on bills protecting debtors from creditors, the Old Spectator challenged: "Let him, I say, produce those Journals, and he can show his honourable name in the negative." His popular credentials were of various colors.[21]

Print was serving many purposes in the political public sphere, as both a record of public service and a vehicle for the monitoring and critique of that service. But Stoddard felt obliged to print a disclaimer following the Old Spectator essay. The printer's code might put some opinion beyond the pale, and it also provided ample opportunity for the careful management of opinion, as in Elkanah Watson's fabrication of his exchange on the virtues of paving in 1792. Certainly the *Gazette* would have been read with papers from Albany and New York City, which provided far more space for deliberative opinion and often printed items from Columbia's writers. But these metropolitan papers were not quite as readily accessible. Thus Chancellor Robert R. Livingston from Clermont wrote to his brother Edward in the summer of 1795, urging that he get certain essayists published in the New York *Herald,* "which is the only paper that has a country circulation." The county newspapers would develop as truly energetic, if often abusive, sites for deliberation and debate only as they began to multiply at the turn of the century and be put to the purposes of formal party organizations.[22]

ELECTORAL PROCEDURE

What was more apparent in the first years following the ratification of the Federal Constitution was a settling of prickly issues of electoral procedure. How were particular private individuals to be set before the public for election? What were the appropriate procedures of nomination, of publicity?[23]

In 1787 the complaint lodged by Honestus against the "Hudson slate" revolved around the purported identities of the gentlemen attending this nominating meeting; claiming to represent the majority of districts, they had represented only four. Stemming from a "partial invitation," this was a "private meeting," an "imaginary assembly," and composed of invisible men whose names were not presented to the public. In 1788 the nominations for assembly and the ratifying convention had a similarly opaque quality. Meetings of unnamed but "respectable citizens" proposed slates of candidates to the public, for the most part without any recommendation other than to their "characters." In a minor if telling departure, two of the notices announced the meeting locations: the Antifederalists had met at Captain George Phillips's in Claverack; one of the Federalist meetings was at Colonel Matthew Scott's in Spencertown. In Albany, first the Anti-Federal Committee and then the Federalists had been more aggressive, publishing detailed arguments, platforms, and slates supported by lists of subscribers.[24]

In 1789, with the first congressional seats and the governorship at stake in the March and April elections, the Federalists took the initiative, publishing the nomination of Robert Yates for governor in a signed letter from a statewide committee, following the Albany County Federalist and Antifederalist nominations, duly signed by committees. The Federalist meeting, attended by "some gentlemen" from Columbia, nominated Peter Silvester of Kinderhook to Congress, who let it be known that, though he declined the nomination, he would serve if elected, as he would be early in March. With the congressional election brought to a successful conclusion, the Columbia Federalists ventured into print with a detailed account of their meeting's nomination of governor and lieutenant governor, senators and assemblymen, complete with a precise location ("at the house of Capt. Isaac P. Van Valkenburgh, situate on the public road between Kinderhook and Claverack"), their chair and clerk (Peter Silvester and Matthew Jenkins) announced in boldface, and twelve-member assembly nomination committee formally identified by town. The Antifederalists were able to get in only a couple of short notices but announced that "upwards of one hundred Freeholders" had met to nominate George Clinton, senators, and assemblymen under the chairmanship of Peter Van Ness.[25]

Thus the spring of 1789 brought formal party electioneering in print to Columbia County. This sudden elaboration of nomination procedure was matched by that of electoral notification in the first tabular array of votes by candidate and township at the March congressional election, finally published in the *Gazette* in late April. These were the essential electoral formalities that would prevail in the decades to come: publicized meetings at prominent locations, elected chairs and secretaries, lists of committee members who would support candidates. While they marked the 1789 election as a break with the past, these efforts could not be sustained annually. Off-year elections for the assembly into the late 1790s retained the limited and opaque form of the traditional nomination, often simply emanating from "a number of electors." Behind the scenes the gentry struggled to shape the lists to suit their interests. The surviving issues of the *Gazette* for 1792 record the meeting of the Hudson Committee of Correspondence working to elect John Jay as well as a large meeting for Jay in Canaan, and rumors had circulated that the grand jury would support either Yates or Clinton. A county committee supporting Clinton coordinated with the Rensselaer County committee to support a common Clintonian senate slate. But in a stepwise progression, the relationship between print and politics had been established, and the 1795 and 1798 campaigns for governor — if not without controversy — saw announcements of planned meetings, formal printed resolves, longer and longer committee lists, and increasingly routinized election returns.[26]

A system mandating election by large districts and entire counties bred jealousies over the privileges and perquisites of representation, requiring careful consideration of "just claims" and the development of a rotation by towns. As late as April 1799, the Hudson Federalist committee had to warn Peter Van Schaack that Kinderhook's failure to unite behind a declared list "has produced little good for the federal interest, as respects members of the Assembly." Kinderhook would be left "destitute of a candidate" that year, but it was imperative that Columbia Federalism "form itself into a compact body [since] then it will be irresistible." Such a "compact body" — a strong Federalist party organization — would indeed emerge in the first years of the next century.[27]

The growing publicity of politics drew a range of responses, from the hostile to the satirical. Henry Van Schaack, now established in Pittsfield over the border in Berkshire County, used his perch in Massachusetts to comment on New York's politics to his friend and congressman, Theodore Sedgwick of Stockbridge. Through the 1790s Henry and Peter Van Schaack continually begged Sedgwick for copies of Philadelphia papers and badgered him about the formation of postal routes from the river through Kinderhook and Lebanon to Pittsfield. In February 1795 Henry was worried about Jay's coming election and wrote Sedgwick an extended comment on the place of print in Columbia County politics.

> If the federalists in Columbia have prudence to resist the temptation of publishing meetings I will insure them good effects from the publications of their opponents — It is *anti-republican* to advertise a *caucus* — and so the people will think, when those meetings, and the aristocratic resolves of those meetings, are properly animadverted upon. But the truth is my friend . . . it would produce the most salutory effects to let the opposition meet and publish, and for our side to expose the resolves and meetings in the public papers.

In December 1797 Van Schaack complained to Sedgwick that a paper was being started in Pittsfield: "I am sorry for it, especially if the Editors are Anti which I believe is the case." Apparently he would have been "sorry for it" even if the editor had been a good Federalist. Van Schaack would have preferred a world without newspapers, in which his influence and connections would have counted for more, in which political meetings were held unannounced. Outside this perfect world, the press should be used to ambush the opposition.[28]

Others were taking a more lighthearted approach, suggesting a certain comfort, indeed boredom, with the unfolding of political routines in print. During the spring 1793 congressional campaign a clever essay circulated through the river papers, comparing the various candidates to horses on the track: Peter Van Ness as "Lofty" was "long-legged and jumps far but rather too high and can't gather quick"; Peter R. Livingston as "Peacock" had "little else to recommend him but his *blood* as his is really out of the *old Caladonian mare* . . . his *courage* is not the best, nor does he *carry himself well*"; Ezekiel Gilbert of Hudson as "Phoenix" would carry the day: though "not well prepared for the race" and "of the New England breed, if well kept, will acquit himself handsomely in the Federal race." Two years later it was the nomination process that was the butt: the *Poughkeepsie Journal* leavened a long list of election notices with an obvious spoof under the headline of "Reconciliation!!!": Jay and the Federalist slate had been nominated "at a meeting of about three electors of the county of Dutchess, held in an open field . . . [with] but one dissenting voice."[29]

The satires of 1793 and 1795 indicated how serious the question of electoral procedure had recently been. In 1789 two controversies had roiled the political waters in Columbia County. Peter Van Ness held seats in the senate and on the county bench, and after his vote against the ratification of the Constitution Federalists were not willing to tolerate such egregious plural officeholding. And in the spring 1789 election for governor, Clintonians and Federalists alike were scheming to have votes from Livingston, Kinderhook, Canaan, and Hillsdale rejected on the grounds that polling places were moved. Van Ness eventually resigned from the bench, and the election irregularities were overlooked so as to spare mutual embarrassment. But in the spring of 1792 a procedural controversy erupted across the state that seemed to threaten civil war. Returns in the election for governor from the three western counties of Otsego, Clinton, and Tioga had not been delivered to the election canvassers in New York City in the manner stipulated in the state constitution. Rather than being delivered by the county sheriffs, they had been carried by a former sheriff, a clerk, and a private citizen. This violation of the mandated procedure allowed the canvassers to throw out these votes, about 1,000 total, giving Clinton a majority over John Jay of barely 100 votes of an approximate total of 16,700.[30]

As soon as the canvassers' decision was announced, Federalists began making "an appeal to the people." Judge William Cooper of Cooperstown in Otsego County led a petition calling for "immediate legal or legislative interference," and Albany County Federalists recommended a "general convention" of the counties of the western senate district. Federalists in Columbia County had worked especially hard to elect Jay, and on premature news of his election they had celebrated with cannon fire at Hudson; they rose up in righteous indignation. In the *Gazette* An Independent Elector announced to the "the Freemen of the County of Columbia" that the grounds of consent in the revolutionary settlement were in grave doubt. The Clintonian canvassers had "without just cause proscribed three whole counties and disenfranchised 1200 freemen of a most sacred right." If Clinton were to hold his office, the "Freemen" were told, it would prove "that American Liberty is a mere sound; That elections are mere puppet shews, by which the people are to be juggled out of their liberties, and then to be taxed to pay the jugglers for their tricks, and that our constitutions are nothing but certain characters impressed on paper, pleasant to be read, but . . . not to be understood by the vulgar." Ulster County Federalist Ebenezer Foote demanded that "Clinton must quit the Chair, or blood must and will be shed, — and if no innocent blood was to flow, I would not care how soon it began to run."[31]

The deciding ballots rejected on procedural grounds, Federalists were withdrawing their consent in government: routine politics was giving way to crisis, and rebellion seemed to lie on the horizon. Meetings in Columbia were held in mid-June, Thomas Frothingham chairing a Hudson City meeting and William Powers and Jacob R. Van Rensselaer chairing a county meeting at the new city hall in Hudson. John Jay, holding federal circuit court in Bennington as Supreme Court justice, made a ceremonial progress down the Hudson Valley. Met on the Rensselaer County line by a troop of Federalist gentlemen, Jay was escorted through Kinderhook to Claverack, where at William H. Ludlow's mansion house on the Hudson road "they were regaled with a glass of wine" before riding into the city to salutes from Frothingham's artillery and an "elegant entertainment" at Kellogg's Hotel.[32]

Through the summer and into the fall Stoddard printed essay after essay on the crisis in the *Gazette*, as did Powers in Poughkeepsie and William Wands in his new Lansingburgh *American Spy*, condemning the canvassers' decision against Federalist Jay. The controversy spilled over the state line to Stockbridge, where Theodore Sedgwick's printer, Loring Andrews, printed a long series of essays from Federalists in Canaan. In September Stoddard printed a forty-five page pamphlet, *The Rights of Suffrage*, by Plain Sense, detailing the evidence in the election and defending the Federalist call for a convention against the Clintonian charge that "under the specious mask of a redress of grievances, their real objects are a dissolution of the government and a subversion of the constitution." Here lay a fundamental problem for the Federalists: despite the apparent justice of their claim, their challenging the constituted procedures of the canvassers, calling for conventions, and even the marching of militias brought to memory the recent Shaysite disorders in Massachusetts. The more cautious among them were concerned that a new, fragile constitutional structure was being undermined. John Jay hoped, he told the Columbia Federalists assembled at Kellogg's Hotel, that their "efforts to maintain and preserve our constitutional rights, will not cease to harmonize with that order and decorum." Alexander Hamilton wrote from Philadelphia that New York should "beware of extremes" and steer clear of the dangers of "the convention and the bayonet." "It is not for the friends of good government to employ extraordinary expedients which ought only be resorted to in cases of great magnitude and urgent necessity." This conservative impulse to preserve the routines of constitutional government seems to have restrained Theodore Sedgwick of Stockbridge from intervening in print. Peter and Henry Van

Schaack were writing to him all summer and into the fall and winter, hoping that "your printer" in Stockbridge would publish on the issue, and hounded Sedgwick for "your long thing . . . on the New York dispute." But by January, when he apparently produced the long-awaited essay, Peter had to write, "There is a Tide in human affairs, and the Document . . . did not arrive until the cause began to ebb."[33]

The tide in the Otsego crisis turned with a countervailing response from Clintonian Republicans high and low. As we have seen, on a rainy June day in Van Schaack's Kinderhook, Lieutenant John A. Van Buren addressed a militia muster, toasting Clinton, "the laws of the state," and "the just and wise decision of the late canvassers." The Van Buren circle must have had a good laugh when letters in the New York papers called the Van Schaacks, so active that summer in the Federalist interest, "two infernal tories who were both within the enemy lines" during the late war. At least two major series of essays defending the decision of the election canvassers ran in the *Hudson Gazette* as well as in the *Albany Gazette* and the New York *Daily Advertiser*. One series was written by Robert R. Livingston himself as Cato; frustrated at his failure to land a federal appointment and increasingly alarmed both at the Federalists' interventionist policies and at their affinity for England, the chancellor was moving into the ranks of the emerging Republicans. The other was by a pseudonymous Columbianus, who in his final essay in the September 20 *Albany Gazette* expressed the Clintonian Republican critique of the Federalist "appeal":

> In some governments different from our own, when the cord of power is drawn so tight that nature revolts at the oppression, "an appeal to the people," in the true sense of the words, may sometimes be made with propriety: but, in a representative government, where every act of government is the act of the people, to talk of "an appeal to the people" is nonsense. They are random words, used by superficial politicians and designing men, to distract society and throw all into confusion, in hopes of partial advantages.

Thus, for Columbianus, some Federalists, unhappy with the operation of electoral procedure, were looking to use the tactics of Revolutionary politics to achieve an outcome in what had become the routine cycling of representative government.[34]

By the late fall of 1792 it became clear that a convention would not be called, and Federalists rested their hopes in a legislative inquiry that occupied a great part of the spring 1793 session. As the assembly opened the session in December, petitions on both sides of the issue began to arrive, at least ten from Columbia County alone, two from Federalist meetings and eight from Republican. Matthew Adgate attempted without success to have one of the Republican remonstrances written into the assembly journal. He with the other Republican assemblymen from Columbia voted with the majority to absolve the election canvassers of impropriety or corruption and to pursue the investigation of Federalist Judge William Cooper for "improper conduct" at the 1792 Otsego election.[35]

THE CANAAN DEMOCRATIC SOCIETY
AND THE PUBLIC SPHERE

These votes were part of a wider political reality in Columbia County that had endured since the ratification. Clintonians, now evolving into Republicans, prevailed in Columbia well into the 1790s. Matthew Adgate, the perennial radical of the previous decade, after being elected in the spring of 1788 to the ratifying convention and to the ensuing 1789 house, would serve in five sessions through 1795. The Columbia Clintonian delegation perpetuated the tradition of Revolutionary service: of the five voting to absolve the canvassers in 1793, four had served on Revolutionary committees, and Benjamin Birdsall of Hillsdale had been a lieutenant colonel in a Dutchess County regiment at Saratoga. Only Federalist Jared Coffin, a Hudson Lodge Freemason, voted against the Clintonian canvassers. Indeed, until the Columbia Federalists gathered into a "compact body" in the 1799 election, Columbia's Clintonian Republicans maintained an overwhelming majority in the county's delegation to the assembly, and the Federalists increasingly managed to win seats in the senate and the United States House of Representatives.[36]

Their strong base in Columbia's assembly electorate enabled these Clintonians to continue the radical politics of the 1780s. Thus in February and March 1791 Matthew Adgate, supported by Stephen Hogeboom, attempted to block the chartering of the Bank of New York and, failing that, to limit its charter rights. In the winter of 1794, a year after the Otsego crisis, the Canaan Clintonians made a notable contribution to the political public sphere, founding one of the seven Democratic Societies to be established in New York State.[37]

The previous year had seen the arrival of Citizen Edmond Genêt from France and his triumphal progress to Philadelphia, chartering privateers and encouraging the rise of what Federalists condemned as Jacobin "self-created societies." Within months Genêt would feel the threat of Robespierre's Terror and settle down in America as a gentleman farmer. Marrying George Clinton's daughter Cornelia, he eventually took up permanent residence at Cherry Hill, fifteen miles north of Kinderhook in the town of Greenbush. His influence was distantly felt in Kinderhook in February 1793, when Barent Vander-poel presided over a meeting that diplomatically toasted both "the glorious revolution in France" and the Federalist John Jay. It was more directly felt in the founding of a Democratic Society, in February 1794, in the town of Canaan.[38]

Only a very few of the Canaan men who formed the Democratic Society are known, but they were grounded directly in the politics of the Otsego crisis and the longer tradition of King's District radicalism. The chair of the society's opening meeting was Colonel Philip Frisbie, member of the 1793 assembly. One of the clerks, Jonathan Warner, had been a leading subscriber of one of the five Canaan petitions submitted in defense of the election canvassers in December 1792 and once the adjutant of the Seventeenth Albany County Militia, commanded at Saratoga by William B. Whiting, who led one of the other 1792 Clintonian petitions. The other clerk, Moses Younglove, had endured a painful captivity at the hands of tories and Iroquois after the battle of Oriskany and remained for his long life an ardent Republican. None of these founders of the society was a member of Canaan's Federalist-dominated Unity Lodge.[39]

Their purposes were expressly political. The Democratic Society announced in its constitution, printed in the *Hudson Gazette* on February 20, that it would pursue "a political intercourse and association, for elucidating, as far as is in our power, the Rights of Man." As one among a network of "societies formed for political investigation," it would defend "the observance of the Democratical form of republican government," standing against both "a powerful combination in Europe" and "in these states the growing establishment of pride, formality, inequality, political heresy, and a baneful and servile imitation of sovereign and corrupt nations." In due form, officers were to be chosen, meetings called, correspondence established with other societies, and each member sworn to uphold "a government of open justice and equal rights." The following July, apparently after considered debate, the Canaan Society voted a set of resolves asking the legislature for a reform of the court system, complaining of the high judicial fees, the "extraordinary delays of the decisions," and "the intricate and antiquated formalities" and "obsolete phraseology" of the law. It complained of "the vast accumulation of books required, many of them written in dark ages and corrupt government." The society wanted "a new code of laws and rules in plain English, full concise and unequivocal."[40]

The Democratic Society was the target of considerable Federalist hostility. The Federalist Stockbridge *Western Star* published the society's constitution in May but followed it up with a satirical poem set in ballad form: "Because our vigilance alone / Can keep and hold what it hath won . . ." The society's members were accused of being "dictators" of county nominations, while they lashed back against "Lawyers and public functionaries" who assumed that they alone were "fit candidates." While they were attacked by "the lordly and corrupt," the Canaan Democrats pointed to England, where "the more enlightened there are forming societies for further information, investigation, and reform." That September one of their number defended the society's restricted membership, perhaps only seven or eight men, in the pages of Elihu Phinney's *Columbian Mercury*. "More than a house-full cannot deliberate": the society "would fondly have others" of all persuasions, including "Aristocratical" and "Tory Societies," form their own circles; there they could "all freely discuss and publish as we do or as they might choose, that the views of each might be made manifest and bear their proper weight with a proper and orderly people."[41]

In February 1795, during the run-up to the contest between Jay and Yates for the governorship, Henry Van Schaack wrote to Theodore Sedgwick that the Canaan Society was "almost, if not quiet." He was very premature in his assessment. In early March the society met in "a full annual meeting" and then published its anniversary address in the *Gazette*. It was confident now that a "general interest" was securing the people from "fear, corruption, and fraudulent artifice"; a general "revival and diffusion of letters [had] ushered in genuine philosophy," and "the press hath more and more exposed the ancient abuses, exhibiting in full view all the attractive rights of man, and hath awakened his attention to them as to almost abash the wiley advocates for corrupt precedent." It closed its address with an exhortation to the people, "Be up and doing . . . each in his particular sphere and manner, whether as members of private associations for aiding the general good, or merely as members of the social whole." The next October it gathered to hear an oration condemning the Jay Treaty and defending its mission "of a general dissemination of political information and virtue."[42]

With this address the Canaan Democratic Society faded from view, after a career of perhaps twenty months. Federalists condemned it and its fellow societies as self-created and even "traitorous," but the societies had expressed in clear and concise language the establishment of a political public sphere. The public sphere was a place of association and deliberation, publication and reading. It was a place where opinion was shaped and transmitted to representative government for informed lawmaking; it was the locus of the practice of express consent. The Canaan Democratic Society most clearly manifested the deliberative ideal of the public sphere—sprouting up around the society throughout Columbia County. Deeply grounded in the Revolutionary political culture of public meetings and a coercive consensus, the society perpetuated these values in its concern for equality and hostility to formality. And it carried forward from this Revolutionary experience a powerful understanding of the relationship between consent, deliberation, and governance. But, in its vision of a competing multiplicity of political societies meeting, discussing, and publishing in the public sphere, it had begun to develop an understanding of the plural structures of liberal democracy. Consent would be forged in competing debate and deliberation in the public sphere.[43]

4

Persuasion and Civil Boundaries
1780s–1790s

Heidelbergh Catechisms, Translated for use of the reformed protestant Dutch churches, in the state of New-York, to be sold at this office.

—*Hudson Weekly Gazette,* May 18, 1786

To the Public. Theophilus Vosburgh, having in the Hudson Gazette of the 2nd instant, represented to the public, that I the subscriber his wife had eloped from him, and thereby forbidding all persons to trust me; I have been induced to inform the public in my turn; that true it is I have left his place of abode; I did it from no other motive than that of self-preservation and want of necessary sustenance to myself and a small infant; I have born the cruel treatment of this hard hearted tyrant for a long time with patience and fortitude. . . .

JENNY VOSBURGH. Kinderhook, August 15, 1792.

—*Hudson Gazette,* August 16, 1792

Twenty Dollars Reward. Ran away from the subscriber on the 7th Day of June instant, a negro man named SIMON, about five feet seven or eight inches high, twenty five years of age, is very black, walks very upright, is very spry and active, speaks good English and Dutch, was brought up to the farming business. . . .

Abraham Van Alen, Kinderhook Landing, June 16, 1796.

—*Hudson Gazette,* June 23, 1796

I was Called upon by Gen. Jacob R. Van Rensselaer, accompanied by Mr. [Elisha] Williams, and informed that a report was in circulation upon the Manor, that he had said on the floor of the House of Assembly . . . "that the tenants were not fit to govern themselves, and deserved to have a Master"—that this report was doing him great injury in the matter of his reelection.

—Martin Van Buren, writing in Sorrento, Italy, in the summer of 1854,
describing events of the summer of 1811

Hannah Goes Van Buren lived in the shadows of the deliberative civil life that would so preoccupy her husband Martin. Indeed, in many ways, she lived her life in the shadows of consent. When she was born, early in 1783, her father, John D. Goes, was an outlaw in Kinderhook, living under the continuing order of banishment. In her youth she might have shared in some of the "natural boldness" that Colonel Johann Friedrich Specht observed among the women of Kinderhook, perhaps expressed when she and Martin were secretly married in Catskill in February 1807. But she apparently set such boldness aside when she began householding, in Kinderhook briefly, then in Hudson, and finally in Albany, where from 1812 she raised her three sons, slowly giving way to tuberculosis, until her death in 1819. As a married woman, she stood in the shadow imposed by legal coverture, since in giving her free consent to marriage her rights of contract and property were subsumed in her husband's identity. She was described as shy and retiring; perhaps a childhood speaking primarily country Dutch did not prepare her to shine in town society in Hudson and Albany. And in this childhood she would have known slaves, three in her mother's house and six at Martin's father's tavern in 1790, three of whom were still held in 1800. Did she know Simon, who escaped from her cousin Van Alen's in 1796? In her own household Hannah would have given orders to a man named Tom, who escaped into Massachusetts in 1814. When Tom was found in Worcester ten years later, Hannah's widowed husband offered to sell the right to his labor for fifty dollars, if a Mr. Hammond of Berlin in Rensselaer County "could get him without violence."[1]

When he wrote these words, Martin Van Buren was in Washington, having served three years in the United States Senate for New York and was only eight years away from his nomination as Andrew Jackson's vice president. He stood at the very center of the nation's deliberative public sphere, about to forge one of its most enduring institutions, the Democratic Party, on the model of the Regency, the party machine that he had built in New York, which in turn was forged in the experience of his legal and political apprenticeship in the county of Columbia. Hannah stood barred from this deliberation. Her life, in its public silence and invisibility, in the qualities of her household experience, might stand as an emblem of a much wider silence and invisibility. The runaway Tom's life, in flight from slavery in Columbia, is even more shrouded by invisibility. Such invisibilities, however, were being challenged in subtle yet profound ways by an emergent quality of the public sphere. If the public sphere was the domain of deliberation and constituted lawmaking, it was also increasingly the arena of a more fluid and multivocal persuasive culture. Americans excluded from constitutional roles would find their way into public space in this arena of persuasion. But even here their paths into public were complicated by the control of this persuasive space by men of property and power.

BOUNDED CONSENT IN CIVIL SOCIETY

The open enactment of political opinion—as the practice of express consent in a deliberative public sphere and its translation into binding and legitimate law—was both a consequence of the revolutionary settlement and a reason for its stability. But this deliberative public sphere was also a bounded, limited space, hedged in both by constitution and by custom. Decision making beyond the household was restricted to the independent owner of productive property; such had been the common custom in the colonies, which was perpetuated in the state constitution written by the New York convention in 1777. Electoral voice in public was explicitly limited to male freeholders worth twenty pounds or at-will tenants of holdings worth a minimum of forty shillings, and this was simply to vote for members of the assembly and for congressmen; to vote for state senators or the state governor one had to be a freeholder owning at least one hundred pounds in property. By this measure, if those qualified to vote in assembly elections had increased from perhaps 45 percent to about 60 percent, only a quarter of the adult inhabitants of Columbia County were qualified to vote for assemblymen, and fewer than a fifth for senators. In his address to the legislature in November 1800, Governor John Jay articulated the central importance of land in defining civil status. He was concerned about the rights of "infant freeholders," whose land by law might be sold by guardians. But "valuable civil Privileges" were, he noted, "conferred exclusively on that class of Citizens who are Freeholders"; and, when orphaned children's land was sold, "their civil rights, as freeholders of those lands, [were] extinguished."[2]

Martin Van Buren himself, in the bitterly contested 1804 election, had his qualifications to vote for governor challenged by the Kinderhook Federalists on polling day. Here he faced a boundary of property; Hannah Van Buren and her female peers faced a more formidable one of gender. Men might transcend the limits of wealth, but women were permanently excluded from the sacred circle of deliberation. And chattel slavery, enduring in the state of New York until 1827, imposed a third and even more formidable boundary, excluding slaves from any civil status. These civil boundaries of property, gender, and slave status were pervasive in the early Republic. Everywhere, except in the state of Vermont, a minimal property ownership was required before men could vote. Everywhere women, though citizens, were excluded from rights in the market and in politics. In great parts of the Union, slavery condemned persons of African origin to effective civil death.

TABLE 4. *Assembly and Senate Voters and Population in Columbia County*

	1801 Electors	1800 Estimated Population	Proportion
Assembly and Congress			
Adults	3,811	13,316	28.6%
Adult whites	3,811	12,531	30.4%
Adult males	3,811	6,550	58.1%
Adult white males	3,811	6,168	61.8%
1800 taxpayers	3,811	4,159	91.6%
State Senate and Governor			
Adults	2,582	13,316	19.4%
Adult whites	2,582	12,531	20.6%
Adult males	2,582	6,550	39.4%
Adult white males	2,582	6,168	41.9%
1800 taxpayers	2,582	4,159	62.1%

Sources: 1800 MS United States Census; 1801 voters from 1855 *New York State Census,* ix; 1799–1800 Tax Lists, NYSA.

In Columbia County, and elsewhere along the Hudson, two additional boundaries cut through civil society. One was of legal consequence. Tenancy had more profound implications than simple distinctions in wealth. Tenants could make no permanent claim to improvements that they might make to their land, and this incapacity extended from private to public realms. Life-lease tenants had been included in the electorate since 1701, but, even so, the Manor towns mustered fewer voters qualified for either the gubernatorial or assembly elections, and fewer qualified to sit on juries. A second boundary in civil life peculiar to this region was grounded in inherited ethnic culture. Most of the older settled households in this region were of Dutch and German descent, and their children into the first decades of the nineteenth century grew up speaking English as a second language. Some of their parents could speak English only with great difficulty, and many were illiterate. If ethnicity and language had no status in law, they were a boundary of consequence in an English-speaking world, limiting one's efficacy in the public sphere. Limited efficacy, limited agency, meant a limited autonomy, even a dependency on others for mediation in public. This linguistic barrier was complicated by subtle and powerful differences in traditions about the nature of "civil" and "public" among the Dutch-, German-, and English-speaking of various sorts. Some of the boundaries in civil society, thus, were maintained by those seemingly excluded.

Whatever their source, however, these boundaries in civil life imposed limits on the autonomy and agency of individual will. Slaves, women, and men of lesser property stood unambiguously outside the sphere of public deliberation, barred from the conversations shaping law that would be binding on their circumstance. Excluded from deliberative equality, they were consequently excluded from consent and thus any confirmation of governing legitimacy. Thus they posed a grave problem for the assumption that the new American governments ruled by the consent of the governed. Men of property and thus independence of will were surrounded by men and women with neither, and without any articulated agreement to assume the obligations and to abide by the principles of American public life.

Threatened by the potential for insurgency, the men of the deliberative center could fall back on force. Indeed, the laws that they discussed, and indirectly approved in elections, gave them the authority to deploy force to defend private property and the general society. Routinely in sanctions of the courts and on several occasions in the mobilization of militia, they would indeed deploy lawful force against manifestations of civil disorder and dissent. But the legitimacy of the new republican governments mandated the minimum use of force; the men of Columbia County would have found the secret to their stability in John Locke's *Two Treatises on Government* in his discussion of tacit consent. In the original compact and in routine deliberation and voting, men granted their express and overt consent to the obligations of their government. But, in accepting the strictures of ordinary life, others not privy to formal politics gave their tacit consent to the conditions of their governance.

The building of tacit consent, then, stood outside the domain of deliberation, in a wider and far more complex but informal politics of persuasion. This politics of persuasion is as ancient as society itself; in its basic and essential form, the direct and symbolic representation of a governing person or institution in public achieved the cultural persuasion necessary to establish a social peace based on hierarchy and deference. In the Hudson Valley the grand houses and personal deportment of the landlord gentry, with the ritual humiliation written into the terms of their leases of land, were only the most conspicuous and powerful of an array of persuasive realities and symbolic representations working to elicit a tacit consent. But tentatively in the 1760s, and then driven by the accelerating expansion of the institutions and practices of the public sphere from the 1780s, this domain of persuasion progressively became far more complex. The expansion of commercial and associational life meant that there would be many more avenues to the wealth required to compete in this persuasive politics, and the spread of print meant that the experience and structure of persuasion would change fundamentally as well. Cultural constructions in print, compared to the cost in wealth and time required by traditional representations of wealth and power, were cheap, quick, and potentially dramatic. Coded language and a constricted discourse, set in authority-laden, sanctioned forms, would elicit tacit consent in the uncritical reader, an acquiescence to hegemonic interests wrapped in the language of the "public." Conformity to norms of respectability and refinement was requisite upon actors in the deliberative domain and upon the acceptable members of the broader civil society. But, if print comprised a cultural defense of the boundaries in civil society, it assumed literacy and encouraged a capacity for an interior, interpretive life. The simple act of reading might contribute to tacit consent, but it was an act in civil life and an act driven by the will of the actors, who might not have a claim to political deliberation. Literacy would undermine the ancient boundary between independence and dependence. The door was opening to counterpersuasions, respectable subversions, in the public sphere.[3]

PRINT AND PERSUASION

At the center of the informal politics of persuasion in the public sphere stood the printer-publisher, the cultural gatekeeper in the young Republic. Ashbel Stoddard's printshop, despite its unfortunate destruction by fire in 1793 that sent showers of sparks and burning paper over the little city of Hudson, was the nerve center of the persuasive public sphere in Columbia County. Besides the *Gazette* itself, Stoddard certainly printed pamphlets and broadsides that served the function of political deliberation. But the great bulk of printing undertaken at his press and books sold from the shelves in the front of his shop had little direct bearing on the politics of the day. They were devoted to acculturation: introducing the rising generation to the codes of civility and the public sphere. With ministers and schoolteachers, parents and magistrates, Stoddard worked to inculcate an appreciation, indeed a conformity, to rules of improvement and sensibility that would allow the obedient to take their appointed places in this corner of the Republic and in a wider Atlantic culture.[4]

Some of Stoddard's imprints contributed to a stream of entertaining and improving chapbooks coming off American presses. His earliest surviving imprints, from 1786 and 1787, include *The Life and Adventures of Ambrose Gwinnett, The Narrative of Elizabeth Wilson,* Benjamin Franklin's *Way to Wealth,* and a long poem, *The Returned Captive;* these were among the best-sellers of their day. Each about individual agency and moral choice, these little books spoke to a society in great uncertainty. *Gwinnett* was an old tale of a young man who escaped an English noose for a murder he did not commit; for infanticide, Elizabeth Wilson paid that price on a Pennsylvania gallows. "John," returning from years of Indian captivity, had to rebuild his life; Franklin offered advice on how "everyman" might build his own life. Indeed, the great bulk of Stoddard's printing and his sales of wholesale imprints from New York and Albany were in some way didactic, devoted to the improvement of the virtues of children and youth. Estimated by pages printed, about a quarter of his own production was devoted to religious imprints and more than a quarter to imprints for children and schools. Some of these categories overlapped, as did Ezra Sampson's 390-page *Beauties of the Bible,* a selection from both testaments "with various remarks and brief dissertations . . . particularly for the use of schools, and for the improvement of youth," which Stoddard brought out in 1800 in the first of at least eight Hudson editions. Occasionally he invested in educational printing ventures at Albany presses, such as Nathaniel Dwight's *Geography,* published by the Websters in 1796, and Caleb Bingham's *Astronomical and Geographical Catechism,* put out by their competitor Loring Andrew in 1797.[5]

By 1801 Stoddard was printing his own edition of Noah Webster's *New England Primer,* which he stocked in his shop at least as early as 1787. Stoddard's relationship with Webster must have begun at the office of the Hartford *Connecticut Courant,* where Stoddard apprenticed with Webster's cousins Charles and George and where Webster published first the *Primer* and then his more ambitious *American Spelling Book,* the first part of his *Grammatical Institute . . . Designed for the Use of English Schools in America.* Stoddard was advertising Webster's *Spelling Book* in the spring of 1786 and that August began to publish a long-running series of ads for the *Grammatical Institute.* In these instructions on pronunciation, spelling, and grammar, followed by rules of elocution, collections of dialogues, and assorted orations, Webster was attempting to reform the linguistic base of common speech in the public sphere. He hoped "to diffuse an uniformity and purity of language in America — to destroy the provincial prejudices that originate in the trifling differences of dialect . . . — [and thus] to promote the interest of literature and the harmony of the United States." His goal was a common uniformity, a national language, which he hoped would set a new standard and displace established texts that originated from English authors, "too large and expensive for the body of the people to purchase."[6]

In December 1787 Stoddard signed on to another Webster venture, the *American Magazine.* Published in New York and offering original essays and selections from the European press, Noah Webster was attempting to emulate the best British literary publications and to reach a more refined audience. Stoddard's efforts to attract subscriptions for Webster in Hudson could not keep this venture from failing, but the literary magazine did prove a popular enduring regional genre; Stoddard's son William would publish the most successful of these, the Hudson *Rural Repository,* from 1824 to 1851. While he continued to stock Webster's schoolbooks, Stoddard would strike out on his own, printing in 1795 one of the treatises that Webster had hoped to supplant, Hamilton Moore's *Young Gentleman and Lady's Monitor, and English Teacher's Assistant* (which Stoddard had sold at his bookstore in 1793), followed in 1798 by another, William Enfield's *Speaker; or, Miscellaneous Pieces.* In the interval, he put out a local production, *An Introduction to the Art of Reading,* composed by a recently deceased local minister, Bildad Barney, which Stoddard protected with a copyright filed at the federal district office in New York City. These three imprints also shared the distinction of being the longest that Stoddard attempted before venturing Sampson's *Beauties of the Bible.* Here the risks inherent in large volumes were offset by a strong, steady market in schools; Stoddard would issue the *Monitor* again in 1809. All of these and similar works coming off the presses in Poughkeepsie, Troy, Lansingburgh, and Albany were set to the same broad purpose that Webster was attempting to nationalize: the careful channeling of the young into the proper forces of speech and deportment. Stoddard took this project to some length in his 1795 edition of Moore's *Monitor,* commissioning a series of engraved plates from Albany bookseller and jeweler Christopher Hutton. Hutton's plates were designed to illustrate the *Monitor's* concluding section, "Elements of Gesture," which prescribed the body language and deportment appropriate for each of the various classes of oratory. Matters of art, the arrangement of the body was not to be left "to nature."[7]

Printing for a county soon to be hailed for the power and conviction of its legal oratory, Stoddard was contributing to the construction of cultural boundaries in civil society. Those who had been trained in the polite refinements could stand easily inside these boundaries; those who had not would have to struggle. Martin Van Buren, the son of a tavernkeeper, struggled throughout his life with his lack of a classical education; his handwriting would always be a wild scrawl, in sharp contrast to that of the academy-trained gentry. But he did spend a few years in the Dutch Reformed consistory school in Kinderhook, and some of his oratorical skills at the bar might have been shaped by an encounter with Stoddard's *Monitor* and assimilating the outward manifestations of linguistic and bodily refined uniformity that signaled membership in an American civil society.[8]

TABLE 5. *Subscriptions to Imprints in Columbia County, 1786–1800, by Town*

| Town (Taxpayers in 1800) | Subscriptions (Taxpayers per Subscription) | | | | | |
| | Decile of Valuation | | | | | |
	1	2	3	4	5–10	Total
Hudson (433)	6 (1.8)	6	4	1	8	25
Canaan (597)	18 (1.5)	8	7	1	5	39
Hillsdale (579)	6 (6.3)	2	0	0	1	9
Chatham (423)	9 (2.6)	1	1	3	2	16
Kinderhook (461)	11 (2.4)	3	3	0	2	19
Claverack (497)	14 (2.2)	3	2	2	2	23·
Livingston (912)	3 (18.2)	2	0	0	0	5
Clermont (156)	5 (3.0)	0	0	0	0	5
Germantown (91)	0 (0)	0	0	0	0	0
Overall, Columbia County (4,159)	72 (2.9)	25	17	7	20	141
Percent of all subscribers	*51.1*	*17.7*	*12.1*	*5.0*	*14.2*	*100.0*

Note. Subscriptions are to imprints from New York City, Albany, Hartford, and Stockbridge.

TABLE 6. *Subscriptions to Imprints in Columbia County, 1786–1800, by Genre*

Valuation Decile	History and Belles-Lettres	Law and Commerce	Religion	Overall
1	10 38%	50 60%	12 39%	72 51%
2	7 27%	12 14%	6 19%	25 17%
3	3 12%	8 10%	6 19%	17 12%
4	2	4	1	7
5	2	1	2	5
6	1	2	1	4
7	1	2	0	3
8	0	3	1	4
9	0	1	1	2
10	0	1	1	2
Total	26	84	31	141 100%

Note: Imprints included are from New York City, Albany, Hartford, and Stockbridge.

The lists of men from Columbia County who subscribed to books printed in New York, Albany, Hartford, and Stockbridge give a small sense of the distribution of print across the county's social landscape. Some were subscriptions promoted by Stoddard in the pages of the *Gazette;* others followed other channels, such as local ministers. These were volumes of some cost and consequence: Jonathan Edwards's *History of the Work of Redemption* and *Treatise concerning Religious Affections,* the 1792 compilation of the *Laws of the State of New York,* histories of the "rise and progress" of the United States by William Gordon and William Winterbotham, Joel Barlow's *Vision of Columbus* (printed in Hartford), *The Writings of Thomas Paine* (put out by the Websters in Albany in 1792), and Rousseau's *Dissertation on Political Economy.* Robert R. Livingston, standing at the height of genteel refinement, alone signed for a *French Prosodical Grammar.* Ashbel Stoddard himself signed many of these subscription lists, buying the 1792 *Laws,* Newton's *Dissertations on the Prophecies,* twelve copies of Paine's *Writings,* and six of William Watson's *Treatise on the Law of Partnership.* In all, 116 subscribers to nineteen imprints can be identified on the 1800 tax lists. Fully half of the subscribers were in the wealthiest decile of the county valuation, and almost 70 percent were in the top two deciles, though the subscribers of religious and historical-belletristic texts were not quite as wealthy as those buying the *Laws* and legal treatises.[9]

If it was present, print was still relatively rare and expensive, and this raises questions as to its power to persuade. Expensive in themselves if not too costly to transport up the river, volumes such as these were items of considerable regard. Visiting Abraham Staats in Kinderhook in March 1790, Alexander Coventry covetously noted that he "saw a book," Edmund and William Burke's 1757 *Account of the European Settlement in America,* that Staats had borrowed from William Van Ness of Claverack. In great measure, encounters with the refinements of print would have been through such borrowing. Even newspapers, the most common item of print, must have been in short supply, constantly borrowed or read in the shared quarters of taverns and reading rooms.[10]

An exercise in the hypothetical distribution of newspapers in Columbia County illustrates the problem. In June 1801 Stoddard reported to Noah Webster that each week he printed 650 issues of the *Gazette.* The previous year the federal census had counted 35,322 inhabitants, 13,316 adults, and 6,168 adult white men; the county had listed 4,159 taxpayers, 3,811 assembly voters, and 2,582 senate voters. Quite clearly, the *Gazette's* 650 issues were spread thinly across this landscape. With the relative wealth of the book subscribers in mind, however, a possible distribution pattern can be constructed for Stod-

TABLE 7. *Subscribers to Imprints in Columbia County, 1786–1800, by Ethnicity*

Subscriber Decile	English Surname	Dutch or German Surname	Total Subscribers
Wealthiest	49 45%	23 70%	72 51%
2d–10th	55 51%	10 30%	69 49%
Overall	108 100%	33 100%	141 100%

Notes: Taxpayers in the wealthiest three deciles of the 1800 valuation generally were assessed at or above $1500. (See analysis of slaveholding in Chapter 5.)

Imprints included are from New York City, Albany, Hartford, and Stockbridge.

Sources: Imprint subscription lists; 1799–1800 Valuations of real and personal property, Columbia County, NYSA.

dard's *Gazette,* suggesting a scenario dividing the county into regular and irregular readerships. Of Stoddard's 650 papers, we can assume that 50 would have made their way out of the county, many as exchanges with other printers, leaving 600 papers for more than 35,000 people. Typically, subscriptions in the rural regions were shared in "squads" of four subscribers, who shared an issue weekly. Some merchant and gentry subscribers, of course, might not have bothered to share their issue, choosing to save their papers for future reference. We can propose a hypothetical regular subscription of 400 issues of the paper, each issue shared among three households. In these twelve hundred households, encompassing almost 30 percent of the population, there would have been about 10 adults per newspaper, and perhaps 25 men, women, and children. This regular readership in the "respectable part" of society would thus have included both men and women, who would have a reasonable chance to spend a half hour a week glancing through or closely reading the paper in the moderately private circumstances of parlor, chamber, or kitchen.[11]

The other 200 newspapers in this scenario would have been shared among the remainder of the population, and most commonly in the public subscriptions available in taverns. Among this plain or rough sort, few women would have commonly seen the paper. It would have been the adult white men, frequenting the neighborhood tavern, or the hotel while in Hudson on business, who would have seen the paper reasonably regularly, though they would be sharing it with perhaps 20–25 of their peers. Shifting the numbers slightly to 500 private subscriptions and 100 public increases the possible regular readership to just more than a third and raises the number of adult white males per public paper from 25 to 40. A sprinkling of out-of-county papers, in gentry houses and local taverns, would have leavened these numbers somewhat.[12]

TABLE 8. *Imprints Subscribed by Columbia County Purchasers, 1786–1798*

	Subscriber Link	
	Town[a]	1800 Tax List[b]
HISTORY AND BELLES LETTRES		
Barlow, *The Vision of Columbus,* 1787	7	5
Gordon, *History of the Rise, Progress, and Establishment of the Independence of the United States of America,* 1789	3	1
Paine, *The Writings of Thomas Paine,* 1792	17	10
Gay, *French Prosodical Grammar, or Reading Book,* 1795	2	1
Winterbotham, *Historical, Geographical . . . View of the United States of America,* 1796	3	1
Rousseau, *A Dissertation on Political Economy . . . A Treatise on the Social Compact,* 1797	8	7
Pickering, *Letter . . . to Mr. Pinckney,* 1797	1	1
LAWS AND COMMERCE		
Laws of the State of New York, 1792	106	69
Watson, *A Treatise of the Law of Partnership,* 1795	16	11
Jones, *Jones's English System of Bookkeeping,* 1796	1	1
Lee, *The American Accomptant,* 1797	3	3
RELIGION		
Edwards, *A History of the Work of Redemption,* 1786	9	2
Edwards, *A Treatise concerning Religious Affections,* 1787	31	12
Newton, *Dissertations on the Prophecies,* 1787	19	7
Linn, *Sermons Historical and Characteristical,* 1791	7	5
The Whole Genuine and Complete Works of Flavius Josephus, 1792	5	1
Watson, *An Apology for the Bible . . . Addressed to Thomas Paine,* 1796	1	0
Fraser, *A Collection of Select Biography; or, The Bulwark of Truth,* 1798	4	4

[a]All subscribers who can be reasonably identified as living in one of the nine towns in Columbia County in the 1790s.

[b]All subscribers linked to towns who can also be identified on the 1800 tax list.

Even if men did get to the tavern, a great many would have been very irregular in their encounter with print. The tavern was a place of many distractions: reading was jumbled with rough entertainments. Alexander Coventry and his brother William, prosperous young men in Hudson, noted the gambling, cockfights, dancing, turkey shoots, brawls, and affairs of honor that unfolded in Hudson taverns in the 1780s and 1790s. Passing through the county in 1804 and detained at the ferry landing south of Hudson, the Reverend Timothy Dwight wrote acerbically of this tavern culture:

> It is a peculiar characteristic of the ignorant and vicious part [at the landings on the Hudson] to feel that their settlement intimately resembles great trading towns. . . . They employ themselves in copying the fashions, follies, and vices of the cities. To be first, and excessive, in fashions; to make a parade in midst of poverty; to be pert; to gamble; to haunt taverns; to drink; to swear; to read newspapers; to talk on political subjects; to manage the affairs of the nation and neglect their own.

These might have been the circumstances of the men at the Catskill Ferry landing, seen through the eyes of the Pope of New Haven, who clearly did not think much of the claim to deliberative practices by the "vicious part" at the landing. But, in general, setting aside Dwight's more caustic comments, the quality of reading for men without newspaper subscriptions would have been less than ideal. For the women and children comprising their households, many illiterate or only barely literate, reading would have been even more restricted, to the Bible, the almanac, and the *Primer*.[13]

As such, it would be hard to argue that print at this juncture could exert a consistent persuasive power directly on a large part of the population of Columbia County. Before the era of truly mass-printing (which would emerge several decades later), print would operate somewhat indirectly; the persuasion was in some measure convincing the privileged of their right to govern. They in turn, culturally reinforced by this encounter with persuasive print, would have to continue to practice a politics of cultural representation. But, if print's persuasive power did not have a uniform reach, it was in growth and transition. With the arrival of the press in Hudson and the other river towns, the popular encounter with print was beginning to change. An irregular readership was not necessarily a stagnant readership, and many of these readers struggled against the limits of their situation.

One such reader was the young Jesse Torrey, born in New Lebanon to a middling family in 1787. By his own account, in 1817, Torrey was continually reading, borrowing books from a local lawyer who "kindly invited me to make as much use of his excellent library as I wished." In 1804, with the assistance of

Doctor Moses Younglove, recently a stalwart of the Canaan Democratic Society, Torrey founded "the New Lebanon Juvenile Society for the Acquisition
of Knowledge," a free library. He clearly saw the tension between the availability and the cost of print. "The printing press is the main engine, and books
are the rapid vehicles for the general distribution of knowledge." But, despite
the "prodigious" decline in the cost of books over four centuries, he would
write, "but few comparatively can meet the expense of private libraries." Moving to Pittsfield, to Philadelphia, and to Washington, in a career as a doctor, an
antislavery activist, and apparently the first promoter of free libraries, Torrey
grounded his life's worth on building civil institutions to bridge this gap.[14]

Literacy, borrowed books, and fluid extensive reading all provided Jesse
Torrey with his ticket beyond the village of New Lebanon. He was, of course,
like his contemporary the young Martin Van Buren, one of the white men
in Columbia County destined for a higher place in the public sphere. But
Torrey's path toward a condemnation of slavery as "a *black,* accumulating,
threatening-thundercloud," in his 1817 *Portraiture of Domestic Slavery, in the
United States,* suggests the directions in which literacy might move the reader.
Literacy and print were an avenue into civil society; the act of reading was
a civil act. Persuasive print, mediating between individual circumstance and
a wider society and nation, might channel the reader into tacit consent. A
reader might well assimilate persuasion on its own terms, uncritically being
molded and guided toward a sense of place and position, of civil limitations.
But the civil capacity of literacy and the civil act of reading were a double-
edged sword. A critical reading in the wider domain of print might also lead to
challenges to these civil limitations and to creative persuasive interventions,
such as Torrey's, that would ultimately demand attention in the deliberative
public sphere.[15]

ETHNICITY: THE DUTCH AND THE GERMANS

Both deliberation and persuasion in the public sphere required a common
ground of linguistic understanding. Classical styles of literary construction
could and did impose linguistic barriers in the public sphere, barriers that
might be simultaneously mitigated and reinforced by interventions such as
Webster's *Institutes* and Stoddard's *Monitor.* The construction of Webster's
"uniformity and purity of language in America" would include more people
in the national conversation but also would exclude all the more powerfully
those who continued to avoid conformity.[16]

These issues were complicated by the diversity of national origins and language represented in Columbia County and the surrounding region. Indeed,
Columbia's white population was probably among the most ethnically di-

verse and divided in the entire nation. Until the incursions of Yankee squatter settlements in the eastern hills in the 1750s and 1760s, this had been a region in which the English language had been virtually an alien tongue. Along the river, from Kinderhook though Claverack to Livingston and the East Camp (or Germantown), Dutch graded into German, reflecting the settlement streams running south from Dutch Fort Orange (later Albany) and north from the Palatine German refugee community settled at German Camp and Livingston Manor in 1711. Into the early nineteenth century, these peoples comprised distinct and coherent ethnolinguistic communities, speaking High and Low Dutch and various shades of German, deeply rooted in Reformed Dutch and German Lutheran confessions. The Dutch had created a distinctive form of civil life in the seventeenth century, not yet erased by a century of contest, first with Anglo gentry and then with floods of Yankee immigrants. Germans, arriving as impoverished war refugees in the early eighteenth century, maintained their own suspicions of the public domain. By 1800 they were no longer the majority but comprised almost 40 percent of the county population, the largest concentration in any of New York's counties. The Dutch and German presence was felt across many aspects of county life, complicating a public deliberation and persuasion about which they felt a great ambivalence and in which their ethnic culture was barely recognized.[17]

There had, of course, been a long history of interethnic relations in New York and along the Hudson. The Livingstons were Scots married into the Dutch aristocracy of the Van Rensselaers and themselves fluent in Dutch, and they spoke English at home and Dutch in the formal settings of colonial governance. The linguistic boundary between the English regime and the Dutch and German farming communities had given them authority as cultural mediators and brokers and made them well versed in translinguistic political communication. When the Livingstons orchestrated a meeting to protest taxation in January 1781, they made sure that "every Resolution which was entered into was first read in English and then explained in Dutch before the question was put." In 1788 the Federalist committee had the Albany printers produce the new Federal Constitution in Dutch; in the spring and summer of 1798, as the XYZ Affair was raising Federalist hopes, Peter Van Schaack wanted translations of the screeds written by the Federalist pamphleteer William Cobbett. Writing two members of Congress in Philadelphia, he asked for "two or three German Porkupines, and Bloody Buoy in the German language." He was promised a German edition of "Cannibal's Progress." His representative wrote, "I believe them calculated to produce a good effect among the People"; Van Schaack replied, "I will reimburse you when we meet, and in the mean time I think I can make good use of them."[18]

If accommodations were made for the Dutch and Germans at moments of political crisis, however, they seem to have been utterly neglected in the routine proceedings of the emerging public sphere. The linguistics of power seemed to have shifted with the Revolution. In February 1780 John Beebe, sleighing down from the King's District to Albany, stepped into the assembly hall. He "saw with Sattisfaction that that body was principly Compos:d of English men," and "reflected back on the State of affairs in this Government ten years ago when Publick affairs were conducted by Dutch who look:d Down with Distain on those that are now Set at the helm." Charles Webster in Albany, as did Stoddard in Hudson, initially avoided distributing his papers into the old Dutch and German districts, sending a postrider up through the King's District into New England. More tellingly — according to local anecdote — though it was suggested that he should print part of his paper in Dutch, "there being many citizens who could neither speak nor read English," Webster maintained a strictly English-language newspaper, as did all of his colleagues in the other Hudson River towns.[19]

Stoddard did regularly advertise the Heidelberg Catechisms, but in translation into English. Dutch and Germans, though they comprised almost half of the population, were otherwise practically invisible in the regional print culture. In one of the few moments when German traditional culture appeared in local print, the *Gazette* in 1788 carried an ad for Spoor's English School, which offered instruction in "German text" along with "court hand" and "print hand." The two constitutions printed in Albany, the occasional broadside, a funeral sermon and a catechism printed in Catskill and Kingston for the Reverend Petrus van Vlierden of Saugerties: these constituted the sum total of non-English publication in the entire region. By 1812 even Van Vlierden was having his sermons translated into English. The presses on the eastern shore of the Hudson produced only English-language texts, and the newspapers in Troy, Hudson, and Poughkeepsie did not even advertise German- or Dutch-language texts. Newspaper references to Dutch and German culture were very few, comprising only a few short complimentary notes and stories on Dutch industriousness and agricultural skill, obviously framed for an English audience, and the occasional quite vicious mockery of Dutch or German dialect. Uniformly migrants from New England, the editor-printers were attuned to an English-speaking and -reading public, and their printing never deviated from the terms of the Anglo–North Atlantic cultural circuit. Eventually Dutch- and German-speakers would have to read their papers if only to read the legal notices and scan the columns of postmasters' letter lists, but they would receive little or no accommodation from the printers.[20]

Of course, they might not have wanted any. The Germans and Dutch were noted for their insularity. The merchants at Hudson found negotiating in a bilingual situation unnerving; while they spoke English only, groups of farmers in their stores maintained a linguistic shield, consulting among themselves in Low Dutch before making a counteroffer. To some, they were backward, by the standards of English civility. An English traveler, William Strickland, passing from Hudson through Kinderhook in the fall of 1794, complained that the Dutch had never "stepped out of the paths of their ancestors or made improvements of any kind; they never have had any schools, throughout the State, except one at Albany, or given any education to their children, whom they say it ruins; many of the principal people among them can neither read, write, or cypher; tho' the lowest man in N: England is master of all of them." Washington Irving, who spent a summer with the Van Nesses in Kinderhook in 1809, captured this clash of English and Dutch cultures in "The Legend of Sleepy Hollow," where a Yankee schoolteacher found himself immersed in "a drowsy, dreamy" world in which "his rustic patrons . . . apt to consider the costs of schooling a grievous burthen, and schoolmasters as mere drones."[21]

Certainly there was some learning among the Dutch and Germans—Strickland notwithstanding—as the Reformed churches had sponsored grammar schools since the seventeenth century. But pockets of illiteracy persisted in these towns until 1840, reflecting, perhaps, an older generation who had missed the universal education mandated in 1812. People in these Dutch and German towns were also much less likely to have occasional imprints, such as sermons and July Fourth addresses, published at presses like Stoddard's. What seems particularly likely is that literacy, particularly English literacy, was graded with wealth in these ethnic communities, with local leading families continuing to play the role of cultural brokers for their communities. Thus, while just more than a quarter of the book subscriptions from the county were from Dutch and German households, mostly in Kinderhook and Claverack, almost three-quarters of these were in the wealthiest decile of the tax valuation, in sharp contrast to the subscribers of English background, among whom the wealthiest tenth accounted for fewer than half of these subscribers.[22]

The common folk among the Dutch and Germans were certainly not completely illiterate, as Strickland had it, but comprised their own reading community, attuned, not to the emerging bourgeois public sphere, but to a tradition of religious, indeed Pietist, reading that had strong continuities with patterns of literacy that emerged with the Reformation. Thus, while Alexander Coventry found that Abraham Staats had borrowed Burke's *Account of the European Settlement* from William Van Ness, he also found a German, Dr. Tully, reading the New Testament, presumably in German. Across the river in Lunenburgh (later Athens), at the center of the upper Hudson Lutheran parish, the Reverend Wilhelm Berkenmeyer by his death in 1751 had built up a circulating library of more than 350 German texts, predominantly theological but including philosophy, science, and geography. Among these same pious German Lutherans, Berkenmeyer's successor, Johannes Christopher Hartwig, enlisted more than fifty subscribers to the 1751 Philadelphia edition of Johann Arndt's *Des hocherleuchteten Theologi*. Presumably, libraries similar to Berkenmeyer's, if perhaps smaller, existed in Kinderhook, Claverack, and Livingston households, built on correspondences reaching downriver to New York and Philadelphia. Dutch and German household Bibles, psalmbooks, and other religious texts came up in the river trade, and local stores in country neighborhoods likely offered prayer books, psalmbooks, chapbooks, and pamphlets in Dutch and German. When Andries Lowe of Claverack died in 1800, his will, written in German, left his son Jacob a loom, cows, "and also my Bible, Christian Sermons, and all of my books."[23]

Ethnic and Pietist culture had stood behind some of the strands of neutral and loyalist sentiment during the Revolution. The Kinderhook loyalists were as much defending an ordered hierarchy in their old Dutch district as they were the king. Echoing pacifist traditions that ran deep in the sectarian tradition, Martin Krum, the leader of a Lutheran secession from the Claverack Dutch church in 1776, refused to bear arms in the patriot militia and was banished with Peter Van Schaack and John D. Goes; he, like them, managed to return after the war. Pietist sentiments underlay a controversy in the mid-1790s that pitted the Germans of the Churchtown Lutheran church against the emerging public sphere. In 1791 they had hired John Frederick Ernst to serve their congregation and that of the Lunenburgh church across the Hudson. Ernst was a patron of the English-speaking public sphere. Organizing a celebration at the refitting of the church organ in Lunenberg in 1792, he had Stoddard publish in English the hymns sung that day. Four years later Stoddard published another Ernst production, a long prayer given and anthems sung at the opening of the Masonic Hall in Hudson, in December 1796. By then, however, the Lutherans at Churchtown were in turmoil; many were saying that Ernst, "on account of his membership with the Freemasons, . . . stood in league with the Devil." Communion was suspended until Ernst's departure for a seminary on the Otsego County frontier. He defended himself on the terms of the public sphere but was aware that he was violating the norms of German Pietist culture; he had "joined the Society from a Desire of Knowledge and removing Ignorance. . . . I've broken in my Boat the Ice of Prejudice, as no other German Minister in this Country is initiated to my knowledge." Writing in another publication in defense of Masonry, he warned a Pennsylvania merchant, "Don't let it come to the hands of unlearned or prejudiced Germans and others who would deal with it, as Swines with Pearls."[24]

The Dutch as well as the Germans had a long history protecting their ethnic culture from intrusion and change. With their language, the Dutch retained a strong memory of the distinct legal forms of civil life that had developed in the seventeenth century. Some of these memories were quite raw. Local Dutch families had played a leading role in advancing the cause of Jacob Leisler against English authority in Albany in 1689; the suppression of the rebels and the burgeoning fortunes of the landlord families who had opposed them must have rankled for decades, perhaps informing Kinderhook's contrarian Dutch loyalism of the 1770s. A related resistance to religious Anglicization was manifested in the unique relation of churches on this stretch of the Hudson to the schisms that swept the Dutch Reformed in the eighteenth century. Urban Dutch merchant families in New York had accommodated to English influences, and a popular Dutch diaspora into New Jersey was drawn to Pietist revivalism that led down a different path to New Light ecumenism. But the Dutch churches in Columbia County avoided both these paths. Relatively insulated from elite English culture except through the landlord families and some merchants, the Dutch Reformed in Kinderhook, Claverack, and Livingston had resisted popular Pietism in calling antirevivalist Johannes Fryenmoet to their joint pastorate in 1756 (Claverack would be among the last churches to join the American Dutch Reformed Synod, in 1815).[25]

The survival of the German and Dutch languages and the advance of English might well have varied along lines dividing public from private, and change must have come in a jagged, contradictory mosaic. By the turn of the century, if not well before, it must have been abundantly clear that the language of public affairs — of commerce, court, and politics — would be English. The Schaghticoke Scientific Society, formed by young men of Dutch families in 1799 to the north in Rensselaer County, legislated this understanding when it voted to conduct all its business in English. Although Dutch and German were still heard in agricultural labor, in household prayer, and from some pulpits into the 1820s, church records began to shift to English slightly sooner. In Taghkanic on the Livingston Manor, this transition came in the fall of 1803 and was shaped by civil initiatives: English was adopted by the Lutheran Church as it incorporated under state law and as legislation was introduced under Republican sponsorship to separate the neighborhood from the Manor as a new town. But this was a long linguistic and cultural transition, which would take decades. At the end of the eighteenth century, however, the German and Dutch communities retained enough coherence to allow many of their members, if not all, to live in certain isolation, perhaps insulation, from the emerging persuasive public sphere. This aloof, perhaps critical, isolation in traditional ethnic cultures must have represented a certain withholding of a grant of consent.[26]

SLAVERY AND THE AFRO-DUTCH

If the efforts of the Dutch and German at maintaining a cultural isolation hint at a withholding of consent, they had living among them a people denied that very option. African peoples had been held in slavery along the Hudson since the 1630s, and their condition was the definition of civil exclusion. Slavery was deeply entrenched in New York State, and slaves counted among the dependents excluded from the privileges of civil deliberation. Uniquely, however, they were seen as beyond persuasion, and subject directly to force. As elsewhere in the early Republic, it can well be said that slave and free along the mid-Hudson stood in a relationship of undeclared war.[27]

Columbia County was not the epicenter of slavery in the region. Although its proportion of total population in slavery, almost 6 percent, was larger than in Dutchess County to the south and in the future Rensselaer County to the north, Columbia's commitment to slavery was overshadowed by Ulster County across the river to the south, where almost 10 percent of the population was enslaved in 1790, and in Kingston and several other towns along Esopus and Rondout creeks, where the enslaved comprised 17–18 percent. Across the river in the towns of Catskill and Albany slaves made up 15–16 percent of the population. If it lagged behind these other upriver centers of slavery, Columbia followed New York's ethnic geography of slaveholding. Slaves were concentrated in the older river towns, held for the most part by the Dutch, the Germans, and the Anglo-Dutch landlord elite. Kinderhook, Claverack, and Clermont led the county with 10–13 percent enslaved. Clermont was adjacent to Rhinebeck, another center of Livingston landlord influence, which, with the Dutch town of Fishkill, was one of two centers of slaveholding in Dutchess County. To the north, the river-facing neighborhoods of the eastern district of Rensselaerwyck, inhabited by Dutch tenants of the Van Rensselaers (later set off as the towns of Schodack and Greenbush), might have approached the levels of slaveholding in Dutch Kinderhook. In sharp contrast, the Yankee-settled hill towns along the Massachusetts border contained virtually no slaves. In Columbia County, in Hillsdale and Canaan, slaves counted for less than 1 percent of the population, matched or nearly so to the north in Stephentown and Hoosac and to the south in Amenia and Pawling.[28]

The result of this differential slaveholding among ethnic whites was a sharply contrasting social geography of slavery for African Americans. In Dutch Kinderhook, where roughly a quarter of the white households in 1790 owned slaves, more than six blacks in ten lived in groups of at least five of their peers. Uphill to the east, in Yankee Canaan, where fewer than 3 percent of the households in 1790 reported slaves, fewer than a third lived in groups of five or more. In some cases, slaveholdings along the river compare with those that might be found in a county in the southern tidewater. Robert Livingston, the third lord of the Manor, ruled a literal plantation, with some of his forty-four slaves working at his ironworks at Ancram. A few of the slaves at Ancram Furnace and some of the older domestic slaves serving at the manor house on the river might have come directly from Africa or from Antigua and Jamaica on slaving voyages that Robert and his father, Philip, had helped to finance. At Clermont, the widow Margaret Beekman Livingston had fifteen slaves, and her son Chancellor Livingston nine. In Kinderhook, Colonels Abraham and Philip Van Alstyne held groups of eighteen and sixteen slaves, followed by Peter Van Ness, Cornelius Van Schaack, and other Van Alstynes, Van Alens, and Vanderpoels, each holding ten or eleven slaves. Various Van Rensselaers and Ten Broecks in Claverack, Hudson, and Clermont also had slaveholdings in this range. Slaves in these numbers made a considerable contribution to a farm economy: women in the kitchen and the dairy, men working with horses and cattle, plowing, and harvesting, and some working in the flour mills and on river sloops.[29]

In such circumstances of larger African numbers, a certain cultural distance and certain social autonomy might well develop. If so, however, it was deeply enmeshed within the prevailing Dutch context of their enslavement. Slaves in the region erected horse and cattle skulls as birdhouses, perhaps an African custom. But they were also remembered at Claverack for cooking the Paas cakes at the Easter festival observed by the Dutch. By the late eighteenth century the Easter celebration of Paas and the Pentecost celebration of Pinkster seven weeks later were becoming as much African as they had been Dutch. In Kinderhook, where the Dutch minister, Isaac Labagh, held six slaves, the assignment of pews in the Reformed Dutch church in 1795 included a reservation of bench 24 "vacant voor de swarte vrouwen." The advertisements for runaways that Ashbel Stoddard printed in the *Gazette* testify to a slave acculturation: Abraham Van Alen's slave Simon spoke "good English and Dutch" when he disappeared from Kinderhook Landing in 1796; another runaway, advertised from Coxsackie across the river, spoke "good English, High and Low Dutch"; another in 1801 "bred in a Dutch family speaks both Dutch and English." Slaves would have honed these language skills in their circulation in and between neighborhoods, sent to the store by their master, or engaged in small-scale commerce of their own. One traveler reported that slaves could give more reliable travel directions than their Dutch masters.[30]

Explosive tensions lay just below the surface of these close relations. Slaves in New York Colony had a long history of insurgency, manifested in these decades not only by runaways but by outright violence. Dr. Alexander Coventry of Hudson, himself a slaveholder, ministered to an injured slave-catcher in April 1787: John Van Valkenberg, "one of the most powerful men I ever saw," had received a deep knife wound in his thigh in a struggle to recapture a slave couple, who had escaped over the border into Massachusetts, "where Negroes are free." But there were more direct and systemic threats of rebellion, perhaps manifestations of secret societies and communications among the blacks along the river. In 1775, as the Revolutionary struggle got under way, slaves in Kingston were caught conspiring to burn the town, and a slave in Poughkeepsie was burned at the stake for torching a house and barn. The Albany County Committee heard rumors of meetings among the slaves and passed resolves that colonial laws restricting slave movements be enforced. In 1793, as news of the Haitian Revolution filtered up the river, a slave murdered a leading citizen in Kingston, and three slaves in Albany were convicted in a conspiracy to burn the city. In Columbia County events such as these had not happened since 1715, when John Dykeman had been murdered on Livingston Manor for selling a slave's child to the West Indies. But, as the county was being formed and for years later, the *Gazette* regularly printed news of black transgressions and possible secret combinations: a Negro was stopped in Hartford with a horse stolen "near Hudson's River"; three blacks were arrested in Albany with counterfeit money; one of the three horse thieves sentenced to hang at the first court in Claverack was John Davis, "a Negro man." In 1789 rumors were circulating through the county taverns that a mixed-race gang—the Johnsons—encompassing whites, blacks, and Indians, was hiding out in the Kinderhook pine woods, living in "little huts" and stealing from local farms.[31]

The rumors of the Johnson gang in the Kinderhook woods powerfully encapsulated the civil status of people of color on the late-eighteenth-century Hudson. They were excluded from civility; they lay outside the privileges and protections of civil society. They most commonly appeared in the public sphere as civil transgressors, as criminals or runaways, and as the civilly dead, subject to sale as chattel property. This civil exclusion was confirmed and perpetuated in the spring of 1785, when a bill for the abolition of slavery failed in the assembly. But the debate over abolition in 1785 also hinted at new attitudes and prospect for change.

Opposition to slavery had first surfaced in the constitutional convention of 1777, where the delegates approved a resolution enjoining "future Legislatures of the State" to abolish slavery so that every inhabitant of the state could eventually "enjoy the privileges of a freeman." In 1781 slaves serving in the army were freed, but the convention's challenge for a general act of abolition was not taken up until early 1784. That spring a bill for gradual abolition was introduced by Senator Ephraim Paine of Amenia in Dutchess County, where antislavery sentiment was building among the many Quakers living in the towns along the Connecticut border. Paine reintroduced his bill in the senate in February 1785, where it quickly passed, but it encountered considerable resistance in the assembly. Immediately rejecting Aaron Burr's proposal of immediate abolition, apparently a deflecting tactic, the assembly proceeded to vote a bill of gradual emancipation, which imposed severe limits on that freedom, including a denial of rights to vote, to sit on juries, and to intermarry. Neither Matthew Adgate nor Jacob Ford, representatives from the Yankee hill towns Canaan and Hillsdale, respectively, owned any slaves. While they opposed Burr's motion for immediate abolition, they struggled to get the best possible outcome for freed slaves. Ford introduced failing motions to ensure their rights of suffrage and marriage. Ford and Adgate were vindicated when the Council of Revision rejected the bill for its exclusion of Negroes, mulattos, and mustees from the vote, which threatened to create a "class of disenfranchised and discontented citizens" that, if blood was to be the measure of suffrage, would eventually amount to "many millions." Despite its flaws, however, Ford and Adgate, with William Whiting in the senate, voted to override the council's veto, but the council was upheld by assemblymen who had consistently opposed the abolition bill throughout that spring. Walter Livingston, one of the heirs to Livingston Manor, voted against the abolition bill and, in consequence, might have faced an insurgency in his own house. In June 1785 he angrily dismissed a free black woman Flora from his service and vindictively charged her for clothing that he had supplied in years past; "her insolent behavior" might well have been to challenge him for his vote against abolition in the assembly.[32]

Doors to the future were beginning to open, slowly, for the African Americans of the mid-Hudson. Hints of these openings might also be found in the *Gazette,* which started printing in the spring of 1785, and in some of the other papers started by emigrant Yankees in the river towns. Thus, while Stoddard regularly printed runaway advertisements in the summer of 1786, on June 15 he published prominently on his front page a sentimental account of "The Slave" — "presented . . . with his liberty . . . sunk senselessly upon the ground" — and on the second page, an account of an Italian merchant's son, imprisoned among galley slaves in France; the next April he gave notice of a Columbia College oration against slavery. The language of sensibility was beginning to be mobilized against slavery, the first manifestations of a long campaign of persuasion in the public sphere toward abolition.[33]

If it was not being abolished, the day-to-day and year-to-year experience of late-eighteenth-century slavery in New York was certainly changing. Within certain bounds, there was room for a limited expression of consent — and dissent. Alexander Coventry discovered that he could not really just purchase a slave as a chattel but had to negotiate with him. Thus in July 1786, when he tried to buy a slave across the river at Catskill, he was rebuffed by a "very proud" black man of "haughty mein" who "preferred not to leave his old mistress, and so she would not sell him." In March 1789 Coventry was asked to solve a family quarrel: a slave of one of the Van Alstynes complained that "his mother and he could not agree; he told his master he must have another house to live in," and he was sent to see Coventry. This relationship also did not work out, and in April Coventry found himself in competition with his brother William for the allegiance of Cuff, a slave in the Van Keuren household. Cuff initially "wanted to live with" William, but Alexander eventually persuaded him to "agree to live with me"; Coventry and Van Keuren "tossed up" a coin to settle on a price of seventy-seven dollars for Cuff's labor. Thus slaves could negotiate the terms of their labor within certain circumstances. Cuff demanded time off to observe both Paas and Pinkster, for which Coventry gave him permission and, perhaps, a written pass.[34]

We can assume Cuff attended a Pinkster celebration in Kinderhook; at Paas he had gone "over the creek" separating Kinderhook from Hudson. It is possible, too, that some Columbia County slaves might have occasionally participated in the Pinkster festivities in Albany. A weeklong celebration in early June, Albany's Pinkster started with troops of slaves marching through the streets and continued with the sale of special food and drink by wandering hucksters and at booths set up on Pinkster Hill at the old fort above the city. Here the festivities culminated in a whirl of all-night dancing and reveling, presided over by an African "king" in a British officer's scarlet tunic.[35]

This, like African-American celebrations throughout the late-eighteenth-century North, was a classic carnival, a symbolic and temporary inversion of social norms in which the least would rule for a day or a week. As such, Pinkster was ostensibly part of an older, traditional world of rulers and ruled, in which inhibitions were thrown off and roles reversed, perhaps in a reinforcement of traditional norms. Such a role reversal may well have reinforced traditional norms, as powerfully stated when three slaves convicted of arson in 1793 were hanged on Pinkster Hill. But, in the case of New York's Pinkster, this carnival might have been less traditional than transitional. Africans had long participated in Pinkster with the Dutch, but the Dutch withdrew from this traditional festival after the Revolution. It is possible that a newly African Pinkster was linked in some way with the 1785 debate over abolition. If abolition was not voted in 1785, the Pinkster rituals yet gave over to slaves a place in public, on the edges of civil society if not in the formal public sphere. It is at least suggestive that Walter Livingston dismissed his free servant Flora "for her insolent behavior" only two weeks after the traditional Pinkster date. Just as carnival and even riot were legitimate means of political expression for disenfranchised whites in the monarchies and empires of the wider Atlantic world in the eighteenth century, now they were given over to the disenfranchised slaves in post-Revolutionary New York.[36]

WOMEN AND THE PUBLIC SPHERE

Hannah Goes was almost twenty-four years of age when she and Martin Van Buren eloped to be married in Catskill in February 1807. She was perhaps slightly older than her female peers on their wedding days and had thus experienced something of the independence of unmarried American women that Alexis de Tocqueville noted twenty-five years later. This independence before marriage was all the more grounded in her mother's widowed circumstance. John D. Goes had died in 1789, and Maria Goes headed a household in the next decade holding slaves, listed in the tax valuation and the census, and in 1795 rented a seat in her own name in the Dutch Reformed church in Kinderhook. Her father dead six years since, we can imagine Hannah sitting with her mother, perhaps in the red or gray wraps that Hessian Colonel Specht noted the Kinderhook women wearing in 1777.[37]

Death thus provided one avenue to civil visibility lost in the feme covert status of married women. Married women were virtually invisible in the civil domain, their property and any power of contract conveyed to their husbands. In 1787 the legislature opened another avenue to civil visibility in passing an act granting the right of divorce in cases of adultery; here the guilty party was forbidden to remarry, but the guiltless was allowed to remarry "as if the party convicted was actually dead." Women could, and did, exercise rights of petition and pursue claims to justice in the state court of equity over which Chancellor Robert R. Livingston presided, often meeting at his Clermont estate, a court that also had the power to determine the facts in cases of divorce. But unmarried, married, widowed, or divorced, no women in the state of New York could participate in the deliberative public sphere that governed their circumstances. At best they might appear in celebrations of national Independence or of the Constitution, rendering female assent to masculine prerogative. Even here Columbia County did not stand out at the moment of national origins: no women were mentioned among the "citizens of Hudson," "principal gentlemen," and "most respectable characters of the neighborhood" who gathered to celebrate the Federalist Fourth in Hudson in 1788. Six weeks later the women of the village of Lansingburgh, just to the north in Rensselaer County, marched in their own parade, carrying the Constitution as a banner.[38]

Herein lay an ambiguity that would drive a powerful political struggle that would take almost a century and a half to be resolved. White women occupied a profoundly indeterminate place in civil society. They were certainly not slaves, yet they had no place in public deliberation. If they had rights in property, they lost them in marriage. If law protected them from violence, they were still highly vulnerable. But, if they were excluded from the deliberative public sphere, American women would come to occupy a central place in a persuasive public sphere, by virtue of their literacy and their location in an emerging American moral universe. As of the 1780s and 1790s, however, this new place in public was only beginning to take shape. And, in Columbia County, women's place in public was profoundly shaped by the different ethnic and religious traditions that formed the basic ground of the cultural landscape of the mid-Hudson region and that provided a ground for women's agency. These traditions in turn shaped their encounter with civil society in the years to come.[39]

Sitting at their bench in the Dutch church, Hannah Goes and her mother would have exchanged occasional glances with other women of note in Kinderhook. Among them, Caterina Kittle stood out. In the summer of 1777, as British armies approached from the north, Caterina's husband, Andrus, had sided with the loyalists, while she had—in words of her petition to the Council of Safety—"ever during this unhappy war been friendly and well affected to the American cause." Afraid that the property that she had brought into the marriage, already sequestered as part of Andrus's estate, would be confiscated by the Revolutionary government, she had petitioned the council in December 1777 for relief. She was well supported by her neighbors, who testified that they had "frequently heard" the two "in discourse ... upon public matters" and that Caterina "always evinced the most steady attachment to this country." Exactly what happened to Andrus is not clear, but the Kittles did not lose their property. In March 1779 the Kittle house and land were listed in Andrus's name, but by November it was in that of "Caty, w of Andries." Caterina appeared in the 1790 census as the owner of a slave and in 1795 as a former holder of a pew in the Dutch church.[40]

Dramatically announcing her consent in the new Revolutionary government, Caterina survived the "ruin and destruction" that she had seen in her husband's "unnatural" actions to maintain her property and place in Kinderhook society. Maria Van Buren, Martin's mother, took another route into the civil public. A Goes by birth and married into the Van Alen family by her first marriage, Maria seems to have quite self-consciously pursued a strategy of protecting landed interests in a town where conflicting overlapping patent grants perpetually threatened the prosperity of Kinderhook households. Apparently not trusting her tavernkeeping husband, she ensured that three of her Van Alen and Van Buren sons received educations that would prepare them for the law, an American law in the English tradition that would have to be asserted to protect Dutch property in Kinderhook. Her youngest, Martin Van Buren, briefly attended the local Kinderhook village academy before, at age fourteen, being apprenticed to the law with Peter Silvester, where he spent six humiliating years, living in a back room at Silvester's office in Kinderhook village.[41]

These women were working in a long tradition of female authority and even autonomy. Traditional culture among the Germans and the Dutch had once been the ground for considerable female communal authority and, among the Dutch, command over property. Into the middle of the nineteenth century Dutch and German women retained their maiden names in church records, an aspect of a wider conservative preservation of ethnic tradition and languages by women in household and church. If inheritance patterns followed those in rural Ulster County, Dutch women in Kinderhook had continued to preserve something of the ancient control over family property. Caterina Kittle and Maria Van Buren invoked quite different claims to the emerging civil society, but to the end of maintaining inherited property and the ethnic traditions adhering to that property. Caterina, in particular, might have successfully asserted her political status distinct from that of her husband, but she did so from the position and prerogatives of a Dutch housewife. If Dutch and German women claimed public status, they did so within the terms of their ethnic culture, terms that did not translate easily into the reformulated civil society of the early Republic.[42]

Thus the mosaic of ethnicity and gender was conditioned by, and conditioned, experiences in civil society and the public sphere that had a generational dimension. The ethnic traditions that gave Dutch and German women communal authority were old and attenuating, remembered and followed by an aging generation. Dutch and German women of this older generation might well have been illiterate in English and their reading limited to traditional confessions, catechisms, contemplative works, and doctrinal tracts. But, as their children's reading skills in Dutch faltered, the presses stood ready to advance their acculturation: the Heidelberg Confession was being published in English in New York City as early as the 1760s and by 1782 in Albany. Abraham Hellenbroek's *Specimen of Divine Truths* had been appearing in English in New York since 1765, Kingston by 1801, and Albany by 1803. Occasionally they were advertised in the Hudson papers: Stoddard advertised the Albany *Heidelbergh Catechism* in the late 1780s but had given up by 1793; Johann Georg Zimmermann's *Solitude,* published in New London in 1806, was advertised in Federalist papers in Hudson and Troy. Between 1812 and 1818 a minor rush of German and Dutch works in translation appeared from Hudson presses. Mostly catechisms and religious instructionals, they were issued mainly by the independent Federalist offices of Ashbel Stoddard and William Norman. These English translations were apparently an effort to hold young Germans and Dutch to the content if not the language of their tradition; in the long run it appears that this effort to maintain a separate space in the public sphere was not particularly successful.[43]

Nonetheless, women of the Dutch and German traditions attempted to maintain a certain distance from the English-speaking public sphere. They seem to have comprised a distinct and isolated reading community, most likely not members of the regular readership of the *Hudson Gazette*. If the Dutch and German population in 1800 comprised as many as 40 percent of the county's people, we can extend that regular readership much further into the ranks of the English-speaking population; perhaps as many as half of the people of English tradition lived in households with regular access to the *Gazette*. Women among the English-speakers, most from New England but many emigrants from the lower counties and Long Island, would have constituted an important readership for the products of the press and the bookshops in Hudson.

A comment dropped by Alexander Coventry in March 1786 suggests the stakes involved in literacy. Noting the beauty of a girl from a local German family, Coventry wrote, "Were she brought up with good educational advantages, and surroundings of city society, she would make a fine woman." Later that night he had a pleasant and "enjoyable" walk home with an English girl, who was "a little inclined to sentimentality." Without political or economic rights, women's claim to civil society was narrowly dependent upon conformity to the strictures of polite convention and refinement, a conformity that might be attained, or at least approximated, through "good educational advantages" and the reading that it made possible. When Stoddard printed Hamilton Moore's *Young Gentleman and Lady's Monitor* in 1795, it was for the young "lady" as much as the young "gentleman," and essays on the advantages and disadvantages of good and bad educations were followed by an essay, "Learning a Necessary Accomplishment in a Woman of Quality or Fortune." If men were to conform in language and body to public codes of respectability, this conformity was an emblem of consent, indeed citizenship, for American women. This conformity was part of the persuasive dimension of the public sphere. Showing their consent in conformity to persuasion, the conforming might also have it in their power to persuade.[44]

Between 1814 and the early 1830s, Ammi Phillips, an itinerant painter living in Troy, painted portraits of members of middling families across Columbia County, which hint at the central place of reading in specific women's lives in Columbia County in the early Republic. One of his frequent conventions, though out of fashion among sophisticated urban portraitists, was the emblem of literacy. Husbands were painted as men of affairs, grasping letters addressed to them, or—as in the case on Leonard Ten Broeck of Clermont—a copy of the *Albany Argus* boldly asserting an affiliation with Van Buren's Regency. Wives and daughters, from the ten-year-old Catherine Dorr of Chatham to Anna Maria Gebhard, the elderly wife of the Dutch Reformed minister in Claverack, were pictured gently holding small books, of a size typical of novels, prayer books, or pious advisories. Some of the evidence is inscribed in the books themselves. Phebe Woodward and then Betsy Vale successively signed a copy of Samson Occom's *Choice Collection of Hymns,* published in Hudson by Ashbel Stoddard in 1787. Nabby Keith was similarly possessive of two sermons on the death of Washington, preached at Spencertown village in Hillsdale and published by Stoddard in 1800. Here and there letters and diaries tell us what particular women were reading. In the spring of 1788, Katherine Hogeboom in Claverack made sure that her suitor in New York City, General Samuel Webb, sent along current and back issues of a literary magazine to complete her series. Eighteen years later Charles Foote, a young law student in Kinderhook, wrote to his sisters on their reading; the girls had been reading a history of China—he urged them to move on to English history, poetry, and Pope's *Essay on Man.* Julia S. Ludlow of Claverack was among the subscribers to Thomas Brown's *Account of the People Called Shakers* in 1812; twenty-five years later her daughter Mary Frances did at least a thousand pages of reading, interspersed with visits and sewing, in one very cold winter month. Occasionally the newspaper editors would allude to the special place of reading in women's lives. Thus in 1797 Stoddard inserted into the *Gazette* a request that, with the rising cost of paper, the women of the county should be saving rags: "All the books we read . . . depend on the saving of rags . . . let it be the perquisite of some little girl in the family to have the rags. Hang up a little bag in some convenient place . . . a pound or two of rags will make a volume of Sermons or the History of Cecelia." Five years later in the spring of 1802, Stoddard included a brief sketch of a girl named Lucy, "who cared not a farthing for a newspaper," and let it be known that all they were good for was "to tell us the marriages and deaths of our acquaintance, that is all that I read in it, except the Poet's Corner."[45]

These small windows onto women's reading hint at some essential patterns. Pious reading would have been common to women of all ages and ethnicities, but Katherine Hogeboom's reading of a magazine was part of the broader Anglicization of the younger generation among the more prosperous Dutch. Pious or secular, historical or sentimental, all women's reading depended upon the mediation of men in the marketplace, the printers, editors, and booksellers who produced and sold the volumes of sermons or Fanny Burney's *Cecelia; or, Memoirs of an Heiress* and chose the content and blocked the pages of type for the county newspapers. In this mediation there was a hierarchy of print accessibility grounded on cost and connections: for every Katherine Hogeboom, who could get her magazines sent up from New York City, there were hundreds of Lucys, whose only frequent exposure to printed text would have been in cheap, locally produced primers and psalmbooks and the weekly "Poet's Corner," a fixture in papers throughout the country, typically on the upper left-hand corner of the back page. The wives and daughters of the more prosperous householders might purchase books of local or regional printing in Hudson or might borrow books from the emerging circulating libraries, either those being established in Hudson and the other leading river towns or from the larger libraries operating out of New York City and advertising in the local papers. Across the countryside women would be supplied less adequately at local stores and taverns or by peddlers. Despite the role of wealthy patrons and wandering peddlers at either end of the spectrum of supply, the printer-booksellers of the leading river towns played a central gatekeeping role in shaping the content of this hierarchy of accessible print.[46]

The investments of the printers suggest something of the English reading habits of the regional reading community. Setting aside the repeated printings of primers and readers, there were thirty-three best-sellers produced by the presses in Hudson, Poughkeepsie, Troy, and Lansingburgh between 1785 and 1819 (defined as titles printed two or more times). Of these, following the nine printings of Washington's *Farewell,* eight of Ezra Sampson's *Beauties of the Bible,* and six of Isaac Watt's *Psalms,* Susanna Rowson's *Charlotte Temple* tied for fourth place with, suggestively, *The Clerk and Magistrate's Assistant* and Joseph Lord's *Military Catechism.* Both subordinate to the charismatic and religious foundations of the Republic, the sentimental stood in symmetric opposition to the instructional texts of court and militia, female-inclusive ritual contrasted with the exclusively male.[47]

Ashbel Stoddard's press was the source of many of these sentimental best-sellers, even before he reprinted *Charlotte Temple* in 1803. Since the late 1780s he had been developing the moral-sentimental formula that structured the plot of *Charlotte Temple,* as it had those of the foundational novels, Samuel Richardson's *Pamela* and *Clarissa.* This formula situated female experience in a narrative of adversity and tribulation, in which a woman's exercise of virtue and self-control were literally matters of life and death.

Just as Charlotte died for failing "to resist the impulse of inclination," Stoddard's publications were strewn with women wrestling with moral failings. In 1786 he had a story from true life, that of Elizabeth Wilson's execution for infanticide following illegitimate birth, complete with her confession. In the 1791 *Harriet; or, The Vicar's Tale,* complete with pillars of white marble on the Yorkshire moors, a mother and daughter go to their graves, done in by sexual encounters with designing men. The two stories in Stoddard's *Hour's Amusement,* another best-seller printed three times between 1793 and 1818, presented a tamer version of the same formula for younger ears: in the first, Mrs. Goodman's "generous action meets its own reward"; in the second the arrogance of "Miss Haughty" leads directly to her demise. In another best-selling staple of the Stoddard press printed four times between 1796 and 1829, *Death and the Lady,* a lady of fashion bargains with Death for "a little longer time to live and reign"; the appended *Bride's Burial* recounted a groom's loss of his "turtle dove." When in 1801 Ashbel Stoddard began to devote the entire back page of the *Gazette* to a "Bouquet" of poetry and prose, he opened with a two-part story with this positive outcome of the sentimental formula. Miss Williams, faced with the death of an unknown benefactor, resolutely refused any claim to charity, earning a reward of one hundred pounds per annum from the dead man's brother.[48]

The sentimental formula of the contest of virtue and tribulation would structure women's reading for decades to come. Perhaps it reached its climax in the work of Susan Warner in 1851, who used the Columbia County hill town of Canaan, from which her father had removed to prosper and fail in New York City, as the backdrop to *The Wide, Wide World.* Here the heroine Ellen Montgomery builds self-discipline in a situation of domestic suffering. The sentimental formula, it has been argued, allowed the forging a sense of female agency in its action: women, faced with powerful forces of fate or the vicious male, determined their own outcomes by force of character. The sentimental, thus, provided a means of imagining and reimagining the relationship of personal circumstance and a wider women's experience in the confines of domesticity. But the formula was not always complete, particularly in early years of printing along the upper Hudson. If the rhetorical power of the sentimental novel from *Pamela* to *Charlotte Temple* to *The Wide, Wide World* was grounded in an account of female agency through virtue (or its failure), the absence of this side of the formula would convey a more ambiguous message. Looking over the corpus of public print depicting women, the textual balance between the forces of tribulation and the agency of virtue would tilt strongly toward accounts of tribulation.[49]

This imbalance between accounts of female virtue and the force of tribulation was much more apparent in the metatext of the newspapers and almanacs making up the bulk of available reading. Certainly, there were positive depictions of women, beyond the rhapsodies on love and romance that must have drawn Lucy and other young women to the "Poet's Corner." A wife poetically consoled her bankrupt husband in a 1786 *Gazette,* men and women were equal in marriage (according to a 1787 "Matrimonial Creed"), ladies in the "Poet's Corner" declared for virtue and extolled Washington, women's cloth manufacture was an example of economy to the national government, the deaths of children and mothers were mourned. But these positive images were counterbalanced by negative, in both proscription and description. Through the 1790s editors presented a characterization of women as extravagant spendthrifts, with Stoddard lecturing the "feathered young ladies" of Hudson and the Troy papers regularly urging that both "extravagancies in female dress" and "petticoat government" be restrained. In the summer of 1802 the Hudson *Balance, and Columbian Repository* almost gleefully included items on girls' stealing feathers from their mistresses and of a woman caught stealing corn; two years later the editors provided the details of a female swindler in Vienna.[50]

More commonly, however, the depiction of women's experience in the news columns was dark and threatening, the everyday manifestation of the tribulations comprising half of the sentimental formula. Here the depiction of women's misfortunes verged on the sensational, even voyeuristic, in a sense confirming the utter powerlessness of the feminine in gothic literature. Murdered women made up the bulk of these reports, poisoned by their lovers, bludgeoned by slave rapists, even shot by other women; others were robbed and raped. Some were the objects of domestic abuse; one of the Livingstons was unfit for office, Hudson Freeholder declared in 1799, because he frequented cockfights and horse races, was a seducer and adulterer, and had

for several years past immured in a dreary dungeon his own wife, a woman before marriage, ornamented with every accomplishment of nature and art — but alas she is now insane; whether she came so by a train of melancholy reflections, is only left to conjecture. He constantly resists to permit any person, even those of her own sex, to visit her, and she is left to the *kind care* of himself and his negroes.

Other female tribulations were more exotic. Polly Cooly in 1793 returned to Saratoga seeking her family, penniless and widowed after eighteen years of Indian captivity and frontier life on the Ohio. Further afield, the editors made sure that the public knew of a woman's epileptic fit in Bordeaux, a woman possessed in Jehra, five women executed for witchcraft in Patna, the massacre of black women on Antigua by British troops. The *Rural Casket,* a weekly published briefly in Poughkeepsie in 1798, included a detailed account of the physical and social constrictions in the lives of Chinese women. As part of a Federalist cultural campaign against Virginia, the Hudson *Balance* published an essay on the purchasing of wives for tobacco at early Jamestown; it also found it necessary to publish a long article on the female slave trade among the Circassians, but so did the Republican Kingston *Plebeian.* The depiction of women's powerlessness and affliction had no partisan boundaries.[51]

Thus Lucy perhaps had good reason to restrict her reading of the newspapers to the "Poet's Corner" and notices of local marriages and deaths. The endless parade of female tribulation elsewhere in the newspapers must have been unsettling and disturbing for female readers; at least in the "Poet's Corner" adversity was tempered with romantic love and assumptions of female virtue. If Lucy read the marriage and death announcements, she avoided the routine, prosaic notices about women in public distress in the body of the paper. The advertising pages carried a regular stream of elopement notices and ads of the sale of slaves, framed in the same printer's boxes as ads for commodities for sale and notices of lost animals. Husbands whose wives had eloped published their names and announced that their debts would not be covered. Even more prosaically, black women — "wenches" "well acquainted cooking and all household business" — were available for purchase in Columbia County and advertised in the newspapers, well past the passage of New York state's act of gradual emancipation. Occasionally, black women were listed among the slave runaways month after month. These women, leaving matrimony or domesticity or simply being of color, were outside the privileges and protections of civil life; they had no claim to the assumption of virtue that shielded white women in domesticity. The newspapers were unrelenting records of the dangers besetting women in the public world, dangers against which private moral virtues at best provided a slim bulwark.

In June 1786 Stoddard had reprinted a "Scene" from the *Worcester Maga-*

zine in which a Dr. Pull had articulated a keen understanding of the role of the press in a deliberative polity. In this same scene Dr. Pull's wife had weighed in for an equal place in deliberative space for women of the new Republic: "The women could write in this great news-paper and so have a chance to speak their minds upon public matters as well as men—I always thought it a hardship that we should not be able to speak our minds as well as they—men will talk about having more sense—if they have, Let them show it—What good does it do? What signified to have sense like my husband and never speak it?" Thus Mrs. Pull made her mind known, in the context of the political struggles in Massachusetts leading to Shays's Rebellion. But such female claims to deliberative speech were few in the contemporary press, and most, like this, would have had a tone of satire to them. Women's place in the public sphere of the early Republic was in the persuasive rather than the deliberative, and even here they were to be the subjects, not the agents, of persuasion.[52]

Unsettling as it might have been, the persuasive outcomes of the depiction of women in public print might not have been entirely hegemonic. Whether or not they gave women agency, these accounts could be read as a metanarrative on the boundaries in civil society and the boundaries of consent. This narrative reminded its audience that women, despite their emerging public role as repositories of republican virtue, were situated on the edges of civil society and constantly under threat of force. This was not necessarily an audience of women: the readership of newspapers in particular would have been predominantly male. Another aspect of this boundary was invoked in the captivity narratives, as women moved between white and Indian spaces. Thus this was a literature as much about women as for women. The incomplete rendition of the sentimental formula in the newspaper had its own place in the wider culture of sensibility: here men in the public sphere were reminded of the narrow boundaries of their world and the dangers that lurked around its edges and in their own behavior. Thus the construction of women in print marked the dangerous boundaries of civil society. Women coerced were women denied consent, most fundamentally where their consent was most prismatically focused, in sexual relations and in marriage.[53]

The collapse of civility into force was not just hypothetical. The same spring 1787 session of the legislature that voted the divorce bill also passed an act to punish rape, prescribing the penalty of death for anyone convicted of "ravish[ing] a married woman, or maid, or any other woman." The penalty was also extended to anyone coercing a woman into marriage "against her will" for the purpose of acquiring her property. More commonly, marriages broke down in violence. In March 1790 Peter Van Dyck wrote to an apparently very concerned circle in Kinderhook about the violent collapse of a marriage in

Albany, where a local doctor in a jealous rage had beaten and horsewhipped his young wife. Entirely devoted to this affair, the contents of Van Dyck's letter would have been privately circulated in a gossip network in Kinderhook, but other such marital breakdowns entered the public sphere. Thus in August 1792 Jenny Vosburgh presented her situation "To the Public" on the third page of the *Hudson Gazette:* fleeing the "daily cruelty" of her "hard hearted" husband, she had taken refuge at her father's house. Nine years later it was Sukey Pease of Hudson publishing in the *Gazette*. She began in a self-conscious consideration of how she should appeal "to the Public": she had "this long time been contemplating the method I should to inform you of the base and cruel treatment I have received from my perfidious and cruel husband," who accused her "of deceiving him in her former marriages." Detailing her two years of tribulation, she closed with a direct effort to persuade: "For this some time past I feel myself transported with an Idea, that an all wise Being will see fit to shower a blessing upon him, direct him in the paths of virtue, and open his eyes to his errors, he then will become a kind husband, an affectionate father, and a true Christian."[54]

Women publishing such notices in the *Gazette* were responding to injustices, in both their married lives and in their husbands' prior notices of their departure. But they were taking conspicuous action in the public sphere. These responses, defending personal virtue and hoping for reconciliation, were the earliest female voices in public print to appear in Columbia County. These voices were heard within a wider culture of sensibility, a narrative that explored the boundary between civility and force and that queried the terms and practices of consent in the new Republic. This culture of sensibility comprised one of the grounds upon which a more organized female agency would emerge in the new century. In the shorter run, however, its political potential was much more limited.[55]

TENANCY AND CIVIL SOCIETY

In the summer of 1811, as tensions mounted in the town of Livingston, "a report was in circulation on the Manor" that summarized the political conditions of the tenants who held land under leasehold in Columbia County. Colonel Jacob Rutsen Van Rensselaer of Claverack, one of county's leading Federalists, was said to have announced that spring "on the floor of the House of Assembly . . . 'that the tenants were not fit to govern themselves, and deserved to have a Master.'" Even if he had not uttered these exact words, they had a ring of believability, and Van Rensselaer was worried about his reelection to the legislature: tenants of the manor voted for representatives to the assembly, even if many could not vote in elections for governor and state senators.[56]

Van Rensselaer's reported words evoked an ancient stigma of dependency. Propertied independence comprised yet another boundary in the layers of inclusion and exclusion in Columbia's civil society, and the county's tenants had long been seen as less than full and independent citizens. American culture placed profound value on the status of propertied independence, linking it with the capacity for self-governance and autonomy. Those adult white males who were merely tenants occupied an ambiguous status, more limited than freeholders, but certainly higher than women in coverture, children, servants, and slaves. Tenants of the great landlords would have to struggle for such autonomy as long as they remained in the leasehold system on the manor towns.[57]

Governance involved deliberation, either in the halls of government or in the public sphere. The meaning of Van Rensselaer's imputed words was plain: lacking personal autonomy, like women or slaves, tenants were not fit to sit in deliberative forums. Indeed, the tenants failed to gain much of a hearing in the assembly in 1811; the failure reflected their difficulties in gaining much of a foothold in civil society and the public sphere, either deliberative or persuasive. If property ownership conveyed status as a citizen, the institutions of civil society provided the means of citizenship. But, as dependents, the tenants were not admitted into these civil institutions and thus into deliberative processes. Similarly, they lacked the capacity and experience — the social capital — to participate effectively in the domain of persuasion. Lacking a purchase on civil society, the tenants periodically found their only political recourse in violent insurgency.[58]

The first and fundamental foothold in the deliberative public sphere was the franchise, and here the tenants suffered a double liability. The 1777 constitution restricted voting for the assembly, and for the senate and the governor, to freeholders of twenty pounds and one hundred pounds, respectively, and the tenant towns mustered fewer voters relative to their population than the freehold towns: in 1800 roughly 70 percent of the white males over the age of twenty-six in the manor towns of Livingston, Clermont, and Claverack would have been voters, versus 80 and 100 percent in freehold Canaan and Hillsdale. In the ensuing censuses the tenant towns had conspicuously fewer electors qualified to vote for the senate than their freehold counterparts. Those tenants who could vote were constrained by what Abraham Lansing of Albany called "the Baneful Manor interest": Livingstons and Van Rensselaers made sure that their tenants voted in accordance with their wishes, increasingly resorting to coercive tactics. They threatened to enforce leasehold contracts to the letter of the law and used special ballots — Stephen Van Rensselaer's were on silken paper — to ensure that their tenants toed their electoral line. And they

TABLE 9. *Property, Jury Pool, and Assembly Voters, 1798–1800, Columbia County*

| Town | Personal Property, 1800 Valuation | | Taxpayers/1798 Jury Pool[a] | 1800 White Males over 25/1800 Assembly Electors[b] |
	Total	Per Capita		
Hudson	$109,642	$150	443/125 28%	577/351 60%
Canaan	90,132	140	597/268 45%	842/689 82%
Hillsdale	75,171	115	579/269 46%	604/646 107%
Chatham	69,125	146	423/168 40%	516/395 77%
Kinderhook	118,924	156	461/190 41%	611/427 70%
Claverack	142,899	147	497/202 41%	587/428 73%
Livingston	119,888	111	912/109 12%	979/685 70%
Clermont	32,387	141	156/64 41%	152/112 74%
Germantown	16,202	122	91/39 43%	100/78 78%
Overall, Columbia County	774,370	135	4,159/1,434 34%	4,968/3,811 77%

[a]Jury lists were not complete lists of the freeholders in a given town, but those eligible in a given rotation. It is likely that the pool in the given years comprised about half of the potential eligible freeholders.

[b]Estimated from the 1795 census, assuming a 4 percent increase in all towns.

Sources: see Table 10.

and their leasehold agents made their presence felt at the polls: the younger Livingstons were "out attending the election" in the neighborhoods on the Manor, Robert reported in April 1788, and "had good success yesterday at Millers, today at Takkanick, tomorrow at Ancram." The effectiveness of these tactics became apparent when newspapers began to report election results by towns: in 1790 only 4 voters of 378 on the Manor dared to vote against the family candidate for Congress, John Livingston. The contested 1792 governor's election saw equally skewed results in Rensselaerwyck and Livingston for the opposing candidates, and both sides condemned what Columbianus called the power of "a tyrannical landlord" over "the trembling tenant": the Van Rensselaers driving out the tenant vote for their relative, Justice John Jay, and the Livingstons for their ally of the moment, George Clinton.[59]

Beyond the vote lay the deliberative institutions of the state: the courts and the legislature. Here, the tenant towns were weakly represented, overwhelmed by the landlord families. On the Upper and Lower Manors, the Livingston family held the vast majority of appointments to the county courts and terms served in the legislature, senate, and Congress through 1821. Tenants had difficulty even being nominated for office, despite the developing consensus that party nominations should rotate among the several towns of a county. While the Federalists could find assembly candidates in Republican Canaan, Hillsdale, and Claverack and regularly carried the eastern towns of the Manor, Granger and Gallitan, their county committee before 1813 never nominated a single assembly candidate from the Manor towns, secure in the landlord influence — and the Republicans made only seven nominations. The grand juries convened by the superior court were another avenue toward county recognition, but here too the property qualifications for service excluded tenants: almost 50 percent of the 1800 taxpayers in Hillsdale and Canaan were listed on a surviving grand jurors list for 1798, compared with fewer than 12 percent for the Livingston Manor.[60]

The tenant communities thus had only a weak and tenuous place in the deliberative life of Columbia County. This political isolation had its corollary in a wider civil society, and specifically the limited articulation of the persuasive public sphere. Timothy Dwight, riding along the Columbia turnpike through the northern section of the Manor to the Catskill ferry in 1804, expressed a caustic opinion of the civil improvements in this region. Complaining of "ordinary and ill repaired" houses and "wretched" taverns, Dwight noted that, over eighteen miles of road, "not a church, nor a schoolhouse was visible." Dwight's observations, if perhaps jaundiced by his New England sensibilities, do suggest that neither Tocqueville's ideal of civil life nor the earl of Shaftesbury's ideal of sensibility and civility was being met in the Manor towns. Three years after Dwight passed through, a Methodist meeting was stoned in Copake; a decade later a woman was murdered in Ancram as a suspected witch. The Manor was a rough, wild place, in which an exclusion from and a certain avoidance of the improving refinements of the public sphere fed, and fed upon, each other.[61]

Freemasonry could have been a vehicle for associative improvement on the Manor. The grand master of the New York Grand Lodge, Chancellor Robert R. Livingston, living nearby at Clermont, certainly could have enabled the founding of lodges in the Manor towns. But lodges in the tenant towns were few and short-lived. One, the Washington Lodge, was founded during Livingston's tenure, in 1790, and included men of note, but not of the great landlord families, in the Manor neighborhood along the river. It was led by Phillip Hoffman, who had political aspirations and a long family history of hostility toward the Livingstons: Chancellor Livingston's estate manager,

William Wilson, might have joined the lodge to keep an eye on him. After the Washington Lodge collapsed sometime soon after 1800, Masonry lapsed on the manor until a lodge was warranted at Clermont in 1813; a third was established in 1824 in Taghkanic but had disappeared from the Grand Lodge records by 1827.[62]

The failure of Masonic brotherhood to flourish on the Manor might be ascribed to ethnic antipathies. The Lutheran church at Churchtown on the Claverack-Livingston Manor border had forsaken Communion in 1794–1795 when the minister, John Frederick Ernst, had joined the lodge at Hudson. But there were some English sprinkled among the Germans in the Manor towns, who were indeed a primary constituency for Masonic association. Among these English, there was a blatant frustration of Masonic aspirations: it is the lodge that was not warranted that is perhaps the most interesting.

By June 1798 there were approximately eighty lodges in the state of New York, all but ten warranted under the hand of Grand Master Robert R. Livingston; twelve lodges were warranted in 1798 alone, the year that Livingston ran as the Republican candidate for governor. Thus Benjamin Birdsall, Jr., of Copake might have had every expectation that his petition of June 1798 to establish a lodge in the eastern end of the Manor would receive quick attention. Birdsall came from a notable hill town family with established Masonic connections. His father, Benjamin, Sr., had abandoned Quaker roots to serve as a colonel in the Dutchess County Militia during the Revolution before settling in Hillsdale; he had been a founding member of the Temple Lodge in the town of Northeast in Dutchess in 1785. But when Benjamin, Jr., submitted his petition to the Grand Lodge in New York, his alone among seventeen petitions considered that session was tabled. "Referred to the Grand Master," Robert R. Livingston of Clermont, Benjamin Birdsall's petition for a lodge warrant was never granted.[63]

The Livingstons of the Upper Manor, the owners of the land of the Copake neighborhood, like their neighbor Jacob R. Van Rensselaer of Claverack, steered well clear of popular Freemasonry. If some of them joined the elite Holland Lodge in New York City, they did nothing to encourage Masonic fraternity among their tenants. Certainly Grand Master Livingston did nothing to advance Masonic privileges to Birdsall's Copake petitioners; indeed, his cousin Henry W. Livingston, owner of the east Manor lands where Birdsall was a rising figure, might have intervened to have the lodge petition set aside. In the style of oligarchic politics that the Claverack Rensselaers and the Manor Livingstons practiced, a civil association of any sort might undermine the patrician authority of the landlords. And, as we shall see, Birdsall's lodge petition was indeed embedded in a project to undermine that authority.[64]

By the time that Tocqueville raced along the Hudson River in the summer of 1831, Freemasonry had lost its pride of place, and the country was entering upon a new and explosive phase of evangelical Protestant revival. Religion was central to Tocqueville's vision of American civil life. "Religion in America," he wrote, "takes no direct part in the government of society, but it must be regarded as the first of their political institutions." Religion was, Henry Highland Garnet of Troy would tell the American Antislavery Society in 1840, "the basis of civil society." Indeed, the entire Second Great Awakening, beginning in the 1780s, was an extended elaboration of the new American configuration of public sphere and civil society. Denied their ancient legal grounding for metaphysical authority in the Revolutionary disestablishment of religion, American evangelical churches quickly became primary institutions in the persuasive domain of the public sphere. Proliferating religious associations organized a mobile people, tempered and channeled popular energies, and gave them voice in the public arena.[65]

Columbia County and the east Hudson region were certainly swept by the denominational proliferation of the Second Great Awakening; by 1810 dozens of new churches already had been formed in towns throughout Rensselaer, Columbia, and Dutchess. But this was a patterned mosaic of religious institution building, and the Manor towns lagged far behind the other parts of the region. Measuring back from the relatively comprehensive benchmark of the 1845 state census, towns in these three counties that had tenant majorities in 1821 had far fewer churches per population than did either manufacturing towns or the freehold-majority farming towns. Five of these six tenant-majority towns were once part of the old Upper Livingston Manor: Taghkanic, Copake, Ancram, Gallitan, and the landlord base on the river, Livingston. In 1845 there was a total of seven churches in these five towns. The three Dutch Reformed churches, at Linlithgo in Livingston, at Gallitan, and at West Copake, were all formed by the 1750s, and the Pict Bush, or Manortown, Lutheran Church in Livingston was formed in 1764. These four churches, with the Lutheran church at Churchtown just over the Claverack line (formed in 1718), served the people of the Upper Manor towns until 1832, when a Methodist church was formed in Copake, followed in 1842 and 1844 by two Methodist branches in West Taghkanic and East Ancram. In summary, for every 2,928 people living in these five tenant towns in 1840, one new church was formed over the seven decades following the Revolution, whereas in the other fourteen towns of Columbia County one new church had been established for every 749 people residing there in 1840.[66]

Some efforts were made much earlier, however. In 1807, three years after the Reverend Mr. Dwight had passed through on his way west, a Methodist exhorter named William Swayze was invited by a convert to raise a revival in the Copake neighborhood south of the turnpike, in "what was called Livingston's Manor," in hopes of reforming "the destitution and wickedness of the place." At his second effort the meeting was "attacked by a volley of stones, dashing against" the walls of the house; at the third meeting "a large, respectable congregation, from the neighborhood of the Hudson turnpike" attended and formed a Methodist class over the town line in south Hillsdale. It would be another twenty-five years before the Methodists organized in Copake, and more than thirty-five years before they could organize in Taghkanic and Ancram.[67]

The hostility toward the Methodists in Copake and their long delay in forming classes and churches on the Manor might possibly have had a ground in leasehold politics. In 1793 the region's leading Methodist, Freeborn Garretson, had married Catherine Livingston, a sister of Chancellor Robert R. Livingston of Clermont, forging an important landlord connection to the Methodists. Many years later, in 1842, the Methodist chapel in West Taghkanic village was built on land donated by Julia C. Livingston, a granddaughter of Robert Cambridge Livingston, who once owned the entire northern section of the Manor. But an association of the landlord family with the Methodists would not have extended to Presbyterian and Baptist churches, which were forming in the hill towns to the north of the Manor, or to the Quakers, with numerous meetings just over the county line in Dutchess. Certainly ethnicity played a role; the Dutch and German families on the Manor were comfortable with their ancient versions of the Reformed tradition and, like their freeholding relations elsewhere in the region, were unlikely to take up the confessions of British churches, whether magisterial or radical in origin.[68]

But such a rejection would not have been the case for the peoples of English origins filtering onto the Manor east from New England or north from the lower counties of New York (the Birdsalls derived from a Long Island family via Dutchess County). Clearly the circumstances of the life lease discouraged the investment in permanent religious institutions that was taking place elsewhere in the county, the state, and the nation. As Benjamin Birdsall and a committee of tenants on the Livingston lands would argue in 1811, in a petition to the legislature, insecurity of tenure led to an attenuation of public life. "Owing to the business of the tenure by which they [the tenants] hold their lands," they wrote, "the exercise of common prudence forbids any lasting or valuable improvements on the same." The result was "destructive of the interests of the community." In an extreme manifestation of this insecurity, many people on the southern sections of the Upper Manor would not even bury their dead locally in rented land but carried them south into Dutchess

County or to a graveyard in Ancram known as the Free Ground, apparently so called because it was "free" of manorial obligations.[69]

This detachment from public institutions extended to those of the communicative public sphere. The towns with larger numbers of rural tenants were the last to get local post offices that would connect them with the outside world, the last of these post offices being established in 1826 and 1827. These places were less likely to sponsor the occasional sermon or Fourth of July oration at the county press than were the towns with large freehold majorities; tenant-majority towns such as those carved out of the Upper Manor never did. And these were also towns with gaping pockets of illiteracy. Thus in the 1790s, when all Masonic petitioners could sign their names, a few other signed documents coming from the Manor towns indicate that very large numbers of tenant farmers could not. Almost half of the more than two hundred petitioners against the Livingston Manor land claim in 1795 apparently signed with an *X*, as did half of the twenty-two men signing a 1798 agreement not to cut wood for sale on Henry Livingston's lands. The same inability to sign extended to the churches in these tenant towns: almost half of the eighty-seven subscribers to the 1790 regulations of Saint Thomas's Lutheran Church in south Claverack, many of whom lived on the Manor, and three of the eight officers of the Reformed Church at West Copake signed the church articles of incorporation in 1803 with an *X*.[70]

These rates of illiteracy were roughly comparable with those to be found in most of the South in the 1840s. By the 1840s universal common schooling had reduced illiteracy on the Manor to traces, but discernible traces nonetheless (see Tables 10, 11). Thus in 1840 the old Yankee settlements of New Lebanon, Canaan, Austerlitz, and Hillsdale had among them 110 illiterate white adults, just more than 1 percent of the total white population; in the four towns of the old eastern Manor there were almost 350, or about 5 percent. Residual illiteracy in 1840 correlated inversely with another kind of literacy (as recorded in the 1799 valuation of personal property for the county). The measurement of time was already a hallmark of a wider cultural literacy, and in 1799 the ownership of watches varied with urbanization — and the numbers qualified to vote in assembly elections, a rough proxy of tenancy. The freehold towns, which had higher literacy in 1840, had the largest number of cheaper watches taxed in 1799; the tenant towns, with higher illiteracy, were noted for the value of gold pocket watches in 1799, presumably the property of the landlord families.[71]

On the wider issue of literacy, it is difficult to differentiate the impact of tenancy from that of ethnicity. Tenants were often Dutch, but frequently German, particularly on the life-lease patents of the Livingston Manor, and in

TABLE 10. *Property and Timepieces, 1799, and Literacy, 1840, Columbia County*

Town	Personal Property, 1800 Valuation		Value of Timepieces per $1000 in Personal Property			Illiterate White Adults as Proportion of White Population in 1840
			Watches			
	Total	Per Capita	Gold	Other	Clocks	
Hudson	$109,642	$150	$8.70	$13.50	$9.80	1.6%
Canaan	90,132	140	0	10.80	4.90	.8%
Hillsdale	75,171	115	1.30	13.60	5.80	1.6%
Chatham	69,125	146	0	9.90	2.30	1.4%
Kinderhook	118,924	156	5.50	7.10	4.40	2.8%
Claverack	142,899	147	4.20	5.00	5.60	3.7%
Livingston	119,888	111	5.00	5.80	3.00	3.4%
Clermont	32,387	141	7.70	6.70	7.40	1.3%
Germantown	16,202	122	0	10.40	7.40	1.5%
Overall, Columbia County	774,370	135	4.10	8.80	5.40	2.5%

Sources: 1798 Jury List for Columbia County, NYSL; 1799 Columbia County Valuation of Personal Property; 1800 Assembly Returns; 1795 Census of Electors; 1800 U.S. Census; 1840 U.S. Census.

Censuses of electors, by county and town, taken in 1790, 1795, 1807, 1814, and 1821 were recorded in *NYAJ*. For Columbia County, see *NYAJ*, 14th sess., 1791, 14, 19th sess., 1796, 32, 31st sess., 1808, n.p., 38th sess., 1815, 239, 45th sess., 1822, 11. The return for 1800 has apparently not survived, but the county aggregates were published in Franklin B. Hough, ed., *Census of the State of New York, for 1855*... (Albany, N.Y., 1857), ix. The county figures indicate that the county's assembly voters increased by roughly 4 percent. Using this figure, I have estimated the number of assembly voters in each town.

The Columbia County grand jury pool lists for 1797 and 1798 survive in the New York State Archives in "Lists of Freeholders qualified to serve as jurors, 1789–1821" [J4011]. These lists did not include men who had served recently, and thus were not inclusive of the total freeholders in a given town, but they suggest that freeholding status was highest in hill towns Canaan and Hillsdale, and lowest in urban Hudson and landlord-controlled Livingston.

TABLE 11. *Religious Culture and Adult White Illiteracy in 1840: Rural Towns in Three Counties*

Church Presence in Towns	No. of Towns	Adult White Illiteracy Rate		
		2.2%–3.7%	3.8%–8.7%	Overall
Presbyterian or Congregational; no Dutch Reformed or Lutheran	11	2	0	2 15%
Dutch Reformed or Lutheran	23	5	5	10 43%
Baptist, Methodist, and Quaker only	9	3	5	8 89%
Presbyterian or Congregational	18	3	0	3 17%
No Presbyterian or Congregational	25	7	10	17 68%
Dutch Reformed or Lutheran; no Presbyterian or Congregational	8	1	3	4 50%
Dutch Reformed or Lutheran, and Presbyterian or Congregational	7	1	0	1 14%
Dutch Reformed or Lutheran, and Baptist; no Presbyterian or Congregational	8	3	2	5 62%
Overall	43	10	10	20 46%

Notes: To provide a broader sample, this and the following tables include Rensselaer and Dutchess counties as well as Columbia. Except in Table 14, they exclude these counties' towns that had the most extensive manufacturing as of 1840 (Hudson, Stockport, Troy, Lansingburgh, Schaghticoke, Poughkeepsie, Fishkill, and Pleasant Valley), defined as towns where employment in manufacturing in 1840 was greater than 9 percent of the total population.

Sources: Population and adult white illiteracy from *Sixth Census; or, Enumeration of the Inhabitants of the United States . . . in 1840* (Washington, D.C., 1841), 100–101, 116–117, 120–121; churches from *Census of the State of New York, for 1845* (Albany, N.Y., 1846), n.p., plus Methodist churches formed in Taghkanic and Ancram in 1842 and 1844.

TABLE 12. *Sponsorship of Publication in Rural Towns, 1780s–1819, in Three Counties*

Church Presence in Towns	Towns in 1840	Publications Sponsored, 1780s–1840	1820 Population per Publication
Presbyterian or Congregational; no Dutch Reformed or Lutheran	11	20	1,295
Dutch Reformed or Lutheran churches	23	16	3,307
Baptist, Methodist, and Quaker only	9	2	8,512
Presbyterian or Congregational	18	28	1,670
No Presbyterian or Congregational	25	10	4,907
Dutch Reformed or Lutheran; no Presbyterian or Congregational	8	2	5,786
Dutch Reformed or Lutheran, and Presbyterian or Congregational	7	8	2,608
Dutch Reformed or Lutheran and Baptist; no Presbyterian or Congregational	8	6	3,413
Overall	43	38	2,522

Sources: Publications from Evans and Shaw-Shoemaker series. Rural towns and churches: see Table 11. Population from *Census for 1820* (Washington, D.C., 1821), n.p.

general these non-English peoples had lower levels of education and literacy. But it does appear that tenancy more significantly shaped the pattern of residual illiteracy in these towns in 1840 (see Tables 11, 13, 14). The most important determinant of literacy in the rural Hudson Valley seems to have been the presence of churches in the wider Reformed tradition, most importantly the British Reformed churches of Congregationalists and Presbyterians but also the Dutch Reformed and Lutheran, if to a lesser extent. The presence of these Reformed churches was associated with low residual illiteracy in 1840; their absence, with higher residual illiteracy. Reformed traditions thus encouraged the founding of schools and the emergence of a reading public. The British Reformed churches were entirely absent from the tenant-majority towns, and here the sectarian and traditional Dutch and German institutions apparently did not reach enough children. If illiteracy was not uncommon in the Dutch and German freehold communities, it was worse in the tenant towns, where a

TABLE 13. *Religious Culture in the 1840s and Land Tenure in 1821: Rural Towns in Three Counties*

	No. of Towns in 1840		
	Land Tenure in 1821		
		Freehold Majority	
Church Presence	Tenant Majority	Moderate	High
Presbyterian or Congregational; no Dutch Reformed or Lutheran	0	5	6
Dutch Reformed or Lutheran	3	7	8
Baptist, Methodist, and Quaker only	3	5	1
Presbyterian or Congregational	0	6	12
No Presbyterian or Congregational	6	14	5
Dutch Reformed or Lutheran; no Presbyterian or Congregational	3	3	2
Dutch Reformed or Lutheran, and Presbyterian or Congregational	0	1	6
Dutch Reformed or Lutheran and Baptist; no Presbyterian or Congregational	0	6	2
Overall	6	20	17

Notes: Tenants with perpetual leases must have been entered as freeholders, since the Rensselaer County towns where most of the land was under perpetual lease do not show a tenant majority. Thus the "Tenant Majority" category is probably a "Life-Lease Tenant Majority." The result is to highlight the Livingston-owned lands, where the life leases were predominant. Land tenure in towns formed after 1821 are calculated from the parent town. Freehold majorities: Moderate: 1.1–1.6 freeholders for every tenant in 1821. High: 1.7–3.6 freeholders for every tenant in 1821.

Sources: Rural towns and churches: see Table 11. Land tenure in 1821 from *NYAJ*, 45th sess., 1821, Appendix, 11, 13, 41.

TABLE 14. *Land Tenure, Population, and Measures of Civil Life, 1775–1840: All Towns in Three Counties*

	Rural Towns, 1840		
	Land Tenure, 1821		
			Freehold Majority	
	Manufacturing Towns, 1840 (8)	Tenant Majority (6)	Moderate (20)	High (17)
	Number of Instances (Proportion)			
Individuals appointed to county civil office, 1780s–1821	116	7	77	84
Population in 1820 per individuals appointed	252	1,572	534	521
Terms served in New York Assembly and Senate, U.S. House of Representatives, and New York Constitutional Conventions, 1780s–1821	313	46	296	274
Population in 1820 per terms served	93	239	139	160
Individuals elected	94	17	114	113
Population in 1820 per individuals elected	311	647	360	387
Terms per individual	3.3	2.7	2.6	2.4
Lodges by 1826	7	2	11	12
Popuation in 1820 per lodge founded since 1785	4,175	5,501	3,737	3,644

TABLE 14. *Continued*

		Rural Towns, 1840		
		Land Tenure, 1821		
			Freehold Majority	
	Manufacturing Towns, 1840 (8)	Tenant Majority (6)	Moderate (20)	High (17)
		Number of Instances (Proportion)		
Rural towns sponsoring occasional publications, 1785–1819		0	7	12
Total publications		0	10	28
Adult White Illiteracy in 1840 by town				
2.2%–3.7%	1	1	8	1
3.8%–8.7%	3	4	4	2
Total (2.2%–8.7%)	4 (50%)	5 (83%)	12 (60%)	3 (18%)
Post office				
By 1800	5	0	4	3
By 1812	1	1	5	7
Total (to 1812)	6 (75%)	1 (17%)	9 (45%)	10 (59%)
After 1812	2	5	11	7
Churches in 1845	78	11	75	93
1840 population per church in 1845	720	1,009	575	490
Population in 1820	29,224	11,003	41,108	43,734
Population in 1840	56,202	11,061	43,098	45,548

Notes: Includes all towns in Rensselaer, Columbia, and Dutchess counties; the eight manufacturing towns are Hudson, Stockport, Troy, Lansingburgh, Schaghticoke, Poughkeepsie, Fishkill, and Pleasant Valley. Freehold majorities: Moderate: 1.1–1.6 freeholders for every tenant in 1821. High: 1.7–3.6 freeholders for every tenant in 1821.

general failure to make "improvements" resulted in particularly poor schooling before 1812. Such neglect would seem to explain the residual illiteracy rates in 1840.[72]

The question of tenant literacy and engagement with the public sphere was politicized early in the new century. In 1807 the Republican county committee nominated for the assembly Fite Miller, a noted tavernkeeper on the road through the Manor at Taghkanic village in the town of Granger. A tenant of the Livingstons, Miller had been active in local politics since at least 1792, but he had not signed the 1795 protest against the Livingston claim. Nonetheless, the Federalist Hudson *Balance, and Columbian Repository,* which made a great show of literary pretense in the mode of Joseph Dennie's *Port Folio,* made his candidacy the topic of great derision. Reproducing his marks *FM* and *X* on a lease and on loan notes in a wood block print on their editorial page, the editors assailed the Republicans for putting up such a candidate.

> When it was first made known, that Mr. Fite Miller was nominated as a candidate for member of the Assembly by the democrats of this county, it was intimated in the Balance, that he could neither read nor write. The fact has never been contradicted in print.... And now, may we be permitted to ask, Why was Mr. Miller put in nomination for member of Assembly? It is not denied that Mr. Miller is an honest man, and a good farmer; and as much may be said of a thousand others in this county; but he is altogether uninformed and illiterate—he cannot even write his name. Why, then is he dragged from his obscurity, and offered as a candidate for an office, which, were he to obtain, would but render his weakness conspicuous, and expose his ignorance to the world. It is one of the most cruel and abusive tricks of jacobinism.... But, after all, if Mr. Miller will submit to become the dupe and the tool of faction, let the electors take up the subject with all the spirit and firmness of independent freemen, and decide, whether Mr. Fite Miller, and his fellow candidates, shall be permitted to set their black mark and seal on the liberties and honor of our country.

Two years later the succeeding Federalist paper in Hudson, the *Northern Whig,* carried on in a similar vein, publishing a parody of a Republican convention, in which the chair, Peter Pennyloaf, signed with an *X,* and condemning the Republican Hudson *Bee* as "the production of mean, illiterate and unprincipled fellows."[73]

Indeed, it was a mark of Federalist political culture in the decade following their defeat to mock the opposition as uncultured and illiterate, but these satirical jabs had a special sting in Columbia County, where literacy and the freehold had such a distinctive geography. The county's middling gentry were almost compulsive about the emblems of literacy when they sat for the portraits in these decades. Almost uniformly, they sat clutching books, letters, newspapers, or inscribed canes, which gave testimony to their direct connection to the material vehicles of the public sphere, in sharp contrast to most of the portraits of the great landlord families and, indeed, the occasional tenant farmer.[74]

It was Benjamin Birdsall, Jr., of Copake, frustrated in his ambition to get a lodge warrant in 1798 and now a middling figure among the county Republicans, who fully articulated the linkages between education and civil society, literacy and the tenant condition. In a long letter published in the Hudson *Bee* in August 1811, Birdsall attacked the Livingstons for holding their tenants in a state of uncivilized ignorance. Reviewing the colonial origins of the Manor, the Livingstons, Birdsall argued, had taken "a people uneducated and untutored in many of those acquirements that exalt or enlighten the human understanding" to work their "newly and self acquired territory." In this feudal condition all rights political and civil were denied the tenants.

> All of their essential rights, privileges and immunities were monopolized, and even the distinguishing characteristic of the free man from the slave was buried in oblivion. They were bought and sold at the election of their lord. It was in these times that their tenants experienced in profusion life leases with their slavish appendages. . . . It was in a state like this that a set of people, uneducated in the laws of their country and totally ignorant of their rights and liberties, were prevailed upon by their humane and generous lords to acquiesce under a claim not valid and without foundation. But a prohibition by their lords and masters of the common bounties of nature was not all, for such was their jealous disposition of their title to the manor, that they absolutely considered a state of ignorance and servile dependence as the essential rampart of their title. The fact is notorious that for many long years they even forbid the introduction of an English school, the last and only means given man by which he can acquire a knowledge of his rights and duties as a member of civilized society. Every means which the power of their ingenuity could invent has had recourse to, to place an immoveable barrier between their tenants and every source or avenue of information through which they might be led to discover the impositions practiced upon them. And by this sacrilegious and unparalleled aggression on the rights and liberties of their tenants, acquire by a long acquiescence under their claim a perfect, absolute and indefeasible title.[75]

There it was: the tenant, denied the benefits of "an English school," had no "knowledge of his rights and duties as a member of civilized society." A clearer statement of the political consequences of the building of social capital in civil society would be difficult to find. And, in a stunning confirmation of Birdsall's complaint, the August issues of the *Bee,* where his letter appeared, and the Federalist *Northern Whig,* which was quick to condemn his effort, bore literally no other presence of the people of the Manor towns. In one issue of the *Bee* alone there were more than 250 printings of names from every other town in the county, advertising goods, mentioned in land proceedings, sued for debt; another 100, roughly, appeared in the *Northern Whig.* Some were women, and several runaway notices inscribed black men's names — for better or worse — in the public prints. Dutch and German names were sprinkled through, probably almost in proportion to their numbers in the population. But not one of those noticed was a resident of the Manor towns. Tenancy sealed off these people from the public life of the county, and seemingly from citizenship itself.[76]

II

Extending the Settlement

5

Land Politics in Columbia
1781–1804

I John J. Acmodrey testify That in the Fall of the year 1786 I was in company with Dr. Hamilton of Hudson and Ethan Allen, when they conversed about the affairs of Wyoming; and they both explicitly declared it was the design of them and their associates to. . . . erect a new State. . . . Afterwards I was at Hillsdale and heard Doctor Caleb Benton avow explicitly the same design. . . . The [New] York Lessees, as they have been called, were in this scheme, and to do their parts towards carrying it into Execution. . . . Col. John McKinstry (who was closely connected with Dr. Hamilton, Beach and Franklin) told me that it was their design to declare a New State in the fall of that year.

> — Pennsylvania depositions on the Susquehannah Company

Sir,

. . . I approve much of bringing suits against refractory tenants on the western part of the lot. . . .

The general Complexion of the Affairs of the Manor is very inauspicious. An Explosion seems to be inevitable, and when it does happen, I trust it will be on an occasion, where no blame can possibly be imputed to us. The Measure of Iniquity seems to be full, and when the Crisis arrives, I hope there will be nothing to exempt Guilt from its merited Punishment. . . .

I am Sir yr most obedt serv.

Peter Van Schaack

> — Peter Van Schaack, Kinderhook, to William Wilson, Clermont, October 6, 1797

———

Martin Van Buren's conception of political parties in perpetual civil struggle would be his lasting legacy to the American political system. Ambiguously situated between state and ordinary life, the party would be an enduring institution in American civil society, occupying an imperfect but evolving arena of deliberation and, indeed, a ground of persuasion. But party did not emerge de novo in Van Buren's political imagination. Throughout the country partisans had begun to align in two opposing camps over the 1780s and 1790s. Equally important, these alignments were particularly competitive in the county of Columbia. Indeed, if Van Buren would be the first to fully articulate the necessity of party in American politics, it was due in no small measure to the world in which he was born.[1]

This was a world where dramatic civil struggle during the Revolution led to an equally charged politics in the ensuing decades. The transition from Revolutionary to routine politics was fundamentally complicated by the question of landownership. Even before the peace was signed, the colonial struggle over land was reignited in Columbia County, and it would fuel a volatile politics of Demo and Aristo for decades to come. Emboldened by Revolutionary mobilization, squatter settlers and leasehold tenants challenged the claims of the rentier gentry, whose dependence on leasehold rent was driven in turn by the division of estates and by losses in the speculative market. An undercurrent of insurgent violence at times boiled to the surface: again almost uniquely in the state of New York, armed force frequently supplanted political deliberation in this particular county. Quite explicitly, these eruptions of violence were treated as challenges to the legal settlement of the state as it had emerged from the Revolution: gentlemen wrote nervously as the war came to a close of "the danger we run of a *second Vermont,* to spring up in our western limits." Over these decades, however, the stark confrontation of Demo and Aristo nonetheless was blurred by the emergence of political coalitions, shaped by the post-Revolutionary elaboration of civil life. If the Livingstons feared the "end of distinction between men," the political peace of the county and the state required the accommodation of lesser men and the settling of their most fundamental needs. The revolutionary settlement would have to be extended to achieve this peace. But this settlement struggle was hard fought in Columbia County, and, if the first cycle of the post-Revolutionary politics of land came to a close by the turn of the century, it left an enduring mark on the county's political culture. Columbia County had in the Jeffersonian era one of the highest levels of political mobilization in the entire state of New York and probably the country as a whole.[2]

The emergence of new institutions in civil society, mediating between the practices of colonial oligarchs and popular committeemen, both brought civility to county politics and contributed to the resolution of many—but not all—of the land struggles that threatened the civil peace. The outcome was a developed set of political practices and routines linking committees, candidates, and constituencies that Van Buren and his contemporaries would inherit and fine-tune in the coming years and decades. But those who continued to be excluded from this settlement would continue to be a source of violent insurgency.

The lands in greatest contention in Columbia County lay along the higher hill country on the eastern edge of the county. In the southeast, along the broad and fertile valley of the Roeliff Jansen Kill at Copake and Ancram, the Livingston Manor lands had long been let in life leases, in which a tenant's tenure would last the life of three lessees' names in the lease. Just to the north of the Livingston lands, John Van Rensselaer, the proprietor of Claverack, had clear claim to the lowlands east of the river, but in the eastern hills (appropriately renamed Hillsdale) his patent had been challenged for decades by settlers at Nobletown and Spencertown, who based their claim on purchases made from Mahican Indians who had abandoned these ancestral lands and gathered at Stockbridge, over the mountains in Massachusetts. In the northeast, in the King's District (soon to be renamed Canaan), a tangle of overlapping New York patents had been challenged by New Englanders settling under several similar Indian titles. In all of these places there had been flashes of violence in the closing decades before the Revolution, and such violence would erupt repeatedly in the decades following. In each case, however, the settling of land disputes and the subsidence of civil violence were dependent upon the construction of political coalitions and the elaboration of the new institutions of civil society.[3]

KING'S DISTRICT, CANAAN, THE VAN RENSSELAER CLAIM, AND THE WESTENHOOK PATENT, 1750S–1790S

Political settlement was achieved most easily in the north, in the old King's District. Here the claimants to three New York colonial patents competed with settlers occupying the land under deeds bought from the Mahican Indians at Stockbridge. Two land claims, dating to the first years of the eighteenth century, those of the Claverack Van Rensselaers and of the holders of a huge Westenhook Patent (including several of the Livingstons), covered overlapping territory from the hill country east of Kinderhook to the Housatonic River in Massachusetts. In the 1760s these vast and indeterminate claims were reconciled in a division of sixteen huge lots. Several of these Van Rensselaer and Westenhook lots were cut through by yet another claim, called the Mawighnunk Patent, which in 1743 had granted most of the valley lands of Wyomanock Creek to a group of New York City merchants and Kinderhook men, including Cornelius Van Schaack, a fur trader with interests running into the hills to the east.[4]

In the 1760s and 1770s the Kinderhookers, led by Cornelius's sons Peter

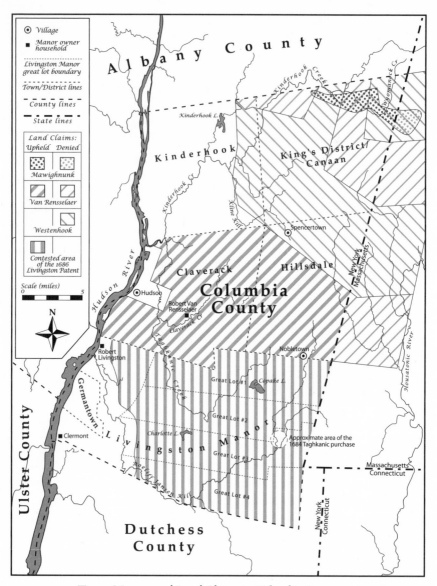

MAP 3. *Towns, Manors, and Land Claims in Columbia County, 1780s–1802.*
Drawn by Jim DeGrand

With the exception of most of Kinderhook and Germantown, eighteenth-century Columbia County was dominated by the land claims of the Van Rensselaers and the Livingstons. A branch of the Van Rensselaer family, which held a vast manor on both sides of the Hudson River around Albany, the Claverack Van Rensselaers claimed most of the lands in Claverack proper and central and southern Hillsdale. They also unsuccessfully claimed lands well

into Massachusetts and in the northeast corner of Columbia County. Here they were con-
tested by the proprietors of the Westenhook Patent, granted in 1705 to a group that in the
1770s was led by some of the Livingstons. The Van Rensselaers and the Westenhook propri-
etors settled their competing claims in 1763, but in 1773 all of these lands were surrendered to
the crown as the King's District, the Van Rensselaers receiving a confirmation to their Clav-
erack-Hillsdale claim. From 1743 a third group, including the Kinderhook Van Schaacks,
had another competing claim to land in the northeast—the Mawighnunk Patent, running
along Lebanon Creek and over the mountains into Massachusetts; this claim would not be
settled until 1802.

Livingston Manor dated to 1686, when Robert Livingston received a manor patent from
Governor Dongan. Two years earlier he had purchased two parcels from Mahican Indian
families, 2,000 acres along the Hudson River and the western Roeliff Jansen Kill and 600
acres to the east at Taghkanic meadows; the 1686 patent granted the intervening lands, for
a total of 160,000 acres. In 1710 the rights to 6,000 acres were repurchased by the crown to
settle a group of Palatine German refugees, in what was known as the East Camp and,
later, Germantown. At Livingston's death in 1728 the rest of the manor south and west of
the Roeliff Jansen Kill was set off as the "Lower Manor" (named Clermont in 1788), and
the remainder of the estate became the "Upper Livingston Manor" (and the town of Living-
ston in 1788). On the death of Robert Livingston III in 1790, the large eastern section of the
Upper Manor was divided into four "Great Lots." For almost a century, from the 1750s to
the 1840s, insurgent groups challenged the legality of the Upper Manor Livingston title to
land held solely under Governor Dongan's 1686 patent, mostly in these Great Lots.

---

and Henry Van Schaack, hoped to extend the bounds of their district eastward and began to provide legal counsel to the New England families at the
settlements of New Canaan, New Concord, New Britain, and Spencertown,
building a wider alliance against the Van Rensselaers and the Westenhook
patentees. Early in 1772 Peter Van Schaack was instrumental in having nearly
the entire region east of Kinderhook established as the King's District and,
apparently, in having Matthew Adgate and William B. Whiting appointed
as justices of the peace for the new district. A committee, meeting at New
Canaan two days after the act's passage, wrote warmly to Van Schaack, thanking him for his "care and asiduity for this public good" and promising that
they would "upon every Occasion be Happy to Testify to you how much we
are Obliged for what you have done for us."[5]

Van Schaack's intervention did improve the settlers' circumstances, in
some measure. Pressed by the governor, Van Rensselaer surrendered his claims
in the King's District in February 1773. But the Westenhook patentees continued to advance their claim, both in the colony courts and on the ground.

Surveyors sent to map their lands in September 1773 were challenged and fired on by "a number of persons dressed in Blanket habitts." The New Britain settlers condemned the gentry patentholders as men "who hesitate not to enrich themselves by depriving others of the Fruit of their Labor, and raise their Fortunes on the Destruction of the Poor." Late in 1774 the King's District squatters sent one of their leaders, James Savage, all the way to the Board of Trade with a formal legal claim against the Westenhook patent. In February 1775, literally as the Continental Association was being distributed for signature in Albany County, the board considered Savage's testimony as well as a petition from several former army officers also making claims on the region. Their decision, rendered in March and delivered to the Privy Council on May 25, vacated the Westenhook claim and granted lands to the officers, with the stipulation that they be laid out "without prejudice to the present occupancies (now under actual improvement)." Awaiting this decision, the people of the King's District held back from the earliest Revolutionary mobilization, declining to form committees before news came of the fighting at Lexington and Concord.[6]

Thus the Board of Trade decision came too late for a definitive result; and, as the Revolutionary war unfolded, the people of the King's District worried about their title to the land. After a May 1778 meeting, the district submitted a petition to the second sitting of the assembly, asking for a confirmation of its titles. Though it was introduced by the governor himself, the petition was buried in committee until February and then set aside to be considered "as soon as other public Business will permit." But, when legislation regarding the King's District was finally passed in the summer of 1782, it created even more upheaval. On July 25 an act passed with an article purporting to ease the "Fears and Uneasiness prevail[ing] among the Inhabitants of King's District" that many of their lands had never been formally granted. The article stipulated that land titles conveyed under either the state or the colony outside the bounds of "any grant or patent" would not be "impeached." Despite the fact that a petition to the senate from New Lebanon apparently had opened deliberations on this article, its reference to colonial grants and patents threw the people of the district into even greater anxiety.[7]

Their anxiety was rooted in part in the complexities of familial politics among the Van Rensselaers. The lands of the Van Rensselaers at Claverack proper and their family claims into the eastern hills were held by John Van Rensselaer under the doctrine of entail, in which landed property by law must be inherited whole and undivided. John Van Rensselaer had inherited these lands and land claims in 1740 from his father, Henry, as a "tenant in tail." In 1763 John had "docked" the tail, allowing him to alienate certain lands, presumably giving some land in Claverack to his younger son, Robert, who married and settled in Claverack in 1765. But in May 1782 John, anticipating his death in February of 1783, made a will assigning the better part of the Claverack estate to his grandson John Jeremiah (son of his eldest son, Jeremiah, now deceased). The residue of the estate, much of it in Hillsdale, would go to his four surviving children, Robert, Henry, James, and Catherine, who would hold their property as tenants in common.[8]

Catherine's connections led to a powerful circle that further intensified fears in the King's District. Catherine Van Rensselaer had married Philip Schuyler, and their daughter, Elizabeth, had just married Alexander Hamilton, who was then studying for the bar in Albany. Rumors began to circulate that Philip Schuyler, standing to manage Catherine's inheritance on the old patroon's death, had had a hand in the language of the July 1782 King's District legislation. Schuyler, on his part, acknowledged in April that he had indeed supported the article's language in the senate but announced that he had no intention of reviving the Van Rensselaer claim surrendered nine years before. John Van Rensselaer's will was filed in May 1782, after the end of the legislative session, in which the senate had passed a bill outlawing the practice of entailing family estates, which had been stalled in the assembly. The will soon had to be changed by codicil, because that July, early in the next session, the assembly finally passed the entail bill.[9]

The Revolution had divided the King's District people from their Kinderhook ally Peter Van Schaack, who had come to their aid in 1772 but had been exiled to London since 1778; the continuing threat to their lands must have suggested the potential value of an old alliance. Van Schaack had old connections with the Schuyler orbit, as he had been a college friend of their political ally John Jay. Such connections would be useful in the King's District households, if they could get beyond the passions of the Revolution. The people of the district had suffered at the hands of tory bands during the war, and in May 1780 and May 1783 the district meeting—presided over by Matthew Adgate and Philip Frisbie—passed resolutions against the restoration of the loyalist property. Thus it was a significant departure—but one grounded in an old alliance—when "a very considerable Number of Inhabitants" from the district joined others from Claverack, Hillsdale, and Kinderhook in March 1783 to petition the senate that "certain of the persons, adherent to the King of Great Britain . . . may be permitted to return."[10]

Among the loyalists who would benefit from a pardon would be the Van Schaaks of Kinderhook, whose connections ran deep in the hill towns. The impetus for a changing attitude toward the loyalists was led by Major Jacob Ford of the Red Rock settlement in north Hillsdale, who recently had given long service in the Revolutionary militia. As early as the fall of 1781 Ford voted in opposition to Adgate and Frisbie to suspend the sale of loyalist property; on February 7, 1783, he introduced to the assembly the legislation that successfully dissolved the Commission on Conspiracies. A year later, this time with Adgate supporting him consistently on a series of roll calls, Ford introduced legislation to overturn the exclusion of the former tories, both voting against the disenfranchisement of tories that their Clintonian allies had pushed through. The law allowed Henry and David Van Schaack, among others, to return to the state without fear of retribution. Peter Van Schaack remained in exile in London until June 1785, when he took ship for New York and was met at the dockside by his old King's College friend John Jay. He arrived in Kinderhook on August 23. The following May his citizenship was formally restored by an act of the legislature, and he reopened his legal practice in Kinderhook village.[11]

In less than a year Van Schaack was deeply involved in land politics. In March of 1787 Henry Livingston wrote to his cousin, Robert R. Livingston, about the failure of the Federalist county meeting to arrive at a consensus on assembly candidates for the spring election.

> I am sorry to inform you it was all in vain. The Hudsonians appear to join the eastern Districts and form a private conversation with Peter Van Schaack. He would not agree upon an equality of representation unless we would take up Mr. Ford for the Eastern Districts, which we could not agree to upon any terms. So that nothing was effected save a discovery of our private sentiments. ———— Claverack, part of Kinderhook, and part of the 2 Eastern Districts, will join us provided we undertake John Bay, Mr. Powers, and Mr. John Livingston, which we told them we would consider of. — and I believe it will be the best representation we can get. . . . The Van Schaacks are interested in the Westenhook patent, and they fear if *Ford* is not in, the powerful claimants may by their influence, get their *just rights.*

These "powerful claimants" were the Livingstons, who had not given up hope on the Westenhook patent and found their way blocked by a competing axis among their fellow Federalists. Commenting on the Livingston efforts in local politics, Peter Van Schaack wrote to Schuyler, "The Westenhook Petition has had an admirable Effect to cement this union." Van Schaack was now a pivotal figure in an alliance between new men in new settlements and the Schuyler-Hamilton connection; Livingston aspirations to revive the Westenhook claims in Canaan were being undermined by the renunciation of such claims by the Schuylers.[12]

Heretofore Van Schaack's ally Jacob Ford, if a militia major of some re-

PLATE 8. *Peter Van Schaack (1747–1832), Kinderhook.*
Courtesy, Collections of the New-York Historical Society

nown, had no standing among the valley gentry: he had been condemned by Hamilton as one of "the Leveling Kind," and later in life he would put his political experience to work among the Baptists of the Shaftsbury Association. But he was now a firm Federalist, as was his colleague William Powers, James Savage's brother-in-law, in the wider Schuyler-supported opposition to the Livingston-Westenhook interest. A merchant with an extensive trade along the border, Powers was a rising man in the Canaan settlements and would serve in the assembly and state senate before his untimely death in 1795; he was also among the men who formed the Unity Lodge in 1789. Meeting first in December 1786, the Masons at Canaan petitioned for a lodge in 1788. Among them were men who had been members of the Union Lodge in Albany, and over the coming decade the Unity Lodge Freemasons, led by Powers, would forge a strong connection with Albany Federalists. This Masonic connection would underlie the land settlement as unfolded in Canaan.[13]

Among the nominations that the Federalists put forward in the spring of 1788 for assembly and for the federal constitutional ratifying convention, John and Henry Livingston would have to share equal billing with Ford, Powers, and Van Schaack, however much it galled them. "Distinctions among men" destroyed Federalist chances in Columbia County in 1788. John Livingston quit his nomination after a fight with the upstart Hudson Federalists, and the ticket was further damaged by insults General Robert Van Rensselaer of Claverack gave to Colonel Isaac Goes of Kinderhook. Van Schaack was so disgusted with the conflicts among the Federalists that he too would have withdrawn, but for the intervention of Philip Schuyler. Van Schaack wrote his misgivings to Schuyler, stressing the fears in the hill towns: there could not be "any antidote applied to the Eastward, where the ill fated Controversies about their lands make this [election] in their Idea a Contest *pro Aris et Focis* [for altar and hearth]." The Federalists were indeed defeated in both the assembly and convention races (Van Schaack wrote, "The popular tide was against us"), and their loss was in great measure due to the hill town fears about land rights. An observer wrote sarcastically from the Poughkeepsie convention to the *Hudson Gazette* in July, "When the subject of the Federal courts comes doubtless some of the inhabitants of King's and Hillsdale districts will attend, that they may be able to determine how far the controversy respecting their lands will be affected by the judiciary power."[14]

In the end, the Federalist connections forged through Peter Van Schaack seem to have resolved the threat to land titles in Canaan. The Westenhook patentees never seem to have pressed their claim, which had been fatally wounded by the March 1775 Board of Trade decision and apparently further complicated by the stipulations of the enactment of town government passed in 1788. But in the end a special act of the legislature was required, and Federalists played a key role. In March 1791 Philip Schuyler brought a bill on land sales from committee to the floor of the senate, where Samuel Jones, a Federalist from Queens County, moved the addition of a clause stating that all properties "in the town of Canaan, in the county of Columbia, now possessed by any person or persons, shall be, and hereby is granted to the respective possessors of such lands." Among the majority supporting the measure was the Federalist Stephen Van Rensselaer, the new patroon of Van Rensselaer lands to the north and a prominent member of Albany's Master's Lodge since 1786; among a small minority opposing was Philip Livingston, a Westenhook inheritor. The act moved unopposed through the assembly to the approval of the council and the governor's signature.[15]

Thus was the issue of land settled in most of the town of Canaan. Two intersecting schemes contributed to this outcome. The Federalists continued to hope that they could erode the strength of the old committeemen, who, with the exception of Ford, were now becoming Antifederalists and Republicans under the leadership of Matthew Adgate. In 1792, Peter Van Schaack rejoiced that "Proceedings in the populous town of Canaan [were] very favorable to Mr. Jay," referring to the town committee's unanimous nomination of John Jay and Stephen Van Rensselaer for governor and lieutenant governor. Van Schaack must have had a role in a letter in the *Gazette* purporting to be from Jacob Ford, which reminded the people of Canaan of their long struggle for land titles and related that Jay had advised James Savage before he took ship to London in 1775.[16]

Elite Federalist willingness to sacrifice tenuous colonial claims to gain votes in Canaan was matched by popular Federalist institution building in Canaan itself. The Federalist-dominated Unity Lodge, formally warranted in September 1788, spawned a daughter lodge at New Concord in 1796, where, similarly, Federalists prevailed. After their involvement in unsuccessful if creative efforts to have the legislature approve lotteries to build a Presbyterian meetinghouse and fund an academy, Unity Masons clearly had a role in getting a federal post office established in New Lebanon village in 1794, the first in the county east of the river towns; both postmasters appointed in the 1790s were masters of the lodge. So too was Federalist Elihu Phinney, settled in the town since the mid-1780s, who started a printing press in 1794, briefly publishing a newspaper, the *Columbian Mercury*.[17]

But the bubbling of Federalist civil activism in Canaan had its Republican counterpart in the Canaan Democratic-Republican Society, which in the end narrowly prevailed over the Federalist efforts. Canaan voters might have begun to move toward the Federalists, but a persistent if slim majority was never weaned away from the Revolutionary popular tradition, manifested in Clintonian, Republican, and eventually Jacksonian party building. In 1792, a considerable vote for Jay almost closed the gap with Clinton, but about sixty of these Federalist voters withheld their vote from Van Rensselaer, evidence of an enduring distrust of the patroon to the north. In 1798 and in the decades following, the Federalists often achieved narrow victories in Canaan, and the town ran up an impressive record for voter turnout in all types of elections.[18]

In some considerable measure, this contested politics was a product of Federalist efforts to settle the volatile issue of land in the old King's District. But it also was a symptom of a wider truth: the Canaan people were deeply engaged, if not always successfully, in the civil institution making of the post-Revolutionary public sphere. In the end, if all of the specific processes at work are not completely clear, the story of the settlement in post-Revolutionary Canaan provides an illustration of how civil institutions served as a flywheel between people and polity, a means to influence and connections but also mobilizing social capital in the dynamic of interest and lawmaking power that ran between locality and legislature in the early Republic.[19]

COMPANIES OF ADVENTURERS

Thus was a revolutionary settlement effected in most of Canaan. To the south, in Hillsdale and on Livingston Manor, the deaths and estate distributions of John Van Rensselaer and Robert Livingston would set off further struggles over land and revolutionary settlement. These would be far more contested than in Canaan, bringing a rising tide of insurgent violence and even blood-shed, and they would not be settled until the 1840s.

But, before these local struggles began to unfold, men in Columbia County joined in a wide-ranging scramble for land on the frontier, a scramble pro-foundly implicated in the wider revolutionary settlement. These ventures in-volved nearly everyone of some ambition and capital in the county; former militia officers, in particular, were notable in their number. This statewide politics of land effected a democratization of distributive politics, a democ-ratization of greed, in the post-Revolutionary decade, as men of rough and simple origins joined the scramble for land that had once been the exclusive domain of the colonial magnates. Land had long been the coin of politics in New York, and Governor George Clinton worked to manage this post-Revolutionary distribution to achieve the same consolidation of power in the state of New York that Alexander Hamilton on the federal level would achieve with the Bank of the United States.[20]

Failure to meet the demand for land threatened to reopen Revolutionary violence: such was the challenge from quasi-military "companies of adven-turers" that Clinton confronted in the 1780s. Fears of unconstitutional vio-lence were palpable early in 1788, as fears were raised of "the horrors of civil war," the destruction of "our liberties by dragooning the legislature," of fac-tions wanting "the people to go to the senate and enforce their demands with the point of the bayonet." As much a manifestation of the explosive post-Revolutionary tensions in Columbia as they were of conditions in the new na-tion at large, the coalitions emerging from some of these ventures formatively shaped the emergence of New York's Republican "interest" in the 1790s. If land promoters were seen by many as a corrupting force in New York politics, they were viewed by many others as advancing a popular cause. In a county where relentless population growth competed with a grasping rentier class to make land an ever scarcer commodity, men who could secure land grants, to be sold on reasonable terms to farming families, might well be popular on election day. In so doing, they began to build the coalitions that would structure the local Republican Party as Martin Van Buren came of age in the late 1790s.[21]

In 1782, as the feudal inheritance system of entail was being abolished, the New York legislature began to work out a policy to carve up the lands in their sovereignty occupied by native Iroquois, Revolutionary enemies and allies alike. On July 25, 1782, in the same land bill that promised security for the King's District titles, a Military Tract was laid out in the western Iroquois lands, though few soldiers of the New York Line or militia would ever take up their bounty rights there. These were the lands of the Seneca, Cayuga, and Onondaga, who had actively supported the British cause.[22]

Few from Columbia County seem to have taken up these military patents. Rather, many of them made more direct efforts to get western land, including that occupied by the friendly Oneida, just west of the Mohawk Valley. Many of these were reasonably modest grants: Israel Spencer was granted 200 acres on the Susquehanna in 1783, Jacob Ford received a grant of 350 acres in 1790, and Philip Frisbie shared rights to two lots in Tioga County with ten other men. One of the earliest petitions in this regard was submitted by Matthew Adgate of the King's District on September 1781, a request that was referred to the committee deliberating the formation of a land office. The land office, formed in 1785, would allow for sales of both small and large tracts, opening the state's sovereign lands to both individual farmers of some means and large-scale operators. Matthew Adgate—the leader of the popular radicals in Columbia throughout the war years and then a stalwart Antifederalist and Republican into the 1790s, voting against the Federal Constitution in the Poughkeepsie convention and sitting a record twelve terms in the assembly between 1776 and 1795—reaped a large reward from his connection with Governor George Clinton. In the summer and fall of 1791, in land transactions passionately condemned by Federalists, a number of Clinton's political associates were given large grants of land. Adgate alone received three grants totaling almost 90,000 acres; sometime after 1800 he moved to live with his son Asa on some of his land up the Champlain Valley in Essex County, where he died in 1818. For others the sale of forfeited loyalist estates opened the way to land acquisition. Colonel Henry Livingston bought 13,000 acres in the Susquehanna Valley, Henry Platner and Peter Weismer of Claverack bought 1,400 acres in the Whiteborough holdings in the Susquehanna Valley in 1785, and Platner also bought 350 acres of Sir William Johnson's old holdings in the Mohawk Valley in 1784.[23]

The expansion that would make these western lands valuable depended upon ventures to finance and construct canals, ventures that would take decades to come to fruition, and were bound for failure in the 1790s. Two great canal-building enterprises were chartered in 1792, as the Western and the Northern Inland Lock Navigation companies. Controlled by Philip Schuyler, the Western Company planned a channel from the upper Mohawk Valley to Lake Oneida, which would eventually be the key to western land development. One Columbia Federalist, Walter Livingston, was involved in this western project. The Northern Company, which would be similarly unsuccessful in building a canal from the Hudson to the lakes, attracted a few leading Columbians who would gravitate toward the Republicans in the 1790s: Robert R. Livingston, Henry Livingston, Peter Van Ness, and Matthew Scott.[24]

Canal projects would eventually open up western lands in New York and beyond, but in the 1790s they were beyond the capacities of even the greatest combinations of wealth in the state. And in Columbia County many smaller fry — and some of the great men too — were given to even more suspect ventures. Their efforts would concentrate on the swath of Iroquois lands running from the lakes down into the Susquehanna River valley. Matthew Adgate's 1781 petition had requested permission to purchase land from the Oneidas, and late in 1784 Philip Frisbie, also of the King's District, was one of the partners in the huge Harper's Purchase south of there on the Susquehanna. Adgate's petition was tabled, and the Harper's Purchase scheme was invalidated, as the state attempted to assert authority over the western lands. Here the state's sovereignty was challenged fundamentally by a huge Massachusetts claim and by the superior authority of the Confederation government in Indian affairs. But the machinations of companies of men such as these posed an equal threat, particularly when they were inspired by the success of Vermont, where the Green Mountain Boys led by Ethan Allen had successfully carved a new state out of the sovereign, if disputed, territory of the old province of New York. In the summer of 1784 such a venture was already under way in the Wyoming Valley, along the Susquehanna River in Pennsylvania. Here Connecticut settlers, some the survivors of loyalist massacres of summer of 1778, were being organized into a militia by Colonel John Franklin to resist the assertion of Pennsylvania authority. The following year, in July, the old Susquehannah Company of Connecticut was reorganized in Hartford, the proprietors reasserting Connecticut's old colonial claim and offering a half share proprietorship to "every Able bodied and effective Man" approved by the committee and willing to "repair to Wyoming" and defend the company claim.[25]

The speculator leadership and the half share rank and file were all part of the same westward flow out of Connecticut that had populated the contested eastern towns of Columbia County and Dutchess County to the south, since the 1750s and 1760s. In 1785 some of the Columbia towns, particularly Hudson and Hillsdale, became the forward bases of the new Susquehannah Company, and Columbia County men leading players, particularly in the armed struggle that soon developed.

Foremost among these, Dr. Joseph Hamilton of Hudson balanced a long connection with the western lands with a calculated understanding of the demands of civil life. Hamilton's father had invested in both the old Susquehannah Company and in the Hampshire Grants, moving his family from the eastern Connecticut town of Lebanon to Sharon in the northwest. Born in Lebanon and married in Sharon, Joseph Hamilton established himself in Hudson at its founding, where his physician's practice was known for his doses of calomel, bark, and brandy and for his success at smallpox inoculation. In July 1785 Hamilton was appointed to the standing committee of the revived Susquehannah Company and immediately made his mark by recruiting the support of Ethan Allen himself with a gift of twelve shares of company stock. His tavern in Hudson rapidly became the vital link between the Wyoming settlements and the nominal company headquarters in Hartford, and Hamilton made full use of his place in the new city. By the time he signed the petition to the Grand Lodge to warrant the Hudson Lodge in December of 1786, Hamilton was a regular patron of Ashbel Stoddard's press. Stoddard was regularly publishing the minutes and notices of the company in the *Gazette,* following the lead of the Hartford *Connecticut Courant.* Meeting with Ethan Allen earlier that fall, Hamilton must have arranged for Stoddard's publication of *An Address to the Inhabitants of Wyoming,* signed by Allen, John Franklin, and John Jenkins that September, the first surviving political broadside from Stoddard's press. That March, at the close of a long letter discussing their strategy and urging Franklin to "preserve rule and good order" in the Wyoming settlements, Hamilton had written to John Franklin about the importance of the press to their project. Demonstrating a sharp understanding for the ways in which public opinion could be shaped, Hamilton stressed, "We must constantly do in the Public Prints and every where else, otherwise we bring the resentment of the Public upon us."[26]

If Hamilton and his associates wanted to gain legitimacy in the public sphere, it was because they were preparing for sterner measures. As Hamilton wrote to Franklin, they were about to "Strike a man in the Streets in view of the Public." The company leadership was planning a full-scale rebellion against the state of Pennsylvania to defend the settlements and speculations in Wyoming, and their plans were inspiring others in Columbia County to follow suit with plans of their own.[27]

In March 1787, Doctor Caleb Benton of Hillsdale published a notice in the *Gazette* calling "the proprietors of the old Indian settlement at Cawannisque" to a meeting at James Bryant's Hillsdale tavern. This was the first public manifestation of a new project, grandly called the New York Genesee Company of Adventurers. Benton had been involved with the Susquehannah Company since at least November 1786, and he and Bryant would be deeply involved in the affairs of the new Adventurer company, which attracted eighty shareholders, about thirty from Columbia County. In November 1787 and January 1788 Benton and two other leading Genesee Adventurers, John Livingston of the Manor and Ezekiel Gilbert, the Hudson lawyer, signed two leases with the Iroquois deeding all their vast lands in central and western New York to the company for 999 years.[28]

These leases were key elements of a wider plan that had been secretly discussed since the fall of 1786, when Ethan Allen and Joseph Hamilton met in Hudson. Behind their plan to defend the Susquehannah claims, they seem to have envisioned a new state analogous to Vermont, encompassing the entire region from the Susquehannah Purchase north and west "as far as the British lines." With the Susquehannah Company preparing for a defense against Pennsylvania authority, leading men among the Adventurers were ready for stern measures in the late summer of 1787. Prominent among them were Colonel John McKinstry and Captain Benjamin Allen, both recently moved from Hillsdale to Hudson, who appeared at Tioga to meet with Franklin and Jenkins. They were, informants said, "forming a plan to Oppose the laws of Pennsylvania being Carried into Execution" and "to erect an independent state." McKinstry was said to have declared that they were "fully Determined to defend the Cause of the Half Sharemen Even to force of Arms" and that "General Ethan Allen would be there in a fortnight with a number of men for their assistance." He and Benjamin Allen had brought two casks of powder for the defense of Wyoming. Things heated up even further in late September and October. After issuing warrants for the Wyoming and Adventurer leaders, the Pennsylvania authorities arrested John Franklin as well as Asa Starkweather, a Hillsdale schoolteacher who had been carrying letters from Hamilton to Franklin, including a constitution for the proposed new state drawn up by William Judd, a Connecticut lawyer.[29]

When word of these arrests arrived at Tioga, John McKinstry gathered twenty men and marched south to Wyoming. Here he acted on a promise made some weeks before when, with Benjamin Allen and Zerah Beach, another Susquehannah militant from Amenia in Dutchess County, he was the first among more than sixty signers of a "Combination" pledging their honor and property that they would devote their "utmost exertions for the protection and defence of each other in the possession of the Lands" in the Susquehannah Purchase. In June 1788 Timothy Pickering, the Pennsylvania commissioner, was kidnapped and held for a month as a hostage for Franklin's release. Pickering was taken by what the Pennsylvanians called "a Bandity here called Halfshear men or wild Boys"; McKinstry and his associates were widely thought to be the prime movers.[30]

Later in the summer of 1788, as New Yorkers uneasily adjusted to their ratification of the Federal Constitution, these same men brought violent confrontations to the northern stretch of the Susquehanna country. That February the New York assembly had soundly rejected the Genesee Adventurers' petition for recognition of their leases of Iroquois land and quickly passed an act authorizing the state Indian commissioners to enter into land negotiations with the Iroquois. After preparations and meetings running through the summer, early in September 1788 the state commissioners negotiated a huge purchase from the Oneidas at Fort Schuyler, both to preempt the incursions of the Adventurers and to secure, free of federal intervention, the route of Philip Schuyler's proposed canal. In June and July 1788, just as they were apparently involved in Pickering's kidnapping, John McKinstry and "the Committee of Hudson" had been working to disrupt the coming Fort Schuyler conference. Caleb Benton spread misinterpretations of the governor's message, and John Livingston offered bribes to dissuade Iroquois sales to the state. In September they reportedly took stronger measures at their camp on Seneca Lake at Canadesega (present Geneva). Cayuga and Seneca warriors reported to the missionary Samuel Kirkland that "they had been kept in a continual state of Intoxication and Dissipation for Three weeks to prevent their going on to the Treaty." Arms and threats were also deployed. "Dr. B[enton] and Colo. M[c-Kinstry] had between twenty and thirty Riflemen in Arms for twenty-four Hours." They "gave out severe Threats" to two white men "for being Enemies to their Party and Friends to the Government, in perswading the Indians to attend the Treaty at Fort Schuyler, and they were ordered off the Ground or to abide the Consequences." That November McKinstry was under indictment in Pennsylvania for attempting to erect a new state; by the following summer he, Benton, Allen, and five others were being hunted by New York authorities on similar charges of "treasonable Practices."[31]

John McKinstry would evade these charges and live to a ripe old age in Columbia County. His escapades in 1789 brought his decades in the field to a close. The son of an Ulster immigrant, McKinstry had marched in 1757 from the bleak frontier town of Blandford, Massachusetts, in the failed relief of Fort William Henry. By 1767 he had taken up land in Nobletown, apparently on a lease from John Van Rensselaer; by 1770 he was a captain in Van Rensselaer's militia regiment. In the spring of 1775 he raised his own company of Nobletown men and marched to the siege of Boston; taken into Patterson's Berkshire regiment of the Massachusetts Continental Line, McKinstry's company fought at the disastrous Battle of the Cedars in May 1776. Resigning in December 1776 and returning to Nobletown, he was in the spring of 1778 both elected to the Claverack Committee of Safety and appointed a major in Colonel Peter Van Ness's Ninth Albany Militia. In the fall of 1780 he was back in active service. With William B. Whiting and David Pratt of the King's District, McKinstry was one of the commanders of the advance party of patriot militia that marched from Albany in October 1780 to drive Sir John Johnson's raiders from the Mohawk Valley. After General Robert Van Rensselaer failed to send men across the Mohawk to the aid of the defenders of the Stone Arabia settlement, and actually rode off to Fort Plain to have lunch while men were being massacred north of the river, McKinstry reputedly broke his sword, swearing that he had no use for such a weapon while Van Rensselaer remained in command. Later that afternoon McKinstry and his men were part of the attack that turned the British left flank at the brief battle at Klock's Field, west of Stone Arabia.[32]

John McKinstry thus served long and hard in the Revolution and emerged with hopes of advancement. Perhaps he was more determined than most, but he was among an extensive network of former and active militia officers in the New York Genesee Company of Adventurers. In Columbia County, the colonels of three of the five Revolutionary militia regiments were involved, usually with several junior officers. From the Ninth Albany, McKinstry brought along his brother Charles as well as Benjamin Allen. Both had been lieutenants in the wartime rosters, and in 1786 Charles was a major and Benjamin a captain in the Hillsdale regiment; Caleb Benton was the regimental surgeon. From his later service with Willett's Levies, John McKinstry brought along Lieutenant Peter Loop; in 1786 Loop was a captain in the Hillsdale regiment and deeply involved with the Susquehannah Company as well as with the Adventurers.[33]

The closing episode of McKinstry's Revolutionary service hints at the specific motivations of the officers among the Adventurers: unfulfilled expectations of a reward in land. After commanding a garrison of Willett's Levies at Saratoga in 1781, McKinstry was given papers to raise a regiment of his own. Recruiting went slowly, but McKinstry gave up only when he was told by Governor Clinton that the legislature would not include him and his men in the offer of a recruitment bounty of the unappropriated western lands that would be known as the Military Tract. Such exclusion was the common denominator of almost all of the former officers among the Adventurers. Only three received land in the Military Tract: among them, Major John Graham of the First New York Line received lots in Ulysses and Cincinnatus townships.

But at least twenty former officers did not, since most of them had served only in the militia, rather than the line. And at least nine of them had served as majors and colonels in the militia, including four who had been in action at Klock's Field in October 1780: John McKinstry, Robert Van Rensselaer, William Whiting, and Abraham Cuyler of Albany. Writing in the *Gazette* in February 1788, Justice reminded the public of their services: the Genesee men were not "the mushrooms of the hour, but men who have considerably contributed to the liberty we now enjoy."[34]

Justice was responding to the accusations leveled by A Citizen several weeks before in the *Gazette,* who saw a secret cabal to defraud the state by "unconstitutional" means. A Citizen revealed a careful coalition building in the company's plans. "In order to stop the multitude, they have received a few of the common people into their association," he wrote, but "they have gone farther . . . [and] endeavoured to interest a number of influential people in their plan." If men like McKinstry and Benton played important roles in the field for the Adventurers, they were men of action rather than influence. Indeed, McKinstry's was only one of several military networks among the Adventurers, and that of the least influence in the politics of the new state. They were overshadowed by the real powers in the New York Genesee Company, a select group of assemblymen, senators, and powerful county officials who worked to achieve a legislative recognition of the company's claimed leases.[35]

Exactly how much these gentlemen knew about McKinstry's frontier activities is an open question, but in the fluidity of the late 1780s it seems that some were willing to entertain the possibility of alternative political outcomes in a final revolutionary settlement. These gentlemen Adventurers included eleven former assemblymen, three sitting in 1788, two former senators and one sitting senator, the county clerks of Albany and Columbia, the treasurer of Columbia, and four of six judges of the new Columbia County courts. Among them were General Robert Van Rensselaer (the Columbia County clerk), his brother Judge Henry Van Rensselaer, and Henry Platner (a captain from the Eighth Albany, which the Van Rensselaers had once commanded), involved in a wide array of land ventures. Another Adventurer network linked Colonel Morris Graham of Dutchess County, an assemblyman in 1788, who variously had commanded three regiments of militia and levies, with Colonels Benjamin Birdsall and Henry Livingston. Graham's brother John had connections with former fellow officers in the Second New York Line, including Major Peter Schuyler, assemblyman in 1784 and a senator from 1787 to 1792.[36]

Peter Schuyler and John Livingston, Henry's brother, occupied the central positions in this web of connections among the Adventuring gentlemen. Schuyler had been appointed a commissioner of Indian Affairs in June 1783 and might have been hatching the plan for the landgrab with John Livingston as early as the fall of 1784, when Livingston began to attend the meetings of the commission. Perhaps uniquely among the Adventurers, Livingston had no record of military service and had actually declined reelection to the committee of safety in August 1776. But he began attending the state commissioners' meetings with the Iroquois in 1784 and then served in the assembly for Columbia for three years, 1786–1788.[37]

These gentry Adventurers were a distinctly different set of men from the likes of Benton, McKinstry, Hamilton, and their following among the company officers of the local militia. Indeed, the Genesee Adventurers forged an odd alliance between what Henry Livingston had only recently called the Aristo and the Demo. While John Livingston was active in the western negotiations and made sure that his name was on the Livingston leases, it is not completely obvious how he and others of his gentry circle of "influential people" established working relations with "common people" like McKinstry and his followers.

Here it appears that Freemasonry was the civil glue that linked these two orbits together at several critical points. Masonic affiliation was often a continuation of military brotherhoods, but in this case it was a critical supplement. Men at the center of the western land schemes of the mid-1780s appear to have used new Masonic affiliation to make up for the lack of senior militia patronage as an avenue into a higher orbit of influence.

Benton, Hamilton, and McKinstry were indeed all "common" men. Caleb Benton and Joseph Hamilton were recent settlers from Connecticut, with no connections to the local gentry. John McKinstry, a pre-Revolutionary immigrant from a remote Scots-Irish settlement in the Berkshires, had served in the Continental Line, but in that of Massachusetts rather than New York. He later had been a major in the Albany County militia and a lieutenant colonel in the levies, but his militia regimental colonel, Peter Van Ness, would have nothing to do with either the Susquehannah Company or the Adventurers. While Van Rensselaer patronage was at work in his militia commission before the Revolution, McKinstry had endangered his ties with the Van Rensselaer family when he broke his sword in mutinous rage on the afternoon of the engagement at Klock's Field in 1780.[38]

Thus it is striking that all three of these men of action established Masonic fellowship with key gentlemen of influence in the mid-1780s. In February 1785, Caleb Benton ventured up to Albany to be initiated in the Union Lodge, where the powerful Matthew Visscher, clerk of Albany County, sitting assemblyman, and soon to be a fellow Adventurer, was the lodge treasurer. Visscher seems to have been the vehicle to Benton's entry into Albany circles, where a number of men of influence, including Senator Peter Schuyler, would be deeply engaged in the company's plan. In Hudson, Masonic connections were built in as part of strategies of migration from the New England border region. Joseph Hamilton, originally from Sharon, Connecticut, was one of the first initiates in the Temple Lodge in Northeast, Dutchess County, before he joined the petition for the Hudson Lodge in 1786. McKinstry had established Hudson's first tavern when he moved there from Hillsdale, and it was here that the Hudson Lodge was organized in December 1786.[39]

In his lodge room he and Hamilton were on fraternal terms with Ezekiel Gilbert, a fellow Connecticut emigrant of somewhat higher station, a Yale graduate and the trusted attorney enlisted by John Livingston to negotiate with the Iroquois and to move the company's petition through the legislature. Livingston worked in a set of horizontal affiliations of kinship and high-level officeholding, but the Masonic affiliations of some of his political peers like Gilbert and Visscher secured vertical connections to lesser men, who in turn had their own orbits of influence. Thus the understandings of the lodges, while not encompassing large numbers of the Adventurers, provided an essential vehicle in the political process. Lodge affiliation worked to bridge the deep chasm between Aristo and Demo in the Adventurer coalition, linking circles of gentry of some county and state influence and authority with circles of more ordinary men, tavernkeepers, farmers, and carpenters who were also militia officers and thus themselves leaders in their own neighborhoods of men of even less property and connection.[40]

By the spring of 1788 the Adventurers' plans were in shambles. That February the legislature had annulled the two 999-year leases that the company had negotiated with the Six Nations and with the Oneidas, and the governor and the board of commissioners were laying the groundwork for a treaty meeting at Fort Schuyler, preferably to take place before the new national Constitution might take effect: the federal Constitution's provision of federal supremacy in treaty relations between American citizens and American Indians was an important consideration in George Clinton's Antifederalist stance. John Livingston attempted to revive their fortunes by packing the county's Federalist assembly slate with members of the Genesee Company: himself, William H. Ludlow of Claverack, and their attorney, Ezekiel Gilbert. When the Hudson committee, probably supported by Peter Van Schaack, opposed his nomination, preferring Seth Jenkins, John Livingston fought hard and, when outvoted, refused to cooperate with any "person unfriendly to his family." William Wilson, attending the Federalist meeting for John's skeptical cousin Robert R. Livingston, had his eyes set on constitutional ratification and was "sorry however to see this business so much blinded with another matter which appeared to me foreign to the purpose. . . . It seemed to be as much a meeting of the Associates in the Indian Purchase as any thing else and indeed this gave a bias to the whole." John Livingston's tantrum contributed in some measure to the Federalist defeat in Columbia County in the April elections. He headed west into the Iroquois country that summer with Gilbert, Benton, and McKinstry, where they directed a plan that threatened the constitutional settlements of established states and the emerging Republic. While New York debated the new federal Constitution, they intervened in Pennsylvania affairs and at Buffalo Creek negotiated a new understanding with the Iroquois for lands east of the recent Phelps-Gorham Purchase. Back in the county the following spring, Livingston was more successful at the polls, engineering his own and Gilbert's nomination and election to the 1790 assembly. Three years later Gilbert would be elected to Congress as a Federalist, the county's first congressman.[41]

Gilbert shared Masonic membership with an emerging stratum of Columbia political figures who had no deep local connections of kinship or affiliation. Following William Powers of Canaan's Unity Lodge, and a Federalist of the competing Schuyler–Van Schaack orbit, Gilbert was the second Freemason to be elected to the New York assembly. He also shared with Powers the distinction of being the first men elected to the assembly who had no background in the Revolutionary committees or the militia. Conversely, John McKinstry was one of only two Revolutionary militia colonels in the county who joined a Masonic lodge, the other being Benjamin Birdsall, also of Hillsdale. Both had been colonels of the levies, raised late in the war, and both had moved recently, McKinstry from Hillsdale to Hudson and Birdsall north from Quaker Ridge in Dutchess County to Hillsdale. Generally, Freemasonry in Columbia County was an affair of younger men, but without strong local connections McKinstry and Birdsall both seem to have joined lodges to advance their somewhat tenuous positions. While McKinstry hosted the formation of the Hudson Lodge in 1786, Birdsall had maintained his connections in Dutchess in joining the Temple Lodge in Northeast. Again, Masonry provided an associational milieu in the building of a political understanding.

Early in 1789 Benjamin Birdsall became the legislative point man for the Genesee Adventurers' claim. The state was demanding that all three of the Iroquois leases be returned, and apparently neither John Livingston nor any of his close associates was willing to take on the task. So Benjamin Birdsall, with James Bryant, the town supervisor of Hillsdale, was sent to meet with the Indian commissioners at Albany on February 14, 1789, where they turned over the documents to be held by the governor "until the further order of the board." The following September (while the state considered plans to arrest

Benton, McKinstry, and Allen) the Adventurers held a grand gathering at Hudson, where they reputedly spent as much as twelve thousand pounds for arrangements and gifts to visiting Iroquois dignitaries. Apparently encouraged by a certain ambiguity in the state's position and armed with native confirmations of the July 1788 agreement, Birdsall carried further petitions to the assembly in 1790 and 1791, which approved and then rejected a ten-mile-square grant of land to the Genesee Adventurers.[42]

Two years later, as a member of the assembly himself, Birdsall would play a final and successful role in the saga of the New York Genesee Company. But by then he and others among the Adventurers had also played a pivotal role in an entirely different thread in the politics of land, civil society, and revolutionary settlement in Columbia County.

A PETITION, A MURDER, A TRIAL, AND A CLOSE ELECTION: HILLSDALE AND THE "GREAT AND MIGHTY RUMPUS," 1789–1792

The death of John Van Rensselaer of Claverack Manor in February 1783 might have raised fears of tenancy and disposition in the King's District, but it led to open civil violence in Hillsdale. Known as East Claverack, the recruiting territory of the Ninth Albany Regiment was set aside as the district of Hillsdale by legislation introduced by Jacob Ford in March 1782. Four months later the doctrine of entail, the legal bulwark of landed oligarchy, was abolished, and the Van Rensselaer land in Claverack and Hillsdale devolved to John's various children, including Catherine, wife of the powerful Federalist Philip Schuyler. The stage was set for an epochal struggle over land and the meaning of the Revolution.[43]

Even before the Van Rensselaer family could begin to assert its claim, the Hillsdale people began to petition the legislature. In February 1784 Simeon Rowley with James Spencer, who had filed a similar petition in 1772, led a petition asking for an inquiry into John Van Rensselaer's 1773 patent of confirmation for the east Claverack lands. Matthew Adgate, the popular leader in Canaan, introduced the petition from committee, urging that it be heard, and it was approved by the assembly, pending concurrence in the senate. Philip Schuyler, sitting in the senate, ensured that this concurrence was not forthcoming; he was opposed by only three senators, among them Adgate's neighbor Colonel William Whiting. A year later, in the spring of 1785, Whiting again urged that the senate accept a petition from Hillsdale to reconsider their nonconcurrence and was again outvoted. In the intervening October, Schuyler had begun to bring actions for the ejectment of Simeon Rowley and several others in these Hillsdale lands.[44]

These cases were still pending in January 1789, when the legislature received the first of two new petitions from Hillsdale, asking that the 1784 proceedings be reconsidered. Signed by more than two hundred men, the first petition condemned the "iniquitous conduct" of the "rapacious" Governor Tyron in making the 1773 confirmation to Van Rensselaer, to the "manifest injury of some hundred families of Loyal subjects to the state of New York," threatening the "valuable improvements" and "worldly substance that by many years hard Labour they had honestly acquired." Later that month Simeon Rowley tendered yet another petition from Hillsdale, reiterating these points and noting that settlements had originally been made "by Virtue of legal Indian Purchases licensed and authorized according to the Practice of the General Court of Massachusetts Bay." Five of the Hillsdale petitioners were directly threatened by the legal proceedings being brought by Philip Schuyler, but the rest were clearly threatened by future suits. They were led by Colonel Benjamin Birdsall.[45]

Birdsall thus made his entry into legislative politics on two fronts in the 1789 session. In February, when he represented the Adventurers in delivering the Iroquois leases to the board of commissioners, his name was already before the assembly as the leading name among more than two hundred signatures on a petition against the Van Rensselaer claim to lands in Hillsdale. Perhaps his willingness to take on the unpleasant task of returning the leases was in hopes of assembling support for the Hillsdale cause. Such an effort, however, would have been blocked by the powerful players among the Adventurers and their family connections who would be materially injured by the overturning of the Van Rensselaers' 1773 confirmation. Most directly, these included Robert and Henry Van Rensselaer of Claverack and, indirectly, Peter Schuyler of Albany, Philip Schuyler's brother. Birdsall's petition, read in the assembly on January 23, disappeared in committee in the 1789 session, where Philip and Peter Schuyler sat in the senate and various Van Rensselaer cousins sat in the assembly. Simeon Rowley's petition was delayed a year and then suffered a similar fate in an assembly committee headed by John Livingston, the leader of the Company of Adventurers but also soon to inherit large tracts of lease land in the Manor. Livingston's committee reported against the petition, arguing that "the validity of grants and all other titles to land" were matters for the "Courts of Justice," not the interposition of the legislature; the assembly agreed by a large margin.[46]

Benjamin Birdsall was one of five Adventurers to sign the Hillsdale petition against the Van Rensselaer title, but these Hillsdale men were among the less influential in the roster of the New York Genesee Company. If they had local connections, the 1789 petitioners had few links out to centers of power.

Among these five Adventurer Hillsdale petitioners were John McKinstry's brother Charles, Benjamin Allen (who had signed the 1785 senate petition), and Ambrose Latting, respectively a major and the captains of the first and seventh companies of the Hillsdale regiment of militia, formed in 1786. Five other company officers were among the petitioners. Concentrated in the southern half of the town, the petitioners included members of the new Baptist church, organized in May 1787 at old Nobletown center. Ambrose Latting, a carpenter and housewright, was elected clerk of the church and engaged to build the Baptist meetinghouse. He was one of seven church members to sign the petition, and eight other signers would join the church over the next decade. Since this was the only church for miles around, presumably many other petitioners attended. A considerable number of the petitioners, at least forty, were inhabitants of Claverack itself, and at least twelve lived to the south on the Manor.[47]

It must have given a healthy sense of public affirmation when the Shaftsbury Baptist Association, bringing messengers from seventeen Baptist churches in three states, met at Ambrose Latting's new meetinghouse in the summer of 1789. But political connections to the county leadership were few. Other than several officers of church and militia, Benjamin Birdsall was the 1789 petitioners' sole figure of authority. He had been a justice of the peace since 1786 and would be elected to the assembly for three years in the 1790s. Another petitioner, John McKinstry's brother Charles, would later follow a similar path after his election as town supervisor in 1791. And they had Masonic affiliations; Birdsall and McKinstry were both early initiates in the Temple Lodge in Northeast in Dutchess County. Both, with others among the petitioners, would petition to form a lodge in south Hillsdale in 1803. Birdsall and Charles McKinstry would have had visiting privileges in Hudson, where they might meet with Ezekiel Gilbert, the attorney for John Livingston's company (but also in the ejectment suits being brought against some of the Hillsdale petitioners), who was elected to the assembly in April 1789. But Birdsall's Masonic and Adventurer connections did little good in 1789, when he and his Hillsdale neighbors had only four failed petitions and the growing threat of dispossession to show for their political labors against the Van Rensselaer claim to their farms.[48]

By the fall of 1790 the Van Rensselaers, and particularly Philip Schuyler, had a plan for Hillsdale. In November Schuyler published an open letter to the occupants of his wife's claimed lands. At "a considerable sacrifice to my interest," he was prepared to sell farms to occupants, offering mortgages to be paid in full with interest by May 1796, or to reopen leases with rent due for all of 1789 and the ensuing years. Decisions were to be made by March 1,

1791, but the Hillsdale people would not abandon their challenge to the Van Rensselaer claim so quickly. In November 1788 an anonymous committee, following the example of Joseph Hamilton and the Susquehannah Company, had gone to the press, publishing in the *Gazette* a short notice opposing the Van Rensselaers' title. Being very careful "to manifest our loyalty to the state, and all subjection to good and wholesome regulations of the same," the committee announced that it would oppose the Van Rensselaers' "clandestine claim, with a fixed and resolute determination to defend ourselves at the risque of our lives or fortunes, unless there is an authentic and indisputable title produced." In February 1791 another unknown group of subscribers wrote up an agreement, enforceable by a justice of the peace and two freemen, to share the costs of any suits brought by the various heirs of John Van Rensselaer.[49]

Such associations for mutual aid were common throughout the Confederation and new Republic in the 1780s. Generally, they were entered into for the protection of their members from the collection of debts and taxes; in the Susquehanna country, in Vermont, and on the Maine frontier such associations were formed for reasons similar to those in Hillsdale: the protection of land from the claims of patent proprietors. Such associations often moved beyond the financial support offered in the 1791 Hillsdale agreement to violent resistance to the enforcement of contract law. The Hillsdale people had plenty of examples close at hand. Men from Hillsdale — John McKinstry, Caleb Benton, Benjamin Allen — were involved in the defense of the Susquehannah Company claims against Pennsylvania; these same men, with Benjamin Birdsall, Charles McKinstry, Ambrose Latting, and others of their Hillsdale neighbors, were variously involved with the affairs of the Adventurers, who were bringing force to bear outside the law in the Iroquois country. Just to the east, Berkshire County in Massachusetts had been rocked by debtor violence in Shays's Rebellion. The neighboring town of Egremont, where the Nobletown people had taken refuge after the attack of British troops in 1766, was a hot spot for the Shaysites. Among those indicted in Massachusetts after the rebellion were two men from Hillsdale families; from Egremont the indicted included two nephews of one of the leaders of the 1766 Nobletown refugees as well as Matthew Van Gelder, from a part-Mahican family that had been involved in the riots against the Livingstons in the 1750s. Late in the rebellion, the Massachusetts rebels had encamped to the north in the King's District, and Governor Clinton had mobilized the Columbia County militia to root them out.[50]

Such was the background to the events in southwest Hillsdale in October

1791, when force was brought to bear against the law. In the middle of the month, a Columbia County deputy attempted to hold a vendue "sale of some effects taken by execution in favor of the Rensselaers" at Jonathan Arnold's farm in south Hillsdale near the Claverack line. Harassed by the assembled crowd, he rode back down to Claverack, and the following Saturday, October 22, Sheriff Cornelius Hogeboom rode out to hold the sale. Waiting long into the afternoon for the deputy carrying the execution papers, Hogeboom was about to return to Claverack when a band of seventeen men, "blacked" or "painted and in Indian dress," appeared on Arnold's signal. After a volley of shots from the "Indians," Hogeboom lay mortally wounded on the Claverack road.[51]

Hillsdale long had a reputation as a violent place: in 1776 people in Claverack complained of a threat of rioting in Spencertown; more than a century later the town was remembered as a place "not safe for a man to ride through," and the Hillsdalers as a "rough and somewhat lawless people." If so, its condition was a symptom of its marginal status in the state of New York, literally at the boundary of the wider political and civil society. Such marginality had been demonstrated in recent years by its inability to get distributive redress through law. In the murder of Sheriff Hogeboom, Hillsdale's "lawlessness" took a political expression, literally social banditry and verging on civil war. The case might have been the same in New Lebanon and Canaan, but a successful building of local civil institutions and regional political alliances brought a distributive settlement, manifested in March 1791 in the easy passage of the legislation protecting land titles in the old King's District.[52]

Such a settlement was not yet in sight for Hillsdale, and the portents seemed grim. Two days after the murder, Henry Livingston wrote from Ancram in the Manor to his brother Walter in New York City that the "Matter" of the Van Rensselaer claims in Hillsdale "will be brought to a crisis." On October 31, Governor George Clinton issued a proclamation announcing rewards for the capture of five named rioters, augmenting a subscription fund established in the county on October 24. The murdered sheriff, Cornelius Hogeboom, had been a man of influential connection; his brother, Lawrence, had been among the Federalists elected to the assembly in 1786 and had preceded Cornelius as the first appointed sheriff of the new county. On November 8 the governor with the Council of Appointment made a ceremonial visit to the courthouse in Claverack to appoint John C. Hogeboom as sheriff in the place of his murdered father, appointing a special commission of the court of oyer and terminer to sit at Claverack at the end of the month to open proceedings against suspects, who were already being tracked down. The following January, perhaps reflecting on recent events in Massachusetts, Clinton denounced the Hillsdale riot in his opening message to the new legislative session as "a daring outrage . . . against the laws and authority of government." Henry Van Schaack wrote confidently from Pittsfield to Theodore Sedgwick in Philadelphia, "Weak as the government has been there, it will be found that the State of New York has energy enough to execute a number of the perpetrators of this atrocious murder — This murder is universally detested by the people of both States, and I fancy the like of it will not happen again in this quarter of the United States." Governor Clinton was pleased with "the judicious and spirited exertions" of the Columbia County courts, which brought indictments at the special session of the oyer and terminer. But the friends of order were not to see the justice they sought, as the process of a political settlement in which Clinton was deeply involved began to intercede.[53]

On February 7, 1792, the court reconvened, a grand jury was charged, and the prisoners were arraigned and tried over three days in four trials: Thomas Southward on a first degree charge of murder and the others on charges of murder in the second degree; seven were charged together, with individual trials for John West and Jonathan Arnold. The verdicts of the February court were, as the bemused editor of the *Poughkeepsie Journal* put it, "contrary to the general expectation." Thomas Southward's case came first on February 9: after hearing three witnesses for the state, a prisoner's deposition, and fourteen witnesses for the defense, the jury deliberated and returned a verdict of not guilty. The three subsequent trials followed the same course; the defendants and five others indicted but not tried were bound on recognizance in case of an appeal, and the court adjourned.[54]

Nicholas Power, the Federalist editor of the *Poughkeepsie Journal*, was quick to publish a scathingly sarcastic piece condemning the Hillsdale verdicts.

> Happy Hillsdale! Thrice glorious nook! . . . has dared to stand forth and crush the monster Restraint . . . Hillsdale will be that long wished for city of refuge, whither, from every part of the empire, those whose souls are too big for trammels may resort: and form a society, the scourge and terror of those dastards, who rank decorum, law, and government, among the class of public felicities.

"Restraint" was the fountain of "public felicities," this essayist announced, and Hillsdale had set both aside. An uncivil place, Hillsdale stood outside the definition of civil society as a space protected by law, in a zone of unregulated force. In a sense it was that already, and that marginality, that exclusion, had shaped the new town's failure in the political arena and the eruption of violence that had led to the trials. But this author in the *Journal* also saw a larger plot.

> At last, my friend, the great and mighty rumpus is over, and all the pageantry of Governor, council, proclamations, and courts adjourned and non-adjourned, are vanished and gone, like that "baseless fabric of a vision."

For, if the Hogeboom verdicts challenged "contrary expectation," they had a political purpose that would work to achieve important outcomes for Columbia County. The trials were indeed a "great and mighty rumpus," the beginnings of a general political settlement for Hillsdale in particular and the county in general. The acquitted defendants in the Hogeboom murder trials were humble men, but they had patrons in strategic places in the court, patrons with political plans.[55]

Among the accused, Thomas Southward would remain in Hillsdale to be counted on the 1800 valuation, where he ranked in the bottom fifth, another of the accused would rank in the middle, and Jonathan Arnold would be in the top fifth. Most of the others would move on by 1800, to Ulster, Albany, Cayuga, and Chenango counties. Two were old enough to have been listed in the Revolutionary militia: Jonathan Rodman in the Hillsdale regiment, Thomas Southward apparently in the Dutchess militia. Only one had signed the 1789 petition. Five defendants indicted but not tried were men of some substance, three ranking in the top fifth in 1800, and three signing the 1789 petition. They were also among the twenty-three defense witnesses who spoke for the accused, eight of whom were petition signers. Four militia officers stood as witnesses for the defendants, including Captain Benjamin Allen and Major Charles McKinstry. Thomas Southward's trial, the first undertaken, and the only one with a charge of first-degree murder, set the tone for the following trials: the fourteen witnesses for Southward included five 1789 petitioners and two Adventurers, most importantly Colonel John McKinstry himself.[56]

The defendants had similar good luck with their jurors, despite the fact that two of the latter from Hillsdale seem to have tried to avoid the proceedings. Oliver Teall, two years a member of the Hillsdale Baptist church, was a day late to the sitting of the grand jury; Ambrose Latting was among five petit jurors fined for failing to attend the court. But the defendants had many neighbors and sympathizers on the juries. Where only two of the twenty-one grand jurors sitting in February were from Hillsdale, the defendants had better odds with the petit juries. Of twenty-nine men on the jury pool, ten were from Canaan, nine from Claverack, and seven from Hillsdale; five had signed the 1789 petition, including two from Claverack. The seven men from

Hillsdale had a somewhat disproportionate presence on the jury panels. As 24 percent of the pool, they got 31 percent of the seats on the juries, including four of the twelve on the critical Southward trial.

Above the juries sat the judges on the bench. If the judges could not determine the pool, they could shape the jury panels and certainly the overall tone of the trials. While eighteen county judges were involved in some manner in these proceedings, variously appointed to the special commission of oyer and terminer and attending the November and February courts, they did not treat the proceeding in the same fashion. John Livingston complained five days after the close of the trials that only Peter Van Ness, Cornelius's Hogeboom's brother-in-law, who sat on the court in November but not February, had "behaved well in the case of the prisoners." The rest, he condemned for a lax enforcement of the law. The four county judges who attended all five days of this "great and mighty rumpus" had histories of opposing the interests of the great families. Peter Van Schaack of Kinderhook, though a committed Federalist, had, since the 1770s and his recent return from loyalist exile, opposed the interests of the Claverack Van Rensselaers when it came to the eastern lands. The other three were the leading Clintonian politicians in Canaan, the old King's District. Judges Matthew Adgate and William B. Whiting had similar records, most recently supporting the Hillsdale petitions in the 1784 and 1785 legislatures. Whiting had also defended the claims of the Harper purchase of Oneida lands, in which Philip Frisbie, another consistently attending judge, had an interest. Adgate and Frisbie were certainly thinking ahead to the upcoming April elections, when both the governorship and the assembly would be at stake. Both of them, with Judge Israel Spencer, would be candidates for the assembly, and Hillsdale represented a large bloc of votes, traditionally popular or Antifederalist, which should not be alienated.[57]

Looming above the proceedings was the electoral interest of Governor Clinton himself, who in consultation with the presiding justice, Antifederalist John Lansing, had called the court into session. Political sentiment at the court was certainly flowing toward Clinton. John Livingston wrote a few days later, "At our late Grand Jury—it was declared by all except one that they would support Judge Yates—if he declined Clinton was the man and that they would support him with all their influence agt. every other person." But Yates, a moderate who had narrowly lost for the Federalists in 1789, had already just told Philip Schuyler that he would not run a second time. Thus the cynical Federalist might well see in the entire Claverack court proceedings a "great and mighty rumpus" designed to shore up support for the Clintonian interest.[58]

Governor Clinton was more deeply involved in another simultaneous effort to solidify his political base, one that would be condemned as corrupt for decades to come. Authorized in March 1791 to sell "waste and unappropriated lands," the land commission appointed by the governor sat from April to December. There were a few winners, and a few losers, in Columbia County. In late April, Adgate, with Frisbie and their neighbor Aaron Kellogg, bid too low for a twenty-five-thousand-acre parcel in the Chenango townships 4, 5, 8, and 9. But in two meetings November and December Adgate was awarded three tracts in the Mohawk Valley and east of Lake Champlain, totaling almost ninety thousand acres, for the price of about ten thousand pounds, perhaps explaining why he missed the first session of the court of oyer and terminer. The previous August Robert C. Livingston, one of the sons of the Upper Manor, was awarded one of the Chenango towns, comprising twenty-five thousand acres. His second application, for a massive half-million-acre chunk of the Adirondacks, was rejected. So too was an application from his brother Walter, asking for "all the unappropriated lands south of the Oneida Lake, purchased from the Oneidas and of the Onondagas and the Cayugas."[59]

These Livingston transactions, successful or not, spelled a turning point in the politics of Columbia, moving the county from a Federalist majority back to the Clintonian Republicans. The Livingstons had all been advocates of the federal Constitution and opponents of Clintonian popular politics, but some of them were beginning to shift by 1791. All of them were extremely con- *earlier* cerned that they were being marginalized by the Federalist coterie encompassing Philip Schuyler, John Jay, Stephen Van Rensselaer, and Alexander Hamilton; locally this alliance was making inroads into the northern county towns. Robert R. Livingston, the chancellor, was increasingly insulted at not being recruited for national office and moving toward an aristocratic agrarianism similar to that of the tidewater gentry who would form one wing of Jefferson's Republican coalition. Historians have long found it suggestive that Thomas Jefferson and James Madison made a northern trip together in the spring of 1791, a few months after Alexander Hamilton's Bank of the United States was signed into law. Meeting at Ellsworth's Boarding House in New York City with the likes of Aaron Burr and Robert R. Livingston, with whom Jefferson might have exchanged notes on the ravages of the Hessian fly, they passed through the Manor, Claverack, Hudson, and Kinderhook, where they spent an uncomfortable night on May 25.[60]

The Upper Manor Livingstons could be bought. Federalists complained that Robert C. Livingston had "recently become a friend and advocate" of Governor Clinton, explaining his grant in the Chenango region. Clinton had reason to worry about the Livingstons. In 1786 New York had to make a massive cession to Massachusetts in western New York, and in January and February 1791 Robert C. Livingston and his brother John were in Boston, attempting to wrangle a grant from the Massachusetts General Court. Walter's application for Iroquois land seems to have been submitted in coordination with John Livingston's longstanding efforts. The resolution of this struggle began to unfold during Clinton's trip to Claverack in November, when he stopped twice to visit John Livingston at the Manor. John wrote to Walter on November 13 that the "Governor in his way up did me the *honor* to stop and breakfast and on his return staid and supped." After small talk and perhaps expressions of mutual disdain for the Hillsdale rioters, conversation turned to the west, particularly the Seneca lands around Niagara. Clinton seemed to hint that Livingston might be able to make a claim: "The lands at Niagara are ours by conquest," he told Livingston, and "no excuse can be made about extinguishing the Native Claim." John wrote expectantly to his brother Walter, "The approaching Election may do as much for us in this business as anything whatever"; the governor "cannot play off and on" forever.[61]

Three months later, just after the Hogeboom murder trials, the Livingstons were still toying with Clinton, John writing, "Perhaps it would be well to push the land business at this moment," proposing that Henry "could ask Clinton in a way that would not give offense . . . but not to pledge himself in such a way as Clinton can have any hold on him." If Walter thought this a viable approach to the land commission, John would "send in proposals for the land in another name." By April, while their estranged older brother Peter threw in with Jay and the Federalists, John, Walter, and Henry had declared for Clinton and were "using their utmost" to advance his election in the county.[62]

In Kinderhook, Peter Van Schaack was complaining that Clinton was shoring up his "precarious foundation" by "seeking refuge in forced and unnatural Coalitions."

> Various surmises are made respecting the grounds of the Coalition (not less unnatural than that of North and Fox in 1783) between Mr. C. and the L. Family; People cannot be brought to believe but that there is some concealed Quid pro Quo, in this Bargain and that the "Dignity and Interest" spoken of, are not those of the state, but of the high contracting parties in reciprocity.[63]

The "pro Quo" was certainly delivered on election day, and the "Quid" would indeed come later. As Peter Livingston had predicted earlier in the month, the influence and efforts of John, Walter, Henry, and Robert R. did "carry considerable" in the Manor towns. Livingston and Clermont had voted for Federalist choice in 1789, Robert Yates, and against Clinton, 313 to 34; in 1792 they cast 384 votes for Clinton and 5 for Jay.[64]

The crisis over the mishandled votes in Otsego County unfolded over the next several months, and Clinton's margin stood at just more than one hundred votes statewide. As this margin was more than covered by the seismic shift to Clinton in the Livingston tenant vote, the Federalists made as much noise about the "dependent creatures of the landed interest" as did Clintonians about tenant votes in Stephen Van Rensselaer's domains around Albany. This was only part of the story: the early 1790s saw a surge of participation in politics.[65]

The overall turnout of one-hundred-pound freeholders qualified to vote for the governor in Columbia held steady from 1789 to 1792 at about 92 percent, but this was significantly higher than the statewide turnout of about 70 percent. The big change in the 1792 vote in Columbia came in the turnout of voters in the twenty-pound freeholder category, qualified to vote in the assembly election (see Figures 1, 2). Estimated turnout in the three assembly races between 1789 and 1791 did not break 50 percent, and had dropped to less than 40 percent in 1791. In 1792 it jumped to more than 60 percent and would retain this level until the election of 1800, when it topped 75 percent, holding roughly level through the War of 1812. In Columbia County at least, the "great and mighty rumpus" of electoral politics took an important shift in intensity during the crisis year of 1792, in the wake of the trials of the Hillsdale rioters. A new and enduring electoral configuration emerged that year and held until local and national crises at the end of the decade. Federalist support surged in the city of Hudson, and in Canaan about seventy-five voters shifted to the Federalists from their former popular allegiances, reflecting the Federalist role in the land settlement of 1791 but not overcoming the strong base of Clintonian support in Matthew Adgate's old King's District. In Claverack and especially Hillsdale there was a strong countermovement toward Clinton, as the struggle over the eastern Van Rensselaer title reached a crisis in 1791–1792. But the shift in Livingston and Clermont was the most striking and obvious, as tenant voters humbly did the landlords' bidding and switched their votes to Clinton.[66]

The result was indeed Van Schaack's "unnatural coalitions" and the solidification of Columbia's Republican interest. For six years after 1792, Republican assembly and senate candidates would be sent to the legislature on the basis of the paradoxical alliance of Republican voters most numerous in Canaan, Hillsdale, Claverack, and Livingston Manor. And here the curious position of the Republican Livingstons was particularly apparent. While they could deliver hundreds of tenant votes, they could not determine candidates, because, to win, such candidates would have to be popular in Canaan and Hillsdale. Thus, in order to keep the Federalist Schuyler–Van Rensselaer "clan" at bay, the Livingstons had to settle for slates that they could barely stomach. In 1791 Henry Livingston had written that Stephen Hogeboom and Peter Van Ness could not support his brother Walter for the state senate, since they had prior commitments to Matthew Adgate. Livingston "sincerely regret[ted] that two such gentlemen are opposed to us, when they must know, that the Senators of the State government are the only persons who represent the Landed interest, and they being both proprietors of Lands cannot have great faith in such a representative as Adgate."[67]

Three years later, Henry wrote to Walter about two proposed slates for the assembly, settling on one including Adgate and Birdsall as "the list we shall support." He was unhappy with their choice, writing, "I don't like the list, but it is the best of the two, and both are very bad." In 1796, William Wilson, the chancellor's estate manager, received communications that the Kinderhook committee saw "no other prospect of success than exerting ourselves in favor of Mr. Adgate," while John Bay, the Claverack attorney, debated the strengths of John McKinstry for "the republican interest," eventually deciding, "If we take Col. McKinstry . . . the town of Hillsdale will be unanimous for our Ticket." McKinstry indeed did win in 1796, and, while Henry Livingston's lackluster endorsement did not translate into tenant votes in 1794, in 1792, 1793, and 1795 Adgate, Birdsall, and others of "the republican interest" received landlord support—and won the Manor by lopsided majorities. In aggregate, these compromises meant that between 1792 and 1798 the Manor, with Clermont and Germantown, would send six Republicans to the assembly while Canaan, Hillsdale, and the county town of Claverack sent a total of twenty-four.[68]

This was, however, a compromise grounded on mutual interest, and the wider context of the "Quid pro Quo" that Peter Van Schaack had suspected in April 1792. The Clintonian Republicans elected to office from 1788 to 1800 were notable for their origins in the Revolutionary committees and militia, and only in the latter half of the 1790s were they likely to be members of Masonic lodges (see Tables 1, 2). They were also deeply involved in the continuing land politics, as were the Livingstons themselves. In particular, these Republican politicians were disproportionately represented among the shareholders in the Susquehannah Company, as revived in the mid-1790s, laying claim to large tracts, even entire townships, in Pennsylvania. A seat in the New York assembly might give leverage to their running challenge to Pennsylvania law.[69]

However, the Columbia delegation elected in 1792 also began to have marked success in the realm of distributive politics within the state. If the county lay on the verge of civil war in the winter of 1791–1792, the members of the 1793 legislative session enacted a sweeping set of laws that brought a political settlement to almost all corners of Columbia. Paradoxically, in a year when the state of New York stood on the verge of a constitutional crisis, deeply divided on the issue of the Otsego ballots for governor, Columbia County crossed the boundary between the crisis politics of revolutionary settlement and the routine politics of interest and development.

THE COUNTY SETTLEMENT, 1793

The transition from settlement to routine in the politics of New York State stretched over an entire decade, from the concerted efforts by Alexander Hamilton to overturn popular control of the assembly in 1785 to the election of John Jay in 1795. Governors George Clinton and John Jay presided over two distinctly different approaches to public policy. Clinton, with a much-democratized legislature, governed the state from what has been called the "Revolutionary Center," meeting potential popular unrest with public initiatives that worked to stabilize the new government and, broadly, arrive at a viable popular settlement of the Revolution. Clintonian policy worked to dispossess loyalists and restrict their rights of citizenship and established a system of county loan offices to provide credit; it legislated comprehensive town and county government and public money for road and bridge construction. These initiatives were of a public nature, statewide in their application or authorizing public commissions in certain regions. Clintonian policy was distributive, but of authority as much as resources, in the public interest of "good police." The grants and sale of state lands, though leading certainly to private profit, could be justified under these terms of public interest, since access to new western lands would bring prosperity to ordinary citizens and the state in general.

Despite the fact that Clinton's public intervention managed to steer the state through the economic crises of the 1780s, unlike Massachusetts to the east, conservatives and Federalists complained that these public initiatives were expensive and a threat to the interests of private property. The era of John Jay's Federalist governorship, 1795–1801, brought a decisive shift in the nature of distributive politics in the state of New York, from a politics of revolutionary settlement through public authority to a politics of development through state-chartered private corporations. Emerging in strategic centers in the latter years of Clinton's governorship, there would be a veritable explosion of chartered corporations during Jay's administration.[70]

The first hints of this new direction came in 1789 and 1791, when conservative forces orchestrated the state incorporation of existing entities in New

York, the New York Society Library in 1789 and the Bank of New York (operating since 1784) in the spring of 1791, at virtually the same time that Hamilton's proposal for a Bank of the United States was being debated in Congress. The Columbia Antifederalists in the 1789 assembly did nothing to oppose the confirmation of the colonial charter of the New York Society Library, but Adgate and Stephen Hogeboom did try to block the incorporation of the Bank of New York in the spring of 1791. The next year brought important initiatives advanced by Philip Schuyler's interest in Albany. Although there was some debate whether they should be public or private, Schuyler's proposals for building northern and western canals were enacted by the 1792 session without notable opposition. Schuyler was also behind a pair of literary and banking institutions proposed for Albany. Columbia assemblymen split on the bank.[71]

Among the Columbians, Jacob Ford and James Savage of Hillsdale and Canaan opposed and Jared Coffin of Hudson and Henry Livingston of the Manor supported the Bank of Albany. Unlike their colleagues from the hill towns, Coffin and Livingston both had interests in two other matters before the legislature. The first was introduced two days after the Bank of Albany vote, when Thomas Jenkins and Stephen Hogeboom introduced a bill to incorporate the stockholders of the Bank of Columbia at Hudson. A week later the assembly voted to approve An Act for the Relief of Benjamin Birdsall and His Associates. Broad and overlapping constituencies stood to gain from the bank bill and the land bill, in which past met the future in New York's politics of interest.[72]

The Birdsall bill represented the last serious hope of the New York Genesee Company of Adventurers. After the state forced it to give up its 999-year lease with the Iroquois, the Adventurers continued to agitate for land. After negotiating with the state for the company in 1789 and 1790, in February 1791 Benjamin Birdsall introduced a petition for a new ten-mile-square land grant for the company's members; that April he was elected to the 1792 assembly with fellow Adventurer Henry Livingston. The Birdsall bill came before the assembly as a petition on March 3, a mere four weeks after the Hogeboom murder trial, and was approved by the assembly on March 30. Neither Birdsall nor Livingston voted on the bill in which they had such an interest, but three of their Columbia colleagues supported it. Sent to the senate, the Birdsall bill was postponed to the next year. The bank bill faced a similar postponement. Henry Livingston wrote to Samuel B. Webb that, while "it is certain Policy of this State to encourage the rising growth of that small but industrious City, all will be done by the members of our County," but "the only fear I have is want of time." The petition, published in the *Gazette* on March 15 and debated at the Hudson City tavern on March 17, was sent down to New York too late in the session and died in the assembly, which by April 1792 was buried in an investigation of the grants made by Governor Clinton's land commission.[73]

Sitting from November 1792 to March 1793, the next legislature was clogged with weighty investigations, both on the question of the handling of the Otsego County ballots, upon which hung both the governor's election and the close election of John Livingston to the senate, so clouded by his sudden switch to the Clintonians. But, nonetheless, the 1792–1793 session achieved great things for the county of Columbia. Its delegation was shaped by the new alliance of the Manor and the hill towns: Adgate, Birdsall, Coffin, Stephen Hogeboom, and Samuel Ten Broeck were all elected with overwhelming support from the Manor as well as from Canaan and Hillsdale; Philip Frisbie won with support in Hudson. The necessary reciprocal support in Canaan and Hillsdale for John Livingston was more restrained. With the exception of Federalist William Powers of Canaan, who voted to exclude Livingston from his seat in the senate and abstained on the Birdsall bill, these county members would work together to advance many of a host of petitions that flooded the assembly and senate from Columbia early in the sixteenth session, which began on November 6, 1792, nine months to the day after the opening of the Hogeboom murder trials.[74]

On December 7, almost a month before the Otsego controversy was settled, Jared Coffin reintroduced the Bank of Columbia bill; on December 12 the Birdsall-Adventurer petition was recommitted from the previous session. Both would move easily through committees and readings on the floor to enactment: the Birdsall bill, granting a tract of land "equal to ten miles square" to the eighty Adventurers, by February 4, and the Bank of Columbia bill by March 5. Both bills received unanimous support from the county delegation and passed with opposition mainly from the lower Hudson, New York City, and Long Island.[75]

But these were only the most important of the flood of Columbia petitions to the legislature. On December 10 and 26, 1792, six petitions were read asking for an investigation into the Van Rensselaer title. On December 13 Colonel David Pratt, who in 1780 had led the county militia with John McKinstry at Klock's Field and the previous spring had sat as one of the judges at Claverack, led a petition to confirm titles in Hillsdale north of the bounds of John Van Rensselaer's claim. The same day, eight petitions arrived from Canaan, Claverack, and Livingston supporting the Otsego canvassers; on December 28 another arrived from Canaan in opposition. Hudson asked for highway money

and the power to inspect shoe leather and to pave its streets; a petition regarding conflicting land patents in Kinderhook was revived from the previous session.[76]

The marks of the county tragedy, of "the great and mighty rumpus," and
of Peter Van Schaack's "Quid pro Quo" were written all over these county
initiatives. Between February 1792 and April 1793 constituencies in almost
every corner of Columbia County gained tangible benefit from the deliberations of court and legislature. The Hogeboom murder suspects, among them
four Hillsdale 1789 petitioners, were acquitted or not prosecuted. A bank
was established in Hudson, Clintonian assemblymen voting unanimously for
an institution that soon would be a bastion of Federalism. Four of the early
directors had been among the Hogeboom judges. Thirty Columbia men were
granted shares in a vast tract of frontier land in the Birdsall act; they included
five who had signed the 1789 Hillsdale petition, six judges and three witnesses
at the Hogeboom trial, and four of the incorporators of the Bank of Columbia. Hogeboom trial judges were successful in other efforts to secure land.
Colonel David Pratt's petition for confirmation of titles in north Hillsdale
was approved, and two years later Israel Spencer led a successful petition for
a special grant of land in Otsego County. In Claverack, a local petition for
funding a road and bridge near the courthouse was rejected in committee at
the request of John C. Hogeboom, the twenty-five-year-old son of the murdered Cornelius, recently appointed sheriff in his father's place. In Kinderhook, problems deriving from a series of divisions in the ancient De Bruyn
patent were settled for the time being in special legislation. Abraham Van
Buren joined a petition supporting the settlement; early in his career as an attorney in the Columbia courts his son Martin would have to renegotiate this
controversy. Hudson got the authority to appoint an inspector of shoe leather
and to pave its city streets.[77]

Perhaps there was nothing truly remarkable in the achievements of the
members for Columbia in the sixteenth session. Such coalition building was
the stuff of routine legislative politics. But the number of legislative outcomes
was not routine, nor was the historical moment. In the winter of 1791–1792
the county had been on the verge of civil war, with armed insurgents challenging the agents of the law. So too civil war seemed to threaten the entire
state in the summer of 1792, as Federalists loomed on the brink of violence
in their frustrations with the procedural legalisms of the Clintonian canvassers. By the end of the year it was clear that constitutional procedures, rather
than bayonets, would prevail in settling the election, and at the same time the
Columbia County delegation went to work moving bills that would advance
the interests of their various constituencies. Challenges to a revolutionary

settlement were not yet completely dead in Columbia County: the following November John Livingston himself, with Caleb Benton, again was stirring the pot, circulating a proposal that the counties from Otsego west should, it was charged, "immediately shake off all Dependence from the State of New York, and support their Independence by Force of Arms." In the west, agitation for a new state simmered for another few years. Closer to home, Livingston would soon face similar sentiments among his tenants on the Manor. But for the majority, the routine politics of deliberative and legislative compromise had been decisively established.[78]

The outcome, if incomplete, certainly did establish an enduring pattern, a settlement of sorts, in the county's politics. The new Republican coalition between the Livingstons on the Manor and the old popular leadership would establish a tight grip on the county's representation in assembly and senate, if Federalists prevailed in the larger congressional and state senate districts of which Columbia was a part. The county had elected five Republicans and one Federalist to the sixteenth sitting of the assembly and, apparently satisfied with the outcomes of that session, sent virtually uniform Republican delegations to the next six sessions. Similarly, the county's one-hundred-pound electors opposed Federalist John Jay in the 1795 governor's election but swung to his camp in 1798, when crisis in both nation and county suddenly undermined the majority supporting the Republican coalition in Columbia. Nonetheless, for seven years this coalition held the allegiance of the county electorate, consistently beating the Federalist assembly slate at the spring polls. If they did not yet function as a formal party, these men were associated in an increasingly routine tradition of county leadership meetings, meetings shaped by the tradition of the Revolutionary committees, the parallel meetings of grand juries and county supervisors, and the diffuse influences of lodges and land companies. And, throughout the 1790s, when they met in Kinderhook, men like Matthew Adgate, John Bay, and Benjamin Birdsall were watched by Abraham Van Buren's sharp-eyed, red-haired, growing young son.[79]

The wider lessons of the county's political settlement were surely part of Martin Van Buren's education, and he would inherit the consequences of its paradoxical tensions. The wider context of this settlement lay in the emerging fabric of new institutions of the nineteenth-century public sphere — the bank, the lodges, the *Gazette*. But it also lay in a specific accommodation with a feudal interest; a Clintonian-Republican alliance of popular men and aristocratic landlords, of Demo and Aristo, was flawed and unstable from the start, even if it was mediated by the new institutions. It was perhaps particularly remarkable that it lasted for so long. If a great family, the Livingstons of Upper and Lower Manors, were an important part of this coalition, they were only that, their influence and interest contained by an assemblage of men of lesser social status but of equal or greater political weight. Martin Van Buren would come of age just as this "unnatural Coalition" came apart, and his understanding of American party politics emerged from the furious if futile efforts he and others made in the decade following to rebuild the Republican interest in the county of Columbia.

THREE STRUGGLES AND CIVIL ASSOCIATION: 1794–1804

If the county at large achieved an omnibus political settlement in the legislation of the sixteenth session in 1793, several very contentious issues could only be papered over. The central conflicts over land were not resolved: three colonial patents, covering thousands of acres of land, were still in effect, and they would require settlements of their own. Though most of the occupants' titles in the town of Canaan had been confirmed in the 1791 legislation, one patent remained on the books. The Mawighnunk Patent of the Van Schaacks and their associates remained a threat, if unenforced, to the independence of the settlers along the Wyomanock Creek as far east as New Lebanon village. In Hillsdale, the Van Rensselaer title to the lands *south* of the region covered by David Pratt's petition survived intact, the most significant setback to the county's initiatives in the sixteenth session. And on Livingston Manor the uniquely burdensome terms and practices of life-lease tenancy had been preserved intact through the Revolution, and a rising generation of landlords, hoping to maintain a rentier style of life, were about to encounter the social and political expectations of the Revolution.

In Canaan and Hillsdale the final land settlements were achieved through a deliberative politics shaped by the aggressive construction of civil institutions. On the Manor the failure of these essential features of civil life to take hold brought three cycles of protest and armed violence over the next fifty years.

A Turnpike, the Royal Arch, and the New Lebanon–Mawighnunk Settlement, 1794–1800

In Canaan and in Hillsdale, the final settlements of land titles unfolded with the elaboration of civil institutions, new developmental initiatives, and the widening of the public sphere itself, set in the broader context of Federalist preeminence during John Adams's presidency and John Jay's governorship. In some small measure, the extension of the revolutionary settlement would follow the spread of the United States Post Office. In 1786 private post offices had been established in Livingston Manor, Claverack, and Kinderhook, along the old post road just inland from the Hudson River. If these early post offices reflected the pre-Revolutionary political geography, new realities determined the distribution of post offices in the 1790s. By 1791 the Livingston Manor post office had been replaced by one in Clermont, with the chancellor's estate manager, Dr. William Wilson, as postmaster. In July 1792 the city of Hudson got a post office, run by Federalist merchant Cotton Gelston, and within two years the Claverack post office had closed. The Kinderhook post office, at the landing, served a large hinterland, but there were insistent demands for better service between the river and the upcountry. Thus, in December 1794, Ephraim Hunt was named postmaster at New Lebanon village, serving routes from both Albany and Kinderhook heading over the mountain east to Hancock and Pittsfield in Massachusetts. Three years later Federalist James Bryant, a tavernkeeper and clothier in old Nobletown village and a leading Genesee Adventurer, was appointed the Hillsdale postmaster for the route running from Hudson east over the state line to Egremont and Great Barrington.[80]

These early hill town post offices were, in more ways than one, the vehicles of a wider, national public sphere. They brought distant communication, letters and newspapers, into emerging village centers, key points of local congregation in a region of scattered neighborhoods divided by a rough rolling topography. And the early post offices in New Lebanon and Hillsdale were also tightly linked to the early Masonic lodges. In New Lebanon, Ephraim Hunt was the master of the Unity Lodge when he assumed the postmastership. Resigning early in 1795, he was replaced by Federalist Eleazer Grant, the organizing master of the lodge. In Hillsdale, James Byrant was an early member of the Vernon Lodge, warranted in 1803, as were his two successors serving through 1806, Jacob Bogardus and Joseph Jewett. To the south, on the Upper Manor, there would be neither lodges nor post offices until the 1820s. And, in varying degrees, lodges, post offices, and turnpike initiatives would shape the final revolutionary settlements in Canaan and Hillsdale. There would be no such constellation of civil initiative and public settlement on Livingston Manor.[81]

The Jay years saw a remarkable attention to the physical infrastructure of the public sphere. Libraries and academies, in particular, were encouraged by state charters and support, and funding for common schools was the subject of great debate (these will be considered in the ensuing chapter). Starting in April 1797, the legislature began to incorporate turnpikes. The first two ran west from Albany to Schenectady and Cherry Valley. The third and fourth turnpikes, chartered in 1798 and 1799, were to run east, through Columbia County. The third turnpike ran from Greenbush opposite Albany to the springs at New Lebanon, and then past the Shaker settlement at Mount Lebanon to the Massachusetts border.[82]

This Rensselaer and Columbia Turnpike was the joint venture of eleven men, all but two Federalists, many of them Masons, in New Lebanon and neighboring Stephentown and Schodack. Nathan Hand, once a master of the Unity Lodge, introduced the bill in January 1798; the other four Unity Lodge Masons included Postmaster Eleazer Grant. Elisha Gilbert, who both hosted the lodge and had been a member of the Canaan Democratic Society, was named a turnpike commissioner. Federalist John Tyron, who took over the New Lebanon postmastership from Grant in 1800, was to keep the eastern set of corporate books. When the legislation had to be reenacted in 1799, John W. Schermerhorn, a turnpike incorporator and a Unity Mason from Stephentown, introduced the bill; Elisha Gilbert chaired the cōmmittee charged with the revision.[83]

In the intervening year, in October 1798, New Lebanon was the site of another early institutional innovation. That March a grand chapter of Royal Arch Freemasonry was established at Albany, with De Witt Clinton as the grand high priest and Thomas Frothingham of Hudson as the grand king. The Royal Arch was a branch of "ancient Freemasonry" and was the first step in a wild proliferation of Masonic degrees that would flourish in nineteenth-century America. A Royal Arch chapter had been established at Hudson, as an extension of the lodge itself; in October 1798 the grand chapter established an introductory Mark Master Mason's Lodge at New Lebanon. By January 1802 more than eighty men had been advanced in the Lebanon Mark Lodge, among them Eleazer Grant, Elisha Gilbert, his son Elisha, Jr., and Nathan Hand, the original turnpike petitioner.[84]

These institutional initiatives as well as the action of the Canaan Democratic Society in 1794 and 1795 provided the essential backdrop to the settlement of the Mawighnunk Patent claim between 1799 and 1801. Gilbert's house, where the Unity Lodge met for more than fifty years, looking over the Wyomanack Valley (Lebanon Creek), where lowland property rights were overshadowed by the holders of the old patent, who included Peter Van Schaack of Kinderhook. Though their claim to the patent had long been dormant, the Mawighnunk patentees decided to bring suits for recovery of land in the October 1799 circuit court, winning the two cases that they brought. By the time the assembly had met late the following January, Van Schaack's surveying party had been ambushed and roughed up by a band of men in New Lebanon, leading Governor Jay to complain in his opening address of the "daring opposition . . . made in the County of Columbia, to the judicial authority of the state." Whatever happened, Jay noted that "the ordinary means of surpressing" these "offences" were "inadequate"; he urged "that the regular administration of justice . . . be not interrupted," and that "whatever may be the claims or rights of contending individuals, it is their duty to meet each other in the proper courts, and peaceably acquiesce in the justice of their country." Within days Samuel Jones and others of New Lebanon did just that, petitioning the legislature for the right to personally address the charges raised by the governor, which had been detailed in a series of affidavits before the house. Jones's petition was followed by a succession of petitions from others, asking for access to these documents and complaining that Attorney General Josiah Ogden Hoffman had blocked their efforts to mount an official investigation of the Mawighnunk patent title. After the attorney general finally rejected the assembly's efforts to order him to open the case, a bill introduced by John W. Schermerhorn passed on April 7, 1800, in which the patentholders and the New Lebanon occupants agreed to submit their disputed claims to legal arbitration by commissioners appointed by the legislature. The commissioners were "to hear and examine all disputes and controversies between the said parties . . . and finally to determine such disputes, controversies, and claims, according to law and equity, which determination shall be absolutely binding."[85]

This legislated settlement brought trusted men to intercede in a volatile situation. Hosea Moffitt of Stephentown and Jacob Ford of north Hillsdale were among the five commissioners, who included the renowned jurist Tapping Reeve of Litchfield. The Canaan possessors were led by a familiar group of names. Elisha Gilbert, Eleazer Grant, and John Darling (another Unity Mason) were the first three listed, followed by Samuel Jones's in-law, Moses Younglove, five years earlier the clerk of the Democratic Society, when Gilbert was a chair. All told, the Canaan possessors signing the agreement included six of the turnpike incorporators, including the retiring and newly appointed postmaster and twenty-four Masons, nineteen of whom had or soon would join the Lebanon Mark Lodge. Five were Federalist committeemen and six Republican, including three of the six known members of the Democratic Society.[86]

In New Lebanon, thus, a sudden burst of violence over land had rapidly moved into the legislative arena. Participation in civil institutions of various kinds underwrote the confidence in deliberative proceedings that shaped the Mawighnunk settlement. The direct democracy of Revolutionary committees and militias, of town meetings and county juries, had been leavened over the previous decade by Masonic lodges, a short-lived newspaper, a post office, at least one political debating society, and the rise of competing political factions. Four times, in 1782, 1791, 1798, and 1799, public benefit had been successfully achieved through legislative deliberation. The people of New Lebanon had worked assiduously to construct the local manifestations of a public sphere. Now, in 1800, the last vestige of land struggles that stretched back to the 1750s was finally and absolutely settled by a legislatively mandated set of procedures in a settlement anticipated and facilitated by institution-building efforts in civil society.

The South Hillsdale–Van Rensselaer Settlement: Lodges, Churches, and Turnpikes, 1793–1808

The settlement in Hillsdale involved many of the same civil institutions as in New Lebanon, but appearing in a different order and without quite the same local impetus. The 1793 sixteenth session brought only a partial settlement for the Hillsdale people. The act that followed the 1793 petition of Judge David Pratt had clarified the conditions of land tenure *north* of John Van Rensselaer's confirmation of 1773. But four other petitions that year had demanded an inquiry into the circumstances of confirmation itself and of the status of the *south* Hillsdale lands, as had the 1789 petition. It was on these lands that Sheriff Hogeboom had been shot in October 1791. On March 2, 1793, Clintonian Jonathan Havens of Suffolk County reported on the petitions for an inquiry into the Van Rensselaer title. The various petitions, he summarized, argued "that there is little prospect of having the said controversies determined in the ordinary course of law" and asked for the legislature to "interpose, and take such measures as may appear most proper for restoring tranquility to that part of the country." But, after reviewing the documents the committee had found that — though the struggle over the title was indeed "of a nature so alarming" as to require legislative attention — it was not "able to determine what measures ought to be adopted by the Legislature, in order to quiet the disturbances which have arisen in the said county." The committee proposed a general review of the title in the next session, but nothing seems to have come of their recommendation.[87]

But the wider logic of the 1792 election result and the 1793 sixteenth session did open a staged process of settlement in Hillsdale. In some measure, this began as a settlement for — perhaps a co-optation of — strategic members of the Hillsdale leadership. Thus on December 29, 1789, about eleven months after he led the signers of the Hillsdale petition, Benjamin Birdsall bought 234 acres of land, including his "old dwelling house," from Henry I. Van Rensselaer, an associate in the New York Genesee Company. Perhaps this was a sale on favorable terms, to buy Birdsall's influence among the Hillsdale people and undermine their opposition to the Van Rensselaers and to solidify his role as point man for the Adventurers. Indeed, including Birdsall, three of the five Genesee Adventurers who signed the 1789 petition against the Van Rensselaers would buy or mortgage land from the Manor family. Birdsall's neighbor John Collin also bought land from Henry I. Van Rensselaer in 1789, the first of six purchases from various members of the family over five years. According to his grandson, he was both "a pacificator among the people" and "on terms of intimacy with the Van Rensselaers"; his grandson thought that his purchases of land were bound up with his efforts "to settle the controversy between the occupants of lands in Hillsdale under Massachusetts titles and the Manor Claims." So, too, Charles McKinstry had land from his brother David but in 1802 bought a parcel from Catherine Schuyler.[88]

The events of 1792 and 1793, however, did not make an immediate impact on Philip Schuyler's evolving strategy of getting control of his wife's lands. As he had done since 1784, in July 1792 he brought four new suits against relatively poor and obscure men, isolated from the center of resistance in Hillsdale, hoping to establish a test case, including one against a Claverack signer of the 1789 Hillsdale petition who had stood surety for rioter John West that February. Four more cases, all in Claverack, were introduced in January 1793. Here the local settlement of 1793 began to come into view. The defendants' attorney, John Bay, a leading member of the Republican interest, seems to have been successful in stalling action in court, including a critical delay by the sheriff in filing critical papers. This was John C. Hogeboom, the son of the murdered Cornelius but also a rising figure in the local Republican interest himself and perhaps not eager to rile the Hillsdale voters. In October 1795 Schuyler was ready to find a way out and entered into a contract with another Hogeboom, Peter of Hudson, to sell his wife's interest in the Claverack Van Rensselaer lands. Peter Hogeboom, who had sold land to the Hudson proprietors, had been a director of the Bank of Columbia, and was deeply involved in the Susquehannah Company, was to start payments in February 1796. But by November 1797 he had defaulted, and Schuyler was forced back to the law. Here his son-in-law, Alexander Hamilton, took charge, bringing forward a flurry of cases against the Hillsdale people. The result was the relatively quick resolution of the struggle.[89]

Starting with the 1793 prosecutions, Schuyler and now Hamilton pursued a complex challenge to the Hillsdale occupants called a "writ of right," an ancient English procedure that required a full historical review of the competing claims to proprietorship. It was on these terms that the 1793 cases had been advanced, and Hamilton in September 1799 began in Robert R. Livingston's court of chancery, bringing a total of twenty-four cases. The first of these was heard in the October 1801 circuit at Claverack, and a second the next July: in both Hamilton prevailed, successfully turning back the argument posed by Theodore Sedgwick that all Hillsdale once had been part of the abandoned Westenhook Patent. Faced with endless court trials and certain defeat, the

Hillsdale occupants agreed to a legislative resolution, sending what Schuyler called "a deputation from the People occupying the Claverack estate, with full powers to negotiate an adjustment," to meet with Schuyler and Hamilton in Albany on October 28, 1802. Hammering out details with their new attorney, Josiah Ogden Hoffman (recently the state attorney general), Hamilton was able to engineer passage of an act of settlement within a week of introducing a petition to the senate in March 1803. That October a commission of arbitrators, men of considerable legal position in New York, met at Claverack, and by March 1804, 101 Hillsdale occupants received deeds to their land, with six years to pay off mortgages. The Van Rensselaers might have received as much as fifty thousand dollars in mortgage payments and obligations, and they owed more than six thousand dollars in legal fees.[90]

Fifteen years separated the 1789 petition, with its 211 signers, and the 1804 arbitration and its 101 Hillsdale grantees. Many of the 1789 petitioners were now dead or had emigrated to the west; Hillsdale had grown by only two hundred inhabitants over ten years, to a peak population of forty-seven hundred in 1800, and would lose population or barely maintain itself for decades to come. Only a third of the 1789 petitioners were still in Hillsdale to be counted on the 1800 valuation; of these, only a third were among the 1804 grantees. Some of the 1789 petitioners had received deeds and mortgages from the Van Rensselaers, though in only a few cases, such as John Collin's, did these early transactions appear to influence political affiliations. Birdsall and others remained strong Republicans and would have provided little comfort and assistance for the Van Rensselaers in Hillsdale. There was also a strong core of leadership for the 1803–1804 Hillsdale grantees, of whom 9 had been involved in the 1792 Hogeboom murder trial, and 15 served on Republican committees in Hillsdale by 1807: there were no known Federalists among these last to settle with the Van Rensselaers.[91]

The first name on the 1804 settlement, and clearly the leader, was Captain William Tanner, a shoemaker in Green River who had been both a witness and a surety at the 1792 trial and was already a Republican of note in the county, with a wide range of civil connections. Tanner had joined the Hudson Lodge in the early 1790s, and in April 1803 he and two other 1804 grantees, with Colonel Benjamin Birdsall, had signed the petition asking that the Grand Lodge warrant a Masonic lodge in Hillsdale. All told, at least nine of the 1804 grantees or their sons joined this new Vernon Lodge over the next few years. In Canaan civil institution building contributed to the settlement; in Hillsdale, the route was opposite, as movement toward the final settlement seems to have encouraged civil institution building, an initiative that soon moved to turnpikes.[92]

Hillsdale's first encounter with a turnpike had not been a happy one. In the spring of 1799 a group of Hudson men, many involved in the Bank of Columbia, had introduced a bill in the senate that led to the incorporation of the Columbia Turnpike, to run from Hudson through south Claverack and Hillsdale to the Massachusetts border. Only after gaining their charter did they begin to approach affected people in Hillsdale. Those on the route, John Collin among them, quickly signed over rights-of-way in the expectation of a greater volume of traffic past their doors; Collin would hold more than a tenth of the total shares in the turnpike by 1811. Others in Hillsdale were not so happy, forcing their way past the new turnpike gates and threatening lawsuits against the company. Legislation passed in 1800 reduced the gates from six to three; a turnpike plan providing free passage to those who would "cease to be excited themselves and will avoid fomenting excitement in others" might have calmed some of the tension in Hillsdale. By 1803–1804 the turnpike was apparently operating routinely, perhaps encouraging Benjamin Birdsall in the spring of 1804 to serve as a commissioner for a turnpike in Chatham. At the next session William Tanner led a petition to incorporate a turnpike to run through north Hillsdale into Chatham and then, three years later, joined two initiatives to build turnpikes running from his Green River neighborhood toward Claverack and Hudson. While Tanner was the most deeply committed, he was joined by at least seven other veterans of the struggles with the Van Rensselaers, including David Pratt (the judge in 1792 who engineered the 1793 north Hillsdale legislation), Oliver Teall (the Baptist and 1789 petitioner who arrived a day late at the 1792 grand jury), Major Tyler (a 1792 juryman and a 1804 grantee), and Charles McKinstry (a 1789 petitioner and 1792 witness).[93]

Thus in the new century the Hillsdale people were moving beyond the old land struggles and into the new era of institution building. David Pratt, an incorporator with Tanner of the 1805 Hillsdale and Chatham turnpike, in 1803 had been elected a trustee of the old Spencertown church, newly incorporated as Saint Peters Presbyterian. Similarly, in early June of 1803, two months after the legislature passed the Van Rensselaer settlement, a new Baptist congregation, made up of many of the protesting families in the southwest Hillsdale neighborhood where the sheriff had been shot, was set off from the east Hillsdale church. And one of Tanner's fellow commissioners for the Hillsdale and Chatham turnpike, Horace Jones, was the leading petitioner and first master of the Charity Lodge, warranted in Spencertown in June 1808 on the recommendation of the older Canaan and Vernon lodges. Thus the settlement of the Van Rensselaer claim seems to have led the way to the construction of new institutions in Hillsdale. Again the distributive outcomes of public deliberation, here in these contested hill towns constituting a final revolutionary settlement, were tied to new initiatives in civil society. If they did not anticipate, and perhaps facilitate, the settlement, as they did in Canaan, these initiatives must have been shaped by a realization that local improvements would no longer be threatened by rentier dispossession, a threat that had hung over the Hillsdale settlements for fifty years.[94]

Between 1800 and 1804 Canaan and Hillsdale saw the final negotiated settlement of the ancient leasehold system and the colonial land grants that had shaped it. In the same years, something similar was beginning to unfold in Claverack itself, the heart of the Van Rensselaers' Lower Manor. John Jeremiah Van Rensselaer, who had inherited the better part of the Claverack lands from his grandfather John in 1782, was by 1794 hopelessly in debt and forced to sell more than thirty-three thousand acres of tenanted farms to a New York merchant, Daniel Penfield. Moving to Hudson, Penfield perpetuated the leasehold traditions of the old Manor until 1801, when he began to sell his land in fee simple and to issue mortgages. In 1806 he sold the remainder of his land to another New Yorker, John Watts, and moved west to found a town in Ontario County. Perhaps not coincidentally, the Columbia Lodge of Freemasons was warranted in Claverack in the spring of 1803, led by Republican Killian Hogeboom, newly appointed as the county clerk. The era of Federalist landlord control in Claverack was beginning to fade.[95]

Nothing like such a resolution would unfold to the south on the Livingston Manor in these years. Rather, both routine politics and civil institution building would fail, and the Manor would descend into a period of strife and violent insurrection, neither the first nor the last of its kind.

Civil Failure and Crisis in the Livingston Manor, 1790–1800

Tensions on the Manor began to mount with the death of the old "Third Lord," Robert Livingston, Jr., in late November 1790. As with the death of John Van Rensselaer of Claverack, Livingston's death meant a partition of a vast estate, and it reopened questions about the legality of the Manor title that had been suppressed since the strife of the 1750s. Since his eldest son, Peter R., was hopelessly indebted, Robert had broken the entail on the Manor in 1771 and in May 1784 divided the bulk of the property among his four younger sons, Walter, Robert C., Henry, and John. They inherited four "Great Lots" running east-west through the central and eastern sections of the Manor, and home lots looking out over the Hudson River. Peter and his brothers fell into a protracted quarrel over the division of the estate, contributing to the doubts about the Manor title.[96]

Symbolic challenges to landlord hegemony broke out almost immediately.

Henry reported to Walter that "on Christmas Eve," less than a month after Robert's death in 1790, the Linlithgow "Church was robbed of all the Black Cloth which we put up for mourning." By October 1791, about two weeks before Sheriff Hogeboom was killed, questions were being raised about the legal basis of the north boundary of the Manor, and Henry wrote to Walter, "The Nobletown and Egremont people are tampering with our people to resist us." If he was confident on October 8 that his allies "in that quarter" would "keep all quiet," he was not so on October 24, when he wrote that "the people are very much distressed" and might "revolt" if forced to pay back rent. Pressed by their father's creditors and by Walter's shaky investments with William Duer (the New York financier who failed so spectacularly the next spring), the brothers had "printed letters" posted in the Manor, offering terms for the payment of back rents. Since the tenants were so far behind in their rent, John was considering accepting cattle in payment, to be sold at Hudson for the West Indian trade.[97]

Livingston titles to the unimproved lands of the eastern section of the Manor were the first to be challenged. Starting in the summer of 1791 tenants began to clear some of the Manor woods for farmland while the Livingstons hounded their surveyor, John Wigram, to complete surveys of the Manor. In the fall of 1792, when the Livingstons brought suits against the woodcutters, the tenants hired two lawyers, John Bay of Claverack and his former student, Ambrose Spencer of Hudson, to defend them.[98]

Where Bay was a leading Antifederalist, Ambrose Spencer sided with the Federalists when he settled in Hudson, joining the Hudson Lodge and getting appointed city clerk. While he had done some legal work for Walter Livingston, who had fled New York upon Duer's bankruptcy and whose affairs were now in crisis, Spencer turned decisively against the Livingstons in the spring of 1793. By the spring of 1794 he and other Federalists, in an ironic reversal driven by the new Republican "unnatural Coalition," were trying to gain votes on the Manor by promising to secure tenants title to Livingston land.[99]

It is possible that they had a hand in the petition submitted by the tenants to the legislature in March 1794. Andrew Wheeler, kin to some of the rioters in 1777, led the petition and demanded an inquiry into the Manor title, arguing that "in *fact*" certain of the Livingston lands belonged to "the people of this state." Within a week the committee had its report ready: the members were "of opinion, that the said allegations are true, and that the people of this state have a title to a considerable portion of the said lands, in the town of Livingston." They recommended an immediate survey. Henry Livingston was amazed that "Spencer's influence was greater than John's," his brother in the senate. Spencer apparently had other plans afoot. One of the committeemen was Dirck Gardinier, once a Kinderhook tory and now a Federalist elected to the assembly with Spencer in 1793. A month after his committee delivered its dramatic verdict, Gardinier was meeting with Livingston tenants, promising them, John reported, that "the next year they will have the land." Henry reported that Spencer had got the Federalist county committee to nominate for the assembly one of its tenants, Peter Bishop, a justice of the peace. Both Bishop and Gardinier racked up more than 250 Federalist votes in the Manor, but the "unnatural" Republican slate, led by Adgate and Birdsall, reluctantly supported by the Livingstons, and garnering hundreds of votes in Claverack, Hillsdale, and Canaan, prevailed in the election.[100]

The survey proposed by the assembly committee was not authorized, and the next January a second Livingston tenant petition was sent to the legislature. Possibly written by Spencer, the tenants' lawyer, the petition of Petrus Pulver and more than 250 cosigners detailed the "false and fraudulent pretences" under which two separate Livingston grants had been extended from 2,600 acres to more than 175,000 in a confirmation granted by Governor Thomas Dongan in 1686. They closed their petition with a complaint and an exhortation: their tenancy was "upon Terms and Conditions oppressive and burthensome to the last degree, unfriendly to all great exertions of Industry and tending to degrade your Petitioners from the Rank the God of Nature destined all Mankind to move in, to be *Slaves* and *Vassals*." This time John Livingston attended the committee meeting, controlled by his Republican allies, and made sure that the tenant petition was stopped cold. Once again, as with the Van Rensselaer lands, the assembly was unwilling to disturb property rights on this scale. The family had "been in the uninterrupted possession of the said Manor for more than one hundred years," and it "would be improper in the State to resume lands for any real or supposed defects in the original grants." There would be no investigation, and the petition was formally dismissed. John Livingston wrapped up the session by maneuvering a bill settling the issue of the gore of land along the north bounds of the Manor, which, he wrote, would "prevent much expense—and give me a handsome property for my fatigue."[101]

Thus in the spring of 1795 the Manor tenants were shut off from legislative redress. Over the next eighteen months the struggle moved into the courts. The Livingstons pursued ejectments of a number of tenants, and both sides developed their strategies for the court. Alexander Hamilton resisted efforts of both sides to recruit his legal expertise. "His talents in general and particular knowledge of the Livingston title," Spencer argued to Theodore Sedgwick of Stockbridge, made him "the most proper man on earth to be engaged by us." Sedgwick himself joined the suit against the Livingstons, perhaps because his father-in-law, General Joseph Dwight, had been a strong supporter of the Massachusetts title—and the border rioters—in the 1750s and 1760s. The opportunity for this arch-Federalist to attack the turncoat Republican Upper Manor Livingstons might well have been an added motivation. The cases were heard in circuit court starting late July 1796 and, despite Sedgwick's assistance, were resolved in the Livingstons' favor by November; an appeal to the court of errors produced a similar unanimous opinion for the validity of the Livingston title by the spring.[102]

Rebuffed in legislative and judicial arenas, the tenants turned to ritual violence. Henry wrote to Walter on March 13, "The Peace that we hoped from our decision in the court of Errors has vanished." It had been reported that militants "were determined to hold the land by force," and now flag- and chainmen surveying the land of a recently dispossessed tenant were fired on by a band in the woods; later in the month it was rumored that some from Nobletown were among them. Bands of men were mustering in disguise, as they had six years before in Hillsdale when Sheriff Hogeboom had been killed. Now they drew on deeper sources. Mahican Indians had long been involved in the border struggles on the side of the tenants and squatters, to whom they had sold titles in the 1750s. White and Mahican rioters had assaulted the Albany County sheriff in 1755 with an "Indian Yell and other hideous noise"; in 1766 the Mahicans at Stockbridge asked the authorities in both Boston and Albany that mercy be shown to the people of Nobletown. Thus in March 1797 the militant tenants held a night meeting at which, Henry reported, "they had Quinto an Indian dance." Rebuffed by civil authorities at every step, the Manor tenants, now "insurgents" in the Livingstons' communications, symbolically put themselves outside a civil society that offered them no distributive solutions. Disguised, armed, and in the woods, they signaled their alienation from that civil society and their long affiliations with the Mahican world in this Indian ritual.[103]

While the conditions of tenancy—and a common culture of resistance—characterized all three of the disturbances on the Manor in the eighteenth century, the events in the 1790s centrally involved a constituency quite different from that of previous uprisings. For the most part, the ranks of the rioters of the 1750s and 1760s had drawn upon immigrant New Englanders and upon men dependent on New England civil authority, particularly that of Massachusetts. The rioters in 1777 were neither recently settled Yankees nor longtime Manor tenants, but recent immigrants without local connections and susceptible to the recruitment of British agents. But the petitioners in 1795 and the rioters lurking in the woods in the years following were for the most part tenants of the Livingstons, a mixture of Dutch, German, and

English ethnicities. Where they had personal or familial experiences in the Revolution, it was with either militia service in the Tenth Albany Regiment or with the delinquents fined for refusing to serve, not with the rioters of 1777. The Revolution had raised expectations of autonomous independence broadly across the Manor of Livingston; the resistance of the 1790s was thus the first to be grounded in the tenant population at large. The turn to Indian ritual and guerrilla violence in the late 1790s marked the radicalization of previously quiescent families and a considerable collapse of faith in civil institutions.[104]

For the next two and a half years a state of low-level civil war smoldered in the eastern sections of the Manor. Squatters continued to cut in the woods and to build houses on occupied lands, encouraged, in the northeast section of the manor, by hopes that the boundary separating Livingston from Claverack and Hillsdale would be redrawn. Tenants who took up repossessed farms under a new Manor lease were harassed. Sometime in the spring of 1797 one such new tenant, Peter Loucks, was taken out one night and whipped; in August he was severely wounded with buckshot. Henry Livingston's agent was fired on in the road, and shots were aimed at Livingston himself at least twice. A constable and deputy sheriff, serving warrants, were captured and whipped by men in disguise. Then in the spring of 1798 houses and barns started to burn, including Henry Livingston's coal houses at the Ancram ironworks, torched on May 11. The arson continued into the spring and summer of 1799; Henry's meadow fence was burned in May, and a dispossessed tenant's house in August.[105]

The Livingstons took recourse in the law and the state, with important implications for local politics. In June 1797 Henry claimed to have "about 12 of our insurgents" under indictment, and over the next six months plans for surveys, ejectments, and dispossessions went forward. William Wilson, now a justice of the peace, was asked to "collect any testimony of the conduct of our insurgents." The next winter the state government began to take action. On February 22, 1798, Governor John Jay, in a message to the senate, asked for a resolution condemning tenant rioting on Livingston Manor, writing that the "first and obvious principles of civil society, certainly demand, that individual citizens be, without partiality, protected in the enjoyment of their property and other rights." Within two days the house and senate passed a concurrent resolution, calling for the enforcement of laws on the Manor and (in an echo of 1787) authorizing the governor to order the militia of the surrounding counties to support the sheriff of Columbia. Jay's proclamation of March 1, condemning the "numerous combinations of individuals in the town of Livingston" and calling out part of the county's militia, was published in the *Hudson Gazette* on March 13, 1798. The following August "commissions of Rebellion" were being issued against certain of the militants.[106]

The intervention of the state seems to have inspired the transition from shootings to arson in the Manor resistance and at the same time brought something of an effort to reduce the tension. In early March, while he could not see "that the proclamation has had any effect on our insurgents," Henry Livingston was of the opinion that it might not "be prudent" for him "to institute any more suits." Peter Van Schaack, now an attorney for one of the Livingston families, organized a general meeting with the tenants in April. Slowly, though there would be continuing meetings and sporadic arson, tenant resistance began to fizzle out. In November 1798, twenty-one of Henry's tenants, including six 1795 petitioners, promised not to cut on his private woodlot. By the following April Henry was comfortable with "the principles that the more we settle with[,] the weaker the opposition," a plan that Peter Van Schaack was pursuing the previous winter. The fire in August 1799 presumably was the last act of the Manor insurgency. Van Schaack displayed ambivalent opinions about the policies of his Livingston employers, as suggested by his 1797 letter warning of an inevitable "explosion" on the Manor and adamant that the "blame" for "Inequity" not fall on his shoulders. In August 1799 he knew that "a Remnant of the former Combination may still exist" but recommended that, "by easing off a little, now that the Law has been carried into Execution, you could reconcile the Parties to their fate."[107]

The intervention of the state of New York in the Livingston Manor controversies was also bound up in a wider political struggle. John Jay's message to the legislature followed a petition by the Upper Manor Livingstons on February 17, 1798, asking the state's protection from "a spirit of opposition . . . excited among some of the Tenants" on the Manor, now manifested in "acts of violence." What was striking was not that the state intervened but that it took its time doing so, and only after the Livingstons' humble petition to the sitting Federalist governor. Here was another quid pro quo, in reverse. In 1792 John Livingston had bargained with George Clinton; now he bargained with John Jay. And the outcome was another political reversal: the Upper Manor Livingstons, beset by insurgency, abandoned their Republicanism and threw their support to Jay and the Federalists in the spring 1798 election. With Henry's assistance, John Livingston ran as a Jay Federalist for the senate; though he won three of every four votes on the Manor, he lost the election. After losing the Manor vote 245–31 in 1795, Governor Jay himself split the 1798 vote, losing 114–112. At the April 1799 election the Federalist assembly candidates won in the Manor and across the county for the first time for almost a decade; in 1800 and 1801, as they would for most of the next two decades, the

Manor voted at least two-to-one for Federalist candidates. A "gentleman in the County of Columbia" summed up the results of the new arrangement in June 1799: the titles to landed estates were being upheld in court, and the ringleaders of the opposition were being fined and imprisoned. "Thus in a moment is the County of Columbia (at this time truly Federal) changed from the most turbulent County to as orderly a one as any in the state."[108]

As the Upper Manor Livingstons gravitated toward Federalist power in 1798, they also abandoned their pretense to the aristocratic Republicanism that had forced them into "unnatural Coalitions." John and Henry Livingston, as Adventurers in the late 1780s, had consorted with men of mean station to pursue their ends of land acquisition and, in consequence of this bargain, had been forced to accept a marginal place in the Republican interest in the mid-1790s, delivering votes but not determining slates or even policy. And the Manor struggle pitted the Livingstons against some of their former fellow Adventurers. One of these was Ambrose Latting, the Baptist carpenter in south Hillsdale, who had signed the 1789 Hillsdale petition and received land in the Birdsall grant. In September 1797 Henry Livingston was trying to discount rumors that "Mr. Lattin of Nobletown" had hired men to drive off his tenants "and to injure me"; a year later he was certain that Latting had led "a large meeting of those rascals" at Peter Pulver's. Latting's interest might have been in the contested gore lands between Hillsdale and Livingston, but he had extensive connections among Baptist and Republican south Hillsdale families — Birdsalls, Jordans, Morehouses. All had opposed the Van Rensselaers, in a struggle obviously parallel to that on the Manor. Peter Bishop, the Livingston tenant and justice of the peace recruited by Ambrose Spencer as a Federalist candidate in 1794, was another former Adventurer now ranged against the Livingstons. Bishop had signed the 1795 Pulver petition, and John Livingston reported that Bishop had said that he knew the Livingstons had "good title" but that he and the other militants were "determined to bring us to their terms." He had also subscribed to the Websters' edition of Thomas Paine's *Writings,* evidence of his radical politics.[109]

Behind Bishop was Ambrose Spencer, the leading young Hudson Federalist attorney who in 1796 had both argued the tenants' case and been appointed to the senate at the election of John Williams to Congress. Spencer and Bishop had a Masonic connection; Spencer was a founder of the Hudson Lodge and Royal Arch Chapter, and Bishop's and Spencer's brothers were members of the Temple Lodge in Northeast, Dutchess County, where Colonel Benjamin Birdsall and Charles McKinstry of Hillsdale were also members. Spencer entered into a common interest with McKinstry's brothers and others in Hillsdale when he invested in Susquehannah Company titles in early 1795. He maintained his connections with his family in Northeast and was visiting his father's in July 1797, when a band of thirty mounted men "armed with clubs" rode down to the Dutchess line and ran off one of the Livingston tenants. "This blasted force," Henry complained, then rode by Livingston's house "and after passed some small distance gave Three Cheers." Henry Livingston was convinced that the militants had "consulted" with "Mr. Ambrose Spencer, the Senator," at his father's house "the Evening before and the day of this transaction."[110]

By July 1797 Ambrose Spencer was already beginning his own political conversion, moving from Federalist to Republican as the Upper Manor Livingstons made the reverse passage. The circumstances of Spencer's partisan reversal were debated by New York's political historians for generations; by one account his "apostasy produced a profound sensation in political circles." In April 1798 he had completed the transition and beat John Livingston in the senate race as a Republican. With him came a number of Hudson Federalists: Elisha Jenkins, Thomas Frothingham, David Lawrence, Jared Coffin, all Hudson Lodge Freemasons. Spencer would be a close ally of De Witt Clinton, the nephew of the Revolutionary governor who was about to emerge as central power broker in New York politics and had just helped to establish the grand chapter of the Royal Arch that Masons in Hudson and Canaan were flocking to join. Exactly when Spencer made his decision to switch political affiliations was a point of great controversy. The strong suspicion was that, ambitious for higher office, he began his break with the Federalists when Governor Jay appointed Samuel Jones as the first comptroller of the state on February 15, 1797. A month later Spencer bitterly condemned Jones's triumph in a letter to Samuel Webb in Claverack: "The die is cast and old Jones is appointed Comptroller, I wash my hands of it—and may those who have contributed to his appointment, live to regret it. . . . We shall adjourn in a fortnight, for which thank God." Four months later Spencer met with the Manor militants at his father's house in Northeast.[111]

One of the two leaders of "this blasted force," and as such a familiar of Ambrose Spencer, was Benjamin Birdsall, Jr., son of Colonel Benjamin of Hillsdale. These events were thus the wider circumstances around the younger Benjamin Birdsall's failed petition of May 1798 to the Grand Lodge of New York for a Masonic lodge to meet in the eastern part of the Manor. Birdsall's Masonic petition was thus closely linked with his leadership of the Manor resistance. His leadership in the field and in petition was a reflection, if a pale one, of his father's, a colonel in the Revolution elected to the assembly from Dutchess in the 1780s and Columbia in the 1790s. The younger brothers of Benjamin, Jr., and even his sons, rose further than his station of tenant farmer: his brother George would be a doctor, and brother James a lawyer and congressman in Chenango County; his son Benjamin III a major in the regular troops during the War of 1812, and son Samuel, a lawyer trained by Martin Van Buren, a congressman. In his lodge petition, in his leadership of the tenants in 1798, and again in 1811, Benjamin, Jr., was struggling to achieve a comparable station in life, without success.[112]

Years later Benjamin, Jr., would describe himself to Van Buren as having devoted his "good offices and dedication" to the settlement of the "disputes, disturbances, and controversies" among the "tenants and possessors" on the Manor lands of Robert C. Livingston in the summer of 1798. Birdsall claimed that he had "used his influence and advise[d] the said tenants and possessors to settle the said differences and did spend much time, money, and was at great pains to promote by his good offices and mediations the said settlement." Some of these efforts might have gone into a petition being circulated in March 1798, which might have been the one that Birdsall and others submitted to the assembly a year later regarding the Hillsdale-Livingston boundary. That month ejectment proceedings were in the works against Birdsall, but he seems to have settled his accounts with Peter Van Schaack by December 1798, apparently in an agreement signed with Henry Livingston at the Claverack court in November. The following August, Birdsall intervened on behalf of Peter M. Pulver, possibly the "Petrus" of the 1795 petition. Henry Livingston wrote to Van Schaack that, while he was installing his own tenant on the dispossessed Pulver's farm, "Birdsall came there and behaved in a scandalous manner . . . if he and Pulver come to you do not believe them." Two years later, the "disturbances" on the Manor having died down or gone underground, Birdsall was in court with both William Wilson and Henry Livingston, as he began to promise to pay back rent on his farm.[113]

The two Benjamin Birdsalls, father and son, would in 1803 sign the petition for the Vernon Lodge in Hillsdale, as would others in the eastern Livingston holdings. This initiative, however, if it was part of the closure of revolutionary settlement in Hillsdale, was evidence of its failure on the Manor. The events of the 1790s on Livingston Manor led to stalemate and deadlock. The Livingstons were set upon maintaining their grip on both the land and the political will of their tenant dependents.

In his message to the legislature on the Manor troubles, Governor John Jay had articulated the classical definition of civil society as it had taken shape in the early modern era: civil society was the domain of ordinary life and property protected by law in a legitimate nation-state. But, throughout the early Republic, this definition of civil society was rapidly becoming too limited to describe the relationship of a people with its government. In Canaan and

Hillsdale, across the county, and indeed in much of the nation as a whole, certainly the northern states, a dynamic was emerging between deliberative and distributive politics and the various forms of civil life that Tocqueville would examine in *Democracy in America*. Local institutions of civil society formed the connective tissue between the needs of the people and the deliberative processes of governance. Men of small property and local reputation rode this connection into the nineteenth century.

Most notably, one such was Ambrose Spencer, whose transition to Republicanism in alliance with the rising De Witt Clinton would make him state attorney general, justice, and chief justice of the state supreme court and one of the most celebrated legal figures of the New York bar in the first half of the nineteenth century. Unsuccessful in harnessing the flywheel linking governance and social life, Benjamin Birdsall and his fellow tenants on the Manor would struggle with their rents and dream until, a decade later, they met another rising star in New York law and politics, Martin Van Buren. In September 1801, as Birdsall and others on the Manor adjusted to the failure of their struggle in the 1790s, Van Buren was beginning a career in American politics, borrowing money to attend the Republican district convention about to meet up the river in Troy. In this career, which would crystallize key formations in the structure and culture of American political life, Van Buren was shaped by a county's arduous history of struggle over the meaning and settlement of the American Revolution.

6

Boundaries, Sympathies, and the Settlement
1785–1800

The Negro's Complaint:

A SONG

To the tune of Homer's Ghost.

By W. Cowper, Esq.:

... Deem our nation brutes no longer,
Till some reasons ye shall find
Worthier of regard, and stronger,
Than the colour of our kind.
Slaves of gold! whose forbid dealing
Tarnish all your boasted powers,
Prove that you have human feelings
Ere you proudly question ours.

    —*Hudson Gazette,* Nov. 25, 1788

    Albany 24th March 1798

    Dear Sir

    I have nothing very material to write you at Present, I must however inform you that a Bill has passed the House of Assembly yesterday for the Gradual abolition of Slavery. . . . The Greatest objection I have to the bill, is that the expences arising on such as are to [be] Liberated by this bill, is to be Defrayed By a partial tax.

    —Samuel Ten Broeck, Albany, to William Wilson, Clermont, Mar. 24, 1798

    23d Aug. 1799

    Sir

    I have received yours of the 21st Inst. Pulver must abide the fate he has provoked. I have had an application from Mr. Birdsall Junr. in his favor but I have referred the business to you. who knew my Disposition to Senity. . . .

    I am glad to hear of Mr. and Mrs. Crawford's intended Visit to the County. . . . . A general view of the affairs of the Manor [is] much more favorable than perhaps they had reason to expect, is all that occurs to me at present. . . . Bye the bye, our academy will soon be on a respectable Footing under the auspices of a Gentleman of Character and Abilities bred at the University of Glasgow. Would not this be an eligible situation for one at least of Mrs. Crawford's Sons . . . ?

Your Obed. Servt

    P V Schaack

    — Peter Van Schaack, Kinderhook, to William Wilson, Clermont, Aug. 23, 1799

MARTIN VAN BUREN, THE CULTURE OF SENSIBILITY, AND THE SHAPING OF ANTEBELLUM AMERICAN POLITICS

In the 1780s and 1790s education, the primary vehicle of a culture of sensibility in the early Republic, stood on somewhat shaky ground in the town of Kinderhook. Traditionally the schools were conducted in Dutch on the authority of the Reformed Church, and a final transition toward instruction in English came only haltingly. In the fall of 1777 Andrew Carshore, recently deserted from General John Burgoyne's defeated and interned army, started an English school in Kinderhook village, but in 1780 he was lured away to Claverack to teach in the new Washington Seminary, where many of the county gentry sent their sons, and some of their daughters, for an academy education. In 1792 the Kinderhook Reformed consistory acted to improve the level of education in the town, selling a parcel of land to build a new school for students advancing beyond the primary level. Three years later, when the state began to provide modest funding to local common schools, the Kinderhook Academy announced that it was ready to accept students, to be guided through the "classics" and the "sciences" by the Reverend John Egan, "late of Trinity College Dublin." How long Egan stayed on is unclear. In 1797 the consistory's new institution was incorporated by the state as the Columbia Academy, and by July 1798 the academy was housed in a building with a cupola. But that March the trustees could only report to the legislature that they were having trouble "obtaining a good and able instructor" and that their fifty-eight "scholars" under an "English teacher" were studying geography and the basics of the common school curriculum.[1]

Thus Peter Van Schaack, presumably one of the new academy's trustees, was greatly relieved eighteen months later when he could write to William Wilson, discussing the waning troubles on Livingston Manor, "Our academy will soon be on a respectable Footing under the auspices of a Gentleman of Character and Abilities bred at the University of Glasgow." This "Gentleman of Character" was the Reverend David B. Warden, who in 1798 had left revolutionary Ireland under threat of British arrest. By 1800 Warden was well enough established at the academy to put on quarterly exhibitions of his students' work, but apparently his political inclinations crossed those of arch-Federalist Kinderhook village, and he soon left for Kingston.[2]

The improved standards that state incorporation and a series of short-tenured Irish scholar-instructors might have brought to the academy in Kinderhook probably had a most limited impact on Martin Van Buren's education. Noted as a bright student in the village common school, Van Buren had advanced to the consistory school — by one account at age eleven — where he did manage to learn some Latin and make "considerable progress in the various branches of English literature." If the school used J. Hamilton Moore's *Young Gentleman and Lady's Monitor,* available at Stoddard's Hudson print-shop by 1793, Van Buren would have had some training in rules of deportment and speech that marked polite society. Van Buren might have been under Egan's instructorship briefly, but he would not have benefited from Warden's teaching, since in 1796 at the age of fourteen and probably at his mother's insistence he began his apprenticeship in the law with Federalist Peter Silvester and his son Francis. For the rest of his life Van Buren deeply felt his lack of an advanced education; decades later he wrote that it was "a source of regret" that he had not followed the New England tradition of working briefly as a school teacher so that he might go on to college. In Kinderhook, Peter Van Schaack had been the first to go to King's College (now Columbia University), followed by one of Martin Van Buren's employers, Francis Silvester, and by the Van Ness sons, with whom Van Buren would practice briefly, who had studied at the Washington Seminary in Claverack before going to King's College. John P. Van Ness, whom Van Buren would know decades later in Washington, had distinguished himself at King's by winning a Premium of Eloquence and had his winning oration — on the nature of rebellion — printed at Albany. Among his allies and adversaries at the Columbia County bar in the coming years, Ambrose Spencer, Jacob R. Van Rensselaer, and Thomas P. Grosvenor had all gone to Yale; Elisha Williams had studied law with the legendary Tapping Reeve of Litchfield, Connecticut. In the years to come Van Buren often "felt the necessity of a regular course of reading . . . to sustain me in my conflicts with able and better educated men" and would perpetually feel insecure about his deportment and presentation. In 1831 the newspaperman James Gordon Bennett, traveling with Van Buren by stage on the Utica road, found him "formal" but "nothing grand or imposing," a man who had "no appreciation of wit or satire — or learning — or fancy."[3]

Although he would work hard to adopt the trappings and demeanor of a man of the world, Van Buren was at heart a plain man of plain purposes. If one of his contributions would be to bring an easy sociability to American politics, his was not the highly polished sociability of the eighteenth-century gentry, where a carefully crafted mask of politeness hid intense animosities. Van Buren spent a lifetime fashioning his self to have the greatest effect, with the least friction, upon those around him. Though challenged at least once, Van Buren would never participate in the contemporary culture of honor and the duel. If his mother pushed him into the law, to follow in Peter Van Schaack's footsteps as a defender of local Dutch landholdings in an English legal system, Van Buren might well have inherited his easy, noncombative sociability from his father, tavernkeeper and militia captain Abraham Van Buren. He would refine this quiet, accommodating, yet purposeful demeanor in Albany and Washington, where it would become the defining vehicle of the deliberative politics of routine interest. The clash of both distributive contest and considered principle would be muted and tamed in Van Buren's style of pragmatic civility.[4]

Van Buren's political persona was a central feature of the new middling political culture that was emerging across the post-Revolutionary North. In Columbia County his brand of civility came too late to mediate the eighteenth-century contest between Demo and Aristo, patrician and plebeian, here so particularly intense. In the county and on the wider stage of nineteenth-century American politics this mode of civility would not play much of a role in *extending* the revolutionary settlement; indeed, it might well have helped to slow the extension of the bounds of citizenship beyond the ranks of white men of minimal property. Locally, this extension of the settlement had been achieved to the degree that it would be for decades to come; the land struggles of the 1780s and 1790s, always tinged with the threat of regime-challenging violence, had brought the promise of personal independence to the people of Canaan and Hillsdale and even Claverack. Only in the Livingston region would the old struggle continue, and here Van Buren would play an ambiguous role at best (discussed in Chapter 9). As with his wider political generation on a wider national stage, Van Buren's role was to consolidate and defend the legacy of the Revolution for its principal beneficiaries. He would take up the political inheritance of the Revolution — and its settlement as achieved for white men by the turn of the century — to fine-tune the practices and institutions of liberal politics. Starting in 1801, Van Buren would begin to play a direct and vital role in routinizing these practices and institutions in Columbia County, the formative background to his similar role in state and national politics.

While the effect of Van Buren's political civility was to establish the culture of the American political party, his purposes were conservative. The defense of the Revolutionary legacy required a jealous, monitorial oversight of the state and the rights of the people. The conservative minimalism of Van

Buren's political consolidation derived from two sources. First, his own *Inquiry into the Origin and Course of Political Parties in the United States,* written in the 1850s, credited the emerging definition of the republican principles as articulated by Thomas Jefferson as the touchstone of his political culture. But also, quite clearly, his worldview was shaped by the enclosed ethnic world of Kinderhook, by the sense of a people set apart that had fundamentally shaped the loyalism of his father-in-law, John D. Goes. Far into the nineteenth century the New York Dutch were noted for their conservatism and their unwillingness to entrust government with any significant powers of social and economic action. In some measure this ethos was grounded in the Old Testament traditions of the Dutch Reformed Church; it was also an ethos formatively shaped by the imposition of an alien government in the English conquest of 1664, further embittered by the ethnoreligious struggles between Dutch-German Leislerians and Anglo-Dutch anti-Leislerians in the 1690s. In the era of Andrew Jackson's and Martin Van Buren's presidencies, the New York Dutch would be rock-solid supporters of the minimalist policies of the Jacksonian Democratic Party.[5]

Arrayed against them in the 1830s and 1840s would be first the Whigs and then the insurgent forces of political antislavery. In great measure this was an ethnic division, Whigs and abolitionists coming overwhelmingly from the New England migration that, in the 1790s, was beginning to flood into central New York; its earliest manifestations were in the Yankee settlements in Columbia County's eastern hills, at Nobletown, Spencertown, New Canaan, New Concord, New Britain, and New Lebanon in the 1750s and 1760s. If the division between Whig and Democrat lay forty years into the future, the roots of the positive and negative liberalism that informed this contest were being shaped in the 1790s. More precisely, the culture of positive liberalism was being forged in Columbia County and elsewhere in the early Republic, against which negative liberalism would coalesce. Out of the culture of positive liberalism, compounded of threads of disinterested benevolence, sentimental sympathies, and interventionist improvement, would emerge a narrow but growing channel for the extension and enlargement of the American revolutionary settlement.[6]

Positive and negative liberalism involved more than competing definitions of the role of government in society and economy. These opposed deliberative positions were embedded in different understandings of the problem of consent and coercion in civil life. Both were equally grounded in understandings inherited from a republican past. Negative liberalism flowed naturally from classical republican assumptions about a society and a polity shaped by sharply defined status boundaries, in which the explicit consent of the independent householder was the sole determinant of public action. Beyond this field of deliberative consent lay a wider field of assumed dependence and potential coercion: wives, children, servants, and slaves were to tacitly accept their subordination as part of an immutable and essentially patriarchal order of things. The ethos of positive liberalism had its origins in efforts to understand and to reinforce this wider field of subordinate tacit consent. Early-eighteenth-century thinkers located women's subordination in a weaker nervous system; sympathy for female sensibilities would reinforce their subordination. In the early American republic, and most importantly among the Congregational ministers of the New Divinity newly seated throughout New England, a polity without a monarch required a virtuous people, and a virtue and a people broadly defined. Virtue might inhere in the independence of propertied men, but it was just as critical that the dependent be equally virtuous. In the virtue of dependents lay subordination and a tacit consent to the shape of society.[7]

But the culture of sympathy and the requirement of a universal virtue brought a series of demands and challenges. They both focused attention on those members of society outside the circle of independent property and explicit consent and raised questions about status, capacity, and justice. Sympathy itself, the recognition of a common humanity in a suffering and subordinate other, would undermine the ground of that subordination. If one had the capacity for virtue, was it just to hold others in a subordination? Where would the boundaries hold, once one began to sympathize with the powerless and to develop a sensibility to the coercion of potentially autonomous individuals? And what was required of the individual, once such a sensibility had been achieved?[8]

In sum, the imperatives of sympathy and virtue underlay a mode of middling civility that gave priority to continuing improvement and reform, rather than simply either to a polite maintaining of the bounds of respectability or to a jealous monitoring of popular rights. The amelioration of injustice and unacceptable conditions of life required public action. Indeed, it involved the expansion of the field of rights themselves, and in New York State this meant the lawmaking deliberation of assembly, senate, and council. During the 1780s and particularly the 1790s these bodies considered and eventually legislated funding for schools, the establishment of libraries, incremental changes in women's rights in property, the reform of the criminal code, the end of imprisonment for debt, and the gradual abolition of slavery. In each, the imperatives of disinterested reform were balanced against the weight of established interest. However, reform had no necessary natural constituency as did interest. It required careful preparation, careful persuasion, to achieve a legislative outcome. On the widest level, reform required a cultural transformation, or at least a sufficient shift toward sensibility and sympathy, to overcome entrenched traditions and interest. The persuasion that would achieve this shift unfolded in the public sphere, in the civil institutions of print and association that in the wake of the Revolution had begun to spread across the state of New York. But the reach and penetration of the public sphere was in the 1780s and 1790s a spotty and patchy thing, thickening and widening only slowly, and not all were equally shaped by its influence. In Kinderhook, while Peter Van Schaack and his fellow trustees worked throughout the decade to put their academy on "a respectable Footing," it seems likely that Martin Van Buren missed by several years the wider influences of an improved academy education. He certainly avoided the influences of Van Schaack's own abolitionist sentiments. Similarly, the county's political record of reform and improvement in the 1790s was halting and incomplete. As such, however, it may more clearly illuminate the political work of cultural persuasion in the late-eighteenth-century American public sphere, as it worked more broadly across the state to incrementally advance the revolutionary settlement.

SENSIBILITY AND PERSUASION IN EARLY COLUMBIA

The development of a public language of sensibility and sympathy in Columbia County was a necessary but difficult process. Deeply divided by ethnicity, by Revolutionary experience, and by the tangle of countervailing interests that threatened the fabric of the revolutionary settlement, violence in civil affairs was not just possible but real. In the face of these threats cultural authorities across the county mobilized a language of benevolence and unanimity. Common feeling would bind the people together in face of divisive particular interests.

On December 27, 1786, the Reverend John Camp addressed a group of Freemasons, assembled for the annual Masonic Festival of Saint John the Evangelist, at his meetinghouse in New Canaan. Camp lectured his audience on a theme that would be repeated in dozens of Masonic orations in New York State: the "most sublime virtue" of men in Masonic fraternity was love. Fraternal love was a "regulator, it is a golden rule, an unerring COMPASS." Love was "the union which cements" society at large, through which "peace and friendship is purchased for individuals, families, societies, cities, states, kingdoms, empires, earth and heaven." Without love all social connections would be dissolved, and "the earth and heaven, with the vast expanded universe, would burst asunder and break out into horrible convulsions, and thereby produce a chaos of the wildest uproar, anger, hatred, revenge, and rage." Illustrations of such "chaos" lay close at hand, and in recent memory, for these Masons. While

PLATE 9. *Heart and Hands Mural. Unity Lodge, New Lebanon. Circa 1800.*
Private Collection

they celebrated Saint John in the closing days of 1786, the rebellion raging to the east in Massachusetts must have reminded them of the darkest days of New York's Revolution. Love would engender sympathy: it would open "our bowels of compassion to the miserable," Camp told the Masons at Canaan; it would extend "our liberal hands to their relief." Two and a half years later, in June 1789, the delegates to the Shaftsbury Baptist Association, meeting at the Reverend Stephen Gano's new church in Hillsdale, used a circular letter similarly to urge harmony and union. Mindful of the autonomy of the member churches, they felt the need to remind them: "All communities formed among men, are under certain bonds of union to their own society . . . if one member is indulged in the breach of this combination, why not another?" Elder Gano, with Lemuel Powers of Stillwater, was asked to "travel somewhat at large," to attend the meeting of the Philadelphia Association and then to head south to enter into "fellowship" with the new associations being formed in Virginia.[9]

Such aspirations for a national union had been given persuasive form throughout the year before, as the Federalist press mobilized the language of sentiment behind the Constitution. Ashbel Stoddard's first invocation of the culture of sensibility was in his proposal in the *Hudson Weekly Gazette* in 1785: he was certain that the absence of "an impartial NEWSPAPER" had been "very sensibly felt" in the new city of Hudson. In the spring of 1788 he had invited anonymous contributions, seeing it "necessary for every man of abilities to declare his sentiments." Earlier that year the county grand jury had used the paper to "declare our sentiments.... THE preservation of the UNION of these states (effected after a struggle scarcely paralleled in the annals of mankind, and attended with an expense of so much blood and treasure) we conceive to be a duty incumbent on every citizen of America." In September, Stoddard published the full account of the Federalist parade in Albany, with the organizing committee's notice: "Pervaded with sentiments and principles favorable to good government and mutual conciliation, we are happy that we can now with propriety, not only congratulate our immediate constituents but every class of citizens, on the accomplishment of an event so ardently wished for by America in general; and under the joyful prospect of its encreasing the peace and happiness of our common country."[10]

No matter how much Federalists might try to impose an affective uniformity, "sentiment" was by its nature variable, as synonymous with opinion as with feeling. By the early 1790s, claims to unanimous feeling in the political invocation of sentiment were stretched even thinner than in the ratification year. In 1792, John Jay's Fourth of July progress through the county to the Hudson docks was decked with the trimmings of Washington's national tours of the previous years, but the context of the Otsego election crisis gave it an obviously partisan edge. Nonetheless, the language of sentiment was invoked to the point of absurdity. Mayor Seth Jenkins wanted to express the citizens' "sentiments and sense of injustice" at Jay's defeat; Jay in turn "felt the full force of the generous sentiments which this anniversary inspires." Jay was "very sensible of the honor" bestowed by the people of Hudson, and he made sure that "the gentlemen of the neighboring towns" knew of his "high and pleasing sense of the attachment and attentions with which they have honored me." Two years later the Democratic Society of Canaan turned sentimental patriotism to the uses of the rising partisan opposition. Concerned that "patriotic vigilance can alone preserve what patriotic valour has won" and that "the supineness of one generation, too frequently destroys the liberty, bought by the noble ardor of the preceding," the Canaan Democrats wanted to "animate and inspire the rising generation with sentiments, worthy of the hearts of the heroes of the American revolution." A year later they celebrated the failure of "the attempt to restrict the general freedom of sentiment in consequence of partial insurrection," meaning here the Federalist response to the Whiskey Rebellion. They were certain that a "respectful attention to prevailing *sentiments* and wishes of their sovereign," the people at large, ought to allay any fears the administration might have of popular associations such as their own.[11]

Though the democratic societies hoped to develop a system of collective, national deliberation, they achieved only a form of persuasion. Indeed, throughout the 1790s and into the ensuing decades the county experience of national politics lay less in a deliberative than in a persuasive domain. Cloaked in sentimental patriotism, if increasingly bifurcated, and acted out in the distant city of Philadelphia, the grand affairs of the nation had an almost surreal quality for the great majority of county voters. Certainly Stoddard's *Gazette,* with the other newspapers of the river landing towns, religiously printed the proceedings of Congress and selections of national laws. But even the middling-to-senior leaders in the county, whose letters tend to survive, rarely discussed national events in their correspondence in any detail. National affairs loomed largest in the communications of local congressmen and their contacts in the county, but local letters to Philadelphia might complain as much of the lack of information as they would discuss national affairs. Men of national standing in the county in the 1790s numbered fewer than the fingers on a single hand: three congressmen and Chancellor Livingston, who had been a Continental delegate and the foreign secretary to the Confederation and was a future ambassador to France. If congressional elections were generally well attended, only very occasionally did petitions sent to Congress provide a more direct role in national deliberations. As Madison had planned, national representation in large districts meant that the actual affairs of Congress were insulated from popular involvement.[12]

The result was that for most Americans national affairs inhabited a domain of persuasion rather than deliberation in the public sphere, in a framework of political *culture* rather than political *action.* The encounter with the nation was bound up in the ritual of reading the news, including accounts of July Fourth celebrations that some of the readers had attended. Divorced from formal deliberation, national politics as persuasive culture could include many more than the constitutionally enfranchised; divorced from the direct calculus of immediate interest, the politics could be suffused with affect, emotion, feeling, sentiment. Experienced as persuasion, the affairs of the nation became matters of personal identity and sensibility. Thus William W. Van Ness's conversion to Federalism began when he confronted the minister in Claverack with a copy of Paine's *Age of Reason,* only to have the Reverend Mr. Gebhard, as the story was told, unceremoniously put the book *"behind the back-log of his fire."* Then the dramas of the French Reign of Terror had their effect, perhaps in a subtle alchemy with Van Ness's courtship of Jane Bay, the daughter of the Jeffersonian lawyer with whom Van Ness was clerking, whom he married in 1795. As James Kent remembered it years later, "Van Ness's democracy was somewhat shocked by the execution of Louis 16th, and it was converted into warm indignation . . . when the horrid and unmanly murder of Marie Antoinette was perpetrated."[13]

Print was the centerpiece in this battle for affective identity. We can imagine teenagers William Van Ness and Jane Bay reading newspaper accounts of the royal executions in Claverack parlors and imagine ensuing emotional debates in their circle of friends. Such catalytic sentimental experiences would have triggered a political slippage for many individuals. The *Gazette* and other newspapers juxtaposed affairs of nation and the world at large with admonishing anecdote and sentimental verse, which provided the ground for evolving linkages between the domains of persuasion and deliberation, grounded in an unspoken resonance between sentiment as loving union and sentiment as informed opinion. In public print the language of "sentiment" was becoming a thing of partisanship, moving toward a synonym of "opinion," its connotations of "feeling" gradually attenuating. The transition would never be absolute, and throughout the 1790s the term would retain its emotional import as partisans saw their "sentiment" as the only true understanding of the common interest of the nation. But sheer repetition of a conventional term would work to conflate political sentiment with partisan opinion.

But sentiment and sensibility certainly retained more powerful referents than opinion: empathy, sympathy, and benevolence. Understandings of "union" and "fellow feeling" had a reciprocal relationship with sympathy and benevolence: feelings of sympathy with others in the wider union would overcome particular interest; common fellowship would encourage common benevolence. If accounts of the execution of the French queen might have worked Van Ness's conversion to Federalism, Jesse Torrey's abolitionism might have had its spark in a reading of William Cowper's "Negro's Complaint" or of Samuel Miller's "Discourse . . . for Promoting the Manumission of Slaves," published in the *Columbian Orator,* a popular school reader. Sensibility to injustice and iniquity—to violations of consent—would demand amelioration.

Sensibility thus might have a long reach: if sensibility could be mobilized into ameliorating reform and lawmaking, the shape of the revolutionary settlement would be reconfigured. Here the relations of these emotional exchanges were complicated, because the boundaries of union were indeterminate and almost by definition included those excluded from formal politics. As political sentiment became mere opinion, an alternative politics of sympathy also began to emerge, first in the persuasive arena of the public sphere, then moving into the domain of deliberation and lawmaking. If national deliberation was experienced as persuasion, literary persuasion might lead to public deliberation and to a formal politics of improvement and reform, establishing the ground for an ethos of positive liberalism and slowly and incrementally changing the shape of the revolutionary settlement.[14]

FROM PERSUASION TO DELIBERATION: LEGISLATING SENSIBILITY, 1795–1797

A politics of sensibility did emerge in New York in the mid-1790s. Between 1795, when state funding for schools was first voted, and 1799, when An Act for the Gradual Abolition of Slavery finally passed, the legislature considered a stream of proposals for reform and improvement, measures that would fund common schools, incorporate libraries, reform the criminal code, free debtors from prison, free African Americans from slavery. These efforts, based in shifting coalitions of both Federalists and Republicans, forged the ground upon which wider nineteenth-century reforms would develop.

Politics during much of George Clinton's governorship had centered on addressing the distributive interests necessary to achieve a public settlement and recovery from revolution. But, if succeeding years saw a new sympathetic attention to society's dependent and disenfranchised, this new politics was not untouched by questions of interest. During John Jay's administration, a politics of reform coincided with a politics of development, as the new model of state incorporations for internal improvements superseded the older model of public authorities. The boundary between benevolent reform and the new improvements was sometimes indistinct. The new banks and turnpikes shared a corporate form with new institutions of benevolence: academies, libraries, missionary societies. Their advocates sometimes also claimed that they were vehicles of benevolence themselves, that certainly both were agencies of improvement. And, if interest was thus given a benevolent purpose, benevolence itself was limited by interest. The call for disinterested reform was always conditioned by a calculus of cost, whether it be cost in taxes or cost to the interest of the owners of the freedom of others. Such considerations complicated and limited the emergence of a politics of sympathy in Columbia County.

In its 1795 and 1796 sessions the New York legislature acted to develop the basic infrastructure of sensibility across the state. Schools and libraries were essential institutions of public improvement and refinement, but before the mid-1790s New York had done little to provide for their public encouragement. By a 1784 act reconfirming their colonial status, schools were maintained by the trustees of local churches; it would only be in 1812 that a fully structured common school system would be established. In one Columbia town, the lack of a local church had led to establishment of the state's first publicly funded school in March 1791. Clermont had been carved off from Livingston Manor in 1787, but until the 1830s the people of Chancellor Livingston's little town attended church variously in Livingston, Germantown, and Rhinebeck. The petition for this first public school in the state to the 1791 assembly coincided with a flurry of local institution building. The Washington Lodge was warranted in nearby Johnstown under Grand Master Livingston's hand in September 1790, and in November 1791 one of these Masons, Livingston's estate agent, William Wilson, was appointed local postmaster. In the intervening March, Livingston, Wilson, and four others were given special legal authority to spend the town's unused poor tax funds to build a schoolhouse and hire a schoolmaster. This close attention to local improvement might well have helped to forestall any serious antirent sentiment in this little town, as compared with the turmoil that was to overrun the Upper Manor in the years to come.[15]

The Clermont initiative might well have been influenced by the writings of William Livingston, the chancellor's cousin. The chancellor had begun his legal career in William Livingston's law office in 1768, where he must have read his cousin's journal of essays, the *Independent Reflector*. In 1753, as the founding of King's College was being debated, William Livingston had written in the *Reflector* "The Advantages of Education, with the Necessity of Instituting Grammar Schools." Citing the *"Scotch"* and their "little Country Seminaries," he had argued, "Knowledge among a People makes them free, enterprizing and dauntless; but Ignorance enslaves, emasculates and depresses them." He proposed "that an Act be passed for the building and establishing two Grammar Schools in every County, and enabling the Inhabitants, annually to elect Guardians over them, and Impowering the Assessors to raise" taxes for their support.[16]

This Presbyterian Party plan had not been enacted in the colonial assembly, control of which the Livingstons contested with the Anglican De Lanceys. But it was enacted for Chancellor Livingston's Clermont in 1791, and in a first approximation for the state in the spring of 1795. Starting in 1793, Governor Clinton and the state regents began to argue for public support for "the lower branches of education" in grammar schools, which had been "greatly neglected." In 1795 he urged "early and decided consideration" of school support in the populist terms that had characterized his settlement politics for the past decade. Though provisions had been made for the incorporation and support of academies, their influence was "principally confined to the children of opulent," and "a great proportion of the community is excluded from their immediate advantages."[17]

When the school bill did come to the floor of a now-Federalist-controlled 1795 assembly, it was limited and constrained by interest: schools cost money. Still working in the post-Revolutionary climate of an active state government, Clinton's Republicans marshaled support behind efforts to spend higher amounts of state funds; the Federalists for the most part worked to limit these expenditures. But these partisan lines were not solid, and Columbia's Republican delegation was divided, voting for and against Federalist efforts to reduce state funding or to require matching local assessments.[18]

The next year the newly elected John Jay did not make education a priority in his governor's message, as the state's relationship toward local civil life shifted away from Clinton's public initiatives. The Federalist-controlled legislatures of 1796 and 1797 amended the school law to spread the funds to academy students doing the common school curriculum, and then to restrict the use of state funds to the payment of master's salary. A similar parsimony was evident when the legislature passed a general act for the incorporation of libraries in the winter of 1796. Individual libraries had successfully petitioned for confirmations, as did the New York Social Library in 1789, or for new charters, as in Albany in 1792 and Lansingburgh in 1794. In 1796, when a petition from Stephentown, adjacent to New Lebanon in Rensselaer County, was submitted for the incorporation of a library, the assembly drafted a general law to allow libraries to establish themselves as corporations.[19]

Nothing in the law offered state financial support. The model was a state-chartered private institution founded for public benefit, such as a bank. Libraries had been linked with bank initiatives in previous years: more loosely in New York City in the 1780s, and quite specifically in the parallel Schuyler initiatives for a bank and a library in Albany in 1792. In Hudson, Ashbel Stoddard formed his own private subscription library in 1793, the same spring that the Bank of Columbia was chartered. In the late 1790s the spread of incorporated libraries anticipated the sudden explosion of turnpikes. Stoddard led the formal incorporation of the library in Hudson in March 1797; the Hudson library trustees would be among the leadership of the Bank of Columbia and of the early turnpikes running east from the city as well as of later corporate ventures. In Stephentown, whose petition had led to the general library incorporation law in 1796, the corporation model by 1801 had spread to a special trusteeship for its schools and a local turnpike. Rather than the public committees entrusted with state-sanctioned funds that had characterized Clintonian initiatives, Federalist policy made the chartered corporation—granting public authority but not money to discrete private groups—the model of a reformed relationship between state and civil society across New York and the preferred vehicle for an array of commercial and cultural projects. It was thus under Federalist auspices, and a limited but privileged enactment of state authority, that a wider category of the institutions that Tocqueville would see as foundational to American civil life began to proliferate in the state of New York.[20]

Under the Federalist legislature this corporate form was also moving into the religious domain. In 1798 the Northern Missionary Society was established by laymen and ministers in Albany, Lansingburgh, and Troy to "propagate the gospel" among the Indians and the white settlers of New York's frontier; the year before, the Columbia County ministers of the Reformed tradition had formed a similar institution with their brethren across the state line in Berkshire County, their interstate alliance apparently explaining their failure to seek incorporation. While the Federalists refused to incorporate groups of mechanics, when the Republicans regained control of the legislature in 1801 they incorporated a mechanics' mutual aid society in Albany, the state's second after New York's, followed several years later by incorporation of similar societies in Hudson, Troy, and Poughkeepsie. Educational or commercial, religious or mechanical, all were part of the leading edge of a wave of organized charity and benevolence that would crest thirty years later in the era of Tocqueville's visit to America.[21]

If any one man personified the Federalist fusion of commerce, benevolence, and state delegation to authorized voluntary societies in the early 1790s, it was Elkanah Watson, a wandering Yankee improver who settled in Albany in 1789 after spending some years in England, France, and the Carolinas. While primarily a merchant, Watson dabbled in land speculation, promoting a village across the Hudson (which he named Bath), and in manufacturing, helping to establish a glassworks west of Albany, the second manufactory in the state to receive a charter of incorporation. Watson immediately began to churn out essays for the Websters' *Albany Gazette,* a number of which would have been reprinted in Stoddard's paper in Hudson. He campaigned for a host of improvements to the conditions of civil life in Albany: for paving the streets and sidewalks, banishing the old Dutch house gutters jutting into the city streets, establishing a city coffeehouse and a "public hotel." Watson also wrote as the Northern Centinel, advocating moving the state capital to Albany, urging the construction of canals and turnpikes, and attacking Clinton's land distribution of 1791. He appears to have been responsible for the stream of essays slipped into the river town papers extolling "the utility of inland navigation" in quasi-sentimental terms, particularly in the United States, which was "so well watered" as "to have been formed by nature for a most Intimate union." His attack on Clinton's land dealings attracted the attention of General Philip Schuyler, and together in the year following they advanced three bills in Albany's interest, establishing the Bank of Albany, the Western and the Northern Inland Lock Navigation companies, and the Albany Library.[22]

Watson split with Schuyler in 1793 over the management of the canal company and the bank, and by 1795 he had joined the Republicans; he would eventually settle in the idyllic Jeffersonian retreat of Pittsfield in the Berkshires, raising merino sheep and organizing cattle shows and county fairs. Leaving an increasingly hostile Albany in 1797, he took his family first to New York and then in 1798, to avoid the peril of yellow fever, briefly to Poughkeepsie. Here, he later wrote, "having nothing to do, I devoted myself to Raising up their drooping academy—and exciting a Spirit for a turnpike road," writing about both in the *Poughkeepsie Journal*. As much as he extolled the benefits of communication, Watson was also a tireless advocate of education. In 1792, apparently writing on the passage of the bill to support (now) Columbia College as well as academies, he stressed that "much remains to be done." Echoing Noah Webster, he saw the nation-building potential of common schooling: "Should our wise lawmakers extend their arms to embrace literature as one their first objects—the Germans—the Dutch—the Yankies—will lose all local prejudices and distinctions and find themselves consolidated under the dignified name of Americans, possessed of the same language, genius and education." After the passage of the 1795 school act, he wrote in the *Albany Register,* "Of all the laws passed by our legislature since the revolution that for establishing Free schools will probably have most benefitial tendency—It will dispel ignorance, the bane of republics."[23]

Watson's essays might well have set the tone in the upper valley, but they were only a part of a wider campaign by the editors from Albany and Lansingburgh to Hudson and Poughkeepsie to keep the issue of education before the public. The *Federal Herald* in Lansingburgh published endorsements of Webster's *Institutes* for use in schools and a graduation oration from Boston; a correspondent in Canaan sent a letter to Stoddard's *Gazette* by a young girl to demonstrate "that the fair sex are as capable of improvement by a good education, and proper learning, as the men." The *Register* published a long essay on the difficulties of instructing the young. As the school bill moved toward passage in 1795, Federalist editors made it their own. A week before the 1795 school bill passed, the Federalist Lansingburgh *American Spy* declared, "Public schools will assuredly be fatal to private political clubs!" That summer the paper published the entire act, covering the entire first and most of the second page of their July 7 issue. Stoddard in 1793 had announced the opening formation of a subscription library in republican terms: "Circulating Libraries tend to diffuse general information among a community at large; on which depends peace and security of republican government." Echoing these themes, as well as the *Spy*'s Federalist strictures, Stoddard in December 1795 invoked the republican functions of education in an editorial to close the year. Following a notice of the "harmony and brotherly love" exhibited at the Hudson Lodge's Saint John celebration, Stoddard situated the school act in a review of the blessings of "peace and good order," as the nation had avoided both colonial tyranny and slavery and domestic riot and rebellion. Without mentioning the rioting over land that continued to threaten in the county's eastern hill towns, Stoddard reminded his readers that the Shays men "in the North and the *whiskey boys* in the South" had both shaken "the fabric of the constitution." But education would have stayed their hand.

> Had the minds of the people been properly enlightened by education, they would have taken a view of their own constitution and the superior advantages they enjoyed; had they turned their eyes toward other nations, viewing the despot on his throne having the lives and properties of his subjects in his own hands, they would sat down under their rulers, thanking their God that they were born in a land of freedom.
>
> Knowledge is the parent of virtue and religion, ignorance, of vice and impiety. When knowledge is wanted in a nation religion will scarcely be found. So that a republican government founded upon virtue cannot subsist without a general diffusion of knowledge. Hence we see the propriety of encouraging schools and seminaries of learning. From these originate the supports of republican government.[24]

The Federalist editors thus had some conservative uses for education. As, first, French revolutionary Jacobinism and then American political societies and the Whiskey Rebellion drove the Federalists into a sense of foreign and domestic embattlement, they saw schooling as a prop for government, a vehicle of religion, a bastion of good order. Republicans had a different construction of virtue in the Republic and of education. Virtue lay, not in deference, but in participation. When William Wands, the Federalist editor of the Lansingburgh *American Spy,* counterpoised public schools with "private political clubs," it was in response to the Democratic Society of Philadelphia's resolution: "Public schools are well calculated to teach men their rights and secure the blessings of independence and republicanism." The Canaan Democratic Society expressed similar sentiments at its March 5 meeting: "The revival and diffusion of letters ushered in genuine philosophy," through which man "gradually deserved his rights, appreciated his dignity and broke his fetters."[25]

AMBROSE SPENCER AND REPUBLICAN-MASONIC HUMANITARIANISM

It was on these expansive and participatory terms that Elkanah Watson, recently converted to Republican principles, hailed the 1795 school act. This Albany Yankee was swinging toward the radical vision being articulated by a group of young Republicans, particularly in New York City. Inspired by the French Revolution and the new doctrines of the rights of man, these men were advocating a new vision of a reformed America that rested on the widest implications of sensibility and sympathy. Universal rights transcended particular interests; sympathy and sensibility were a vehicle to this understanding. All barriers to autonomous rights were to be swept away. In New York City, the Tammany Society meeting late in 1794 announced the core themes of this radical Republican vision: "The Empire of Philanthropy," "The Genius of Universal Emancipation," and "Humanity." Their increasingly specific program encompassed "A speedy abolition of every species of Slavery throughout America," "A happy melioration of our Penal Laws, respecting criminal punishments and imprisonment for debt," and "the establishment of Public Schools." Young Republican politicians and intellectuals—prominently Samuel L. Mitchill and De Witt Clinton—gave orations before a series of societies in New York City in these years that extended this optimistic vision; Clinton saw "the principle of benevolence" building "schools of virtue," striking off "the shackles of slavery," abolishing "the horrid instruments of capital punishment." Addressing the Ulster County Republican Society gathered on the Fourth of July, radical Paineite Phineas Hedges invoked the language of sentiment and sensibility. Why had "the doctrine of the equality of man . . . been so long hidden from the human race?" The "cunning and wicked"—"lost to every sentiment of justice"—had long "unfeelingly domineered" the "weak and ignorant." A series of events, importantly "the invention of Printing" and "the discovery of America," had set the stage for a new order of things. In the American states "our sensibility is not wounded with the extreme poverty of European despotism," but Hedges subtly had to remind his audience, some among them slaveholders, that "a greater part of man are groaning under an insupportable tyranny," many "pining under the galling chain."[26]

In Columbia County the man who best represented and acted upon this optimistic culture of reform was Ambrose Spencer of Hudson. Spencer was an exact contemporary of Watson, and both were Yankee emigrants into the

Hudson Valley, though Watson had grown up in Plymouth and had apprenticed with merchant John Brown in Providence, and Spencer was from an ironmaking family in northwest Connecticut and had attended both Yale and Harvard. Studying the law in Sharon, Connecticut, and in Claverack, Spencer settled in Hudson in 1788. Broad-shouldered, more than six feet tall, and noted for his hard-driving energy, Spencer made a quick impact in Hudson. Joining the Hudson Lodge in 1789, he was immediately appointed clerk of the city, a position he held until 1804. Elected to the 1794 assembly as a Federalist, he immediately served his constituents in attempting to get the courts moved to Hudson from Claverack. In the same session Governor Clinton had challenged the legislature to review the criminal code, and Spencer watched as the assembly inconclusively opened a discussion of corporal and capital punishment in which he would take a large part in subsequent sessions. For the past several years Spencer had also been representing the Manor tenants against the Livingstons, perhaps helping to write the Wheeler petition of March 1794, and trolling for Federalist votes. But, if he seems to have been playing a political game with the tenants in 1794, his experience as their advocate over the next few years might truly have been transformative. Spencer lost when he ran as a Jay Federalist for the state senate in 1795, but he gained a seat the following January, just as he was organizing the tenants' case against the Livingstons, when he replaced John Williams of Washington County, who had been elected to Congress.[27]

Once in the senate, Spencer immediately came into conflict with Samuel Jones, the powerful conservative Federalist lawyer from Queens. Tradition had it that Jones's appointment in February 1797 to the new position of comptroller enraged Spencer to the point that he abandoned the Federalists for the Republicans. These animosities had a history. In the 1796 session the two were continually at odds on the issue of criminal code reform. Philip Schuyler had been converted to the cause of prison reform while in Philadelphia, and Spencer carried Schuyler's bill for legal reform into the assembly; Elkanah Watson claimed to have "inundated" the legislature with petitions in support of the bill. Early in February, Jones opposed Spencer's motion to build one rather than two prisons, and Spencer opposed Jones's motion to maintain the death penalty for burglary, house burning, the rape of a child, and counterfeiting. So it went on, vote after vote, issue after issue, from February into March. Spencer's most important triumph was to establish the principle that acquittal would be a bar to further prosecution. Although he lost the tenants' court case against the Livingstons in the fall of 1796, Spencer continued to advance the legislative agenda of reform — and to oppose both Jones and his Federalist colleague Peter Silvester of Kinderhook — in the senate. In 1798 he worked to reduce the scope of capital punishment and to abolish imprisonment for debt, which measures he successfully pushed through the following year. In the midst of this session he publicly defected to the Republicans, and in the April elections he successfully defended his seat in the senate, running on a ticket headed by Robert R. Livingston's unsuccessful gubernatorial candidacy.[28]

Spencer had not been able to sway the Columbia delegation in the assembly to consistently support the prison bill, and some of this resistance seems to have been grounded in the cost of the project. Whipping and hanging criminals was cheaper than keeping them in an expensive prison for years at a time. Federalist appeals to taxpayer interest seem to have swayed the county in the 1798 election. Both Livingston and Spencer lost in Columbia that spring, and Spencer won his senate seat thanks only to strong Republican votes in Rockland, Orange, and Ulster. The Columbia County Federalists had pilloried the cost of the new initiatives in a broadside, *To the Public,* printed up in mid-April by Ashbel Stoddard in Hudson, written in the form of a dialogue between a "senator" and a "farmer." When the "farmer" asked why "our Treasury is so empty at present," the reply of the "senator" placed the blame on the entire array of reforms legislated in the previous four sessions. If the treasury was bare, it was due to "the large sums of money which have been appropriated by the Legislature within the last few years for the establishment of schools — opening roads — building bridges — cutting canals and improving our inland navigation, and erecting a state prison, etc." Governor Jay "had nothing to do" with this "expenditure," which had "been zealously promoted by most of [his] leading opponents." In the April election, Robert R. Livingston, standing reluctantly as the Republican candidate for governor, won only an unenthusiastic vote in the Manor towns, plus considerable majorities in Hillsdale and Claverack; Spencer took Hillsdale, Claverack, and his hometown of Hudson. Columbia's Republican assembly delegation survived, but for the last time before an epochal shift to the Federalists took hold in the 1799 election.[29]

If he was moving away from the political mainstream of the county, Ambrose Spencer's conversion to Republicanism brought him into a rising constellation in New York public life, one that hitched its fortunes to improvement and reform. Robert R. Livingston had a shaky alliance with the young New York City politician, De Witt Clinton, who in 1798 won his own seat in the senate along with Spencer. Clinton and Spencer worked well together, and, after the decisive Republican victories in April 1800, they won seats on the powerful Council of Appointment, where they led a three-to-one Republican majority and launched a purge that shaped politics in New York for decades. These events signaled the end of Federalist power in New

York and opened a personal alliance that would endure for decades, sealed in Spencer's sequential marriages to two of Clinton's sisters. In this connection, Spencer was a key part of a Clermont Livingston-Clintonian alliance that would prevail in the two ensuing gubernatorial elections and then collapse in the struggle to charter the Merchant's Bank in 1805.

Livingston, Clinton, and Spencer were also tied by a Masonic connection that ran as an undercurrent among these Republican reformers. The chancellor had been grand master of the New York Grand Lodge since 1784; Clinton had been a member of the Holland Lodge in New York since 1790; Spencer joined the lodge in Hudson in 1789 and served as junior warden in the early 1790s. Clinton was already one of Livingston's "political friends" when he was appointed junior grand warden in 1795, which led to the senior grand wardenship in 1798. In this capacity, Clinton toured the state in the spring of 1799, collecting contributions to the Masonic charitable fund and warranting a host of new lodges. "The interests of Masonry in the Northern and Western parts of the state progress with the population of the Country," he reported, and "the Grand Lodge is respected and its authority almost universally acknowledged." The year before, in March 1798, Clinton had founded Royal Arch Freemasonry in New York and sat as its first grand high priest; in 1806 he would begin thirteen years' service as grand master of the Grand Lodge.[30]

In their various ways and degrees, each of these men was committed to a vision of improvement and benevolence. Robert R. Livingston was continually pursuing such improving projects, variously agricultural and scientific. In the spring of 1798 his distraction over the politics of his bill to develop Robert Fulton's steamboat might have contributed to his loss of the gubernatorial election. The steamboat bill was introduced by Samuel L. Mitchill of New York and advanced in the assembly by De Witt Clinton, both of whom must have seen the steamboat as an extension of the Republican vision they had articulated in the mid-1790s. Spencer presumably stood with the unanimous vote in the senate supporting the steamboat bill while he was struggling to advance other avenues of reform. Some of his energies were supported in the climate of opinion in his circle in Hudson.[31]

As a small commercial city, Hudson stood out by the early 1790s for its densely elaborated array of civil institutions. It was a microcosm of late-eighteenth-century "town society," with its newspaper, library, bank, Masonic lodge, and hotel and with its streets of small shops where merchants and artisans engaged in a hothouse of commerce. Here the ideas of the day, such as were being advanced by New York City's Republican intellectuals, could be discussed and debated. But the pressures of an intensifying economy seem to have borne down upon at least some of Hudson's struggling men, and here reform proposals had a particularly immediate salience.

After the New York banks discounted the exchange value of the Bank of Columbia's notes in 1799, a city banker wrote to William Wilson at Clermont: "The moneyed people here are very fearful of the Solidity of our Country Banks both at Hudson and Albany. . . . Small merchants are very apt to overtrade themselves, and unless they are restrained might go to some unpleasant lengths[;] this is the reason of the discredit of the Hudson bank." One of these small merchants might have been Thomas Frothingham. A Hudson merchant soon to be involved in the Columbia turnpike, Frothingham in January 1798 headed up a petition to the assembly asking that the legislature take up the issue of the "more ample and speedy relief of persons confined for debt." Frothingham was probably not an imprisoned debtor, as was William Schermerhorn, who wrote a similar petition from the Columbia County jail a month later. Nothing would happen this session, though Spencer protested; the next year he introduced such a bill in the senate and, assisted by Clinton, worked to pass it on the most generous terms possible.[32]

Frothingham was a central figure in a circle of Spencer's close associates in Hudson who made the same migration from the Federalists to the Republicans in the late 1790s. Like Spencer, all of them were Freemasons in the Hudson Lodge, and several were members of the Royal Arch chapter established in Hudson before March 1797, first meeting with Clinton's Grand Chapter the following year. Thomas Frothingham, who in 1788 had fought off the "ignorant antis" at the Federalist July Fourth celebration in Hudson, stood as a Republican assembly candidate in 1800; in March 1798 he had been appointed grand king of the Grand Chapter of the Royal Arch, second to Clinton himself. The Hudson Republican committee in the spring of 1798 was chaired by Jared Coffin, elected to the assembly as a Federalist earlier in the decade; among the other Republican committeemen that year, David Lawrence had been on the Federalist committee in the early 1790s. Coffin was a member of the Royal Arch chapter, as was Elisha Jenkins, the Republican candidate for Congress, and his cousin Robert Jenkins. Both Jenkinses were trustees of the Hudson library, and more than probably all of these men with their families were members of this library. Spencer, Elisha Jenkins, and Thomas Frothingham were also Presbyterians, but their connections to a politics of reform brought some of Hudson's numerous Quakers to the Republican column.[33]

All of these men would benefit, some immensely, from their new politics. With Ambrose Spencer becoming a pivotal member of the Council of Appointment in November 1800, they suddenly were showered with civil positions. Elisha Jenkins, the county treasurer from 1798 to 1801, was appointed state comptroller on the expulsion of Samuel Jones. Jared Coffin was elevated to a common pleas judgeship. David Lawrence became the city recorder, Thomas Frothingham the city clerk, and Robert Jenkins the city chamberlain, the county treasurer, and eventually the mayor of Hudson. Spencer himself, an associate district attorney since 1796, became the attorney general of the state in 1802 and then a supreme court justice in 1804, where he would sit for nineteen years, four as the chief justice. Ambrose Spencer and Elisha Jenkins, banding together with, among others, Elkanah Watson, John Tayler of Albany, and the chancellor's brother-in-law Thomas Tillotson, would drive through the legislation for a Republican-controlled New York State Bank in 1803. Watson did so well in this venture that in 1807 he was able to retire to the life of a gentleman farmer in Pittsfield, living in grand style in Henry Van Schaack's old mansion on the road to Lenox. Before he retired to the Berkshires, Watson invested in a glassworks in Rensselaer County with Frothingham, Jenkins, and a number of Albany Republicans.[34]

In 1807 Watson was described in an Albany newspaper as "once a *federalist* — afterwards a *professed* republican — and now a *quid*." Such would be the direction that Spencer's career would take: from Federalist origins through the Jeffersonian enthusiasm to the moderation of northern middling entrepreneurs, eventually finding political expression in national Republicanism and the Whig Party. Here lay the roots of the nineteenth-century politics of improvement in the state of New York, of an activist definition of the relationship between government and civil life, a positive liberalism, which has had a long and powerful reach in American political life.[35]

But in the late 1790s improvement among these young New York Republicans was born of an exhilarating youthful utopianism. Certainly these visions of improvement were inspired by the French Revolution (an inspiration perhaps somewhat tarnished by the end of the decade). There is also some reason to suggest that Freemasonry played a minor but not insignificant role in shaping the sensibilities behind this benevolence. Such was the message of De Witt Clinton to the men of the Holland Lodge in 1794. "Our Institution asserts," he argued, "the natural equality of mankind," and it drew upon the highest human capacities, "the best sympathies of the heart . . . , the most enlightened properties of the head." Though the path was difficult, Freemasonry led to "a course of active virtue," requiring its brethren to carry "into action" "the beauties of charity and benevolence." Clinton and the other New York Republican intellectuals laid out such a "course of active virtue": the abolition of all forms of inequality and coercion, the vestiges of a backward colonial past. Ambrose Spencer was certainly following this course in his assault on the harsh penalties of the old criminal system, whether they be corporal or capital or the irrational imprisonment for debt.[36]

The election of the reformist Republicans from Hudson accounts for the small surge of Masons holding elective office from Columbia at the turn of the century. There are also other intriguing suggestions of the interplay of Masonic sentiment and Republican activism scattered across Columbia County. The subscriptions for the Albany printing of the voices of radicalism in the 1790s — Thomas Paine and Jean Jacques Rousseau — provide one such hint. In 1791 Charles and George Webster issued a prospectus calling for subscribers for a multivolume edition of the *Writings of Thomas Paine*. Published over the next several years, the Websters' edition of Paine was subscribed to by at least seventeen men in Columbia County, of whom five were Masons. The Paine subscribers also included the old popular leader Matthew Adgate of Canaan as well as Peter Bishop of Ancram and the Temple Lodge and Phillip Hoffman of Clermont and the Washington Lodge, both of whom would challenge the Livingstons in the mid-1790s.[37]

It was a measure of the political calm of the first years of the decade that the Federalist Websters would put out an issue of Paine. In 1797, well after ideological lines between radical and conservative had been sharply drawn, the Republican printers in Albany, Barber and Southwick, were making a dramatic political statement when they published by subscription Rousseau's *Dissertation on Political Economy;* they also put out in that year an issue of Paine's *Agrarian Justice.* Only eight people in Columbia County can be found among the subscribers to Rousseau's *Political Economy,* all of middling circumstances. Four of the eight were from Canaan, led by Moses Younglove, one of the old warhorses of the Democratic Society. Three of the eight were Freemasons. One was a sea captain from Hudson, Judah Paddock, of whom we shall hear more. The other two were Unity Lodge Masons and Republican committeemen from Canaan who, with Younglove, were in 1800 deeply involved in the land struggle over the Mawighnunk patent.[38]

Canaan Masons were also involved in another controversy that tested the sympathies of the Canaan people. By 1800 the Shakers had established their communal village on the slope of the mountain above New Lebanon Village, on the new turnpike road to the town of Richmond, Massachusetts. Many in New Lebanon and Richmond felt, however, that certain young men and women among the Shakers were being held against their will and better interest; in March 1800 they got up a petition of complaint to the New York legislature. David Patterson (one of the Rousseau subscribers in Canaan) and three other Unity Lodge Masons were among the sixteen signers who were Canaan taxpayers. But the Masonic leadership, among them the turnpike incorpora-

PLATE 10. *Mount Lebanon Shaker Village. Circa 1840.* From John W. Barber and Henry Howe, *Historical Collections of the State of New York . . .* (New York, 1842)

tors and the great majority of the Mawighnunk occupants, did not join this campaign against the Shakers and might have opposed it; the petition was led by the Congregational ministers in Canaan and Richmond and seems to have been centered in the churches. In May a committee of three, including Justice Eleazer Grant, one of the founders of the lodge and the turnpike, examined the young people among the Shakers and found no grounds for complaint. Sixteen years later David Patterson joined a quite different petition, asking that the Shakers be exempted from both military service and the payment of militia fines. Joined by at least thirteen Masons who had been taxpayers in 1800, including a number of "past masters" of the lodge, Patterson signed a petition describing the Shakers as "a peaceable, industrious, charitable, and moral people," asking that they be exempted from both military service and the payment of militia fines. By 1816 and perhaps before, there seems to have been an affinity between Masons and Shakers in Canaan.[39]

TWO REPUBLICAN LIBRARIES, A SCHOOL, AND THE LIMITS OF SENSIBILITY

Chancellor Robert R. Livingston's Clermont provides another window onto the workings and the limits of the politics of sensibility as practiced by Republican Freemasons. Here we have surviving details on both the intellectual climate and the practical outcomes of the institution-building efforts of a group of Republican Masons, in the form of catalogs of private libraries and the attendance records of local schools in the wake of the 1797 revision of the school act.

In 1791 Livingston, the grand master of the state, joined two Masons from the recently warranted Washington Lodge to found Clermont's grammar school, the first secular school in the state. One of these Masons, the school's overseer, Dr. William Wilson, the postmaster and consistently a Livingston-faction Republican, took the time in 1801 and again in 1807 to write out catalogs of the books in his own library, apparently recording his books as they stood on his shelves. Wilson had a remarkable collection of the works that made up the Enlightenment understanding of benevolence and sensibility. The earl of Shaftesbury's *Characteristics of Men, Manners, Opinions, Times,* the foundational discussion of civility in public life, stood between Montesquieu's *Spirit of Laws* and John Locke's *Thoughts on Education.* On another shelf Laurence Sterne's *Sentimental Journey through France and Italy* was grouped with Locke's *Essay on Human Understanding,* Hugh Blair's *Lectures on Rhetoric and Belles Lettres,* and another copy of Montesquieu. Adam Smith's *Theory of Moral Sentiments,* the era's seminal analysis of the workings of sympathy and sensibility, in 1801 sat with Gershom Carmichael on Samuel von Pufendorf and a Latin text of Virgil; by 1807 Smith and Carmichael had migrated to sit with Sterne's *Sentimental Journey,* down the shelf from Smith's *Wealth of Nations,* Shaftesbury, William Winterbotham's history of America, William Preston's *Illustrations of Freemasonry,* and Thomas Paine's *Age of Reason.* Wilson apparently did not have a copy of Edmund Burke's essay on refinement, the *Philosophical Enquiry into the Origins of Our Ideas of the Sublime and the Beautiful,* but it was available in the library of his patron, Chancellor Livingston, who would have had to borrow Smith's *Moral Sentiments* from Wilson. While both Wilson and Livingston had copies of Paine in various forms, neither owned Rousseau's *Dissertation on Political Economy.* Both Wilson's and Livingston's libraries were well supplied with the classics of the moderate Enlightenment without stepping over the bounds into a truly radical vision.[40]

Such was the intellectual milieu of Clermont's senior commissioner of schools as he served under the regulations of the new school act. Though he failed to provide a report to the assembly of the progress of Clermont's schools and of school attendance in time for their March 1798 report, Wilson did keep very detailed records of the progress of education (see Table 15). Two schools had been established in Clermont, and, in addition, children from Clermont also attended a school in Germantown and two schools in Livingston. Apparently in preparation for the March 1798 report, the Clermont schools listed students' names, the date they began at a given school, their days of attendance, and whether they were studying reading, writing, or arithmetic (the reports from the Germantown and Livingston schools were less detailed). The ninety-four Clermont children in the Clermont and

TABLE 15. *School Attendance in Clermont and Germantown, March 1797–March 1798*

Place on Tax List	No.	Avg. Days Attended No.	Rate	No. Studying Reading	Writing	Arithmetic

Clermont Children in Clermont and Germantown Schools, 1797–1798

BOYS

Place on Tax List	No.	No.	Rate	Reading	Writing	Arithmetic
Deciles 1–3	23	136.8	44.0%	4	4	5
Deciles 4–10	29	141.6	44.8%	17	9	1
Not linked	18	93.2	36.3%	7	8	2
Slave	1	60	19.1%	1	0	0
Total	71	126.6	42.3%	29	21	8

GIRLS

Deciles 1–3	12	160.9	46.0%	3	6	0
Deciles 4–10	4	112.5	31.0%	2	1	0
Not linked	6	61.0	18.7%	3	3	0
Slave	1	107	28.6%	1	0	0
Total	23	123.9	35.8%	9	10	0
Grand total	94	125.9	40.0%	38	31	8

Germantown, Livingston, and Rhinebeck Children in Clermont Schools

Boys	24	79.9	29.1%	4	16	4
Girls	8	47.3	18.2%	4	4	0
Total	32	71.7	26.5%	8	20	4

Notes: Percent attendance is calculated from the dates at which students were noted as admitted to the school. The data on numbers of students studying reading, writing, or arithmetic were not recorded for the returns from the Germantown school. The connection of a student to the 1800 valuation is approximate, based on common last names. In fifteen cases where there are multiple last names on the valuation matching that of a given name, I have averaged the deciles of the possible candidates to roughly place students into these two large wealth categories.

Sources: School attendance records, March 1797–March 1798, Clermont Schools No. 1 and No. 2, Germantown School No. 1, in box 41, folder 22, WFP-UM; 1800 Valuation of Property, Town of Clermont, NYSA.

Germantown schools accumulated 11,840 days of attendance, for an average of 126 days per student, surpassing Hudson's 107 days per student and far exceeding Kinderhook, which reported only 53 days per student. On average, Clermont students attended school 4 days out of 10 between March 1797 and March 1798. But attendance varied somewhat among different groups of students. Boys from families both rich and poor in Clermont attended about 44 percent of the total year, girls about 36 percent.[41]

But, much more important, girls were vastly underrepresented, comprising only a quarter of the total students. And, while girls from reasonably prosperous households were not quite so poorly represented and had the best attendance record of the entire system, girls from poorer families were almost completely missing from the schools and had relatively poor attendance records. Equally revealing, only boys, and particularly boys from the wealthier households, had advanced to the study of arithmetic: girls of all backgrounds and probably ages were restricted to reading and writing. Almost universally, girls attended only if they had brothers in attendance; the few girls attending schools without siblings might well have been under the wing of a cousin or neighborhood family. The distinctions of gender and supervision of family were apparent among Wilson's three children, who attended School No. 1, in the care of schoolmaster Seth Curtis. Seven-year old William H. Wilson attended better than six days in ten over the course of the year; his sisters Frances and Mary, aged ten and six respectively, attended about four and a half days out of ten. William would prepare for a doctor's life; Frances and her younger sisters, Mary and Eliza, would attend schools in Hudson, Albany, and Dutchess County, where they would combine formal studies with lessons in embroidery, dancing, deportment, presentation, and sensibility from the *Young Gentleman and Lady's Monitor*. But the most striking evidence from the Clermont attendance records is the virtual absence of girls from poor families in the schools of this small section of the early Republic.[42]

This virtual absence of poor girls extended to the slave children of Clermont as well. Virtual but not total, since Wilson's neighbor Dr. Thomas Brodhead sent his slave girl Bett to School No. 1, where she was learning to read, as was Dien, a slave in one of the Minkler households. But slavery was a hard reality in Clermont and throughout Columbia County. In 1800 there were ninety-five slaves in Clermont: three were held in William Wilson's household. Wilson had held three in 1790, two of whom, Sylvia and an unnamed boy, he had bought in the previous year. When Sylvia gave birth to a boy named Isaac in 1803, Wilson did renounce his right to the child's labor, which, by the 1799 act for gradual emancipation, he might have claimed until the child's twenty-eighth birthday. But he did not free his adult slaves, and as of the 1810 census, eleven years after the passage of the emancipation act, there were two slaves and one free person of color in his household. On January 25, 1811, Wilson bought another slave, described as a "Negro Boy named Sharp aged about Twenty years a slave for life"; Wilson's eighteen-year-old daughter, Mary Ann, witnessed the sale. Somehow, this young Scots immigrant to the Hudson valley found it inconvenient to conduct his household affairs without enslaved labor.[43]

Here then lay the limits — and the great moral crisis — in a politics of sensibility and sympathy in Columbia County and throughout the nation at large. Wilson had grown up in Scotland, he had ready at hand what must have been two of the best private libraries in the entire region, fully stocked with the best of the Enlightenment and the literature of sensibility, but he could not find it possible to live without slaves. Perhaps he and his family were uncomfortable with their decision to run a slave household. But it would appear that Wilson, as did his patron, the chancellor, who held twelve slaves in 1800 and five in 1810, flinched at the ultimate test of the politics of sensibility in the early Republic.

LEGISLATING SYMPATHY:
GRADUAL EMANCIPATION, 1787–1799

The entire county flinched at this ultimate test: emancipation. Indeed, many actively resisted. Extending the revolutionary settlement beyond the bounds of white manhood would take more than a century of struggle in the nation at large. It would require a reimagining of the people who lay beyond the bounds of political citizenship, a process of collective persuasion that would have to reach a critical point before legal change could unfold. Sympathy would have to trump interest. The first halting steps toward extending the revolutionary settlement to people of color were being taken in the state of New York, but in Columbia County this would be particularly contested. The struggle to abolish slavery in the 1790s reveals the limits of a politics of sympathy and sensibility in this county and in the mid-Hudson region in which it lay.

Despite the best efforts of the popular assemblymen from the border hill towns, Matthew Adgate and Jacob Ford, the antislavery initiative of 1785 had fallen short. In the ratification year, change seemed on the horizon. After several years of stalemate, the legislature had passed a ban on the exportation of slaves out of the state in the spring of 1788, and newspaper editors along the upper Hudson saw change in the air. Readers of the monthly magazines published in New York and Philadelphia, such as Noah Webster's *American Magazine* that Stoddard advertised in 1787, would frequently have encountered essays on race and slavery, but they were less frequent in local news-papers. In the late summer of 1788 the upper Hudson printers apparently decided to bring this magazine content to their weekly papers. In May and June, Stoddard in Hudson and John Babcock in Lansingburgh published a few British critiques of the slave trade, the 1788 anti-exportation law, and an extract from William Cowper's antislavery poem, "The Task."

Then, following the federal ratification in Poughkeepsie and the celebra-tory parade in Albany, where Stoddard and Babcock marched with Charles R. Webster as representatives of the printers' trade, there was an explosion of material both informative and sentimental on the issue of slavery. On Au-gust 25 Webster devoted two columns in his *Albany Journal,* composed for the surrounding counties, to the proceedings of the Scots Presbyterian General Assembly and the British House of Commons on the slave trade. From the middle of August into September, Stoddard in the *Hudson Weekly Gazette* printed an account of the new antislavery society in Philadelphia, which, turning "their attention to every species of slavery," was concerned about the enslavement of American sailors on the "Algerine" coast, a subject of some anxiety among Hudson's sailors and shippers. He printed a report on the efforts of the New York Manumission Society to establish a school for the children of freed slaves, more news on the British slave trade debate, and the rescue of free blacks kidnapped in Boston and sold into slavery in the West Indies. One of the rescuers, "a sensible fellow, and a free-mason," had used his Masonic connections to secure their freedom.[44]

John Babcock in the Lansingburgh *Federal Herald* was probably the most assiduous in his efforts, publishing a stream of essays and poems on slavery throughout the fall of 1788. In his first two September issues, immediately following his final description of the parade celebrating the Constitution in New York City, Babcock printed a remarkable account of "a poor African . . . on the fertile banks of the Mohawk." "Faint and weary with toil," his wife murdered by slaveholders, he had "experienced a life of sorrow"; his "transient hopes" of freedom were "blasted," since "the council of this state have deter-mined that we shall continue slaves." Dissuaded from suicide, "he spoke," the white writer noted, "with a sensibility that surprised me." Later that month it was a long poem on the "distresses which the inhabitants of *Guinea* experi-ence at the loss of their children to the slave trade"; the following June it was a graphic description of a slave muzzle. And in October and November Stod-dard, Babcock, and Nicholas Powers in the Poughkeepsie *Country Journal* all published various excerpts from William Cowper's new poem, "The Negro's Complaint." Stoddard closed with the "Negro" admonishing white slave-holders, "Prove you have human feelings, Ere you proudly question ours!"[45]

Antislavery sentiment and argument could also be found in the printers' bookshops. By August 1789 Stoddard was advertising copies of Thomas Clarkson's *Substance of the Evidence . . . on the Slave-Trade,* published that same year in London; he carried this volume down to the end of the 1790s. In July 1799 he put into the *Gazette* a notice of Mungo Park's newly published *Travels in the Interior Districts of Africa,* highlighting black scholarship in Arabic; William Wilson had a copy by 1801. More important, Part III of Noah Webster's *Grammatical Institute,* available in Hudson by 1786 and used in the region's schools at least into the end of the next decade, contained a long excerpt from Thomas Day's 1776 London letter on slavery. Day, an associate of Joseph Priestley and an English sympathizer of the American Revolution, placed slavery in a class of human behavior tending "to interrupt the personal security of individuals, or deprive them of those things which they have acquired by their industry." Stoddard's 1795 edition of William Enfield's *Speaker* included a more sentimental piece, "Liberty and Slavery," by Laurence Sterne.[46]

Handed from child to child, these materials were put to use in the public sphere. The debating society in Hudson tackled the slave trade in 1786. Eleven years later, in the winter of 1797, the young men of a Polemical Society upriver at Schaghticoke struggled with the question, Whether "the practice of slavery be considered human or inhuman?" With some older men admitted as spectators, the "subject was warmly espoused on both sides." "The discussions were lengthly, and the arguments forcible." The vote condemned the slave trade, fourteen to four. At Union College in 1801 William Wilson's eldest son Alexander was assigned the oration topic "Is domestic slavery justifiable on the principles of morality and the good of the state?" An undated school exercise perhaps written by one of his siblings dissected the legal grounds for slavery: captivity, self-sale, and birth.[47]

Probably the most dramatic expression of antislavery thought in the county was written into Peter Van Schaack's correspondence with John C. Wynkoop in Kingston on the eve of the 1792 election. George Clinton's supporters were using Federalist John Jay's association with the New York Manumission Society to turn slaveholding voters to the Clinton ticket. Van Schaack, a college friend of John Jay, shared his abolitionist sentiments. While Federalist Wynkoop, in heavily Clintonian and slaveholding Ulster County, had given up on the contest, Van Schaack, reporting from Kinderhook, was more optimistic.

The manumission business is here as with you made an engine of to tarnish the illustrious character of Mr. Jay, but I trust its pernicious effects will in great measure be defeated. People are already coming to their senses and feel the impropriety of opposing a man so unexceptionable upon grounds so questionable at least, if not wicked. They consider that if it should really be true that they should not have an absolute right to convert a part of God's rational creatures into Brutes.

Van Schaack knew something of slavery: he held three slaves in his household in 1790, and four in 1800. But he saw the prospect for emancipation—gradual if not immediate—gaining ground in Kinderhook.

As to the Injustice of Slavery I presume that none among you is so hardened as to deny it; as to the Inexpediency of a general manumission some worthy Characters among us maintain it with some force of argument, but I do not find any who do not contemplate a gradual manumission as a desirable object.

Reaching back into recent revolutionary history, Van Schaack teased his friend in Kingston from the perspective of a former loyalist.

I hope the County of Ulster and especially the ancient town of Kingston is not less enlightened than the little Village of Kinderhook; and that the Whigs will not have to receive lessons of Liberty from the Tories. But this would not be the only paradox arising out of this subject for while slavery can have no Existence in the *Venal and corrupt* Island of Great Britain, it is cherished and advocated in the free country of America: thus while the Americans invite the slavish Europeans to quit their native country and repose in the sunshine of Liberty here; the unfortunate Africans have to fly from this free country to regain their liberty in England where a free-born American cannot so much as breathe.

But Van Schaack's comments also painted a darker picture of the attitudes of his slaveholding neighbors in Kinderhook.

Some indeed there are whose avarice induces them to deny "that these Creatures so black and with such flat noses" are part of the Human Species and these I suppose will by and by trace up their origin to a different source from that of our first Parents. Paradise reproves that Noah would not admit such creatures into the Ark. Minds like these will easily be brought to conclude that the poor black wretches are not contemplated by the Supreme being in the Decalogue and particularly that it would be no transgression of the Sixth Commandment to destroy one of them any more than to slaughter a Bullock. I really do not see how these consequences can be avoided by those who maintain the legitimacy of Slavery.

Clearly, a pseudoscientific racism was emerging in the villages and farms of Columbia County and providing a potent barrier to the working of human sympathy.[48]

That April John Jay swept the city of Hudson, 252–22, but only narrowly took Van Schaack's Kinderhook, 156–124. Otherwise, Clinton won the county by more than 2–1, the high point of Clintonian politics in Columbia. Some of this Clinton vote certainly rested in his new coalition with the Livingstons, but some might well have rested in slaveholders' anxieties about their property. The truth was, despite the play of antislavery sentiment in the print public sphere, there was great resistance to emancipation in Columbia County and elsewhere along the Hudson River. Indeed, the high tide of antislavery activism had already crested, and, as the state painfully moved toward the most limited abolition of slavery, actors in the deliberative domain in Columbia County did all that they could to slow the process.[49]

The actors in the persuasive domain also seem to have tempered their zeal for the antislavery cause after their burst of enthusiasm in the wake of federal ratification. Certainly Stoddard did continue to place items in the *Gazette* that would turn one's thoughts to questions of racial bondage: in 1790 the formation of the Society of the Friends of the Blacks in revolutionary Paris, in 1791 an extract from John Ledyard's voyage up the Nile, in 1793 an advertisement for Phillis Wheatley's poetry, in 1797 items on the slave trade, in 1799 extracts from Mungo Park's travels, the regular inclusion of "Clarkson on Slavery" in his long lists of books for sale. But throughout the decade these hints of antislavery sentiment were counterbalanced by the steady flow of advertisements of slaves for sale and notices of runaway slaves.[50]

But in the early 1790s unfolding events in the French West Indies, which were of particular importance to Hudson's sailors, began to paint a picture, not of racial harmony, but of racial violence. In November 1791, in the same issue with the governor's proclamation against the Hillsdale rioters, Stoddard published the conclusion of the recent agreement between "the white citizens of Port au Prince and the citizens of colour"; by the following March he was printing reports of fighting and massacres in Haiti. The vicious struggles in the islands would be fare in the region's papers throughout the decade, pushing aside the sentimental pieces. And these distant dangers had local echoes in late 1792 and 1793, perhaps inspired by news from Haiti arriving with ships in the island trade. First, in November 1792, Colonel Cornelius D. Wynkoop, a distant cousin of Van Schaack's friend in Kingston, was murdered by an angry slave. Then, a year later, the city of Albany narrowly escaped destruction by fire at the hands of several blacks, possibly part of a wider plot, given the copycat fires that plagued the city in the months following. In Albany, printer

Charles R. Webster of the *Albany Gazette* was called to the stand to testify against one of the accused slaves. Three years later a Hudson sea captain was murdered by a slave.[51]

Writing in March 1792, Van Schaack had felt secure in the face of West Indian violence.

> One would imagine that the present tragical scenes in the West Indies would be an awful admonition . . . , scenes which by-the-by have been predicted long since by those who have opposed this horrid practice. . . . I wish this may not prove a presage to our Southern neighbours.

Van Schaack hoped that "the laudable exertion of the Quakers" meant "that something like this does not also threaten us." But, in fact, the Quakers' antislavery exertions had not achieved much and had recently been given a serious setback. After failing to pass a gradual emancipation law in 1785, the legislature banned the export of enslaved persons from the state of New York. But in 1790 even this limited advance was compromised. Matthew Clarkson, a member of the society seated from New York City, introduced a new bill for gradual abolition in January, which was narrowly rejected. In Columbia the division over Clarkson's bill was between the Manor and the new Yankee settlements: John Livingston, whose brother Walter had opposed the 1785 gradual abolition bill, opposed Clarkson's initiative, which was supported by Ezekiel Gilbert of Hudson and James Savage of Canaan. But even these Yankee votes turned a month later, when they supported a bill introduced by an Ulster representative to permit the export of slaves who had been convicted of crime.[52]

Blocked in 1790, antislavery advocates abandoned their legislative effort for six years. In the 1795 session the issue of race had reemerged with a motion on the state school bill to support the Manumission Society's school for free black children in New York; Republican Elisha Jenkins of Hudson voted to support the provision, against the majority in the assembly. In November, after the passage of the school act and election of John Jay, the Manumission Society drew up a new petition to the legislature. The following January James Watson of New York, perhaps acting on the request of Jay, introduced a bill for gradual abolition, which the house agreed to consider. But, when the bill came up for consideration, the house voted first that children of slaves would not be born free, and then voted that emancipation without compensation would violate the property rights of slaveholders — interest here trumping sympathy. Then the legislation stalled. Again, the majority of the Columbia delegation was proslavery. The county vote divided between "Yorker" and "Yankee" sections: the four representatives from Kinderhook,

Livingston Manor, Claverack, and Clermont voting in the interests of slaveholders, those from Yankee Hillsdale and Canaan for emancipation. But even Colonel Benjamin Birdsall of Hillsdale, after four antislavery votes, voted to require slaveholders' compensation. While the progress in the abolition effort would develop with the redistribution of representation toward new frontier regions, the doubling of representation in Columbia County in 1791 had only doubled its proslavery vote.[53]

In the next few years, as the state moved toward enacting emancipation, Columbia's legislative defense of slavery would intensify in the face of a slowly emerging consensus for abolition. In 1797 antislavery efforts turned to the senate, which throughout the session delayed consideration of an abolition bill. After championing the cause of prisons and criminal reform in the 1796 session, Ambrose Spencer of Hudson voted with the minority to keep abolition on the agenda; he was opposed by his nemesis Samuel Jones as well as by Peter Silvester of Kinderhook. Spencer would repeat this vote in April 1798, after the house had established a new consensus and passed a bill for gradual emancipation.[54]

As the assembly was seated on January 2, 1798, for the twenty-first session, the basic decision had been made: there would be a bill for gradual emancipation, based on votes in the assembly from the new counties in the Mohawk Valley, the southern tier, and the Champlain country, recently settled by migrating New Englanders. When abolition finally did pass, it would be driven by a bipartisan coalition of western Federalists and western and downstate Republicans, and opposed by mid-Hudson legislators, most strongly slaveholding Republicans. Abolition would be enacted by Jayite Federalists and reformist Republicans like Clinton and Spencer, and opposed by men of interest, traditionalists within the Republican ranks. Where popular Columbia assemblymen like Adgate and Frisbie had voted for emancipation in 1785, sentiments were quite different in 1798 and 1799, and the new antireform majority of the county's Republican assemblymen, elected as and by slaveholders, worked assiduously to block change of any kind.

In 1798 the issue was who would bear the cost: the slaveholders, the state, or the slaves themselves. The shape of opinion in the house was measured on February 3, when a bill guaranteeing former Quaker manumissions that had not met the exact standards of the law passed by a vote of 45–33. The majority Republican delegation from Columbia established its posture with this vote, voting 5–1 against the measure; Elisha Jenkins, representing Quaker constituents in Hudson, was the sole dissenter. Several days later the abolition bill was introduced and sent to a committee on a vote of 59–34.[55]

Then in four days in late March the assembly hammered out a new compromise on slavery: slaves born after July 4, 1799, would be free after terms of service, slaveholders would not be compensated, slaveholders would be required to register all slave births, and the towns of these births would be responsible for any child paupers among the freed slaves. Members of the Columbia delegation worked furiously to improve the outcome for slaveholders, as part of a coalition including representatives from Albany, Ulster, and Queens counties. Killian Hogeboom of Claverack introduced motions to require special taxes on free blacks to pay for paupers and, that failing, to make any paupers the responsibility of the state at large. On the question of the length of service required of slave men born after July 4, 1799, Peter I. Vosburgh of Kinderhook proposed thirty-five years, and Hogeboom proposed thirty; the house settled on twenty-eight. When the final vote on the bill was taken, John C. Hogeboom of Claverack, the chair of the drafting committee, demanded a roll call, seconded by Samuel Ten Broeck of Clermont. Of the county representatives voting in the slaveholding interest, only Caleb Benton of Hillsdale, now essentially a Livingston minion, stayed quiet through the proceedings. Elisha Jenkins of the city of Hudson voted consistently to advance the progress of emancipation on the best possible terms for the slaves.[56]

On March 24, two days before the final vote, after the struggles over paupers and service, Samuel Ten Broeck had written to William Wilson in Clermont about the Republican nominations for the April 1798 election and to tell him that the abolition bill had essentially passed the assembly. He was unhappy about the tax burden imposed on the slaveholding towns. "Whether it will pass the Senate I cannot say," he told Wilson. It seems likely that he had a pretty good idea that it would not, and ten days later, indeed, the senate refused to take up the bill that year. The question then rolled over to the 1799 session, where the assembly passed a new bill by early February. Killian Hogeboom, Samuel Ten Broeck (who again moved that the bill be rejected), and his cousin Peter of Claverack all voted against the bill; Elisha Gilbert of Canaan and John and Charles McKinstry of Hillsdale all voted for abolition. The house had already passed a bill reforming imprisonment for debt and in mid-March would vote to abolish it, with the near-unanimous support of the Columbia representatives.[57]

The senate rejected the bill to end imprisonment for debt in short order, but Hudson's Ambrose Spencer took up both the debtor reform bill and the gradual emancipation bill, both of which had been languishing for weeks. Spencer intervened in the debate on emancipation with a motion to forbid the manumission of slaves who were "superannuated and unable to gain a livelihood by labor," which failed; he voted with the majority to reverse the assembly and make paupers the responsibility of the entire state, as Ten Broeck had hoped the year before. By early April both bills had become law as well as a measure to raise a direct tax to support the state's common schools.[58]

In 1802, and finally in 1804, New York's gradual emancipation law was further refined; acting to reduce expenditures, the state support for free black paupers was abolished. Again the majority of Columbia's delegation, led by Samuel Ten Broeck and including Martin Van Buren's half brother, James I. Van Alen, did what they could to protect the interests of slaveholders. In the senate Spencer took the opposite side in 1802, but in 1804 he was replaced by John C. Hogeboom, who voted to preserve the state support for the costs of free black paupers.[59]

So ended Columbia's role in the main phase of the abolition of slavery in the state of New York. Thirteen years later, at the urging of Governor Daniel D. Tompkins, the legislature set July 4, 1827, as the final date of emancipation for all slaves in the state. But, in the county of Columbia, the persuasive language of sensibility and sympathy had failed to assemble majority opinion for abolition. Increasingly, the representatives and senators chosen by the voters of the county worked to slow the arrival of emancipation and then to minimize its cost for slaveholders. Here persuasion in the public sphere could not overcome the entrenched interests of slavery.

A CENSUS OF SLAVERY AND FREEDOM IN 1800: THE VARYING INFLUENCE OF THE PUBLIC SPHERE

It might well be argued that interest drove the votes on emancipation among Columbia's legislators and electorate. Non-slaveholders in Columbia County, as throughout the state, especially in the new settlements to the west and north, had no interest in paying for the support of former slaves, old and young, who would be turned out onto the roads by manumission. The antislavery legislators in Columbia came almost universally from the new Yankee towns of Canaan, Hillsdale, and Hudson, where slavery was much less entrenched; the pro-slaveholder legislators to the same degree were from Clermont, Livingston, Claverack, and Kinderhook, where slaves had long been a fundamental part of the agricultural economy (see Table 16). The legislators themselves held different numbers of slaves. The sixteen in the proslavery group had held forty-two slaves in 1790 and by 1800 held seventy-eight. John and Walter Livingston together held twenty-one in 1800, the Hogebooms sixteen, and Samuel Ten Broeck and James I. Van Alen twelve each. The antislavery legislators had far fewer slaves, sixteen in 1790 and fifteen in 1800. There were, then, direct stakes involved in the resolution of slavery in Columbia County.

But, if interests were so obvious, there are suggestions that other forces

TABLE 16. *Antislavery and Proslavery Legislators from Columbia County, 1785–1802*

| | Voting Record | | | |
| | Antislavery | | Proslavery | |
	No.	Proportion	No.	Proportion
Individual legislators				
Federalist	2	14%	4	25%
Republican	12	86%	12	75%
Freemasons	8	57%	5	31%
Participants in turnpikes or banks	3	21%	8	50%
Representatives of Kinderhook,				
Claverack, Livingston or Clermont	1	7%	15	94%
Representatives of Canaan, Hillsdale,				
or Hudson	13	93%	1	6%
Book subscribers	11	78%	8	50%
Imprints subscribed to	17		12	
TERMS SERVED				
Federalists	2	10%	7	28%
Republicans	17	90%	18	72%
Freemasons	13	68%	6	24%
Participants in turnpikes or banks	4	21%	24	40%
Representatives of Kinderhook,				
Claverack, Livingston, or				
Clermont	1	5%	24	96%
Representatives of Canaan, Hillsdale,				
or Hudson	18	95%	1	4%
Book subscribers	15	79%	17	68%

Note: Average valuation in 1800 of antislavery-voting legislators was $4,478; of proslavery legislators, $6,080.

were also at work. The antislavery legislators were not completely devoid of an interest in slavery. Two had a significant number of slaves in 1800: Charles McKinstry held five, and Ambrose Spencer himself held three. Each of these men was voting against his simple financial interests, but both also had deep connections to the emerging public sphere in which the language and politics of sensibility and sympathy were unfolding. Both were also Freemasons, an identity that, after geography, most sharply distinguished antislavery from proslavery legislators. To a large degree the division over slavery was one of ethnoreligious and historical experience, dividing households of the old "Yorker" Dutch and German traditions from households of various in-migrant English-speaking traditions. But engagement with, or disengagement from, the institutions of the new public sphere, with the various energies of change and reform running through it in the 1790s, also shaped positions on slavery in the 1790s. Columbia's pro-slaveholder politics was rooted in the large proportion of households where English was not the primary language, which were in many ways insulated from or resisted the print and association of the public sphere and the culture of sentiment and sensibility that it carried. Conversely, antislavery commitments encompassed both the improving ethos of the riverfront city and the populist militance of the eastern hill towns.

The legislators provide one window onto the county's commitment or opposition to slavery. The county's households themselves, making private political decisions in their slaveholding and their employment of free people of color, provide a second snapshot (as measured by the federal census and tax valuations of 1800, a year after passage of the gradual abolition law), set against their many civil affiliations.[60]

The federal censuses of 1790 and 1800 record the beginnings of change. Slavery was already beginning to decline in Columbia County in 1800, falling to 1,500 slaves from 1,623 in 1790, and free people of color increased from 55 to almost 500. In 1800, Columbia's slaves were held in 530 white households, comprising one-eighth of the taxpayers (and one-tenth of the census-enumerated households); two-thirds to three-quarters of these slaves were held in households assessed at more than $1,500 and were particularly concentrated in the towns of Kinderhook, Claverack, and Clermont. Columbia's small but growing body of free people of color was distributed among three different kinds of households. Just fewer than one-half lived in slaveholding households; probably recently manumitted, they might well have been living with family members still enslaved. The other half of Columbia's free people of color lived in households for which there was no recorded slavery as of 1800. A smaller group, about 100 people, lived in twenty-two free black

TABLE 17. *Columbia County Households, Slaves, and Free Blacks, 1800*

	Households			
	Rated at over $1,500 in the 1800 Valuation	On the 1800 Valuation or the 1800 Census	Free Black on the 1800 Census	Total
Total Slaves in				
White households with slaves only	657 63%	339 73%		996 66%
White households with both slaves and free blacks	380 37%	124 27%		504 34%
White and black households with free blacks and no slaves	0	0		0
Other white households with no resident blacks	0	0		0
1800 total (households on census and valuation)	1,037 100%	463 100%		1,500 100%
1800 total (valuation only)	1,037	321		1,358
Total Free Blacks in				
White households with slaves only	0	0		0
White households with both slaves and free blacks	148 63%	45 32%		193 40%
White and black households with free blacks and no slaves	86 37%	97 68%	104 100%	287 60%
Other white households with no resident blacks	0	0		0

TABLE 17. *Continued*

	Households			
	Rated at over $1,500 in the 1800 Valuation	On the 1800 Valuation or the 1800 Census	Free Black on the 1800 Census	Total
Total Free Blacks in (continued)				
1800 total (households on census and valuation)	234 100%	142 100%	104 100%	480 100%
1800 total (valuation only)	234	98	23	355
Total Households				
White households with slaves only	265 25%	213 5%		478 9%
White households with both slaves and free blacks	95 9%	38 1%		133 2%
White and black households with free blacks and no slaves	52 5%	76 2%	22	150 3%
Other white households with no resident blacks	669 62%	4,086 93%		4,755 86%
1800 total (households on census and valuation)	1,081 100%	4,413 100%	22	5,516 100%
1800 total (valuation only)	1,081	3,072	6	4,159

Note: Census households estimated from the 1790 census ratio of 6.43 total population per household.

households, 13 located in Hudson city. A larger group, almost 150 people, lived with non-slaveholding white families.[61]

What were the conditions of freedom for these people, in the year following the act for gradual emancipation? Clearly it was a matter of a gradation of liberty, rather than pure presence or absence. The act itself freed only the children of slaves born after July 4, 1799, and required that they serve lengthy indentures. These children would have been recorded as free, and at least some of the free blacks in the slaveholding households must have been these infants, born into a halfway house between freedom and slavery. Even if they had been manumitted already, older blacks were often required by their acts of manumission to serve out terms of indenture as part of a system of compensation. Such terms worked to the benefit of slaveholders, as they tied former slaves to service and good behavior, subject to civil action. Thus many free blacks living in slaveholding households must have been bound under these indentures. Many of the free people living in non-slaveholding households likely were also working out indenture arrangements, hired out from slaveholding households.[62]

Unfortunately, only the most tangential hints of such arrangements survive, hidden behind the census record of slavery and freedom. Thus a slave named Coeradt Maass listed in Hudson in 1800 was recorded in the census, perhaps hired out, but living alone. In the same year, Judah Paddock, master of the ship *Oswego,* left the port of Hudson for Ireland and Cape Verde with a crew of twelve, including "black man Jack of Hudson" and "a black man Sam of Philadelphia." Jack was apparently part of Paddock's household, since, when they were wrecked on the Barbary Coast, he made a special effort to save some Irish fabric for Mrs. Paddock, swearing, "My mistress shall wear these gowns yet." Weeks later, the shipwrecked company having been captured by Arabs, Jack and Sam were taken into the internal African slave trade: "The poor negroes wept bitterly, and, for our own part, we were sorely afflicted with the parting," Paddock wrote. "We never saw them more."[63]

A Freemason, and recently a subscriber to the Albany edition of Rousseau's *Dissertation on Political Economy,* Paddock wrote in the language of sympathy, but his sentiments might have had a wider currency. He was from one of the Nantucket Quaker families who settled Hudson, though he himself was apparently not an active Quaker. The Hudson Quaker households employed a particularly noticeable concentration of free people of color and held virtually no slaves; among them Peter Barnard's rather poor household stands out in housing both a slave and a free black. Peter's wife, Hannah Barnard, a noted leader in the Hudson Meeting, was on a celebrated mission to advance a peace testimony in England, and there had to have been special conditions tied to the slave in their household. Fifteen years later we have a hint at the indenture system, when George Holcomb, a young farmer in Stephentown, went down to Peleg Spencer's in Canaan to hire a black man named Solomon, noted for his knowledge in distilling. Spencer let Holcomb "engage" his "hired negro" to still brandy from cider for fifty cents a day, with "extra wages" for Solomon. The "black boy" whom a Methodist itinerant encountered raking by the Columbia Turnpike in Hillsdale in 1807 (and questioned on the state of his soul) also might have been working off an indenture of some sort. In Albany in June 1817, George Holcomb "fetched a free black boy home to live with me" in Stephentown; this "Negro John" might also have been working off an indenture.[64]

Even if they were working off indentures, however, free persons of color living in non-slaveholding households were necessarily removed from the traditions of slavery. Across Columbia County the social geography of these people was markedly different from that of their peers living in slaveholding circumstances. More than two-thirds of the free blacks living in free households were located in the Yankee towns of Hudson, Hillsdale, and Canaan. Importantly, these free households were not old slaveholding families; of the 903 slaves held in 1790 by families recorded in 1800, only 11 had been in the free households of 1800, versus 892 in the slave households (see Table 18). The free blacks living in slave households were concentrated in the older, Dutch-dominated towns along the river, particularly Kinderhook and Claverack, and in households where slaveholding was a tradition. We cannot begin to recover the experience of Columbia's free people of color living with non-slaveholding whites in 1800. Many must have been hired on indentures, but many must have been employed as free laborers; perhaps Solomon, living in Canaan at Peleg Spencer's, had moved from one status to another. Whatever tensions and coercions ran through these early nonslave interracial arrangements, they marked a significant departure from former institutions.[65]

The state and federal surveys of the county in 1800 reveal the sociology of slavery and freedom in Columbia at this transition. Here, to control for household wealth, it seems best to focus on the 1,081 households assessed at higher than fifteen hundred dollars, roughly the top three deciles of the valuation, who owned or lived with the majority of Columbia's black population.[66]

Looking at investment in slavery itself, a familiar pattern emerges when we compare the wealth and slaveholdings of distinct groups of households taxed at more than fifteen hundred dollars (see Table 19). The great landlord Livingston and the Van Rensselaer families, the proslavery legislators, the pew-holders in the Kinderhook Dutch church, the members of the Washington Lodge in Johnstown on the Manor, directors of Hudson banks living in Clav-

TABLE 18. *Slaveholding in 1790 by White Households on the 1800 Valuation and 1800 Census*

	No. of Households in 1800	White Households, 1800, That Had Slaves in 1790	No. of Slaves in 1790
White Households on 1800 Census Rated at More than $1,500 on the 1800 Valuation			
White households with slaves only	265	101 38.1%	374
White households with both slaves and free blacks	95	45 47.4%	193
White households with free blacks and no slaves	52	4 7.7%	8
White households with no resident blacks	669	46 6.9%	115
All Other White Households on the 1800 Census or the 1800 Valuation			
White households with slaves only	213	41 19.2%	100
White households with both slaves and free blacks	38	7 18.4%	15
White households with free blacks and no slaves	76	2 2.6%	3
White households with no resident blacks	4,085	49 1.2%	95
Total	5,493	295 5.4%	903

erack and Livingston, all stand out as the most-committed slaveholders in the county. Dutch farmers in Hudson owned far more slaves than their English-origin counterparts or than artisans and merchants in Hudson. The investors in the Susquehannah Company and the Genesee Company of Adventurers were strong slaveholders. Particularly striking, slaveholding was quite strong among the men who subscribed to special orders of books printed in New York and Albany, with the sole exception of the subscribers to Rousseau's *Dissertation*. Apparently slaveholding and book subscription both appealed to the same sense of personal assertion. So, too, the known Federalist and Republican committeemen and candidates, in aggregate and relative to their fellow townsmen, tended toward higher levels of slaveholding. Only Hud-

TABLE 19. *Slaveholding and Property: Columbia County Households Assessed at Greater than $1,500 in 1800*

	No. of Households	Average Assessed Property	No. of Slaves	Property per Slave
County total	**1,081**	**$2,854**	**1,037**	**$2,975**
Republicans total	120	$3,556	190	$2,246
Federalists total	147	$3,901	286	$2,005
Proslavery legislators	13	$6,893	66	$1,358
Antislavery legislators	12	$4,428	10	$5,313
Freemasons total	105	$2,862	72	$4,174
Washington Lodge, Livingston	7	$2,485	16	$1,087
Other Freemasons	98	$2,889	56	$5,056
Turnpike incorporators	72	$4,634	131	$2,547
Bank directors and cashiers	32	$5,170	68	$2,433
Directors, Claverack and Livingston	8	$8,695	55	$1,265
Livingston families	12	$8,503	63	$1,620
Van Rensselaer Family	7	$5,958	34	$1,227
Genesee Adventurers	18	$8,971	75	$2,153
Susquehannah Company	7	$5,980	29	$1,444
All book subscribers	91	$5,365	239	$2,043
Hudson city	**123**	**$3,414**	**90**	**$4,666**
Republicans	18	$3,274	10	$5,894
Federalists	19	$3,525	16	$4,186
Dutch farmers	34	$3,653	46	$2,700
English farmers	21	$3,751	5	$15,756
Merchants	21	$4,626	14	$6,939
Artisans	20	$2,268	4	$11,340
Esquires	4	$4,312	6	$2,874
Library Society	9	$3,564	2	$16,036
Hudson Lodge	17	$3,374	11	$5,215
Fire companies	12	$2,780	1	$33,359
Mechanics Society	7	$2,125	1	$14,872
Quakers	9	$4,210	0	
Presbyterians	7	$4,758	7	$4,758
Episcopalians	6	$4,038	6	$4,038
Bank directors and cashiers	24	$3,995	13	$7,375
Turnpike incorporators	23	$4,216	28	$3,463

TABLE 19. *Continued*

	No. of House-holds	Average Assessed Property	No. of Slaves	Property per Slave
Canaan (excluding Shakers)	**167**	**$2,664**	**27**	**$16,480**
Republicans	14	$3,229	4	$11,302
Federalists	18	$3,907	14	$5,024
Canaan Democratic Society	4	$4,410	2	$8,819
Mawighnunk settlement, 1800	29	$3,142	5	$18,225
Not Mawighnunk settlement	138	$2,564	22	$16,083
Freemasons	34	$3,194	9	$12,065
Hillsdale	**102**	**$2,614**	**34**	**$7,842**
Republicans	17	$2,652	5	$9,016
Federalists	9	$4,920	13	$3,406
Petitioners against Van Rensselaer title, 1789	30	$2,913	13	$6,723
Occupants, Van Rensselaer settlement, 1804	22	$2,355	11	$4,711
Chatham	**133**	**$2,691**	**100**	**$3,579**
Hill town[a] Congregationalists	44	$3,159	15	$9,266
Hill town Baptists	15	$2,439	0	
Hill town Methodists	4	$3,980	4	$3,980
Kinderhook	**153**	**$3,550**	**317**	**$1,713**
Kinderhook Dutch Reformed pewholders, 1795	52	$4,659	173	$1,400
Claverack	**169**	**$2,907**	**241**	**$2,038**
Livingston	**185**	**$2,243**	**147**	**$2,823**
Republicans	10	$3,325	19	$1,750
Federalists	23	$3,456	52	$1,528
Livingston families	10	$7,259	51	$1,423
Petitioners against Livingston title, 1795	38	$1,984	9	$8,377
Not petitioners, not Livingston families	137	$1,949	87	$3,069
Lutheran and Dutch Reformed deacons and elders	19	$1,941	5	$7,374
Washington Lodge Masons	6	$2,515	13	$1,161
Other Freemasons in Livingston	12	$2,040	5	$4,897
Clermont	**24**	**$3,678**	**52**	**$1,697**
Germantown	**25**	**$2,313**	**29**	**$1,994**

[a]Hill towns include Chatham, Hillsdale, and Canaan.

son and Hillsdale Republicans had smaller slaveholdings than their towns at large.[67]

Among this relatively prosperous group rated at fifteen hundred dollars or more, householders who owned no slaves in 1800 had a very different profile from the slaveholders'. The Hudson Quakers and Baptists in the hill towns of Canaan and Hillsdale stand out as entirely avoiding slaveholding, followed by the known members of the hill town Congregational churches. These would be the core constituencies of abolition in the coming decades. But close behind them were two rather different groups whose slaveholding behavior is rather less easy to predict. *First* and foremost, the members of the associations of the emerging urban public sphere in Hudson—the fire companies, the Library Society, the Mechanics Society, the Hudson Lodge—all avoided slaveholding. Indeed, Freemasons across the county, even if we include the slaveholding Masons of Livingston Manor's Washington Lodge, ranked well below the county average for slaveholding. *Second,* and particularly surprisingly, the men who struggled with landlords and patentholders in the 1780s and 1790s were weakly invested in slavery, relative to wealth. The Hillsdale petitioners of 1789, the Livingston petitioners of 1795, the Mawighnunk-Canaan occupants of 1800, all ranked low on the spectrum of slaveholding groups across the county; the signers of Petrus Pulver's 1795 petition were the least likely of any group, relative to wealth, to own slaves on the Manor of Livingston. All three of these anti-landlord groups ranked below the antislavery legislators themselves in this leading stratum of wealth.

Equally important, most of these same categories of white households, involved in different ways in the public sphere, also stand out among the fifty-two *free households,* white households that included free people of color but no slaves (see Table 20). Hudson Quakers led the list of free households in 1800: fourteen free blacks lived in six Quaker households that held no slaves. Similarly, all of the free blacks living with members of the fire companies, the Mechanics Society, and the Hillsdale and Canaan Baptist churches lived in such free households. So, also, two-thirds of the free blacks living with the land petitioners in Hillsdale and in Livingston and with the Hillsdale occupants in the final settlement with the Van Rensselaers were living in non-slaveholder households. Particularly striking for their distribution, the county's Masonic households also stand out as places where free people of color lived without the immediate daily presence of slavery.

There were some very familiar names among the heads of these fifty-two free households. In Hudson, they included merchants Thomas Jenkins, a founder of the city and the bank, and David Lawrence, who both turned from Federalist to Republican with Ambrose Spencer. Elisha Jenkins, Spen-

TABLE 20. *Residence of Free Blacks in White Households Assessed at More than $1,500, Columbia County, 1800*

	White Households				Free Blacks in Free Households
	Total	"Free"	Blacks in	Free Blacks in	
County total	**1,081**	**52 5%**	**1,271**	**234 18%**	**86 37%**
Republicans total	120	11 9%	243	63 25%	19 30%
Federalists total	147	9 6%	351	65 19%	14 22%
Proslavery legislators	13	0 0%	72	6 8%	0 0%
Antislavery legislators	12	1 8%	15	5 33%	1 20%
Freemasons total	105	14 13%	103	31 30%	21 68%
Washington Lodge, Livingston	7	0 0%	18	2 11%	0 0%
Other Freemasons	98	14 14%	85	29 34%	21 72%
Bank directors and cashiers	32	8 25%	99	31 31%	13 42%
Bank directors, Claverack and Livingston	8	0 0%	64	9 14%	0 0%
Turnpike incorporators	72	10 14%	174	43 25%	16 37%
Livingston families	12	0 0%	72	9 13%	0 0%
Van Rensselaer Family	7	0 0%	41	7 17%	0 0%
Genesee Adventurers	18	4 22%	90	15 17%	7 47%
Susquehannah Company	7	0 0%	31	2 6%	2 100%
All book subscribers	91	5 5%	279	40 14%	5 13%
Hudson city	**123**	**19 15%**	**149**	**59 40%**	**39 66%**
Republicans	18	4 22%	22	12 55%	7 58%
Federalists	19	3 16%	30	14 47%	6 43%
Dutch farmers	34	1 3%	55	9 16%	6 67%
English farmers	21	3 14%	10	5 50%	4 80%
Merchants	21	8 38%	39	25 64%	14 56%
Artisans	20	2 10%	8	4 50%	2 50%

TABLE 20. *Continued*

	White Households				
	Total	"Free"	Blacks in	Free Blacks in	Free Blacks in Free Households
Esquires	4	1 25%	8	2 25%	2 100%
Library Society	9	1 11%	5	3 60%	1 33%
Hudson Lodge	17	5 29%	23	12 52%	9 75%
Fire companies	12	6 50%	10	9 90%	9 100%
Mechanics Society	7	1 14%	4	3 75%	3 100%
Quakers	9	6 67%	14	14 100%	14 100%
Presbyterians	7	0 0%	11	4 36%	0 0%
Episcopalians	6	1 17%	8	2 25%	2 100%
Bank directors and cashiers	24	8 33%	35	22 63%	13 59%
Turnpike incorporators	23	6 26%	53	25 47%	11 44%
Canaan (excluding Shakers)	**167**	**4 2%**	**33**	**6 18%**	**4 67%**
Republicans	14	0 0%	4	0 0%	0 0%
Federalists	18	1 6%	15	1 7%	1 100%
Canaan Democratic Society	4	1 25%	3	1 33%	1 100%
Mawighnunk settlement, 1800	29	0 0%	5	0 0%	0 0%
Not Mawighnunk settlement	138	4 3%	28	6 21%	4 67%
Freemasons	34	3 9%	12	3 25%	3 100%
Hillsdale	**102**	**12 12%**	**60**	**26 43%**	**18 69%**
Republicans	17	3 18%	10	5 50%	4 80%
Federalists	9	1 11%	20	7 35%	1 14%
Petitioners against Van Rensselaer title, 1789	30	4 13%	25	12 48%	8 67%
Occupants, Van Rensselaer settlement, 1804	22	1 5%	14	3 21%	2 67%

TABLE 20. *Continued*

	White Households				Free Blacks in Free Households
	Total	"Free"	Blacks in	Free Blacks in	
Chatham	133	3 2%	121	21 17%	4 19%
Hill town[a] Congregationalists	44	5 11%	27	12 44%	7 58%
Hill town Baptists	15	1 7%	4	4 100%	4 100%
Hill town Methodists	4	1 25%	5	1 20%	1 100%
Kinderhook	153	4 3%	359	42 12%	6 14%
Kinderhook Dutch Reformed pew-holders, 1795	52	1 2%	195	22 11%	1 5%
Claverack	169	7 4%	300	59 20%	12 20%
Livingston	185	3 2%	147	12 8%	3 25%
Republicans	10	1 10%	21	2 10%	1 50%
Federalists	23	0 0%	55	3 5%	0 0%
Livingston families	10	0 0%	56	5 9%	0 0%
Petitioners against Livingston title, 1795	38	2 5%	12	3 25%	2 67%
Not 1795 petitioners, not Livingston family	137	1 1%	91	4 4%	1 25%
Lutheran and Dutch Reformed deacons and elders	19	0 0%	6	1 17%	0 0%
Washington Lodge Masons	6	0 0%	15	2 13%	0 0%
Other Freemasons in Livingston	12	1 8%	6	1 17%	1 100%
Clermont	24	0 0%	58	6 10%	0 0%
Germantown	25	0 0%	32	3 9%	0 0%

[a]Hill towns include Chatham, Hillsdale, and Canaan.

cerite and antislavery assemblyman, had owned a slave in 1790 but had no blacks, slave or free, living with him in 1800. Senator Ambrose Spencer himself, the leading opponent of the slaveholding interest, did have three slaves in his household in 1800, but this circumstance might have had its own story behind it, given that he had tried and failed to have a clause added to the 1799 law forbidding the manumission and abandonment of elderly "superannuated" slaves. In Claverack and Canaan there were distinct clusters of Freemasons among these heads of free households. In Claverack two young Esseltyne brothers, both Masons in Hudson since at least 1796, headed households with free blacks and no slaves; their older cousin Gabriel had some years before sent a slave girl to learn her letters at the Washington Seminary.[68]

In Hillsdale and in Livingston free householders included some of the leading figures in the resistance to the county's great landlord families. Ambrose Latting, recently a thorn in the side of Henry Livingston, had just died at the age of fifty: his widow, Joanna, a member of the East Hillsdale Baptist Church, headed a household that included four free blacks. William Tanner, the shoemaker in Green River who signed the 1789 petition, joined the Hudson Lodge, and led the Republican resistance to the Van Rensselaers early in the new century before helping to organize three different turnpikes, was also a free householder in 1800, living with two free people of color. And then there were the Birdsalls, Masons and Republican leaders. Colonel Benjamin Birdsall was from a Quaker family that had settled in eastern Dutchess in the 1750s; he had been disowned by the Oblong Monthly Meeting for his Revolutionary service. By 1800, after years of involvement in the Genesee Company and the resistance to the Van Rensselaers, his Quaker roots might have shaped his employment of a free black, rather than a slave, in 1800. And just to the south in the Copake neighborhood on the Manor, fully embroiled in a struggle with the Livingstons that would endure for more than another decade, Benjamin Birdsall, Jr., was also a free householder, employing one free black and no slaves.[69]

Again, it is impossible to penetrate the quality of experience in these interracial households where the traditional structures of slavery were falling away. It is entirely possible that the freed men and women in these households were working under extremely difficult conditions only marginally removed from slavery. Yet these experiences were in civil fact fundamentally different from slavery: their service was limited by civil contract and could not be transferred to their children. They were working in circumstances that would begin to allow them to accumulate sufficient property to achieve a purchase of minimal civil autonomy as independent householders. And, given the particular focus of this new form of interracial household in the orbits of both the web of public associations and the militant settlement struggles over land, it seems safe to argue that these engagements with the new forms of the public sphere were shaping a departure from the racial configurations of the past.

If a politics of sensibility, with its connotations of benevolence and improvement, even perfection, was born on the literary currents of the late-eighteenth-century public sphere, it did not prevail in this conservative region. The majority opinion in Columbia County, expressed in vote after vote for proslavery legislators in the late 1790s, was to slow or stall the abolition of slavery in the state of New York. But, among certain specific circles most closely engaged with this emerging public sphere and its prevailing culture of respectability, benevolence, and improvement, a new attitude toward race was incrementally taking shape. Among these specific households the sentimental language of abolition expressed in Cowper's "Negro's Complaint" might well have contributed a persuasive resonance to the leading edge of racial transformation in Columbia.

III

Politics and Exclusions

7

Party and Corruption

THE COLUMBIA JUNTO AND THE RISE OF
MARTIN VAN BUREN, 1799–1812

I had for some time before been entrusted with professional business, and, as a zealous politician, represented my county at the age of nineteen in a District Convention held at Troy, which nominated John P. Van Ness for Congress. . . .

So poor were both of us, that when I went to Troy to sustain his nomination, I had to borrow the amount necessary to defray my expences.

— Martin Van Buren, Sorrento, Italy, 1854

On the subject of the Merchant's Bank it is vain to expect silence. . . . Little was apprehended, twelve months ago, that a fallen faction, too small in our public councils to fear and respect, should in the very next legislature acquire an irresistible ascendancy. . . . How powerful, how irresistible, O gold, is thy influence. . . . Beware of bribery, beware of selling votes, and beware of bartering and trafficking with the public rights for money.

— Aristides, Hudson *Bee,* Apr. 23, 1805

The Feds undoubtedly will make a vast many votes — Our Friends at first startled at the proposition . . . [but] the spirit has extended through our ranks throughout the county . . . *we had no other course left but to meet them on their own ground* — I cordially despise the practice but I think under existing circumstances necessity directs us to it — we only neutralize the effects of their corrupt conduct.

— Martin Van Buren, Hudson, to De Witt Clinton, New York City, Apr. 19, 1810

Though he remembered it slightly differently a half century later, Martin Van Buren was about two months shy of his nineteenth birthday when he was sent from Kinderhook to the Republican meeting of electors in Troy in September 1801. He had already lived a life steeped in politics. His father's tavern, where he must have watched the sale of loyalist property in the summer of 1788, continued to host Republican meetings through the 1790s and into the new century. But the young Van Buren particularly remembered the embarrassment of being as shy of money as he was in age. The teenage son of a now less than prosperous tavernkeeper, he must have needed something to spend on his wardrobe, to say nothing of the stage fare required to make a respectable arrival in the village of Troy. If he was too poor to pay his way, his family was also too poor to send him out of town to clerk with a Republican lawyer. Apprenticing with Peter and Francis Silvester, Van Buren learned lessons in fashion as he endured the sneers of a local Federalist gentry whose animosity ran back to Kinderhook's Revolutionary divisions. When he returned from Troy, indeed, the Silvesters made their displeasure apparent, cutting him off from finishing his clerkship in their office. Promised support from the Van Nesses, Van Buren ventured on to clerk in New York City; by the time he passed the bar and returned to a Kinderhook partnership with his half brother, James I. Van Alen, he owed three hundred dollars to various creditors.[1]

In the coming decades Martin Van Buren would compensate for his humble origins. He would be known for his fastidiousness — even flashiness — in dress; not for nothing would he be known as the "Little Dandy." He was said to have attended the Columbia courts in a smart green coat, buff breeches, and white-topped riding boots; in the late 1820s he attended church in Rochester in a beige swallowtail coat, orange cravat, gray vest, and white duck trousers. At five foot, six inches, Van Buren's moderate height might have driven his clothing choices. But his consuming work at the presentation of respectability, perhaps not always successful, also spoke of his position in the county's political sociology. Van Buren was always conscious of his precarious place as a poor man's son in a rich man's world. Abraham Van Buren had not prospered, and Martin would be faced at the bar by men with university educations, often representing the interests of landed families desperately working to maintain their claim to aristocratic preeminence. Of any place in the early American republic, at least in its northern states, the culture of class in Columbia County came the closest to mirroring that of contemporary rural England, with its rentier gentry, living off an income produced by a dependent tenantry.[2]

But Columbia was a far more complex, contested place, with lowland Dutch freeholders, hill town Yankee squatters, and manor town German tenants challenging the rentier class. Van Buren's father and many of his freeholding neighbors in Kinderhook had joined with the Yankees in the popular politics of the Revolution. Van Buren's political creed ran back to the popular men — the Demos, as Henry Livingston had once called them — and he faced the Aristos in court and in the political arena. But Van Buren and his generation would forge a new political style between the extremes of Demo and Aristo, a pragmatic style of public life that empowered men of middling station by virtue of their bourgeois respectability. Quite literally, the material presentation of self and the printed representation of society, governed by conventions of respectability and civility, gave men like Van Buren authority in the public sphere.[3]

PARTY, FACTION, CORRUPTION

To confront the great rentier gentry, such rising men had to develop practices and patterns of cooperative organization, of partisan loyalty and coherence that by the mid-nineteenth century would comprise a particularly American vehicle of the routine expression of popular consent. In retirement in the 1850s, in his *Inquiry into the Origin and Course of Political Parties in the United States,* Van Buren recorded his interpretation of "the Civil Revolution of Eighteen Hundred." Opposition to the "money power" and "monarchical institutions" advanced by the Federalists "served to weld the members of the old Anti-Federal party and the Republicans . . . into a thorough union, which became permanent." Their guiding principle was the "safety of republican government," and their means "a steady adherence" to "a caucus system" that could realize the sovereignty of the people at large against the workings of private interest and "personal factions." When he wrote that "the old Republican party attained a degree of vigor and efficiency superior to that of any partisan organization which had before or has since appeared on the political stage," he was certainly influenced by his own memories of the very special circumstances of his political apprenticeship in Columbia County. And, if the Jeffersonian Republicans in Columbia County took the arts of partisanship in organization and press to great heights, they were matched by the county Federalists.[4]

In great measure, Republicans and Federalists in Jeffersonian and Madisonian Columbia met on the same middling ground of an emerging new American politics, a ground of partisan practice and procedure that here had been developing since the close of the Revolution, with its politics of committee and coercion. Partisanship was already being played on a field of bourgeois civility that tempered, if it did not eliminate, the raw contest of Demo and Aristo. But it was the enduring tensions between aristocracy, the people, and this mediating civility in Columbia County that shaped both Van Buren and his contribution to the place of party in American civil life. If Van Buren would be hailed as the architect of party in America, his architecture was the unique product of a particular local political history.[5]

As Van Buren rose beyond county politics to serve in Albany and then Washington, that history was compounded of a violent past and a treacherous, segmented present. By the time Van Buren was old enough to vote, politics in New York was complicated by a byzantine factionalism among Republicans. In 1804 Van Buren would split with his Van Ness patrons when they supported Aaron Burr's schism with the Clinton-Livingston alliance. In 1805 he would side with the Clintonians when they divided with the Livingstons, and after 1812 he would side with Daniel Tompkins's Bucktails in their struggle with De Witt Clinton, eventually building the Democratic Albany Regency, while the Clintonians became a nucleus of the New York Whigs. In each instance Van Buren opposed a smaller Quid Republican faction that was flirting with a practical alliance with Federalists, who stood in a statewide minority after the end of Jay's term in 1801. This swirl of faction complicated and compromised the expression of popular consent, injecting an opaque layer of intrigue into ideally transparent deliberations in the public sphere. Through all this factional intrigue, Van Buren moved carefully and deliberately to rise to the leadership of New York's Democratic Party and eventually to the presidency of the United States. In doing so he developed a powerful understanding of the role of structured parties in the expression of the people's sovereign consent.[6]

Underlying the rumble of segmenting factions in the opening years of the century was another fundamental threat to the expression of consent. Political corruption, both in its reality and as a rhetorical device, suddenly emerged in a multiplicity of forms. Newspapers were secretly funded; voters were bought or coerced; legislators were bribed. Almost immediately a narrative of corruption emerged as a vehicle of the election campaign, with party and press assuming the role of civil monitor in the public sphere. A particular conjuncture in the state's political history shaped this emergence of corruption politics in New York. The entire era of the early Republic comprised an epoch when a mercantilist, activist vision of the developmental purposes of the state overlapped with the emergence of an organized and communicative partisan politics. In the interests of achieving a revolutionary settlement and meeting the aspirations of the people, the state legislature threw its authority behind hundreds of incorporated associations seeking to provide credit, to build roads and bridges, to promote literature and the arts, to manufacture cloth. And from roughly the election of Thomas Jefferson this political process was shaped by a partisan structure, in which parties and their factions deployed competing newspapers to advance their causes and to undermine their opponents. The new developmental politics intersected with a now ancient tradition in New York: politics had long been a means for the unalloyed pursuit of interest and wealth. Once the prerogative of a small stratum of oligarchs, the Revolution had democratized the politics of interest. Now open to a host of new players, against whom many of the old players vainly attempted to bar the door, a democratized politics of distribution marshaled the incorporating power of the state for public and for private good.[7]

Partisanship created an imperative for decisive action. As the routines of post-Revolutionary, postsettlement politics emerged, these players began to understand the implications of the cyclical unseating of legislators and governors: those in power in one year might be gone the next, at the whim of the electorate. By 1801 and 1802 it was quite clear that power — and the opportunity to use it — was a fleeting thing that might evaporate at any April election. Thus suddenly emerged both the imperative to make hay while the sun shines and to expose one's opponent's less than legitimate haymaking practices.

Such opportunistic politics were practiced throughout the state, but they had particular salience in Columbia County. In the eyes of their Republican opponents, with some considerable justification, the Federalist Columbia Junto of Elisha Williams, William W. Ness, and Jacob R. Van Rensselaer ran a well-oiled "engine of corruption," basing a new electoral advantage on the votes of tenant dependents and leading an alliance of Federalists and Republican Quid schismatics to drive through the legislature a series of new bank charters. On the other hand the mainstream party Republicans were not entirely clean themselves. But on balance it was Federalists and Quids, seeing the developmental and financial advantages of state-chartered corporations, who used the most questionable tactics to achieve their ends.[8]

In Columbia County, then, the young Martin Van Buren would be faced with wily and powerful opponents who creatively used every possible means to reestablish and maintain the political preeminence of great wealth, what he and Jackson would later call the "money power." He would learn as much from his opponents as from his allies, which would stand him in good stead in the decades to come. And, if in these years he was drawn to the edge of a corrupt politics, he and his peers in the democracy would build their party on the principle of severing the corrupting ties between government and society. But the years between 1800 and 1820 saw an unprecedented explosion of fears, accusations, and realities of political corruption in the state of New York. As much as any other place in the state, including New York City, Columbia County was the epicenter of this politics of corruption, as New Yorkers began to make the transition from a crisis politics of revolutionary settlement to the routine politics of liberal interest.[9]

During his mid-teenage years, while clerking with the Federalists Francis and
Peter Silvester, Martin Van Buren began his public career by taking civil cases
in the local justice's courts, where bar qualification was not required. In this
"almost incessant employment" he developed a wide and enthusiastic following in the endless drama of property disputes in Kinderhook. According to
legend he would stand on a chair or table while addressing the justices of the
peace, the local juries, and others attending court, usually at a tavern; after one
hard-fought victory in a land dispute he was carried out on his clients' shoulders to the cheers of his supporters. As he was "entrusted with professional
business," we can assume that he began to have a hand in politics as well, since,
when he went to Troy in September 1801, he was already "a zealous politician."
In 1799 the Kinderhook Republicans had met at his father's tavern, and presumably they did the same in the spring of 1800, when Martin turned his precocious energies to organizing for the April assembly election.[10]

The 1800 assembly election in New York was of great importance. The
assemblymen would vote that November for slates of presidential electors
committed to Federalists John Adams and Thomas Pinckney or Republicans
Thomas Jefferson and Aaron Burr. With these high stakes party committees
in New York City, and perhaps elsewhere in the state, carefully prepared for
the four days of voting with public meetings and canvass lists of voters. The
result of the effort in Columbia County was to expand turnout in the assembly election from roughly 60 percent, where it had stood since 1792, to 70 percent, a level below which it would rarely fall until after the War of 1812 (see
Figures 1, 2).[11]

These electoral energies were only one element of a wider and decisive transition in Columbia politics. Throughout most of the 1790s Republicans had
controlled the assembly delegation, but they had recently lost their hold on the
county electorate. In April 1799 the Federalist county committee had taken a
stern line with its contending factions, writing to Kinderhook, "We hope that
Federalism will form itself into a compact body." Such unity would mean that
"then it will be irresistible." Their efforts, the defection of the Upper Manor
Livingstons back to Federalism, the aftershocks of the XYZ affair, the Quasi
War with France, and Burr's chartering of the Manhattan Bank succeeded in
winning the first assembly election in a decade for the Federalists, doubling
their vote from what it had been three to four years before. With the spring
1800 election the Republicans almost recovered their lost ground, increasing
their vote by 32 percent to the Federalists' 18 percent, regaining lost voters in

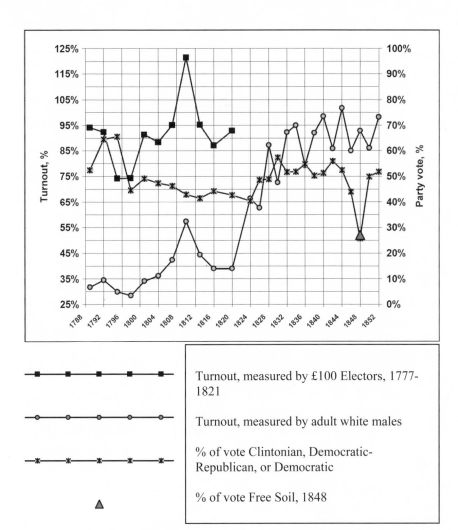

FIGURE 1. *Turnout and Party Vote, Elections for Governor, Columbia County, 1789–1852*
Given the scale of "vote making" in the 1810 vote for governor, when the total turnout comprised almost 125 percent of the legal electorate, the scales on the left (turnout) and the right (party vote) are not the same.

Hillsdale and Canaan and finding new converts in Hudson. But the Federalists prevailed by a narrow margin of fewer than two hundred votes, and on November 6 the county delegation cast a united, if futile, vote for Adams and Pinckney electors.[12]

Four months later, in March 1801, another election cycle commenced, with George Clinton standing for the Republicans against the Federalist

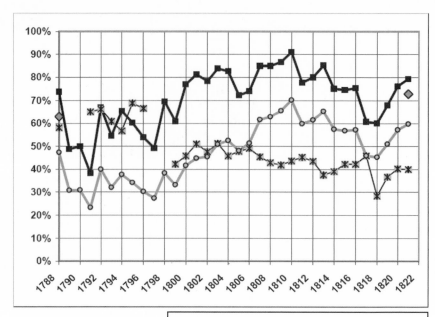

	Turnout, measured by legal assembly electors, 1777-1821
	Turnout, measured by adult white males
	% of vote Clintonian, Democratic-Republican, or Democratic
◇	Turnout, by adult white males, in elections for delegates to the 1788 and 1821 constitutional conventions

FIGURE 2. *Turnout and Party Vote, Elections for Assembly and Constitutional Conventions, Columbia County, 1788–1821*

The assembly returns for 1789–1790 and 1797–1798 do not survive, so the turnouts for Congress were used here as a rough estimate of assembly turnout, since the qualifications for voting for representatives and for congressmen were the same. The results for Congress and the assembly were different, however. Federalists were elected to Congress in each of these elections, Federalists and Republicans elected to the assembly in 1789–1790, and Republicans winning in 1797–1798.

Stephen Van Rensselaer in the race for the governorship. In Columbia County there was a further intensification of effort by both parties, both now organized behind statewide party committees. After the state committees issued addresses to the people, town committees began to meet in late February, culminating in April in massive county meetings, fully reported in the *Hudson Gazette*. The Republicans led off on March 31, meeting at Lawrence Hogeboom's in Claverack to announce their support for Clinton and to nominate four of six assembly candidates. They then reconvened twice, on April 9 and 13, to finalize the assembly slate and to nominate senators. But, most important, the *Gazette* provided the space to list the entire slate of town committees as a general county "committee to promote the election of the above candidates," a list of 120 names that was the equivalent of about 10 percent of Clinton's vote across the county that spring. The Federalists followed on April 10 at Jacob Mowl's tavern in Claverack, announcing their support for Van Rensselaer and their nominations for senate and assembly but also including a huge list of 141 members of committees of correspondence and election, about 13 percent of the total Columbia vote for Van Rensselaer later that month.[13]

Such meetings might have been held the previous year, but they were unprecedented in the surviving run of the *Gazette;* never before had so many relatively ordinary men had their political allegiances published in the public prints. The practice was repeated that fall, when a congressional seat opened up, and the Republicans put up John P. Van Ness against Hezekiah Hosmer of Hudson in the election that sent Van Buren from Kinderhook to the congressional meeting in Troy. The Federalists could not quite match their total of that spring, listing a county committee with 63 names; the Republicans were cut back to 110. By contrast, the meeting that Van Buren attended in Troy was simply a meeting of Troy Republicans, not a general county meeting. Columbia's partisan efforts brought results, particularly in the regular state elections: turnout in the county election for governor jumped from 74 percent in 1798 to 91 percent in 1801, and turnout in the assembly election rose to more than 80 percent. The turnout in the off-cycle congressional election, however, was a more modest 40 percent.[14]

The sizes of both the published committees and the electoral turnouts were new in Columbia County's history, and they were enduring, unique in the region, and distinctive in the state at large. Between 1800 and 1816 Columbia's turnout in assembly and governor's elections averaged 80 percent and was consistently the highest in the region and, perhaps, the state. By comparison, to the north in Rensselaer County the largest published county committee lists comprised at most 3 percent of the electorate, as they had in Columbia in the 1790s; to the south Dutchess County produced only one list comparable to Columbia's, a Federalist committee list in the 1816 governor's election (see Table 21). Turnout for the assembly elections in Rensselaer lagged slightly behind Columbia at about 73 percent while in Dutchess County the figure hovered at only slightly more than 50 percent, with deep troughs in off-year elections. Columbia turnout for governor's elections also stood out, by comparison with most of the state (see Figure 3).[15]

If the Columbia Federalists stopped publishing their committee lists after 1803, the Republicans published long lists of town delegates to county conventions at critical junctures over the next two decades, growing to include 22 percent of the party's voters in 1811 and 34 percent in 1820. This Republican activism was clearly an effort to stem the tide of resurgent, militant, and enduring Federalism in Columbia County. Where the Federalists were in retreat across most of the state after 1800, in Columbia they secured a solid and enduring majority support, sweeping all assembly elections in the first two decades of the new century except those in April 1801 and 1803, and all congressional elections except those in 1800, October 1801, and 1806. Republicans contested vigorously each one of these elections; the Federalist margins of victory were typically very narrow, and the turnouts very high.

This struggle, formative for Van Buren's political worldview, hinged on the issues of charters for banks and turnpikes and increasingly was colored by the national and international politics of embargo and war. But it also clearly had its roots in the uniquely unsettled political climate in Columbia since the end of the Revolution. Nowhere else had enduring colonial patterns of tenancy and engrossing land patents survived on the scale that they did in Columbia County, and nowhere else had the problem of landownership engendered such intense political struggle. To the south, in Dutchess County, settlement revolved around the tory estates in the southern sections of the county, which were settled by the legislation of the mid-1780s. To the north, in what became Rensselaer County in 1791, rumblings of potential unrest among the people taking up land on Stephen Van Rensselaer's vast holdings were quieted in 1788–1789 by his very generous terms of perpetual leases, forgiven rent, and outright grants for local schools and churches, terms that fifty years later would bring renewed troubles when this Good Patroon died in 1839. Thus in both Rensselaer and Dutchess the settling of the politics of land and independence brought a wider stability by 1789. Politics over the next two decades would reflect this settlement; run by select groups of county gentry hungry for office, elections would generate relatively little interest and relatively low turnouts. The circumstances of partisan politics in Rensselaer and Dutchess seem to have been the norm across much of New York State, where Jefferso-

TABLE 21. *Size of Published Countywide Party Committees, 1792–1834*

Year	Place	Electoral Contest	No. of Committee Members, Proportion of Party Voters	
			Federalist	Republican
1792	Rensselaer County	Governor	26 3.6%	
1795	Columbia County	Governor	21 3.6%	
1798	Columbia County	Governor	28 3.7%	26 3.1%
1801	Rensselaer County	Governor	43 2.8%	
1801	Columbia County	Governor	152 13.1%	129 10.8%
1801	Columbia County	Congress	62 11.3%	110 10.2%
1803	Columbia County	Assembly	129 7.4%	109 6.0%
1804	Columbia County	Governor		104 8.9%
1806	Columbia County	Assembly		85 4.9%
1807	Rensselaer County	Governor		71 4.6%
1808	Columbia County	Assembly		168 9.3%
1811	Columbia County	Lt. Governor		274 22.9%
1816	Dutchess County	Governor	206 11.3%	
1816	Rensselaer County	Governor	49 2.4%	38 2.7%
1819	Rensselaer County	Assembly		44
1820	Rensselaer County	Assembly	61 2.4%	51 3.6%

Year	Place	Electoral Contest	Clintonian Committees	Democratic Committees
1820	Columbia County	Governor	212 12.5%	413 32.7%
1821	Columbia County	Convention		76 3.8%
1821	Columbia County	Congress		48 2.5%
1826	Rensselaer County	Governor	117 3.3%	82 2.7%
1834	Columbia County	Governor		419 11.0%

Note: The county committees listed here are only those which included lists of delegates, with the exception of the 1834 Democratic convention in Columbia, which simply recorded that 419 delegates had attended.

Sources: Columbia County: Hudson *Gazette,* Mar. 26, 1795, Apr. 24, 1798, Apr. 14, 21, Sept. 22, 1801; Hudson *Balance,* Apr. 19, 1803; Hudson *Bee,* Apr. 19, 1803, Apr. 10, 1804, Apr. 15, 1806, Apr. 19, 1808, Apr. 19, 1811, Mar. 14, 21, 1820; Hudson *Columbia Republican,* Jan. 9, Apr. 17, 1821; Kinderhook *Columbia Sentinel,* Oct. 16 1834 (total number only).

Rensselaer County: Lansingburgh *American Spy,* Apr. 20, 1792; Troy *Northern Budget,* Mar. 4, 1801; *Troy Gazette,* April 21, 1807; *Troy Post,* Apr. 16, 1816; Troy *Northern Budget,* Mar. 5, 1816, Apr. 20, 1819, Feb. 8, 1820; *Lansingburgh Gazette,* Apr. 11, 1820; Troy *Budget and City Register,* Oct. 26, 1826; Nomination Broadside for John D. Dickinson of Troy and assembly candidates (Clintonian), Oct. 16, 1826, AAS.

Dutchess County: *Poughkeepsie Journal,* Apr. 10, 1816.

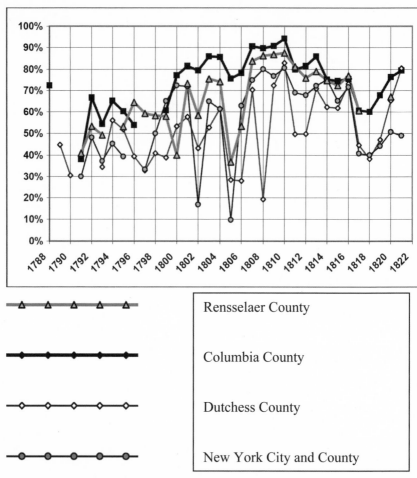

FIGURE 3. *Turnout in Assembly Elections, Columbia, Rensselaer, and Dutchess Counties and New York City and County, 1788–1821*

Between 1800 and 1813, turnout in assembly elections was higher in Columbia County than in virtually any other country in New York State; this figure thus compares Columbia with adjacent counties and New York City.

nian politics has been described as an elite affair of little interest to the average voter.[16]

But things were obviously very different in Columbia County, where the revolutionary settlement was — for some — still a matter of doubt. Clearly, the intensity of party politics in Van Buren's Columbia had its roots in decades of mobilization around the issue of landed independence. Some among the gentry still hoped to restore a remembered deferential past. Writing in 1795, not quite midway between the pivotal elections of 1792 and 1800, Henry Livingston had hoped that Samuel B. Webb of Claverack could aid in this project:

> Pray let us all join in [supporting] one Man. . . . I am sure the [Van Rensselaer] family at C[l]averack, and our [Livingston] family aided by the Gentlemen of the County Could do much in bringing about such a union, that this distracted County could again have peace.[17]

But such hopes of political harmony were doomed, at least through the traditional terms and practices of oligarchy that the great families were desperate to defend. As the political center of gravity moved from crisis to routine, there were certainly elites interested in managing politics on both of the opposing sides. But the long struggle over a revolutionary settlement in Columbia County had made for a precocious development of the rhetorical and organizational vehicles linking elites and electorate, and the boundary between the two was porous and open. By 1801 the young Van Buren and even some of the young men who would make up the Federalist Junto were already stepping across that boundary. While the Junto used the new civil vehicles to restore traditional oligarchical power, Van Buren and the county Republicans used the same vehicles to carry on the old popular resistance to landed oligarchy, even as it evolved into the money power.

THE RISE OF THE PARTISAN PRESS AND FEDERALIST SATIRE: THE *BALANCE,* THE *BEE,* AND THE *WASP*

This intensification of partisanship in Columbia County was followed by a revolution in the newspaper press in Hudson. Ashbel Stoddard had had the county to himself and the *Gazette* since 1785 and in 1800 and the spring of 1801 impartially published the proceedings of both coalescing parties. But Stoddard's unchallenged command of the market in Columbia was overturned in 1801 and 1802, when two new papers were established in Hudson, driving his *Gazette* out of business by the end of 1803. A new configuration of print in the public sphere was rapidly emerging.[18]

On May 21, 1801, three weeks after the spring election, a troika of editors published the first issue of the *Balance, and Columbian Repository.* The *Balance* would emerge as the county's banner Federalist paper, but the editors moved cautiously in their first number. They set a witty tone in their opening editorial, "To the Public," defending their title, which had appeared to some, they reported, as equivocating: "You are aiming *to balance between the parties,* and will be veering to one side or the other, as may best suit your own interest." Not so, the editors retorted: "In these days of political ferment, while the public mind has resembled *the crater of Etna,* moderation has been deemed cowardice." They would stand for moderation, defend the nation's interests, watch the development of "public measures" as "watchful and faithful centinels," but they would respect the "ancient *sedition law,* which says '*thou shalt not speak evil of the ruler of thy people.*'" As one of the editors wrote to Noah Webster six weeks after the paper commenced, they hoped to "render our paper a standard of truth, in the cause of *good order,* unbiased by the flimsy theories of demagogues and disorganizers."[19]

The *Balance* editors also had higher aspirations. "Gentlemen desirous of engaging in political investigation and discussions" were invited to offer contributions, but the editors also hoped that they would receive "Moral and Literary original Essays." The *Balance* would be edited for an audience in the Augustan "republic of polite letters" rather than the American republic of engaged voters. The editors conceived of the *Balance* as a "well conducted literary newspaper," formulated to "accommodate a variety of tastes and palates." The paper contained very little in the way of the traditional anecdotal news and the excerpts from legislative journals that took so much space in other papers. Rather, it was filled with persuasive opinion pieces in regular sections: "Original Essays" on social questions, ardently Federalist "Political" critiques of the Democrats, "Monitorial" and "Agricultural" sections of moral advice, "The Wreath," with literary offerings, and the "Editor's Closet." The editors gradually fine-tuned the paper's appearance, starting with a redesign in January of 1802 to a short-column, eight-page format on the model of an English literary magazine. Working to completely divest itself of the taint of commerce, in January 1803 they banished advertisements to a separate sheet called the *Balance Advertiser*. At the close of the previous year's run they printed an ornate title page and an annual index, to facilitate the private binding of annual volumes. While they published limited election material, including the Federalists' committee list for the special fall 1801 congressional election and the April 1803 assembly election, by 1805 the *Balance* was segmenting most of these Federalist election materials into specially printed handbills. The editors were very proud of their innovations and pilloried Stoddard when he criticized their departures from tradition: "For such a *pitiful printer* as Ashbel Stoddard to insert in his Gazette, strictures upon the mode of arranging a newspaper, is as ridiculous as it would be for a *Bear* to tell a *Dancing Master,* that he does not handle his feet gracefully."[20]

The *Balance* editors were even more contemptuous when a third paper was established at Hudson. For several years Charles Holt of New London had run one of the most influential Republican papers in New England, the *Bee;* when the Connecticut Federalist magistrates had the opportunity, they had him jailed under the Sedition Act in September 1799. Despite his persecution,

Jefferson passed him over for a federal printing contract that might have salvaged his finances. Thus he jumped at the opportunity when he was offered a five hundred dollar subsidy to move his paper to Hudson, where he began printing the *Bee* in August 1802, in a second-floor office above the store where the city's "Democratic club" met, on benches and chairs around "a red-hot stove, in an atmosphere blue with tobacco smoke."[21]

Starting on July 7, the *Balance* office began to issue an occasional paper of political satire titled the *Wasp*. The *Wasp*'s editor, publishing under the pseudonym of Robert Rusticoat, Esq., was sworn to protect his "Gentle reader" from the "clan of unprincipled adventurers" editing the "democratic presses." Until recently, "the vicinity of Hudson's River, has been tolerably free from these reptiles," he trumpeted. "But of late they begin to thicken around us." Rusticoat stood against Jeffersonians of any stripe disturbing the peace of the valley. "The WASP is declared to be at enmity with the BEE," he declared. "Wherever the BEE ranges, the WASP will follow ... [and] will only strive to displease, vex and torment his enemies. . . . He will never accede to the philosophical doctrine, that 'We are all WASPS — we are all BEES.'"[22]

Holt ignored the stings of the *Wasp* in his first issue of the *Bee* on August 17, opening with a long essay, "Domestic Manufactures," a favorite Republican theme, from the Philadelphia *Aurora* and attributed to Benjamin Franklin, the patron saint of the Republican printers. In his address to his readers, Holt wrote of "the publication of a republican newspaper as the most effectual method of propagating republican opinions and supporting the republican doctrines and administration of our government." His proposals, which had circulated weeks before, read like a mirror image of those of the *Balance,* announcing that his "object" would be to uphold "republican institutions" and "to detect and expose falshood and error, and defend the truth against the open or insidious attacks of its enemies."[23]

Both the *Balance* and the *Bee* were part of a wave of new newspapers that established New York State's partisan press after the turn of the century. Despite the flurry of six new Republican papers launched across the state in 1799–1800, there were only two cities — New York and Albany — with competing partisan papers in 1800. Another nineteen towns like Hudson had a single paper, typically Federalist-leaning. But, by 1810, eighteen New York cities and county seats supported two or more competing party papers, of a total of thirty-five towns and cities with papers. Many of these competitive locales were along the river north and south of Hudson. To the north, in the twin villages of Troy and Lansingburgh, there were four papers by 1803: the Troy *Northern Budget* (which featured a woodcut of Franklin as its masthead) and the Lansingburgh *Farmer's Register* speaking for the Republicans against Federalist *Gazettes* in both villages. The Federalist *Poughkeepsie Journal* was briefly challenged by an *American Farmer* in 1798 and then in 1801 by the *Guardian,* which was transformed into the *Political Barometer* in 1802. In Kingston the Federalist *Ulster Gazette* was challenged by a Republican *Plebiean;* in Catskill it was the *American Eagle* and the Catskill *Recorder.* Nearby in Massachusetts, the Republican *Sun* was established in Pittsfield in 1800 to challenge the Federalist *Western Star,* printed in Theodore Sedgwick's Stockbridge, and by 1810 was opposed in Pittsfield by the Federalist *Berkshire Reporter.*[24]

Almost overnight the rise of these papers brought the end of the era of the single paper printed for a given county, with its moderate Federalism shared by others up- and downriver, sometimes forged in apprenticeships in Hartford, as with the Websters of Albany and Ashbel Stoddard. Where the Websters were able to make the transition and carried on their *Gazette* for several decades, Stoddard, faced with two new papers, could not. As the *Balance* and the *Bee* drained off committed Federalists and Republicans in Columbia's climate of intensifying partisanship, Stoddard ceased publication of the *Gazette* in late December 1803, selling his newspaper business to the *Balance* but continuing to print in Hudson for years, doing a good business in religious and educational imprints.[25]

Some very special circumstances surrounded the establishment of the *Balance* in Hudson. All of these papers had some pretenses to literary production. Charles Holt included "literary patrons" among the prospective readers of the *Bee;* the *Barometer's* editor, Isaac Mitchell, a teacher at the Poughkeepsie Academy, printed long serial narratives, including his own gothic tale, "Alonzo and Melissa." They all sniped at one another incessantly in their editor's columns, as they did at the banner partisan papers, the *New-York Evening Post* and the Philadelphia *Aurora.* But, among the towns along the Hudson, the editors of the *Balance* and the *Wasp* were unique in their deployment of literary style as a political weapon against their opponents. Their physical form as literary magazines, the high and moral tone of the *Balance,* and the slashing satire of the *Wasp* all stood in self-conscious contrast to the more traditional forms and styles of other papers. In separating out moral edification, commercial advertising, and political satire, the editors effectively targeted particular interests of particular audiences. The *Balance* also conceded the general delivery of political news and information to the New York papers that arrived every Wednesday with the southern mail and to the Albany papers. Their production was, thus, eminently cultural; they sought to be a vehicle for persuasive influence rather than a means of deliberative debate.

The *Balance* office initially was run by three editors, each apparently responsible for a particular side of the business. George Chittenden might have been the printer and in charge of the *Advertiser;* he dropped out in 1804 to work as a bookseller and to make paper. Ezra Sampson, the senior editor, had been an army chaplain in the Revolution and the minister of a church in eastern Massachusetts before moving to Hudson in 1796, where he preached in the Presbyterian church when needed. Later he would write religious texts for schools, such as *Beauties of the Bible* and *The Youth's Companion;* he was responsible for the moral and didactic tone of the *Balance* proper. The political side of the enterprise, and particularly the attack satire of the *Wasp,* was the work of the "Junior Editor," Harry Croswell.

Croswell was one of a family of printers from Hartford who settled across the river in Catskill in the early 1790s. His older brothers, Thomas and Mackay, had started the *Catskill Packet* in 1792; Mackay had apprenticed at the Hartford *Connecticut Courant* before working as a journeyman in Philadelphia. Harry Croswell apprenticed in the *Packet* office before briefly coediting the Catskill *Western Constellation* with his brother Mackay in 1800–1801. This venture led the Croswells in opposite directions. McKay established this new paper on Republican principles, and his son Edwin would carry on the tradition and be recruited in 1823 by Van Buren's Regency to edit the state Democratic banner paper, the *Albany Argus.* But Harry, at age twenty-three, moved in the opposite direction, crossing the river to write and push type for the Federalists at Hudson. In doing so, he made a decisive break from his family in Catskill. After running the *Balance* in Hudson, he moved the paper to Albany to try to bring his "Augustan" style to the state capital (briefly putting out the *Republican Crisis* as well). When by 1812 he had failed in these ventures, he retooled himself as an Episcopal clergyman and presided over Christ Church in Hudson in 1814 before taking up a post in a wealthy parish in New Haven, where he preached for more than forty years. In this very conservative career, Harry Croswell might well have considered on occasion how his position stood in extreme contrast to that of his great uncle, Andrew Croswell, who had been a radical New Light itinerant in the Great Awakening of the 1740s. When the *Wasp* put the epigram "To lash the Rascals naked through the world" on its masthead, one has to assume that these were Croswell's sentiments about his family as much as about the Jeffersonians in general.[26]

Exactly how Harry Croswell came to Hudson to help found the *Balance* is not entirely clear. Certainly, at age twenty-three and alienated from a not very prosperous printing family, he did not have the capital to start up a newspaper. Nor did the senior editor, Ezra Sampson, who was listed about a third of the way down the Hudson valuation of 1799. Clearly, the *Balance* was a sponsored paper, as were most of the new Federalist papers being founded at the time. There is no question that the paper was founded at the invitation—and on the cash subsidy—of the county's leading Federalists and must have involved the mobilization of Upper Manor Livingston money by attorneys Elisha Williams, Jacob R. Van Rensselaer, and William W. Van Ness, for two decades the troika of the Columbia Junto. Where the Republicans met around a wood stove in Dayton's general store, the Federalists assembled "in the best furnished apartments" at one of Hudson's taverns. These men represented the legal interests of the Claverack Van Rensselaers, long-ardent Federalists, and the Upper Manor Livingstons, reconverted to the faith in 1798. It seems highly likely that the *Balance* had its genesis during the pivotal election year of 1800 in either one of these tavern apartments or the drawing rooms of the Van Rensselaer and Livingston mansions, as the Federalists consulted on how to maintain their new but tenuous hold on county politics and to restore "peace" on their terms to a "distracted County," as Henry Livingston had put it in 1795.[27]

The pivotal figures in this Federalist revival, Van Rensselaer, Williams, and Van Ness, were all a decade or more older than Van Buren but too young to have served in the Revolution. They were part of a generation of "Young Federalists" shaped by the backlash against the French Revolution and willing to aggressively pursue means new and old to assert power over a rising democracy and gain place and wealth for themselves. In January 1801 Williams and Van Ness met at the Albany Tontine Coffee House with Federalists from throughout the state to establish a statewide network of county committees.[28]

The oldest member of the Junto, Jacob Rutsen Van Rensselaer, was the son of General Robert Van Rensselaer, the "lord" of Claverack, the commander of the county militia brigade during the war, and the first county clerk. Jacob R. Van Rensselaer graduated from Yale in 1787 and might have clerked in Albany, possibly for Abraham Van Vechten: both were named among the incorporators of the Albany Library in the spring of 1792. That same summer, however, he began to be active among the Columbia Federalists as the clerk of the Otsego protest meeting, then served on county committees for John Jay's election in 1795 and 1798, and was elected to the assembly for the first of many terms in the April 1799 election. He followed close in his father's footsteps, receiving a landed inheritance in 1798, and was active in the claiming and sale of Van Rensselaer lands in Hillsdale. In 1803 he began to build an ambitiously designed mansion house east of Claverack village, financed in part by his speculations in western lands and his directorship in the Bank of Columbia, in which he and Elisha Williams were developing a controlling interest.[29]

Elisha Williams was one of the Connecticut Williams clan, born in Pomfret in 1773. He studied law first with Tapping Reeve in Litchfield and then clerked briefly with Ambrose Spencer in Hudson before being admitted to the bar in 1793. For the next six years he practiced law in Spencertown, in northwest Hillsdale, where by 1795 he was on the committee of correspondence for John Jay. In April 1800 he was elected to the assembly, beating his Hillsdale neighbor, the shoemaker William Tanner, by a narrow margin; that December he had moved his practice to Hudson, where he became a permanent fixture in Federalist politics (as he was already in the county courts). Williams, "perfectly erect and corpulent," was known for his "brilliant wit" and his "majestic and dignified appearance." He preferred wealth to public position: wielding a "controlling political influence," he "dictated who should go to Congress, but would never consent to be a candidate for that office himself." One of his designees was his brother-in-law, Thomas P. Grosvenor. In 1800 Grosvenor was studying in his office; he took the bar in 1803 and joined the Junto as a junior partner. After two terms in Congress he settled in Baltimore, marrying Mary Jane Hanson, sister of the arch-Federalist Alexander C. Hanson, the editor of the Baltimore *Federal Republican,* whose fanatical politics led to a violent siege of his office by Baltimore Republicans in 1812. This connection between two of the country's most rabidly Federalist circles soon faded, however, as Grosvenor, his wife Mary Jane, and Alexander Hanson were all dead by 1819.[30]

The third member of the troika, William W. Van Ness, resembled Elisha Williams in manner and deportment, but Martin Van Buren in his origins. Two years younger than Williams, he was a big man, of "a commanding presence, almost a colossal form, and a voice marvellous for its strength and for the music of its intonations." "Sober minded men were carried away with the fascinating effervescence of his public utterances and the brilliancy of his conversation." He was perhaps the closest of the three in circumstances to Van Buren. The older brother of Peter Van Ness of Kinderhook, his father, William, was a prosperous but otherwise undistinguished Claverack farmer. William W. (unlike his Kinderhook cousins) did not attend college. Clerking with Republican John Bay, Van Ness reversed Van Buren's rejection of the Silvesters' politics and converted to militant Federalism. By 1799 he was representing the Livingstons in court and active on Federalist committees; he would be elected to the assembly in 1804 and 1805, before he was appointed to the supreme court in 1807 by Governor Morgan Lewis.[31]

If Martin Van Buren learned anything from his Federalist opponents, it was at the hands of these three men of the Columbia Junto. After years of struggle to maintain their hold on power in the county and influence across the state, Van Ness would be a principal with Williams and Van Rensselaer in the Bank of America scandal that would drive them from power after 1821. The *Balance* was probably their first project together. In 1800 and 1801, in their late twenties and early thirties, they were already or were soon to be appointed directors of the Bank of Columbia, supplementing their emerging dominant place in Federalist politics. Presumably they brought cash advances from the Claverack Van Rensselaers and the Upper Manor Livingstons. Certainly these young Federalists were the kind of men with whom Sampson would have consulted in editing the *Balance* and who—with other "gentlemen of the County"—would have made literary contributions to both the *Balance* and the *Wasp*. In 1806, as Hudson's urban primacy over rural Claverack was finally confirmed with the relocation of the county courts to Fourth and Warren streets, much the same cast of characters was involved in the incorporation of an academy in Hudson, after a campaign in the *Balance*, contested by essays in the *Bee*. Overwhelmingly Federalist in complexion, the incorporators of the new Hudson Academy included Ezra Sampson and Harry Croswell of the *Balance* and Elisha Williams and William W. Van Ness of the Junto.[32]

In their literary efforts the Columbia Federalists were situating themselves in an ancient belletristic tradition that had its most notable American manifestation in the work of the Connecticut Wits, including Joel Barlow's *Vision of Columbus*, to which they had enthusiastically subscribed in 1787. Ashbel Stoddard had attempted to work in this tradition of literary Federalism when in February 1801 he began to run a section of poetry and prose called "The Bouquet," covering his entire fourth page. In July 1801 he began a long-running series of material excerpted from Joseph Dennie's Philadelphia *Port Folio*, which stood at the head of this genre of publishing, a literary expression of an elite alienation from a crass world in which the rising democracy threatened classical values. If they too mirrored the style of the *Port Folio*, the *Balance* editors were happy to mock Stoddard's "Bouquet" as a desperate effort to save his paper from "a *deep decline.*" Through the vehicle of the *Wasp* they were able to tap into a cognate vein of political satire that ran back to Swift, Pope, and Gay and that had been a stock in the manuscripts circulated in the colonial "republic of polite letters." This satirical play was deeply rooted in New York gentry circles, locally manifested in Peter W. Yates's mockery of the Albany committee in 1775, and it would enter the literary canon with Washington Irving's *History of New York* (1806) and his Burrite prose poem *Salmagundi* (1807).[33]

The *Wasp* in particular was produced as a print departure from this manuscript-based tradition of political satire, and it is not difficult to imagine the men of the Columbia Junto feeding "Robert Rusticoat" with ideas and scraps of doggerel for these occasional issues, eye candy for Federalist gentlemen and followers alike, designed to forge fellow feeling in their performance in drawing rooms and public houses. In the late 1780s and the 1790s a romantic literary politics of sensibility had been mobilized to advance the cause of emancipation and, more generally, the opening of the bounds of civil life, through the vehicle of sympathetic understanding. Now an older Augustan literary politics of wit and satire was redeployed to shore up the cultural boundaries circumscribing Federalist definitions of the legitimate political voice in a wider civil society.

THE CROSWELL TRIAL

Harry Croswell's satirical jabs took him onto dangerous ground. His primary targets in the *Wasp* were his fellow printers, Republicans Charles Holt of the *Bee,* Isaac Mitchell of the Poughkeepsie *Political Barometer* (whom he mocked for comparing himself to Hudibras and M'Fingal), Phinehas Allen of the Pittsfield *Sun,* and Benjamin Austin of the *Boston Chronicle.* But he also went after grander prey. In his fourth issue, August 12, 1802, he published "A Few 'Squally' Facts," accusing Thomas Jefferson of undermining the Constitution. Then in his seventh issue, September 9, he printed a brief paragraph contributed by Thomas P. Grosvenor, stating that Thomas Jefferson paid Virginia printer James Callender "for calling Washington a traitor, a robber, and a perjurer" and "for calling Adams, a hoary headed incendiary; and for most grossly slandering the private characters of men, who, he well knew were virtuous." In the same issue Croswell mocked the state attorney general as drunk with "Power and pride"; in subsequent issues he attacked him as "the Turncoat-General." This was Ambrose Spencer, who had abandoned Federalism in 1798, and had been made attorney general in February 1802, after completing his term as senator. Still a resident of Hudson and deeply involved in local Republican politics, Spencer was looking for a chance to strike back at the Federalists, and Croswell seemed to offer a golden opportunity. Spencer himself appeared on January 10, 1803, at the Claverack courthouse to secure indictments for seditious libel against Harry Croswell and, later that year, against both Ezra Sampson and Thomas Grosvenor.[34]

The Columbia Federalist leadership leaped to Croswell's defense. Van Rensselaer, Williams, and Van Ness appeared as counsel to defend Croswell at the Claverack court, under Republican Morgan Lewis, on January 10; in July 1803 they were joined by Abraham Van Vechten of Albany, and their arguments in defense of freedom of the press were carefully covered in the *Balance.* Despite Philip Schuyler's opinion that Croswell was a disgrace who "produces Immorality by his pernicious example," Alexander Hamilton agreed to serve on the defense when Croswell, convicted of publishing a libel in July, had his case heard on appeal in Albany before the supreme court in February 1804.

Hamilton, aided by Van Ness and others, won Croswell's freedom in a performance that emptied both houses of the legislature.[35]

Van Buren, coming up from New York to Kinderhook, attended the July 1803 trial. He reported, "Van Vechten spoke with his usual energy and Talents but it is a tribute due to Spencer to say that in point of argument and solidity he was excelled by none." But he felt that Republican Justice Morgan Lewis's "charge of the Court was extremely severe" and heard that he had attempted to bring indictments against New York City printers on similar grounds. The Croswell case was a problem for Republicans everywhere, since it seemed to be repeating the Federalists' abuse of the press with the 1798 Sedition Act. Charles Holt, who had suffered imprisonment after his own conviction in 1799, was conspicuously circumspect in the pages of the *Bee* for the duration of the trial. The issue in question involved whether the printing of a true fact, however unpleasant to an officeholder, constituted "seditious libel." It had in traditional English common law as codified by Blackstone, and these were the rules applied against Republican printers under the Federalist Sedition Act. The presiding justice at Claverack in January and July, Morgan Lewis, was a Republican and a close relation and ally of Robert R. Livingston, then negotiating the Louisiana Purchase as Jefferson's ambassador in Paris. When the Federalist lawyers attempted to delay the proceedings to call Callender from Virginia as a witness, Lewis invoked Blackstone's rules and instructed the grand and petit juries to consider only whether Croswell had indeed published the text in question in the *Wasp*. This narrow construction allowed the New York Federalists to distance themselves from the 1798 Sedition Act by championing the doctrine that "truth" ought to be accepted as evidence in defense against charges of libel, that any other standard would impose prior restraint upon the press's informative function.[36]

All through the spring and summer of 1803 the *Balance* covered the trial in detail and editorialized against "previous constraints" on press freedom; in April it printed a huge countywide committee list for the support of William W. Van Ness and other Federalists for the assembly, under the slogan, "Huzza for the liberty of the press!!!" This was, however, the last year when the Republicans squeaked into office: Van Ness lost to his Claverack neighbor Stephen Miller by fewer than thirty votes. A year later, after his February 1804 appearance with Hamilton for Croswell at the supreme court in Albany, Van Ness led a field of Federalists in the spring assembly election, beating the Republicans by three hundred votes. That same spring Federalist James Emott of Albany had introduced a bill to allow truth as a defense for libel, which was rejected by the Council of Revision. In the following session William Van

Ness brought this drama to a close. His Act concerning Libels, passed in April 1805, would shape New York's libel law for the rest of the century.[37]

HAMILTON'S DEATH, FACTIONAL POLITICS, AND A CORRUPTED PRESS?

The Croswell trial of 1804 was a critical juncture in the history of the public sphere in Jeffersonian New York, but for Alexander Hamilton it was but an episode in an accelerating train of events that would lead to his fatal encounter with Aaron Burr at Weehawken in July. In October 1803, three months after Croswell's initial conviction, Hamilton was at the Claverack courthouse, representing Schuyler and Van Rensselaer interests against the people of southern Hillsdale, in company with Abraham Van Vechten, Peter Van Schaack, and Jacob R. Van Rensselaer. In February 1804, when he represented Croswell in Albany, the Hillsdale commissioners were finalizing their report on the Van Rensselaer claim, which Hamilton began to review in March and continued to monitor during and after the 1804 election, which pitted Morgan Lewis against Aaron Burr for the governorship. That July Hamilton met Burr for an affair of honor. When the Van Rensselaer legal accounts were settled, Hamilton's charges were paid to his widow, Catherine Schuyler Hamilton.[38]

Hamilton's death at the hands of Aaron Burr was a direct consequence of the collapse of party politics in the state of New York. Defeated in 1800 and 1801 for control of the assembly and the governorship, the Federalists would not consider running a candidate in 1804. The absence of an effective opposition threw the New York Republicans into factional schism (as it would the national Republicans in 1824). A lifetime later, in a passage that must have reflected his youthful experience, Van Buren reflected on the role of factions in the national election of 1824:

> In the place of two great parties arrayed against each other in a fair and open contest for the establishment of principles in the administration of Government which they respectively believed most conducive to the public interest, the country was overrun with personal factions. These having few higher motives for the selection of their candidates or stronger incentives to action than individual preferences or antipathies, moved the bitter waters of political agitation to their lowest depths.

These words could as easily have been written of the politics of New York and Columbia County in the age of Jefferson and the era of Van Buren's emergence.[39]

In February 1804, Governor George Clinton declined renomination to the governorship and then was nominated in Aaron Burr's place to run for vice president with Jefferson. Justice John Lansing of Albany was proposed as a means of uniting Republicans and Federalists against Burr, but Burr had already begun discussions that led to his nomination for governor. The remaining Republicans, an alliance led by the Clinton family and the Clermont Livingstons supported by Ambrose Spencer, countered with the nomination of Justice Morgan Lewis. Hamilton had opposed Burr's presidential aspirations in 1800–1801, and he now stood against his election as governor, counseling Federalists to avoid an alliance with the Burrites. After the election, in May and June, rumors flew concerning what Hamilton had said about Burr to whom; Burr demanded an explanation and an apology, Hamilton refused, and the path led to pistol shots on the New Jersey shore opposite Manhattan. That spring the young Martin Van Buren split with his new patrons the Van Nesses, who were adhering to Burr's faction; Van Buren's former friend William P. Van Ness had served Burr as a second in his fatal duel with Hamilton.[40]

With Hamilton dead, New York Federalists were even weaker, and Republican factionalism ran wild. Burrites, shorn of their leader by Jefferson's prosecution over Burr's purported Western Conspiracy, remained a lurking presence, and Governor Lewis quickly lost the support of the Clintonians and Spencer's following and fell into a Quid alliance of convenience with the Federalists. The Clintonians, led by De Witt Clinton and Ambrose Spencer, would gain power again in 1807, but their anointed figurehead, Governor Daniel D. Tompkins, developed a following of his own, split with Clinton and Spencer in 1812, and retained the governorship until he was elected Madison's vice president in 1816. In this schism of 1812 Van Buren would hitch his star to Tompkins and his Bucktail faction.

The collapse of the Federalists after 1801 meant that Jeffersonian New York would not continue a possible route toward a statewide institutional party politics, seemingly developing from the late 1790s to 1801. Rather, a factionalism based on interest, family, and personality deeply rooted in the New York political experience reasserted itself. In Columbia, this factional politics was manifested overtly in the governor's elections of 1804 and 1807 but played a complex role behind the scenes, as state assembly and senate slates were matched with electorates. Here party organization was uniquely strong and enduring, as the county Federalists prevailed in the assembly elections and forged alliances of convenience with centralist Quid factions of the Republicans. Importantly, and perhaps paradoxically, this fluid partisanship developed just as the press was suddenly expanding. This new press brought an aggressive new political style—a vigorous effort to appeal to the public—to control the flow of information and the construction of opinion. But this style was mobilized both for party and for faction, faction that represented particular propertied interests and was shaped by a flow of subsidies that some saw as corruption.

The early *Gazettes* of the 1780s and 1790s were relatively independent in their finances, if Federalist in inclination. They lived and died on their advertising, job printing, and bookselling. When Ashbel Stoddard sold out his *Hudson Gazette,* he and his son William continued in the printing line for decades, churning out religious and educational publications. But, with the advent of the heightened partisanship of the turn of the century, newspapers along the Hudson were increasingly funded, at least at the outset, by wealthy men or groups of men seeking to control and direct the construction of public opinion. The Clermont Livingstons seem to have been the most aggressive in this regard, probably funding the Poughkeepsie *American Farmer* in 1798, possibly the Poughkeepsie *Guardian* in 1801, certainly the *Barometer* from 1802. They also must have provided the five hundred dollars in start-up money to Charles Holt, the New London printer imprisoned under the Sedition Act of 1798, who moved his *Bee* to Hudson in 1802. Holt wrote to William Wilson, the manager of Clermont, in August 1802:

> In regard to Messr. Livingstons accounts, I did not conceive warranted by gratitude or justice to make any charge for papers against a family from whom I had received so liberally. Whether I am endebted to Messrs R[obert] R., R[obert] L[eroy], and E[dward] P. Livingston, or ———, I cannot tell, though I was told (by Judge B[rockholst] Livingston) that they are all of one family. If you think proper, you may present the enclosed accounts, or withhold them.~~~and if they wish or expect their papers continued you will please inform me.[41]

By 1805 Holt and the *Bee* were bitter enemies of the Livingstons and their kinsman, Governor Morgan Lewis, having switched to the patronage of De Witt Clinton. In April 1805 the Federalist *Balance* jeered that Holt's *Bee* was recently

> extremely zealous in support of Morgan Lewis, and the party attached to him. It was then printed with old and worn-out types.... The Bee *now* rancourously opposes and attempts to depreciate the men with whom Gov. Lewis ranks. It is *now* printed with new types, lately procured from New-York ... Now, then let the dronish insect talk of *bribery* and *corruption.*

The following year and into 1807 the Clermont Livingstons, in support of Governor Lewis, funded the publication of the *Republican Fountain* at Hudson and the *Republican Crisis* in Albany, the latter edited by Isaac Mitchell, formerly of the Poughkeepsie *Barometer*. To the north, in Lansingburgh, it seems likely that the establishment of Francis Adancourt's *Farmers' Register* in 1803 had something to do with the settling of Edmond C. Genêt, a fellow Frenchman and Clintonian, at nearby Greenbush by 1804, after his marriage to George Clinton's daughter, Cornelia. The *Farmers' Register,* the Hudson *Bee,* the *Albany Register,* and the New York *American Citizen* were certainly among the papers about which Robert R. Livingston complained when he wrote to his brother Edward of De Witt Clinton's presidential aspirations in 1806. Clinton, in Livingston's opinion, hoped "thru the medium of corrupt printers to maintain his influence here and by the weight of this state to [press?] the United States to overlook his inexperience and total incompetence for so weighty a change."[42]

The rise of a political press in New York thus raised a series of questions about the terms of opinion formation in the public sphere. There were great suspicions on all sides about the sources of funding for these papers and the role of these funds in shaping the flow of information and persuasion to the public. In short, the press seemed, not free, but corrupt, available to the highest bidder. Seeing opposing papers as polluted agents of partisan chiefs, opponents sought to silence them through legal action.

The grounds for action were not, however, corruption, but its public face. Ambrose Spencer's prosecution of the Federalist Croswell saw Republicans recycling the Federalist tactics of 1798: their case against Croswell rested on the traditional view, derived from Blackstone, that the publication of truth might be a breach of the peace and "tranquility of society" if it gave rise to political passions. Spencer's associate George Caines spoke of the dangers of "the civil incendiary" kindling "the flame of party spirit." But Republicans would not pursue state legal action again, after the Croswell trial. Rather, for all their noise about "truth in evidence," the Federalists were ready to bring civil libel accusations against their Republican opposition, but so were the various Republican factions, particularly the Lewisites. Thus in May 1803 Hamilton's *Evening Post* recommended that Federalists bring private suits against the Republican printers "to bring them down from their daring flights of effrontery in slander." That spring James Cheetham of the Republican *American Citizen* was battling thirteen such suits, and over the following decade dozens of libel suits were entered against newspaper editors in a form of vicarious dueling that indeed often degenerated into literal violence in the streets.[43]

Whether a given paper was secretly sponsored by a wealthy partisan or coterie or simply supported by a readership and advertising that were Federalist or Republican, it could no longer be the public voice of the whole community.

Rather, it was a voice in public dependent on a particular interest and violated old assumptions of print neutrality. Thus the editors were caught in a spiraling contest grounded in the partisan demands of their sponsoring public and the prepartisan claims of their opponents. Building and holding a committed readership required defining a boundary between reader and other—one virtuous and one corrupt. But attacking one's opponents as corrupt might well trigger accusations of slander and suits for libel. At the same time, a paper's survival increasingly would come to depend upon printing contracts with the state and the county courts. Thus mobilization of readers as voters would ensure the survival of the paper; an electoral loss might well lead to a paper's demise.[44]

In essence, eighteenth-century republican assumptions were colliding with nineteenth liberal realities. Partisan advancement of interest was suddenly becoming a reality, but the same partisans could play on classical assumptions of a common interest. At the heart of the matter lay corruption, the violation of public procedure for private gain, the problem of transparency in government. If so, the shape and content of corruption were also in flux, shifting and changing with every passing year.

CLASSICAL AND LIBERAL MODES OF CORRUPTION

A consideration of the political sociology of corruption might start with Alexis de Tocqueville, who rushed past Columbia County one night in early July 1831, headed on a steamboat for Albany. In *Democracy in America*, Tocqueville described two broad modes of political corruption observable in the Atlantic world. In aristocracies, men of status and wealth corrupted the electorate to gain and retain power in government; in democracies, where there were too many voters to buy, the powers of government—and the rewards offered by wealthy interests—corrupted elected officials. If corruption violates the legitimate relationship between public power and private society, Tocqueville saw in the move from aristocracy to democracy a reversal in this relationship. In the classical context, power corrupts society; in the liberal context, society corrupts power. Specifically, this is a violation of public trust in two key arenas: routine administration and transparent decision making. These arenas and their relationships to civil society in its various modes need careful consideration.[45]

The United States, and perhaps especially Columbia County, lay on the cusp between these two modes of corruption in the era of the early Republic, as politics lurched away from the crisis politics of revolutionary settlement toward the settled patterns of routine governance. The era of revolutionary settlement was politically unstable, tinged with threats of political violence and the reality of or potential for constitutional upheaval and unstructured by enduring partisan institutions. During this era of settlement, corruption retained its eighteenth-century connotations, reshaped by the politics of national identity. Corruption had less to do with interest than with treason, retaining its connections with early modern fear of the powers of monarchs and prime ministers to corrupt legislatures and electorates. Only after the settlement had been achieved would a liberal politics of party, interest, and corruption emerge. The politics of corruption was a dimension of the emergence of a liberal politics of distributive interest, which did not take place until the central issues of the Revolution were settled.[46]

Tocqueville's aristocratic mode of corruption thus was that feared by the classical republicanism of the eighteenth-century. We can include in its definition not just the bribing of voters, the corruption of an electorate to gain access to office and power, but the Walpolean corruption of parliaments and legislatures by prime ministers and governors that had so worried British-Americans before the Revolution. This corruption of society by power also worried some New York Federalists in the early 1790s, faced with the enduring and popular governorship of George Clinton. Thus in 1791 Federalists saw a corrupt project under way to build a political coalition in the cheap land sales known as the Macomb purchase; Alexander Hamilton saw Clinton's apparent malfeasance driven by a "narrow and perverse politics" rather than a violation of rules of "probity." These and other land deals that Clinton orchestrated in these years had more to do with aristocracy than democracy, aimed at buying political support rather than lining his pockets. The Macomb land scandal allowed anti-Clintonians to exploit classical fears of the corrupting powers of the executive, most notoriously in a broadside issued in Federalist Kinderhook just before the election that claimed that Clinton was treasonously conspiring to sell the state's north country to the British government. Classical fears were similarly circulating in Virginia circles as Hamilton advanced his own proposals for establishing a national bank and a national policy on industrial development. In New York these fears of an executive's reaching for power were confirmed in the Otsego crisis following the 1792 election, when the gubernatorial ballots of a majority anti-Clintonian county were thrown out on procedural grounds, providing the margin for Clinton's reelection.[47]

At both the state and national levels these eighteenth-century "spectres of Walpole," threatening executive tyranny, ironically set the stage for the emergence of the nuclei of formal opposition seeking popular support: in New York the Federalist supporters of John Jay, and in the country at large, given a boost by the Alien and Sedition Acts, the Democratic-Republican supporters of Thomas Jefferson. In New York, Jay's administration, running from his victory in 1795 to Clinton's final reelection in 1801, stood as an era of transition. Three orderly elections in 1795, 1798, and 1801, accepted as fair and legitimate, calmed fears of executive tyranny that had animated many in the final years of Clinton's long Revolutionary governorship. On the other hand, until 1800, when De Witt Clinton rode Jefferson's electoral victory into control of the Council of Appointment and thus the entire range of state patronage, partisan organization across the state was minimal. Opposition newspapers were few and in both 1798 and 1801 made no claims of corruption in the administration of the state.[48]

Classical concerns about corrupting of executives had long since abated in America by the early 1830s, and Tocqueville saw in democratic America a pettier form of administrative corruption, where officeholders would "pillage the public purse and . . . sell the favors of the state." This we might call a nineteenth-century "liberal" form of corruption, in which corruption was pursued for simple monetary interest rather than for the accumulation of power, in the classical formulation of corruption as the road to tyranny.[49]

In great measure such administrative corruption was endemic, particularly where placeholders depended more on fees than salary for their compensation, as in New York at the turn of the nineteenth century. Here Peter R. Livingston might congratulate his brother Walter in 1785 on his new customs post, wishing him "much joy with your new Office and health and strength to enjoy and improve it to your family's advantage." William Wilson could write sarcastically to Edward P. Livingston in 1802, "My neighbor Hoffman is a justice of the peace and is selling law for a living." Similarly, Charles A. Foote, a law student in Peter Van Schaack's office in Kinderhook, wrote to his father in 1805, "A politician is the servant of the people, and must put up with a great deal of buffeting for the privilege of picking their pockets."[50]

In some measure the entire administrative system of the state under the constitution of 1777 encouraged a corrupt system of influence, as local notables worked to support the election of their peers, who would in turn elect the Council of Appointment, the body of four senators who with the governor approved all appointments to civil and military offices in the state. If this corruption was implicit, contemporaries were certain that other corruption was more explicit: officeholders were violating their administration of public accounts for personal private gain. The Clermont Livingstons suffered a great blow when Edward Livingston was convicted of mishandling funds as mayor of New York in 1803; in that same year the local Federalists complained bitterly about Captain John C. Ten Broeck's loss of the federal customs inspection in Hudson. In 1804 the Burrite and Federalist presses exposed the number of offices held by the Livingstons, the Clintons, and their connections, and indeed the division of these two great Republican clans the year following rested in De Witt Clinton's anger that his relations were losing the spoils of office to the Livingstons. Five years later Sheriff John C. Hogeboom was targeted by Hudson Federalists for his handling of county funds, and then in 1810 the Albany papers began a campaign against state comptroller Elisha Jenkins, who they claimed had made loans from the state school fund on very easy terms to his family and connections in Hudson. After the War of 1812 Governor Daniel D. Tompkins would suffer, accused of mishandling state accounts.[51]

These accusations of corruption and private gain at public expense were carefully timed for maximum impact, published in the party press in the weeks and days before general elections in an attempt to attract and hold the attention of the voters. In some cases these were clearly smear campaigns, as in the attack on Hogeboom, which was admitted months later to have been trumped up. But in May 1809 Jacob R. Van Rensselaer could write from Hudson to Federalist Ebenezer Foote in Delaware County:

> Our opponents are completely overthrown and until they can procure new leaders they will never rise, the attack on John C. Hogeboom has essentially impaired [him and?] will eventually destroy his influence[.] He has been the prominent man of that party here and his place cannot be supplied[.] When the fact of extortion shall be fully proved on himself in a Court of Justice the public confidence will be withdrawn from him and he will sink into the insignificancy from which he never ought to have emerged.

A great company, rightly or wrongly, were called to justify their public accounts in Jeffersonian New York. As the routines of partisan rhetoric emerged, the behavior of officeholders emerged as a natural and easy narrative for editors and politicians to develop. Here a deep-rooted American suspicion of the private avarice of royal placeholders was intensified by the endless scramble for advantage in the marketplace. The experience of this scramble for individual gain in the economy made it easy for Americans to suspect that private individual interest was corrupting the public trust and power granted to men by civil appointment. Such concerns easily superseded older ones about the classical corruptions in the quest for pure power. As were all Americans, officeholders were seeking a way to wealth, or at least a stable competency, what contemporaries called "the bread of office."[52]

The drive to "pillage the public purse" was thus a central dimension of the corruption that the people of New York saw running through their political system. But a second key mode of corruption can be extrapolated from Tocqueville's observations on the sale of "the favors of the state," the systemic corruption of public decision making by which collective problems led to political solutions. This process assumes and requires inclusive participation and attention to rules, implied and constitutional, intended to achieve equitable, disinterested results. The wider lawmaking arena was clearly more important in Jeffersonian New York than the formally administrative-bureaucratic one, since New York may be seen as a preadministrative state, in which the better part of public problem solving was achieved through distributive legislation.[53]

FACTIONS, BANKS, AND THE
CORRUPTION OF THE LEGISLATURE

The relationship between public and private, and thus the ground for corruption and its perception, began to change markedly during the Jay years. Under George Clinton, the state government itself functioned as a vehicle of distribution and development. Public committees, authorized by the legislature, built roads and bridges or lent money in the same manner that the state regulated citizenship or established town governments. Federalists established a new relationship between governmental authority and society at large: the granting of public authority to private corporations. Although there were important precursors before 1796 in the early banks chartered in New York, Albany, and Hudson, in the early canal companies, and in a few academies, the Jay years saw an explosion of chartered corporations: academies, libraries, turnpikes, banks, turnpike companies. This sudden shift toward granting limited public and financial authority to discrete self-perpetuating groups of individuals can be measured roughly in Columbia and the adjacent counties of Dutchess and Rensselaer. Before 1796 only one private corporation, the Bank of Columbia in Hudson, was incorporated in these three counties, more than counterbalanced by law after law devoted to public loan offices, roads, bridges, and village, town, city, and county governments. Starting in 1796, academies for classical education were chartered in each of these counties, followed by libraries (under a general act), and then six turnpike corporations and the Farmer's Bank in Troy between 1798 and 1801. This rising curve of state incorporation was not unique to the mid-Hudson, and it continued unabated in the years to come. Importantly, it coincided with the rising numbers of newspapers in New York State, especially newspapers directly competing with one another in a given town or county.[54]

Stakes in this reconfiguration of state authority, partisanship, and civil institutions were enormous, and they offered a ripe field for political entrepreneurs. New York was in the midst of the opening stages of its Herculean economic development, which would make it the pivot of the wider national economy by the 1830s. This process required credit and capital, and state-chartered banks were the vehicles of that credit, and political connections (as well as kinship) were vital means of individual access to that credit. By 1793, three banks in New York City, Albany, and Hudson placed credit firmly in the hands of Federalist commerce; their collective capitalization of $1,420,000 was challenged in 1799 by Burr's Republican Manhattan Company capitalized at $2,000,000. In the last legislative session of Jay's governorship the Federalists chartered the Farmer's Bank in Troy and Lansingburgh, bringing bank capital under Federalist control up to $1,720,000. Although the 1802 legislature was dominated by turnpike issues, the politics of banking occupied the next three sittings of the legislature, in a politics of unrestrained group interest.[55]

The proliferation of chartered corporations in the Jay years marked the onset of New York's nineteenth-century politics of state power and economic action, but without organized parties or competing newspapers the nineteenth-century politics of corruption lay in abeyance. Charges of corruption were not a central feature of politics during Jay's governorship, perhaps in some measure because of the lack of competing partisan papers outside New York and Albany. The Federalist inclination of the press had made it hostile to Clinton during the final years of his administration; this inclination meant that few editors would have much negative to say about Jay, and there were very few Republican papers to focus an opposition voice. Thus, even after the national expansion of the Republican press between the Sedition Act in 1798 and Jefferson's election in 1800, only New York City and Albany had competing local presses. Not yet clearly attached to organized parties in the 1790s, New York's papers did not yet instinctively see projects of corruption in the months before elections, and without party competition there might indeed have been less corruption to expose. Such would not be the case in the years to come, and the press itself would be an agent in this very corruption.[56]

That restraint ended with the election of 1801. In the spring the Republicans deployed the general terms of the classical narrative of corruption in their gubernatorial campaign against Stephen Van Rensselaer, who was supported by "the corrupt admirers of monarchy" and the "seaport nobility." In Columbia County the wave of support for the old Revolutionary hero, George Clinton, narrowly elected a Republican assembly slate. These assemblymen included Dr. Moses Younglove of the hill town of Canaan, who led a phalanx of ideological Old Republicans in the spring 1802 session of the assembly against the Jayite model of developmental distribution, in an aggressive effort to perpetuate the radical vision. In the heat of this struggle Younglove would articulate a model of corruption that harked back to classical definitions, a model of corruption that would soon fade into the background as the new partisan politics of corruption emerged in full form in the following year.[57]

In the legislature's first extended struggle over the powers of incorporation, Younglove with a group of downstate Republicans voted consistently to restrict the power of turnpikes and to oppose their continuing establishment. In particular, they vehemently opposed the powers of turnpike corporations to appropriate timber and gravel on private land adjacent to their roadways, even if the owners gave their permission. Clashing with blocs of Federalists and entrepreneurial and moderate Republicans, these ideologues also voted overwhelmingly to ban theatrical productions. Where others strongly supported a loosening of the New York Social Library charter, these men split. They were united in opposing militia fines for Quakers. Thus on a wide array of public issues, this group of Republicans expressed a minimalist vision, seeking to restrict the powers of governmentally sanctioned civil associations, to enforce ancient moral standards, and to defend the rights of individual dissenters.[58]

Some of the motivations behind these votes were articulated in a series of letters in the *Albany Register,* signed by Civis and attributed to Moses Younglove by his opponent, Elkanah Watson, once again in Albany promoting a variety of improving schemes. Writing in the midst of the turnpike debate in the assembly, Civis-Younglove announced on March 2, 1802, "The Legislature ought to check the great increase of this kind of Corporation." However "well-intentioned," Civis believed "their tendency hostile to sound republican maxims." He was not concerned with petty corruption, but with "despotism": the insidious and systemic corruption that the "opulent" would be the stockholders, the more numerous would "pay toll," and society would be divided "into two orders of opposite interests." In chartering more turnpikes the legislature would "multiply authorities beyond the reach of legal controul, and thus narrow at once the sphere of liberty and legislation."[59]

Watson challenged Younglove a week later in the *Register.* Younglove's argument had included implicitly the host of libraries and charitable societies recently incorporated by the state; were their powers a threat to the state? Civis's reply was unequivocal:

I hold it clearly anti-republican, to perpetuate any of these corporations, and bind posterity to their will and interest . . . it is not only turnpike corporations only that excite my apprehension—we are continually incorporating companies of various description. . . . In this we follow the monarchical monopolizing plan of Britain; and as in Britain these corporations will in some things have a common interest in preferring a partial to the general good. Our fathers, and we, have heretofore done without them — and I had rather enjoy LIBERTY and EQUAL RIGHTS in the old plain way, under some inconveniencies, than sacrifice them at the shrine of Monarchical improvements.

Younglove as Civis spoke a monitory language that harked back to the circular letters of the Canaan Democratic Society, which he established in 1794 and carried into 1795 with three other Canaan democrats, Matthew Adgate, Jonathan Warner, and Elisha Gilbert. The society's constitution had condemned a "growing establishment of pride, formality, inequality, political heresy, and a baneful and servile imitation of sovereign and corrupt nations" and "corrupt proceedings" in elections; it had spoken of the common interest in the "conduct of those in public trust" and warned that "corruption hides her guilt in a specious closet of artful intricacy."[60]

In the spring 1802 assembly, Younglove was in a position to act against the corporate agents of this general social corruption and to defend the classical republican principles as he learned them in the Revolutionary crisis. His language anticipated that of Andrew Jackson, for whom Younglove would stand as a presidential elector in 1828. More immediately, over the next decade, others were more willing to cry "corruption" without condemning these instruments; corruption lay in one's opponents' means of access to state authority, not in the access itself. Rather than a general violation of "republican maxims," corruption was part of the give-and-take of legislative and elective politics.[61]

Although he would remain a figure in Republican circles in Columbia County for many years, Moses Younglove served his only assembly term in 1801–1802. In the April 1802 election the Federalist slate won by a margin of about 150 votes, led by its standard-bearer, Henry W. Livingston, who also narrowly beat John P. Van Ness for a seat in the Eighth Congress. The next session of the legislature saw the contest over state-chartered corporations raised to a new level. Petitions presented to the 1803 legislature asked for charters for two banks and a bank branch in Albany. A group of prominent Republicans, including, among others, Ambrose Spencer, Elisha Jenkins, and Elkanah Watson, urged the state to incorporate a new State Bank of Albany; two groups of Federalists wanted a charter for the Albany Mercantile Company and approval for an Albany branch of the American Exchange Company. Columbia's Federalists, with some occasional dissensions from the representative from Canaan, voted to stall the Republican State Bank and advance the Federalist Albany Mercantile Bank. By the end of March the outcome was apparent: a Republican legislature had approved the State Bank at a capitalization of $460,000 and had vetoed the two Federalist initiatives. As the election approached, the issue of corruption suddenly emerged as a campaign issue.[62]

The first time that more than one bank was proposed in a given session for a single city, the bank struggle of 1803 set off an editorial battle in Albany between the Federalist *Albany Centinel* and the Republican *Albany Register*. The *Centinel* printed pieces blasting the State Bank of Albany's aborted plan to write a monopoly over the Onondago saltworks into its charter. The backers of the State Bank had also on March 25 published a "remonstrance" against the Albany Mercantile Bank; this too was a target of the *Centinel*'s contempt. Meanwhile, in New York, James Cheetham in the Clintonian *American Citizen* attacked the unsanctioned establishment of a new Merchant's Bank by a coalition of Federalists and Burrites, and it was rumored that the Exchange Bank was a front for Burr, who had recently been ousted from the Manhattan Company.[63]

Then around April 20, a week before the upcoming assembly elections, the Albany County Federalist Committee published a pamphlet, complete with appended affidavits, entitled *A View of Certain Proceedings in the Two Houses of the Legislature, respecting the Incorporation of the New State Bank*. Its authors "look[ed] with astonishment at the corrupt and scandalous scene exhibited among the member of the Legislature." Not only had it been proposed that the State Bank should monopolize the western salt springs and be capitalized as a specifically Republican institution at a high capitalization, but legislators had been bribed with distributed or reserved bank shares. Where the Republicans in 1801 had claimed that "corruptions of monarchy and aristocracy were creeping into the government," the Federalists had proof that the "sanctuary" of the legislature had been violated by "corruption."[64]

The response of the Republican *Albany Register* was defensive yet telling. On April 19 it had warned its readers of Federalist electioneering plots, of "numerous progeny of *fabrications*," of "snares and traps." The Federalists were spreading lies and "slander" in a "spirit of calumny." "They seem to think that the propagation of an idea so dishonorable to the founders of that Law, will promote the success of their Ticket." On April 22, the editor reported that the Federalist *View* was in circulation, blatantly "calculated to impose absolute falsehoods on the public, to serve electioneering purposes." Why else would it be "ushered in at this late day," the *Register* asked, noting the parallel with 1792, when in the closing days before the election Federalist broadsides had accused Clinton of attempting to sell northern New York to the British and of having an interest in Macomb's purchase? In Hudson, the *Balance* was consumed with the Croswell trial — "Liberty of the Press!" — and with the firing of Federalist John C. Ten Broeck from his customs post, leaving it to Stoddard's *Gazette* to publish the Federalist *View* from the *Centinel*.[65]

Perhaps the Federalists cut it too close; perhaps their affidavits would never have been very convincing. Across the state the Republicans easily prevailed in the April elections; in Columbia the Republican assembly slate was elected by the narrowest of margins. The press war over the corruption charges, having spread quickly down the Hudson from Albany to New York City, just as quickly subsided. The issues of credit and political publication would not disappear, but converged in the ensuing sessions of the legislature. The 1804 and 1805 sessions would struggle with the problems of expanding the terms of political speech and capitalized credit while the specter of corruption hovered over their proceedings.

William W. Van Ness of Claverack had been narrowly defeated in his April 1803 bid for the assembly; thus the Federalist bid to revise New York's libel law was introduced in early February 1804 by an Albany associate, James Emott. The assembly's discussion of this bill was delayed for several days in mid-February by Croswell's final trial before the Supreme Court, as the arguments for the defendant by Van Ness and, particularly, Hamilton emptied both house and senate chambers. Then through the end of February and into March both houses debated first the libel law and then petitions for incorporating a Merchant's Bank in New York and the Albany Mercantile Company.[66]

The Republicans were combative. A critical core of Republicans voted against loosening the terms of libel defenses — granting juries powers to determine fact and law in particular — and against new Federalist-supported banks. Here a committee reported that the previous legislature had determined that there were sufficient credit facilities in New York City and recommended legislation to restrict unauthorized banking associations, a measure aimed at the Merchant's Bank, which had been operating without a charter for almost a year. This restraining act was indeed passed, but with a proviso giving the Merchant's Bank another year "to intrigue" with a new legislature, as one observer put it. The four Republicans from Columbia, apparently under the pressure of their narrow mandate, split on the bank legislation: Colonel Benjamin Birdsall and Samuel Ten Broeck supported the restraining act, which restricted the activities of unincorporated banks like the Merchant's Bank; they were opposed by Stephen Miller and James I. Van Alen (Van Buren's half brother) in the assembly and Stephen Hogeboom in the senate. The Columbia Republicans were similarly divided on the Federalist libel bill, Van Alen again voting with the Federalists. The Republican majority, supported by Birdsall and Miller, voted to restrict a defense against libel to writings that were signed by their author, a provision that the *Balance* condemned. The bill was delayed in the senate and submitted too late for review by the Council of Revision; its delay that spring was the ground for a spate of accusations in the *Balance,* the *Bee,* and the New York party press in general.[67]

Elected to the assembly in spring 1804, in the first of a string of continual Federalist victories that would run to the collapse of the Columbia Junto in 1821, William W. Van Ness played a central and controversial role in the 1805 session. Again the issues were banks and libel. That February 12, voting with a large majority not to attempt to override the council's belated rejection of the 1804 libel bill, Van Ness "gave notice, that on some future day he would move" another libel bill. This 1805 bill avoided the stipulation of a signature and exactly repeated language that Hamilton had used in Croswell's trial — truth would defend from libel accusation if "published with good motives and for justifiable ends." It passed into law without great controversy early that April and set a shaping precedent for American libel law. Over the previous month, however, the legislature had been mired again in accusations of bribery and corruption.[68]

That February the Merchant's Bank had once again petitioned for incorporation, this time in the senate. Debates ensued, and by March 13 the senate had engrossed the bill, but immediately cries of corruption exploded from a core of antibank Republicans. Certain senators were said to have been bribed for their votes by the bank's agents; it was, Elisha Jenkins wrote that day to De Witt Clinton, "the most bare-faced corruption that ever disgraced a Legislative measure"; even "the Yazoo measure," in which a bribed Georgia legislature had sold a vast territory in 1795, did "not even furnish an exception." On March 16, before the assembly even opened the subject of the bill, certificates alleging the exchange of bank shares for votes for the bill were read into the record, and a struggle ensued to form a committee of investigation. Once again, William W. Van Ness was the first on his feet on the sixteenth, making an "elegant" speech to oppose any investigation, on the eighteenth managed to get himself onto the committee, and on the twentieth was instrumental in sidetracking the inquiry. By the twenty-third the Merchant's Bank bill — fully supported by Van Ness's Federalist colleagues from Columbia — had passed the assembly by a vote of fifty-two to thirty-two and was on its way back to the senate, to pass into law on the twenty-sixth.[69]

The Federalist press gushed over Van Ness's performance: the *New-York Herald* announced that he had "done wonders" and had "excited the admiration and applause of all." Clintonian Republican James Cheetham in the *American Citizen* was not so sanguine: "Whether he had bribed others or himself received a bribe, I cannot say, but it is certain that he has unhappily disappointed all who heard him that once thought him an honorable man." As was Jabez Hammond when he wrote his classic history of New York politics four decades later, Cheetham was convinced that "Mr. Van Ness of Hudson" was the primary manager of the bill, advising and commanding the "common soldiery" of the bill's supporters. Both Cheetham, in the *American Citizen,* and Charles Holt, in the Hudson *Bee,* invoked "the maxim of Sir Robert Walpole, that *'every man has his price,'*" and Holt twice reminded his readers of the Yazoo scandal. Cheetham also trumpeted that "a charter obtained by *bribery* and *corruption* is necessarily void" and proposed an "*appeal to the* PEOPLE" if the bank passed the test of the state supreme court. For these and other comments, Federalist Abraham Van Vechten of Albany, who recently had represented Croswell in his libel defense, introduced a resolution for Cheetham's prosecution on a charge of libel, which easily passed both houses. In the assembly on April 5, the bank's proponents equally easily beat back a proposal to retroactively apply the protections of the new libel law to Cheetham's prosecution.[70]

Van Ness had apparently returned to Hudson to manage the coming election and did not vote on Cheetham's exclusion from the libel law. Van Ness's role in the Merchant's Bank affair had wider implications of which the Columbia County Republicans were well aware. He had effectively established himself as a statewide power broker, leading a rump group of Federalists into a new and growing breach in the ranks of the Republican Party. In the previous years the Republican mainstream had hived off a small Burrite faction, which had decisively lost the 1804 governor's election. In 1805 the issue of the Merchant's Bank led to another division, since Governor Morgan Lewis and the Livingston interest supported the bank against the opposition of Clinton and Spencer, who saw a threat to the interests of the Republican Manhattan Bank. By the spring of 1805 the Republicans were utterly divided, and, in Hudson, Charles Holt aligned the *Bee* with Clinton while Croswell's *Balance* had pleasant things to say about Morgan Lewis, the Livingstons, and Stephen Hogeboom, who had voted for the bank in the senate. The 1807 election would pit Clintonians against Lewisites allied with Federalists and the residual followers of Aaron Burr. But in 1805 the Columbia Clintonian Republican leadership was convinced that Federalist Van Ness was the kingpin of this emerging factional alliance. It urged the Republican electorate to make every effort to turn him out of office. Curtius described him in the *Bee* as the "bold yet subtle leader of the united bands of Burr and Hamilton whose pliancy of principle and opinion has conducted him prosperously thus far in his political career." "Under his fostering hand," he argued, "the Merchants' Bank" had been pushed through the legislature by a coterie of "monarchists, tories and refugees." Writing in the *Bee*, "One of You" laid out the picture in all its ramifications:

> Federalism . . . too feeble to act as a party . . . builds all its hopes on fomenting dissensions among republicans, by the subtlety and intrigues of a few federal members from two or possibly three counties. It remains with the citizens of Columbia, to determine whether she will give to this flagitious and desperate little band a powerful, artful and inveterate leader, bent on dividing and destroying the whole republican strength of the state, or redeem her reputation for attachment to good principles. . . . Before the genius of republicanism, spreading light and knowledge in its course, civil and ecclesiastical oppression has vanished, and the hydra of federalism hides its manifold and pestiferous head, while freedom, peace and plenty hail the recurring year. . . . Why, then, can it be that in Columbia county a federal majority should ever be found? . . . Why send [Federalist] members to the assembly to eke out a nominal minority?

Despite the Republican efforts, Van Ness easily won his seat again in 1805 and in 1806. After the 1807 session he landed a place on the supreme court bench, in exchange for "his exertions to re-elect uncle Morgy," the *Bee* sarcastically noted.[71]

After his elevation to the state bench, Van Ness's leading place in Columbia's electoral politics was inherited by his associates Elisha Williams and Jacob R. Van Rensselaer. Williams would play a central role in the years to come in the state's banking politics, most notoriously with Van Ness and Van Rensselaer in the Bank of America scandal. Closer to home, they managed the Bank of Columbia in the city of Hudson, which — according to a local historian some decades later — dropped "sound business principles" and "was used as a political engine." In 1807 Williams himself described the bank in these terms to a colleague: "As we have 13 fine federal Directors . . . you have no great reason to fear that it will be brought to subserve the cause of Democracy."[72]

Well before 1807 it was clear to all that the boundaries between state authority, factional interest, and the wider institutions of civil society were thin at best. If civil society stood as a flywheel between the people and the legislative authority of the state, the hidden and not-so-hidden hands of small groups of "designing men" were controlling its levers. The factions that splintered across New York's political landscape had public voices, sometimes secretly funded, in the newspapers that proliferated in the years after 1800. In Hudson in the spring of 1807 there were three papers competing for readership: the nominally Federalist *Balance*, the Clintonian *Bee*, and the Lewisite *Republican Fountain*, sponsored by the Clermont Livingstons. Factional interest was equally grounded in competing banks; indeed, banking and credit were increasingly the underlying root of political action. In New York City banks were seen as engines of electoral control. Writing in 1806 of New York City in the 1790s, James Cheetham was certain of

> the pernicious effects of Banking institutions upon the freedom of elections, while they were confined within the hands of a single party.... Even the affluent merchant would reluctantly oppose the wishes of Directors whose smiles were gold, and whose favour was essential to the success of commercial enterprizes. It was impossible to resist so formidable an engine.

In 1807 the Hillsdale Republican meeting, echoing the language of the anti–Van Rensselaer petitions of the 1780s, resolved that "the divisions which at present subsist among the republicans of this state, have been fomented by designing men, for the sole purpose of enriching themselves, to the injury of the great body of the people." Politics, it seemed, was a vehicle, not for a public good, but for a variety of competing private goods, pyramids of economic power and political influence centering on banks. Despite radical concerns about designing men, a group of the Columbia Clintonian Republicans decided to round out their structure in February 1808, petitioning for a bank of their own, the Bank of Hudson, perhaps hoping that the simultaneous petition to recharter the Federalist Bank of Columbia would fail. Both banks were approved in a wave of rechartered passing the legislature, as Jefferson's Embargo slowed the state's — and the county's — economy.[73]

FEDERALIST LANDLORDS AND ELECTORAL CORRUPTION

If the commercial collapse of the Embargo years would ratchet up the stakes of New York's politics, they were already high: Federalists expected no quarter from their Republican opponents and gave none in return. These stakes revolved around the increasingly complex linkages between politics and personal prosperity, stakes that made public life volatile and violent. The Clintonian-Lewisite division over the Merchant's Bank set off a veritable explosion of public and private actions for libel. Many were aimed at party printers, others at the authors of libel themselves. In this fluid, sparring world, the problem of "truth" became increasingly complicated, verging onto a slippery terrain of corrupt distortion and outright falsehood.[74]

Alexander Hamilton, seeing himself the great constitutional statesman, had taken on the Croswell case so that truth might stand against corruption, classically defined. In the tradition of a jealous watchful republicanism, a truth-bearing press would stand against creeping tyranny. Hamilton saw virtue, rather than a breach of the peace, in exposing Jefferson's alleged misdeeds and in thwarting an attempted cover-up by state Republican officials. The Blackstone tradition, in which truth might be treasonous libel if it led to partisan violence, might be manipulated into a vehicle of corrupt distortion and incipient tyranny.[75]

Other Federalists, less statesmen than political operatives and increasingly desperate after Hamilton's death, were perhaps not so principled. Or perhaps they saw the need for a little "holy lying" for "the *Good Old Cause*." Where the Federalist press claimed the protections of the new libel law, invoking "truth" at every step, the Republicans saw a continuing system of lies and dirty tricks, running back to the Federalist efforts in 1792 and 1803. The Columbia County Federalists seemed particularly given to electioneering trickery. In 1805 William Tanner of Hillsdale, one of the Republican assembly candidates, had to publish a series of affidavits denying that he had blacked his face and joined the rioters who had killed Sheriff Cornelius Hogeboom in 1791. When the Federalists accused another Republican candidate — Fite Miller of Granger — of illiteracy in 1807, it was only one of a host of "fibs" and "crooked stories" emanating that year from the united front of Federalists and Lewis-ite Quids. The next year the county Republicans were overjoyed at defeating a Federalist effort to accuse them of ducking an unpublicized debate challenge by packing the meeting; in the early winter of 1810 Elisha Williams and Jacob R. Van Rensselaer had to publicly disclaim their accusations that John C. Hogeboom, the Republican sheriff and assembly candidate, had corruptly mishandled the county funds. The *Bee* mocked their opposition's "rare morality":

> These are all harmless and honorable electioneering tricks, because they are to support the good cause of quid federalism . . . the means may be detestable, and the end commendable . . . good federal folk, in the good quiddical cause, may swear as many plumpers as they please.[76]

The stakes of the electoral battle were clear to all, as New York's Federalists attempted to hold a minimal purchase on the political process. Columbia County, with Albany, Oneida, and Ontario, provided the last bastion of consistent Federalist voting in a Republican state; the survival of the Federal interest and its revival with the unpopular Jeffersonian Embargo policies depended upon the efforts of these county politicians. The Columbia Junto would reap its rewards — and seal its eventual downfall — in 1812 and 1813, with a special loan to the Bank of Columbia by the newly chartered Bank of America and the elevation of Jacob R. Van Rensselaer to the speakership by a temporary Federalist majority in the assembly.

But it would appear that interest was only part of the mix of motivations that impelled the Columbia Federalists. They also harbored a powerful psychological need to maintain control and dominance. These were men who were desperately threatened by any challenges to their authority and honor, quick to anger, and quick to resort to violence. Charles A. Foote, a young law student in Kinderhook, reported to his father that John Livingston had flown into a rage when his son Robert LeRoy—mocked in the *Bee* as "Crazy Bob"—was narrowly defeated for Congress in 1806, and Foote predicted a similar explosion if the county Republicans won the 1807 assembly election. Foote learned the consequences of this anger the hard way when he and some friends were foolish enough to laugh at Jacob R. Van Rensselaer from a window casement as he was riding through town. Striding into the house, Van Rensselaer called him "an impudent puppy" and a "d——d rascal" and started to horsewhip him, not realizing that he was the son of a fellow Federalist leader. In Hudson, Federalist Elisha Williams assaulted Republican printer Charles Holt for an article in the *Bee,* knocking him down in front of his office. Martin Van Buren was challenged to a duel by a Federalist legal opponent in 1811. Upriver in Albany, heated exchanges about imputed statements by Edmond Genêt of Greenbush in March 1807 led to a series of street brawls: Federalist Solomon Van Rensselaer attacked Elisha Jenkins of Hudson from behind, striking him in the back of the head with a heavy cane; in return Van Rensselaer was hunted down and assaulted by Albany's leading Republicans.[77]

Such violence was, of course, not uncommon in the politics of the early Republic. Certainly political violence had a popular dimension in the volunteer companies organized in Hudson: the Hudson Greens, in green-feathered black hats and green uniforms, comprised the Federalist contingent; the Wigton Artillery, in red-feathered black caps and blue uniforms, the Republican. Kept apart by the separate partisan celebrations of the Fourth of July, these men certainly came to blows on occasion in Hudson's streets and alleys. But here in the Hudson Valley, as in the slave South, there was more than a tinge of aristocratic presumption behind such political violence, and the other "means" to political ends. In the affair of the Merchant's Bank, and later the Bank of America, the Columbia Junto was accused of forms of corruption that Alexis de Tocqueville would call "democratic." Seeking favorable treatment, private interests in a democracy would corrupt various officeholders—legislators, judges—to achieve their ends. But it also appears that the Columbia Junto established and maintained its grip on electoral politics by means of what Tocqueville would call aristocratic corruption, the purchase or coercion of the electorate itself.[78]

Electoral corruption focused on the manor lands of the Livingstons and took two broad forms, the coercion of and the "making" of voters. Throughout the eighteenth century Livingston Manor had operated as a pocket borough, automatically electing the announced Livingston candidate to the legislature. The 1777 constitution eliminated the privileges of this old manorial representation, forcing the Livingstons into countywide assembly elections, but by the end of the 1780s the Manor had emerged as a decisive engine in county elections. Quite simply, starting in 1789 the massed votes of the Livingston tenants often determined elections in Columbia County. In 1792 Peter Van Schaack had detected the *"quid pro quo"* of an "unnatural coalition" between the Livingstons and George Clinton, and this coalition had contributed to the Republican control of Columbia's assembly delegation down through 1798. The Upper Manor Livingstons returned to the Federalist fold in 1798, and from 1800 the overwhelming Federalist votes on the Manor, in Germantown, and increasingly at Clermont began consistently to carry elections for Federalist candidates (see Figures 1, 2).[79]

Though they narrowly lost the 1801 elections, the Federalists regained their control in 1802. In the days after the election Republican candidate Ambrose Spencer was panicked at their impending loss and wrote an angry letter to William Wilson. Spencer detected "great exertions and the most abandoned deception": a rumor apparently had circulated that he was doing legal work for the Federalist Upper Manor Livingstons. While reports gave the rest of the county to the Republicans, "the Manor has destroyed us." Spencer won 1,315 votes in the northern towns and only 141 in the "lower towns," compared to an 1,122–552 split for the leading Federalist, Samuel Edmonds of Hudson. William Van Ness's first election in 1804 was similar: north of the Livingston region he was beaten by his closest Republican rival, Colonel Benjamin Birdsall, 1,441–1,155; in the Livingston towns he won 817–213. The Federalist vote in the Manor towns thus determined the string of Federalist victories in 1800, 1802, and 1804–1808 and contributed to these victories from 1809 on, when Madisonian policies of embargo and war turned other sections of the county against the Republicans.[80]

As the *Bee* put it in 1806, tenants were "induced" to vote the landlord's ticket "by those means which the tenants of Livingston's Manor are too well acquainted with." When he had first arrived in 1802, new to the county and obliged to the Clermont Livingstons for patronage, Charles Holt had been hesitant to attack the landlord interest in the *Bee*. In 1803 he published an essay by A Plain Farmer, announcing that the Federalist candidates — "Messrs. Van Ness and Co." — had been chosen at a closed meeting "on the Manor," clearly at one of the Livingston houses. In 1804, when the votes from the Upper Manor towns determined the county's majority for Federalists in the assembly and Aaron Burr for governor, Holt was much bolder, noting caustically in the *Bee's* election roundup the decisive role of "an increased requisition of the feudal posse in the manor of Livingston, marshaled and conducted by the two Messieurs Livingston and Van Ness." But in 1805, no longer obliged to Clermont, Holt's *Bee* fused the rhetoric of legislative and electoral corruption in bold, slashing attacks on aristocracy and dependency.[81]

On April 23, Holt published essays condemning "the tools and panders of corruption" and urging the county to vote to deny them their "bold and subtle leader," William W. Van Ness. On April 30, the *Bee* kept up the drumbeat of the "conclusive testimony of *bribery* and *corruption*" and turned to the theme of the corruption of the electorate. Attacking one of the Livingstons running for the assembly, Scrutator pointed to the "well known" effects of "the tenure of the inhabitants of the manor of Livingston, and the species and degree of influence exercised upon them at elections by their landlords." He then directly compared tenants with slaves, sharing dependency and civil death.

> In Virginia the negroes are not permitted to vote for their masters; much less are they obliged to. But if they were they would not vote more uniformly in favor of their owners than the tenants of Livingston's manor, with the exception of a few virtuous, honorable, and independent citizens.

Despite the odds of their "combat against the influence of manors and wealth and influence of family, against the most powerful local aristocracy in this state," Curtius urged the county Republicans: "To the polls . . . ye who believe our government is better than a monarchy . . . that all men are born equal and have equal rights; especially, ye who believe that a republic can exist without king, or nobility, or aristocracy." A year later the *Bee's* assault on Crazy Bob kept up the rhetorical assault. The Livingstons were a family "claiming more than their ordinary share in government": "In three of our towns they hold and exercise as complete dominion over the inhabitants as the overseers of plantations in Virginia." In 1807 the *Bee* mocked "the republicanism of the landlords of hundreds of life leases, whose tenants vote only as the proprietors will, and are brought to the polls in posse comitatus to support federalism." In the wake of another defeat at the polls Holt put the county's unique politics into wider perspective.

> The republicans of Columbia will not be discouraged by their defeat in the late election. There are not manors of Livingstons or Rensselaers in every county, but freemen enough in the state to preserve the government from the hands of the landlords and every other species of aristocracy.

The message was clear to those that would hear it: Columbia County politics was in the hands of an alliance of "corruptionists" who would buy a legislature to charter a bank, lodged in elective office by aristocratic families preying on a dependent, slavelike tenantry.[82]

THE EDUCATION AND TRIBULATION
OF MARTIN VAN BUREN, 1807–1812

It was in these years, and in this climate, that Martin Van Buren emerged from legal and political apprenticeship. His rise was intimately connected to the fortunes of his half brother, James I. Van Alen. In the summer of 1803, trying to evade binding commitments to the Republican Van Nesses and Aaron Burr, Van Buren returned from New York City to Kinderhook and quietly studied for the bar in Van Alen's office. In November, about two weeks before his twenty-first birthday, he made a quick trip to the city to take the bar and then entered into a partnership with Van Alen. Van Buren brought a quick wit, intense diligence, and a wide connection to Van Alen's well-established practice, and within a year he had reached an income of more than $3,000. He calculated that he would be worth $120,000 by the time he retired. He must have assumed a considerable body of the office caseload, as Van Alen in 1804 was appointed county surrogate, charged with administering the local affairs of probate and wardship. Van Buren continued to have time for society, however. As a young lawyer he mixed easily with the young men studying with Peter Van Schaack, and in the fall of 1805 he briefly met with them in a Kinderhook Law Society, of which he was elected the examiner; a year and a half later, just twenty-four years old, he was admitted to the bar of the New York supreme court, approved to practice with the most accomplished lawyers in the state.[83]

His political career followed a similar path, after he navigated the factional shoals of the Clinton-Burr division. After working for John P. Van Ness's nomination in 1801, he had to separate himself from the Burrite Van Nesses: when he made his Clintonian allegiances public at the polls in April 1804, his right to vote was challenged by Peter Van Ness and Peter Van Schaack, "arm in arm," now allied in support of Aaron Burr. Standing up to his former patrons, Van Buren was subjected to a humiliating challenge to his right to vote in the governor's election, a challenge that required him to swear in public that he was of age, not a felon, and the holder of a two hundred dollar freehold estate. On the last count, Van Buren could not have been entirely truthful; his freeholder status rested in his law partnership with his half brother, Van Alen, who would have had to lend him the money if the challenge had been pressed

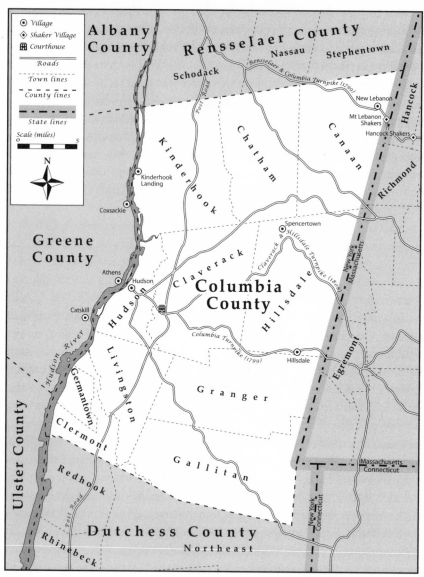

MAP 4. *Jeffersonian Columbia, 1803–1818*. Drawn by Jim DeGrand

For the fifteen years between 1803 and 1818, Columbia County's civil geography did not change. The town of Chatham had been incorporated in 1795, and in 1803 Clintonian Republicans succeeded in separating two towns from Livingston: Granger and Gallitan. A Federalist legislature in 1814 would rename these towns Taghkanic and Ancram. In 1818 three new towns were chartered, Austerlitz taken from northern Hillsdale, New Lebanon from northern Canaan, and Ghent from Kinderhook, Claverack, and Chatham. Finally, in 1824, two new towns were formed out of the old Upper Manor, Copake from the east section of Taghkanic and a new Gallatin from the west section of Ancram.

further. The beneficiary of the practice in the spring of 1804, the custom of "making voters" on election day would loom ever larger in Van Buren's political calculus over the next eight years.[84]

The next April, Van Buren was chosen as secretary, first of the Kinderhook Republican meeting, and then of the county meeting in Hudson. His half brother, Van Alen, apparently forgiven for his votes for the Merchant's Bank in 1804, was nominated at this meeting for the assembly. Van Alen and the Republican slate lost their bid in 1805, but only by 150 votes. The tables turned in the spring of 1806, if only in the congressional race. Van Buren apparently had a role greater than town convention delegate to the county meeting, since Van Alen was chosen as the Republican candidate to run against Robert Leroy (Crazy Bob) Livingston for the county seat in Congress. One of his Federalist colleagues in the Kinderhook Law Society, Charles A. Foote, wrote sourly to his father of Van Buren's rising position.

> The election in this County will go very hard. I fear the whole democratic ticket will succeed, at least their congressman. Our candidate is very *weak,* and his opponents are indefatigable. The exertions of the whole party and particularly that little imp of jacobinism M. Van Buren, are almost incredible. What makes the probable success of Van Alen more mortifying is the accession it will bring to the already intolerable impudence of that fellow, who will then have this county completely under his thumb, for strange as it may seem he is the life of democracy here and its acknowledged head.

Two weeks later Foote had to write the "mortifying" news that—though they lost the assembly race—the Republicans had carried Van Alen into Congress by a microscopic four-vote margin, an outcome determined by crossover votes in Kinderhook that had Van Buren's fingerprints all over them. Van Buren was himself elected to the humble office of Kinderhook fence viewer, where he maintained his close relations with these voters. But he had his hand in county politics and in January 1807 was a key player on the General Corresponding Committee supporting Daniel D. Tompkins for governor. Though neither Kinderhook nor the county cast a majority vote for Tompkins in April, Van Buren received his reward from the Council of Appointment the next winter. In Albany in February 1808 lobbying for the charter of the Republican Bank of Hudson, he was appointed surrogate of Columbia County, in place of his half brother, now in Washington.[85]

He and Hannah Goes had been secretly married in Catskill a year before, soon after he was admitted to practice at the supreme court; by February 1808 they were already parents. By the end of the year he had moved his family from the quiet village of Kinderhook to noisy Warren Street in Hudson, near the courthouse newly relocated from Claverack. Forging a path from country to city that millions would follow, Van Buren would return to an ancestral Kinderhook only to rest and reinvigorate. But his life was focused on a march toward urban prominence. From Hudson he managed the affairs of the Republicans while attending to his practice and the surrogate's duties, from here won a seat in the state senate in the spring 1812, and from here with Hannah and their three young sons would move to Albany in 1815, after he was appointed the attorney general of the state. His rise had been rapid. Except for Edward P. Livingston, the young scion of the Lower Manor at Clermont whom he displaced in 1812, Van Buren at age twenty-nine was the youngest man yet elected to the state senate from Columbia County.

Van Buren's election to the senate, however, was not determined by Columbia County votes, where he won only in Hillsdale, Canaan, and in a new town on the Manor named Granger. For years Republicans had been elected to the senate from Columbia, but only as part of the Middle District, which stretched down into the Clintonian strongholds of Ulster and Orange Counties, and it would be from these southern counties that Van Buren gained his slim majority. After 1807 Columbia's Federalist edge became a solid majority, driven in part by demographic and economic forces far beyond the county Republicans' control. Between 1800 and 1810 the county lost about 7 percent of its free population, the decline particularly pronounced in Claverack, Kinderhook, and Hillsdale. Only Hudson had seen a moderate growth of about 12 percent, but the Embargo had already sounded the death knell to its booming economy. Hudson's economy was based on its hinterland, and as elsewhere in the northeast the closing of American seaports to agricultural exports, here particularly into the West Indian trade, dealt a blow from which the region would never really recover. If populations would stabilize somewhat in the next decade, they dropped again in the 1820s, as people from Columbia headed to the west in great numbers.[86]

Economic decline and emigration explain a considerable amount about Columbia's increasingly conservative voters. But there were other forces at work. The county's rate of voter turnout, as has been discussed, was very high, perhaps abnormally high (see Figure 1). Oddly, the county shared these distinctions with New York City and also shared a very low rate of growth in electors qualified to vote for governor by virtue of a one hundred pound freehold. Urban poverty, exacerbated by the Embargo, underlay the slow growth in the numbers of governor's electors in New York; in Columbia County population stabilization and the onset of a decline played a certain role. But turnout, conversely, was extremely high.

There was another dimension to the distortions of electoral politics in these two counties: the making of voters. New York City was already notorious for the fabrication of Republican voters, temporarily qualified to vote for governor or for assembly, by means of temporary deeds and loans in what was called the "fagot" or "tontine" system. Such was increasingly the case in Columbia, though here they were mostly Federalist. The county's low rate of expansion of qualified electors, quite different from the newly settled counties in the state's west and far north, mean that the high turnouts were probably not caused by new voters. Rather, they reflect a symbiotic combination of political intensity and voter fraud. The high voter turnout in Columbia County was a symptom of a uniquely intense partisan culture, and perhaps a uniquely corrupted one.[87]

Starting with the Burr-Lewis election in 1804 a distinct pattern began to emerge in township voting in Columbia County, as roughly measured by the ratio between the votes cast in the election for governor and the number of one hundred pound freeholders listed on the various electoral censuses (see Figures 4–5). In 1804, the Federalist Livingston families of the Upper Manor threw their influence behind Aaron Burr's nomination and apparently manufactured voters wholesale in the town of Livingston, the Manor town on the river where most of the landlord families lived. In the 1807 election, which pitted Clinton-sponsored Daniel Tompkins against Morgan Lewis, connected by marriage to the Clermont Livingstons, the vote-making practice seems to have spread from the town of Livingston south into Clermont and Germantown. By April 1810 the pattern was clear to the Republican leadership, and temptations were overwhelming. If the Federalists had inaugurated voter fraud, the stakes in the 1810 election impelled a Republican imitation.[88]

On April 19, 1810, Martin Van Buren wrote a detailed note to De Witt Clinton. "The Feds undoubtedly will make a vast many votes," he reported, and the county Republicans had decided that *we had no other course but to meet them on their own ground.*" The Republican county committee had initially rejected the idea of making voters: "Our Friends at first startled at the proposition and voted me down in Committee with some degree of warmth." But when confronted with the numbers, and "the extent to which the Feds intended to carry it," the committee had agreed, and "they are now if anything too zealous in the business, the very men who were the warmest opposers are now constantly [teasing?] me on the subject, the spirit has extended through our ranks throughout the county." Van Buren closed his letter on a pained note: "I cordially despise the practice but I think under existing circumstances necessity directs us to it — we only neutralize the effects of their corrupt conduct."[89]

Nine days later Van Buren, "once more with shame," described to Clin-

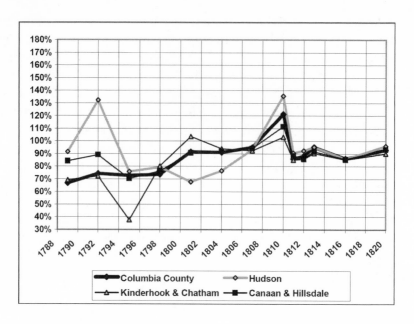

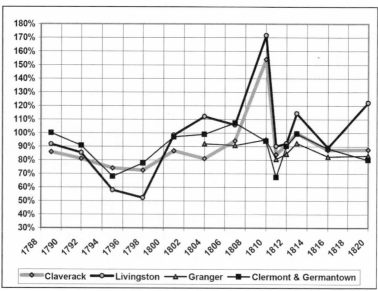

FIGURE 4. *Town Turnout in Governor's Elections, 1789–1820*

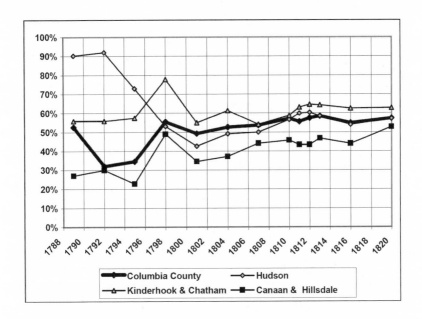

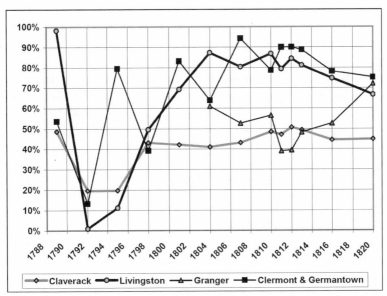

FIGURE 5. *Town Votes for Federalist Candidates for Governor, 1789–1820, Lieutenant Governor, 1811, and State Senator, 1812*

 The town of Livingston was divided into Livingston, Granger, and Gallatin in 1803. For the 1804–1820 elections, the votes in Granger are shown here, and Gallatin is combined with Livingston.

ton the outcome of this "corrupt conduct." The Federalists had made 400 votes to the Republicans' 200 votes and had carried the county again, by a 527 majority. Once again the Livingston domains led in the number of manufactured voters, both in the town of Livingston itself and in the Outer Manor town of Gallitan, where "Robert LeRoy Livingston [Crazy Bob] this morning admitted to me that he had made 190 — Elisha Williams was there during the whole election to fill up the Deeds." The Federalists had also done well in making fraudulent voters in the city of Hudson, while the Republicans had done better in Claverack but had been thwarted in Chatham. Here, Van Buren reported, "Our friend Dorr after he made about a Dozzen got one of the *Judas Breed* into his Camp who gave up his deed to the Federalists — this broke us up there." Van Buren was certain that the circumstances in Columbia were unique: "I am satisfied that this county has been principally the seat of their operations in this way — all other accounts [from other counties] are favorable." In part Van Buren blamed the vestiges of New York's colonial past, when royal governors had notoriously trafficked in land: "I am sorry for Columbia but have done all that I could — King George has issued too many pattents for us." But he also blamed weak-willed members of the Republican county committee: "If some friends had laid off some scruples earlier we would have reduced their majority to about 250, which is all they are honestly entitled to."[90]

Elisha Williams's correspondence in these years provides a window onto Federalist rationalizations. In the spring of 1809 he described the new county Federalist organization, revitalized by the opportunity provided by the Embargo. The county was divided into committees and wards, the names of all voters recorded and divided into classifications: "The faithfull are rendered faithfull still — the bad are counteracted as much as possible in their views and actions — and the doubtful are plied by every *honest means* if peradventure they may be saved — What mortals can do will be done by us." A year later, in the midst of preparations for the fraud-filled 1810 campaign (during which he spent days in the Manor towns "filling up deeds"), Williams was more expansive in his definition of "means." After a discussion of questions involving patronage appointments in Delaware County, Williams chided Ebenezer Foote for his unwillingness to step outside the straight and narrow for the cause of Federalism:

In this cursed crooked world there is much to be done that such men as yourself won't do. . . . [If] you reduce the federal party to that standard of purity which you would proscribe for it — it would retain one fourth of its present numbers, if our institutions are worth preserving, we must preserve them by use of such means as alone can sustain them, and we must not drive from our party every immoral man. Their votes may save our country and it is our duty to obtain them if possible without doing an dishonest or dishonorable act.

Though the focus of his discussion was the need to satisfy office seekers and not specifically a justification of vote making, Williams's argument clearly spells out a rationalization for electoral corruption. The preservation of "our institutions" was a higher cause that justified the "use of such means as alone can sustain them," and the votes of "every immoral man" were such means. "If possible" did not exclude the occasional (or even the systematic) "dishonest or dishonorable act." The Junto leaders were well convinced of the higher, absolute morality of the Federalist vision that drove them. The year before, Jacob R. Van Rensselaer had written to Foote to condemn a moderate Lewisite Republican:

No middle course can be pursued. He must be the humble devoted tool of Clinton, Spencer, and Co . . . or . . . must unite with those whose only object has been . . . to draw forth the best talents in our country and promote her happiness and prosperity. There is no middle ground.[91]

Federalist willingness to pursue any means necessary foundered on Republican numbers across the state. In the 1811 legislature following the bitter and corrupted 1810 election, Van Rensselaer, Grosvenor, and the two other Columbia Federalists fought desperately to stave off a Republican bill that mandated stricter surveillance of the polls. The Act to Prevent Frauds and Perjuries at Elections required that a voter swear that he had not "become [a] freeholder fraudulently, for the purpose of giving my vote at this election, nor upon any trust or understanding, express or implied, to reconvey such freehold during or after this election." Specific funding was authorized that the act "be published in all the newspapers printed in the state"; in Columbia, at least, it seems to have had an effect, and the most obvious signs of electoral fraud subsided.[92]

THE BANK OF AMERICA AND THE LEGACY OF CORRUPTION

Thus, as Van Buren wrote in his *Inquiry* decades later, faction "moved the bitter waters of political agitation to their lowest depths." If blatant electoral corruption subsided after 1811, its legislative variant certainly did not. There was little middle ground in the winter and spring of 1811–1812, when, as rumors of war with Britain consumed public attention, the Bank of America was proposed in the New York State legislature. Governor Daniel D. Tompkins announced his opposition in terms that spoke to the minimalist definition of corrupting interest: "The interests and the sentiments of the great mass of our constituents are opposed to the further incorporation of banking institutions." While the Columbia Republicans met in Claverack to oppose "establishment of a *British bank* in the city of New York," the Columbia Federalist leadership quietly went to work to move the passage of the bill on terms favorable to its collective "prosperity." As he testified in 1820 at the Van Ness hearings, Elisha Williams, acting as unelected lobbyist, "was in Albany during the greater part of the winter session of 1812" and "advised my political associates to promote the institution." The Bank of America would retain the foreign capitalization of the defunct Bank of the United States and act as a Federalist counterbalance to the Republican Manhattan Company. To this end Williams signed a secret contract to transfer the deposits of the Bank of Columbia from the Merchant's Bank to the new Bank of America, an arrangement that by May of 1813 involved a massive loan of $150,000 to the Bank of Columbia and payment of $20,000, to be divided among Williams, Van Rensselaer, and Van Ness. Whether or not Williams was directly involved in an alleged wider scheme to corrupt the legislature is not clear. When these charges were leveled in the assembly after the third reading of the bill, his brother-in-law Thomas P. Grosvenor, then a Federalist assemblyman from Hudson, was one of several to testify that they knew of no "improper attempt to influence the vote of any member, either for or against the bank."[93]

Nonetheless, the accusations gave Tompkins the opportunity to prorogue the legislature until after the April election. Tompkins's prorogation drew support from Republicans throughout the state; the Bank of America — a "six million dollar bank" — was an overbearing institution that corrupted by its sheer scale, and the means to its passage were corrupt. The ever-watchful Republicans in Canaan condemned both the "baneful influence of large monied institutions" and the threat to "public morals" and "confidence in republican legislation" posed by bribes of stock allegedly offered to certain assemblymen. The secretary of this meeting, Elam Tilden, had already written darkly to Tompkins that he saw "the finger of Napoleon" in the bank bill and applauded the prorogation: "When arguments the most reasonable and forcible, will not convince, force ought to be applied to save the commonwealth."[94]

Elam Tilden, married to Moses Younglove's adopted daughter, was very much the inheritor of the traditional republicanism that Younglove expressed as the old warhorse of the Democratic Society and as Civis in his 1802 paper duel with that "bold projector," Elkanah Watson, on the subject of turnpikes. Twenty-five years later Tilden would be Martin Van Buren's country adviser during the great banking crisis that would so shape his presidency. But in 1812, while he took public stands against the great Federalist banks, Van Buren was not yet ready to assume the mantle of this hypertraditional republicanism. In 1811 and again in 1812 he was named a director of the Bank of Hudson, and he had long been a close confidant of John C. Hogeboom and others among a group of entrepreneurial party Republicans. The next year, as a freshman state senator, he chaired the committee reporting in favor of a Middle District Bank for Kingston and Poughkeepsie. In the spring of 1812, however, he was reported to have spoken in a county meeting against the Bank of America as "a proposition fraught with danger to the public weal." As he remembered it, "[I] had exerted myself, as far as I could, to arrest the bank mania of the times."[95]

That spring Van Buren was nominated to the state senate, but only after a nasty struggle with a host of factions, including the Kinderhook Van Nesses, the Jenkins clan of Hudson, and the Clermont Livingstons. Although these factions combined against him at the mid-March county meeting at Bement's Hotel in Hudson, Van Buren prevailed on the first ballot. Edward P. Livingston was nominated by a rump convention in Claverack; as Van Buren remembered the "severely contested" election, he was opposed by "the entire federal party, the Lewisites, the Burrites, and the supporters of the Bank of America . . . a project they were well satisfied would be opposed by me." The election stood undecided for two weeks, and news came on the fly. Early in May Van Buren took a steamboat passage to attend the courts in New York, smiling his way past the taunts of the Livingston faction celebrating at the hotel. As he was passing Catskill, a rowboat brought the certified return from Delaware County, which put him over the top by two hundred votes, to the dismay of William W. Van Ness, who met the Hudson boat at the New York docks.[96]

The next November Martin Van Buren rode up to Albany, "jauntily" dressed "more like a sportsman than a legislator," to take his place in the senate, rooming at Baird's boardinghouse on Market Street. He now had finished his political apprenticeship. He certainly had more to learn over the next decade or so, as a state senator and attorney general, before he began to turn his hand to rebuilding a national party as a new United States senator. But in a decade in Columbia County he had learned many lessons, lessons that — if not fully articulated — seem to have shaped his future role in American politics. These lessons involved the structure and purposes of party.[97]

Van Buren's decade of political apprenticeship was one, not of bipolar party politics, but of multipolar factional politics. If ostensibly the Columbia Republicans stood united against the Federalists, in reality they were deeply divided among themselves. Along a gradient of opinion and interest the Republicans in the county and across the state had aligned themselves behind factional chieftains, in pyramids of affiliation and patronage. Whether it be Burr — or Livingston-Lewis, Spencer, Clinton, Tompkins, or more local men — the leaders of these factions put personal advancement on a par with, if not ahead of, any collective program of a party. "It is a mortifying circumstance," a correspondent had written of Peter Van Ness of Kinderhook to William Wilson in the spring of 1800, "that measures must fall a sacrifice to the will and caprice of this man." Twelve years later Wilson and other Republicans were under pressure to declare for Edward P. Livingston against Van Buren, and they declined on grounds of regularity of party procedure: "As a committee from this town, we agreed to support Mr. Van Buren, and consequently cannot with propriety advocate a counter nomination." The committeemen had articulated a fundamental value of party structure: the collective decisions of town committee, county meeting, or state convention would take precedence over any personal connection or factional imperative. They might not have acted on their decision, since it carried little weight among Clermont voters, who voted eight to one for Livingston. Party regularity was a virtue recognized but not always manifested in Van Buren's Columbia.[98]

By the time Martin Van Buren rode up to Albany in November 1812, war with Great Britain had been declared, only further complicating factional questions weighing upon his mind, questions that bore upon the very purposes of party. For all his remembered "exertions" against "the bank mania of the times," Van Buren owed his rise in the party and his senate nomination to De Witt Clinton, who had signaled his approval of his nomination that spring. Although Clinton opposed the Bank of America, he had not made his position public, because he hoped to gain Federalist support among New York City merchants for his proposed presidential candidacy against James Madison, on a platform of peace with England. In this Clinton put himself into enduring confrontation with Governor Tompkins and into a temporary spat with his brother-in-law, Ambrose Spencer, formerly of Hudson, to whom Van Buren was also obliged. Van Buren was forced into the awkward position of successfully engineering Clinton's presidential nomination in the Republican caucus while speaking in favor of Madison and party loyalty in time of war.[99]

Five months later, in March 1813, after a confrontation with Clinton over the irregular election of Federalist Rufus King to the United States Senate, Van Buren again negotiated the shoals of factional retribution and established a public benchmark for party regularity, by nominating Clinton to another term as lieutenant governor on the assumption that he would not accept "unless he was sincerely desirous to act with us in the future." Clinton lost, and Van Buren — hailed a healer of party — was awarded with the chairmanship of the committee to write the election address to the people, published serially late in March in the *Albany Argus*.[100]

Echoing his recent experiences in Columbia politics, Van Buren opened the 1813 state address by warning his "Fellow-Citizens" of the "seductive wiles and artful blandishments of the corrupt minions of aristocracy"; they were to "exercise the elective franchise — a right which in every other country has been destroyed by the ruthless hand of power, or blasted by the unhallowed touch of corruption." He certainly did not mention the role of this "unhallowed touch" in Columbia's recent politics, but that "touch" in the immediate affairs of the legislature would have been apparent to all Republican voters that spring. That February the senate considered a petition from the Bank of America that a payment to the state be rescinded; Van Buren spoke at length to oppose the revision. Later he wrote that the two days' recess spent attending the funeral of Chancellor Livingston at Clermont had provided the margin for the passage of this bill on March 8, certainly eased by the election of Junto manager Jacob R. Van Rensselaer to the speakership of the assembly.[101]

Thus when Van Buren wrote in mid-March of the "corrupt minions of aristocracy," he was still in the midst of a struggle with such "minions" that ran back to the Bank of America charter, the corrupted elections of 1807 and 1810, the Merchant's Bank controversy, and the very fabric of Columbia politics since its turn-of-the-century counterrevolution had returned oligarchs to ascendancy. The purpose of party was to represent the people in their resistance to such corruption. In his experience of his first decade of politics, Van Buren might have been driven to learn too well certain lessons about the purposes of party, lessons that would stand in the way of other definitions of popular government.[102]

Partisan contest in the early Republic, and specifically in Columbia County, arose out of two broad definitions of the relationship of civil society and the state, which would shape the fundamental themes of American political life for centuries to come. In the eighteenth century these might have been defined as variations on republicanism; in nineteenth-century New York these postures have been defined as positive and negative liberalism. One was an improving, advocating, problem-solving orientation in civil life. Identifying problems in social life and opportunities in the quest for prosperity, many men in post-Revolutionary New York reflexively turned to the legislature for grants of incorporation — for counties, towns, and cities, for libraries and academies, for roads and bridges, for banks and manufactories. In this state-sanctioned improvement, these men, typically Federalists and entrepreneurial Republicans, saw their bold projects building up a developed society, a civilized world. Their publicly sanctioned institutions and the newspapers that promoted them were key building blocks of civil society as they defined it. Conversely, ancient traditions of "jealous" watchfulness and vigilant monitoring informed an older and equally powerful definition of civil society — a definition forged in early modern struggles with absolutism. In this mode, civil society was fundamentally monitorial and watchful, alert to the signs of the corruption of the public trust. Certainly all Americans might and did engage in this monitorial role of civil society, scanning the papers for signs of bribery and malfeasance. But it was a select group of ideological Old Republicans who were sure that the sole function of civil society lay in its monitorial role, and they stood as the most vigilant in their conviction of the corruptions lurking behind every project of improvement.[103]

Corruption was real in the state of New York, but particularly in the county of Columbia, in the years of Van Buren's political emergence. A real aristocracy stood behind it. Its money power reached into the press, the legislature, the electorate. In the *Balance* and *Wasp* it funded first an Augustan mode of satire designed to exclude the people by cultural means. Later in the decade, Federalist enthusiasm for societies for benevolence and moral reform — the Hudson Academy, the Berkshire and Columbia Missionary Society, the Hudson Missionary Society, the Columbia Moral Society, the Washington Benevolent Society, the Columbia County Auxiliary Bible Society (of which William W. Van Ness was the first president) — might have seemed to corrupt morality and religion themselves.[104]

To Federalists and ensuing generations of evangelical reformers and Whigs, these civil institutions — eminently Tocquevillean — were vehicles of the improvement, the perfection, of society at large. But to Old Republicans and an ensuing generation of Jacksonians, they were only part of a vast conspiracy to subvert the sovereign consent of the people. Suspicion of these expansive purposes in civil society not only resonated with a monitorial watchfulness but was also rooted deeply in both the sectarian resistance to a blending of state and religion and the enduring Dutch and German hostility to civil projects impinging on the autonomy of the traditional household. All of these minimalist notions of civil society were present across great reaches of the early American republic. But Columbia County, with its violent history of class struggle and ethnic tension and its obviously successful reassertion of oligarchic power under the cover of the new civil institutions, provided the ground for a particularly potent minimalist synthesis. The Democratic-Republican

Party would stand as permanent pillar in civil society, like Montesquieu's intermediate institutions, protecting the people, not from the state itself, but from the corruption of the state by the money power. The most able observer of this synthesis, Martin Van Buren, would carry it far beyond the bounds of Columbia County.[105]

Female Interventions

Sunday Janry 6th [1788] . . . . I was prevented from reading till late in the Morning but retired as soon as I could. Read the solemn service of our Church, and afterwards a Sermon of Mr. Sousang translated by my Grand papa. . . . I was now obliged to set some Hours with a Young Gentleman on a Visit. . . . I spent this evening in the parlour, and after Supper, retired to my room. I now read the 6 Chap. of Revelations. This Chap. is all mystery, and leaves upon the Mind a sense of the weakness of human understanding.
   — Catherine Livingston, at Clermont, Jan. 6, 1788

Mother Lucy always used correct and proper Language in speaking, and not use clipped, or low, vulgar words, or expressions. Taught us to call persons and things by their proper names and not use nicknames to the meanest. . . .

   She had a great degree of discerning Light, by which she perceived the state not only of individuals, but of different Orders, so that her speech was adapted to their State. She often spoke in the meetings of the Church, and of the Orders. I heard her speak several times in the young Believers' meeting, well adapted to their state. She was the best Female Speaker I ever heard.
   — Calvin Wright's description of the Shaker eldress
      Mother Lucy Wright, of Mount Lebanon

HANNAH BARNARD AND THE QUAKERS
IN THE PUBLIC SPHERE

On November 23, 1802, the Hudson *Balance, and Columbian Repository* closed a six-month series, "Education," with an appeal that "the fair daughters of Columbia . . . co-operate in supporting and perpetuating the national independence." The author, Senex, was certain that "on the purity of *their* morals and the prudence of *their* conduct, the weal and permanence of this infant republic and the hopes of generations to come are essentially depending." All year long the *Balance,* directed by its senior editor, the Reverend Ezra Sampson, had carried on a campaign to guide the lives and morals of the "daughters" of the county of Columbia. That January the editors had announced a "new and improved" format, which was "intended for the improvement equally of both sexes." The paper would "contain strictures on female education and manners: the virtues and foibles of women will occasionally be pointed out, and their character scanned with a *brother's* eye." Throughout the year the editors fulfilled their promise, with item after item of "strictures" that delimited the virtues of "women of a domestic turn who hav[e] no ambition to shine in crowds." But Senex's concluding essay put the message in the starkest terms. The "daughters of Columbia" must "govern their passions": "A turbulent, passionate woman, while she renders herself disgusting to all around her, is usually the wretched victim of her own impotent fretfulness and rage: but a sedate and quiet mind possesses peace and conciliates favour. No ornament is so beautiful in a woman, as that of a 'truly meek and quiet spirit.'" Women would do best if they emulated the "ancient Romans," who "deified *silence,* and adored it as a goddess."[1]

Turbulent women, aspiring to public place, should be silent: this was the Federalist *Balance*'s unmistakably antifeminist message. This message certainly could be found in print everywhere in the early Republic, but in Hudson in the late fall of 1802 it would have had a powerful and specific resonance. Between December 1801 and June 1802 the Hudson Monthly Meeting of Friends, whose membership encompassed about a third of the city's households, had been wracked with controversy. Over these seven months Hannah Barnard, a recognized minister in the Hudson Meeting who had undertaken a three-year itinerant ministry in Ireland and England, was investigated by a committee for publishing her doctrinal disputes with the London Yearly Meeting. Silenced as a minister in January, she was disowned formally by the Hudson Meeting in June. Decades later she would be celebrated by a city historian as "an extraordinary woman, one of the most gifted of her day . . . possess[ing] great power of language [and] a remarkably inquisitive turn of mind . . . a woman of much thought and extensive reading." In 1802 Barnard was condemned by the Hudson Meeting for "giving way to an aspiring, exalted mind . . . clouded in her understanding, and led away by the spirit of delusion." In their editorial decisions throughout the year, the editors of the *Balance* obligingly echoed the understanding and spirit of the Hudson Monthly Meeting's disownment of this "extraordinary woman."[2]

Hannah Barnard's controversy with the Quaker authorities in London and Hudson centered on questions of interpretation; her troubles began with her challenges to doctrines of scriptural infallibility. As a good Quaker, confronted with the horrors of civil war in Ireland and the stresses of wartime England, she refused to accept biblical history as a divine commission of war for the Israelites. Her authority for her interpretation lay in her "extensive reading"; time and again she drew upon John Foxe, Robert Barclay, William Penn, Anthony Benezet, Alexander Geddes, and Edward Evanson to support her arguments in London and Hudson. She was, as Gorham Worth wrote in 1850, "'read out of meeting' for having herself read too much." Accused by the Hudson committee of disseminating the doctrines of "pernicious book[s]," Barnard forced the members to admit that they had not read these texts. She urged the committee to read and judge for themselves: the books were "open to any person's criticism." Her investigators, she argued, should also recognize

> the necessity of applying a public remedy, if they thought it a dangerous book; for I told them, it was utterly in vain to attempt to keep the matter a secret, or stop the general current of free enquiry: they might with as much reason expect a person could, by spreading out a hand, collect a swarm of bees, which were flying in the air, and press them down into a hive.

Here Barnard was articulating, in a powerful vernacular metaphor, the values of open discourse in the public sphere, a discourse that she had in some measure forged. Her troubles in London had deepened when she had contributed to a doctrinal tract published without the meeting's authority, and in Hudson she continued to assert herself in print. In December 1801, when asked by the Hudson committee to avoid "attempting any thing in a public manner at present," she sharply inquired whether "they alluded to printing my sentiments." Assured that they were thinking about her "speaking as a minister," Barnard nonetheless refused to be "bound" from "a faithful declaration of my sentiments, either in a public, or a private manner." Some time that winter her position was published in a pamphlet printed by Ashbel Stoddard, editor of the *Hudson Gazette*. Denied access to the documents bearing the actual charges against her throughout the trial, Barnard complained that the proceedings were "irregular" at best, conducted in "great ignorance of the first principles of impartial judicial proceedings."[3]

Hannah Barnard's controversy thus encompassed central problems in the ideal functioning of the public sphere, in which opinions should be freely shaped and freely expressed in an open discourse. Her controversy brought a potent female challenge to the boundaries defining that public sphere and a wider civil society in Columbia County. But it also exposed countervailing vectors of the life of women in the public sphere in the early American republic. If women were to stand as exemplars of virtue for the new Republic, they were not to raise their voices in public. Women were acted upon, culturally interpreted, and subjected to hegemonic persuasion as to their rightful place in the world. But some women were finding a transformative agency of their own, turning that weapon of persuasion to their own uses.

In both of these vectors the wider Anglo-Atlantic culture of sensibility played only an ambiguous role, perhaps especially in the segmented and conflicted world of Columbia County. On the wider stage and over the longer period, the expression of sensibility and sympathy in the public sphere was building a metacommentary on the boundaries between consent and force in civil society. By the 1830s it would contribute to a wave of reform across the northern United States, and across the century to come it would contribute to entirely new modes of gender relations. But in the short term, and in this particular place, the wider culture of sentiment and sensibility had little immediate purchase on the public. Despite the halting spread of an infrastructure of sensibility in schools, lodges, and libraries, a literary campaign for the abolition of slavery had not been particularly effective in blunting the forces of interest and ethnic tradition to turn minds and votes against slavery. Indeed, over the course of the 1790s, Columbia's legislators increasingly voted to defend slaveholding interests, with certain notable exceptions.

This outcome certainly constituted a defeat for a politics of sensibility in Columbia County, and such a defeat seems to have contributed to Federalist cultural politics, deploying satire to maintain boundaries around citizenship and the public domain.[4] In any event, one certainly gave way to another in Columbia County at the turn of the century, with the decline of Stoddard's *Gazette* and the advent of Sampson and Harry Croswell's *Balance* and Croswell's *Wasp*. This, with the advancing partisanship and indeed corruption of formal politics and the wider counterrevolutionary currents in the Anglo-Atlantic world, certainly chilled the climate for female interventions in the public sphere. But such interventions were already unfolding in these years, as Hannah Barnard's controversy with the Hudson meeting attests. She and at least two other women of note would in different ways set themselves against the prevailing cultures in Columbia County, in subtle forms of female insurgency in the public sphere. All three of them would base their authority in public, however, on an old but reinvigorated tradition of female testimony protected in radical Protestantism. Each would take a critical posture toward the practice of reading that comprised women's distinguishing action in the public sphere. Positioning themselves within and against the persuasive domain that women occupied in their exclusion from the deliberative, each was set against the culture of sentiment in subtle and important ways. They represented a particular generational experience of women born in the decade before the Revolution, and they each forged in practice or example new spaces for women in public. But it was not clear whether the conservative milieu of Columbia would allow their specific initiatives an enduring central place in the coming century. Boundaries in civil society were well defined and hardening.[5]

BOUNDARIES FOR WOMEN: SATIRE AND SENTIMENT

As throughout the new Republic, women in Columbia County occupied a symbolic role in the public sphere. Occasionally, a Mary A. Wilson might witness the purchase of a slave, the signing of a deed, or the drafting of a will. But, in the intensifying political domain, Hannah Van Buren's invisibility was closer to the norm. This not to say that women, particularly in gentry families, were not participants in political conversations. In May 1788, coming home from a "Solitary walk," Catherine Livingston was informed by her brother "of a disagreeable peice of public news." That same summer Samuel B. Webb began showering Kitty Hogeboom with letters describing the Poughkeepsie ratifying convention, militant Federalism in New York City, and his own role in Washington's inauguration and carefully reviewing the details of electoral strategy in 1789, as the Federalists attempted to unseat Governor George Clinton. But even such a grand dame as Catherine's mother, Margaret Beekman Livingston, presiding at Clermont in 1789, failed utterly in her attempt to turn the tenants against Clinton, writing dejectedly to her son the chancellor, "I am very sorry you have not kept your intention of being here at the Election . . . I was so unsuccessful in my application among your Tenants when I last applyed to the them that I have given up all thoughts of going among them."[6]

Younger women might express their politics through the company that they kept and the promises of marriage that they made. Such expressions of consent were grist for the newspaper wars. A "FAIR CORRESPONDENT" in the *Albany Register* in 1794 wanted "all REPUBLICAN BACHELORS" to "adopt the *American* and *French* COCKADES, in the shape of *Hearts*," since she and "her *fair co-patriots* of Albany" were determined that only Republicans "shall enjoy their smiles." The Hudson *Balance* in 1807 published the resolves of a mock meeting of "uncommonly fierce-looking . . . Democratic Republicans of the region of Public Good" who had voted that *"Republican Young Men* marrying *Republican young women only"* would *"promote the prosperity and happiness of our common country."* But such political marriages were no joke; they ranged from the union of Federalist Thomas Grosvenor with Mary Jane Hanson of Baltimore — and Edmond Genêt with Cornelia Clinton — to the tangle of Republican marriages linking the Younglotes, the Jones, and the Tildens in Canaan or those binding together the Van Burens, the Goes, the Hogebooms, and the Cantines of Kinderhook, Claverack, and Catskill. William Wilson of Clermont suffered at the hands of matrimonial partisanship in 1805. Rejected by a woman in Rhinebeck, Wilson was told by her brother in-law, a close friend, that

> Her sole and conclusive objection was yr Politics!! Your Whig Principles, and fixt adherence to Whig Men and Measures formed the only bar of that *Party's* declining the connexion contemplated!! . . . I should never think that her bigotry and fanaticism should extend so far, tho' I know that she was a violent *Briton* . . . Let her go, in God's name — tis all most probably for the best — I should be sorry to see any friend tied to any woman, ever so rich or so fair, even a sister, who would carry her weakness, or folly, or Tyrant principles to such a ridiculous length.[7]

For their political scruples, the women of Columbia and the region were briefly recognized at the political celebrations of the Fourth of July. Starting in the summer of 1801, Federalists, Republicans, militia companies, and the Mechanics celebrating American Independence raised toasts to "the daughters of Columbia" and the "American fair." Both Federalists and Republicans routinely raised their glasses to the women of the county and the nation at the close of their seventeen toasts, one for each state of the Union. The message was the same throughout: rather than any reference to the "rights of woman," all of these male assemblies invoked a literal sexual and reproductive political economy. Just as the county Federalists in 1804 wanted the "smile of approbation for the brave, and their hearts for the virtuous," the Hudson Republicans in 1811 hoped that "all the charms that nature hath bestowed on their form, be heroically withheld from every base designing knave that dares oppose his country's rights." The Mechanics Society in 1803 hoped that they would "never become the mothers of bad citizens," and the Hudson Volunteers in 1807 hoped that "a green coat and an honest heart [would] ever find favor in their eyes."[8]

These toasts to the "American fair" were reported in the new publishing climate that followed the 1800 election. By the late summer of 1802 printers in Hudson were publishing three papers, and factional politics was spawning new papers up and down the river, in Poughkeepsie, Kingston, Catskill, Albany, Lansingburgh, and Troy. On balance, the gendered messages in these papers, particularly if their primary purpose was political, were similar. But in multiplying the number of papers, the forces of factional competition were beginning to open print to different audiences. In a process of trade specialization, older printing offices, abandoning politics to the new printers, were the most attuned to women as readers — and authors.[9]

The *Balance*, an intensely partisan Federalist paper, had announced a commitment to a female audience from its opening issue, but this was a commitment to an intensely ideological proscription, a persuasion aimed at a wider hegemony. Ezra Sampson and Harry Croswell, the *Balance* editors, expressed satisfaction that "American ladies . . . take no violent part in the political feuds of the nation" and found it self-evident that voting was not a natural right, for that would include women. They buttressed their demand that the "daughters of Columbia" confine themselves to domesticity, with attacks on the influence of "vicious and futile books," fears about the corruptions ensuing from too extensive "female education," and a campaign against female profanity. In late July 1801, soon after they began publishing and probably by prior arrangement, the *Balance* editors began a series by "Alfred," or "John Bunyan," critiquing the acquisition policies of the Hudson Library, particularly as it fed the "mania for Novel reading," and attacking the trustees' decision to purchase William Godwin's *Political Justice*. By September Alfred had got to Godwin's doctrine that "the institution of marriage is a system of fraud" and complained that the trustees were even stocking a novel, *The Vagabond,* that was a secret vehicle of the "pernicious tendencies" of Godwin's thought. In the same issues, "The Restorator" began first to attack "genteel" female education and moved on to assail "the writings of Mary Wolstonecraft and the radical understanding of *the rights of woman.*" "One of the Trustees," in turn, wrote in the *Gazette* that Godwin's *Political Justice* was "not a chap-book" and would not be excluded from the library. As they brought this series to a close and over the next year, the *Balance* editors featured moralist Hannah More's strictures against "NEW PRINCIPLES" being disseminated in "monstrous compositions," and sprinkled their pages with snide comments about Mary Wollstonecraft's domestic failings and sexual downfall.[10]

Despite a promising beginning, the equally partisan Hudson *Bee,* edited by Republican Charles Holt, was not really much better. The opening issue of the *Bee,* in August 1802, made a few gestures toward Hannah Barnard's recent controversy, with an essay on the "Rights of Women" prominently situated below the opening prospectus, followed on page 4 — perhaps ambiguously — by a poetical "Eulogy on Matrimony" and an essay "The benevolent Quaker," on Warner Mifflin. But Holt's paper never devoted much space to women as an audience, and by the following spring, when a women's benevolent society was formed in Albany, the *Bee* was sounding much like its arch-rival the *Balance:* Holt wrote condescendingly, "Though we exclude the softer sex from the affairs of state and the enterprises of war, we cannot deny them the luxury of doing good in a humbler sphere."[11]

But a subtly different tone unfolded on the pages of Ashbel Stoddard's

Gazette in its final years of publication as the city's traditional public print. Anticipating the impending establishment of the *Balance* that spring, Stoddard invested in a new supply of type and on February 17, 1801, launched "The Bouquet," covering the fourth page of the *Gazette* with poetry, polite commentary, and sentimental literature. The first two numbers featured "The Story of Miss. Williams" by a "Mrs. Griffiths," a cliff-hanger sentimental romance in which an orphan girl earned a hefty annual settlement for exhibiting selfless virtue. Here and throughout the offerings of "The Bouquet," the message might have been similar to that of the *Balance*'s strident demand for quiet and submissive virtue, but the medium of narrative, female action, and female voice was decidedly different. If in late 1801 Stoddard had published a satire on radical thought that included Paine, Godwin, and "novel books," early in 1803 he reprinted in the *Gazette*'s "Bouquet" a two-part defense of Mary Wollstonecraft's religious beliefs from a London magazine, developed in a careful consideration of her published writings. On February 16, 1802, Stoddard began to reprint the Samuel Saunter series of the "American Lounger," from Joseph Dennie's *Port Folio,* exactly one month after Dennie began the series in Philadelphia. The "American Lounger" was modeled on the Edinburgh *Lounger,* edited briefly by Henry Mackenzie, the author of *The Man of Feeling.* In settling on the "Lounger," Stoddard made a careful decision to balance Federalism and a female audience. If the "Lounger" set himself against the driving political and economic competition of the day, Dennie made sure in his first number to announce that he hoped "to attract the attention of the fair," and he expected "assistance, from the pen of many an ingenious female." Echoing the tones of his inspiration, Mackenzie, the "American Lounger," wrote in comforting tones on questions of domestic sensibility and social sympathy, in sharp contrast to the harsh, ideological antifeminist posture of the *Balance* editors, who would never invite any "ingenious female" to enter the public sphere. Ashbel Stoddard was finding a new niche in print as his moderate Federalism lost its hold in an increasingly partisan world.[12]

WOMEN AS AUTHORS, WOMEN AS READERS

Unfortunately for Hannah Barnard, one such "ingenious female," her controversy with the London Yearly Meeting, and its sequel in Hudson, coincided with the rising conservative onslaught against Mary Wollstonecraft's radical message of the rights of women. Thus the *Balance* opened its campaign against Godwin and Wollstonecraft as news of Hannah Barnard's struggle with the London Quakers was becoming common knowledge on the streets of Hudson. By the summer of 1801, copies of the *Appeal to the Society of Friends,* which spelled out her pacifist position against the testimony of the London

Meeting, would have been in circulation among the Hudson Quakers. When The Restorator concluded his series in the *Balance* condemning "she, who is ever prating about her rights, and the dignity of the sex" on October 1, his essay was quite fresh in the minds of his readers when Hannah Barnard returned to Hudson several weeks later. Importantly, it was Ashbel Stoddard of the *Gazette,* rather than the *Balance* editors, who was willing to publish her account of her trial in London.[13]

Echoes and hints of the Hannah Barnard controversy swirled through the little city over the winter of 1801–1802. Around the time that he must have published the account of her London trial, Stoddard inserted a barely fictionalized Hannah Barnard into his ongoing war with the *Balance:* a "Susie," aunt of the Lucy who would not read newspapers. After attacking "the contagion of vicious books" and the "blasphemous speeches" of "lewd and infidel mothers" in the same week that Barnard was silenced by the Hudson Meeting, the *Balance* editors ran an essay by Philander condemning swearing by one of the young ladies of Hudson. Stoddard's answer came in the voice of "Aunt Susie." She was "a person of good natural abilities, improved by an excellent education. . . . Education and habit rendered her a strenuous advocate for religion and its institutions . . . hers was not a speculative belief, but was founded upon rational investigation," and she "had seen much of the world . . . on a tour of England." Putting "on her spectacles to read the Balance," Aunt Susie quickly scanned the Philander essay and, in a voice that might well have been Hannah Barnard's, announced, "This paper has an extensive circulation, its influence may be great, one ought to be very particular how they attack characters, especially the female, in a public paper."[14]

This fictional Hannah Barnard was apparently as far as Ashbel Stoddard could go in the pages of the *Gazette.* Hannah Barnard's controversy was probably fraught with danger for a printer under new competitive pressures: too close an identification with her cause might bring a collapse of advertising by Hudson's many Quaker merchants. Thus he, apparently, did not report directly on her quarrel with the Hudson Meeting in the *Gazette.* Her *Considerations on the Matters of Difference* with the London Friends was published under the fiction of a male authorship, and Stoddard did not publish the details of her struggle with the Hudson Meeting, leaving her to send them to London. But the next year Stoddard broke the barrier against female authorship in the public sphere, publishing the first two imprints credited to women from a Hudson press: Stephanie Genlis's *History of the Dutchess of C——* and Susanna Rowson's *Charlotte Temple,* the signature work opening the entire tradition of domestic novels by American women writers.[15]

These were not the first female-authored works to be published in the river towns north of New York City, but they marked an important moment in the emergence of woman's voice in the region's commercial print. Previous imprints by women from the Hudson River towns were essentially anonymous or published within the bounds of a traditional understanding of gender, charity, and religious voice. In 1794 the Catskill press in which Harry Croswell was apprenticing published a "pastoral drama" by a Lady in Connecticut based on the poetry of Hannah More, and in 1796 and 1797 three books were printed by Albany presses, of which only one, *American Cookery,* was female-attributed on the title page, to Amelia Simmons, "an American orphan." In 1798 two short pamphlets issued from presses in Poughkeepsie and Troy expressed very traditional women's religious voices: one an account of a vision of Christ by a Quaker woman in Beekman, carefully noting the witness of "divers persons"; the other was Naomi Rogers's *Verses, Composed upon the Awful and Sudden Death of Oliver . . . Hall of Stephentown.* The seminal departure was made in 1797 by a press in Mount Pleasant in Westchester County, boldly publishing *The Italian,* a classic sentimental gothic novel, under the authorship of "Anne Radcliff, author of the Mysteries of Udolpho." In 1803 Stoddard crossed the great divide between traditional masked female authorship and commercially announced female authorship. Genlis's *Duchess* was "written by herself," but *Charlotte Temple* was credited on the title page to "Mrs. Rowson." Needless to say, the *Balance* press never published any title authored by a woman.[16]

The events of 1801–1802 in Hudson — the emergence of competing papers, the Barnard controversy, the dueling constructions of women and the public sphere — marked a significant transition in the construction of gender in the region's print culture, perhaps a point of slippage between republican and liberal frameworks for print and authorship. With interesting implications for the structure of the public sphere, the market pressures generated by the rise of party paradoxically opened the door to women's voices in public. The sudden emergence of press competition during John Jay's second term as governor impelled Stoddard and other printers in the other towns along the river to look for new markets, bringing a new specialization in the region's press (see Table 22).[17]

Before 1801, the printers in the four river towns east and south of Albany had typically issued a weekly newspaper, like the *Gazette* of Federalist inclinations, and a thin stream of broadsides, pamphlets, and tracts. The bulk of these imprints were divided among current affairs, history, school books, and religious material, often collections of the Psalms and hymns. Inasmuch as

TABLE 22. Nonserial Imprints by Partisanship, Printing Office, and Genre, 1785–1819

	Almanacs	Adventure
FEDERALIST NEWSPAPERS THROUGH 1806		
Hudson Gazette, 1785–1800	216	226
Lansingburgh *Federal Herald,* 1788–1790	0	0
Lansingburgh *American Spy,* 1791–1797	0	0
Lansingburgh *Tiffany's Recorder,* 1793–94	0	0
Poughkeepsie Journal, 1785–1806	334	34
Total pages	550	260
	14%	17%
FEDERALIST NEWSPAPERS, 1798–1819		
Lansingburgh Gazette, 1798–1819	530	0
Troy Gazette, 1802–1812	140	236
Troy Post, 1812–1819	172	0
Hudson *Balance,* 1801–1808	0	0
Hudson *Northern Whig,* 1809–1819	0	0
Total pages	842	236
	21%	15%
FEDERALIST BOOKSELLERS, 1801–1819		
Penniman, Parker, Bliss, Lansingburgh/Troy	0	0
Ashbel Stoddard, Hudson	828	210
William Norman, Hudson	76	0
Total pages	904	210
	23%	13%
Poughkeepsie Journal, 1806–1819	548	133
	14%	9%
REPUBLICAN NEWSPAPERS AND PRESSES, 1795–1819		
Lansingburgh/Troy *Farmer's Oracle,* 1796–1798	36	185
Lansingburgh/Troy *Northern Budget,* 1797–1819	456	423
Troy *Farmer's Register,* 1807–1819	176	0
Hudson *Bee,* 1802–1819	202	0
Hezekieh Steele, Hudson, 1807–1813	36	106
Poughkeepsie *Republican Journal,* 1795–96	0	0
Poughkeepsie *American Farmer,* 1798–1800	36	0
Poughkeepsie *Political Barometer/Republican Herald,* 1802–1819	104	0
Poughkeepsie *Dutchess Observer,* 1815–1819	36	0
Total pages	1,082	714
	28%	46%
Grand total pages	3,926	1,553

Note: "Current Affairs" includes imprints relating to law, commerce, and trades.

Masonic Books	Current Affairs and History	Children and Education	Polite and Sentimental Literature	Religious Material	Total
149	715	1,353	257	1,118	4,034
0	16	0	50	364	430
0	36	300	0	64	400
0	793	24	0	176	993
10	463	0	105	22	968
159	2,023	1,677	412	1,744	6,825
39%	16%	8%	8%	8%	10%
12	97	1,095	0	329	2,063
24	1,092	926	304	664	3,386
0	208	2,710	0	988	4,078
0	238	1,029	0	1,135	2,402
0	568	0	0	816	1,384
36	2,203	5,760	304	3,932	13,313
9%	18%	27%	6%	19%	20%
0	1,716	4,884	873	2,252	9,725
0	272	1,695	730	3,743	7,478
0	1,396	744	562	3,189	5,967
0	3,384	7,323	2,165	9,184	23,170
	28%	34%	43%	43%	35%
104	2,886	6,430	1,415	1,750	13,266
26%	24%	30%	28%	8%	20%
0	30	60	300	0	611
0	468	40	0	2,375	3,762
0	740	31	0	147	1,094
0	201	84	0	330	817
0	0	0	102	297	541
0	0	24	0	0	24
0	46	0	0	19	101
107	210	0	300	1,241	1,962
0	60	0	0	46	142
107	1,755	239	702	4,455	9,054
26%	14%	1%	14%	21%	14%
406	12,251	21,429	4,998	21,065	65,628

women were already consumers of religious books, presses attended to these needs, but in fact the early presses, relative to later presses, focused on reading primarily shaped by a male audience: current affairs, history, and small but suggestive clusters of adventures and Masonic pamphlets. After about 1800 the presses producing political newspapers appear to have divided this market, with Federalist presses maintaining a considerable amount of educational printing and the Republican presses particularly notable for male-oriented reading: adventures, almanacs, and Masonic pamphlets.[18]

Beyond these partisan editors a third set of printer-booksellers either persisted or emerged, Federalist in inclination and culture but typically not printing a newspaper. Among them were Ashbel Stoddard, who abandoned the *Gazette* in December 1803, Obadiah Penniman, who established himself in Lansingburgh and maintained an association with printers Parker and Bliss, and William Norman of Hudson. In Hudson, with the exception of Hezekiah Steele's brief print production, the overall pattern is clear. The three political presses of the *Bee,* the *Balance,* and the *Northern Whig,* between 1801 and 1819, produced about a third of the volume in nonserial imprint pages produced by the independent printers Stoddard and Norman and produced absolutely nothing in the line of polite and sentimental literature. In 1824 the commitment of the moderate and independent Federalist press to a female-inclusive audience would be institutionalized when Stoddard's son, William, launched the *Rural Repository,* which would publish for a respectable female readership into the 1850s.

Though the picture is a bit more blurry, newspaper advertisements broadly support these impressions. The Federalist newspapers regularly carried ads bearing long lists of books; by and large, in the Republican papers these lists were few, far between, and quite skimpy. If *Charlotte Temple,* "with a few other novels," was listed in the Republican Troy *Northern Budget,* it was one of sixty-two novels and romances available at the Federalist Penniman's Lansingburgh Bookstore, at the "sign of Shakespeare's Head." The Hudson *Bee* carried booklists for Peter Cole, a Republican merchant, in 1802 and 1803 but by 1807 was running ads for Norman and Stoddard, which also appeared in the *Balance* and its successor, the *Northern Whig.* In Poughkeepsie, Federalist printer and bookseller Paraclete Potter gave no advertising patronage to his Republican opponents at the *Political Barometer,* who attempted with marginal success to open their own bookstore in 1810. In 1804 the longest book list in the *Barometer,* all of fourteen imprints, featured radical religious texts on consignment from the Republican press of Moffitt and Lyon in Troy.[19]

There were, of course, some exceptions to this pattern of gender, print, and partisanship. In Poughkeepsie, Paraclete Potter took over the Federalist *Poughkeepsie Journal* in 1806 but also developed a huge trade in educational materials and sentimental literature, producing the highest page count of imprints of any press in these four towns. Among the Republicans, the exceptions seem to prove the rule. Luther Pratt, who began the Republican-leaning *Farmer's Oracle* in Lansingburgh in 1796, made a promising start on works that might attract a female audience, printing an abridgment of Richardson's *Pamela, Love Triumphant* (an advice book), and Robert Dodsley's play *The Toy-shop* — but he failed in 1798. The printers of the Republican Troy *Northern Budget* had a considerable list of sectarian religious imprints: half of this material comprised the collected works of Benjamin Gorton, a local millennialist; Matthew Adgate's personal interpretation of the Bible, *The Northern Light;* and the minutes of the Shaftsbury Baptist Association. In Hudson, Hezekiah Steele, a Republican printer and merchant, produced an edition of Rowson's *Charlotte Temple* in 1808, neatly matched the next year by the *Memoirs of Stephen Burroughs,* and Steele was out of business by 1813. This record of Jeffersonian printing addressed to female inclusive audiences was, simply put, very thin.

Here it was nonpartisan, if culturally Federalist, printer-booksellers who focused overwhelmingly on religious and educational materials and on a smaller but distinctive body of sentimental and polite literature. If the rise of republics in the Age of Revolution worked to gender public space and exclude women from the formally political, then it seems that the intensification of partisanship in the Hudson Valley opened to women, in new ways, the persuasive domain of the public sphere. At the partisan extremes, an Augustan satirical mode defined the more intense Federalism, represented by the *Balance* and the *Wasp,* and a monitorial civil vigilance characterized the Republican press of the *Bee.* In the cultural space between these extremes lay a moral sentimentalism produced by a cadre of moderate Federalist printers. Over the course of the coming century the first of these cultural modes would fade into a bitter, genteel obscurity, and the second would become the essential voice of the party press. The third would open an important place for women's persuasive voices in the public sphere.[20]

GOTHIC STORIES, PERSONAL CONSENT, AND A "CITY OF SCHOOLS"

The neglect of sentiment in the Republican *Bee* did not necessarily extend to the entire spectrum of Jeffersonian editors. Indeed, just to the south in Poughkeepsie, Republican Isaac Mitchell, editor of the *Political Barometer,* offered a significant exception: *The Asylum; or, Alonzo and Melissa,* which he published in serial form between May and October 1804. Destined to be a minor classic far into the nineteenth century, the story of Alonzo and Melissa was one of a number of similar stories published in the *Barometer*. Mitchell followed the typical form, including departments on page 4, which might attract a young gender-mixed audience: "The Trifler," "The Minstrel," and "The Legend." Within months of his first issue he inaugurated a series of romances under the rubric of "The Legend" with a story of his own, "Albert and Eliza," which he reprinted the next year in the Kingston *Plebeian,* which he coedited with Jesse Buel, where he might have published another story, "Melville and Paulez." In the *Plebeian* "Albert and Eliza" was followed by "The New Chevalier," "Maria — An Affecting Tale," and an excerpt from Benjamin Frere's 1801 *The Man of Fortitude,* which he titled "The Haunted Castle." In the *Barometer* it was followed by "The Shield of Expectation," "Edric of the Forest," "History of Peroudou; or, The Bellows Maker," and "Schabraco — A Romance" before launching into the serialization of his magnum opus "Alonzo and Melissa — A Tale," between June and October 1804.[21]

In a note to his readers following the last installment, Mitchell defended himself against his critics. While some would complain that "the scenes are hurried over with too much rapidity for the *contour* of a perfect Novel," Mitchell was more concerned about the characters he had to leave out, the "important events of the American War" omitted, and the travels in Europe foreshortened; he promised a "projected" enlargement. This story would be published in expanded form as a two-volume novel in Poughkeepsie a year before his death in 1812. He also asserted that his novel was "not unfriendly to religion or virtue." He saw its wider theme as the importance of "a firm reliance on Providence . . . in the gloomy hours of affliction." But he also felt that he had "copied nature" in his dramatic account, which he hoped would "not fail to interest the refined sensibilities of the reader."[22]

Afflictions there were, in spades, in both "Alonzo and Melissa" and its predecessors in the *Barometer*. In particular, the question of the condition of female consent in the contract of marriage was the central problem running through these romances. In each, these conditions of female consent were threatened by villainous figures. Betrothed to Eliza, Albert disappeared on a voyage to Europe: courted by a string of suitors, Eliza was almost raped by one, and another (himself the product of an illegitimate liaison of an English nobleman) was finally revealed to have hidden the information that Albert had been taken into slavery by Algerine corsairs. The humble bellows-mender was used by spurned suitors in a ruse to trick the beautiful Aurora of Lyons into a degrading marriage with this poor French artisan. "Schabraco" presented a torrid tale of murder, robbery, and a woman's kidnapping in Sicily.[23]

In the romance of Alonzo and Melissa, readers of the *Barometer,* closely following the 1804 governor's election, would have recognized less exotic sources in this tale's villains. Set in western Connecticut during the Revolution, Melissa was separated from her Alonzo, recently ruined at the beginning of the war, by her father, Colonel Bloomfield. In Bloomfield and his chosen for Melissa, Bauman, both gentlemen of considerable "independent fortune," the *Barometer* readers would not have had much difficulty seeing Aaron Burr, or even perhaps Benedict Arnold, Connecticut-born aristocrats now both notorious, or any of the speaking aristocracy of Connecticut Federalism. To keep her from Alonzo, Bloomfield confined Melissa in a gothic castle set somewhere between the Long Island Sound and the northern wilderness, haunted by ghosts who turned out to be a band of tory smugglers; she was aided by her father's oppressed but virtuous tenants. Both Alonzo and Melissa were novelistically raised from the dead and finally united after many tribulations on land and sea. In the end, Melissa successfully thwarted patriarchal power and asserted her right to freely grant or withhold consent to marriage.

While he saw a superintending Providence, Mitchell was more interested in "copying nature," distorted as it was by a gothic imagination. He tried to argue that the story contained no "indecorous *stimulants*" or "inexplicated incidents," but the tone throughout was redolent of the supernatural, here mustered to intimidate a virtuous young woman. It has been argued, and rightly so, that the supernatural gothic genre deployed such tales as a metacritique of illegitimate authority and coercive power, perhaps even Calvinist predestination. Inequalities of gender, age, and wealth — all overturned by the assertion of personal independence and autonomy — were variously grist for the gothic mill.[24]

"Alonzo and Melissa" was written by a Republican editor and published in a Republican paper. A book by Ann Radcliffe — the paradigmatic author of the supernatural gothic — was published by a similarly Republican printer to the south in Westchester County. The gothic romance was more broadly connected with the wider radical sentiments of the Revolutionary decade of the 1790s, and it was roundly condemned by Federalist and clerical authorities. Specifically, "Alfred," in his series in the 1801 *Balance* attacking the Hudson Library's recent acquisitions, singled out William Godwin's *Caleb Williams,* now seen as the pinnacle of a radical political gothic, for "inculcat-[ing] principles, wholly subversive of social order." Next to *Caleb Williams* on the library shelf, "Alfred" found another classic gothic novel, *The Monk,* by Matthew Lewis, "as complete a system of seduction as ever fell from the pen of Rochester." Mitchell's literary efforts were as much Croswell's target in the *Wasp* as was Holt's *Bee*. Conversely, after Mitchell put the *Barometer* to work for Dutchess native magnate Morgan Lewis in the Merchant's Bank crisis, he was mocked in the *Bee:* "All the labor and ingenuity of the author of Alonzo and Melissa, Melville and Paulez, Albert and Eliza, ... and every other writer of romances in the state, cannot convince the public of the propriety of 'countenancing ... bribery and corruption.'"[25]

Copies of the *Barometer* making their way into Columbia might well have been a major source of the gothic supernatural in this county. Perhaps gothic novels were indeed on the shelves of the Hudson Library in 1801, but the city booksellers did not advertise them in the Hudson papers. Ashbel Stoddard carried issues of Mackenzie's *Lounger,* the touchstone of the moral sentimental, for sale in the early 1790s, but neither he nor the other Hudson booksellers regularly carried Godwin's *Caleb Williams* or any of the other key texts of the gothic supernatural. While the Albany Library had copies of Radcliffe's *Mysteries* and "Woolstancraft's Letters" in 1797, neither Robert R. Livingston nor William Wilson — perhaps not surprisingly — had either in their collections. In Hudson, Mitchell's literary page had its closest analogue in Stoddard's "Bouquet," but this was a proximity within a wider sentimental genre. The moderate Federalist Stoddard clung to gentle moral sentiment and published the occasional admonition against novel reading, and the Republican Mitchell ventured into the more controversial waters of the gothic supernatural.[26]

Isaac Mitchell was, however, an oddity among the ink-stained Republican editors of the Hudson Valley. He would offer his services to increasingly Quid-centrist Morgan Lewis, first in Poughkeepsie and then in Albany, following a line of patronage that seemed to conflict with the political thrust of his romances. He also was not that ink-stained: he was primarily an academy teacher, not a printer. In the early 1800s he taught at the Dutchess Academy, founded in 1792 and revived by Elkanah Watson in 1799. The employment of this writer of romances in this academy seems to hint at subtle differences in the gendered public culture among the leading towns along the river, differences that might have had long shadows.

Mitchell's employment at the academy was consonant with his Republican sentiments, since the early trustees were divided almost evenly between parties, and Elkanah Watson saw his involvement in 1799 as part of his own brand of improving, entrepreneurial Republicanism. Two decades later, while Federalists outnumbered Republicans among the men who in 1821 invited Emma Willard to found her Female Seminary in Troy, the first classes of stu-

PLATE 11. *Catherine Van Slyck Dorr (1804–1892). Chatham.* Private Collection

In 1814 traveling artist Ammi Phillips painted miniatures of all of the children in the Dorr family. A physician in Chatham, Russell Dorr was, like William Wilson, a Jeffersonian and a Freemason and a sometime inventor and manufacturer of cloth-shearing equipment. When his estate was inventoried in 1824, his library included Locke, Rousseau, and Franklin as well as Jesse Torrey's Portraiture of Domestic Slavery. *Catherine, at the age of ten, was more likely holding the* Columbian Orator, *Murray's* Grammar, *or the* Moral Instructor, *all listed in Dorr's inventory. By the time that her father had died, Catherine had probably read Isaac Mitchell's gothic* Alonzo and Melissa.

dents appear to have been drawn from a wide cross section of Federalist and Republican families in Troy and Rensselaer County. A politically neutral ground, Willard's seminary would be a focus of civic attention and pride in Troy, one student writing in 1823 that lectures there were "for the convenience of the girls and the people of the city come here to attend them."[27]

If female academy education was a matter of civic pride in Columbia County, it was firmly in the hands of conservative Federalists, first in Claverack and Kinderhook, and then in the Junto project of the Hudson Academy, which in April 1806 established a "Young Ladies School." The entire project of academy education was intensely politicized in Hudson. The general law for incorporating academies had led to a failed effort in the spring of 1796 for a county tax to support an academy in Hudson, and for the next decade the town was served by a series of short-lived private, select schools. In February 1805, just as Republican governor Morgan Lewis was advocating a land fund to support common schools rather than academies, which passed in April, a consortium of Federalists met to set in motion plans for the private Hudson Academy, a building to be funded by subscription shares. While the *Balance* campaigned for improved education from 1801, the *Bee* in 1805 argued that "the establishment of an academy at the present time" was "highly inexpedient," invoking Montesquieu for the position that "a public is preferable to a private education." Fall examinations at the Hudson Academy seem to have commenced in 1807 and must have been grand Federalist rituals, presided over by the Junto leaders, rounding out the cycle of the Federalist calendar. Conspicuously, however, Ashbel Stoddard, and not the Junto's *Balance*, produced the most forthright advocacy of female education, the first letter in an 1804 reprint of *A Series of Letters on Courtship and Marriage*.[28]

The experience of the Republican Wilson family of Clermont confirms that female education was not politically neutral in Columbia County. After his wife died in 1801, Wilson sent his oldest daughter, Frances, to Mrs. Bell's, a small school that relocated from Hudson to Albany in the fall of 1802. In 1806, as Frances was finishing at Mrs. Bell's in Albany, Wilson sent his second, Mary, to the Pleasant Valley School in Dutchess County rather than to the new "Young Ladies School" in Hudson. In 1810 he toyed with sending his third daughter, Eliza, to Sarah Pierce's Litchfield Female Academy, but in the end she too went down into Dutchess, to another female academy in Isaac Mitchell's Poughkeepsie. None of the Wilson children would go to the Federalist academy in Hudson.[29]

In the long term, unfolding over the next half century, it would be Willard's Troy and Mitchell's Poughkeepsie that would far outstrip the little city of

Hudson in building enduring traditions of institutions of female education. Perhaps it was simply a matter of size, and perhaps economy, but Hudson would never begin to match the achievements of the other towns along the river. As of 1845, there were no "female seminaries" in Hudson, but five in Troy and Poughkeepsie. The premier institution was in Troy, where Emma Willard's Seminary was for decades the national epicenter for the education of young women. Its graduates ventured far to the west and south, building a national culture of women's learning. By the 1830s Poughkeepsie was known as the "city of schools," at least three devoted to female education: the Poughkeepsie Female Seminary, the Female Collegiate Institute, and the Cottage Hill Seminary. The earliest school for girls was the "Boarding School for Young Ladies," started in 1801, where Eliza Wilson apparently was educated. These schools must have been nurtured by a civic culture that encouraged women's education; certainly the Quakers of Dutchess County also deserve significant credit in this regard, and the old Dutchess Academy must have been a formative influence.[30]

It might have been a symptom of this particular civic culture that Poughkeepsie was also a city that had once supported an eccentric Republican academy teacher-editor who wrote and published gothic romances. By the 1840s, Lydia Booth, the principal of the Cottage Hill Seminary, had begun to convince her rich but childless uncle that the city might support a major women's college. Perhaps Booth had briefly attended Mitchell's Dutchess Academy; she and a covey of Van Kleeck cousins did go east to attend Sarah Pierce's school in Litchfield, where they would have studied under a countervailing Federalist climate. Whatever the mix of long-term influences in Poughkeepsie, they had a permanent outcome. In January 1861 the legislature would grant Lydia Booth's uncle, Matthew Vassar, a charter to establish a women's college in Poughkeepsie.[31]

Such long-term institution building was not to be in Hudson. Here, and in Columbia County in general, the particularly contested civic culture forged in the Jeffersonian era seems to have impeded such female improvements. Ashbel Stoddard, in his quiet, limited way, provided a voice for women in print and thus in public in the simple moral sentiments that he advanced at his press and that his son would advance in the *Rural Repository*. But the political and economic power of both the Federalist Junto in Hudson and the opposing "popular tradition," expressing a stridently ideological antifeminism in the *Balance* and a masculine populism of the Republican *Bee*, built a series of barriers and pitfalls against the entry of women into the public sphere. Apparent throughout the early history of Columbia County, forces were at work to limit rather than to facilitate the entry of an excluded group into civil society. Perhaps inevitably, the entry of women into public in Columbia took the form of insurgency, of dramatic challenges to the routines of civil life.

THREE WOMEN INSURGENTS
AND COLUMBIA'S BOUNDARIES

In these decades, three leading women forged three very different paths into the public in Columbia County. If in some measure they acted out the struggle for personal autonomy that lay at the core of the subversive gothic, they would have never accepted the analogy. The era of the early Republic from the 1780s to the 1820s was a unique transitional world, where the androgynous spirit of early modern evangelical culture intersected with the radical spirit of the Enlightenment salon. This was a world in which, metaphorically speaking, Anne Hutchinson met Mary Wollstonecraft. But in their self-conscious efforts to build new public spaces for early-nineteenth-century women in Columbia County and beyond, these three women drew their energy, not from literary culture, whether sanctioned or subversive, but from the radical sectarian religion of a sterner, older generation.[32]

Though they probably never met, and might have been only vaguely aware of their respective efforts, Lucy Wright, Catherine Livingston, and Hannah Barnard shared a generational and cultural impetus. They were all daughters of the late-provincial era, born at Clermont, on Nantucket, and in Pittsfield between 1752 and 1760. They all emerged as important figures among three radical sectarian movements in Columbia County in the 1780s and 1790s: Lucy Wright organizing the Shakers at Mount Lebanon in the old King's District; Catherine Livingston undergoing a lonely conversion to Methodism at the Clermont manor house, leading to her marriage to Freeborn Garrettson in 1793; and Hannah Barnard rising to authority in the new Hudson Meeting of Friends. Each of these women, "turbulent" and "disorderly" in her own way, might have drawn some vicarious energies from the wider insurgent spirit of this decade. They each challenged the republican ideal of motherhood in some way: Lucy Wright as a Shaker was childless; Catherine Livingston, married in her late thirties, had only one child; and Hannah Barnard had two, who were in their early twenties when she set out for Ireland and England in 1798. Rather than evading the English-language public sphere, as many Dutch and German women seem to have done, each of these radical women had to actively come to terms with the authorized centers of civil society in their world. They all created spaces and boundaries for female counterpublics, and they all used print in different ways to achieve these ends.[33]

Lucy Wright, the Shakers, and the World

Lucy Wright was one of the earliest American converts to the Shaker dispensation, forged from the mystical celibacy of the French Camisard Protestants and the English radical sectarian tradition and brought to America by Ann Standerin Lee and her brother, William. Though she settled at Watervliet near Albany in 1774, rumors spread in later years that Mother Ann Lee had been a drunken camp follower with General John Burgoyne's army. The early English Shakers had little local impact until the "dark day" in the spring of 1780, May 19, when the smoke from fires burning to the north and west blotted out the sun in the hills east of the Hudson, seemingly auguring the end times. A religious revival, a "New Light Stir," that had been running among the Baptists in neighboring parts of Massachusetts had spread recently to the King's District. After Mother Ann Lee began to preach the new Shaker faith in an itinerancy across New England, local King's District households as well as others dislocated and on the move began to be attracted to her millenarian message; many set up squatter farms on the contested lands of the Westenhook and Mawighnunk patents on the Massachusetts border. When Ann Lee and others of the earliest Shakers were imprisoned in Albany and Poughkeepsie that summer on charges of being secret tories, Lucy Wright, then still living with her husband in Richmond, sent gifts; a year later she was entrusted to lead the Shaker sisters at Watervliet while Ann and other Shakers set off to the east for a two-year mission into New England. Building upon the charismatic foundations laid by Mother Ann Lee, she would be the critical force in stabilizing and entrenching the United Society of Shakers at Mount Lebanon and across the breadth of the country until her death in 1821.[34]

In announcing and living out a theology of dual-gender divinity, realized on earth in the coming of Christ and in the Second Appearing of Mother Ann Lee, a Fourth Dispensation, the Shakers stood at the radical edge of Protestant belief and practice. After a harrowing series of childbirths and a life of marital abuse, Ann Lee had a Manichean vision that the way to mystical perfection lay in absolute celibacy: the two sexes were not to meet in the "flesh." The Shakers' challenge to gender hierarchy and norms of gender relations, the greatest that American society had ever seen, would face violent resistance from without and even within.

It would meet its first resistance where the Shaker gospel first spread to an American audience. Shakers in New Lebanon were subjected to riotous arrests and to probing inquiries. Shaker conversion would be most dramatic among the Baptists and was a function of an intensifying patriarchy among the Baptists, for whom an older tradition of female preaching and authority was disappearing. Their impact on local institutions was devastating: the preachers in both New Lebanon churches, Joseph Meacham of the Baptists and Samuel Johnson of the Congregationalists, were converted with many of their laity when Mother Ann Lee brought the message to the King's District in the spring of 1780, and their societies did not recover for more than a decade.[35]

The Shaker message might well have encouraged others in New Lebanon to establish a particularly male form of association. Three men of note came "in a friendly manner," Shaker tradition records, to question Mother Ann Lee on her religious beliefs in her mission to New Lebanon in 1780. All three, Eleazer Grant, Elisha Gilbert, and Dr. Isaac Averill, would be among the earliest members of the Unity Masonic Lodge; the first two were founding lodge masters. There seems to have been a broad affinity between Shakers and Masons in a tradition of radical perfectionist mysticism. Years later, an apostate's history recorded that some Shakers believed that "the church was in much the same order as the Free Masons were, only they were *travailing downwards,* but the church was *travailing upwards.*" The "same order" that Shakers and Masons were "in" was that of a claim to a mystical restoration of the ancient Hebrew temple; the distinction lay in their differing relation to the public sphere of civil society. The Freemasons were a fundamental part of the popular Enlightenment that occupied this public space; the Shakers rejected that same public space and its civil corruption. There were also critical questions of gender authority at stake.[36]

The sharp boundary separating the world, flesh, and the devil from the Shaker Holy City served to insulate Shaker gender relations from the insults of contemporary American civil society. The enduring, bounded separation that defined a space of equality between the sexes in Shaker societies was shaped in no small way by Lucy Wright's managing care. Born in Pittsfield, Massachusetts, in 1760, "she was a leading character among the higher class of young women" and recently married to a merchant in Richmond, when she and her husband were drawn to the Shaker gospel in 1780, in the wake of the New Light Stir among the local Baptists. By the time that she was renamed Lucy Faith in 1785, she had distinguished herself as "a leading caretaker among the sisters" at Watervliet, and, after the deaths of, first, Mother Ann in 1784 and, then, her successor, James Whitaker, in 1787, Lucy rose to a shared first eldership with Joseph Meacham, formerly the preacher in the New Lebanon Baptist Church; they served as the "Mother" and the "Father." In his final days in August 1796 Meacham, writing that Lucy was "one whom I esteem my Equal in order and Lot," proclaimed that "as both the man and the woman have Equal Rights in order and Lots and in the Lord and Government of the Church," she would be the "Elder, or first born after my departure." While the

Shakers would eventually establish a gender-balanced leadership, Lucy Wright in 1796 assumed sole authority over the Shaker world, and until her death a quarter century later she was arguably the most powerful woman in America.[37]

Working in coeldership with Joseph Meacham, Wright had begun institutionalizing a society separate from the world. In September 1787 they began to gather most of the scattered Shaker families in the King's District, across the Hudson Valley, and in Berkshire County at the Darrow farm on the Boston Road over New Lebanon Mountain, a place of biblical meaning where Mother Ann Lee had prophesied the building of the Shaker New Heaven and New Earth. By September 1788 the first meetinghouse had been raised at Mount Lebanon, and the outlines of the gendered lines of authority that would govern Shaker society for more than a century were established. It might not have been coincidental that the Shaker polity began to coalesce exactly in the months that the Philadelphia convention's Constitution was being debated and voted in the several states of the Confederation, and in the wake of the Massachusetts Regulator movement: both were manifestations of the "world" from which the Shakers sought to withdraw. But, if so, the Shaker elders saw their emerging society as the antithesis of the civil government of the new nation. Shakers both challenged and were persecuted by civil law. As their message began to spread in the summer of 1780, the early Mount Lebanon Shakers were arrested — after interrogation by Matthew Adgate of Canaan — for refusing military service and preaching pacifism; for decades they would be fined for refusing militia duty. Late in 1784 a sympathetic Henry Van Schaack was concerned that Shakers were undermining the rule of law by refusing to press charges against rioters who continued to assault them. But the Shakers had had bad experiences with civil law, in their imprisonment in 1780 and in more recent experience. In 1783, surrounded by a local posse, Justice Eleazer Grant of New Lebanon village had held a disorderly trial of Mother Ann Lee when she passed through at the end of her two-year mission in New England. The Shakers, certain that they had entered a new dispensation, would grant as little as possible to the authority of a corrupt civil law — and a corrupt civil society.[38]

As Meacham and Wright forged the transition from a charismatic, liminal movement to an enduring religious institution, they carefully constructed boundaries between the Shaker Holy City and the world. Their governing structure of three orders, or courts, modeled on the ancient Hebrew temple, established a series of concentric circles around a holy center. The new 1788 meetinghouse was constructed for the first order, or inner court, roughly one hundred unmarried adults of proven spirituality who had no legal obligations of any kind in the world at large. A junior order was made up of young men and women, adolescents, and children who would comprise the Shaker labor force; the outer court, or order, was set aside for older believers, formerly married, who "by living longer after the flesh" would never achieve holy perfection. All swore to covenants separating them from the world, oral in 1788 but written from 1795. And the older Shakers of the outer court, by virtue of both their experience and their corrupted natures, handled all dealings with "the world," insulating the sacred inner order and the novitiates of the junior order from such corruption. Such fears of corruption by the world extended to the senior members; by one account the deacon who was sent to Hudson and Albany to trade "is always considered so corrupted by the spirit of the world that he is not allowed to speak to aney of the members of the church till he has been at home three days."[39]

As equal first elder, ruling over the female wings of the three orders, Lucy Wright was deeply involved in the construction of this communal order, over which she assumed total authority at Meacham's death in August 1796. The process of building a separate communal order was well established, and Wright devoted attention to cultural consolidation and expansion. Under their joint authority, Meacham and Wright had had to suppress the wild dancing and singing that had characterized the early Shakers; Meacham had regularized these dances into the Square Order Shuffle, and Wright brought new dancing forms. Meacham had allowed tonal singing only, to avoid doctrinal influences from the converts' previous churches, and in 1808 Wright approved the reintroduction of verbal singing in Shaker worship. And, most important, Wright set in motion the expansion of the Shaker world. In 1799, after a decade of static membership, she saw possibilities in the opening of a general awakening and authorized preaching and conversion of new members. And in 1805 she sent missionaries to Ohio, where they would found the western wing of the society.[40]

But throughout her first eldership Lucy Wright had to struggle to maintain and assert her authority over the Shaker domain. This authority rested on the doctrine of an absent husband: Ann Lee had once told Joseph Meacham that, as the bride of an absent Christ, "the right of government" over the Shaker dispensation "belongs to the woman." But not all of the Shakers accepted this doctrine, and during the year before Meacham's death discontent began to build among the young men in the junior order, a hostility to the rise of the "goddess" Lucy compounded by what they saw as a life of ease among the powerful leaders of the inner court. Thus in 1795 and 1796, more than twenty young men at Mount Lebanon left the church, several of them suing for back wages. Dissenters at a number of Shaker villages challenged Lucy Wright's authority to govern, complaining at various times from the 1790s

PLATE 12. *Shaker Women Dancing at the Mount Lebanon Meetinghouse.*
Detail from Shakers near Lebanon, State of New York, *circa 1822*. Private Collection

that "wimmin are fools — and . . . men that are willin to have a woman to rule over them," and that they were "weary of petticoat government."[41]

The boundary between Shakers and the world became a struggle over consent. Apostate Shakers complained that the hierarchy surrounding Wright expected a "passive obedience" that brought to mind "the Romish church." Their allies in Richmond and New Lebanon center who petitioned the state in 1800 complained that young Shakers were being kept from their families and under a strict discipline "without the least Consent of their own but what is induced by the active and overawing influence of their superiors who are their sole instructors." Wright's response was to let dissidents go, even settling accounts with some, and to extend the explicit framework of individual consent embodied in signed covenants, making it entirely clear that Shaker membership was a voluntary decision. If the families on the outside worried that their children, "freeborn Citizens," were in "the condition of common slaves," many Shakers — particularly young women — must have experienced the reverse and found an expression of consent against familial power in their decision to join the Shakers. "Overawed" or not, at least two hundred signed covenants pledging property and labor to the church in 1800 and 1801.[42]

Such covenants were all the more important as a new generation of Shaker converts was being settled in a new "gathering order" of "young believers," established in 1799. Both in their youth and their exposure to the world in the 1790s, these young people brought new kinds of cultural pressures to the church. The first generation of Shakers had come directly from the impoverished and isolated circumstances of wartime and postwar rural society. Many among the new generation had been exposed to the expanded print culture of the 1790s, and the younger would have to be educated. Both of these issues posed problems for the boundary around Lucy Wright's domain. While there is no clear evidence of an explicit linkage, it is very suggestive that a society that had gender equality as a central principle also should impose significant barriers against print communication. Lucy Wright seems to have been particularly concerned that this cultural boundary be maintained.

Even before the new generation of converts, Shaker dissenters complained that the Shakers both neglected children's literacy and discouraged reading and the possession of books. Angell Mathewson, who joined the church at the age of twelve in 1782, complained in 1798, "We have no schools — libraries — newspapers — nor books of aney kind accept one testament or bible — for the use of 20 or 30 persons to each book." He claimed that, after the Canaan town authorities censured the Shakers for failing to educate the young Believers, the deacons were "rather mortified" and taught each of the young people to write their names so they could sign the covenants. He and another dissenter, Thomas Brown, claimed that the Shakers burned libraries of books owned by certain early converts.[43]

Thomas Brown and Seth Wells, two of the new generation of converts, left detailed accounts of the problematic relationship of Shakers and the public sphere of print. Brown, who soon left as an apostate, described his encounters with Shaker elders over books and reading in his 1812 *Account of the People Called Shakers*. "Seeing a number of books" in his possession, an elder told him that he "must put away my books and leave off reading, and pattern after my brethren and sisters, to be in union; two-thirds of whom, from year to year . . . don't take a book in their hands, not even the scriptures." Asking for a book among the Wells family, recently converted to the church, Brown was told, "The Elders are here now — we don't want books, we must pay attention to what they teach." Seth Wells had been a teacher at a school in Hudson and would be a leading Shaker at Mount Lebanon to his death in 1847; he told essentially the same story in an 1823 address, "Upon Learning and the Use of Books":

> When I set out to obey the gospel I had a parcel of books of various kinds, perhaps about 30 dollars worth. By the advise of my Elders I put away such as they thought unsuitable to be kept among Believers, and kept the rest, a few in number, principally school books.

Under Wells's direction, Shaker schools would gain a high reputation later in the century, but there is little evidence that the early accounts erred in their assessment of minimal attention to education. The earliest pronouncement on children's education among the Shakers, written in the early 1790s by Joseph Meacham, made no mention of young children and stressed a utilitarian minimalism: "A Vessel Cannot Contain any more than its measure." Apparently schooling was informal at best, even in the first decade of Lucy Wright's administration. Following the March 1800 petition, Justice Eleazer Grant led a three-man committee to investigate the condition of education among the Mount Lebanon Shakers. The first plan for schools came out of a November 1808 meeting. Here "the younger part were . . . instructed to read with propriety [and] soon after this regular schools were established in the different societies for their instruction." The schools established at Mount Lebanon had only evening meetings until 1815, when these were augmented by afternoon instruction; a formal school was established in the north shop in December 1817.[44]

Far into the nineteenth century, however, the 1821 "Millennial Laws," closely grounded on "orders of God" that Lucy Wright had made the structuring principles of Shaker life, imposed strict limits on Shaker reading. While they could not exclude all worldly influences, the Shaker authorities tried to restrict them as much as possible. Newspapers were not to be read after supper on Saturday or on Sundays; no one in a group should read aloud without permission, "as some greater gift might be obstructed thereby." Other articles were more comprehensive in defining the bounds around communication with the world. Any letters received or sent out must be shown to the elders. The sisters and brethren needed permission to leave the community property, and out in the world they were not to buy anything to be brought back into the village. They were not "to see shoes [shows], or any such things as are calculated to attract the mind and lead it away from the love and fear of God." And they were to keep clear of the world's print.

> The Brethren and Sisters are not allowed to purchase nor borrow books nor pamphlets of the world nor of Believers in other families without permission of the Elders. But if the world should offer or urge any of the Believers to take some particular book or pamphlet, it would be better to accept of it than to give offence, but they must not read it until they have shown it unto the Elders.

Seth Wells in 1823 fleshed out the details of a Shaker literary proscription: "Of all descriptions of books I consider the generality of Novels and Romances to be the most pernicious in their tendency, and they ought to be utterly rejected from among Believers." Novels were followed by "books of voyages and travels," and, though he wrestled with these, histories civil and ecclesiastical also fell under his ban.[45]

Mother Ann Lee, of rough working-class origins, had been illiterate and had rejected all forms of writing, and this radical stance against learning had certainly shaped the early Shaker stance on education and reading. But Lucy Wright was well educated: despite the limitations of frontier Pittsfield, she had "acquired an uncommon education . . . she was an excellent reader; a good writer, and grammatical composer," Calvin Green wrote, "and few exceeded her as a judge of propriety and correct style in composition." She was also noted for her "correct and proper Language in speaking," and she worked to reform the use of "clipped, or low, vulgar words" and "awkward mode of speaking" among the Shakers. It is all the more striking, then, that it was not until 1808 that schools were first established, and not until 1820 that they were radically overhauled at Wright's direction by Seth Wells, who introduced a Lancasterian monitorial system. If Wright was as well educated as she apparently was, she did not act precipitously to extend these benefits to her followers.[46]

Seth Wells was also in 1820 asked to assume control of an emerging body of Shaker publications and became "a very able assistant in arranging and correcting the Believers' first Publications." If the rise of Wells to authority in both education and publication in 1820 was obviously an important benchmark, so too were events in 1808. That year had seen the introduction of hymns into Shaker worship, the establishment of the first schools, and the first two in a series of Shaker publications to appear during Lucy Wright's administration. These were the first Shaker publications since Joseph Meacham's *Concise Statement of the Only True Church,* printed in Bennington in 1790. Copies of Richard McNemar's *Kentucky Revival,* printed in Cincinnati in 1807, arrived at Mount Lebanon in July 1808, and *The Testimony of Christ's Second Appearing,* also printed in Ohio in 1808, appeared at Mount Lebanon in January 1809. One historian has argued that Wright was initiating a "publication campaign" when she approved the appearance of the 1808 *Testimony,* which for the first time laid out much of the structure of Shaker theology to the public. Certainly, this and subsequent publications into the 1820s did work to counter the rising tide of apostate literature attacking the Shakers, forging a Shaker view of reality authorized by print. Starting as early as 1810 the Shakers were doing their own printing at Hancock, over the mountain east from Mount Lebanon. But it also appears that Lucy Wright was deeply ambivalent about entering the world in print. She approved the *Kentucky Revival* and the 1808 *Testimony* only after they had been started by others in the western communities, and warned that their publication would create unwanted controversies with the "world." She restricted the 1816 *Testimonies of . . . Mother Ann Lee* to twenty closely guarded copies. And for the last few years of her life Wright refused to authorize even a transcription of "the orders of God," which appeared after her death in 1821 in the "Millennial Laws" only in circulated manuscript and were never committed to print.[47]

Despite her education, then, Lucy Wright carried something of Mother Ann Lee's antistructural charisma far into her ministry. As some of the dissenters complained, hers might have been indeed a closely confining "government," cautiously excluding the influences of the world from her society. Rather than the inscribed word, Lucy Wright depended upon the spoken word. She strove to reform "awkward modes" of speech and to encourage "the simple language of Christ," "the New Tongue." She was herself, in Calvin Green's opinion, "the Best Female speaker I ever heard." "Her manner was energetic and forcible — and without prolixity of words. Her voice was solid and clear, and language plain and distinct, so that her meaning could be easily understood." Her voice was informed by a careful calculus of her audience: "She perceived the state not only of individuals but of different orders, so that her speech was adapted to their state." The voice of the believer, inspired by divinity, might be a vehicle for the "increase of Christ's government and kingdom"; a commitment of words to the page might stifle the opportunity to move toward a "greater gift." In excluding the printed word, the Shakers controlled the boundary between the believers and world, creating the conditions for inspired transcendence and for a new order among women and men.[48]

Catherine Livingston Garrettson and Mystical Methodism

Where Lucy Wright strove to keep her people safe from the world, Catherine Livingston Garrettson was in the world but not of it. The daughter of Chancellor Robert R. Livingston and coheir to the vast landed estates of the Clermont Livingston family, Catherine would rebel against family tradition, abandoning the Dutch Reformed Church to plunge into a mystical Methodist piety and into love with a leading Methodist itinerant. Nurtured in a very private world of reading and writing, her insurgency would be resolved in familial approval; the outcome would shape a subtle but quietist reconfiguration of women's space far-reaching, within its limitations, for the framing of a model of a feminized middle-class respectability.[49]

Catherine Livingston's withdrawal from high society into mystical pietism was bound up in a struggle over personal female autonomy and consent probably not unlike what young Shaker women were experiencing in the late 1780s. Her family, and particularly her imperious mother, Margaret Beekman

Livingston, had refused to allow her marriage to an early suitor sometime in the years just before the Revolution, and this experience clearly had a traumatic impact. By the close of the war Catherine was unmarried at age thirty-one and moving uneasily through the drawing rooms of the highest circles of New York and Philadelphia, attracted and repelled by the proud assertiveness of the "young man of the revolution." The death of her sister-in-law in 1785 induced her "to withdraw from company, and read the Word of God with more attention," and then the death of a sister-in-spirit, Mary Rutherford, in the summer of 1787 led to a personal crisis. That October at Clermont, in the liminal period between the Constitutional Convention and the ratification upon which her family had so much at stake (and while Lucy Wright was working on the first gathering of Shakers at Mount Lebanon), Catherine had a powerful religious conversion experience.[50]

For the next six years, at family estates in Clermont and nearby Rhinebeck, Catherine struggled with her family to assert her new identity as a humble and pious Methodist, the antithesis of the proud, sociable, and respectably orthodox landlord gentry. The vehicle of her personal rebellion was private meditation, prayer, and hours of intensive pious reading, carefully recorded in her spiritual diary. On the third day of the diary in late November she "past my morning with my God" reading a sermon by Henry Scougal, a Scottish Arminian; in the early weeks of December she was deep in the works of John Wesley and Philip Doddridge, interspersed with reading in both Testaments and more from Scougal. Later that month she was reading in translation Herman Witsius, *The Oeconomy of the Covenants,* a Dutch Calvinist who would be a favorite for years; the next May she first noted her reading in another favorite, Carl Heinrich von Bogatzky's *Golden Treasury.* Neither of these works had been as yet published in the United States, so her copies would have come into New York City and up the river as expensive imports. Her reading was otherwise shaped by her family's privileged position. In January 1788 she read a manuscript of a Dutch sermon translated by "Grand papa" (possibly Henry Beekman but probably Robert R. Livingston, Sr.); the following March she "employed a great part of my morning in reading my Grand Fathers Copy Book" of letters, where she was comforted to find "a consistent vein of Piety." Throughout, the demands of the Livingston household were an unwelcome intrusion into her intensely private world. That January the arrival of her brother, Edward, "induced me to forbear reading till the afternoon." One morning the following June after breakfast and a walk: "I retired to my room and Books, and had a pleasant morning . . . [but] was obliged to leave my room to receive some Visitors: and spent great part of this afternoon in company, tho repugnant to my Wishes. After Tea I went once more to that room; where I have so often found peace and holy joy."[51]

Intensive pious reading and meditation would shape Catherine's religious experience for years. This was reading less for unfolding argument than for immediate experience, one means to experiencing the transcendence and immanence of God. Thus in March 1788, reading in Witsius's *Oeconomy,* Catherine "read till I was so overpower'd with the vast subject, that tho' I could not articulate one word, I was carried out of myself in Speechless Wonder, love and Praise." If Lucy Wright had sought this same goal by building barriers against all texts, Catherine Livingston's privileged position at Clermont allowed her the luxury of picking only the most appropriate texts. The intense individual privacy of this mystical experience would be transformed with the appearance of Freeborn Garrettson, a noted Methodist itinerant recently given the task of opening the Hudson Valley to Wesley's movement. Sometime between the spring of 1788 and the spring of 1789 Garrettson preached several times in Rhinebeck, staying with his fellow Marylander Thomas Tillotson, married to Catherine's sister Margaret. Catherine was reading Wesley in the winter of 1787, and by the summer of 1789 she had taken the fundamental step into public by forming the first Methodist class in Rhinebeck, comprising herself and one man from among the Dutch Reformed. Swept away by Garrettson, Catherine met him clandestinely at the Tillotsons; by 1791 she had been ejected from the Livingston house for her challenge to family honor and was living with her in-laws.[52]

After Margaret Tillotson led a campaign among her siblings, the Livingston matriarch relented, and Catherine and Freeborn were married in June 1793. This effort among the Livingston siblings and the ensuing marriage brought a fundamental transition in Catherine's position. She had achieved her immediate goal of union with God and with Garrettson, which perhaps she saw as one and the same. Rather than building an institutional structure in public, Catherine would reconstruct private familial culture in association with male-dominated public institutions. The Garrettsons had one child in 1794, a daughter named for her deceased friend Mary Rutherford, after they had returned to Rhinebeck from a fever-stricken Philadelphia. Catherine then turned from private textual introspection to building "an extraordinary correspondence with a network of like minded evangelical women," what Diane Helen Lobody calls a "circle of holy sisterhood." With Freeborn and with a Livingston inheritance, she fused the Hudson Valley estate tradition with Methodist itinerancy, building a house in 1799 on a site called Wildercliffe, high above the Hudson. Bishop Francis Asbury renamed it the Traveler's Rest, as it became the traditional stopping point for itinerant Methodists. Here, Lobody argues, Catherine realized an elaboration of the goal of Republican motherhood: she became the "ultimate Methodist mother," engaged in a "ministry of hospitality," a "ministry of public domesticity."[53]

While Catherine would be unique in this role, in other ways the boundary between her and her family softened. They turned to religion, even her father the chancellor, a man of the Enlightenment, and they began to patronize new churches. Clermont Livingstons and their Armstrong connections donated land and money to build Methodist and Baptist churches in Rhinebeck and Red Hook. Most prominent among these benefactors was Catherine's older sister Janet, widow of the hero Richard Montgomery, who subscribed with other Livingston sisters to the New York City Society for the Relief of Poor Widows; their sister, Margaret Tillotson, presided over the Albany Relief Society. Catherine was content to support these efforts with letters and donations. As among some of the great families of the Chesapeake, evangelical Methodism turned back the Enlightenment while high social standing cooled the radical ardor of "a boiling hot religion." As such, Catherine Livingston Garrettson's style and persona carrying a mystical experience in a "ministry of domesticity" validated a feminine space in American evangelical religion, one that contributed to the quietist withdrawal by women of upper-middle-class respectability.[54]

Hannah Barnard, the Nine Partners' School, and the Hudson Female Benevolent Society

Where Catherine Livingston Garrettson read and wrote for personal mystical experience, Hannah Barnard read and wrote for linear argument and public purpose. Barnard was both in and of the world. Like Lucy Wright, she carefully modulated her voice to most effectively reach her various audiences. As was her theology, her writing and her public initiatives were this-worldly and optimistic about human capacities, rational and practical in their purposes. The path that she blazed for women in Hudson, like that blazed by Emma Willard to the north in the city of Troy, was grounded in domestic realities yet reached out to establish an autonomous place in the public sphere.

Hannah Barnard's Quaker conviction was critical to her life's work, but it was not that of her birthright. Born in a Baptist family on Nantucket in 1754, Hannah Jenkins converted to Quakerism in 1772 (a few years later and on the mainland she might have become a Shaker); by 1775 she was married to Peter Barnard, a carter by trade. About a decade later they joined the exodus from Nantucket to Claverack Landing. The Hudson Quakers established a preparative meeting in relation with the Dutchess County meetings, and Hannah Barnard immediately emerged as an important leader. In 1786 she began the first of eight consecutive terms representing the Creek Monthly Meeting at the Quarterly Meeting at the Nine Partners, where she must have played a considerable role in the decision to form a Monthly Meeting in Hudson in 1793. Between 1793 and 1796 she was sent three times by the Quarterly Meeting to the Yearly Meeting in New York City.[55]

Here Barnard played a role in forging educational policy. At the Yearly Meeting in May 1795 she was appointed to a committee to oversee a plan for a Quaker boarding school to be established in Dutchess County under the oversight of the Nine Partners' Quarterly Meeting. This was a project vital to the interests of the New York Friends, "the civil and Religious Well-fare of our Society" depending on establishing appropriate institutions for "useful and necessary Learning," shielding Quaker children from "the Custom of the World and its habitudes." In August 1796 Barnard was appointed to a committee charged with "procuring a proper Selection of Books" for the Nine Partners' School and in February 1797 to another charged with drafting school "Rules and Regulations." Thus she probably had a role in drafting the language in the "Sketch" for the school, language that anticipated the Shaker "Millennial Laws." The teachers were to keep a "watchful eye over the children," and particularly over their reading. The teachers were to sit with them in the first-day meeting, "after which they are to read to them, or cause them to read suitable portions of the Scriptures, and sometimes the Writings of Friends, selecting such parts and subjects as are the most instructive and best adapted to their Capacities." But, as among the Shakers, they were to erect barriers between the society and the world.

> They are to be watchful that no improper Books, Pamphlets or Papers be introduced or secreted amongst the children. This being a source of much Evil: and as evil Communications corrupt good Manners, and may be an introduction to those pernicous Books, it is earnestly recommended and enjoined that the Children have as little Intercourse with the Road as possible, either by sending them on errands or otherwise. Care should likewise be taken when there be unprofitable collutions of Neighboring People at leisure seasons, that the order and Quiet of the family be not thereby disturbed."[56]

The Nine Partners' School would endure for decades as an influential institution among the New York Quakers, a seat of innovative teaching and, eventually, abolitionist action. But, by the winter of 1796–1797, Hannah Barnard was already planning her journey to England, and, when she returned in 1801, her struggles with the Monthly Meeting precluded her continuing oversight of the fortunes of this school. If she supported the careful control of children's reading, her struggles with the London and Hudson meetings reveal clearly that she would tolerate no such supervision of adult reading. In her controversy she defended reasoned and informed thought, independent of any confining dogma, and demanded that proceedings be open and accountable to all. Some of this tone would inform her next departure in the public sphere.[57]

Accounts of Hannah Barnard's life typically leap from her struggle and disownment by the Friends in 1801–1802 to her approving of attendance at a lecture by Elias Hicks at the Hudson Friends' Meeting House in February 1819. Hicks, who himself had a role in the Nine Partners' School, would in 1828 lead the Hicksite schism against evangelical Quakers of the persuasion that persecuted Barnard in 1801. Barnard was so exhausted by her struggle with the Monthly and Quarterly meetings that she had foregone a further effort in the Yearly Meeting, where Hicks might have stood up for her in 1802. But in the intervening years before 1819 she was anything but idle. Becoming a Unitarian in principle, she turned her hands to benevolence.[58]

In the years following her struggle with the Meeting, Barnard's Hudson began to thicken with new civil institutions, adding the academy, a growing web of turnpikes, and an insurance company to the banks, the lodge, and the library. In 1806 the Hudson Mechanics Society (including both Ashbel Stoddard and Charles Holt) was incorporated, and the next year a second Masonic Lodge, named Saint Tammany, was warranted in an apparent effort to bridge the partisan gap between Federalists and Republicans. As did the lodge, the Mechanics Society had a purpose of mutual aid and support, associated "for the relief of their unfortunate and indigent members, their widows and children, and other charitable objects." Similar efforts were under way up and down the river: mechanics' societies were incorporated in Albany in 1801, followed by a Columbian Friendly Union Society in 1804, a Saint Patrick's Society in 1807, a Humane Society in 1808. Mechanics' societies were incorporated in Catskill, Troy, and Poughkeepsie in 1807 and 1808. In some of these towns female benevolent societies emerged to more widely support the deserving poor, the earliest formed in New York in 1797, followed by Troy in 1800 and Albany in 1803. These societies were organized by groups of respectable ladies, with the quiet support of leading men. In New York, the benevolent society was studded with Livingstons and other old colonial family names. In Troy the benevolent women were typically the wives of Federalist merchants, members of the Presbyterian church, and linked to an emerging web of improving associations, including the library, the county Bible society, and the Lancaster School Society, formed in 1815 and 1816. In Albany the leadership of the benevolent society was equally well placed, but dominated by Republican rather than Federalist connections.[59]

Hudson was an entrepôt city, a city with its poor, who required benevolence. If so, the city's female benevolent society was not a leader among its peers, as it was established quite late, in the spring of 1811. Probably it was the effects of the continual embargoes on Hudson's oceangoing navigation, impoverishing seaman and their families, that demanded action. The Hudson Female Benevolent Society, "yet in its infancy," published an inaugural notice in both the Republican *Bee* and the Federalist *Northern Whig* on March 22, 1811, and its first report the following April 12. At the head of the list of officers elected for the ensuing year, Hannah Barnard stood as president, as she would stand on all surviving lists through 1817. Like the societies elsewhere, the benevolent women in Hudson encompassed the wives and daughters of leading men in the city, including both Kitty Jenkins, the wife of the Republican mayor, and Lucia Williams, the wife of the Federalist magnate Elisha. Few if any were Quakers, and certainly none were among those who had persecuted Hannah Barnard in 1802.[60]

Indeed, it was Hannah Barnard's presidency of the Benevolent Society that seems most anomalous. A progressive Hicksite Quaker before her time, her theological peers would be leaders of the more radical antislavery societies three and four decades later, and not the more gradualist benevolent societies. In February 1817 she publicly reaffirmed her radical sentiments by advocating the abolition of warfare in the Hudson Forum, a city debating society. A confirmed radical, she also was not a woman of wealth and position. Her husband, Peter, a drayman, had ranked in the middle of the 1799 Hudson valuation; in 1818 Susannah Stone, the new wife of the editor of the Federalist *Northern Whig,* was stunned when he jumped off his wagon, "whip in hand," and ran up her steps unannounced to give her a bridal kiss. While appalled at Peter's behavior, Susannah Stone was fascinated by Hannah Barnard, whom she described as "dignified in appearance and manners, a tall spare person with slim features and lively intelligent dark eyes" who "wrote and spoke very well" and was "visited by the first ladies and gentlemen of the place." Stone "often wished to have learned something of her early years" and how she made such an "incongruous" match. Such a match as Peter Barnard would have been entirely out of place in the benevolent societies up and down the river, but before 1811 the women of Hudson could unite behind no other woman. Apparently Hannah Barnard—standing outside the Federalist and Republican circles and at odds with the Quakers—provided a neutral and even distinguished leadership for the benevolent society, seemingly delayed in its formation by the intensity of partisan contest in Hudson.[61]

The language of the society's first report echoes that of Hannah Barnard's struggle with the Hudson Meeting nine years before. Thanking the "friends of humanity" who had already offered their "patronage," the report stressed the need for more support, "that an institution so honourable to our city, so necessary for the poor, will not be suffered to decay." Two years later, again under Barnard's presidency, the tone was a bit sarcastic: "We hope that exertions so laudable will meet with *support,* as liberal as the *admiration* it has already received."[62]

Hudson was a tough town for charitable enterprises, already feeling the economic pinch that would bring it into permanent decline. By the end of the decade, with a national credit collapse, the local failure of the Republican Bank of Hudson, and political scandal looming over the Federalist Bank of Columbia, this pinch would be a crisis. These economic circumstances shaped one dimension of Hannah Barnard's final foray into the public sphere.

On February 1, 1820, Samuel Clark inserted an ad into his Hudson *Bee* for a pamphlet that he had just printed, Hannah Barnard's *Dialogues of Domestic and Rural Economy, and the Fashionable Follies of the World.* Combining domestic instruction with moral advice, Barnard framed *Dialogues* as a series of conversations between a mistress and young servant, Lady Homespun and Miss Jenny Prinks, with various walk-on parts, followed by an appendix, "On Burns and Their Treatment." Barnard thus appealed to two audiences, young fiction readers and their practical-minded elders, and she protected her work with a copyright. The narrative premise of the main text lay in the need for careful household management, as Jenny was put out to work as a domestic when her father was ruined by her mother's extravagance. Lady Homespun's purpose was to inculcate domestic virtues; recounting her influence over a nearby household, she prided herself in her success in achieving "an important change for the better in that family, in a very short time! neat, rational simplicity completely taking the place of pompous parade." If her purpose was virtue, her means was, not the threat of terminal tribulation, but a light optimism regarding human capacities. She defended her rambling narration, stressing the need to reach a wide audience.

> I have lived long enough to observe the wonderful variety in the structure of the human mind. Some will as fully take an idea, delivered in six words as in nine; others of equal, if not greater strength of intellect . . . require the whole nine, with three more added, to give them the same idea. Now I

write for all who are willing to read; with a wish to be, if possible, clearly understood by all.

She was also concerned that her "fellow christians" would object to a style "too humorous," perhaps "approaching even to levity": this was simply the spice "too afford an agreeable relish." Part of the "relish" — beyond a careful detailing of persons and places and the occasional sarcastic touch — was a happy, prosperous outcome, with the various characters living in a "pattern of domestic and rural neatness and industry," spreading "a benign influence over a large neighborhood." Reflecting her own turbulent history in Hudson's public sphere, Barnard had Lady Homespun announce: "I am fully aware of having advanced some unpopular opinions. They are, however, candidly my own."[63]

The *Dialogues* must have been a project of the late 1810s for Hannah, shaped by her work with the poor of Hudson in the benevolent society. There are flashes of continuity in voice and tone with her polemics against the Hudson Friends; if she did write the little account of Aunt Susie and niece Lucy in Stoddard's *Gazette,* she had long had a bent toward the domestic narrative. If so, she might well have been contributing anonymous essays to the city's newspapers in the ensuing years and possibly to one of the moral and literary magazines that sprouted up in the city after 1811: the *Columbia Magazine,* the *Casket,* the *Spirit of the Forum,* the *Lounger.* But it is more likely that she did not, as all four were venues with which she would have been uncomfortable: the *Columbia Magazine* was the publication of the regional Presbyterian–Moral Society axis, and the other three were short-lived ventures attempting to establish local versions of the young gentleman's magazine and projected just the "genteel airs" and "fashionable folly" that Barnard was seeking to reform. More likely, she carefully crafted her *Dialogues* as an antiliterary intervention, just as it was both implicitly and explicitly antinovel, finding a homespun path between caustic satire and excessive sensibility.[64]

Early in the narrative, Barnard used Jenny's uncle Thrifty to connect the destructive effects of extravagance with the "infernal mischiefs" of "the herd of novel writers" and "the foppish, affected manners" of those who recommended them. When his sister replied that "many novels contain good moral precepts," Thrifty spelled out the argument that the novel was a vehicle for seduction by a young man "with a bad design against some pretty fanciful young girl." If he were such a man, he "would encourage her by all means to read novels: and when she had shed quarts of tears of the Sorrows of Werter, the indiscretion of Charlotte, the tragical end of both them and Albert; with fifty more tales of the same bran[d]; I should not entertain the least fears of their having fortified her against my design."[65]

These sentiments were, of course, those of a woman well into her sixties, who twenty-five years before had recommended that Quaker children be protected from "pernicious books." But they were also those of a woman of recognized intellect, who had risen to positions of leadership, articulated and acted upon a liberal rationalism, challenged the legitimacy of secret proceedings, and forged the first acknowledged secular female domain in the public sphere in this city and this county. In Lady Homespun's words, she had "long laboured for that expansion of thought, which would enable me to estimate what would most likely tend to promote in the best manner, *the good of the whole.*" Her critique of the novel did not stem from an innate conservatism, but from a lifelong effort to forge a serious place for women in the public sphere. It articulated a concern that the print culture of the early Republic, with its construction of women within the confines of mortal adversity and tenuous virtue, had an immobilizing influence. Virtue and adversity were certainly present in the *Dialogues,* but that adversity was toned down, and virtue was made easily achievable through rational action, as Jenny learned the old traditions of household management, writing them into her own "excellent manuscript."[66]

Hannah Goes Van Buren, wife of the county surrogate and of one of the county's most eminent lawyers, a man of note in Hudson, was not a member of Hannah Barnard's benevolent society when it formed in 1811. Six years later her sister-in-law, Catherine Hogeboom, recently married to Martin Van Buren's younger brother, Abraham, would be the only member of the society who came from a Dutch or German household. The daughter of John C. Hogeboom, the Republican state senator so involved in banking schemes, Catherine might well have been among the more Anglicized among her ethnic sisters. But, if women of the Dutch and German traditions avoided the new institutions of the public sphere, it would appear that a strategy of avoidance was perhaps more pervasive in this county. Perhaps it was a cultural osmosis in a county with one of the largest non-English populations in the state; perhaps it had something to do with a particularly virulent partisan contest in these decades. But Columbia County was not a place where women moved easily into the public sphere in the era of the early American republic, if there was indeed any such place. For all of her efforts and real agency in public life, Hannah Barnard's legacy was truncated, leaving nothing like that which would evolve in Troy or Poughkeepsie. Some Columbia women of Yankee roots followed in Barnard's footsteps, such as the members of the Female Charitable Society of New Lebanon, founded in 1814.[67]

The Congregationalist women of this society typified the female associating that would establish the social base for the evangelical reform movements two decades hence. But Columbia County and the Hudson Valley in general would never see the fusion of female activism and reform initiatives that would sweep parts of the state of New York and elsewhere in the Yankee North in the decades to come. The constellation of conditions that might encourage such a fusion was missing in Columbia County. Print provided a limited vehicle for female empowerment, and we can chart the gradual acceptance of a women's authorial voice in this county.

But print was also a double-edged sword, as its persuasive powers inhibited as much as enhanced women's public agency. The three women of note considered here were ambivalent and even hostile toward the sentimental culture that consumed the rising generation. In some measure, each of them founded her assertion of female autonomy on a resistance to the ambivalent messages in the popular culture of sentiment. Each of them enacted versions of a radical sectarianism that had traditionally given women a voice. Given the contested nature of public life in this county, their efforts were each struggles, even insurgencies, to carve out zones of female autonomy in civil society. But, not engaged with the dynamic of sentimental culture and evangelical Calvinism that would shape antebellum reform, the fusion of Enlightenment and radical sectarianism that drove these women's lives would be increasingly anachronistic in coming years and decades. This fusion, an artifact of the close of the revolutionary eighteenth century, would not provide women an enduring purchase on public life in antebellum Columbia.[68]

9

Race, Property, and Civil Exclusions
1800–1821

Among the blessings which a moderate portion of property confers, the right of suffrage is conspicuous: and the attainment of this right holds out a strong inducement to that industry and economy, which are the life of society. If you *bestow* on the idle and profligate the privileges which should be purchased only by industry, frugality, and character, will they ever be at the trouble and pains to *earn* those privileges? No, sir; and the prodigal waste of this incalculable privilege — this attribute of sovereignty — like indiscriminate and misguided charity, will multiply the evils which it is professed to remedy.
— Elisha Williams of Hudson and Claverack, speaking in the
    New York Constitutional Convention, Sept. 24, 1821, defending
    the freehold requirement for voters in state senate elections

[Should] mechanics, professional men, and small landholders, ... constituting the bone, pith, and muscle of the population of the state ... be excluded entirely from all representation in that branch of the legislature which had equal power to originate all bills, and a complete negative upon the passage of all laws[?] ... It was to relieve them of this injustice, and this oppression, that the Convention had been called.
— Martin Van Buren of Kinderhook and Albany, speaking on
    Sept. 25, 1821, supporting the abolition of the landowning
    requirement for voting for senatorial suffrage

THE 1821 CONSTITUTIONAL CONVENTION:
RESTRUCTURING DELIBERATIVE BOUNDARIES

The autumn of 1821 saw a great debate over the structures and boundaries of deliberation in the state of New York. For three months delegates elected from every county in the state met in convention at Albany to revise the constitution of 1777, the framing document of the state's revolutionary settlement. The resulting document ratified the next spring fundamentally altered the shape of government in New York, abolishing the Council of Revision and the Council of Appointment, giving the governor direct appointing powers over the judiciary, and making a host of lesser offices elective by the house and senate. It also addressed the issue of suffrage, in a state where a series of exclusions had limited the vote to men of property in a hierarchy of ranked classes. Impelled by a perceived need to recognize the services of New York's militia in the War of 1812, the delegates voted to abolish the property qualification for white men's suffrage; they retained only a residency requirement coupled with the payment of a tax or with service in the militia or labor on the highways. But, if they greatly extended the deliberative circle for white men, they restricted it for blacks, retaining and increasing the 1777 property requirement for men of color. And if the question of black suffrage was a matter of debate, that of women of any color was rejected out of hand.[1]

Men from Columbia played a considerable role in these constitutional debates. Martin Van Buren, two years widowed and recently elected by the assembly to a term in the United States Senate, was now resident in Federalist Albany, where he stood no chance of election. His chances were equally slim in Columbia County, where the Federalist Junto held an electoral lock unbroken since 1803; he found a place on the Republican slate in Otsego and was duly seated in the convention. Columbia passed over the Republican slate by a three-to-two margin, electing four Federalist delegates. Francis Silvester, Peter Van Schaack's relation and once Van Buren's instructor in the law, had little to say in the convention. But the three leaders of the Federalist Junto, attorney Elisha Williams, Judge William W. Van Ness, and General Jacob R. Van Rensselaer, were repeatedly on their feet, attempting to turn the tide of democratic change and protect the property requirement for suffrage in the state of New York.

Elisha Williams spoke for a wide consensus when he described his understanding of the boundaries in civil society. "It does not follow," he argued in late September,

> that all who are protected by government, or entitled to its protection, are also entitled to a voice in the designation of men who administer that government. All have lives to be protected; but all living are not, therefore, entitled to become electors. All are entitled to civil and religious liberty — the minor as extensively as the adult — the female as extensively as the male — yet they have not all a voice in choosing their rulers; many a female, as well as many a legal infant, is in possession of large estates, but they cannot vote.[2]

Dismissing the deliberative political rights of women and children, the Columbia Federalists — and Martin Van Buren — more carefully debated the rights of two groups of men long marginalized in the civil life of Columbia County: blacks emerging into civil life from the shadows of slavery and white men without the freehold, who included tenants holding land under life lease and perpetual lease from the Livingstons and Van Rensselaers.

The debate on black suffrage was the most revealing. Van Buren entered the convention determined to widen suffrage as well as to enact the structural changes that would allow the emergence of his political machine, to be called the Albany Regency, in the coming decade. Since he thus had to avoid more radical measures that would work against ratification, he was firmly opposed to any language advancing universal suffrage, which would open the door to the black vote — and rejection at the polls. Thus he opposed a motion to strike a requirement of highway service and accused Elisha Williams of advancing amendments that would lead to the constitution's being "rejected by the people." He was "disposed to go as far as any man in the extension of rational liberty" but would not "undervalue this precious privilege." Federalists, led by Jonas Platt of Onieda, professed to seek an equality of condition between blacks and whites behind the bulwark of a relatively high property qualification. In the end it was Judge William W. Van Ness of Claverack who crafted the final compromise, the proviso imposing a $250 freehold property requirement on black voters.[3]

Van Ness also expressed decided opinions regarding the tenant franchise. Some of the strongest constituencies demanding constitutional reform were new settlers in the Genesee Valley and the north country, who held their lands from various land companies under "equitable contracts," essentially mortgages. Van Ness was of the opinion that, under the terms of the 1777 constitution, even if much of the mortgage had been paid, such tenure meant that they could not "vote even for members of the assembly." But they and holders of very long leases should be included in the Federalist definition of the franchise, since Van Ness grudgingly noted that holders of mere life leases, such as on the Livingston estates, had already been defined as freeholders. Williams differed. He extolled the mortgage-holding western and northern settlers as "valuable citizens" who were taming a "wilderness" and who had bravely defended the state in the recent war. But in the final analysis they were not "legal freeholders," and, announced Williams, "virtue and intelligence cannot in every case be insured access to the polls." He then held before the convention the example of the marquis de Lafayette, whose lands had been distributed to the French peasantry during "la grande revolution."

How long, Mr. Chairman, if we yield to this demand, will it be, in all human probability, before those, who now modestly ask no more than a right to govern our property—that they having none themselves to engross their attention, or require their care—will appear armed with the elective power of the state, to *consummate* to us the rich blessings conferred on the vassals of La Grange by the French Revolution? If this surrender be now made, how long before a demand of the property itself may be expected?

While Williams and other Federalists invoked the specter of a propertyless urban laboring class wielding the vote, the land struggles of the previous seventy-five years loomed as a subtext for these Columbia County magnates.[4]

In the end, Van Buren's vision prevailed. White men without landed property but otherwise claiming some minimal place in the civil order of the state would be admitted to elections for assembly, senate, and governor; the result would be a dramatic and enduring surge in vote totals in the landlord-dominated towns. Free black men, on the other hand, would have to own a considerable estate in order to vote. Elisha Williams spoke for the convention at large when he passed over a possible place for women in the polity: "By the universal consent of mankind ... the better half of the whole human family, is at once and utterly excluded from any participation of sovereignty." This new political settlement, adjusted in 1826 when an essentially universal white male suffrage was adopted by popular vote, would endure in the state for the next half century for free black men and for almost a century for all women. One epoch in the history of consent and civil boundaries in the state of New York was coming to an end, and another was beginning to take shape.[5]

The subjects of these attentions, tenants and people of color, had been aggresively confronting civil boundaries in Columbia County for the past two decades. Ambiguously poised on boundaries of civil inclusion, both had struggled in very different ways to transcend these bounds. Among the Columbia tenants, specifically those on the Livingston lands, these efforts encompassed a cycle of politicization, frustration, insurgency, and defeat between 1804 and 1814. Where the story of the tenant struggle in these years involved the public structures and institutions of formal civil society, the stories of blacks were more modest, speaking to the most basic dimensions of civil life.

BLACK COLUMBIA: THE BEGINNINGS OF FREEDOM

In March 1799 the legislature had finally enacted a statute of gradual emancipation for slaves in the state of New York. Freedom came slowly to Columbia, relative to the state as a whole; a quarter of Columbia's blacks were free in 1800, and only a little more than a half by 1820, as against a third across the state in 1800 and almost three-quarters statewide by 1820. Particularly en-

TABLE 23. *Columbia County Black Population, 1790–1820*

	Population				Black Households		Proportion of Black Population	By Household	
	Free Blacks	Slaves	Total	Black	No. of	No. in	Free	Free in White	Free in Black
1790									
New York State	4,654	21,324	340,120	25,978 (7.6%)	—	—	17.9%	—	—
Columbia County	55	1,623	27,732	1,678 (6.1%)	10	43	3.3%	0.7%	2.6%
City of Hudson	27	193	2,584	220 (8.5%)	5	19	12.3%	3.6%	8.6%
Canaan and Hillsdale	11	66	11,248	77 (0.7%)	2	8	14.3%	3.9%	10.4%
Kinderhook and Claverack	17	978	7,923	995 (12.6%)	3	16	1.7%	0.1%	1.6%
Livingston towns	0	386	5,977	386 (6.5%)	0	0	0.0%	0.0%	0.0%
1800									
New York State	10,374	20,613	588,603	30,987 (5.3%)	—	—	33.5%	—	—
Columbia County	480	1,500	35,471	1,980 (5.6%)	22	104	24.2%	19.0%	5.3%
City of Hudson	180	142	3,964	322 (8.7%)	13	71	55.9%	33.9%	22.0%
Canaan and Hillsdale	65	82	9,997	147 (1.5%)	1	4	44.2%	41.5%	2.7%
Kinderhook and Claverack	180	928	12,477	1,108 (8.9%)	4	15	16.2%	14.9%	1.4%
Livingston towns	54	347	9,303	401 (4.3%)	4	14	13.5%	10.0%	3.5%

1810

New York State	25,333	15,017	959,049	40,350 (4.2%)	—	—	62.8%	—	—
Columbia County	850	879	32,370	1,729 (5.3%)	76	337	49.2%	29.7%	19.5%
City of Hudson	194	88	4,048	282 (7.0%)	30	119	68.8%	26.6%	42.2%
Canaan and Hillsdale	127	45	9,123	172 (1.9%)	11	52	73.8%	43.6%	30.2%
Kinderhook and Claverack	397	536	10,683	933 (8.7%)	27	119	42.6%	29.8%	12.8%
Livingston towns	132	210	8,516	342 (4.0%)	8	47	38.6%	24.9%	13.7%

1820

New York State	29,163	10,124	1,372,812	39,287 (2.9%)	—	—	74.2%	—	—
Columbia County	1,008	761	38,330	1,769 (4.6%)	135	653	57.0%	20.1%	36.9%
City of Hudson	290	61	5,310	351 (6.6%)	54	219	82.6%	20.2%	62.4%
Canaan and Hillsdale	131	67	9,753	198 (2.0%)	11	50	66.2%	40.9%	25.3%
Kinderhook and Claverack	490	417	12,528	907 (7.2%)	63	338	54.0%	16.8%	37.3%
Livingston towns	50	102	5,202	152 (2.9%)	5	29	32.9%	13.8%	19.1%

Notes: Chatham and Ghent included with Kinderhook and Claverack. Black population in 1800 calculated from household returns and differs slightly (23 individuals) from the printed return and the manuscript recapitulation.

Sources: U.S. Census, 1790–1820.

trenched in the older Dutch, German, and Anglo gentry neighborhoods running down from Kinderhook through Claverack to Livingston Manor, slavery had never taken deep roots in the new Yankee towns: Hudson, Canaan, and Hillsdale. As of 1800 these were the places where the halfway house of free or apprenticed service in white households was particularly important. The city of Hudson and the Yankee hill towns led the county in "free" white households in 1800, households with resident free persons of color but no slaves. In the hill towns 40 percent of the black population were free and mostly living in white households with no slaves; in the older river towns about 20 percent were free, mostly living in white households with blacks still held in slavery.[6]

Beyond this quasi dependency lay the status of the free black householder, measurable in growing numbers in the census. As of 1790 and 1800 the proportion of blacks living in black-headed households was extremely small, growing from one in fifty to one in twenty. By 1810, after a decade of gradual emancipation, almost one-fifth of Columbia's blacks were listed in black households, and by 1820 the proportion had grown to more than one-third. Again, the city of Hudson consistently led the way, with the population of such independent households growing from about 22 percent to 60 percent of the city's black population between 1800 and 1820. During the 1810s the large black communities in the freehold agricultural towns of Kinderhook, Claverack, Chatham, and Ghent began to develop independent households in considerable numbers while the towns of the old Livingston Manor lagged behind.

An independent household was only one of many dimensions of emancipated autonomy toward which Columbia's blacks struggled in these years. Personal names are a fundamental measure of such a civil autonomy, and slaves had simply a single given name. While most free men and women listed as heads of household in the census had adopted a surname, often apparently that of a former master, through 1810 some were listed by a single given name: Titus, Betty, Little Jack, Black Kane. Toby, listed in Hudson in 1790 was by 1800 apparently "Tobias Wall"; by 1820 all free black heads of household would have surnames.

More important, household independence required employment and, perhaps, property. Slaves had traditionally worked the dairy and cattle agriculture of the Hudson lowlands, and when the 1820 census began to record occupations, the great majority of black households in the country towns listed one or more people working in agriculture. The 1820 census also was the first to record age classifications for blacks; in that year there was a slight disproportion of young black men in Kinderhook and Claverack, suggestive of their role in agriculture, as compared to a decided tilt toward young and middle-aged black women in Hudson, where women would have worked as domestics and men shipped out with the city's fleet in some numbers.

As of 1800, however, the record for property ownership among the free blacks of Columbia is extremely slim. Of the twenty-two black householders listed on the 1800 census, only six had paid taxes in the previous year. Of these, five ranked in the eighth and tenth deciles of the Hudson list; Tobias Wall and Charles Thurston were each charged for a house and lot. These holdings are some of the earliest evidence of black landed property in the county, though these men might well have been tenants. On Livingston Manor the one black on the tax list, John Lawrence, was indeed a tenant farmer. Ranked in the seventh decile of the 1800 Livingston valuation, Lawrence paid taxes on four hundred dollars worth of land and seventy-four dollars of personal property. Three years before, Henry Livingston had asked about him at the end of a letter to his agent, William Wilson. Primarily concerned about the threat of illegal lumbering in his reserved woodlands by his tenants, Livingston closed his letter with a P.S.: "Has Lawrence the Black Man got a lease or agreement?"[7]

Such a minimal claim to property was the essential requirement for stability and the emergence of a black community. Some of these households were remarkably enduring. Of the 5 black households counted in Hudson in the 1790 census, Tobias Wall was still listed in the census in 1810, as was Titus Loosely, taxed in 1800. In Kinderhook, the only free black family in 1790 was headed by Joseph Ripley, who had been freed for his Revolutionary service in a Massachusetts regiment. By 1800 Ripley had moved to Hudson, where he and his family were still living in 1810, when they were one of at least 30 free black households, in a free black population that numbered more than 280. David Ripley, living in Hudson in 1820, was probably a son. John Lawrence, the Livingston tenant farmer, might not have fared quite so well. Taxed in 1800, he might have lost his lease, since he was apparently living in Dutchess County in 1810; by 1820 he was again listed — with a large family — in Ancram, one of the towns broken out of the Manor in 1803.[8]

If Lawrence's hold on civil status was tenuous, that of other men and women of color in the region was even more so. What of Solomon Goomer, listed in New Lebanon in 1820 with a wife and child? He was probably the Solomon who as of 1818 was living at Peleg Spencer's, skilled at distilling. Was he really on his own, or living in a tenant dependency of the Spencers'? And what of the "black man" from whom, in March 1816, George Holcomb bought a small basket for "a peck of corn"? Quite possibly he was an itinerant, and equally possibly kin to itinerant native American peoples who moved through the

PLATE 13. *Shaker Men, White and Black, Dancing at the Mount Lebanon Meetinghouse. Detail from* Shakers near Lebanon, State of New York, *circa 1822.* Private Collection

early-nineteenth-century landscape, utterly outside the protections and obligations of civil society. Solomon Goomer, the only black head of household in New Lebanon in 1820, would have known of David Ginnings, a former slave who had joined the Shakers early in the 1780s with the white family who had freed him, living at Mount Lebanon village until his death in 1850. Which of them, he might have asked, occupied the better situation: Solomon, living on his own but very much on the edge of civil society, or David, living beyond the claim of the world in putative equality of condition with his fellow Shakers?[9]

In sum, despite the facts of emancipation by military service or civil statute, blacks remained a subordinate civil caste, such as the Council of Revision had warned in 1785. Such subordination had been codified in the terms of gradual emancipation and confirmed when the legislature required, in the 1811 law against electoral fraud, that a black voter show "a certificate of his freedom" at the polls. The subtitle of this act was "to prevent slaves from voting." The presence of blacks and the issue of race subsided considerably in the Hudson newspapers, but ads for slaves for sale and about runaways were still evident on the eve of the 1821 constitutional convention. In the courts blacks regularly appeared on the dockets for petty theft, burglary, and horse stealing, but what is as striking are several high-profile cases where blacks appeared as victims. In the summer of 1810 a mulatto named Ezra Rifle was stoned by a mob in Hillsdale; when he died of his injuries, it "made a considerable noise in that part of the county." Tried at the September oyer and terminer, the seven defendants, who had been led by a Republican committeeman, were found not guilty. A white woman accused of poisoning a mulatto child at Kinderhook Landing seven years later did not do so well and was hanged at Hudson in October 1817. Such hangings could attract ten to twelve thousand viewers, almost a third of the county population; for this and other executions, accounts of the trial and confession were printed up for the local readership. If both of these cases probably "made a considerable noise" across the county, there is little indication that the white population of Columbia viewed local blacks as anything but a subordinate caste, subject to racial animosity or a muted language of paternal sympathy.[10]

Subordination in caste might well have been met by secret insurgent combinations, grounded in the traditions of West African secret societies. Such seems to have been the case in New York City, and these traditions of black sociability and resistance might well have existed in the mid-Hudson, manifested in the murders and fires in Kingston and Albany in 1775 and 1793. But, in the 1780s and 1790s, African Americans began to build a place in civil, associational life beyond both the household and the secret society. As of the first years of the nineteenth century, such an institutional emergence was only beginning in New York City, building on traditions of subordination and resistance. White benevolence had established the African Free School in New York in 1789, a few years after the forming of the New York Manumission Society. By an 1810 law, public money was set aside to construct a new building for the African Free School, and in the same year and in 1812 New York City blacks began to form their first autonomous organizations; the New York African Society and the Wilberforce Philanthropic Association would be the first of many mutual aid societies that would serve the black community of New York. But the African Society had roots that ran back in other directions, both to the first black conversions to Methodism in the 1780s and to the West African traditions that informed early black Methodism and lay behind the establishment of a burial society in 1795. In 1796, black Methodists in New York City seceded into an "African chapel" and soon thereafter formed the first black church in the state, the African Methodist Episcopal Zion Church. Building their first meetinghouse in 1801, the AME Zion Church was followed by the Abyssinian Baptist Church in 1807, founded by the Reverend

Thomas Paul, whose son Nathaniel was chosen in 1823 to be the first minister of the new Albany African Baptist Church, the first black church in the upper Hudson.[11]

The Reverend Nathaniel Paul had already begun to make a name for himself in the region; across the river at Stephentown, George Holcomb wrote on July 7, 1822, that he "went to Elder Jones meetinghouse to hear Paul, a black man from Albany preach." But it would be decades before the first black churches would form in Columbia, at Hudson and Chatham. Until then, they would be a small and even dwindling presence in white churches, like the women of color, slave or free, for whom a pew was reserved in the Dutch church in Kinderhook, or Ephraim Pierce's "black girl," whom Holcomb saw baptized in Stephentown in 1818.[12]

Perhaps blacks from Columbia went upriver to the annual June celebration of Pinkster on the hill rising behind Albany. Pinkster had been a Dutch early summer festival, but in the 1780s it had been left to the enslaved "Afro-Dutch," as the white Dutch moved toward Anglo assimilation, perhaps comprising an indeterminate space in public between secret combinations and legitimate civil life, just as the mid-Hudson's blacks stood between slavery and freedom. For three decades Pinkster Day was the key event in the calendar of slaves in the upper Hudson, a carnival of music, dance, and ritual inversion, described in detail in a "Pinkster Ode" published in the Albany papers in 1803. But by the spring of 1811 it had grown into such a disorderly interracial circus that it was abolished by the city council in the interest of respectability.[13]

It might not have been just white respectability that brought Pinkster to an end, however, but also an aspiring black respectability. Pinkster was a celebration that drew rural slaves into Albany, and apparently into the villages along the river, from their scattered dependencies on outlying farms. By 1811, free black families and households had begun to form in Albany and the other river towns. Perched precariously on the edge of independent respectability, on a slim foothold in civil society, these early free black householders might have objected to Pinkster's links to a past life of dependency and slavery in a Dutch world. Five years after the suppression of Pinkster, free black artisans in Albany established an institution of such respectability. Petitioning the legislature, in April 1816 they received an act of incorporation for the Albany School for People of Color, modeled on the New York African Free School. Receiving assistance from the Albany Lancaster Society, founded in 1812 to support education for the white poor, the Albany School would in 1826 meet in the basement of Nathaniel Paul's Albany African Baptist Church.[14]

Where the efforts in Albany were successful in building the ground for a permanent if segregated black school, elsewhere such institution building was less autonomous and more ambiguous in its outcome. In Hudson a similar sequence would unfold, but it took considerably longer and was less successful. A Lancaster Society school was formed in 1817, but it was not until 1828 that the society opened an "African School," which was forced to close in 1833. Writing for the Sunday School Association in Troy in 1817, David Buel announced, "Wherever the people of color enjoy the opportunity of attending Sunday schools, they will wipe off the reproach which has often been cast upon them, of want of capacity." But, by the same year, readers of the papers in Troy, Albany, and Hudson were seeing proposals distributed by the new American Colonization Society, recommending that free blacks be returned to Africa, on the model of Britain's Sierra Leone.[15]

In these same postwar years a white son of New Lebanon village in Canaan emerged as an advocate of colonization, and he wrote with passion of the circumstances of enslaved and free blacks in the American states. Dr. Jesse Torrey, who maintained his ties to his native New Lebanon from Philadelphia, had lived for several months in 1815 and 1816 in Washington, D.C., following the destruction of the city by the British. He was shocked by the sight of slave coffles being marshaled in front of the gutted Capitol, a picture of which — complete with angels of judgment watching from the heavens — he had engraved as the frontispiece for his 1817 pamphlet, *A Portraiture of Domestic Slavery in the United States*. Torrey condemned slavery as "contrary to the precepts of religion, moral justice, and the abstract, natural and political rights of man." He described in particular detail the horrors of the internal slave trade and the kidnapping of free blacks for sale to the South. But if slavery posed a *"threatening-thundercloud"* for the nation, Torrey had only a gradualist prescription for this national "sin": his prescription reflected the torturous path from Revolutionary violence to settled civil procedure that Columbia — and the old King's District, where he was born — had tried to follow over the previous three decades. Simultaneously working on his vision of a national system of free libraries that would be announced in his *Intellectual Torch,* Torrey advocated a gradual amelioration of the conditions of slaves into that of bonded laborers and tenants, combined with the Lancaster program for education that was being adopted in the leading towns along the Hudson Valley.

> Intellectual and moral improvement is the safe and permanent basis, on which the arch of eventual freedom to the enslaved African, may be gradually erected. . . . Let every slave, less than thirty years of age, of either sex, be taught the art of reading, sufficiently for receiving moral and religious instruction. . . . For this purpose, the Lancasterian mode of instruction,

would be admirably well adapted. A well selected economical library of such books as are calculated to inculcate the love of knowledge and virtue, ought to form an essential appurtenance to every plantation.

He did not advocate mass emancipation or colonization of southern slaves, since that would require also the colonization of southern whites, who, he sarcastically wrote, would "perish amidst the desolate cotton and rice fields" without their *"black benefactors."* Free blacks would still need to be protected from the "sacrilegious talons of the numerous hordes of man-stealers," for which he recommended colonization in "some asylum," where they would be followed after an eventual "national ransom of slaves." Failing the intervention of Congress, he expected this to be the work of "beneficent societies," and he included as an appendix the proceedings of the first meeting of the American Colonization Society, chaired by Henry Clay.[16]

At the core of his account, Torrey articulated a powerful sense of the civil boundaries that he thought should define black life in America, taking a stricter line than would even the delegates in the 1821 constitutional convention. As *"strangers in a foreign land,"* virtual "prisoners of war," he would not grant free blacks "a participation in the *civil* privileges of citizenship." But as a fellow human being, the free black had "an incontestible claim to the protection of the laws," to "the enjoyment of his natural and moral rights, . . . the fruits or reward of his own labor, the benefits of mental improvement, and exemption from corporal laceration." But Torrey was also powerfully affected by a story of a slave's being marched past the Capitol, recounted by a former neighbor, Congressman Asa Adgate (the son of Matthew, the leader of the old popular faction in Canaan). As the coffle moved by a group of congressmen, one of the slaves, "elevating his manacles as high as he could reach, commenced singing the favorite national song, 'Hail Columbia! happy land.'" Torrey closed his tract with a hope that the adoption of his program would reverse this desperate sarcasm, so jarring to these two sons of Columbia County.

> Then may the sable Africo-American, who shook his manacles at the conservators of the rights of man, while he was dragged through the city of Liberty, raise his *unfettered* hands, and again exclaim,
>
> Hail Columbia, happy land,
> Hail ye heroes, heaven-born band.
>
> Then, and not till then, may the American Eagle expand his genial wings, and proclaim to an applauding world, with *unalloyed truth,* that

The sons of Columbia shall ne'er be slaves,
While the earth bears a plant, or the sea rolls its waves.

Poetry might thus open the door to a wider civil inclusion for "Africo-Americans" than Torrey was willing to admit in formal prose.[17]

THE 1811 MANOR PETITION

On March 7, 1811, a petition from Henry Avery, Benjamin Birdsall, Jr., and 159 other inhabitants of Granger, Gallatin, and Livingston, towns whose inhabitants still paid rent to the old Upper Manor Livingston families, was read and briefly debated in the assembly of the state of New York. The petitioners couched their objections in terms that echoed both a long history of local struggle between landlord and tenant and broader values held throughout the American republic. They complained that the heirs of Robert Livingston, deceased since 1790, held in private possession title to lands that rightly belonged to the public, "the people of the state." They then called the attention of the assembly to the social and economic effects of the life-lease system prevailing on the Livingston lands. Requiring annual rents and duties, the life lease stipulated that "the premises leased with all the improvements made by the tenants" would revert to the landlord at the death of the three individuals in the lease. The petitioners chose to focus on the assumed relationship of private and public goods on the developing American landscape.

> Owing to the business of the tenure by which they hold their lands, the exercise of common prudence forbids any lasting or valuable improvements on the same and that consequently a tract eminently calculated by nature to form the fairest portion of the country presents a scene precisely the reverse of what otherwise would be[; and is thus] destructive of the interests of the community.

Arguing that the Livingstons rightfully held only 2,600 acres of their claim of "rising of 100,000 acres," the tenant petition "respectfully solicit[ed] that your honourable body" would reopen an investigation into the legitimacy of the Livingston title to the manor lands.[18]

That day the assembly was considering petitions for turnpikes and bounty lands and bills governing manufacturing companies, local taxation, and the purchase of Indian lands, all measures that, like the Manor petition, involved the distribution of the public authority and resources of the state of New York. After some debate, however, the tenants' petition was referred to the state attorney general and surveyor general, who, on April 3, issued a brief finding, grounded on a long report issued after similar protests in 1795, upholding the Livingston claim on grounds of the antiquity of their tenure. While it freely distributed western lands to petitioning individuals and groups and, indeed, settled other large land claims in neighboring towns, the legislature would not intervene in a dispute involving one of the state's most powerful families.[19]

Despite this setback, the tenants' committee continued to press its case in the Republican paper in Hudson, the *Bee*. Over the summer of 1811, Benjamin Birdsall, Jr., still farming in the Copake neighborhood in the Manor town of Granger, emerged as the most eloquent advocate of the tenants' cause. In a long letter to the Hudson *Bee,* Birdsall set the struggle against the Livingstons into the narrative of national history since 1775, calling for an end to "a thirty-six years usurpation and oppression" of the tenants' "inalienable and constitutional rights." "The people on the manor," Birdsall argued, "live in a state of vassalage and servile dependence incompatible with their rights and liberties as Americans, and wholly unauthorized by the constitution of their country." Given these circumstances, they were in his eyes alienated and stateless. Had the Livingston tenants, Birdsall asked, "lost our protection, are [we] no longer Americans and no more to experience the blessings of a republican government"? The ground of governmental legitimacy and popular consent to that government were dissolving fast, Birdsall announced. And, as had the *Bee* in years past, Birdsall reached the inevitable conclusion: tenancy was akin to slavery. "The combined wealth and unconstitutional power of the landlord had become paramount to the law of the land," he continued, and "the connections between right and wrong, between liberty and slavery, was compleatly dissolved."[20]

The fruits of their toil, constitutional rights, the appearance of slavery, even citizenship in the nation: the rhetoric of Benjamin Birdsall and the Livingston tenants in 1811 anticipated the basic points of Jesse Torrey's analysis of the condition of American blacks in 1817. Torrey rejected both slavery and citizenship for American blacks, but he would grant them a minimum of protection under the law as recompense for their labor. The Livingston tenants argued that they were denied even that, in regard to their improvements to their rented farms: they announced their fears that they had no citizenship and were being reduced to slavery. In March they petitioned for their improvements; by August, after the failure of the petition, Birdsall was voicing the more dramatic ideological anxieties. By the next summer some of the tenants had moved from politics to insurgency, taking up arms and firebrands against the Livingston landlords.

As had unfolded in the mid-to-late 1790s, the decade ending in 1812 brought a cycle of politicization, frustration, and outright civil war. Tenants on the Manor, heirs to a tradition of rebellion running back to the 1750s and isolated from the institutions and vehicles of deliberative discourse, were quick to resort to violence when their political initiatives failed. Here, however, these political initiatives had a relatively long cycle of development, a cycle that brings us again to the early career of Martin Van Buren, to the wider efforts of the Columbia Republicans to assert popular power against the rule of oligarchs, and to the efforts of local people to catch hold of the flywheel of civil society linking social circumstance and constitutional polity. The story of this cycle of tenant protest and insurgency thus was bound up with the emerging purposes and agendas of political party and the complex story of the forging of civil life in post-Revolutionary Columbia County.

BIRDSALL AND VAN BUREN: LIVINGSTON TENANTS AND THE COUNTY REPUBLICANS, 1802–1810

This story brought together two then-minor figures in Columbia County, Martin Van Buren and Benjamin Birdsall, Jr. Both were sons of men of the popular wing of the Revolution: Captain Abraham Van Buren, and Colonel Benjamin Birdsall, both of whom probably were in the lines at Saratoga in 1777 and both of whom reached a certain level of prominence in town and county affairs and in George Clinton's Republican coalition. Abraham was certainly the lesser of the two, serving as the town clerk of Kinderhook and hosting Clintonian meetings in his tavern. Colonel Benjamin was a man of great stature in Hillsdale and made something of a mark on the county and the state. After he had led, first, the 1789 petition against the Van Rensselaers and, then, the local men in the controversial Genesee Adventurers, he served for more than twenty years as justice of the peace, was elected four times as a Republican to the assembly, and was elected to the 1801 constitutional convention. The sons, Benjamin, Jr., and Martin, born fifteen years apart in 1767 and 1782, would be intimately connected for several years around 1811 in a failed cause that illuminates some of the boundaries and limitations of civil institution building in the early Republic. In a reversal of their fathers' positions, one would be a neighborhood leader and the other a player on the wider deliberative public sphere, attaching the tenant interest to the purposes of party. But, where Colonel Birdsall had flirted with a challenge to the Revolutionary settlement in his role in the Adventurers and his affiliations with the Hillsdale rioters of 1791, his son would cross the line into open rebellion with the state. Where Captain Van Buren had played only a local role in the patriot and Clintonian cause in Kinderhook, his son would carry his commitment to the new state and nation, and his style of politics far into the nineteenth century.

In the decade leading up to the petition against the Livingston claim in 1811, the younger Van Buren and Birdsall followed convergent paths. Both suffered humiliations at the hands of the Kinderhook Federalist magnates and their wider connections. In 1804, having returned to Kinderhook after eight years of legal apprenticeship locally and in New York, Van Buren was challenged by Peter Van Schaack and his allies when he came forward to vote for Morgan Lewis rather than Aaron Burr in the 1804 election for governor. He would remember the "indignity" of being "compelled to take the oath prescribed by law" and would repay the insult whenever he could in the years to come. In 1804 the younger Benjamin Birdsall was thirty-seven, married for sixteen years with several children, and a veteran of the troubles on the Manor in the late 1790s. In a statement dictated to Van Buren in September 1812, Birdsall claimed that in 1798 he had been granted fourteen years free of rent on a farm in the eastern Great Lot No. 2 on the Manor in exchange for his "good offices and mediations" in arriving at a "settlement" of the Manor "controversies." But by 1804 he had been in and out of court regarding other debts owed to the Livingstons, and in 1808 Peter Van Schaack, who in 1798 had been handling his obligations to the Livingstons, was again pursuing him for these debts; by 1812 they were in the hands of attorney James Vanderpoel, another prominent Kinderhook Federalist.[21]

Thus Van Buren and Birdsall had parallel experiences with the force of Columbia Federalism, and in the first years of the new century the wider entities that they would come to lead began to recognize a convergence of interest. The county Republicans needed to reach out to the tenants to have any hope of regaining the electoral dominance lost at the end of the 1790s; many among the tenants were hungry for the connections in a wider civil life that might help them break the Livingston title and give them freeholds to the land they occupied.

The old Clintonian coalition, now redefining itself through the Hudson *Bee* as the Republican Party in Columbia County, had certainly fallen on hard times. Having swept the assembly elections through most of the 1790s, they had begun to lose after the 1798 election, when the Upper Manor Livingstons ordered their tenants to switch to the Federalists. In the face of this rising tide of tenant Federalism, the Republicans lost the 1799 and 1800 assembly elections. But they managed to win in April 1801, riding the coattails of George Clinton's popularity, which produced a surge of Republican voting in Kinderhook and Canaan. But in 1802 they lost by an average of about two hundred, overwhelmed by a four-hundred-vote margin in the Manor towns. With Colonel Birdsall, Ambrose Spencer was a Republican candidate that year, and on May 1 he sent a scathing letter to William Wilson in Clermont. There were rumors circulating that Wilson, a Republican but also an agent with Peter Van Schaack managing the affairs of the Livingston's Great Lot No. 2, had quietly used his influence to aid the Federalists in their "great exertions" and "most abandoned deception." Reviewing the town votes, Spencer fumed that "the Manor has destroyed us"; Wilson declared any such rumors "a positive and malitious falsehood."[22]

If they were to reestablish their dominance of county politics, the Republicans would have to break the power of the Manor. In the fall of 1802, at a county committee meeting convened at Claverack during the sitting of the superior court, a plan was hatched to arrange legislation to divide the town of Livingston, the old Upper Manor. That winter petitions were circulated, though by February 1803 Spencer was worried that nothing was being done: writing from Albany to a now trustworthy Wilson, he urged, "The object is too important to be neglected; will you take measures, that they [the petitions] be collected and sent up?" Action was swift when the petitions arrived in the Republican-controlled legislature, even though its affairs were clogged with debate over a host of banking proposals. By early March they had been introduced in the senate, and the bill moved out of committee and through a senate and house vote without delay. While the Columbia Federalists attempted to derail the bill, an effort to merge Germantown with Clermont was the only proposal voted down. The resulting law dividing Livingston into three towns was passed in tandem with that incorporating the Republican New York State Bank, perhaps testament to the importance that party leaders placed on its passage.[23]

Thus were born, from party purposes, the towns of Granger and Gallatin (see Map 4). Named for Jeffersonian Republican luminaries, these towns encompassed the better part of the old Upper Manor, and the town of Livingston was reduced to the neighborhoods around the Manor houses on the river. In a fit of partisan revenge, these towns would be renamed for their traditional Manor neighborhoods — Taghkanic and Ancram — when the Federalists briefly regained control of the legislature in 1814. In getting the towns renamed, the Livingstons were attempting to reassert a waning but still potent authority on their Manor lands. Tenants on the Manor had long been virtually cut off from the civil and institutional life of the wider county and state, and this pattern would endure for decades.[24]

The formation of these two new towns by Republican initiative suddenly opened up an avenue along which the Manor tenants might begin to move into the county's wider civil society. Town clerks and collectors would be responsible to county courts and supervisors; the town supervisor would attend regular meetings of the board as an equal. On April 5, 1803, then, the first town meetings in Granger and Gallatin were held, and men were elected to offices ranging from clerk and supervisor down to poundkeeper and fence viewer. The political outcome was immediate. On April 19, 1803, the *Bee* and the *Balance* printed the names of town committees committed to Republican and Federalist assembly candidates, including committees from both towns, among which were men who probably had never before acted on any public stage. A week later the Republican county assembly slate triumphed once again, but by a microscopic fifty-vote margin and for the last time.[25]

The Republican town-building had certainly determined the 1803 election. Republican assembly votes surged in the Manor region, doubling from 140 to about 290 while the Federalist vote stayed put at 550–570. Given the narrow county margin, the 170 Republican votes in Granger might well have been decisive. But Gallatin voted three to one for the Federalists, and the reduced town of Livingston, where the landlord family maintained its river-view estates, seven to one. There was a powerful reservoir of landlord-Federalist power on the Manor, and it would not be denied.[26]

But the ambitious Republicans also would not be denied. By the next March, 1804, Henry Livingston was fuming about a new Republican civil initiative. Benjamin Birdsall, Jr., one of the 1803 Republican committee, with his father sitting in the assembly, was leading a plan to divide the towns again, somehow combining Great Lot No. 2 with the Oblong section of Dutchess County. More threateningly, Birdsall and his associates were also trying to have a new militia regiment established; Livingston was appalled this would come out of the Manor regiment and that "they are to be the field officers." "What do you think of this," he thundered at William Wilson. "Have you been consulted—do you approve of such conduct, in our *Rulers*"? A week later he was still concerned about the proposed regiment as well as a petition being circulated by another Republican, Martinus Miller, a veteran of the 1795 tenant challenge, which petitioned for a grant of all of the vacant land on the Manor. Nothing came of these initiatives, and the 1804 election locked up the county assembly seats for the Federalists in the first of a series of victories that would be unbroken until after the 1821 constitutional convention. In combination with a family commitment to Aaron Burr's independent candidacy for governor, Henry Livingston must have taken up the sword against his local "political enemies," using every trick in the landlord's book, since once again the Manor vote determined the assembly election. About two hundred new Federalists votes were cast, and about seventy fewer Republican; even in Granger, where the Republicans had hoped for a one-hundred-vote margin, a fifty-vote Republican majority had given way to a seventy-vote Federalist majority.[27]

The Republican town-building in 1803 coincided with another strand of civil institution-building. On April 18, 1803, twelve days before the election, a group of men gathered to sign a petition for a lodge warrant in south Hillsdale. Among them, with prominent Hillsdale Republicans like Colonel Birdsall and William Tanner, were men from Granger who had been or would be embroiled in civil initiatives on the Manor. Benjamin Birdsall, Jr., involved wherever he could be, was joined among the Masonic petitioners by Jacob C. Decker, the new town clerk in Granger, and Anthony W. Snyder, a Republican committeeman in 1806. Without local lodges in the Upper Manor towns, failing Birdsall's effort in 1798, men in the towns would find their Masonic fraternity in lodges beyond the borders of the Manor. Though Hillsdale's Vernon Lodge inclined toward Federalism later in the decade, as many as seven Republican committeemen from Granger joined the lodge. Generally, men in Gallatin went south to Temple Lodge in Northeast; a select few joined another new lodge formed in Clermont in 1811.[28]

Freemasonry's links into a wider civil society were greatly prized by some of the local notables in these towns, if we accept the evidence of John Francis Collin, writing in the 1870s about his grandfather, Captain John Collin, who he claimed had played a central role in settling troubles over land in neighboring Hillsdale. Collin wrote that his grandfather

> was a pacificator among the people and did much to settle the controversy between the occupants of lands in Hillsdale under Massachusetts titles and the [Van Rensselaer] claims. He was a prominent member of the Masonic fraternity, and in his social relations was on terms of intimacy with the Van Rensselaers, the Livingstons, the Van Nesses and Alexander Hamilton. Elisha Williams spent some weeks in his family.[29]

Blending the story of his father's and grandfather's generation, and perhaps that of their neighbors the Birdsalls, this 1870s account might have exaggerated the reach of this family's "social relations." However, factual or not, it suggests that the lodge, the seat of Atlantic Enlightenment sociability, was long remembered in the hill towns as an important link to the wider world, providing a connection with leaders and chieftains in the state at large and a vehicle to political outcomes in a wider deliberative arena. These fleeting Masonic affiliations, combined with Republican committee membership, would also provide a common background among the leaders of the reemergent tenant resistance in 1811.

The overarching reality, however, was that these efforts to bring the Livingston tenants into the public sphere were having no results. After 1803, through
to the end of the next decade, the county Republicans would struggle in vain
against the Federalist Junto to elect a slate to the assembly. In the years immediately following their clinching victory in 1804, the Federalists turned to
biting propaganda, in the spirit of the Hudson *Wasp,* which played on the
county land conflicts to beat down their Republican opponents. Thus they
mocked tavernkeeper Fite Miller, a new Granger town official nominated
by the Republicans to the assembly in 1807, as illiterate and unfit for office.
Two years before, they had hounded another Republican candidate, William
Tanner, who they claimed had been among the Hillsdale rioters who had
shot Sheriff Hogeboom in October 1791. David McKinstry (Colonel John
McKinstry's younger brother), a deputy sheriff that day, was called upon to
swear testimony that Tanner was neither "privy to the blacking of the murderers" nor "blacked through the whole course of the event." The events in the
Hillsdale struggle were revisited implicitly in virtually every issue of the Hudson papers and every meeting of the county court following the commercial
collapse in 1807, as the Van Rensselaers began to prosecute Hillsdale farmers
for failing to keep up with the mortgages settled only in 1803 and 1804. Starting in 1806 the lingering controversy over the Merchant's Bank further alienated the county Republicans from any residual Clermont Livingston support.
In the spring election, Robert R. Livingston, Governor Lewis's brother-in-
law and deeply interested in the Merchant's Bank opposed by the Clinton-
Spencer faction, ordered his Clermont tenants to vote Federalist, turning his
back on the moderate Republicanism that he had espoused since the early
1790s. With him, William Wilson temporarily cut his ties with the Columbia
Republicans to support the Livingston-Lewisite Quid faction.[30]

But there were some bright spots for the Republicans. The wider congressional and senate districts of which the county formed one part still consistently elected Republicans, among them Stephen and John C. Hogeboom of
Claverack and James I. Van Alen, Martin Van Buren's half brother. After the
victory of Bucktail Daniel D. Tompkins over Quid Morgan Lewis in the governor's election of 1807, Republicans would control the flow of county patronage as long as the party men held a majority in the house and senate. In
1808 this consistent Republican control paid off for Columbia Republicans:
John C. Hogeboom led the successful chartering of the Bank of Hudson,
a Republican venture that challenged the credit monopoly of the Federalist

Bank of Columbia. On the old Manor, Benjamin Birdsall, Jr., and two other loyal Republicans were appointed justices of the peace. And that February Martin Van Buren was appointed surrogate of the county, with authority over all matters of probate and wardship.[31]

Van Buren owed his rising position in great measure to De Witt Clinton, George Clinton's nephew and the Republican mayor of New York, and over the next few years he was in a regular correspondence, particularly on election matters, in which the Federalist efforts to "make" fraudulent voters on the Livingston domain loomed large. In the 1810 election vote making exploded in Columbia County, as Van Buren reported to Clinton, with the Federalists writing deeds to enfranchise temporary voters in Livingston, Gallatin, and Hudson while the Republicans had met "them on their own ground" in Claverack.[32]

Writing that he "despised the practice," Van Buren emerged from the 1810 governor's election with a very bad taste in his mouth. The Republican county committee had taken a plunge into a sea of corruption and had come up short once again. But Van Buren was looking for a way to "electioneer" in the Manor towns, especially after his mentor Clinton signaled his intentions to run for the lieutenant governorship vacated by the death of John Broome in August 1810. And that December Van Buren's position as county surrogate suddenly offered a unique window through which he might learn more about electioneering opportunities on the Manor.

On December 22, 1810, Henry Walter Livingston, the proprietor of Great Lot No. 1, a long strip of land spanning the northern stretch of the Upper Manor across the town of Granger, died at his mansion house in Livingston. The son of Walter and the grandson of Robert the third lord, Henry Walter Livingston was a popular Federalist leader, who had served in Congress from 1803 to 1807 and recently had been elected on a fusion Federalist-Republican ticket to the 1809 assembly. He had served as secretary to Gouverneur Morris in France in 1793 and 1794; on his return he had married a Pennsylvania heiress, Mary Masters Allen. When his father died in 1797, he and Mary set to building one of the first new Hudson villas, designed in France and facing the Catskills across the river, which he named the Hill. It was here that he died and from here that Mary Livingston faced a turbulent world, "deprived," she wrote in a memorandum book bound in a cover to a French musical score, "of my Friend, my Protector, my Guide . . . without one supporting hand, without one supporting voice."[33]

She would need a "Protector" and a "supporting hand," for the death of powerful landlords had before been and would again be the catalyst for recurrent waves of tenant resistance — and violence. Inheritance by women and children particularly set off the challenges to the Van Rensselaer land in Hillsdale and Claverack in late 1780s and early 1790s. When Robert Livingston, Jr, the third lord of the Manor, died in 1790, leaving his estate to a coterie of adult sons, his tenants simply stole the funeral drapery from the Linlithgow church. But, when his son Robert C. Livingston died in 1794, leaving his Lot No. 2 for division among five young children, the tenants had challenged the Manor title and then resorted to armed violence. The final Anti-Rent struggle of the 1840s, unfolding slowly following the death of the great Stephen Van Rensselaer of Rensselaerwyck in 1839, to be sure, had none of these elements of female and minority inheritance. But the death of Henry Walter Livingston, at age forty-two, certainly left Mary in such a condition. It would seem that in a calculation of the region's minutely tiered status hierarchy, tenants were emboldened to take up the struggle when the great men left their land to their dependents, themselves disenfranchised and of unproven power or benevolence.

Mary Livingston was not entirely without male protectors, and with them she threw the first blow in the coming struggle. Henry Walter died three days before Christmas, and by New Year's Day, Mary with her fellow executors, brother-in-law Robert L. Livingston and Judge William W. Van Ness, had reviewed her personal property — and debts owed — and delivered to the surrogate's office in Hudson an accounting of her estate. In addition to about $1,000 in turnpike stock, she now owned $2,660 in the house and furnishings at the Hill. And Henry was owed more than $2,000 in bonds and notes, $827 in cash, and more than 1,217 bushels of wheat in back rent. Two weeks later they served the first writ for back rent due.[34]

MARTIN VAN BUREN AND THE MANOR COMMITTEE

Nothing particularly marked John Reynolds to be the first target of rent recovery. Apparently from a Connecticut family long settled in the Nine Partners in Dutchess County, in 1799 he had taken up a lease for a 189-acre farm in Great Lot No. 1 on the Manor's boundary with Hillsdale. By the time of the 1800 tax list Reynolds was a man of some prosperity by tenant standards, but his rights to his Manor land were limited to the duration of his life, that of his wife, Polly, and the lives of two women in a neighboring family. In 1806 Reynolds was listed on Granger's Republican committee. On January 15, 1811, Thomas Bay, Mary Livingston's lawyer, served him two writs to appear at the June sitting of the court of common pleas in Hudson for recovery of rent owed since May 1, 1810, "to the sum of four live fat hens and twenty-five dollars in specie."[35]

Presumably Reynolds had hired Martin Van Buren and his colleague Cornelius Miller to represent him some months before the sitting of the June 1811 court. Van Buren, as an attorney, had a new client, but as the county surrogate — and a county Republican — he also had a lot of information. The probate proceedings following Henry W. Livingston's death brought a number of interesting documents into the county surrogate's office. In particular, the lists of persons owing debts and rents to the deceased might well have suggested a plan of action, providing Martin Van Buren with the names of potential clients and voters. Of course, Van Buren and the Republican county committee were already familiar with local Republican committeemen on Great Lot No. 1 and throughout the town of Granger.

While the Federalist *Northern Whig* in Hudson would accuse Van Buren and the Republican committee of stirring up the trouble on the Livingston Manor, Van Buren's version would be that he was approached by a committee of Manor tenants. Anticipating his work on the Manor issue, Van Buren prepared a long document on the history of the Livingston title that he would share with the tenants and that became the basis for a series of tenant manifestos, beginning with the March 1811 petition. The exact details of how this petition was got up are not clear, but by March it had been drafted and signed by 154 men. The petition challenged once again the right of the Livingstons to the lands of the entire Upper Manor, "comprising the towns of Livingston, Gallatin, and Granger." While the Livingstons rested their case on an ancient claim, the petitioners wrote, "Confidently believing that as it respects the rights of the state[,] a claim founded in injustice and supported without right cannot become sanctified or rendered valid by the length of possession which has existed in this case."[36]

The core issues at stake were the conditions of leasehold that these petitioners detested as well as the validity of the title held by the Livingstons. Twenty-four of the petitioners were listed as owing rent or debts to Henry W. Livingston in his probate papers, mostly occupants of his Great Lot No. 1; others can be identified among the tenants on his dead brother Robert's Great Lot No. 2 (see Map 3). More complete evidence would probably show that virtually all were tenants or members of tenant households. Even though the petitioners included men from all three Upper Manor towns as well as Clermont and Germantown, the excitement was strongest in Granger, encompassing Great Lots Nos. 1 and 2, and home to two-thirds of the known petitioners. Most striking, however, was the degree to which the petition was so identified with the Republican cause in Granger, where the effort of the legislature in 1803 had briefly resulted in a Republican majority in this landlord-dominated town (see Table 24). Almost half of the Republican committeemen known

Town Totals

Town	Assembly Voters in 1807	On Republican Committees through 1810	On Federalist Committees through 1810	On Republican Committee in 1811	Freemasons Known	On Political Committees
Gallitan	351	19	20	10	20	14
Granger	376	33	12	34	36	10
Livingston	202	15	25	12	17	7
Clermont	158	47	9	9	4	3
Germantown	97	3	13	3	1	1

Petitioners against the Title (Proportion)

Town	Petitioners					
Gallitan	27 (7.7%)	3 (15.8%)	0 (0.0%)	1 (10.0%)	1 (5.0%)	1 (7.1%)
Granger	87 (23.1%)	16 (48.5%)	3 (25.0%)	20 (58.8%)	6 (16.7%)	4 (40.0%)
Livingston	14 (6.9%)	2 (13.3%)	0 (0.0%)	1 (8.3%)	1 (5.9%)	1 (14.3%)
Clermont	1 (0.6%)	0 (0.0%)	0 (0.0%)	0 (0.0%)	0 (0.0%)	0 (0.0%)
Germantown	0 (0.0%)	0 (0.0%)	0 (0.0%)	0 (0.0%)	0 (0.0%)	0 (0.0%)

Sources: See Chapter 9 and notes and Appendix: Note on County Sources.

to have served in Granger between 1801 and 1810 signed the petition; similar committeemen (and the general population) in Livingston and Gallatin were much less committed. Three of the tenant leaders, Benjamin Birdsall, Henry Avery, and Friend Sheldon, had been appointed justices by the new Council of Appointment led by Governor Tompkins in the spring of 1808, certainly a sign that the Republican powers in the state wanted to extend their influence on the Manor. The signers in Granger comprised almost a quarter of the town's assembly voters; if they were all Republicans, the eighty-seven known petitioners from Granger comprised almost 60 percent of the Republican vote in 1810.[37]

Party politics was one strand running out from these towns to the wider civil life of the county, Freemasonry was another, and membership on party committees and in Masonic lodges overlapped considerably. Such was particularly the case in Gallatin, where a large number of committeemen were members of the Temple Lodge, which met over the county line in northern Dutchess. In Granger a small core of active Republicans and sometime Masons was particularly notable in leadership of the 1811 tenant resistance. The Manor Committee, as it came to be known, was made up of at least nine men, of whom eight were from Granger. Benjamin Birdsall, Jr., a Republican activist for a decade — and, with his father, Colonel Benjamin of the Genesee Adventurers, one of the petitioners for Hillsdale's Vernon Lodge in 1803 — headed the list. John J. Shaver, a Great Lot No. 1 tenant and a Republican committeeman in 1808, was also a member of the Vernon Lodge. Thomas Stevenson, who recently had taken a farm in Lot No. 1, had joined the Temple Lodge in Northeast in 1807 but had transferred his membership to the Warren Lodge in Pine Plains in 1808. John Reynolds and Friend Sheldon, Republican committeemen in 1808, were not Masons but had brothers or cousins in these north Dutchess lodges. And Henry Avery, Republican leader since 1804 and with Birdsall the leading signer of the 1811 petition and the Manor committee letters, would in June 1812 join a new lodge recently formed in Clermont. None of this constituted a secret Masonic understanding linking the tenant resistance leadership. Certainly, they had no such understanding with Van Buren, since he avoided lodge membership throughout his life. Rather, their scattered Masonic affiliations attest to a recurring effort to reach out to a broader set of connections beyond the limiting boundaries of the Manor and its communities.[38]

That March Van Buren carried the tenants' petition to Albany and lobbied hard for several weeks in the capital, pressing the tenants' case with the legislators. But his considerable efforts fell short: Columbia Federalists Jacob R. Van Rensselaer and Thomas P. Grosvenor acted with others to move the issue out of the legislature and into the hands of the attorney general and the surveyor general. On April 3 these officials presented their report, which repeated the 1795 decision and declared that, since any examination would result in a confirmation of title, "every consideration of Law, Justice, and propriety, forbid the inquiry." The next day they passed an act that settled a parallel issue that was brewing regarding the boundary between Granger and Hillsdale. On April 5 news of the legislature's decision reached Hudson, in a short notice in the *Northern Whig*. On April 12 the *Whig* printed a long editorial on the defeat of the petition; condemning the "unprincipled machinations of the democratic leaders of this county" in "superintend[ing] this important business before the Legislature." Martin Van Buren and these county Republicans, editor Francis Stebbins wrote, hoped to excite a spirit of enmity among the people of the Manor against the Livingston family, and to detach them at the approaching spring election, from the political party which they have for years undeviatingly supported.

... Their intention was to keep the business before the legislature, undecided till another session; — to afford themselves the opportunity of electioneering the manor towns during the height of this animosity, and revolutionizing the county.

The Livingstons, for their part, had the decision printed into a broadside, and delivered to the town clerks in Granger and Gallitan.[39]

Returning to Hudson from Albany, Van Buren plunged into the work of the county convention, of which he was secretary, working to support the candidacy of his mentor, De Witt Clinton, for lieutenant governor. Despite the defeat of the tenant petition, Van Buren's efforts had produced a notable result. Thirty-three men signed onto the Granger Republican committee, one of the largest in the county; of these, sixteen had signed the March petition. The convention, meeting on April 15, nominated a slate of assembly candidates, including tenant leader Henry Avery of Granger, and empowered a county corresponding committee, including his associate Benjamin Birdsall and their counsel, Van Buren. On the same day, the seven-man Manor committee wrote from Granger condemning "the false and malicious aspersions" published lately in the *Whig,* and "to inform the public and particularly our fellow sufferers in the lower towns" of their plan to publish a letter describing the "rise and progress of the claim of the Livingston family" and to rebut the arguments of the legislators and the *Whig.* Their letter was published opposite the county resolves for Clinton in the *Bee,* where five of them were listed as Republicans.[40]

At the election a week later, the town, if not the county, was revolutionized. For the first time since the spring of 1803 a majority in Granger voted to support Republican candidates for lieutenant governor and assembly (see Figure 5). Federalist candidates prevailed in Livingston and Gallatin, but with somewhat weaker support than the year before, perhaps a manifestation of the Manor unrest, perhaps because the Livingstons did not bother to make voters for this election. Clinton was elected lieutenant governor, though he lost Columbia by fewer than three hundred votes; Federalists prevailed once again for the assembly by a margin of more than five hundred.

In the days before the election Van Buren had predicted the outcome in a letter to Clinton and was generally optimistic, even cocky, about his role in pressing the Manor petition. "While at Albany I did not believe that the Manor dispute would make so deep an impression as it has." He was pleased

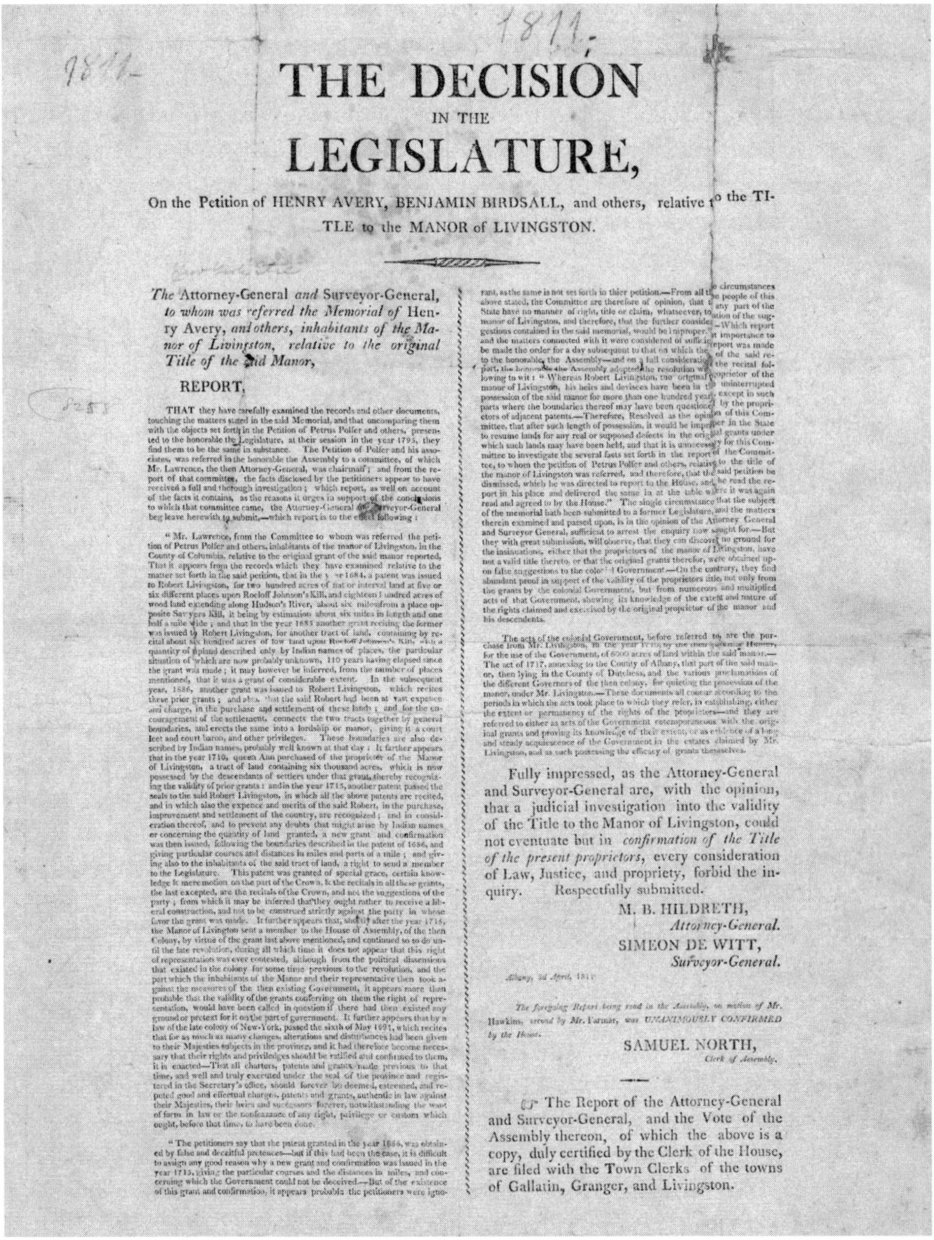

1811–

1811–

THE DECISION
IN THE
LEGISLATURE,

On the Petition of HENRY AVERY, BENJAMIN BIRDSALL, and others, relative to the TITLE to the MANOR of LIVINGSTON.

The Attorney-General *and* Surveyor-General, *to whom was referred the Memorial of Henry Avery, and others, inhabitants of the Manor of Livingston, relative to the original Title of the said Manor,*

REPORT,

THAT they have carefully examined the records and other documents, touching the matters stated in the said Memorial, and that oncomparing them with the objects set forth in the Petition of Petrus Polfer and others, presented to the honorable the Legislature, at their session in the year 1795, they find them to be the same in substance. The Petition of Polfer and his associates, was referred in the honorable the Assembly to a committee, of which Mr. Lawrence, the then Attorney-General, was chairman; and from the report of that committee, the facts disclosed by the petitioners appear to have received a full and thorough investigation; which report, as well on account of the facts it contains, as the reasons it urges in support of the conclusions to which that committee came, the Attorney-General and Surveyor-General beg leave herewith to submit,—which report is to the effect following:

"Mr. Lawrence, from the Committee to whom was referred the petition of Petrus Polfer and others, inhabitants of the manor of Livingston, in the County of Columbia, relative to the original grant of the said manor reported, That it appears from the records which they have examined relative to the matter set forth in the said petition, that in the year 1684, a patent was issued to Robert Livingston, for two hundred acres of flat or interval land at five or six different places upon Roeloff Johnson's Kill, and eighteen hundred acres of wood land extending along Hudson's River, about six milesfrom a place opposite Sawyers Kill, it being by estimation about six miles in length and one half a mile wide; and that in the year 1685 another grant reciting the former was issued to Robert Livingston, for another tract of land, containing by recital about six hundred acres of low land upon Roeloff Johnson's Kill, with a quantity of upland described only by Indian names of places, the particular situation of which are now probably unknown, 110 years having elapsed since the grant was made; it may however be inferred, from the number of places mentioned, that it was a grant of considerable extent. In the subsequent year, 1686, another grant was issued to Robert Livingston, which recites these prior grants; and also, that the said Robert had been at vast expence and charge, in the purchase and settlement of these lands; and for the encouragement of the settlement, connects the two tracts together by general boundaries, and erects the same into a lordship or manor, giving it a court leet and court baron, and other privileges. These boundaries are also described by Indian names, probably well known at that day: It farther appears that in the year 1710, queen Ann purchased of the proprietor of the Manor of Livingston, a tract of land containing six thousand acres, which is now possessed by the descendants of settlers under that grant, thereby recognizing the validity of prior grants: andin the year 1715, another patent passed the seals to the said Robert Livingston, in which all the above patents are recited, and in which also the expence and merits of the said Robert, in the purchase, improvement and settlement of the country, are recognized; and in consideration thereof, and to prevent any doubts that might arise by Indian names or concerning the quantity of land granted, a new grant and confirmation was then issued, following the boundaries described in the patent of 1686, and giving particular courses and distances in miles and parts of a mile; and giving also to the inhabitants of the said tract of land, a right to send a member to the Legislature. This patent was granted of special grace, certain knowledge & mere motion on the part of the Crown, & the recitals in all these grants, the last excepted, are the recitals of the Crown, and not the suggestions of the party; from which it may be inferred that they ought rather to receive a liberal construction, and not to be construed strictly against the party in whose favor the grant was made. It further appears that, shortly after the year 1715, the Manor of Livingston sent a member to the House of Assembly, of the then Colony, by virtue of the grant last above mentioned, and continued so to do until the late revolution, during all which time it does not appear that this right of representation was ever contested, although from the political dissensions that existed in the colony for some time previous to the revolution, and the part which the inhabitants of the Manor and their representative then took against the measures of the then existing Government, it appears more than probable that the validity of the grants conferring on them the right of representation, would have been called in question if there had then existed any ground or pretext for it on the part of government. It further appears that by a law of the late colony of New-York, passed the sixth of May 1691, which recites that for as much as many changes, alterations and disturbances had been given to their Majesties subjects in the province, and it had therefore become necessary that their rights and priviledges should be ratified and confirmed to them, it is enacted—That all charters, patents and grants made previous to that time, and well and truly executed under the seal of the province and registered in the Secretary's office, should forever be deemed, esteemed, and reputed good and effectual charges, patents and grants, authentic in law against their Majesties, their heirs and successors forever, notwithstanding the want of form in law or the nonfeazance of any right, privilege or custom which ought, before that time, to have been done.

"The petitioners say that the patent granted in the year 1686, was obtained by false and deceitful pretences—but if this had been the case, it is difficult to assign any good reason why a new grant and confirmation was issued in the year 1715, giving the particular courses and the distances in miles, and concerning which the Government could not be deceived.—But of the existence of this grant and confirmation, it appears probable the petitioners were ignorant, as the same is not set forth in thier petition.—From all the circumstances above stated, the Committee are therefore of opinion, that the people of this State have no manner of right, title or claim, whatsoever, to any part of the manor of Livingston, and therefore, that the further consideration of the suggestions contained in the said memorial, would be improper."—Which report and the matters connected with it were considered of sufficient importance to be made the order for a day subsequent to that on which the report was made to the honorable the Assembly—and on a full consideration of the said report, the honorable the Assembly adopted the resolution with the recital following to wit: "Whereas Robert Livingston, the original proprietor of the manor of Livingston, his heirs and devisees have been in the uninterrupted possession of the said manor for more than one hundred years, except in such parts where the boundaries thereof may have been questioned by the proprietors of adjacent patents.—Therefore, Resolved as the opinion of this Committee, that after such length of possession, it would be improper in the State to resume lands for any real or supposed defects in the original grants under which such lands may have been held, and that it is unnecessary for this Committee to investigate the several facts set forth in the report of the Committee, to whom the petition of Petrus Polfer and others, relative to the title of the manor of Livingston was referred, and therefore, that the said petition be dismissed, which he was directed to report to the House, and he read the report in his place and delivered the same in at the table where it was again read and agreed to by the House." The single circumstance that the subject of the memorial hath been submitted to a former Legislature, and the matters therein examined and passed upon, is in the opinion of the Attorney General and Surveyor General, sufficient to arrest the enquiry now sought for.—But they with great submission, will observe, that they can discover no ground for the insinuations, either that the proprietors of the manor of Livingston, have not a valid title thereto, or that the original grants therefor, were obtained upon false suggestions to the colonial Government.—On the contrary, they find abundant proof in support of the validity of the proprietors title, not only from the grants by the colonial Government, but from numerous and multiplied acts of that Government, shewing its knowledge of the extent and nature of the rights claimed and exercised by the original proprietor of the manor and his descendents.

The acts of the colonial Government, before referred to, are the purchase from Mr. Livingston, in the year 1710, by the then governor Hunter, for the use of the Government, of 6000 acres of land within the said manor.—The act of 1717, annexing to the County of Albany, that part of the said manor, then lying in the County of Dutchess, and the various proclamations of the different Governors of the then colony, for quieting the possession of the manor, under Mr. Livingston.—These documents all concur according to the periods in which the acts took place to which they refer, in establishing, either the extent or permanency of the rights of the proprietors—and they are referred to either as acts of the Government cotemporaneous with the original grants and proving its knowledge of their extent, or as evidence of a long and steady acquiescence of the Government in the estates claimed by Mr. Livingston, and as such possessing the efficacy of grants themselves.

Fully impressed, as the Attorney-General and Surveyor-General are, with the opinion, that a judicial investigation into the validity of the Title to the Manor of Livingston, could not eventuate but in *confirmation of the Title of the present proprietors*, every consideration of Law, Justice, and propriety, forbid the inquiry. Respectfully submitted.

M. B. HILDRETH,
Attorney-General.
SIMEON DE WITT,
Surveyor-General.

Albany, 3d April, 1811.

The foregoing Report being read in the Assembly, on motion of Mr. Hawkins, *second by Mr.* Yarmar, *was UNANIMOUSLY CONFIRMED by the House.*

SAMUEL NORTH,
Clerk of Assembly.

☞ The Report of the Attorney-General and Surveyor-General, and the Vote of the Assembly thereon, of which the above is a copy, duly certified by the Clerk of the House, are filed with the Town Clerks of the towns of Gallatin, Granger, and Livingston.

PLATE 14. *Broadside Printed by the Livingstons. Posted in Gallatin, Granger, and Livingston following the vote confirming the attorney general's report on the Manor title, Apr. 3, 1811.* Courtesy of the New York Public Library

to report that "the convulsion and agitation there is greater than ever" and that "they are displeased with everybody who has had anything to do with it except me." Anticipating the election result and confirming Federalist suspicions of his motives, he had "now scarcely a doubt that if the Report had been postponed we would have carried our Assembly ticket."[41]

Writing to the Manor committee several days later, he was equally confident in his advocacy of its cause. Pressed by his Federalist enemies, Van Buren told the committee that if he were asked "to attend a meeting of Federalists or Republicans or both to discuss the important subject of the Livingston claim ... either before or after the Election I should and will accept it with pleasure." In early June he and Cornelius Miller acted in defense of John Reynolds's case in common pleas; at the July Fourth celebration in Hudson Van Buren would toast the town of Granger: "She has broke the fetters which bound her to unjust dominion — we hail her emancipation."[42]

"FIRST PRINCIPLES" VERSUS "SETTLED ESTABLISHMENTS"

Within a few weeks Van Buren was more restrained, even pessimistic, about the tenants' case. Writing to the Manor committee on July 28 at their request, he concurred that the Livingston title was suspect and that he had "no hesitation in expressing it as my deliberate opinion that these lands in law and of right belong to the State." But he doubted that the political will existed to challenge the Livingston claim: "Whether the Legislature as the Guardian of the interests of the people will think it just, politic, or expedient to exercise the right which is vested in them it is impossible that I should know — that must depend on their Wisdom and Integrity and on which it would be improper for me to express an opinion."[43]

In essence, Van Buren would represent them in court, but he told the tenant leadership that it would have no other recourse in the formal deliberative arena of the public sphere. His letter would mark a turning point in the tenant cause. Where for years they had worked to build civil engagement, Van Buren's pessimistic review of the tenants' case set the stage for a return to violent insurgency, last seen on the Manor more than a decade before.

On July 29, the day after the committee received Van Buren's letter, Benjamin Birdsall signed and delivered his long discourse on the Livingston claim to the office of the *Bee,* promised to the public on April 19. Published on August 16, his letter covered almost six columns over the second and third pages of the paper. It certainly reviewed "the rise and progress" of the Livingston title and fortunes, apparently drawing liberally from Van Buren's long memorandum on the title, but it also painted a vivid picture of injustice, misery, and citizenship denied on the Manor. In a "distinguished fraud," the family had duped even the British government and had perpetuated since "a thirty-six years usurpation and oppression." "Oppressed and enslaved," the tenants had been denied the right "of an English school, the last and only means given man by which he can acquire a knowledge of his rights and duties as a member of civilized society"; every effort had been made "to place an immovable barrier between their tenants and every source or avenue of information." But what if, Birdsall asked, "a republican government does not possess energy sufficient to protect the rights of its citizens"? What if

> our virtuous rulers say that the honest, the poor and the needy are to apply in vain for justice, that we have lost our protection, are no longer Americans and no more to experience the blessings of a republican government, that virtue and patriotism must fall the victims of falsehood, hypocrisy, craft and meanness, to crouch beneath the yoke of despotism and become the party tool and sport of tyrants[?]

Was it "marvelous that the people, oppressed by these abominable impositions, should rise indignant, that the public ear should be addressed on the occasion"? He closed his letter with more than a hint that the routine politics flowing from the revolutionary settlement would not suffice.

> The crisis has now arrived when the people of the manor have suffered human oppression and impositions as long as it is sufferable, and like the oppressed inhabitants of other countries, when the last particle of good faith in men is entirely exhausted, they must recur to first principles, to the spirit and letter of the constitution, and truth, justice and public virtue, accompanied with prudence and judgment, will ever bear up good men in a good cause — that of asserting their inalienable and constitutional rights.

Thus, though their legal association would continue for several years, there was a philosophical parting of the ways between these two sons of the Revolution late that July. Van Buren stepped up to the outer boundary of deliberative politics and could not "express an opinion"; Birdsall was ready to lead the tenants across that boundary into a "manly" — and violent — defense of rights and "first principles."[44]

Francis Stebbins, the Federalist editor of the *Northern Whig*, however, made no such fine distinctions. On August 16 he claimed that Van Buren had met with a rump group of the Manor committee at Fite Miller's tavern. The next week he printed a long rebuttal to the Birdsall letter, accusing Van Buren of writing it, and pouncing on the language of "first principles," which marked the authors as "apparent despisers of the civil institutions of the state." Invoking "first principles" would destroy the revolutionary settlement: it would

"tear up the settled establishments of society, . . . break down the barriers between right and wrong, between virtue and vice, and expel Justice from its
seat." A week later Birdsall published a second letter in the *Bee,* claiming that
the *Whig* had accused the people of the Manor "of a disposition to excite insurrection": the *Whig* replied on September 6 that it was the "ring-leaders,"
not the tenants, who were of such a "disposition." On August 30 Birdsall
spoke of bringing the title "before a tribune competent to decide upon the
same." But, if the legislature and courts had decided against them, the *Whig*
had announced on September 6, this was "an appeal from the established tri-
bunals of the country, to the people!" "It is, Mr. Martin Van Buren, say what
you will," the *Whig* trumpeted. "It is a spirit of insurrection." No one remembered that only nineteen years before, during the Otsego Crisis, Columbia
Federalists had threatened revolutionary violence against Governor George
Clinton's government.[45]

THE MANOR REBELLION OF 1812

Some among the tenants would indeed turn to insurrection; decades later a
local historian wrote without fear of contradiction, "In 1812 civil war was prevailing in what is now known as the town of Copake." But the turn toward
violence came first in a threat from Federalists enraged at Van Buren's involvement in these and other affairs around the county.[46]

The Federalist *Northern Whig* had in April accused Van Buren of attempting to delay the legislative report on the Manor title as part of the Republican
effort to "electioneer" the Manor towns, to which Van Buren as much as admitted in his April 20 letter to De Witt Clinton. In late August the *Whig,* in
connection with its attack on the Birdsall letter, directly accused Van Buren
of attempting to engineer this delay. These accusations were interwoven with
a controversy with Colonel Jacob Rutsen Van Rensselaer, the powerful Claverack village Federalist, who was certain that Van Buren had been the source
of the rumor that during the debate on the Manor petition he had called the
tenants "unfit to govern themselves." After a heated private and public correspondence on both of these matters, the confrontation got extremely dangerous in the late fall of 1811. During fall sessions of the common pleas and
the supreme court circuit Van Buren represented a number of land cases. On
September 10 he lost his defense of John Reynolds against Mary Livingston's
complaint for failure to pay rent, and Reynolds was assessed the back rents
plus charges. In November he undertook to represent John Collin, Jr. (the
son of Captain John), in a land dispute with Jacob R. Van Rensselaer, and he
won an important case involving the De Bruyn patent, the stretch of land in
Kinderhook that had been in contention for decades.[47]

This string of contests with the Federalist bar nearly led to personal violence. In the final days of the De Bruyn hearing in December 1811, tensions between Van Buren and the opposing lawyer, Federalist John Suydam, boiled over into verbal abuse and published challenges and condemnations. Decades later Van Buren claimed that, at "a large party of distinguished gentlemen of the federal party" hosted by Colonel Van Rensselaer at his Claverack mansion, Suydam had learned "to what extent I was an eye-sore to the Magnates of the County." The Hamilton-Burr affair at Wehawken in 1804 had turned public opinion against dueling, but earlier in 1811 John Armstrong, Jr., of Rhinebeck, Chancellor Livingston's nephew, had fought a duel in the no-man's-land of Boston Corners, perhaps setting a recent local precedent. For five days notes flew back and forth between Suydam and Van Buren via their seconds Thomas P. Grosvenor and Joseph D. Monell, until Van Buren backed out of the confrontation on the grounds that the affair had become public and that Colonel Van Rensselaer was interfering. Suydam posted handbills around Hudson calling Van Buren a coward, and both parties posted bonds with the circuit court promising to keep the peace.[48]

As these affairs were unfolding, the tenants began to divide into two camps. One group, in the face of charges of fomenting rebellion against the constituted authorities and then Van Buren's loss of the Reynolds case in the September sitting of the common pleas, began to withdraw from further involvement. As Mary Livingston put it in December 1811, "A few who were leading persons last year . . . have now prudently withdrawn from all opposition." These included Henry Avery of Granger, who in June 1812 would be admitted into a new Masonic lodge warranted in Clermont. In a lodge membership including a number of leading local Republicans in Clermont and Livingston, Avery was one of only two men to have signed the Manor petition of March 1811. He ran as a Republican for the assembly in 1812 and 1814 and then retired from the public eye until 1821, when he again emerged as a delegate to the Republican county meeting on the constitution and commenced two decades as justice of the peace, in Taghkanic (formerly Granger). In 1842 his son Solomon would lead the formation of the West Taghkanic Methodist Church, built with Livingston patronage. The connections that Avery established in the Clermont Lodge would not be immaterial to an enduring, respectable position in town and county.[49]

While Avery retreated toward Masonic security, a radical core of the tenants persevered, pursuing increasingly desperate steps. In late September, nine days after John Reynolds lost his cases in common pleas, a group of three men led by Benjamin Birdsall was discovered surveying in the northern section of Lot No. 1, near the Claverack line. By December 1811 they and others had formed an agreement to challenge the Livingston claim to a "gore" of land along that northern boundary; they also agreed to hold back their rent and to support one another in event of prosecution. Represented by Van Buren and Thomas Addison Emmett, the Irish republican exile, Birdsall's group sent yet another petition, this time to Governor Daniel D. Tompkins. Tompkins apparently sent contradictory messages to the tenants, then in mid-March 1812 again referred the case to the attorney general, who had rejected the 1811 petition. Mary Livingston wrote on March 20 that "Birdsall and Reynolds have returned home" from Albany "mortified, and disappointed; and the tenants will probably return to their duty, pay their rents which they have withheld, and remain quiet for many years to come." But by the first of April she was again alarmed. Tompkins had not sent the case to the attorney general, and the tenants had "renewed their meetings." "Our affairs thus remain unsettled, which keeps alive the hopes of the tenants till the election is over and induce them to vote for their friends the Democrats."[50]

There were, of course, wider considerations in play in the spring of 1812, considerations that were progressively distracting Van Buren's attention from the affairs of the Manor and affairs of the county itself. Public affairs in New York State that spring revolved around rumors of impending war and the controversial Bank of America, proposed for a New York charter to fill the place of the lapsed Bank of the United States. Van Buren supported Governor Tompkins when he prorogued the legislature after charges exploded that the legislature had been corrupted, which charges eventually would finger the leading Columbia Federalists. Mary Livingston saw the governor's dissolving of the legislature as part of a plot aimed to "unsettle" the Manor, which would seem paranoid if it did not come simultaneously with the commissioning of two of the tenant militants, John Reynolds himself and Thomas Stevenson, as justices of the peace. Further evidence of Republican hopes on the Manor lay in Henry Avery's nomination as an assembly candidate. Potentially, Martin Van Buren might have profited from these efforts, in his sudden emergence as the party candidate for the state senate in the Middle District. But the enthusiasm for party in the town of Granger, so apparent in 1811, began to wane in 1812; if Granger Republicans mobilized for Van Buren, no great lists of names were printed in the *Bee*. But, when it was finally clear in mid-May that he had won the seat, it was also clear that the Livingston Manor tenants had not contributed much to his victory. His political future lay with the strong Republican constituencies in Orange, Rockland, and Delaware, counties where he got 75 percent of the total vote; Columbia County gave him only 42 percent. Even in the town of Granger, the home base of the most militant tenant leadership, he mustered only ninety-five votes to his opponent

Edward P. Livingston's sixty-two. The outcome of the 1812 election liberated
Van Buren from the confined affairs of locality and county, and from then on
he would progress to state and national prominence. But those local affairs
in which he had been so involved had not been fully played out. Once again,
violence would shatter the fragile and incomplete revolutionary settlement in
Columbia, and Van Buren's detachment might well have been a contributing
factor.[51]

In April 1812 Mary Livingston was worried about the election, but she was
more worried about the collapse of deliberation: the tenants had "renewed
their meetings," but they had also "bound themselves by Oath to withhold
their rents, to resist the Sheriff, and to assert their rights with powder and
ball—They threaten violently and the terms 'Murder and Bloodshed' are frequently made use of among them." In May she wrote of a "violent advertiz.
published by the tenants," and she commenced a series of suits for ejectment
against the signers, including Reynolds and Stevenson. Other suits were pending in her name against four others, and her husband's cousin John S. Livingston on Great Lot No. 2 had initiated proceedings against Birdsall in January.[52]

The tenants made one final united appeal to the governor. On June 15, Birdsall, Reynolds, and Stevenson joined with Henry Avery and others who Mary
Livingston thought had "prudently withdrawn" to write and deliver another
petition to Governor Tompkins. In language that echoed Birdsall's letter of
the summer of 1811, the committee opened their letter with an invocation of
the citizens' "solemn duty" to see to the "preservation of the laws and constitution of our country." But the government's failure to act on their behalf
had undermined the people's trust in the legitimacy underlying those laws
and constitution. The committeemen could not "believe that the [govern]
ment has so far lost sight of that solemn injunction the protecti[ion of] the
rights of its citizens, as to receive with cool indifference the remonstrances
of a people who have discharged every duty that the principles of justice or
the constitution could require to give them a hearing." What would be "the
probable result in bearing down a country of people under circumstances and
propositions like these?" they inquired. "It would assuredly produce the belief
that there is no proportion of the Yeomanry of our country however great the
number sufficient to bring to justice the man of wealth however enormous his
offense." Most important, the failure of the government to intervene in the
Manor dispute would "have a great tendency to destroy that good faith in the
people toward their government without which must ever render doubtful its
existence."[53]

In essence, the tenants had withdrawn their consent to governance by
the state; rebellion was imminent. In their minds, the measures taken by the

Livingstons to suppress the tenant protests had "already excited that spirit of res[entment] which frequently produces the most alarming consequences," and "the dispute from its present appearance threatens ere long the total destr[uction of soci]ety the subversion of law and order and every moral obligatio[n]." In no uncertain terms, the committee attributed the impending civil disorder to a failure of the political process and to the collapse of the legitimacy of the state government in the eyes of the people of the manor.[54]

Tompkins could do nothing for the tenants; seeing no recourse in the protections of the state government, some of them took up "powder and ball"—and firebrands. Their targets were Livingston property throughout the Manor—and the county officers enforcing their writs. On the night of June 24, attempts were made to burn the barns of loyal tenants and the Livingston Iron Works in Ancram. John Reynolds, John J. Shaver, and John I. Whitbeck were arrested as the key conspirators and released on bail, on the evidence of Daniel Van Gelder, whom they had hired for the job and whose part-Indian family had been involved in the tenant disturbances of the 1750s and 1760s. On July 3, Mary Livingston's mansion, the Hill, was torched; somehow all of the furniture was recovered, and the blaze died down. Then, on July 30, Deputy Sheriff Charles Truesdale of Hillsdale was sent to eject Daniel Wilkinson from his holding. In a virtual replay of the events of October 1791, when Sheriff Hogeboom was killed a few miles to the north, Truesdale's posse was challenged by a crowd, and Truesdale was shot in the leg by a man he swore was John J. Shaver. Finally, on August 14, the sheriff himself, Republican John King of Canaan, was sent from Hudson with a posse of hundreds to evict Wilkinson, tear down his house, and install a new tenant, here echoing the events of 1754–1755 and 1766. As the *Whig* recounted the affair, a crowd of fifty "malcontents assembled at a place towards a mile distant and in sight"; after the sheriff left, they rebuilt Wilkinson's house and ejected the new tenant.[55]

So the major events of the 1812 "civil war in Copake" came to a close, followed by cycle of prosecution. Mary Livingston continued to complain about "malcontents" trying to refuse rent, and she and her kin continued their policy of evicting troublemakers, ejecting fifty or more at the October circuit court alone. The October court in Hudson, presided over by William W. Van Ness and William Wilson, also brought swift action against a few of the main figures in the recent strife. Some of the charges were for offenses of speech against the civil authorities. During the late summer, Birdsall had persuaded Wilkinson to bring charges of illegal violence against Deputy Sheriff Truesdale, and himself had apparently made similar charges against Van Rensselaer and the sheriff's posse. With a Livingston suit against him, Birdsall was allowed to plead guilty to libel and gave testimony against Wilkinson, who was convicted of perjury and given four years imprisonment. One of the prosecutions was against sympathizers elsewhere in the county. A number of men, mostly from Hudson and Hillsdale and including a number of Republican activists, were fined $15 each for refusing to march with the sheriff's posse in August. John J. Shaver was charged in the shooting of Truesdale but acquitted; he, John Reynolds, and John I. Whitbeck were convicted of conspiring to burn barns and the Livingston Iron Works at Ancram and given thirty days and a $150 fine.[56]

The *Northern Whig* gleefully reported that their counsel, Martin Van Buren, "was taken very suddenly ill and did not come into court again until they were all over." The *Whig* also reported that Jeremiah Shaver, a Manor tenant and a brother of one of the three tried on charges of arson, *"told his brother months ago, that this would be the case, when it came to the pinch, — that that devil of devils would abandon them."* A few prosecutions carried on over the next few years. The next summer, Reynolds was charged with perjury, and in October 1814 he and Birdsall were indicted for conspiracy in the burning of Mary Livingston's house. John Shaver and his wife gave testimony the following summer, but the statute of limitations had run out, and the prosecutions ended. By then, even Mary Livingston was relieved: "At this I rejoice for though their plan was to guard the doors, and consume my Children and myself, had they been hung I should have been much shocked."[57]

One more drama also was being played out, ending with a definitive judicial pronouncement. Justice James Kent, presiding over the October 1813 circuit court in Hudson, brought a harsh and definitive ruling on the title of the Livingstons to the Manor lands, which defined the boundaries and legitimacy of the revolutionary settlement in no uncertain terms. In the spring of 1812 Governor Tompkins had left hanging the issue of the tenant petition regarding the Manor "gore," and late in the year he decided to reopen the case, ordering Thomas A. Emmett (appointed attorney general in August) to launch yet another challenge to the Livingston title. Emmett consulted with Van Buren on the case and decided it was best to delay as long as possible, given the recent string of landlord victories in the courts. In February 1813 a new Federalist Council of Appointment replaced Emmett with Abraham Van Vechten, who pushed to try the case in the October session in Hudson. Emmett and Van Buren attempted further delay, but the case went forward, with a minimal defense by Federalist Van Vechten. After listening to most of the Livingston attorneys' presentations, Justice Kent interrupted and declared that "it was a useless waste of time to proceed any further — that the title of the Livingstons was already established beyond a doubt — *that any man who should hereafter attempt, to question the title of the Livingstons to the lands of the Manor, ought to be considered in the act of rebellion against the laws of the state.*[58]

In the opinion of Justice Kent, the Livingston title was a permanent part of the state's political settlement, and the people of the Manor were to pay their rent — or be scattered to the winds. The Granger Republicans were still defiant and sent Birdsall and Stevenson to the county convention at Claverack in March 1813. But the Granger voters were cowed, and in the May 1813 assembly election they "returned to their duty": the town's Republican majority evaporated, and from 1814 to 1821 the town voted consistently for Federalists. During the Federalists' brief control of the legislature the tenants suffered the further indignity of having the Republican names of their towns, Granger and Gallatin, replaced by their traditional Manor names of Taghkanic and Ancram, in legislation introduced and advanced by their old nemesis, Federalist Jacob R. Van Rensselaer.[59]

REVOLUTIONARY SETTLEMENT, DELIBERATIVE CITIZENSHIP, LEGITIMATE GOVERNMENT

Thus this cycle of tenant resistance came to a close. It was a struggle full of symbol and rhetoric but mercifully short on death and destruction. No one was killed, and the fires were quickly extinguished. If the worst consequences had been only narrowly avoided, the authorities were willing to treat these events as political in nature rather than fully criminal. The intensity of rhetoric on all sides far outran any efforts at revenge, and the proceedings ultimately had many of the qualities of the political settlement of the 1791 Hillsdale indictments. Wilkinson's sentence, which the judge claimed was reduced, stands out as significant, and the court made sure that those refusing service with the sheriff paid a price. Theirs were offenses that directly challenged the integrity of the institutions of the state. But, if the Ancram arson conspirators were convicted, they were essentially given sentences of time served, and Truesdale's wound was never effectively prosecuted.

As in 1791, it would appear that something of an accommodation was reached. Certainly the core issues of tenancy and the title were not addressed. But, except for the Livingstons' prosecution of ejectments, the courts did not act in ways that would exacerbate the situation. For, at its core, the struggle had been political, and the parties had articulated powerful understandings of the potential fragility of the civil life that had evolved since the Revolution three decades previous. The progressive unraveling of political routines in southern Columbia County between 1811 and 1812 had opened a window onto some of the rawest tensions and inconsistencies of the terms of public life in this divided society. And, just as these tensions were being exposed to full view, another route was opening toward a partial resolution.

At the heart of this struggle had been the central premise of deliberative life in the early Republic: as the debate in the 1821 constitutional convention would illustrate, full citizenship and the right to participate fully in the public arena were bound up in property ownership. The rhetoric of rights and liberties was pervasive in the early Republic, but it had a biting edge in parts of Columbia County, where social relations came as close to those of the contemporary English or Irish countryside as did any in America, a point that could not have been lost on Thomas Addison Emmett, the Irish home rule leader, now in exile, who briefly took up the tenants' cause. But, in America, less than full citizenship meant a demeaning dependency, even the shadow of slavery.

Beyond the problem of citizenship loomed the issue of the legitimacy of the government and the consent of the people. Federalists—and many Republicans as well—feared assaults on "settled establishments"; the Manor committee in turn declared that, in upholding the ancient fraud of the Livingston title, the government had lost the "good faith" of the people and that "its existence" was "doubtful." It was ready to withhold its consent. For both Federalists and tenants, the revolutionary settlement of public life in this county was exposed to view and on the verge of collapse. One demanded the security of constituted civil institutions; the other demanded justice and accountability.

The story of the Livingston Manor controversy thus involves property, citizenship, legitimacy, and consent. But it also is the story of a people's failure to gain a foothold in the public life of a county and a state and of the consequences of that failure. Before the nineteenth-century expansion of public life, access to the institutions of civil society was fundamentally tied up with property. Participation in civil society was inherently bourgeois, defining the middling classes against both the propertyless poor and the aristocracy (such as it was in America). But such an aristocracy, or the most potent American manifestation of one, did exist along the Hudson and made claims of superiority over its tenant dependents. And, in striking contrast to the areas where freehold tenure prevailed in Columbia County, access to the institutions of civil society—and access to political power—was amazingly poorly developed on the Livingston Manor. Political party, press, associations, schools: the full spectrum of the institutions of civil society and the public sphere were at issue in the Livingston Manor controversy of 1811–1812. But the issues of property and dependence were not just the grievances underlying the insurgency: they determined access to civil society. In turn that access determined the purchase that the players were able to bring to bear on the political process. Lacking such a purchase, the Livingston tenants turned to violence in the summer of 1812. When the petitioners complained in 1811 of the public consequences of the life-lease system, "forbid[ding] any lasting or valuable improvements," they might well have had in mind the poverty of public improvements, public refinements, and civil life in their communities. This poverty, both private and public, worked in a vicious circle to drive many on the Manor from petition and protest to alienation and insurgency.

Finally, there was the incompatibility of purpose dividing sets of seeming allies. As a political initiative undertaken through committees and petitions was challenged and frustrated, some were willing to both invoke and act upon the rhetoric of "crisis" and "first principles." Dishonored by their tenant status and their effective exclusion from the associational and deliberative practices of civil life, Benjamin Birdsall and the tenant leaders were willing to take desperate — indeed revolutionary — measures. Despite the *Northern Whig*'s wildest claims to the contrary, Martin Van Buren was not willing to go down the road to revolutionary action. His political education had been devoted to finding a middle ground, challenging the corruption and "dominion" of oligarchs while rising in respectability as an attorney and party politician inside the terms of the constitutional settlement of the Revolution. He too was deeply committed to the routine practices of "settled establishments." In 1805, Charles Foote, the young lawyer in training with Peter Van Schaack in Kinderhook who spent considerable time observing the emerging Van Buren, came to this conclusion about the Republicans in general. He did not expect "wild revolution" from American "Democracy," he wrote to his Federalist father. "Democracy on this side of the Atlantic is more of a knave than a fanatic. It has something to lose, and therefore would not push matters to the last extreme. . . . I cannot persuade myself that there is any considerable portion of our inhabitants who would desire to witness the prostration of all government."[60]

But it would appear that Van Buren did not realize the gulf that separated his political understanding from that of the radical tenant leaders. While the county's history had repeatedly shown its dangers, it may well be that he miscalculated the depth of the passions involved in the politics of land and dependency. As the tenants' attorney, Van Buren seems to have seen the tenant grievance as based in a fundamental injustice but also as a simple problem in distributive partisan politics. Throughout the state men petitioned for grants of land, for turnpiking privileges, and for banks, and the legislature acted on their requests. So, too, he might help the tenants obtain a new investigation of the Livingston title and in so doing build up his following in Columbia

County. But land in this region—as he should have well known—was not simply a distributive good but a marker of status and an avenue to citizenship. Apparently he was not prepared for the dimensions of the struggle that he had unleashed, or was, as the Federalists argued, extremely cynical. In any event, Van Buren had no intention of moving beyond the structured bounds of consent and legitimacy implicit in routine settled politics—into the quicksand of a revolutionary challenge to the constitutional government of the state of New York.

DEMOCRACY: WAR, COMMON SCHOOLS, AND THE CANAL

Thus in 1812 Martin Van Buren might not have fully appreciated the degree to which tenancy and its concomitant exclusion from public life comprised a degree of social death, of civil death. In 1821, eight years after Justice Kent lowered the gavel of the state on challenges to the Livingston title, Van Buren would contribute to the constitutional settlement that lifted some of the impediments to the tenants' entry into deliberative life while Kent struggled to retain just these impediments. But race and slavery marked several more degrees of such a civil death, and, at the very same constitutional convention, Van Buren would equally contribute to an erosion of the deliberative rights of free men of color in the state of New York. The first decades of the nineteenth century were setting the broader stage for the new racial divide, where race, rather than property, would become the ground for the inclusion of men in deliberative politics. Such a ground was mandated in New York in the 1821 constitution. In Columbia's story, and probably more widely, the redefinition of political inclusion toward a strict line of race was subtly determined by the events and initiatives unfolding in the years following the "civil war in Copake" of the summer of 1812.[61]

This new direction began to take shape as this brief civil war was on the verge of breaking out. After years of commercial embargo and incipient hostilities, the British government repealed its orders in council on June 16, 1812, and on June 18 James Madison and the United States Congress declared war. Even as the tenant militants were near rebellion against the civil authority of the state, New York was suddenly again a front line against British military force. In the coming months the young state senator Martin Van Buren would have to navigate between his loyalty to a mentor, De Witt Clinton, who was negotiating with antiwar Federalists for support as an independent presidential candidacy against James Madison, and his commitment to the regular party in government, led by Governor Tompkins. By the spring of 1813 Van Buren had emerged as leader of the war party, holding the senate as a Republican bastion against the temporarily Federalist assembly and the Council of

Appointment, writing powerful addresses to the people, and then taking considerable risk in the fall of 1814, after the burning of Washington, in drafting the state's first military conscription act. In the cut-and-thrust over the conscription bill, Van Buren sued the *Northern Whig* for libel when its editor described him as a man "festering to corruption," and came close to a duel with Elisha Williams.[62]

This was a Republican war, and Columbia was a Federalist county. Thus the mobilization of men followed a distinctly political pattern: companies marching to the northern and western fronts throughout the war were led by Republicans; only after September 1814, when New York City was threatened with invasion, were Federalist units mobilized, one led by Colonel Jacob R. Van Rensselaer. In July 1812 Federalists had refused to celebrate the Fourth, and Hudson Federalists led by Elisha Williams and Thomas P. Grosvenor called a county meeting, which produced a massive set of antiwar resolutions that sprawled across two pages of the *Northern Whig*. Williams and Van Rensselaer ran for assembly in the next two years under the label of "Peace Men." Throughout the war the Washington Benevolent Society met in Hudson. From Stephentown George Holcomb joined the society and went over to Hancock and Pittsfield for its celebrations; "to keep out of the way of being called into United States service," he spent fourteen months with his relations in Shrewsbury, Massachusetts.[63]

But Republican towns sent men to war. A squadron of cavalry rode out from Republican Canaan for Buffalo in late August 1812; a composite regiment led by a Republican colonel from Kinderhook, with Republican company commanders from Canaan, Hillsdale, and Clermont, was sent to the northern lakes in September. Echoing the desperate days of September 1777, companies were mustered in September 1814 under Republican captains from Hillsdale and Claverack to march north to stop the British advance down Lake Champlain. William Wilson's son served as an army surgeon during this lake campaign; John C. Spencer, son of Judge Ambrose Spencer, was wounded in the naval battle off Plattsburgh that defeated the British effort; the judge's younger son and namesake, a staff officer, was killed at the battle of Lundy's Lane opposite Buffalo that July. Benjamin Birdsall III, son of the tenant leader and grandson of the Revolutionary colonel, farming land in Watervliet near Albany on leasehold from Stephen Van Rensselaer, raised a company of riflemen in the fall of 1812; his efforts might explain the Columbia court's extraordinary reluctance to prosecute his father that October. After service at Plattsburgh and Sackett's Harbor and combat in the 1813 landing at York, Upper Canada, Captain Birdsall's company in the early spring of 1814 was enlisted into federal service in the new Fourth United States Regiment of Rifles. It saw intense combat at Fort Erie in Upper Canada, where Birdsall received a severe facial wound and was breveted to the rank of major for distinguished service.[64]

With the war came new state initiatives. On June 19, 1812, the day after war was declared, the New York legislature enacted a law that would have far-reaching and permanent consequences for the shape of public life throughout the state. On the recommendation of a commission, the 1812 Act of the Establishment of Common Schools superseded the temporary grants offered to local schools in the 1790s, empowering towns to establish systems of school districts, overseen by elected trustees and the county boards of supervisors, who would manage the construction of schoolhouses and the hiring of instructors, with local funds matched from a permanent state fund. The good intentions of this act would have been difficult to achieve in any year, but, as the war began, they proved impossible. The new state superintendent of schools, Gideon Hawley, reported to the assembly in February 1814 that the towns were not complying, since the 1812 act did not require compliance by towns and counties. In 1814 the legislature, perhaps driven by the certainties of wartime, remedied this flaw, requiring compliance, incorporating the district trustees, and also allowing local inspectors to waive fees for the poor. A note following the law in the annual compilation declared that the legislature's passage of the new school act "reflect[ed] the highest credit on their intelligence, liberality, and patriotism." With the force of law over them, the towns began to comply, calling organizational meetings, laying out districts, and building schoolhouses: the mandated district meetings were first convened in Hillsdale less than two weeks after the new law passed on April 15, 1814. In those years when most of the county's towns sent returns to the state superintendent, their reports suggested that the educational divide between English and German-Dutch areas persisted. The hill towns reported that 90 percent of their children aged five to fifteen were in school, Claverack reported less than 60 percent, and the five towns in the old Manor region to the south reported just more than 75 percent in school.[65]

In the Manor towns the new school laws effected a peaceful revolution of sorts, not unlike that achieved by the formation of new towns in 1803. Perhaps the Manor towns started later than most, but in the fall of 1816 Mary Livingston recorded transactions with two boards of district trustees, elected at meetings beyond her control. In Livingston, she made an arrangement to grant the trustees of District No. 5 a plot of ground fifty feet square for ten years. As a beneficent landlord she subscribed twenty dollars; when she was taxed fifty dollars as a resident, she declared that it was "very unjust as I have no children to be benefited by the School." She had less to say in November

1816 when she gave another lease for a similar plot to the elected trustees of District No. 19 in Taghkanic, on the Hillsdale line; one of the trustees was a long-term, faithful member of the Vernon Lodge in Hillsdale, and another was John Reynolds, the tenant leader whose prosecution in January 1811 had set off the entire Manor struggle. The outlines of a system of local "English" — or "Scotch" — schools envisioned by Benjamin Birdsall in the *Bee* in 1811, and by William Livingston in the *Independent Reflector* in 1753, were finally realized on the Manor in compliance with the Common School Act.[66]

The war and the common schools were major elements of a reassertion of routine politics that had far-reaching implications for the peoples of Columbia in relation to the state. Another was the planning for a western canal, for which state funding was approved by the legislature on June 19, 1812, the same day that the school bill had passed. This was a developmental politics that pitted Martin Van Buren against his old mentor, De Witt Clinton, who had been a canal commissioner since 1810, and who, as the war ended (and he was ejected as mayor of New York by the new Republican Council of Appointment), made the canal his vehicle for building a statewide coalition of Federalists and entrepreneurial Republicans. Despite the obvious need for transportation to the west demonstrated by the logistical difficulties of the war, Republicans opposed the canal for regional and ideological reasons. The strength of the regular Republicans lay in the older areas of the Hudson Valley and around New York City, rather than in the new frontier regions to the north and west. Many of the Old Republican stripe were deeply suspicious of the potentially corrupt blending of public money and private gain that such projects seemed to involve. But to the west the influence of Albany Federalists, the migration of New Englanders, and the need for internal improvements all worked to build support for Clinton and his "big ditch."[67]

Van Buren led the Republican opposition to the canal. He supported the bill passed in April 1814, as the war was going badly, repealing the funding for the canal, and again in 1816 he took the initiative to kill canal legislation that had begun in the assembly. But Van Buren was prospering as the leader of the state senate, and he was shifting his political calculus from his senate constituency in the Hudson Valley to the state at large. The same Bucktail Republican council that ejected Clinton from the New York mayoralty in the spring of 1815 had appointed Van Buren as attorney general, and in July 1816 he moved his family to State Street in Albany. By 1817 Clinton was gaining ground, and Van Buren's emerging hold on state power was insecure. Clinton's advocacy of the canal was increasingly popular, and Tompkins, recently reelected to the governorship, was the nominee for vice president with James Monroe, clearly destined for the presidency that fall. So the following spring Van Buren swallowed his principles and swung behind the canal, for which final funding was approved in April 1817.[68]

Van Buren's reversal brought him into a distasteful alliance with his old enemies. Elisha Williams and Jacob R. Van Rensselaer had led the Federalist assemblymen from Columbia in a united front of support for the canal and had led the county to support Clinton in the 1817 and 1820 elections. The canal was only one in a spectrum of "comprehensive programs" that united the rump Federalists of Columbia with Clinton's rise to power. Some were financial, like the Bank of America, which they had supported together in 1812. A long-term director of the Bank of Columbia, Van Rensselaer had hopes for linking his access to capital to the canal project in a bid for its construction for the sum of ten million dollars.[69]

Other ventures were cultural and persuasive, gentry-led institutions of civic authority. Federalists and the new Clintonians predominated in the county Bible Society, the county Moral Society, the Hudson Missionary Society, and as the trustees of the Hudson Lancaster Society, the latter a favorite project of Clinton himself. Judge William W. Van Ness was elected president of the Bible Society, and Elisha Williams was one of two Federalists on the Hudson subcommittee. Five other Lancaster trustees were in the Moral Society, all Federalists or Clintonians, and three were similarly members of the Missionary Society. These moral-civil associations made a significant contribution to the electoral lock that the Federalists and then the Clintonians maintained in Columbia County in these years.[70]

In the Livingston region, the landlord families and associates built a different sort of institution of civil consensus. Chancellor Robert R. Livingston had long been a leading agricultural improver and must have had a hand in forming an agricultural society in Dutchess County in 1807, which was clearly dominated by the Livingston-Lewisite faction. In 1815 a renewed effort was centered at Livingston's Clermont and given further impetus in 1819 when Clinton encouraged and signed a law offering subsidies for their efforts of "giving every encouragement to enterprize and industry." Among the leading lights in this effort were Edward P. Livingston of Clermont, who had supported the Bank of America and opposed Van Buren for the senate in 1812, and John S. Livingston of the Upper Manor, who had sued Benjamin Birdsall for back rent in September 1812. The group came to be known as the Farmers' Club as well as the Agricultural Society of Dutchess and Columbia Counties; their membership in the early years was restricted to the gentry of the Manor region, Claverack, and neighboring Rhinebeck. After promising William Wilson that he would "use all the influence in my power to favor" the agricultural society bill in the 1819 assembly, Jacob R. Van Rensselaer of Claverack was elected vice president and then president.[71]

In 1819 the *New-York Evening Post,* now a Bucktail paper, hinted that the new agricultural societies were "subservient to the political ambition of a certain individual," namely Clinton. The editor of the *Northern Whig* spurned the "illiberality" of such a thought but had to follow his editorial with a hollow-sounding rebuttal to a charge that his *Whig* was controlled by Clinton's Federalist allies Elisha Williams and William W. Van Ness. In Columbia County in these years the hand of the now Clintonian Junto appeared everywhere; late in 1820 notices for the Bible Society and the Agricultural Society, complete with Van Rensselaer's annual address to the membership, were printed not only in the *Whig* but also in the *Bee,* trimming its sails to the prevailing moderate Clintonianism.[72]

In this so-called era of good feelings, then, a constellation of events and initiatives seemed to be creating a new common field of civil life for the people of Columbia and of the state of New York. War brought new heroes, school districts blanketed the state, and comprehensive projects and institutions large and small seemed to give a new unity of structure and purpose to that common civil life.

Circumstances were, of course, soon to change. The glory days of the Columbia Junto were numbered; they were already mocked by "the Bucktail Bard," attacked in the New York papers, and abandoned by a secession of "High-Minded Federalists" who would land in the Van Buren camp. The Junto would make its last stand in the constitutional convention in Albany in the fall of 1821. Their "comprehensive projects" running back to the Merchant's Bank would provide the ground for Van Buren's ever-sharper articulation of a doctrine of governmental minimalism, rooted in the ancient Republican vision of a monitorial, rather than developmental, understanding of civil society, and a vision to which many in Columbia remained faithful.[73]

RACE, CITIZENSHIP, AND THE ASSASSINATION OF MAJOR BIRDSALL

For the moment, the illusion of unanimity followed an era of partisanship, which in Columbia had led over the doorstep of rebellion in 1812. Those included in this unity, however, were white. African-Americans stood very much in the shadows of mid-Hudson society in these postwar years.

Black New Yorkers served during the War of 1812 as sailors on naval vessels on the lakes and were to be recruited into two regiments of black militia authorized by the state in the fall of 1814. The one apparent celebration of black participation in New York's War of 1812 cut both ways. In 1815 Albany printer Nathaniel Coverly put out a broadside titled *Backside Albany,* commemorating the naval battle of Plattsburgh, with two columns of verse, one in an English ballad form, the other in an imitation of black dialect. If it recognized the role of black sailors in this action, it also mocked and separated their culture, opposing it to the balanced cadences of white tradition. In 1816 the efforts of the Albany black community to found a school — and the subsequent uneven history of black education in Hudson — was testimony to the de facto exclusion of black children from the benefits of the new common schools. And among the wider comprehensive programs of the era stood a formal project of racial exclusion. The affairs of the American Colonization Society were followed in the *Northern Whig,* whose editor, William L. Stone, would in later years chair the New York City society. By 1824 Colonization Society auxiliaries had been established in Hudson and Hillsdale; when the state society was reorganized in 1829, there were delegates and attendees from Hudson, Canaan, and Kinderhook. It was in these postwar years that Jesse Torrey of New Lebanon was rhetorically linking the war with the evils of slavery and arguing that the colonization of free Americans of color would be their protection from a horrifying internal slave trade.[74]

In 1817 Columbia County had a sensational trial and execution involving the murder of a black child; a year later another murder in neighboring Rensselaer County linked war and race in the emerging new climate and brought sorrow to one noted Columbia household. After the close of hostilities, despite his horrible facial wounds, Major Benjamin Birdsall III was retained in federal service as an officer in the consolidated rifle regiment and assigned to the barracks at Greenbush, about twenty miles north of Hudson, opposite Albany. On July 4, 1818, Birdsall appeared in public for the first time without his face bandaged, leading his men in a parade in Albany celebrating the repatriation of the remains of General Richard Montgomery, a Clermont Livingston relation, killed at the gates of Quebec in 1775.[75]

That April Birdsall had enlisted into his company a drifter named James Hamilton, who by his own admission had evaded criminal charges by enlisting at the outset of the war and was again on the run when he reenlisted. Hamilton had served during the war in the same assignments as Birdsall, though in a different regiment, and had been captured after the attack on York, Upper Canada, and had spent months as a prisoner of war. Eight days after the Albany parade, Hamilton had been drinking heavily when a commotion started in the barracks over a man whom Major Birdsall had enlisted that day; he was, Hamilton related, "a *dark colored* recruit" whom he "took to be a mulatto." Hamilton challenged the man on the parade ground and then ran to his barracks for his rifle, swearing, "I am going to shoot that damn'd negro." Instead he accosted Birdsall, stepped back, and shot him. Major Birdsall was buried several days later with full military and Masonic honors. Hamilton was tried, convicted, and then hanged at Albany on November 6, presumably on the old Pinkster Ground above the city. At least three different pamphlets were printed up for the occasion. George Holcomb, down from Stephentown to trade, saw the execution and wrote that "the scene was attended by thousands."[76]

For contemporaries, the "assassination" of a distinguished officer far overshadowed the precipitating confrontation. But the language and behavior of a poor white soldier, a veteran and former prisoner of war but also a vagabond and thief, captures the volatility of boundaries of race and citizenship in this era. Hamilton asked whether the man was "enlisted to go into the ranks or as a waiter," and swore, "He shall never go into the ranks with me — I will not rank and file with him." Confronting the recruit, he remembered saying, "Do you clear off this parade immediately, or I will make you." After a scuffle, the recruit "went away with the major's waiter." Major Birdsall had grown up in a turbulent tenant farming household of Quaker origins where, as a child in 1800, he had lived with free blacks but not slaves. But here, in the eyes of a propertyless soldier, Birdsall was undermining a fundamental civil boundary; membership in the enlisted rank and file and the privileges of the parade ground were markers of his citizenship and off-limits to men of color.[77]

Less than three years later the same issues were being debated in the capital building in Albany, at the constitutional convention, by Martin Van Buren, Elisha Williams, Jacob R. Van Rensselaer, and William W. Van Ness, all either onetime political allies or enemies of Major Birdsall's namesake father and grandfather. At stake in Albany in the fall of 1821 were the boundaries and the configuration of the formal deliberative public sphere, the domain of governance, in the state of New York. Who would participate in government, and how should that government be structured in relation to that body of citizens? Under the grip of a renewed deference to the landed families, a majority in Birdsall's hometown of Taghkanic (formerly Granger) voted in April 1821 against calling the convention, though not by the four-to-one margin of the voters in Livingston, and that July they and the rest of the county followed the now traditional lines of voting to elect the Federalist Junto to the convention. But this delegate election, and the elections in the years immediately following the convention, brought a wave of change to Taghkanic and the landlord towns, effecting something like a political settlement.[78]

Driven through by Van Buren and his Bucktail allies, the abandonment of a property requirement for suffrage led to a surge of voting throughout the county and particularly in the old Manor towns, and most particularly in the voting for governor and state senator, which had the most restrictive requirements under the old 1777 constitution. In 1820, when Clinton defeated Tompkins, there were 2,961 votes cast in Columbia County for governor, 100 or so more than the number in the Tompkins-King race in 1816; four years later in 1824, when Clinton won over the Bucktail Samuel Young, the county total vote had jumped to 5,178. Turnout would climb again dramatically in 1828 to more than 7,000, as Van Buren won the governorship and Andrew Jackson the presidency. The sharpest increases in voting were in the older riverfront towns and on the Manor, most dramatically in Taghkanic, whose increase in turnout was twice that of the county as a whole. And if turnout in Taghkanic more than doubled between 1820 and 1824, its vote for Bucktail Democrats was three times greater by 1824 and five times greater in 1828. By 1832, when the county had finally tipped permanently to the Democrats, Taghkanic was voting four to one for Jackson and Van Buren.[79]

A new order of citizenship for white men thus flowed from the convention of 1821. But for black men, like the unknown recruit assaulted on the Greenbush parade in the midsummer of 1818, such a new order still lay far in the future.

10

Jacksonian Columbia

Few if any of the associations which daily spring up amongst us . . . do not, [as if] by an apparent law of their nature, ally themselves with the dynasty of associated wealth in attempting to defeat, by their united efforts, the end and aim of our free institutions by making the few masters over the many. Thus acquiring in this happy land by indirection and fraud, what is a monarchical government secured by the principles upon which they are instituted, or in other words getting through the efforts of Mammon what is claimed by the grace of God.

— Martin Van Buren, "Thoughts on the Coming Election
  in New York [March 1840]"

As a Board of Managers, we have for the last year, assembled and assembled, for the discussion of our business, with such cheerless and disheartening prospects that we have seen scarcely a ray of hope to light our onward path. . . . Owing to the exhaustion of funds, and pressing embarrassments, [we] deemed it expedient to close the School. Res[olved]. That the School shall be given up.

— Minutes of the Board of Managers of the Hudson Infant
  School Society, Apr. 9, May 18, 1832

Agreeable to previous notice the colored inhabitants of the city of Hudson, convened at the Baptist conference room . . . Mr. Hiram Van Alstyne then addressed the meeting, urging the necessity of acting promptly and with energy, in attempting to . . . . secure the inestimable privilege of having a voice in making the laws by which they were to be governed. It was then Resolved, that a petition be drawn, and signed by all present, circulated among the colored people not present, and sent to the legislature.

— New York *Colored American,* Feb. 6, 1841

In the decades separating the War of 1812 and the Civil War the county of Columbia became something of a backwater. Returning from the west in 1847, one expatriate found Hudson's population "greatly diminished," though more "in character than in numbers." Though it had been "for many years one of the most beautiful and flourishing towns on the noble river whose name it bears," Hudson now suffered an "all-pervading air of listless indolence," but "the surrounding scenery" was "as beautiful as ever."[1]

By the 1820s Columbia, and with it much of the Hudson Valley, was sinking into a quiet and picturesque irrelevance, its population stable or declining, bypassed by the central progress of nineteenth-century America. In the Revolutionary and immediate post-Revolutionary years the county and its region had stood at the leading edge of the energies reshaping civil life in the new nation. Across the northern states it was now overshadowed by the towns and small cities along the new canal to the west and the rivers and lakes beyond, by an explosively expanding New York City, by the intellectual, political, and manufacturing projects emerging in eastern New England.

In some immeasurable degree Columbia's antebellum stasis rested in fundamental conflicts left tangled and unresolved from the decades of the Revolution and the early Republic. New York's constitutional convention of the fall of 1821 had reforged the civil regime, redefining the boundaries around the deliberative arena. Similar constitutional reconfigurations in other states in this same decade mark this watershed between the early Republic and antebellum democracy, a settlement of sorts that would be challenged four decades later in the era of the Civil War and Reconstruction but never fundamentally altered and enlarged until the twentieth century.[2]

Such was the case across much of the nation. But in Martin Van Buren's Columbia the limitations and incompleteness of this epochal transition were more evident than in many places in the new democracy. While the county marked the passing of an era and put an impress on new forms of persuasive culture in the public sphere, leading men pursued an intensified politics of governmental minimalism, directly shaped by decades of struggle with forces working to corrupt that government and to deny the people the benefits of their Revolution. The ancient and unresolved politics of Demo and Aristo would continue to retard the redefinition of civil life. The result was an impasse that reinforced the boundaries around the domain of public deliberation. Excluded groups would have to struggle against particularly great odds, sometimes stepping over into violent means, to have their voices heard in the public sphere.[3]

PLATE 15. *The City of Hudson from the Southeast, circa 1840.* From John W. Barber and Henry Howe, *Historical Collections of the State of New York* . . . (New York, 1842)

THE COUNTY, THE CATSKILLS, AND THE RIVER

Reading death notices in the Hudson newspapers in the early 1820s and reflecting upon the recent history of their county, citizens of Columbia would have sensed the end of an epoch. Men and women who had shaped that history were passing from the scene. On the Upper Manor of Livingston, brothers John and Henry Livingston, the sons of the third lord of the Manor who had led the quite successful effort to uphold the landlord interest in the previous decades, died in 1822 and 1823. Their cousin at Clermont, Chancellor Robert R. Livingston, had died in 1813. In Hudson, Robert Jenkins, the third of the Rhode Island Jenkins clan to serve as mayor of the city, was drowned in November 1819, when he was swept off a river sloop by a boom; he was mourned in the Hudson *Bee* as "a man distinguished for his public usefulness and private virtues." His neighbor, the formidable Hannah Barnard, died sometime in 1825. Among the Shakers, Mother Lucy Wright died in February 1821, during a final visitation from New Lebanon to the Shaker mother settlement at Watervliet, north of Albany.[4]

Emigration was taking others—known locally as the "birds of passage"—to the world beyond the county. Matthew Adgate, the Revolutionary leader in Canaan, had long since emigrated with his sons to the northern Champlain country; he died in 1818. In Hillsdale, the Birdsall family had removed to Chenango County just before the third Benjamin was assassinated at the Greenbush Barracks in 1818; Colonel Benjamin lived another ten years, and Benjamin, Jr., the leader of the Manor tenants, lived on to 1862, into another age. On the Livingston Manor lands, others who had fared even more poorly in the land struggles of the 1790s and years following, many of them tenants whose life leases had expired, moved west in great numbers. Among them was a family of Rockefellers who left Taghkanic for Tioga County in the 1820s; later in the century a grandson would amass a vast fortune in the building of urban America. City life already beckoned. If many from Columbia moved on to the west, others went downriver to the rising metropolis, where the river met the Atlantic. Among those drawn to New York City were members of the merchant Folger family. Frances Folger, once a member of Hannah Barnard's Female Benevolent Society, would be swept up in the early 1820s into a messianic cult led by one Robert Matthews, also known as the Prophet Matthias, and she in turn entangled her in-laws Benjamin and Ann Folger, also Hudson emigrants. William Leete Stone, who briefly edited the Hudson *Northern Whig* and whose wife Susannah was so taken with Hannah Barnard's intellect, assumed the editorship of the New York *Commercial Advertiser* after helping to compile the *Proceedings and Debates* of the 1821 constitutional convention. He would write a lurid exposé of the Prophet Matthias's cult, with particularly harsh words for his former Hudson neighbors, the Folgers. The people of Columbia took many paths out of the early Republic into a wider nineteenth-century world.[5]

New alliances and projects developed among some of these former Columbians, building on old connections. One of these would help to define the region in a wider national culture. Caleb Benton, the young doctor whose Masonic connections had shaped the coalition of Susquehannah Company men and Genesee Adventurers in the 1780s, had moved across the river to the village of Catskill in the 1790s; in the years to come he involved himself in turnpike development west through the mountains. In 1823, two years before his death, he joined a group of men interested in stage lines and turnpiking who were financing the construction of the Catskill Mountain House. Built at Orchard Garden high in the mountains overlooking the valley on land once owned by Elisha Williams of the Columbia Junto, the Mountain House would immediately become the most exclusive vacation resort in the nation. In this venture he was joined by one of the printing Croswells and by Henry McKinstry, the son of his old Masonic brother and Adventurer ally Colonel John McKinstry, who had died the year before in Livingston at the age of seventy-seven. That year William Leete Stone began promoting the new Catskill Mountain House in the pages of the *Commercial Advertiser* and was instrumental in its immediate success among the wealthy Americans and foreigners who now were flocking to Saratoga, as they once had flocked to Lebanon Springs.[6]

As if to fend off a sense of impending marginality, those who stayed behind in Hudson and Columbia in the 1820s plunged into a series of grand events marking the transition from republic to democracy, some looking back to the past, others forward to the new age. In 1822 William Howard Allen of Hudson, a hero of the recent war with Britain, was killed fighting pirates off Cuba; eulogized that winter by a committee carefully drawn to ignore the partisan strife that had wracked the city for decades, he was buried with full military and municipal honors in 1827. In September 1824, in the hero's progress that marked the end of the nation's birth, the marquis de Lafayette took a steamer up the Hudson, stopping at West Point and Poughkeepsie, and spent the night at Clermont, honored with a Masonic procession, a militia muster, and a grand ball. The next day he stopped briefly at Catskill, catching a glimpse of the newly built Mountain House gleaming white high on the western horizon. Lafayette's slow progress toward Albany obliged his entourage to hurry him through the celebrations at Hudson, where ceremonial arches had been built, a dinner laid on at Allen's Hotel, and seventy Revolutionary veterans assembled, among them Warners and Dr. Moses Younglove from Canaan, Ten Broecks from Livingston, Coffins and Prosper Hosmer from Hudson.[7]

Thirteen months later the local people were similarly disappointed at the passage of the fleet of steamboats celebrating the completion of the Erie Canal, linking the Hudson to the Great Lakes and opening the Northwest to New York's commerce. On October 26, 1825, artillery had been fired on the bluffs above Hudson at exactly 11:04 A.M. and 11:46 A.M., as part of a chain of firings running back and forth from Buffalo to New York City marking the final construction. A week later thousands of Columbia's citizens, "snow-white handkerchiefs fluttering briskly in the breeze," watched the fleet of dignitaries sail north past the city, again skipping the "collation provided for the occasion."[8]

As the state celebrated the reconfiguration of its commercial geography, a new self-reflection was emerging that would give the people of New York a fresh public sensibility of time and place. William Leete Stone, representing the printers of New York City on one of the passing steamers, had written the description of Hudson's canal celebration. Among his many other projects, which included the Colonization Society, the Greek revolution, temperance, and accounts of the Prophet Matthias and the Maria Monk "scandal," in the 1830s Stone would begin a series of chronicles of the Revolution in New York, including biographies of Red Jacket and Joseph Brant and an account of the Revolution in the Mohawk Valley in which men from Columbia had played a minor role. Stone's histories, with those that followed in the 1840s and 1850s by his son, William, Jr., and by Benson Lossing of Dutchess County, were among the first to turn the history of the Revolution into popular literature, important elements in the widening stream of imprints in the literary marketplace that was reshaping an American identity in the mid-nineteenth century.[9]

Writing of Hudson's reception of the canal celebration steamers, Stone had waxed eloquent on Hudson's prospect of the Catskills, where there was "no finer view of these lofty mountains," and on the scenery at Mount Merino, south of the city, where Republican Oliver Wiswall of Hudson ran renowned flocks of fine-wooled merino sheep. Stone's celebration of the region's beauties and his promotion of the Catskill Mountain House in the *Commercial Advertiser* contributed to the emergence of the region as an icon in a new American literary and artistic culture. Washington Irving had already begun to construct a national mythology of Dutch culture along the Hudson in Knickerbocker's *History* (1809), and his "Rip Van Winkle," just published in the *Sketchbook of Geoffrey Crayon, Gent.*, anticipated and fueled the wave of interest in its setting, the mountains above Catskill. So, too, James Fenimore Cooper, writing in the year of the construction of the Mountain House, had specifically included the view from Pine Orchard in *The Pioneers,* the first of the Leatherstocking novels. As Irving, Cooper, and Stone were writing about the scenery at Hudson, artists were painting it. Their works had been exhibited in New York and were published in lithographic collections in the early 1820s, and the Mountain House would quickly become the focus of this emerging school. Thomas Cole painted one of the earliest views of the resort in its mountain setting in 1828, and by 1835, when English tourist and travel writer Harriet Martineau spent a week at the Mountain House, he had settled in the village of Catskill and was painting his allegorical masterpiece *The Course of Empire,* in part a commentary on the ruinous development of the Catskills inaugurated by the old Adventurer, Caleb Benton, and his associates. Twenty-five years later, when Cole's disciple Frederick Church bought land on Mount Merino south of Hudson City and built his mansion, Olana, with a mountain view, the Hudson River School of landscape painting was fully established, framing a romantic American aesthetic of the clash of nature and civility.[10]

Columbia thus made some modest contributions to an emerging literary and artistic construction of an American sense of self, romantic in antique tales of heroic Revolutionary struggle and in a wild and raw nature, all far removed from the ugly turmoil of aggressive development in Jacksonian America. Such would have powerful resonances in the nation's persuasive culture. But the man at the center of the transition of civil life in these years would have given little thought to these emerging performances. Later in life Martin Van Buren

PLATE 16. *Martin Van Buren (1782–1862), Kinderhook and Washington, D.C., circa 1822.* Courtesy of the Kinderhook Memorial Library, Kinderhook, N.Y.

would count Washington Irving among his friends and contemplate paintings of the Hudson Valley School on his drawing room walls at Lindenwald, his postpresidential estate in Kinderhook. But in the 1820s he epitomized the advancing world of democratic capitalism from which romantic artists were in retreat. Thomas Cole, an English immigrant of aristocratic sensibilities and Whig politics, would design his *Course of Empire* as a direct critique of the imperial hubris of Andrew Jackson's America that Van Buren would play such a part in constructing over the following decades.[11]

Late in 1821, however, Martin Van Buren was a very busy man, with very big plans. At the end of October, as soon as the constitutional convention completed its deliberations but before it presented its report, he left Albany, first stopping in New York, and arrived in Washington on November 5 to take up the seat in the Senate to which he had been elected by the New York legislature in February. His first visitor was John C. Calhoun of South Carolina. A cordial first conversation bore no hint of a bitter conflict that would develop and fester over the next three decades.[12]

MARTIN VAN BUREN, ANDREW JACKSON, AND A "POLITICAL REVOLUTION"

After twelve years in county politics and nine in state politics, Van Buren was now on the national stage that would carry him to the presidency fifteen years later. He came to Washington with experience, a program, and a plan. His experience with the factional schisms by Aaron Burr, Morgan Lewis, and then De Witt Clinton led him to an early stand for party regularity. Decisions deliberated by duly authorized committees and conventions should guide and structure political behavior; deviance from these principles was a violation of public trust that threatened the foundations of public authority. Such were the principles of the Albany Regency, the New York Bucktail Democratic machine that Van Buren would direct from Washington. His articulation of the importance of procedural regularity had its roots in Columbia's political struggles between Demo and Aristo in the 1780s and 1790s, as people fought over the definition of the political procedures that would provide routine legitimacy to the linkage of the people with state authority. His experience with the effects of schism and irregularity made Van Buren very concerned about the problem of legitimacy that so concerned the post-Revolutionary generation but also about routine effectiveness: parties riven by personal ambition and faction could not effectively prevail at the polls and in the legislature. Such defeats and those brought on by "corrupt means" would bring the illegitimacy of minority rule, as powerful, moneyed, "aristocratic" interests prevailed over those of the people at large.[13]

Van Buren would take the lesson that legitimacy, effectiveness, and justice lay in regular party procedure to its fullest national elaboration in his drive to build a national Democratic Party. But, if Van Buren sought to build a modern institution in the public sphere, his intent was less than transformative. He had not been an unqualified advocate of suffrage extension in 1821, and the Regency would oppose popular election of presidential electors in coming years. More important, he had no intention of expanding the revolutionary settlement to encompass entire categories of people excluded from deliberation or from civil life altogether. As one historian has concluded, Van Buren's thinking "about the darker side of American life, its substantial racial and gender inequities were, at best, undeveloped, always approached through the lens of political caution, and the existing, powerful prejudices of the majority of those he sought to lead." In Van Buren's thinking, any further expansion of the revolutionary settlement threatened to undermine the entire enterprise, and so in 1821 he had played a key role in the erosion of black voting rights at the New York constitutional convention.[14]

In the same years, he saw the country's immediate future threatened by the debate over slavery that had exploded in the debates over the admission of Missouri. Conflict over slavery threatened the Union; party could suppress the slavery debate. "Party attachment in former times furnished a complete antidote for sectional prejudices by producing counteracting feelings," he wrote in his famous letter to Thomas Ritchie, editor of the Richmond, Virginia, *Enquirer,* in January 1827. "It was not until that defense had been broken down that the clamour agt. Southern influence and African slavery could be made effectual in the North." The "natural and benefitial . . . political combination . . . between the planters of the South and the plain Republicans of the North" might be confirmed and preserved "with the substantial reorganization of the Old Republican Party" around regular nominations by congressional caucus or a national party convention "substituting *party principle* for *personal preference.*"[15]

As part of his program to preserve the Union by building a national institution that would freeze in place the revolutionary settlement, Van Buren gravitated toward an increasingly fundamentalist Old Republican vision of governmental minimalism. The southern defense of the local institution of slavery meant that the "planters of the south" would naturally oppose any party proposing to exercise strong federal authority. But his national strategic interest meshed well with his prior experience among the "plain Republicans" in Columbia and in New York and would increasingly shape his advice to President Jackson and his own presidential policies. Though classical Jacksonian rhetoric would not fully surface in his own public writings until the later 1830s, Van Buren's early experience with aristocracy and corruption would form a hard, enduring sounding board for attacks on a "consolidating money power." The illegitimacy of a government deriving from such corruption drove Van Buren's conception of electoral party politics as potential crises rather than simple routine, as a continual constitutional struggle to realize the legacy of the Revolution itself. Such an understanding had deep roots in his apprenticeship in the political culture of Columbia County.[16]

At the opening of the 1820s the archetype of factional division and usurping consolidation, for Van Buren, lay in his nemesis De Witt Clinton. Once his mentor, Clinton had earned Van Buren's enmity by standing as a Federalist presidential candidate in 1812 and then operating outside party structures to advance his vision of an "empire state" built on a fusion of public authority and private profits. But, even more than he despised Clinton, Van Buren despised Clinton's political associates, former Federalists and entrepreneurial Republicans, many of whom would form the basis of the Whig Party in New York. They were "a set of desperadoes," Van Buren wrote in a series of vehement letters to Rufus King in 1820. "Instigated by the hope of official plunder," he was certain that they would "never be content to limit their depredation to the boundaries of the State."[17]

Quite clearly, many of these "desperadoes" were the Federalists of the Columbia Junto. Van Buren's opinions were shared by a growing faction of "High-Minded" Federalists, who in 1819 and 1820 renounced an alliance with Clinton and joined Van Buren's Bucktails. Among them, ironically, was Alexander Hamilton's son, James A. Hamilton, who early in 1819 led a newspaper campaign "to overturn a system of fraud and venality." After almost a year of hints and open attacks, the New York *American* published the details of a corruption of the legislature now some eight years old. The three great leaders of the Federalist Columbia Junto, the paper charged, had demanded a $150,000 loan from the huge Bank of America paid to their Bank of Columbia, with half of the interest as a fee for services, in exchange for their support for it, chartered over Governor Daniel Tompkins's veto in 1812.[18]

The following March, as legislative hearings into the Bank of America scandal got under way, the *American* placed this charge in its widest context. Why, the paper asked, was New York not the first state in the nation? Because the state's "character [was] debased by intrigue and CORRUPTION" stemming from "a few unprincipled and ambitious men."

> Among the intriguers who have kept this state in constant agitation for the last 20 years; the principal are Dewitt Clinton, Ambrose Spencer, William W. Van Ness, and Elisha Williams. These men have also been more

or less concerned in the corruption which has undermined, and almost destroyed, all political morality among us. The two former have never been as openly engaged in corrupt practices as the latter, but are not the less guilty in having connived at and forwarded them. The personal and party friends of Dewitt Clinton in particular have been the most active and efficient agents of corruption; and, acting as his friends, and by his direction, they have repeatedly given their whole party weight to further dishonest measures; as for instance, in the incorporation of the Bank of America. But the great authors, abettors, and agents of corruption are William W. Van Ness, Elisha Williams, and Jacob R. Van Rensselaer, who have been more or less concerned in every party plot in the state, from their first coalition with Burr until their present one with Dewitt Clinton; and in almost every project of corruption, from the incorporation of the Merchants' to that of the Franklin Bank.[19]

Clinton and Spencer, the leaders of the opposing Clintonian faction, were requisite targets in this attack, but the focus of the paper's campaign was the three "authors" of corruption from the county of Columbia: Van Ness, Williams, and Van Rensselaer.

As of 1819 these men — the troika of the Columbia Junto — were still of great and wide influence and power. Van Ness had been justice of the supreme court since the aftermath of the Merchant's Bank affair in 1807, and either Williams or Van Rensselaer had sat in virtually every meeting of the assembly since 1811, playing a central role in the politics of banking and internal improvements, specifically the Erie Canal. In the spring of 1820 Hamilton's New York *American* wrote of both electoral and legislative corruption in reports on Williams's election. In late April the editors "had hoped there was virtue enough even in Columbia county to have saved the State from the disgrace" of his nomination: "We find, however, that we have over-rated the honesty of a certain portion of our electors, who are content, (and who perhaps ought,) to be represented by Elisha Williams." Ten days later, "with pride and pleasure," they related that Williams "was met with hisses at the polls, and was asked if he again wanted a seat in the Legislature, *to get more banks through and finger more dollars.*"[20]

The hue and cry over the 1812 charter for the Bank of America rose as the country sank into its first nineteenth-century depression. While the Federalist Bank of Columbia survived succeeding economic and political crises, the Republican Bank of Hudson went under, its money being refused in the hill towns by June 1819. But rumors had been circulating for years about the circumstances of the Bank of America charter and its subsequent revision. The bank had been chartered over the governor's prorogation, capitalized at six million dollars as a Federalist venture to fill the financial void left by Congress's refusal to recharter the Bank of the United States. Van Ness was said to have declined to run for governor in 1816 for fear of the scandal. By 1819, when calls for an investigation appeared, he was being skewered as "Fallacio" the corruptionist in a series of satirical poems published in New York under the hand of the Bucktail Bard, one of the "High-Minded Federalists" who now put the skills of Addisonian satire to work for Van Buren. Van Ness took the brunt of the attack, accused of violating his oath of judicial office in accepting the bribe to support the bank's charter in the state's Council of Revision, where the governor and justices of the state supreme court reviewed all acts passing the assembly and senate before final enactment.[21]

In the short term, the Junto survived the scandal. The legislative inquiry of the spring of 1820 absolved Judge Van Ness, Williams was reelected to the assembly by a faithful Federalist electorate, and Van Ness and Van Rensselaer were toasted in absentia at the July Fourth celebration in Hudson as men of virtue "assailed by calumny" and "the arrows of persecution." The following June all three, with Francis Silvester of Kinderhook, were elected as Federalists to the constitutional convention. But the era of their total control of Columbia politics and of their far-reaching influence in the state at large was coming to an end. At the convention, their profoundly conservative vision had little or no influence, and they had to watch as the property qualification for white male suffrage was swept away and the high court restructured, unseating the sitting justices. Van Ness's fate was another of the grim passages that marked the new age in the early 1820s. Losing his position on the supreme court, Van Ness opened a practice in New York; then, "afflicted with a disease of the dyspeptic kind," he traveled south for a cure. On February 27, 1823, he died in exile in Charleston, South Carolina, at the age of 47.[22]

Williams and Van Rensselaer managed to hang onto place and position through the crisis. Van Rensselaer, now a general of the militia, took a prominent role in celebrations of Lafayette and the new canal in 1824 and 1825. But, if they were still honored in some circles, they had lost their direct grip on Columbia's politics. Both would reemerge briefly later in the 1820s, but in a politics that had been reshaped by new men and new circumstances, in a politics that looked forward to the Age of Jackson.[23]

This new politics took shape in the mid-1820s. On the one side stood the Republican Bucktail regulars and Van Buren's developing Regency system, standing for minimalism in state government, supporting William Crawford, Van Buren's Old Republican presidential candidate in 1824, and eventually emerging as Jacksonian Democrats in 1828. On the other evolved a shifting coalition of former Clintonians, Federalists, and the occasional Bucktail, taking various names, who stood against the rising power of Van Buren's Regency discipline and coalesced as Adams Republicans and then Whigs, advancing an agenda of manufactures and improvements. Throughout the 1820s this heterogeneous proto-Whig coalition managed to perpetuate something of the old Federalist preeminence at the polls in Columbia, but in 1829 the Jackson party would prevail and establish a tight and enduring grip on the county's politics.[24]

The shifting fortunes of the newspapers in Hudson reflected this evolving political scene. Charles Holt's Hudson *Bee,* the warhorse of Columbia's Jeffersonians, closed its doors soon after a new Bucktail paper, the *Columbia Republican,* was commenced in September 1820, carrying on the competition with the Federalist *Northern Whig.* But doctrinal Federalism was waning fast even in Columbia County. Federalist slates (carefully excluding anyone remotely linked with the old Junto) won in 1821 and 1822, but the Federalists were finally defeated in 1823 by the Bucktails, bringing Columbians of the Jeffersonian tradition back to the assembly for the first time in twenty years. Then 1824, the year of Lafayette's visit, brought the first of two editorial and political revolutions.

At the center of this upheaval was a young lawyer named Ambrose Latting Jordan. Jordan grew up in a Republican and Baptist family in southwest Hillsdale, near the farm where Sheriff Hogeboom was shot in 1791. After clerking for Jacob Rutsen Van Rensselaer, he moved to Chenango and then Otsego County, where he studied and practiced law with several of the Birdsalls and briefly led the local Bucktail Democrats. Returning to Hudson by 1822, Jordan in 1824 joined the Clintonian movement called the People's Party, challenging Van Buren's Bucktail Regency. Assembling support, he bought the *Republican* and turned it to the purposes of the People's movement. While the old Federalist *Northern Whig* soon stopped publication, the Hudson Bucktails responded to Jordan's editorial coup by organizing a new *Hudson Gazette,* a name dormant since Stoddard had stopped publication in 1803. But that November, campaigning on a promise of popular election of presidential electors, Jordan and the People's slate were elected in a landslide to the assembly, and the next year he won a three-year term to the state senate.[25]

If he was named after an old Hillsdale radical, once such a great annoyance to the Livingstons, Ambrose Jordan moved pragmatically toward the vacuum in Columbia's politics. In supporting the democratization of presidential elections, he filled the gap left by the Federalist collapse with a style that his paper celebrated as an "enlightened attachment to the whole theory of our republican institutions" as he gravitated toward more interventionist programs undertaken under the labels of Adams Republicans or National Republicans. In 1827 the old Junto warhorses reappeared on the public stage at Jordan's side, attending a convention supporting Clay's "American System" of governmental support for manufacturing. Elisha Williams managed to get back into the assembly in the November election that year, and Jacob R. Van Rensselaer worked to support the reelection of John Quincy Adams.[26]

This would be their final political rehabilitation. Both Williams and Van Rensselaer suffered continual reverses during the 1820s, most seriously in 1829 when the Bank of Columbia finally collapsed. Both would be dead by 1835, Van Rensselaer after suffering a bankruptcy that forced him to sell his Claverack land and mansion to Williams, who then — ironically — had to convey it to George McKinstry, son of Colonel John McKinstry, who fifty years before had broken his sword and damned Van Rensselaer's father on the banks of the Mohawk. But in the final years of the 1820s these old Federalists briefly stood on a new stage with their political heirs. Following his conspicuous roles in the Lafayette and canal celebrations, Van Rensselaer served with Jordan on the Adams committee in 1828 and with him again as co-vice presidents at the Hudson July Fourth celebration the next year.[27]

In the summer and fall of 1829 the wider Adams coalition had high hopes for a wide range of improvements for the county, to be achieved under their benevolent management. The July Fourth celebration toasted Clay, Adams, the "late lamented" De Witt Clinton, who had died suddenly in February 1828, internal improvements, and the American system. The celebration also took up a collection for the American Colonization Society. Two and a half months later many of these men reconvened to establish the Columbia County Temperance Society; Van Rensselaer addressed the gathering, and Jordan sat as a vice president. Among their number were men who had supported similar benevolent ventures in the Federalist era, the Moral Society, the Bible Society, and the Lancaster Society. Many of them would be subscribers to a new Hudson Infant School Society (heir to Barnard's Female Benevolent Society) being established that same month to instruct the very youngest of the poor in Hudson.[28]

While former Federalists had the longer experience in these benevolent projects, former Republicans of the entrepreneurial stripe were also involved. Elisha Jenkins, who had followed Ambrose Spencer in his shifts from Federalist to Republican to Clintonian, presided over the formation of the New York Colonization Society in 1829 and then was elected to the presidency of the county Temperance Society. Senator Ambrose Jordan, the central figure of the county Adams-National establishment, served a particularly important role for the Infant School Society. With his brother, Allen, and the *Colum-*

bia Republican's printer, Charles Ames, Jordan was a conspicuous member of the Hudson Lodge in the late 1820s as well as a Temperance officer and Infant Society subscriber. He must have been instrumental in the lodge's decision to allow the ladies of the Infant Society to use the lower room in their Masonic Hall without charge, a "noble charity."[29]

The great majority of Columbia's improving elite was surely disappointed that Andrew Jackson had won the presidency, though they might have taken some county pride in Martin Van Buren's appointment as secretary of state, which conveniently had forced him to resign his newly won governorship. They might have taken some solace in holding the county for Adams and for Van Buren's gubernatorial opponent, Smith Thompson, and in managing the election of their slate of assemblymen. But, if they assumed that the county would remain under their benevolent control, the November 1829 election dealt them a mortal blow, when Columbia's voters turned to the "Jackson Republicans." Columbia would send Jacksonians to the assembly until the crisis of 1837 and thereafter, more often than not, into the 1850s. Jacksonian Columbia had arrived.[30]

The force behind Columbia's Jacksonian revolution was John W. Edmonds, a Hudson lawyer whose father Samuel had arrived in the young city after the Revolution with only horse and blanket. Samuel had risen to be a leading man in Hudson, and his son followed; during Lafayette's 1824 visit to the county Edmonds had led the city militia to Clermont as "Col. Edmonds." That September, with the support of a committee of local Democrats, Edmonds had launched the new *Hudson Gazette* and deployed it under the authority of the Bucktail Regency against the Clintonians. In his opening message as the new paper's editor, Edmonds had announced the Van Burenite doctrine of party regularity that echoed back to the county's procedural debates of the late 1780s. The *Gazette* would

> maintain the doctrine that the minority ought in all cases to yield to the majority, and that the great object of the organization of a party is the advancement of principles not men. It will support, with all its power, regular caucus nominations, convinced that hereby the man is obliged to yield to principle, and firmly believing that no other than good can result from a cause which has placed such men as Jefferson and Madison at the head of our government, which has doomed the Adams Federalism to destruction, and which has preserved the triumph of correct principles for years.

Sharing the upper floor of a store on Warren and Second streets with a Democratic reading room, the *Gazette,* Edmonds recounted decades later, "grew in circulation and influence" over the next five years and "was greatly instrumental" in the "political revolution" of 1829 in Columbia.[31]

STANDING AGAINST ARISTOCRACY,
"CORRUPT MEANS," AND THE "MONEYED POWER"

The rhetoric of this "political revolution" echoed that of the county's struggles of the Jeffersonian era. Ever since 1824, when Adams had won the presidency in the House of Representatives with Clay's support and had handed the Department of State to Henry Clay, his opponents had sounded the cry of a "corrupt bargain," and corruption was in the ears of Columbia's voters in 1828 and 1829. Aaron Vanderpoel, who would be on the first Democratic slate sent to the assembly in 1829 and then be elected to three terms in Congress starting in 1833, sounded this tocsin to the "Mechanics and Farmers of Columbia" in September 1828. They were to stand against "the friends of a proud aristocratick and corrupt dynasty"; they were "the bone and sinew of the land, the true salt, that will save the public from taint and corruption." Without any sense of contradiction, Vanderpoel concluded that Jackson was the "only hope" of "the labouring classes of the community" to "save them from the iron oppression of a tyranical and overbearing aristocracy." Four months later the Chatham Democrats celebrated Jackson's victory over "a corrupt coalition."[32]

As first Jackson and then Van Buren sought to restrict central banking in the 1830s, others in Columbia developed the language of "aristocracy" in American affairs. Most notable among them was Samuel Jones Tilden of New Lebanon, a rising young Democrat—a future governor and presidential candidate—whose father, Elam, had seen "the finger of Napoleon" in the Bank of America in 1812 and whose adoptive grandfather, Moses Younglove, had once done battle with Elkanah Watson over the corrupting power of state incorporation. In the early 1830s, while the elder Tilden remained in continual communication with Van Buren in Washington, the younger Tilden took up the pen for Jackson and Van Buren before he even finished with academy studies. His earliest effort, on the tariff, was published in the Kinderhook *Columbia Centinel* in the spring of 1832. That August he drafted an address on the Antimasons and the governor's election that Van Buren, staying at the resort at Lebanon Springs, reviewed and had published in the *Argus*. A month later he gave an address to the Young Democrats in both New Lebanon and Hudson attacking the Bank of the United States and the "moneyed system" in general. If England had once been under the sway of a "hereditary aristocracy," it was now under the control of "a heartless, soulless moneyed power," and this *"modern dynasty of associated wealth"* now threatened the United States. "Are not monopolies and corporations springing up like hydras in every part of the nation?" Tilden asked. "Are they not obtaining an alarming ascendency over our legislative bodies, and over the people themselves?" Corporations had already corrupted the press and the legislatures. Without continuing vigilance of the people behind Jackson's courageous veto, "the rich and aristocratic" would once again line up behind this "centre and stronghold of the money power. . . . till finally, as with advancing time wealth accumulates and poverty becomes more excessive, A MONEYED ARISTOCRACY will hold undisputed sway over this now free and happy people."[33]

Over the next several years Tilden shuttled between New Lebanon, an unsatisfactory semester at Yale, and studies and work in New York City and continued to wield his political pen, tackling the dual threats of South Carolina's nullification and "the corruptions and dangerous tendency of the bank." Finally finishing college, Tilden in 1837 began clerking for Democrat John W. Edmonds, who had just moved from Hudson to New York City. The next February he wrote resolutions and an address to a New York convention of mechanics and workingmen, defending Van Buren's withdrawal of the federal deposits, attacking the threat of a political "monarch and a privileged nobility to regulate our affairs." Van Buren's Independent Treasury, separating governmental funds from the private banking system, would "dissolve an unnatural connection which has exposed politics to influences most corrupt and combinations most dangerous." To do otherwise would be to give way to the power of "concentrated property by monopolies and perpetuities," a "dynasty of associated and privileged wealth" that had already "established an aristocracy more potent, more permanent, and more oppressive than any other which has ever existed."[34]

In 1828 Vanderpoel's "proud aristocratick and corrupt dynasty" was specifically the Adams family; in 1837 Tilden's "dynasty of associated wealth" described a far wider sociology. In Columbia County either rhetoric would have had a particularly powerful resonance. When Van Buren went to Washington in 1821, the attack on the Bank of America corruptionists of the Columbia Junto must have been fresh in his mind, as might have been their corrupt control of the voting on the Livingston Manor, particularly in the 1808–1810 elections. Eventually his presidential order to isolate the federal funds in the Independent Treasury was powerfully directed by these early experiences. Certainly, when he became governor in 1829, he pressed the simultaneous reform of the New York's banks through the Safety Fund system and a strict law "to restrain the use of money in elections."[35]

Early in 1825 Van Buren might well have reflected quietly on the wider implications of these encounters with political corruption in the name of

Columbia's landed dynasties. On February 9, 1825, Stephen Van Rensselaer, the greatest patroon of them all (and Van Buren's Washington messmate), after great hesitation cast the decisive ballot in Congress that elected John Quincy Adams to the presidency, setting the stage for the "corrupt bargain" with Henry Clay. Later that day Van Rensselaer exclaimed to Van Buren, "You saw that I could not hold out!"[36]

There is no evidence, however, that Van Buren ever expressed a link between landlordism and the "corrupt bargain" of February 1825. He was, indeed, assiduous in curbing his rhetoric in his formative decades on the national stage. In July 1832 Van Buren sent James A. Hamilton, his assistant at the Department of State, to the White House to help rework Jackson's veto message, limiting its language regarding the bank. He does not appear to have had a hand in drafting Jackson's famous 1837 farewell, with its powerful account of the threat of the "moneyed power" to the people, the "bone and sinew of the country." In his own inaugural address that same week Van Buren celebrated the "stability of our institutions" and promised to carry on those Jacksonian policies that would "make our beloved land for a thousand generations that chosen spot where happiness springs from a perfect equality of political rights." He said nothing of the forces of "consolidation" or of the "money power" as he accepted the nation's highest office in the spring of 1837.[37]

But the commercial and political crises of that summer and the following years brought to the surface the sharper edges of Jacksonian language in Van Buren's public pronouncements. A short six months after his inaugural, in his special message to Congress announcing the Independent Treasury policy in September 1837, Van Buren set aside his inhibitions, articulating a Jacksonian populism rooted in his early experiences in Columbia that would reverberate through his writings for the next twenty-five years. Before the election he had made clear his opposition to the recharter of the Bank of the United States, but in the autumn of 1837 he was much more militant.

> To these sentiments I have now only to add the expression of an increased conviction that the reestablishment of such a bank in any form, whilst it would not accomplish the beneficial purpose promised by its advocates, would impair the rightful supremacy of the popular will, injure the character and diminish the influence of our political system, and bring once more into existence a concentrated moneyed power, hostile to the spirit and threatening the permanency of our republican institutions.

Elam Tilden, writing to Van Buren only four days later from New Lebanon, apparently had read an advance copy and effused, "It will be like the Morning Star to the democratic party." With this and other encouragements, Van Buren pursued the tension between the will of the people and the "money power" in his public messages for the next three years. That December in his message to Congress he stressed that the "national will is the supreme law of the Republic"; the next year he wrote that Americans were testing the proposition that government rested in the "continual exercise of the popular will." In 1838 he warned the nation "that a concentrated money power is tempted to become an active agent in political affairs" and that no one should expect that "it will ever be found asserting and supporting the rights of the community at large in opposition to the claims of the few." In 1839, as the depression deepened and Whig opposition mounted, Van Buren wrote a long analysis of the "chain of dependence" linking American finances back to "the money power in Great Britain." In conclusion, he warned in stark republican terms that a central bank would establish a dependency of "all classes" upon "privileged associations for the means of speculation and extravagance." Such a groveling dependency would

> nourish, in preference to the manly virtues that give dignity to human nature, a craving desire for luxurious enjoyment and sudden wealth, which renders those who seek them dependent on those who supply them; to substitute for republican simplicity and economical habits a sickly appetite for effeminate indulgence and an imitation of that reckless extravagance which impoverished and enslaved the industrious people of foreign lands.

Such unrepublican desires would replace "those equal political rights" that were "the object and supposed reward of our Revolutionary struggle" with "a system of exclusive privileges conferred by partial legislation." In December 1840, after his defeat by William Henry Harrison, his last message left a warning that "a concentrated money power, wielding so vast a capital and combining such incalculable means of influence," would inevitably "prove an overmatch for the political power of the people themselves."[38]

In the previous March he had developed these themes in a long memo on the coming election. The purpose of this document was to provide guidance to the New York Democrats for the fall, but it also began to develop Van Buren's interpretation of American political history since the founding and of American civil sociology in the late 1830s.[39]

First and foremost, Van Buren was certain in March 1840 that the Whigs had outmaneuvered the Democrats in the recent state elections, which had gone very badly. The party in New York had rested on its laurels while the Whigs had presented "superior activity and better organization," working "all year round, both young and old, in season and out of season." But—in an echo of 1810 — they had also prevailed by "frauds at the election," by both "illegal votes" and "legal votes by illegal means." The great question of the day was, "Shall the will of the people be obeyed or shall it be defeated by sinister and unlawful means[?]" The Democrats would have to stand firm against such "corrupt means." "To preserve and promote the purity [and] freedoms of elections," he urged that "a democratic association be formed in each town in the state." By these efforts, he argued, the party would "oppose associations of men to associations of wealth." His prescriptions for party activity were built around a history of parties in the United States that would eventually be fully developed in his *Inquiry into the Origin and Course of Political Parties in the United States,* published after his death in 1862. At the core of this history lay the establishment of the first Bank of the United States, "the great lever of Hamiltonian corruption," and the challenge by Jefferson and Madison, defending the ideal of political equality and condemning the bank as "hostile to popular rights."[40]

But, beyond this history, his 1840 "Thoughts" developed a revealing commentary on Jacksonian attitudes toward contemporary civil society. The spreading "monopolies and corporate privileges of almost every description," Van Buren argued, threatened to trample "the rights of opinion and the known wishes of a majority of the people." Equally important, a host of other associations were aligned with the Whig opposition: "Nor are Banks the only class of corporation that have from time to time been enlisted in the same service[;] to the prejudice of learning and the dishonor of our literary and benevolent institutions, they are not infrequently made to play their parts in the great drama of resistance to the will of the people." Van Buren then directed his ire at the entire array of civil institutions that Alexis de Tocqueville saw as the foundation of American democracy: he was certain that "the associations which daily spring up amongst us" were automatically allied "with the dynasty of associated wealth," the Whig Party. Years later in his *Inquiry into the Origin and Course of Political Parties* he extended his thoughts with an acerbic comment on the content of the antebellum public sphere: "Any one who visits a common reading-room," he wrote, would note "the remarkable disparity in number between newspapers and other periodicals advocating Democratic principles and those which support the views of the money power and its adherents."[41]

Thus it might be said that Van Buren and Tocqueville arrived at equivalent interpretations of the course of history in the transition to democratic modernity: ancient feudal aristocracies might be destroyed by revolution, but in their place would emerge the web of associated individuals. In Tocqueville's construction, "An aristocracy cannot again be founded in the world, but I think that private citizens, by combining together, may constitute bodies of greater wealth, influence, and strength, corresponding to the persons of an aristocracy." But Van Buren and Tocqueville obviously took different lessons from that transmutation. Tocqueville saw the institutions of civil association as a bulwark against the state, or an alternative form of governance in the absence of a strong state. For Van Buren these institutions, in alliance with a strong state, threatened to undermine the will of the people and the legacy of the Revolution. In the dialect of New York politics, Van Burenites were the "Barnburners," so hostile to corporatons that they were analogous to the farmer willing to burn down his barn to smoke out the rats.[42]

In 1785 Henry Livingston had described the spring assembly election as a "hard tryal . . . between Demo and Aristo." Such had been the political structure of southeast Albany County before the Revolution, and the Revolutionary ground upon which the Demo emerged to contest the Aristo on equal terms, mobilized in committee and militia for national independence and equal rights. But already in the 1780s a web of public institutions in a reconfigured civil society was beginning to intervene in Columbia's struggle between Demo and Aristo. Each side would reach its own accommodation with this new culture of associated respectability, manifested in the papers, societies, lodges, and enterprises spreading from the new city of Hudson. A new configuration of civil society was emerging; an older understanding of an inseparable republican fusion of polity and society was giving way to a liberal understanding of private associations mediating between polity and society. At one time, this new definition of civil life had seemed a threat to the local aristocracy in Columbia. But, well before the 1830s, in Columbia and across the country, Democrats could see the forms of the new liberal understanding of civil society as the vehicles of a new aristocracy.[43]

Van Buren's animus against the "money power" and its "monarchical" aspirations certainly sprang from his early political experiences with both Columbia's aristocracy and the cadre of ruthless young Federalists, proxy warriors in press, court, and legislature for the rentier class, who used every means at their disposal to establish and maintain their grip on power. These men had forged the local links between old landed aristocracy and the new civil institutions. On the eve of the 1840 election Van Buren was forced to revisit these linkages—and humiliations—when in late October he received a letter from a Democratic notable in Hillsdale. The Whig paper in Hudson, the *Columbia Republican,* had dredged up the *Northern Whig's* old claim that Van Buren had abandoned his clients among the Livingston tenants at the 1813 trial; the Democrats were countering by circulating a broadside of an affidavit by John J. Shaver defending Van Buren's legal conduct.[44]

Of course, these events were of only local consequence, though of considerable volatility, as the history of the next few years would show. Van Buren's attack on "the associations which daily spring up amongst us," be they literary, benevolent, or otherwise, leads to a much larger problem, literally a paradox at the heart of America's construction of the public sphere in this settled interval between Revolution and Civil War. Van Buren and the Republican-Democratic tradition at large had reshaped the American public sphere by developing the means to defend popular, equal rights: partisan institutions, systems of political information, and strict codes of procedure. As far back as the rise of the Democratic Societies, New York Republicans had constructed party to monitor the exercise of power and to protect the people's rights. Americans were respected the world over, Van Buren wrote in his 1838 message, because "the rights of our citizens . . . are known to be guarded by a united, sensitive, and watchful people."[45]

But in clinging to this monitorial mode, Van Buren and the Barnburner Democrats had conceded a wide spectrum of public life to their opponents. Where the Democrats vigilantly defended the rights of the people, the Whigs could claim the laurels of reform. Whigs won the state election of 1837 in a landslide, a shocking "political tornado" fueled by the national bank crisis starting the previous August. One of their first priorities in 1838 was to repeal the Safety Fund banking system that Van Buren had crafted in 1829. Designed to stem the tide of corruption in bank chartering, the Regency managers of the Safety Fund had succeeded only in constricting statewide capital formation while channeling charters to Bucktail Democrats. Loco-Foco Democratic radicals, followed by western Antimasons, had been demanding reform of banking for several years, but it was the Whigs — led by newly elected governor William Seward — who took the credit for the new Free Banking Act, finally separating bank charters from the taint of corruption.[46]

The Whigs were, indeed, a party of improving projects. They had a vision of a progressively more advanced commercial and industrial society and, with that improvement, a wider and supportive moral reform; they mobilized two forces to achieve their ends. Tocqueville had seen the institutions of civil society as alternative agents of social action in the context of a weak state, but nineteenth-century Americans knew better. Whigs used these institutions in combination with the power of the state to achieve their ends; they sought through civil action to deploy state power to achieve their improving projects. If the new institutions of civil society had begun to constitute a flywheel between state and society after the Revolution, it was the Whigs who pursued this understanding, what has been defined as a "positive liberalism," pursuing an expansive liberty through the deployment of power. Democrats, led by Jackson and Van Buren, seeing the money power conspiring to undermine popular rights, pursued a policy of "negative liberalism," relentlessly seeking to protect liberty from power. Americans were caught in a paradoxical contest, in which any effort to act upon hard-won rights of self-government was immediately suspect as tending toward corruption, aristocracy, and monarchy.[47]

The result in the 1830s was an intensification of this paradox, perhaps to its apex. Whigs pursued their goal of a complex economy allied with an interventionist state in an explosion of associationalism. Democrats at large seem to have tended toward a suspicion of associationalism, given the taint of the wider connotation of Whig projects. Van Buren ruminated in the spring of 1840 that it was "obvious in my part of the state" that the Democrats had lost the edge in political skills, leaving everything to "their young men," and had "contented themselves with a few spirited meetings at the eve of the election" while the Whigs organized assiduously. Modern theories of civil society suggest that one of the benefits of civil society is the development of "social capital": skills in associated action that lead to wider positive social outcomes. In some measure, it might be argued that Jacksonian Democrats were actually losing "social capital" while Whigs — and others in the wider domain of "literary and benevolent institutions" — were fast developing it. In this wider domain that Van Buren consigned to the Whigs lay an array of long-emerging forces in the public sphere that transcended the simple problem of deliberative politics and distributive outcomes. Bracketed by Van Buren as "literary and benevolent institutions," the wider Whig orbit of improvement and reform encompassed important sites of persuasive culture as well as the politics of sensibility.[48]

LIMITS TO SENSIBILITY, BOUNDARIES TO EQUALITY

In Columbia County in the 1830s, projects of persuasion and sensibility in the public sphere were most obviously manifested in the county Temperance Society and the Hudson Infant School Society, elements of the wider reform movements riding the currents of religious revival that would have such far-reaching influences in American life. In each there was an element of coercive intervention by middling respectability, in each there was the promise of individual empowerment. These were, as we have seen, projects led by the county's Adams men and early Whigs. As there had been since the 1790s, there would be distinct limits on the range and reach of a politics of reform in Columbia County in the 1830s.[49]

Within this range and reach stood the cause of temperance, which by 1833 had taken hold across much of the county. Twenty-five village societies encompassed more than forty-six hundred members; temperance membership was stronger in freehold farming Whig-majority towns and in several Democratic towns (Canaan, Hillsdale, Kinderhook) that had seen a number of new churches established in the preceding years: town clerks and church deacons stood out among the local temperance officers. Membership in these societies doubled from 1832 to 1833, following a local awakening that brought a moderate increase in membership to churches across the region in 1832. The influence of this transformative phase of the Second Great Awakening was far more limited in Columbia and the Hudson Valley than in the other northern regions.[50]

The persuasive and benevolent projects that the Infant and Temperance societies represented were, in their wider northern manifestations, stepping-stones toward powerful redefinitions of society and the individual. At the heart of this new departure lay the "new measures" promoted by Charles Grandison Finney, who since 1824 had been preaching that individuals could have a part in their own salvation; from this optimistic departure the awakened turned their attention to human interventions to perfect the world, first manifested in the temperance movement. In July 1827 Finney had met with Lyman Beecher and other Reformed ministers in New Lebanon, a few hundred yards from the Tildens' farm, in a meeting traditionally seen as formative in the Second Great Awakening. From temperance, forged under the protective wing of the Whig orbit, northern reformers and perfectionists moved on to an array of societal problems, including most importantly the immediate abolition of slavery and the establishment of equal rights for women. These and many other reforms would be advanced well outside the channels of party; certainly the Democrats would have nothing to do with them, but neither would the Whigs.[51]

It was here that the nineteenth-century politics of sympathy, sensibility, and reform stalled in Columbia County and in the wider Hudson Valley, in sharp contrast to the movement's celebrated epicenters in the Burned-Over District of central and western New York, Ohio's Western Reserve, and eastern New England. Abolitionist sentiment was particularly slow to develop in Columbia. The Colonization Society had developed in a moderate way under National Republican leadership, and from the mid-1820s into the early 1830s local societies in Hudson and Hillsdale regularly reported to the national society. But the American Antislavery Society had no such sponsorship, and the classic minimalism of Dutch Yorker culture impeded its growth in Columbia. As of 1836, three years after the explosive growth of temperance sentiment that elsewhere formed the stepping-stone to abolition, there was one lone Female Antislavery Society in the entire county, located in Hudson, apparently the sole outcome of a failed effort to form a county society in 1835.

Another call in 1838 did produce a county society, with officers who had been subscribers and members of the Infant and Temperance societies, but little came of it, other than the establishment of another local society in Spencertown, which managed to send a few petitions to Congress in January 1839 opposing slavery in the District of Columbia and Texas statehood and supporting recognition for Haiti.[52]

Some children of Columbia did play an important role in New York's abolition effort. A few families in Chatham and Kinderhook that had employed free blacks but held no slaves, the "free households" of 1800, produced children who would become abolitionists of note, Elizabeth Cady Stanton and Henry G. Ludlow. They were part of the Columbia diaspora, however, and had no enduring connections to the county's political culture. The antislavery forces in Columbia were pitifully meager, isolated in the old Yankee squatter towns with a few adherents in Hudson City. The county historian writing forty years later could comment sarcastically that there were more officers in the county antislavery society than Liberty Party voters in 1840.[53]

Such limits on a politics of sympathy and reform had been evident at the turn of the century and would be a salient feature of Columbia's conservative political culture for decades to come. Three times between 1846 and 1869 voters rejected proposals to grant suffrage to free black men, in higher proportion than the antisuffrage vote in the state in general. Only in the Yankee freehold towns of Canaan and New Lebanon was there even a strong minority of support for black suffrage in 1846; in 1860 Canaan was the only town in the county to cast a majority for the black vote. Opposition was particularly high in the old former slaveholding towns along the river.[54]

Columbia's antiabolitionist sentiment was supported and articulated in Congress by Aaron Vanderpoel (James's younger brother), a leading Kinderhook Democrat who had once studied with the old Federalist Peter Van Schaack. Vanderpoel held the Eighth District seat in Congress between 1833 and 1841, where he was in close communication with Van Buren. As the struggle over abolitionist petitions developed from 1835, Vanderpoel worked to moderate southern militancy while simultaneously marginalizing the tide of northern antislavery petitions. Straddling the sectional fence, he claimed during the renewal of the gag rule in January 1840 to have "voted to receive their petitions" but then to have voted to "reject their prayer, nail them to the table, mingle them with the rubbish of your garret." He and "the great mass of the North" would, he assured the southern congressmen, "FAITHFULLY FULFIL THE COMPACT" recognizing slavery in the Constitution. Indeed, the abolitionist petitions from Spencertown and neighboring communities in Chatham had not been introduced by a New York congressman, but by John

Quincy Adams of Massachusetts, who relentlessly used hundreds of northern petitions to harass proslavery forces in Congress.[55]

In February 1837, when Adams introduced a petition from nine slave women in Fredericksburg, Virginia, Aaron Vanderpoel rose to speak, making crystal clear the Van Burenite definition of the civil boundaries in the revolutionary settlement, as grounded in what he called the "sacred compact of the Constitution." "The idea that slaves had a right to petition the American Congress," he began, was "too monstrous to justify any labored attempt at refutation," claiming to be more concerned that Adams be protected from any censure that might alienate northern voters. But he felt obliged to "say a few words as to the right of slaves to petition."

> A slave is not a citizen in the eye of the Constitution. His political existence is merged in that of his master. He cannot prosecute in your courts of justice; he cannot petition your legislative assemblies.

Here he paused to note that the assembly in New York had recently rejected the suffrage petitions of free blacks; Columbia's Democratic assemblymen voted with the majority against another petition for black suffrage a month later. He then addressed the question of a universal right of petition.

> Admit that the right of petition is preexistent to, and independent of the Constitution, the question recurs, whether it is not to freemen, and to *freemen alone,* that it attaches. The Constitution secures to the people peaceably to assemble and petition the Government for a redress of grievances. Had any one before today, ever dreamed that appellation of *"the people"* embraced slaves? ... Tell me not then that the right of petition to courts of justice, or legislative bodies, is a universal right; that it is not modified or limited by the laws and relations of society.

For Aaron Vanderpoel, the constitutional settlement forged and reforged in 1777, 1787, and 1821 was beyond debate: he would "no longer discuss" it. There were clear racial boundaries around this settlement, and its privileges were restricted to white "freemen."[56]

Thus when Van Buren celebrated the "perfect equality of political rights" in the American republic three weeks later at his inauguration, Vanderpoel had already reminded the public of the sharp boundaries around that "perfect equality." The Van Burenite Democratic vision of civil society had severe limits: white men were all equal, sharply differentiated from women and persons of color. But these free white men were to associate only for the purposes of defending their rights. All other forms of association were suspect, engines of corruption and coercion by which an illegitimate minority was working to impose the new aristocracy and monarchy of the "money power" or to subvert "free institutions." It has been suggested with some cogency that Van Buren envisioned partisanship in the 1830s, not as a two-party system of legitimate opponents, but as "constitutional," in the sense that three estates of eighteenth-century England had their constitutional place in the "mixed polity." In Van Buren's understanding of the American condition, however, only one party, the Democratic Party of the people, was legitimate, and all opponents were minority consolidationists bent on reestablishing aristocracy and monarchy by new means.[57]

Such a vision was clearly shaped by Columbia's struggles between Demo and Aristo in the post-Revolutionary decades, running down to the various corruptions at work in the legislature and elections at the hand of a Columbia Junto that lent its patronage to the persuasive agencies of "literary and benevolent institutions" in those same years. Except for the Kinderhook Law Society, a debating society of law clerks, which he had joined for a year or so, and some terms as a director of the Republican Bank of Hudson, Van Buren was a member of only one organization: the Democratic Party. Neither he nor any of the leaders of his Bucktail Regency was ever a Freemason. When the Antimasonic movement struck New York, both Moses Younglove (two months before his death) and Elam Tilden, his Old Republican advisers at New Lebanon, suggested that Van Buren might consider absorbing a movement attacking the powerful and secret society of which his arch-enemy De Witt Clinton had long been a grand master. Andrew Jackson's long Masonic affiliation precluded such an alliance for Van Buren, but there was an affinity between the Antimasonic fear of the "Masonic power" and Democratic fear of the "money power"; both drew upon deep-seated republican fears of threats to the rights of the sovereign people.[58]

Van Buren articulated this sense in terms seemingly derived from Rousseau's understanding of the general will, which he alluded to in his *Inquiry*. Younglove and at least three of his neighbors in New Lebanon would have derived such an understanding from their copies of the Albany edition of Rousseau's *Dissertation on Political Economy*, to which they had subscribed in 1797. Van Buren's public statements in the late 1830s were studded with invocations of the "national will," the "popular will," "the will of the people," and the threats to that will emanating from the "sinister and unlawful means" of the "money power" allied with "literary and benevolent institutions" and the "associations which daily spring up amongst us." Strict adherence to the procedures of party, regular nominations of caucus and convention, would protect that "popular will" against the machinations of such designing forces.[59]

But the intensity of Van Buren's notion of the contest of Democrats with the "money power" suggests that the condition of "crisis politics," seemingly settled since the end of the Revolution, lay just below the surface of the routines in which he worked. Self-conscious about being the first president without a direct connection to the Revolution, he constructed one for the party. In his "Thoughts" of March 1840 he drew a sharp and bright line between the Democrats and Whigs running back through the 1790s to the Revolution, a line that must have brought to mind stories of Kinderhook's Revolutionary struggles. If in 1803 Van Buren could joke about the Liberty Pole brawl in Kinderhook, he took a sterner view later in life. The "American people," he wrote, held dear "the republican principles for which their fathers fought." But the parties reflected enduring divisions that called into question the legitimacy—even national identity—of the Whigs. The division "of the people of the U States between two parties" was "undeniably" grounded "in . . . principles and objects, which are . . . identical with those for which the Revolution itself was waged." In Van Buren's account, the "Federalists of 1798" had been almost universally "Tories of the Revolution," but their policies of the 1790s, "excesses and apostacies from the principles of the Revolution," had raised up the "Old Republican Party of the U States," which had been drawn from "the Whigs of the Revolution" who "brought into the political field an enthusiastic devotion to its principles." The partisan struggles of the 1830s, then, were, not routine affairs, but a continuation of the crisis politics of "our glorious revolution." Every election, thus, was a potential constitutional crisis, when the people might lose their legitimate mandate—to control the government—to corrupt and illegitimate tories.[60]

Van Buren's thinking had powerful roots in the political culture in which he spent his earliest years, Kinderhook and Columbia in the 1780s and 1790s, where the politics of tory and whig elided with those of Aristo and Demo. Columbia County had made a troubled and precocious transition to partisan politics in the late 1780s and 1790s, in a milieu in which threats of political violence were numerous and real. Officers of the Revolutionary militias and members of the powerful Revolutionary committees had dominated county politics well into the 1790s, and, when county conventions began to meet in the wake of Jefferson's election, they mobilized large numbers of men. The political practices of the Revolution and the early Republic long endured. Down into the 1850s Columbia Democrats were noted for their at-large conventions, to which towns would send an unrestricted number of delegates. These meetings, the county historian wrote in the 1870s, "popular with the masses," were also "much preferred by the skillful politicians, who were the better enabled to mould and manipulate the public opinion." The meeting to which Van Buren was invited in 1844 was termed the "Mass Convention of

Democratic Electors of the County of Columbia." Mobilizing the electors in unrestricted numbers, these meetings could claim to be polls of the people at large and have a constitutional quality, above and beyond the routines of distributional deliberation. While they certainly shared these qualities with Democrats throughout the county, there was something in Columbia's volatile history of struggle between Demo and Aristo that stood in the way of the emergence of a liberal pluralism.[61]

WOMEN AND JACKSONIAN DEMOCRACY

With this history hovering in the air, and without the civil shelter provided elsewhere by a more self-confident Whiggery, those left outside the boundaries of the revolutionary settlement made only the slowest and most limited gains in claiming a space in public in the antebellum decades. Women, leasehold tenants, and African-Americans had to struggle against powerful countervailing inertia to widen their purchase in the civil society.[62]

The fate of the Hudson Infant School Society may stand as an example of the particularly limited circumstances of women in public in Jacksonian Columbia. In September 1829, forty women, including a few who had been members of Hannah Barnard's Benevolent Society, gathered in great enthusiasm to found a school for children of the poor under the age of six. The Hudson Lodge lent them the lower room in the Masonic hall, and the new society had the support of men of consequence in the city as well as the local Bible Society. When they issued their first annual report in October 1830, the women of the Infant Society announced that they had registered more than one hundred children and that forty or fifty were in regular attendance. They were happy to report that children unable to recite the alphabet when they entered were "now able to read in their Spelling books and Testaments"; the older children had "made great progress in all their studies": they could do the multiplication tables and "have quite a knowledge of geography." The members were a little nervous about their finances, since many of the students could not afford even the smallest amount of tuition, but they had hopes: "Our institution is in its infancy, our treasury is low," and they were getting by on "the noble generosity of strangers, through the influence of one of our dearest and most useful associates."[63]

Their second report was less optimistic. Louisa Macy, the secretary and treasurer, wrote that despite "opposition and embarrassment" they had "struggled through another year," hoping that their report would "awaken new interest, and enlist the feelings of those who have hitherto been indifferent to this useful Charity" and that they would "not apply in vain, to the friends of humanity." In January 1832 they considered running a fair to raise money, and in March they noted collections from the Presbyterians and the Baptists, but "the other societies declined taking up a collection." In April their finances were completely depleted, and the managers were faced "with such cheerless and disheartening prospects that we have seen scarcely a ray of hope to light our onward path." In late May 1832 they made the decision that "the school shall be given up." For the second time in a decade, a public initiative led by the women of Hudson had failed.[64]

The women of the Infant Society chose an inopportune moment to found their institution. Where the Federalist-Clintonian-Adams circle lending support to benevolent reform in Columbia had prevailed in years past, it crumbled in 1829. First, the Bank of Columbia collapsed, sending a financial shock throughout the county and marking the final and definitive end of the benevolent corruption of Elisha Williams and Jacob R. Van Rensselaer, both of whom pledged their support to the Infant Society. Elected a manager of the society in September 1829, Williams's daughter Abigail had to decline. Then in November the Adams men lost the assembly election to the Jacksonian political revolution. After the failure of the bank, Hudson's economy was in crisis, and, though signs of a new beginning were emerging, no one would step forward to save the Infant Society. One of the new Democratic assemblymen, Oliver Wiswall, began the rebuilding that year in establishing the Hudson Whaling Company. Whaling vessels sent out to the Brazilian and South Atlantic grounds and on to the Pacific brought back cargoes of oil and whalebone that would briefly restore Hudson's fortunes. But neither Wiswall nor his two Jacksonian partners were counted among "the friends of humanity" supporting the Infant Society.[65]

Between 1829 and 1833 the Clintonian-Whig orbit did succeed in establishing the temperance movement in Columbia, which certainly recruited a large number of women. But, if the spread of temperance was grounded in the moderate revivals that brought new membership to the county's churches in 1832, the revival made no difference to the Infant Society's fortunes, nor to other reform activities in Columbia that would have mobilized women. The antislavery effort was weak and truncated, though women in Hudson did take the lead in forming the first of two local auxiliaries. A related movement, the Female Moral Reform campaign against prostitution and "licentiousness," also made minimal headway in Columbia, with three auxiliaries formed by 1837 but only one reporting consistently through 1840. The county's three Female Moral Reform auxiliaries were confined in their reach, as they all were rooted in Congregational churches in the hill town villages of New Concord, Spencertown, and Canaan Center, outposts of Yankee-Whig reform sentiment and abolitionism.[66]

The Yankee towns were not, however, absolute bastions of female autonomy. Women's associations here, like the Hudson Infant Society, were situated within a domain of male initiative and sponsorship. A Female Charitable Society established in New Lebanon in 1814 derived its charge from the ministers of the Columbia Presbytery, in their mission of raising money "for the purpose of educating needy pious young men for the ministry." At New Concord, the Female Moral Reform secretary wrote in 1838 that their efforts were failing until the intervention of the Reverend Nathaniel Pine, the local Reformed minister, who that year was one of three men who issued a call for a countywide antislavery society. Even Shaker women increasingly were confined in their public roles. Following the death of Mother Lucy Wright in 1821, the Shaker leadership at New Lebanon was reorganized. After twenty-five years under the leadership of a sole woman, Shaker men asserted themselves, perhaps echoing the masculinizing of the politics of the "world" seen in the recent constitutional convention at Albany. The restructured leadership at New Lebanon would be collective and reflect the gendered division of labor in the wider society. Two male elders would attend to public affairs internal to the Shaker polity and with the "world"; two female eldresses would govern domestic arrangements and the affairs of women.[67]

Another tangent linked these hill towns indelibly to central texts in the rapidly developing women's literature of female sentimentality and stoic resignation. In 1810 Henry Whiting Warner left Canaan for New York City, where he became a prominent merchant and raised a family of daughters in considerable comfort. The themes of rising grandeur and collapsing desolation in Thomas Cole's *Course of Empire* would have had a particularly bitter resonance for the Warners, who might well have known Cole's patron, Luman Reed, a New York merchant who followed a path similar to Warner's, rising to great wealth from humble beginnings in Coxsackie and Hillsdale. While Reed died in 1836, barely even seeing the product of his patronage, Warner lost his fortune in the general economic collapse of 1837–1839, having to sell the farm in Canaan inherited from squatter forebears who had fought long and hard to gain their land. Originally a Federalist, Warner espoused an elite, moralistic Whiggery like that of Thomas Cole; in 1838 he published a conservative discourse on the American polity, *Inquiry into the Moral and Religious Character of the American Government*.[68]

His sudden impoverishment had a powerful impact on his two daughters, Susan and Anna Warner, who struggled to adjust to the reduced circumstances, eventually founding a school on a surviving piece of property on Constitution Island in the Hudson opposite West Point. Retreating behind the walls of an aristocracy of manners, as were their class peers throughout the country, but particularly along the Hudson, the Warners began to write sentimental novels to keep bread on the table. Though she had never liked the rough country world that she had encountered when she visited as a child, Susan Warner set her novels *Queechy* and *The Wide, Wide World* in her grandfather's Canaan. The focus of their narratives was the stoic endurance of a woman of sentiment, borne down by suffering at the hands of callous males. Here the heroine of *The Wide, Wide World,* Ellen Montgomery, built self-discipline in a condition of domestic suffering. The sentimental formula, it has been argued, allowed the forging of a sense of female agency in its action: women, faced with powerful forces of fate or the vicious male, determined their own outcomes by force of character. Working on novels in the 1860s and 1870s, works described by one scholar as conservative evangelical utopias, Susan Warner and her sister Anna spent long visits at the Traveler's Rest with Mary Rutherford Garrettson, the spinster daughter of Methodists Catherine Livingston and Freeborn Garrettson. One has to assume that there were other connections between the quietist mystical piety — and aristocratic withdrawal — of the Livingston-Garrettson connection and the message of stoic domesticity that the Warners perfected.[69]

The Warner sisters most certainly found the cause of their bitterly reduced world in the actions of Jacksonian men of affairs. In all likelihood they would have had biting things to say about their father's county neighbor, Martin Van Buren, whose own father served with their Warner and Whiting relations in the militia at Saratoga and would have met with them frequently in the public affairs of the county both during and after the Revolution. And they certainly knew of his central role in the most celebrated assault on elite female prerogatives of their era. If Jacksonian Columbia gave little space to women in public, the county's most famous native son contributed to this climate of public exclusion in his central role in a national scandal. The Peggy Eaton affair revolved around a beautiful woman and the structure of Jackson's cabinet; it also redefined the gender order of political culture in the national capital.

When he had arrived in Washington in 1821, Martin Van Buren was particularly unhappy with the "amalgamation" of parties that he saw under the hand of President James Monroe, leading to the collapse of the nominating role of the congressional caucus in 1824 and thus to the corrupt bargain. As John Quincy Adams took power, Van Buren set to work to undermine and destroy this entrenched National Republican establishment that had settled into Washington over the past two decades, using his party-building skills, his growing adherence to Old Republicanism, and his advocacy of the man of the people, Andrew Jackson. As Jackson began to settle into the presidency, Van Buren's orchestration of the Eaton affair sealed the transit of power, cultural and political.

Van Buren's role in the Eaton affair and his assault on the Washington establishment had roots running deep into his past, and to Columbia's political culture of Demo and Aristo. Van Buren knew many people when he arrived in Washington, but probably none went back as far as John Peter Van Ness, son of Judge Peter Van Ness of Kinderhook, for whose election to Congress Van Buren had worked so assiduously in the fall of 1801. But Van Ness had thrown away all Van Buren's hard work when he accepted an officer's commission in a local militia regiment and was expelled from Congress early in 1803. By 1821 Van Ness was long married to Marcia Burns, the poised, cultivated, and beautiful daughter of a wealthy local family; the Van Nesses became a fixture in Washington society. John was a man of affairs, president of banks, mayor of the city, and public benefactor. Marcia was one of the leading figures in Washington's glittering and polished women's salon society, which worked quietly and effectively as an informal public sphere in Washington's political culture, shaping the relationships among the men in federal office.[70]

Van Buren and Van Ness might well have formed a cordial relation as fellow sons of Columbia County, but the only surviving scrap of Washington correspondence between them was a curt and testy note from Van Ness in April 1830, involving Henry Middleton, whose wife had once been a popular figure in the Washington salon world. Middleton, from an ancient and distinguished South Carolina family, had served as the ambassador to Russia since 1820. Van Buren, as secretary of state, was recalling him from Saint Petersburg and sending out in his place John Randolph of Roanoke, the aging warhorse of Old Republicanism and a key player in the Richmond Junto that Van Buren had been courting for three years.[71]

The tensions apparent in this relationship reflected a struggle between Jackson and the old order that had been raging in Washington since the spring of 1829. Margaret Timberlake, a woman of great beauty but perhaps low virtue, married John Eaton, soon to be Jackson's secretary of war, on New Year's Day 1829, indecently soon after receiving news of her husband's death at sea, and the Washington respectability refused to recognize her in public. Jackson sympathized with the imperfect Peggy, and Van Buren—without any wife or daughter to influence or restrain him—also sided with her, and against John Calhoun, whose wife, Floride, was a leader of the salon establishment. The result of the Eaton affair, published far and wide across the country, was that Van Buren solidified Jackson's favor, and the established salon culture, a unique vehicle of women's influence in early Washington, was swept away.

Unfolding in exactly the years that the Hudson Infant Society was struggling and failing in its mission of mercy, Van Buren's role in the Eaton affair suggests the wider reach of a Jacksonian barrier against women in the public sphere, a barrier that seems to have been particularly strong in Jacksonian Columbia.[72]

THE ANTI-RENT WAR

By the late 1830s Martin Van Buren should well have been feeling the sense of postimperial desolation that suffuses the final paintings of Thomas Cole's *Course of Empire*. Certainly his loss of the presidency in 1840 was devastating. But he soon recovered sufficiently to carve out his own place in the Hudson Valley landscape, in the form of the Van Nesses' old estate in southern Kinderhook, which he renamed Lindenwald. Lost by the Van Ness family during the 1819 credit crisis, Van Buren had acquired the property in 1839 and had it prepared as a national politician's retreat. He settled in at Lindenwald in 1841, and from there he hoped to launch himself back into the presidency in 1844.[73]

The question of land would shape Van Buren's fortune on the national stage as well as others' lesser fortunes on the regional stage. His ambivalence on the question of the annexation of Texas would undermine his Democratic nomination in 1844, and four years later the unremitting hostility of the Polk administration would carry Van Buren to the unthinkable: a presidential nomination by a movement of dissident northern Democrats and Whigs, the Free Soil Party. Van Buren and the Free Soilers lost across the North in 1848 and lost in Columbia as well. But the Free Soil ticket did comparatively well in the Kinderhook region, the old King's District, and in the towns of Livingston Manor, winning outright in Stuyvesant, New Lebanon, and Taghkanic.[74]

Behind this Free Soil vote in Columbia County lay votes for a native son, but more importantly an era of tumult and strife, the final struggle against the power of the great landlords. The Free Soil movement in New York fed in great measure on the enduring exclusion of farming families throughout eastern New York from access to landownership and from a sense of full inclusion in the privileges of civil society that fee simple ownership of land might bring. Repeating the condemnations of earlier generations of tenants, the Anti-Renters of the 1840s assailed a system that left common leasehold occupants unsecured in and eventually bereft of the benefits of their improving labor on the land, the fruit of their toil. Such insecurity meant that improvements would not be made, and the wider community suffered. Thus when the Hudson *Gazette* complained in 1846 of a "manifest want of interest on the part of our FARMERS in the competition for prizes" at the Columbia County fair, the editor of the Albany *Anti-Renter* wrote of a recent conversation in which

he was told, "The houses, — the farms — the persons — the minds of Columbia farmers are, generally speaking, a full century behind their neighbors in
Dutchess County." The difference lay in "the blighting spirit of Land Monopoly," the *Anti-Renter* thundered, urging its readers:

> Go to the Canada line. Look at the prosperous villages and farm houses
> on the Republican side of it, and then examine the inactivity, hopelessness,
> and neglect exhibited on the British. [Freehold] Goshen and Orange are
> Republican — hence their harmony and prosperity. Hudson and Columbia
> are British — hence their discordance and decay. Root out old Tiger Jaws,
> and then talk of improvement.

Local men were equally militant. Echoing Benjamin Birdsall's manifesto of
1812, Experience wrote from Gallatin to the Albany *Freeholder:*

> Land is the life blood of the community, and therefore, it is the natural
> inheritance of every individual, and all have a natural right to its use. And
> it is the duty of the government to see that the strong, or wealthy, do not
> trample upon the rights of the weak, or poor, by purchasing the whole,
> and thereby making the poor, entirely dependent upon them, for their *first*
> means of sustenance.[75]

The immediate origins of the great Anti-Rent War lay in the year immediately preceding Van Buren's defeat in 1840. Once again, as in 1783, 1794,
and 1811, the death of a great landlord set off a challenge among the tenants.
Stephen Van Rensselaer, the Great Patroon of Rensselaerwyck, died in January 1839, and his heirs inherited great lands and great debts. Van Rensselaer
had built his popularity on his lenient enforcement of rents, but, if his sons
hoped to live the exalted life of the grand rentier, they needed to collect back
rents due. Between the summer and fall of 1839 the Anti-Rent movement
progressed from mass meetings to the melodrama of the Helderberg War, in
which crowds of tenants in the hills west of Albany turned back the sheriff's
posses until they were subdued by the state militia, sent by Governor William
Seward to enforce the law. By 1841 militant tenants were riding through the
hill towns of Albany, Delaware, and Rensselaer counties in arms, dressed as
"Indians," masked with feathers and calico dresses. If one wing of the Anti-
Rent movement, the Land Reformers, was committed to politics through
an associational culture fine-tuned in both the partisan and reform impulse
of the previous decades, another echoed the insurgent violence of 1812, the
1790s, and the 1750s. And, in assuming Indian identities, the Anti-Rent militants signaled their sense of being excluded from routine civil life. The respect-

ability reciprocated, hiding behind a military mobilization that again called the revolutionary settlement into doubt.[76]

Despite Columbia's being the focus of the earlier insurgencies, the Anti-Rent movement came late and was imported from Rensselaer County. The leadership on the east side of the Hudson was centered at West Sand Lake, led by Dr. Smith Boughton of the village of Alps, who was enlisted by the Anti-Renters to carry petitions to the assembly in 1843. In the next year Boughton opened a campaign to spread the message of Anti-Rentism, and, after meeting for several months with committees from the old Manor, in November 1844 he came down to the Manor, speaking with local men in Taghkanic, Copake, Ancram, and Hillsdale.[77]

Two outcomes spilled out from these meetings. First, an Anti-Rent organization was formed that November, the Taghkanic Mutual Association, one of a number of associations being formed that fall, which would be followed by a county organization in 1845. Second, Boughton was invited to return to Columbia in December. Coming soon after a series of confrontations of "Indians" and the county sheriff in the town of Copake, Boughton's appearance opened a drama that seemed to repeat the events of a half century before and blunted the force of the Anti-Rent movement. Boughton spoke in the guise of Chief Big Thunder to a large crowd at Smoky Hollow in southeast Claverack, just a few miles from where Sheriff Cornelius Hogeboom had been killed in 1791. Unfortunately, a young bystander was killed by stray pistol shots on the edge of the crowd, and Boughton was immediately accused of the murder. A wave of hostile opinion surged again several days later when another man was killed by Anti-Renters thirty miles to the north. Boughton and three of his associates were quickly arrested, and Hudson quickly became an armed encampment. A local Law and Order Association was reinforced by militia from Catskill, New York City, and Albany authorized by the new governor, Democrat Silas Wright. The armed might of the state marched out to Claverack and the Manor towns, snuffing out the Anti-Rent Indian militance.[78]

Indicted on charges of robbery and conspiracy against the sheriff's serving of writs, Smith Boughton's show trial at Hudson provided a stage for Columbia men whose stories stretched far into the past. Democrats, many of them linked by a long and tangled kinship, presided over both the trial and the prosecution. Democrat John W. Edmonds sat as the judge, and Attorney General John Van Buren led the prosecution, assisted by Theodore Miller, a son of Martin Van Buren's first legal partner, and by Henry Hogeboom, grandson of Sheriff Cornelius, killed in 1791. Opposing them, in Boughton's defense, stood Whig Ambrose L. Jordan, born in the neighborhood where Sheriff Hogeboom had been shot. During the trial tempers flared, and Van Buren and Jordan literally came to blows in the courtroom, for which they were duly charged and convicted. Less than a decade before, Jordan had stood with Edmonds and against Hogeboom to defend a number of journeyman shoemakers in Hudson on charges of illegal conspiracy to fix wages; their acquittal had been a minor landmark in the development of the right of labor to organize. But, if a county jury had looked favorably on the shoemakers' right to organize in 1836 and had shown considerable lenience to Benjamin Birdsall and John Reynolds in 1812, it was alarmed by "Indian" violence in the 1840s. Boughton was convicted at Hudson and sentenced to life imprisonment by Judge Edmonds; three years later the Finkle brothers of Taghkanic were similarly convicted for resisting a sheriff's prosecution on the Manor, and — relative to the outcomes in 1812 — they received a stiff three-year sentence.[79]

With the suppression of the Indians, the Anti-Rent movement entered into the murky field of New York's factional politics. The Anti-Rent associations organized nominating conventions in 1845 and 1846, which threw their weight to the Whigs. Elected with this new Anti-Rent support, Whig Governor John Young freed Smith Boughton and other Anti-Renters. But doubts quickly emerged over Anti-Rent's new Whig alliance. The Columbia Anti-Renters, inspired by George Henry Evans's land reform movement and the language of Free Soil, moved into alliance with the growing antislavery camp of dissident Van Buren Democrats. In Columbia County, the movement fusing political antislavery and Anti-Rentism was nourished by the *Equal Rights Advocate,* published in Chatham between 1846 and 1848. From thence would come Martin Van Buren's twenty-one hundred Free Soil votes in Columbia in 1848.[80]

Despite his connections to the cabal of Democrats who prosecuted Dr. Boughton, Martin Van Buren, perhaps after reviewing his part in the 1812 proceedings, had taken some creative steps to resolve the Anti-Rent struggle. In October 1844 he wrote to Silas Wright regarding a legal approach to ending the leasehold system by the same means that entail had been abolished in the 1780s: privileges of quasi-feudal ownership might be enjoyed by the current holders but made nontransferable to subsequent generations. This and a series of other creative solutions failed to solve the conundrum of a widely unacceptable form of perpetual leasehold's protection by the constitutional right of property. As Charles McCurdy has demonstrated, New York's political class never found a legal solution to this puzzle. In the end, it would be Justice Henry Hogeboom, grandson of the sheriff killed in Hillsdale in 1791, who passed the final verdict, invalidating the Anti-Rent Act of 1860 as in violation of the doctrine of vested property rights.[81]

By the early 1850s, however, something of an accommodation had emerged on the old Manor lands. The Livingston descendants, with landlords throughout the region, were uncertain of the future legal status of their grants, frightened by the potential for further violence, and spurred by 1847 legislation taxing receipts on rented land, enacted following the report of a legislative commission led by Samuel J. Tilden. The landlords suddenly arrived at the solution that Alexander Hamilton had worked out for the Van Rensselaer claimants to lands in Hillsdale in 1804, in weeks before his death at the hands of Aaron Burr: they began to sell out. In the 1830s the Livingstons had made as many as two hundred land sales to other parties, and between 1845 and 1855 they made almost four hundred more, with a century peak of fifty-one sales in 1847. By 1850 almost four-fifths of the ancestral 160,000-acre Livingston claim had been sold. These sales were financed by mortgages, which put former tenants under a more onerous obligation. But these obligations were temporary, and, as they were undertaken in the late 1840s, there were signs of fundamental change in the old leasehold towns.[82]

Given the insecurity of life-lease tenure, civic institutions had long been very sparse in the old Livingston Manor towns. As of 1845 the Livingston region had by far the fewest churches in the county relative to population, and in the eighty years between 1764 and 1844 only three churches had been formed in the towns on the old Upper Manor. All three were Methodist, two formed as branches of the south Hillsdale church and another in Taghkanic on land donated by one of the Livingstons. But between 1847 and 1855 five new churches were established in these towns: Evangelical Lutheran in Ancram and Taghkanic, Presbyterian and Methodist in Ancram, Episcopal in Copake. Anti-Rent organization and politics seem to have played at least a small role in this institution building. When a meeting was called in Ancram in November 1846 to establish an Evangelical Lutheran church, Abraham F. Miller, active in the Anti-Rent conventions in 1845, served as secretary. Early the next year Anti-Renter Jacob F. Suydam was appointed to the three-man building committee that oversaw the rapid construction of the church building, and in July he was elected a trustee of the new church. In 1848 Suydam proved his local popularity by standing as the Free Soil candidate for the assembly, receiving 150 more votes than did Van Buren in the county's southern district. In 1855 George I. Finkle and John Bain, leaders among the Taghkanic Anti-Renters and elected to local office several times in the 1840s, were among those who founded the Evangelical Lutheran church at center Taghkanic, the first church ever formed at this village. Finkle, kin to the Finkle brothers imprisoned for challenging the sheriff in 1847, chaired the meeting and was elected one of the first trustees of the church. For more than a century Lutheran families on the Manor had gone up to Churchtown, just over the Claverack line, for services. Now, as the long struggle over the lease-hold began to fade away, they and others on the old Livingston domain began to feel secure enough to invest in the basic institutions of American public life.[83]

BLACK COLUMBIA IN THE PUBLIC SPHERE: TOWARD FORT WAGNER

On July 5, 1828, the free "descendants of Africa" in the town of Chatham as-sembled to celebrate the first anniversary of the final end of slavery in the state of New York. If the abolition of slavery in New York had been voted in 1799, it was not until 1827 that the formal status of slave was finally erased from law. Following a salute of fifteen guns, the freed people of Chatham marched in a procession led by their marshal, Thomas Anthony, "mounted and in full uni-form," from a local tavern to a nearby grove of trees. Addressed by David Car-shore, a local white lawyer, they then returned to the tavern for "an excellent dinner." Here there were toasts to emancipation and the "free principles" of the "white people of the State of New York," all conducted with "the utmost order and decorum."[84]

For decades to come black Columbians would celebrate July 5 in meet-ings that echoed the past and expressed increasingly bitter feelings about the present. Beginning only seventeen years after the celebrations of Pinkster had been suppressed in Albany, these gatherings certainly reflected a long tradi-tion of annual assemblies running back into the enslaved past. But by the late 1830s and the 1840s the tradition of African-American assembly turned from celebration to protest. Former slaves in the state of New York demanded the full equality in public life denied to them by the constitution of 1821 as well as the end of slavery across the nation. Working against the material constraints that their minimal civil freedoms allowed, they developed their own voice in the domain of persuasion in the public sphere, demanding a formal place in the domain of deliberation.[85]

These efforts were particularly difficult in Yorker-Jacksonian Columbia. This was the realm of Congressman Aaron Vanderpoel, who was mocked in the New York *Colored American* as "the Kinderhook roarer" for his defense of the gag rule, and of course of Van Buren himself. Van Buren was the quint-essential "northern man, with southern principles," one of the paper's black correspondents wrote after passing through Kinderhook, and his Washington allies were on a par with "the sultan of Constantinople, or the autocrat of St. Petersburg." If the Democratic establishment of the county was ranged against them, Whigs in Hudson might have been somewhat more sympathetic, if only to protect their labor force, acting in 1838 to free a black Hudson sailor from a Virginia jail.[86]

This sailor, Prince Matice, occupied a relatively privileged position in the occupational hierarchy of Columbia's men of color. In 1850 more than four-fifths of the black men in Columbia County still worked as agricultural laborers, and most of the rest as sailors (or "boatmen"), gardeners, or waiters, cooks, and musicians in Hudson's hotels. A distinct surplus of women to men among Hudson's people of color strongly suggests that a considerable number of women were in domestic service. A small number of men worked as barbers. Among these men William H. Greene, of 154 Warren Street in 1851, owned as much as twenty-two hundred dollars in real estate, and Martin Cross, across the river at Catskill, was known to the credit agency Dun and Company as the "King of negroes in this part of the country." But such men of property were the rare exception, and for many of Columbia's blacks the reality was of the grinding poverty of Kinderhook's Guinea Hill, where black families lived in "huts . . . of very rude construction, some them partly underground." Such rural circumstances would have been particularly typical in Columbia. Black population all along the valley was either stable or declining in numbers between 1820 and 1860, but in Columbia, as in Dutchess to the south, these shrinking numbers matched an enduring rural isolation. The contrast was particularly evident compared with Rensselaer County to the north. In Hudson, the county seat of Columbia, the free black population peaked in 1820 at 290 people, and for the next forty years Hudson's proportion of the county's black population never rose above 20 percent. By contrast, if Rensselaer's black population was similarly static, the free black population in the city of Troy grew significantly over these four decades, encompassing more than 40 percent of the county's blacks in 1840 and almost 60 percent in 1860, and Albany's urban concentration of blacks was even higher. Despite being systematically excluded from the better-paying occupations in any of these cities, the relative economic growth and dynamism of Troy and Albany brought black migrants; Hudson's stagnation made it a poor choice.[87]

Population growth or stagnation shaped the path of African Americans in these places into the public sphere. The region's earliest black institutions, Albany's school society and African Baptist church, had been established in 1816 and 1823, and an African Association by 1827. Troy followed in the next decade with an African Female Benevolent Society, a Mental and Moral Improvement Association, and a black Presbyterian church and associated schools all formed in 1833 and 1834. In Columbia such a presence in the public sphere would develop more slowly. While there probably were black societies, no record of them survives; the first black church in Hudson, the Wesleyan Methodists, would form only in 1843, followed by a second in Kinderhook in 1855. Similarly, the black communities in Albany and Troy, inspired by the establishment of the militant voice of the *Weekly Advocate* (subsequently the *Colored American*), published in New York City by Samuel Cornish and Charles Ray, entered the print public sphere in the early 1840s. In Albany, Stephen Myers and others edited the *Northern Star and Freeman's Advocate* (later *The Elevator*); among a series of financially pressed publications in Troy in the 1840s, Henry Highland Garnet, minister to the Liberty Street Presbyterian Church, helped to edit first the *National Watchman* and then the *Clarion*.[88]

But the Hudson black community had access to print and acted upon it. Early in 1837 black Hudsonians probably began to receive copies of the New York *Weekly Advocate* from Martin Cross at Catskill, who had signed on as Samuel Cornish's local agent that January. In September 1837 Cross recorded $10.50 in subscriptions and donations from Hudson, and in 1839 he made contributions to the New York Committee of Vigilance, formed to stem the tide of kidnappings by southern slavecatchers. These first tentative steps beyond the household into public life were bound up with a wider mobilization of African Americans in New York State, galled by residual payments due for manumission by certain freed persons and by their nearly total disenfranchisement under the terms of the 1821 constitution. In Columbia County in 1835 there was a total of fourteen black voters, probably fewer than 4 percent of the black men over the age of twenty-one, where perhaps 90 percent of Columbia's white men were listed as voters; throughout the state the numbers were roughly similar.[89]

This political mobilization began in New York City in the winter of 1837. Hundreds of black men and women signed three petitions — each more than twenty feet long — asking for repeal of residual slave laws, for jury trials for accused fugitive slaves, and for the enfranchisement of all black men in the state. New York City's petitions were followed by others from Albany, Greene County, and elsewhere; Columbia's assemblymen voted with the majority to deny the Albany petition. In the wake of this defeat, further efforts led by Henry Highland Garnet and others in New York stalled until 1839, when momentum began to build for a state convention to meet in Albany in August 1840. When earlier in the 1830s a series of national conventions of African Americans had met in Philadelphia and New York, Hudson had not been able to send any delegates, but they joined the new movement for a state convention in 1840. William Van Alstyne of Hudson was appointed to the convention's committee of correspondence, and he and eight others went up to Albany as delegates. Although none of them was appointed to convention committees, these Hudson delegates were witness to three days of careful deliberation aimed at overturning the 1821 disenfranchisement. At the close of three days of debate, the convention declared the ideal of equality set forth in the Declaration of Independence "consonant with reason and revelation" and that "one of the distinctive and peculiar features of republicanism, is, that rights are to be guaranteed and extended without arbitrary and unnatural distinctions." The denial of such "equal participation in the privileges and prerogatives of citizenship" to black New Yorkers was "a fruitful source of unnumbered and unmitigated civil, literary, and religious wrongs." They saw "great hope for the politically oppressed in the their OWN exertions, . . . appealing to the just sentiments of those in political power." The convention's last resolution was a stirring trumpet call for inclusion in the body politic:

> Resolved, That this country is our country; its liberties and privileges were purchased by the exertions and blood of our fathers, as much as by the exertions and blood of other men, the language of the people is our language; their education our education; the free institutions they love, we love; the soil to which they are wedded, we are wedded; their hopes are our hopes; their God is our God; we were born among them; our lot is to live among them; and be of them; where they die, we will die; and where they are buried; there will we be buried also.[90]

The fundamental purpose of the Albany convention was to revitalize the petition campaign, and by the following February at least fourteen petitions, signed by more than two thousand people, had been presented to the assembly, which once again summarily buried them in committees. Garnet, who had chaired the petition committee, turned his attention to another convention, to meet in Troy in August 1841. The concluding "Address to the Electors" carefully dissected the paradox of inequality in a political community: "If you combine equals with unequals, the whole must be unequal." "The people of our State," they argued "are a whole, made up of individuals, whose relations to each other and to the whole people are indestructably equal." In its "proscription" of forty-five thousand African-Americans the state "inflicts a wound upon herself." By paralyzing "the energies of any portion of the people," the state "breaks in upon the general order, and sends in so far, confusion and disorder into the whole system." The entire fabric of social and political life in the state of New York would be strengthened and invigorated by the grant of the franchise, "that right, the possession of which is the living principle, the main spring of a government."[91]

While the leadership of the convention and the petition movement had rested with the men from New York, Albany, and increasingly Troy, the Hudson black community did its part. At a meeting convened at the Baptist meeting room in the winter of 1840–1841, the "colored citizens of Hudson" were addressed by local men, including one of the local delegates to the Albany convention. Joseph Pell, a Hudson laborer, celebrated the arguments made by Federalists John Jay, Abraham Van Vechten, and Jonas Platt in favor of black suffrage at the 1821 constitutional convention. A petition was drawn up and started into circulation, eventually garnering 82 signatures, quite an accomplishment in a community with perhaps 150 adult men and women. When the petitions failed to move the state assembly, the organizers of the Hudson meeting joined the call for the Troy convention, and four went as delegates, three being designated as a corresponding committee for the county.[92]

As the national convention movement was revived and met sporadically in more distant locations, starting with the 1843 convention in Buffalo, the men from Hudson could not afford to attend; only a few of them were able to attend the 1847 national convention in Troy. Rather, their attention was increasingly devoted to more local ventures in the public sphere. The Wesleyan Methodist church established in Hudson in 1843 certainly had its origins in the flurry of community building that had been at work since 1837; three of its first five trustees had signed the call for the 1841 Troy convention. These Methodists and the suffrage convention activists must have had a leading role in the conventions of the Union Temperance Society in Kinderhook in 1843 and Hudson in 1845, each of which drew as many as a thousand members from New York, New Jersey, Massachusetts, and Connecticut. In 1848 two of the Hudson convention men, Joseph Pell and Chauncey Van Hoesen, with others from Chatham, Spencertown, and Kinderhook, helped to organize the Union Temperance meeting at Great Barrington, over the state line in Massachusetts; the grand marshal, Lewis Jackson of Claverack, had signed the 1841 convention call.[93]

The Great Barrington meeting took up a charge regarding temperance delegated from the 1847 national convention that had met the previous year in Troy. It also must have had an electric, radicalized spirit. The national Troy convention had sounded the alarm against slavery in the South, had issued a report on the need for a "National Press and Printing Establishment for People of Color," and had debated whether it should "recommend to our people the propriety of instructing their sons in the art of war." In New York

State there were equal grounds for militance on the issue of suffrage, which had once again been defeated two years previously, in a statewide constitutional referendum. The lead speaker at Great Barrington was Henry Highland Garnet of Troy, who was increasingly impatient with the civil condition of African Americans both south and north. That spring he had addressed the Troy Female Benevolent Society in a speech, *The Past and Present Condition, and the Destiny, of the Colored Race,* in which he contrasted a glorious African past with a "humiliated and oppressed" condition in contemporary America. By the summer of 1848 this address was at the printers in Troy, as was his powerful *Address to the Slaves of the United States of America,* bound with David Walker's *Appeal,* in which he urged the slaves of the South: "Arise, arise! Strike for your lives and liberties." When Garnet had first delivered his address to the convention in Buffalo in 1843, he had almost come to blows with Frederick Douglass, who still stood for moral suasion and peaceful means. But in 1848 Douglass was of a similar mind, announcing in the *North Star* the imminent publication of Garnet's *Address* and reporting on his role at the Liberty Party convention in Buffalo that June. Douglass also reported that after the convention Garnet was assaulted and thrown off the railway cars, seventeen days before his engagement in Great Barrington.[94]

Shaped by his increasingly militant position and recent traumatic experience, Garnet's address to the temperance meeting in Great Barrington must have had a powerful impact, with enduring consequences. His increasing frustration with American politics, compounded by his assault on the Buffalo rail line, was turning Garnet toward a radical separatism. In the ensuing decade he would turn his back on America, celebrating the founding of the Liberian republic, advocating black emigration, and himself embarking for Britain and then Jamaica. This radical separatist turn must have been on his mind in July 1848, when he addressed the Great Barrington convention, and some among his audience would have taken inspiration from his words. Chauncey Van Hoesen, a whitewasher from Hudson, had been involved in both the 1841 and 1847 Troy conventions, was on the committee of arrangements in 1848 at Great Barrington, and joined the call for a convention in Albany in 1855. In 1870 Van Hoesen would join a movement to found an all-black college in the Hudson Valley to be named after Toussant L'Overture, the great leader of the Haitian republic.[95]

Other Troy delegates from Hudson and Claverack were among the organizers at Great Barrington in 1848, as was a Great Barrington delegate to Troy whose family had connections running back to eighteenth-century Kinderhook. Othello Burghardt was from a clan of African American families descended from a slave named Thomas Burghardt, who had been settled in the

Housatonic Valley by a Dutch farmer from Kinderhook who had been deeply involved in the early land struggles with the Van Rensselaers. Thomas gained his freedom after service in Colonel Ashley's regiment of Berkshire militia; his grandson Othello in 1811 married Sarah Lampman, remembered by her grandson as "a thin, tall, yellow and hawk-faced woman" originally from Hillsdale. This child, born in 1868 and brought up in his Burghardt grandparents' household, was William E. Burghardt Du Bois. In a lifetime in the public sphere, W. E. B. Du Bois would carry Garnet's militance into the second half of the ensuing century; one has to wonder whether Othello Burghardt conveyed to his grandson some of the fire of Garnet's message of 1847 and 1848.[96]

Certainly such militancy shaped the operations of the underground railroad in Columbia County, where stations in Hudson, Chatham, and Austerlitz fed fugitives coming up the river from New York. It also must have contributed to African American action when war finally came. White Columbia, in its Jacksonian conservatism, was ambivalent about the coming of the war; an effort to "raise a full regiment in Columbia county" foundered in the early fall of 1861. But blacks in the county took the first opportunity to join the fight against slavery. Early in 1863 Colonel Robert Gould Shaw of Boston raised the first regiment of black soldiers enlisted for the Union Army, the Fifty-fourth Massachusetts. That spring Shaw had reason to be in Berkshire County, just east of Columbia, since he was courting a Lenox girl, and they briefly honeymooned there before heading south with his regiment. Company A of the Fifty-fourth Massachusetts was raised in Berkshire, and along with a Burghardt cousin—who was killed in the Fifty-fourth's assault on Fort Wagner on the Carolina coast—Columbia men from Hudson and Chatham joined this company as well as Company C. Family connections among the Jacksons, Livingstons, Groomers, Hills, and Van Alstynes linked the ranks of the Fifty-fourth with the men who had organized meetings and institutions in the Hudson black community. Among them were Franklin Livingston of Hudson, whose father had signed the call for the 1841 Troy convention and served as one of the first trustees of the Hudson Wesleyan Methodist Church; he was wounded in the assault on Fort Wagner with Company A. Samuel Jackson, who was living with Chauncey Van Hoesen's family in 1860, served in Company C. All told, twenty-five black Columbians served in the Fifty-fourth Massachusetts, making the ultimate claim for themselves, their kin, and all Americans, to an equal place in civil life in the American republic.[97]

APPENDIX

DRAMATIS PERSONAE

This book introduces the reader to a host of relatively little-known people. This set of minibiographies is intended to sort out some of their identities and relationships.

MATTHEW ADGATE (1737–1818) arrived in the hill settlements from Connecticut in the 1760s. He played a key role in having the King's District established in 1772 and emerged as the region's most powerful populist Clintonian leader during the Revolution and the following decades. Translating his power into land grants, he resettled in the Lake Champlain region about 1800. His son ASA ADGATE (1767–1832) was elected to Congress in 1814.

HANNAH BARNARD (circa 1754–1825), with her husband Peter, a carter by trade, was part of the Quaker emigration from Nantucket that settled in Hudson in the 1780s. She was active in the spiritual and organizational life of the Hudson Monthly Meeting and the Nine Partners Quarterly Meeting, preaching and serving on committees. After challenging the peace testimony of Quakers in London during a trip to the British Isles, she was disowned by the Hudson Meeting in 1802. In 1811 Barnard organized the first women's organization in Columbia County, the Hudson Female Benevolent Society, and nursed it along through hard times for about eight years. She was known for her proto-Unitarian theology, her wit, and her sparkling intellect.

A series of BENJAMIN BIRDSALLS run through this story. Though there are conflicting accounts, they appear to have been father, son, and grandson. COLONEL BENJAMIN BIRDSALL (1743–1828) was born into a Dutchess Quaker family recently removed from Long Island. Expelled from the meeting for his active role in the Revolution — he commanded a regiment of levies — Birdsall settled in Hillsdale, joined the Temple Lodge, and led the petition against the Van Rensselaers in 1789. A pointman for the Genesee Company of Adventurers in the assembly in the early 1790s, he was a leading Republican in the county into the next decade. His son, BENJAMIN BIRDSALL, JR. (1767–1861), was a tenant leader in the Copake neighborhood in Great Lot No. 1 of the Upper Manor. In the late 1790s he was a leader in the tenant insurgency against the Livingstons, after which he became a stalwart of the county Republican committee and the Vernon Lodge in Hillsdale. In 1811 Benjamin, Jr., led a second campaign against the Livingston title, in close association with Martin Van Buren, which resulted in his indictment for conspiracy in 1814. In 1816 these two Benjamin Birdsalls, with a number of other relations, moved west to Chenango County. The grandson, MAJOR BENJAMIN BIRDSALL III (1786–1818), was farming land rented from Stephen Van Rensselaer at Watervliet in Albany County when war broke out in 1812. Raising a rifle company that fall, Birdsall served with distinction in the Fourth United States Rifle Regiment, was seriously wounded, and — retained in federal service — was killed by a soldier at the Greenbush barracks in 1818.

SAMUEL EDMONDS (1760–1826) served in the Continental ranks during the Revolution and arrived in Hudson with little but his name. By the 1790s he was well established in trade, a leading Mason, and trusted Federalist. His son JOHN W. EDMONDS (b. 1799) studied law with Martin Van Buren and started the Democratic *Gazette* in 1824. In the late 1830s he was practicing law in New York City, and in 1845 he was the presiding judge at the Smith Boughton Anti-Rent trial.

JACOB FORD (1744–1837) led companies of Hillsdale militia on a series of campaigns during the Revolution, including Saratoga in 1777 and the defense of Cherry Valley in 1778. In the assembly in the 1780s, he and Matthew Adgate were condemned by Alexander Hamilton as "a couple of New England adventurers . . . of *the leveling kind*." By the mid-1790s the complexities of land politics led him into an alliance with Peter Van Schaack and the Federalists, for which he was rewarded with a county judgeship. Later in life he was a leading member of the Baptist church at Red Rock, Austerlitz.

ELEAZER GRANT (1748–1806), one of the Connecticut settlers in the Mawighnunk Patent, was the quartermaster of the Seventeenth Regiment and then a lieutenant in the New York Line. A founder of the Unity Lodge in 1786, he led a Federalist faction in New Lebanon with WILLIAM POWERS, served as Canaan's first postmaster, and was involved with the Albany-to-Canaan Turnpike. As a justice of the peace he held hearings regarding the Shakers in the 1780s and in 1800.

PIETER MEES HOGEBOOM was born in a family that settled in Claverack in the 1690s. A householder in Claverack by the 1710s, by 1730 he had resettled on Indian land in northwest Connecticut, returning to Claverack in 1748. While in Connecticut his daughter Annatje married Stephen Ashley of Sheffield, Massachusetts, and inherited a young slave girl from her father. After suffering a reign of abuse in the Ashley household, this woman, ELIZABETH (or MUMBET FREEMAN, 1742–1829), enlisting the legal help of Theodore Sedgwick of Stockbridge, won her freedom in 1781. In Claverack, Annatje's nephew STEPHEN HOGEBOOM (1741–1814) emerged as a Republican assemblyman and senator who supported the Livingston Merchant's Bank in 1805; his daughter Catherine married General Samuel B. Webb. His cousin Albertje Hogeboom married Peter Van Ness in 1766; her older brother CORNELIUS HOGEBOOM (1739–1791) was appointed county sheriff in 1789 and in October 1791 was shot dead in the Claverack Road while attempting to serve a writ of ejectment in southwest Hillsdale. Cornelius's son JOHN C. HOGEBOOM (1768–1840) was appointed in his place and soon emerged as a leading county Republican; his daughter CATHERINE married Martin Van Buren's brother, Abraham. His son HENRY HOGEBOOM (1809–1872) carried the family grudge against insurgent tenants far into the nineteenth century, joining Attorney General John Van Buren to prosecute Anti-Rent leader Smith Boughton for a murder that took place within a mile or two of where his grandfather was shot in 1791, and as justice of the New York Supreme Court overturning the new Anti-Rent Act in two decisions in 1860.

GEORGE HOLCOMB (1791–1856) was a tenant farmer in Stephentown, just north of New Lebanon, whose fifty-one-year diary provides a wealth of detail about everyday life in the eastern New York hill towns.

WILLIAM JORDAN (1751–1833) and AMBROSE LATTING (1750–1800) were neighbors in southwest Hillsdale, where their families were members of the Baptist church that Latting built in 1787–1788. Jordan was a regular member of the Republican committees, and Latting was known for his more militant leanings, joining the 1789 protest against the Van Rensselaer claim and leading the insurgency against the Livingstons in 1798 with Benjamin Birdsall, Jr., for which, apparently, he was excommunicated by the Baptists. His namesake AMBROSE LATTING JORDAN (1789–1865) studied and practiced law in Norwich and Cooperstown with various Birdsalls before returning to Hudson to edit the *Columbian Republican* in support of De Witt Clinton. In the 1830s he represented striking shoemakers in a notable case, and in 1845 he defended Smith Boughton at the Anti-Rent trial.

JAMES LANTMAN, or LAMPMAN, was a freeman of color living in Great Barrington in 1800. It is likely that he was the freed slave of the Lampman family of Copake, who had held three slaves in 1790. He might have been the father of SARAH LAMPMAN (1793–1877), described as being born in Hillsdale (just north of Copake), who married OTHELLO BURGHARDT (1791–1872) in Great Barrington in 1811. Othello was the son of Jacob Burghardt, brought from Kinderhook as a slave but freed in Massachusetts with his service in the Revolution; he was a delegate to the National Convention of Colored People in Troy in 1847 and involved in the planning for the 1848 convention in Great Barrington, where Henry Highland Garnet delivered a keynote address. Sarah and Othello were important figures in the early life of their grandson, W. E. B. DUBOIS (1868–1963), America's seminal black historian and activist.

LIVINGSTONS: Two branches of this great landlord family played a dominant role in the public life of Columbia County. They were descended from ROBERT LIVINGSTON, a Scottish immigrant who, arriving in New York City in 1673, made a vast fortune in land and trade. Though intermarried with other of the New York gentry families, his eighteenth-century descendants fell into a series of competing clans, each relatively distinct in its affiliations and united in its politics. In Columbia County, two of these clans were led by first cousins, living on and from the proceeds of what were known as the Upper Manor and the Lower, or Clermont, Manor.

ROBERT LIVINGSTON, JR. (1708–1790), the "Third Lord of the Manor" after the first Robert, owned the entire UPPER MANOR, running from the Hudson River east to the Massachusetts line. His eldest son, PETER R. LIVINGSTON (1737–1794), had been disinherited in 1771, and at Robert's death in 1790 the Upper Manor was divided into a series of east-west–running "Great Lots" (see Map 3). WALTER LIVINGSTON (1733–1797) received the northern Great Lot No. 1, where he had a great house named Teviotdale; when he went bankrupt with the collapse of William Duer's speculations, several complex transactions kept this land for his oldest son, HENRY WALTER LIVINGSTON (1768–1810). Lot No. 2 was given to ROBERT CAMBRIDGE LIVINGSTON (1742–1794), and Lot No. 3 to HENRY LIVINGSTON (1753–1823,) who took up the ironworks at Ancram. JOHN LIVINGSTON (1750–1822), the father of ROBERT LEROY LIVINGSTON (1778–1836; known in the *Bee* as "Crazy Bob"), inherited the southernmost Lot No. 4, where he built a house called Oak Hill. The deaths of Robert, Jr., the third lord, and his son Robert Cambridge set the stage for land struggles of the 1790s, and the death of Henry Walter emboldened the Manor tenants on Lot No. 1 to challenge the Livingston title in 1811. Opportunists in politics, the Upper Manor Livingstons were distrusted by Governor George Clinton during the Revolution but entered into an alliance with the Clintonian Republicans from 1792 to 1798, when they became staunch Federalists.

ROBERT ROBERT LIVINGSTON (1718–1775) held the LOWER MANOR, called CLERMONT, and through his wife, MARGARET BEEKMAN, had extensive land and influence to the south in Dutchess County. During the Revolution, with her husband dead and her eldest son, ROBERT R. LIVINGSTON, JR. (1746–1813), in New York, Philadelphia, and Paris in the service of the Continental government, Margaret was the head of Clermont Manor, including during the fall of 1777, when the house was burned by a British raiding party. Robert R. Livingston, Jr., was one of the most distinguished men in New York State, signing the Declaration of Independence, helping to negotiate the Peace of Paris, serving as chancellor of equity for the state from 1777 to 1801 and ambassador to France in 1801–1804, when he negotiated the Louisiana Purchase. A cousin and son-in-law, EDWARD P. LIVINGSTON (1779–1843), served as his secretary in Paris and for many years in the state senate; in 1831 he escorted Alexis de Tocqueville at the July Fourth celebration in Albany. Robert's brother EDWARD (1764–1836) was mayor of New York when a scandal in the city finances impelled his move to New Orleans, from where he served in the House of Representatives and Senate and then in Andrew Jackson's cabinet. Their sisters appear in this story as much as or more than they do, however. JANET (1743–1828) married General Richard Montgomery, killed at Quebec in December 1775. GERTRUDE (1757–1833) married Morgan Lewis, who served as governor from 1804 to 1807 as the head of the Republican Livingston faction. MARGARET (1749–1823) married Thomas Tillotson, a close associate of Lewis; she was an important influence in the life of her younger sister CATHERINE (1752–1849), who rebelled against the family tradition when she married Methodist itinerant Freeborn Garrettson. The Lower Manor Livingstons, following the lead of the chancellor, gravitated from Federalism in 1787–1791 into a Clintonian Republican stance, becoming one of New York's loose "Quiddish-centrist" factions when Morgan Lewis split with Daniel Tompkins and De Witt Clinton on the issue of bank incorporation in 1805–1806.

JOHN MCKINSTRY (circa 1744–1822) was born in a Scots-Irish family in the hill town of Blandford, Massachusetts, settling in Hillsdale soon after the squatters were driven from Nobletown in 1766. A militia officer by 1770, he took his company into the Massachusetts Line and then served in the Hillsdale militia throughout the war, most notably at the skirmish at Klock's Field. After the war he moved between Hillsdale and a tavern in Hudson, helping to establish the Hudson Lodge and from these bases was deeply involved in the doings of the Susquehannah Company and the Genesee Company of Adventurers, including leading bands of armed men in the western hinterlands. Moving to the town of Livingston, he served briefly in the assembly in the late 1790s. His brothers Charles, Thomas, and David were notables in Hillsdale through 1815, and his sons George and Henry would be involved in affairs in Hudson and Catskill in the following decades.

FITE MILLER (circa 1750–circa 1820) was a tenant on Great Lot No. 1 of the Upper Manor and ran a popular tavern on the road from the ironworks at Salisbury and Ancram west to the Catskill Ferry. In 1780 he was one of a number on the Manor cited by the Albany County Committee for resisting payment of taxes. In 1792 he hosted at his tavern a Clintonian meeting on the Otsego crisis, chaired by William Rockefeller; with the thickening of party organization after 1800 he was a regular member of the Republican county committee. In 1807, nominated for election to the assembly, he was mocked as illiterate by the Federalist *Balance*. While at least a half-dozen Millers signed the 1795 Petrus Pulver petition against the Livingston title in 1795, Fite Miller did not, but in 1811 he signed the tenant petition led by Benjamin Birdsall and Henry Avery, and that August the *Northern Whig* reported meetings of militant tenants at his tavern.

JAMES SAVAGE (1741–1824) was sent by the hill settlers at New Britain to carry a petition to London against the Van Rensselaers. Suspected of toryism when he returned, he was interrogated by the King's District authorities; in the 1790s he was a Federalist assemblyman and state senator. His brother-in-law, merchant WILLIAM POWERS (1745–1796), was similarly suspected of loyalist inclinations and similarly had no public role during the Revolution. An early member of the Unity Lodge, he was the first to be elected to the assembly without Revolutionary credentials, on a Federalist slate in 1787, and rose to the state senate and the Council of Appointment before his death in 1796.

AMBROSE SPENCER (1765–1848) grew up in Salisbury, Connecticut, where his father was involved in ironworking. Graduating from Harvard in 1783, Spencer studied law, established a legal practice in early Hudson, and was a founding member of the Hudson Lodge. He moved from city clerk to the assembly to the state senate as a Federalist, but in 1797–1798, as some of the Livingstons suspected he was conspiring with the tenant insurgents, he shifted into an alliance with Republican De Witt Clinton, including marrying two of Clinton sisters in succession. As a member of the Clinton faction he was named to the Council of Appointment, the state attorney generalship, and then to the state supreme court, stepping down as chief justice in 1823, after which he served a term in Congress. Later in life he was a senior statesmen in the New York Whig Party. His son Ambrose, Jr., was killed at the battle of Lundy's Lane; another, JOHN CANFIELD SPENCER (1788–1855), followed him into the assembly, senate, and Congress, serving for several years in John Tyler's cabinet. He met Alexis de Tocqueville and Gustave de Beaumont in Utica in July 1831 and sat down with them for extended interviews at his home in Canandaigua during the following weeks. Seven years later Spencer wrote an introduction and notes for the first American edition of Tocqueville's *Democracy in America*.

Among the families settling on land in the disputed Mawighnunk Patent in New Lebanon, King's District, one connection stands out. Dr. MOSES

YOUNGLOVE (1752–1829) and SAMUEL JONES (1752–1836) were both in the Revolutionary militia; both would be staunch Republicans. When Young-love and his wife, POLLY PATTERSON, were not able to have children, they adopted their niece, daughter of Samuel Jones and Polly's sister Parthenia. In turn this daughter, POLLY YOUNGLOVE-JONES (1782–1860), married ELAM TILDEN (1781–1842), a merchant from another Mawighnunk family. While Elam carried on a correspondence with President Martin Van Buren in Washington, their son SAMUEL JONES TILDEN (1814–1886) started on his own path into Democratic politics, which carried him to the Democratic presidential candidacy in the 1876 election.

The Kinderhook Van Burens were part of a freeholding and tenant family widely dispersed in Albany and Schodack to the north. The sons of a Martin Van Buren, ABRAHAM VAN BUREN (1737–1817) and MARTIN VAN BUREN (b. 1748) ended up on opposite sides during the Revolution. Abraham served as an officer in the Kinderhook militia, with his cousin HARMAN VAN BUREN and others; Martin became a loyalist after serving in a Ranger company in 1776. Abraham married the widow MARIA GOES VAN ALEN in 1776; MARTIN VAN BUREN (1782–1862), the future president, was their third child. In 1807 Martin Van Buren married HANNAH GOES (1783–1819), the daughter of JOHN D. GOES (1753–1789), one of the Kinderhook loyalists. JOHN ABRAHAM VAN BUREN (1761–1808), a militia officer and a Republican stalwart, was a very close relation.

ISAAC VANDERPOEL (1747–1807) was a prominent landholder at Kinderhook Landing and the adjutant of the Kinderhook regiment when the Revolution started in 1775. By 1777 he was among the disaffected and exiled to the British lines, and he settled at Staten Island, where he commanded a company of loyalist refugees. His land was sold by the state, but Vanderpoel nonetheless returned to Kinderhook, where two of his sons became leading lawyers. JAMES VANDERPOEL (1787–1843) studied law with FRANCIS SILVESTER and served as a Federalist in the assembly; in 1828 he stood as the Jacksonian candidate for Congress. His brother AARON VANDERPOEL (1799–1870) studied with PETER VAN SCHAACK; he served as the county's Democratic representative in Congress, where his speeches in favor of slavery earned him the nickname of the "Kinderhook Roarer." A cousin, BARENT VANDER-POEL (1764–1847), commanded the militia muster disrupted by John A. Van Buren in the summer of 1792.

The Van Nesses were leading freeholders in Claverack. PETER VAN NESS (1738–1804) started as a wheelwright and after a long struggle with the Van Rensselaers rose to be the first judge of the county and a political force in his own right, broadly Republican in allegiance though gravitating toward

Aaron Burr's interest. His sons had minor political careers: JOHN P. VAN NESS (1770–1846) was propelled into Congress in 1801 through the efforts of the young Martin Van Buren but abandoned his seat when he married Marcia Burnes and settled into fashionable Washington life. WILLIAM P. (1778–1826) ended up a federal judge after he served as Aaron Burr's second in the Hamilton duel; Cornelius P. (1782–1852) was elected governor of Vermont and then appointed ambassador to Spain by Van Buren. Peter's brother William was a lieutenant in the Claverack militia during the Revolution; his son WILLIAM W. VAN NESS (1775–1823) studied law with Republican JOHN BAY and married his daughter Jane; in the 1790s he switched to the Federalists and became one of the three leaders of the Columbia Junto. A cousin, JOHN VAN NESS, was tortured and robbed, and his son ABRAHAM killed, by tory bandits during the Revolution.

The power of the VAN RENSSELAER family lay in the fortunes of the Dutch diamond merchant KILLIAN VAN RENSSELAER, granted the "Patroonship" of the lands surrounding Fort Orange (later Albany) in the 1640s. Divided into greater and lesser inheritances in the 1670s, the majority of the Rensselaerwyck claim (Albany and Rensselaer counties) would be held by an "elder" branch of the family, until the death of the "Good Patroon" STEPHEN VAN RENSSELAER in 1839 set in motion the Anti-Rent Wars of the 1840s. In 1649 the Van Rensselaer interest purchased lands south of the Manor proper at Claverack, which fell to a younger branch in 1704. They were developed and expanded by JOHN VAN RENSSELAER (1708–1783), who attempted to transfer his property in entail to his grandson JOHN JEREMIAH; the state of New York quickly passed a law against entail in the summer of 1782. The Claverack lands were inherited in 1783 by a number of John's children, including CATHERINE (1734–1803), who was married to General Philip Schuyler and was Alexander Hamilton's mother-in-law. Her brother ROBERT VAN RENSSELAER (1740–1802) was the commander of the local militia brigade during the Revolutionary war and the clerk of the new county from 1786 to 1801. His son, JACOB RUTSEN VAN RENSSELAER (1767–1835), was one of the three leaders of the Federalist Columbia Junto.

Born in Kinderhook, merchant CORNELIUS VAN SCHAACK (1705–1775) had interests in a sloop on the river, in land grants, including the Mawighnunk Patent of 1743, and in the fur trade running east into the Berkshires. His sons would all be among the Kinderhook loyalists and, later, Federalists. PETER VAN SCHAACK (1747–1832), a prominent lawyer before the war started, went to London but returned, was restored to citizenship, and trained several generations of law students in Kinderhook. HENRY VAN SCHAACK (1733–1823) escaped into Massachusetts rather than take an oath during the

Revolution; he settled in Pittsfield and prospered as a merchant until he returned in 1807, selling his mansion on the Lenox Road to ELKANAH WATSON (1758–1842), the wandering Republican improver. PETER SILVESTER (1734–1808), married to Cornelius's daughter JANETJE, was similarly a lawyer of loyalist inclinations who became a strong Federalist. Martin Van Buren studied law with Silvester and his son Francis in the late 1790s.

WILLIAM BRADFORD WHITING (1731–1796) settled in New Canaan in the hill region and was an important local figure during the Revolution, colonel of the Seventeenth Albany Regiment, a state senator, and then a judge. His adjutant in the Seventeenth was JONATHAN WARNER (1747–1823), an ardent Republican and member of the Democratic Society with Moses Younglove. One of his sons married one of Whiting's daughters; their granddaughters SUSAN WARNER (1817–1885) and ANNA WARNER (1819–1915) would write domestic novels of note in the mid-nineteenth century. William Bradford Whiting was a distant cousin of DR. WILLIAM WHITING (1731–1792), a Revolutionary leader in Great Barrington, Massachusetts, about fifteen miles southeast of Canaan.

ELISHA WILLIAMS (1773–1833) grew up in Pomfret, Connecticut, as the ward of CAPTAIN EBENEZER GROSVENOR. After studying law with Tapping Reeve in Litchfield and Ambrose Spencer in Hudson, he settled in Spencertown to practice law and in 1795 married Grosvenor's daughter Lucy. By 1798 he was a leading figure among the county Federalists and would emerge as the leader of the Columbia Junto. By the time he moved to Hudson in 1800 he was instructing his brother-in-law, THOMAS PEABODY GROSVENOR (1778–1817), in the law. Grosvenor was a junior partner in the Federalist Junto. First elected to the assembly, he served two terms in Congress and in 1815 married Mary Jane Hanson of Baltimore, where her brother Alexander was a leading Federalist editor.

WILLIAM WILSON (1756–1828), a doctor, emigrated from the north of England in the late 1780s and settled at Clermont, where he practiced medicine and Quiddish Republican politics and served as an agent for the Lower Manor Livingstons.

LUCY WRIGHT (1760–1821) was born in Pittsfield, Massachusetts, and in 1779 married Eleazer Goodrich (1751–1812), a merchant in Richmond, Massachusetts. The next year they were caught up in the New Light Stir and then converted by Mother Ann Lee to the Shaker gospel of the "Second appearing of Christ." Renamed "Lucy Faith," she quickly became a close adviser to Mother Ann Lee and on her death worked with Joseph Meacham in the 1780s and 1790s to organize the chaotic Shaker settlements at Watervliet and Mount Lebanon. On Meacham's death in 1796 she become the presiding eldress of the expanding Shaker world. Though her governance was contested by Shaker dissenters, she was clearly one of the most powerful women in America until her death twenty-five years later.

The Printers and Their Newspapers
From the 1780s through the early 1820s four different newspapers of note were printed in Hudson. The first, the *Hudson Gazette*, was established in 1785 by ASHBEL STODDARD (1763–1840) and CHARLES R. WEBSTER (1762–1834); Webster stayed on for a few months before returning to Albany, where he had been involved in printing with his brother George for several years. Stoddard and the Websters were part of a network of printers in the upper Hudson — the Steeles, the Skinners, the Croswells — linked by marriage and apprenticeships in Hartford, more notably at the Hartford *Connecticut Courant*. Stoddard's moderately Federalist *Gazette* had a monopoly in Hudson until HARRY CROSWELL (1788–1858) moved across the river from Catskill in 1801 to establish a vehemently Federalist *Balance, and Columbia Repository,* with Junto money and the editorial assistance of the Reverend EZRA SAMPSON (1749–1823). The next year CHARLES HOLT (1772–1852) was recruited by the Clermont Livingstons to move his Republican *Bee* from New London, where he had been prosecuted under the Sedition Act; the *Balance* editors and the Junto responded with a violently satirical offering, the Hudson *Wasp,* which was published for a year. Holt moved on to New York City in 1809, where he published the *Columbian*; the *Bee* continued under various editors into 1821. The *Balance* editors sold out in 1808, and a new Federalist paper, the *Northern Whig,* was established by FRANCIS STEBBINS (b. 1773), succeeded by WILLIAM LEETE STONE (1792–1844). A new publishing regime emerged with a new political climate in the 1820s, with a Clinton-Adams-Whig paper, the *Columbian Republican,* edited by AMBROSE L. JORDAN from 1824, and a Democratic *Gazette* founded by JOHN W. EDMONDS in 1824. The *Columbian Mercury* was briefly published in Canaan by ELIHU PHINNEY (1755–1813) before he moved on to Cooperstown. Peter Van Schaack, Jr. (b. 1795), published the Jacksonian *Columbia Sentinel* in Kinderhook between 1825 and 1834.

NOTE ON COUNTY SOURCES
The research for this book has involved the reconstruction of individual, family, and community histories in Columbia County between the Revolution and the 1830s. Much of this material cannot be fully cited in the body of the text, so this note is intended to provide a general guide to the most important sources for this reconstruction.

Tax Lists:

1779 District Tax Lists for West Claverack, East Claverack, German
   Camp, Kinderhook, and Livingston, Series (N-Ar)A1201, NYSA; as
   transcribed in the *Columbia,* I–IV (1985–1988); and Arthur C. M. Kelly,
   comp., *Settlers and Residents,* III, part 1, *Town of Livingston, 1710–1789*
   (Rhinebeck, N.Y., 1973–[1989]), 46–56, 238–241.

Tax assessment rolls of real and personal estates, Columbia County, 1799–
   1800, Series B0950-85 (boxes 10–12), NYSA.

Church Records:

I have used the following sources.

Church histories in Ellis, *Columbia County.*

The transcriptions by Royden W. Vosburgh et al., for the New York
   Genealogical and Biographical Society (1912–1921) of the following
   records: "The Reformed Church at West Copake"; "St. John's Evangelical
   Lutheran Church at Manorton"; "St. Thomas's Evangelical Lutheran
   Church, at Churchtown, Town of Claverack"; "The Reformed Church at
   Hillsdale"; "The Reformed Dutch Church of Kinderhook."

Arthur C. M. Kelly, comp. "Gallatin Reformed Church: Members, 1759–
   1899," *Columbia,* VIII (1992).

Records of the East Baptist Church and Society in Hillsdale, NYHS.

Masonic Records

Returns, 1785–1826, from lodges in Columbia, Rensselaer, and Dutchess
   counties, on file at LL-NYGL.

Peacher, "Craft Masonry."

*An Account of the Performances at the Dedication of the Mason-Hall, Hudson,
   on the Festival of St. John the Evangelist . . . Dec. 27, 1796* (Hudson, N.Y.,
   1797).

City Officers, Town Supervisors, Justices of the Peace, County Judges

Stephen B. Miller, *Historical Sketches of Hudson, Embracing the Settlement
   of the City . . .* (Hudson, N.Y., 1862; rpt. 1985), 113–119.

Ellis, *Columbia County,* 73–81, in town histories, 219–416.

Assembly Representatives, State Senators

Franklin B. Hough, comp., *The New-York Civil List, containing the . . .
   Names and Fates of Election or Appointment of the Principal State and
   County Officers, from the Revolution to the Present Time* (Albany, N.Y.,
   1860).

Newspaper Editors

Ellis, *Columbia County,* 17–120.

Milton W. Hamilton, *The Country Printer: New York State, 1785–1830* (New York, 1936), 252–309.

Clarence S. Brigham, comp., *History and Bibliography of American Newspapers, 1690–1820* (1947; Worcester, Mass.,1961).

Printer File, AAS.

Elections

In reconstructing the elections for Columbia and surrounding counties I have had the great fortune to work closely for many years with Philip Lampi, of the First American Democracy Project, located at the American Antiquarian Society. All of the assembly, senate, and gubernatorial elections returns through 1824 analyzed here will be available at the First Democracy Project website, and most are available on Early American Newspapers. The returns used here have been collected by Mr. Lampi and myself from a variety of newspapers, most importantly scattered issues of the New York *Daily Advertiser, Poughkeepsie Journal, Catskill Packet, and Western Mail, New-York Journal, Hudson Gazette* (from 1788 to 1801), Hudson *Bee* (1802–1820), Hudson *Balance* (1802–1808), Hudson *Northern Whig* (1809–1820), Hudson *Columbia Republican* (1821, 1828–1829), *The New-York Annual Register* (1831–1845); the manuscript Book of Election Returns, 1799–1894, on file at the Columbia County Clerk's Office; and the Columbia County Assembly Returns, 1791–1795, 1799, box 41:25, WFP-UM.

The estimated electorate is calculated from the state censuses of electors reported in *NYAJ* for 1791, 1796, 1808, and 1815, and the 1855 New York State Census (for 1801). Intervening years are estimated by a linear interpolation of gain or loss. The town figures for qualified electors do not survive for 1801, so the 1801 town electors are estimated from the county figure and the 1800 census of population.

Militia Records

James A. Roberts, ed., *New York in the Revolution as Colony and State,* 2d ed. (Albany, N.Y., 1898, rpt. 1996), I, 108–119, 132, 228–232, 237–239.

Berthold Fernow, ed., *New York in the Revolution,* vol. XV of John Romeyn Brodhead, E. B. O'Callaghan, and Berthold Fernow, eds., *Documents Relative to the Colonial History of the State of New York* (Albany, N.Y., 1856–1887), 267–270, 273–274.

Hugh Hastings and Henry Harmon Noble, eds., *Military Minutes of the*

Council of Appointment of the State of New York, 1783–1821 (Albany, N.Y., 1901–1902).

Military and Civil Commissions, in Book of Judgments, 1807–1817, Columbia County Clerk's Office.

County Party Committees

While there is considerable scattered information on political affiliation, including nominations and town committee lists published in the papers, the most important lists are the county committees published in the Hudson papers. Some of these list more than one hundred individuals and are unique in New York State at this period (see Table 21). For the county lists, see *Hudson Gazette,* Mar. 26, 1795, Apr. 24, 1798, Apr. 14, 21, Sept. 22, 1801; Hudson *Balance,* Apr. 19, 1803; Hudson *Bee,* Apr. 19, 1803, Apr. 10, 1804, Apr. 15, 1806, Apr. 19, 1808, Apr. 19, 1811, Mar. 14, 21, 1820; Hudson *Columbia Republican,* Jan. 9, Apr. 17, 1821; Kinderhook *Columbia Sentinel,* Oct. 16, 1834 (total delegate number only).

ABBREVIATIONS AND SHORT TITLES

INSTITUTIONS

AAS: American Antiquarian Society, Worcester, Mass.

AIHA: Albany Institute of History and Art, Albany, N.Y.

BHM-GCHS: Bronck House Museum, Greene County Historical Society, Coxsackie, N.Y.

CCHS: Columbia County Historical Society

LC: Library of Congress, Washington, D.C.

MHS: Massachusetts Historical Society, Boston

NYC: New York City

NYHS: New-York Historical Society, New York City

NYPL: New York Public Library

NYSA: New York State Archives

NYSL: New York State Library

COLLECTIONS

DWCP-CU: DeWitt Clinton Papers, Columbia University

EFP: Ebenezer Foote Papers, NYSL

HHCh-DAR: Collections of the Henrick Hudson Chapter, Daughters of American Revolution, 113 Warren Street, Hudson, N.Y.

LL-NYGL: Archives of the Grand Lodge of Free and Accepted Masons of the State of New York, Chancellor Robert R. Livingston Masonic Library of Grand Lodge, New York, N.Y.

MA: Massachusetts Archives volumes, at the Massachusetts Archives, Columbia Point, Boston

MVBP: Martin Van Buren Papers. The microfilm collection compiled by the Papers of Martin Van Buren (Pennsylvania State University, 1969–1987) encompasses material from the Library of Congress and other archives: Philip H. and A. S. W. Rosenback Foundation; Missouri Historical Society; Massachusetts Historical Society.

NYALG: New York (State) Deptartment of State, Applications for Land Grants, 1642–1803 (A0272), New York State Archives (indexed in E. B. O'Callaghan, comp., *Calendar of N.Y. Colonial Manuscripts: Indorsed Land Papers, in the Office of the Secretary of State of New York, 1643–1803,* rev. rpt. [Harrison, N.Y., 1987])

RRLP: Robert R. Livingston Papers, New-York Historical Society

SC-WRHS: Shaker Collection, Western Reserve Historical Society, Cleveland, Ohio

Sedgwick Papers, Massachusetts Historical Society

VSP/LC: Van Schaack Papers, Library of Congress

WFP-UM: Wilson Family Papers, Clements Library, University of Michigan, Ann Arbor, Mich.

WWP-BC: William Wilson Papers, Bard College, Annandale-on-Hudson, N.Y.

Ellis, *Columbia County:* Franklin Ellis, ed., *History of Columbia County, New York* (Philadelphia, 1878)

Goebel and Smith, eds., *LPAH:* Julius Goebel, Jr., and Joseph H. Smith, eds., *The Law Practice of Alexander Hamilton: Documents and Commentary,* 5 vols. (New York, 1964–1981)

NY Laws: New York Laws. Published with various titles

NYAJ: New York Assembly Journal. Published with various titles; through 1784 titled *Votes and Proceedings*

NYSJ: New York Senate Journal. Published with various titles; through 1784 titled *Votes and Proceedings*

Paltsits, ed., *Minutes:* Victor Hugo Paltsits, ed., *Minutes of the Commissioners for Detecting and Defeating Conspiracies in the State of New York,* 3 vols. (Albany, N.Y., 1909–1910)

Peacher, "Craft Masonry": William G. Peacher, "Craft Masonry in Columbia County, New York, 1787–1826," American Lodge of Research, Free and Accepted Masons, *Transactions,* XIII (1977), 320–323, 332–333

Sullivan, ed., *Minutes:* James Sullivan, ed., *Minutes of the Albany Committee of Correspondence, 1775–1778,* I (Albany, N.Y., 1923)

Syrett et al., eds., *PAH:* Harold C. Syrett et al., eds., *The Papers of Alexander Hamilton* (New York, 1962–1987)

NOTES

PROLOGUE

1. *Hudson Weekly Gazette,* Apr. 7, 1785. Within this selection from Price (see the epigraph), the quoted section is attributed by Price as "the words of Montesquieu." According to Bernard Peach, this is actually a paraphrase of extended sections of Montesquieu's *Spirit of the Laws.* See Peach, *Richard Price and the Ethical Foundations of the American Revolution* (Durham, N.C., 1979), 183–184.

2. George Wilson Pierson, *Tocqueville and Beaumont in America* (New York, 1938), 171–184.

3. Ibid., 189; Donald B. Cole, *Martin Van Buren and the American Political System* (Princeton, N.J., 1984), 220–221; John Niven, *Martin Van Buren: The Romantic Age of American Politics* (New York, 1983), 288–289.

4. If Price's legitimate government required the "common consent" of all Americans, such legitimacy is still to this day the focus of continuous struggle. See Eric Foner, *The Story of American Freedom* (New York, 1998); Robert H. Wiebe, *Self-Rule: A Cultural History of American Democracy* (Chicago, 1995); Judith N. Shklar, *American Citizenship: The Quest for Inclusion* (Cambridge, Mass., 1991).

5. For a longer discussion, see John L. Brooke, "Consent, Civil Society, and the Public Sphere in the Age of Revolution and the Early Republic," in Jeffrey L. Pasley, Andrew W. Roberston, and David Waldstreicher, eds., *Beyond the Founders: New Approaches to the Political History of the Early American Republic* (Chapel Hill, N.C., 2004), 207–250.

6. Jürgen Habermas, *The Structural Transformation of the Public Sphere: An Inquiry into a Category of Bourgeois Society,* trans. Thomas Burger (Cambridge, Mass., 1989); Habermas, *Between Facts and Norms: Contributions to a Discourse Theory of Law and Democracy,* trans. William Rehg (1992; Cambridge, Mass., 1996). For analysis, see Craig Calhoun, ed., *Habermas and the Public Sphere* (Cambridge, Mass., 1992); Jean L. Cohen and Andrew Arato, *Civil Society and Political Theory* (Cambridge, Mass., 1992); John Ehrenberg, *Civil Society: The Critical History of an Idea* (New York, 1999), 219–224; Luke Goode, *Jürgen Habermas: Democracy and the Public Sphere* (London, 2005). My commentary can be found in John L. Brooke, "Reason and Passion in the Public Sphere: Habermas and the Cultural Historians," *Journal of Interdisciplinary History,* XXIX (1998–1999), 43–67, and "Consent, Civil Society, and the Public Sphere," in Pasley, Robertson, and Waldstreicher, eds., *Beyond the Founders,* 207–250.

7. Since the 1980s a growing new literature has begun to sketch the history of the emerging public sphere, around the early modern Atlantic world in particular, but in recent world history in general as well. See Johann N. Neem, *Creating a Nation of Joiners: Democracy and Civil Society in Early National Massachusetts* (Cambridge, Mass., 2008); Peter Lake and Steven Pincus, eds., *The Politics of the Public Sphere in Early Modern England* (Manchester, 2007); Tim Blanning, *The Pursuit of Glory: The Five Revolutions That Made Modern Europe, 1648–1815* (London, 2007); Albrecht Koschnik, *"Let a Common Interest Bind Us Together": Associations, Partisan-*

ship, and Culture in Philadelphia, 1775–1840 (Charlottesville, Va., 2007); Paul Starr, The Creation of the Media: The Political Origins of Modern Communications (New York, 2004); Kathleen D. McCarthy, American Creed: Philanthropy and the Rise of Civil Society, 1700–1865 (Chicago, 2003); Hannah Barker and Simon Burrows, eds., Press, Politics, and the Public Sphere in Europe and North America, 1760–1820 (New York, 2002); Jeffrey L. Pasley, "The Tyranny of Printers": Newpaper Politics in the Early American Republic (Charlottesville, Va., 2001); James Van Horn Melton, The Rise of the Public in Enlightenment Europe (New York, 2001); David Zaret, Origins of Democratic Culture: Printing, Petitions, and the Public Sphere in Early-Modern England (Princeton, N.J., 2000); Jeffrey L. McNairn, The Capacity to Judge: Public Opinion and Deliberative Democracy in Upper Canada, 1791–1854 (Toronto, 2000); Victor M. Uribe-Uran, Honorable Lives: Lawyers, Family, and Politics in Colombia, 1780–1850 (Pittsburgh, 2000); Uribe-Uran, "The Birth of a Public Sphere in Latin America during the Age of Revolution," Comparative Studies in Society and History, XLII (2000), 425–457; John L. Brooke, "To Be 'Read by the Whole People': Press, Party, and Public Sphere in the United States, 1790–1840," American Antiquarian Society, Proceedings, CX (2000), 41–118; Victor M. Pérez-Díaz, Return of Civil Society: The Emergence of Democratic Spain (Cambridge, Mass., 1993); David S. Shields, Civil Tongues and Polite Letters in British America (Chapel Hill, N.C., 1997); David Waldstreicher, In the Midst of Perpetual Fetes: The Making of American Nationalism, 1776–1820 (Chapel Hill, N.C., 1997); Mary P. Ryan, Civic Wars: Democracy and Public Life in the American City during the Nineteenth Century (Berkeley, Calif., 1997); John L. Brooke, "Ancient Lodges and Self-Created Societies: Voluntary Association and the Public Sphere in the Early Republic," in Ronald Hoffman and Peter J. Albert, eds., Launching the "Extended Republic": The Federalist Era (Charlottesville, Va., 1997), 273–377; Margaret C. Jacob, "The Mental Landscape of the Public Sphere: A European Perspective," Eighteenth-Century Studies, XXVIII (1994), 95–113; Jacob, Living the Enlightenment: Freemasonry and Politics in Eighteenth-Century Europe (New York, 1991); Keith Michael Baker, Inventing the French Revolution: Essays on French Political Culture in the Eighteenth Century (New York, 1990); Michael Warner, The Letters of the Republic: Publication and the Public Sphere in Eighteenth-Century America (Cambridge, Mass., 1990); Joan B. Landes, Women and the Public Sphere in the Age of the French Revolution (Ithaca, N.Y., 1988); François Furet, Interpreting the French Revolution, trans. Elberg Forster (New York, 1981). On deliberation and persuasion, see Brooke, "Consent, Civil Society, and the Public Sphere," in Pasley, Robertson, and Waldstreicher, eds., Beyond the Founders, 209–211, 227–230.

8. I owe a debt in my understanding of Revolutionary settlements to the basic Weberian framework of structure and antistructure developed in Victor Turner, Dramas, Fields, and Metaphors: Symbolic Action in Human Society (Ithaca, N.Y., 1974), esp. 98–155, "Hidalgo: History as Social Drama."

9. Here it should be apparent that I take a distinctly different view about the function of civil society than did Tocqueville and his contemporary followers. What is particularly striking about civil institutions in post-Revolutionary and even much of antebellum America is, not that they compensated for a "weak state," but that they worked in connection with a quite broad popular understanding that the governments of the American states were problem-solving, improving extensions of the people's will. Americans — broadly Jacksonians — who objected to governmental action also had their doubts about a wide array of civil associations and saw civil society as best fulfilling a monitorial rather than an improving imperative. For various critiques of neo-Tocquevillean thinking, see William Novak, "The American Law of Association: The Legal-

Political Construction of Civil Society," *Studies in American Political Development,* XV (2001), 163–188; Jason Kaufman, "Three Views of Associationalism in Nineteenth-Century America," *American Journal of Sociology,* CIV (1999), 1296–1345; Richard R. John, "Governmental Institutions as Agents of Change: Rethinking American Political Development in the Early Republic, 1787–1835," *Studies in American Political Development,* XI (1997), 347–380; Michael Schudson, "The 'Public Sphere' and Its Problems: Bringing the State (Back) In," *Notre Dame Journal of Law, Ethics, and Public Policy,* VIII (1994), 529–546. For studies that have influenced my thinking, see John Lauritz Larson, *Internal Improvement: National Public Works and the Promise of Popular Government in the United States* (Chapel Hill, N.C., 2001); William J. Novak, *The People's Welfare: Law and Regulation in Nineteenth-Century America* (Chapel Hill, N.C., 1996); Christopher J. Tomlins, *Law, Labor, and Ideology in the Early American Republic* (New York, 1993); L. Ray Gunn, *The Decline of Authority: Public Economic Policy and Political Development in New York, 1800–1860* (Ithaca, N.Y., 1988). The classical statements of this argument include Oscar Handlin and Mary Flug Handlin, *Commonwealth: A Study of the Role of Government in the American Economy: Massachusetts, 1774–1861,* rev. ed. (Cambridge, Mass., 1969); Louis Hartz, *Economic Policy and Democratic Thought: Pennsylvania, 1776–1860* (Cambridge, Mass., 1948).

10. For critiques of Habermas's original formulation, see the following essays: Nancy Fraser, "What's Critical about Critical Theory? The Case of Habermas and Gender," *New German Critique,* no. 35 (Spring/Summer 1985), 97–133; and Fraser, "Rethinking the Public Sphere: A Contribution to the Critique of Actually Existing Democracy," Mary P. Ryan, "Gender and Public Access: Women's Politics in Nineteenth-Century America," Geoff Eley, "Nations, Publics, and Political Cultures: Placing Habermas in the Nineteenth Century," in Calhoun, ed., *Habermas and the Public Sphere,* 109–142, 259–288, 289–339, and Habermas's own self-critique, 422–427. For an important response, see Harold Mah, "Phantasies of the Public Sphere: Rethinking the Habermas of Historians," *Journal of Modern History,* LXXII (2000), 153–182. Habermas's analysis in *Between Facts and Norms* can be read as an elaborate attempt to reconcile these tensions between consent and civil society.

11. I have discussed my thinking on the distinction between deliberative and persuasive processes in the public sphere in "Consent, Civil Society, and the Public Sphere," in Pasley, Robertson, and Waldstreicher, eds., *Beyond the Founders,* 209–211, 227–238, and "Reason and Passion in the Public Sphere: Habermas and the Cultural Historians," *Journal of Interdisciplinary History,* XXIX (1998–1999), 43–67. On the hegemonic dimensions of respectability in the public sphere, see Mah, "Phantasies of the Public Sphere," *Journal of Modern History,* LXXII (2000), 153–182. On civil death, I borrow rather freely from Orlando Patterson, *Slavery and Social Death: A Comparative Study* (Cambridge, Mass., 1982). See also Peter S. Onuf, "'To Declare Them a Free and Independent People': Race, Slavery, and National Identity in Jefferson's Thought," *Journal of the Early Republic,* XVIII (1998), 1–46.

12. Here, see in particular James Brewer Stewart, "Modernizing 'Difference': The Political Meanings of Color in the Free States, 1776–1840," *Journal of the Early Republic,* XIX (1999), 691–712; David N. Gellman, *Emancipating New York: The Politics of Slavery and Freedom, 1777–1827* (Baton Rouge, La., 2006); Markman Ellis, *The Politics of Sensibility: Race, Gender, and Commerce in the Sentimental Novel* (New York, 1996).

13. In some measure this is a study of "subaltern histories," inspired in broad outline by Ranajit Guha and Gayatri Chakravorty Spivak, eds., *Selected Subaltern Studies* (New York, 1988); and

James C. Scott, *Domination and the Arts of Resistance: Hidden Transcripts* (New Haven, Conn., 1990).

14. Pierson, *Tocqueville and Beaumont in America*, 116, 216–225; John C. Spencer, "Preface to the American Edition," in Alexis de Tocqueville, *Democracy in America*, trans. Henry Reeve (New York, 1838), vii; Matthew Mancini, *Alexis de Tocqueville and American Intellectuals: From His Times to Ours* (New York, 2006), 47–48.

15. Henry Livingston, Livingston Manor, to Walter Livingston, New York City, Apr. 24, 1785, RRLP, reel 3.

16. Hudson *Northern Whig,* Aug. 23, 1811.

17. Here I am indebted to Gerald Leonard's challenge, rooted in the "antiparty interpretation," to Richard Hofstadter's interpretation of Van Buren's acceptance of liberal pluralism. See Gerald Leonard, "Party as a 'Political Safeguard of Federalism': Martin Van Buren and the Constitutional Theory of Party Politics," *Rutgers Law Review,* LIV (2001), 221–281; and *The Invention of Party Politics: Federalism, Popular Sovereignty, and Constitutional Development in Jacksonian Illinois* (Chapel Hill, N.C., 2002), critiquing Richard Hofstadter, *The Idea of a Party System: The Rise of Legitimate Opposition in the United States, 1780–1840* (Berkeley, Calif., 1969), esp. 212–271.

18. By elsewhere, I mean specifically Boston and its hinterlands, the Burned-Over District of central-western New York and northeast Ohio, and the Quaker circuit around Philadelphia.

CHAPTER 1

1. Marquis de Chastellux, *Travels in North America in the Years 1780, 1781, and 1782,* ed. Howard M. Rice, Jr. (Chapel Hill, N.C., 1963), I, 196; Harriett C. W. Van Buren Peckham, *History of Cornelis Maessen Van Buren . . .* (New York, 1913), 68–69, 88–89; Donald B. Cole, *Martin Van Buren and the American Political System* (Princeton, N.J., 1984), 9–13; John Niven, *Martin Van Buren: The Romantic Age of American Politics* (New York, 1983), 5–6; Jerome Mushkat and Joseph G. Rayback, *Martin Van Buren: Law, Politics, and the Shaping of Republican Ideology* (DeKalb, Ill., 1997), 4–5.

2. On Abraham's brother Martin, see Peckham, *History of Cornelis Maessen Van Buren,* 68–69; Hugh Hastings and J. A. Holden, eds., *Public Papers of George Clinton . . .* (New York and Albany, 1899–1914), V, 64–66, VI, 399 (petitions from Annatie Van Buren); Sullivan, ed., *Minutes,* I, 519, 520, 679; Paltsits, ed., *Minutes,* I, 181, 183, 189, 197–198, II, 834–835; Lansingburgh *Federal Herald,* July 28, 1788; *New-York Journal,* July 5, 1788; Martin Van Buren, "Thoughts on the Coming Election in New York [March 1840]," MVBP, 18–19. Lindenwald originally was owned by Peter Van Alstyne, one of the Kinderhook tories. Peter Van Ness Denman, "From Deference to Democracy: The Van Ness Family and Their Times, 1759 to 1844" (Ph.D. diss., University of Michigan, 1977), 599 n. 3.

3. William H. W. Sabine, ed., *Historical Memoirs from 12 July 1776 to 25 July 1778 of William Smith, Historian of the Province of New York . . .* (New York, 1958), II, 210, 214, 232.

4. Richard M. Ketchum, *Saratoga: Turning Point of America's Revolutionary War* (New York, 1997), provides the best modern account of the battle (350–425) and of the surrender (426–435).

5. [Johann Friedrich Specht], *The Specht Journal: A Military Journal of the Burgoyne Campaign,* trans. Helga Doblin, ed. Mary C. Lynn and Donald M. Londahl-Schmidt (Westport, Conn., 1995), 102–106. See also Doblin, trans., "The Battle of Saratoga from an 'Enemy' Perspective: Fragments of a Diary from the Lower Saxony State Archives, Wolfenbüttel," *Tamkang Journal of American Studies,* III (1987), 30–33.

6. Sung Bok Kim, *Landlord and Tenant in Colonial New York, 1664–1775* (Chapel Hill, N.C., 1978), 173–178.

7. [Specht], *The Specht Journal,* trans. Doblin, ed. Lynn and Londahl-Schmidt, 106. See also William L. Stone, trans., *Letters of Brunswick and Hessian Officers during the American Revolution* (Albany, N.Y., 1891), 136–144.

8. E. Wilder Spaulding, *His Excellency George Clinton: Critic of the Constitution,* 2d ed. (Port Washington, N.Y., 1964), 83–84; George Dangerfield, *Chancellor Robert R. Livingston of New York, 1746–1813* (New York, 1960), 103–107.

9. Ketchum, *Saratoga,* 437.

10. Peter S. Onuf, "State-Making in Revolutionary Crisis: Independent Vermont as a Case Study," *Journal of American History,* LXVII (1980–1981), 797–815; Michael A. Bellesiles, *Revolutionary Outlaws: Ethan Allen and the Struggle for Independence on the Early American Frontier* (Charlottesville, Va., 1993).

11. My thinking here is indebted to the following studies: Edward Countryman, "Consolidating Power in Revolutionary America: The Case of New York, 1775–1783," *Journal of Interdisciplinary History,* VI (1975–1976), 645–677; Countryman, *A People in Revolution: The American Revolution and Political Society in New York, 1760–1790* (Baltimore, 1981); Michael Kammen, "The American Revolution as a *Crise de Conscience:* The Case of New York," in Richard M. Jellison, ed., *Society, Freedom, and Conscience: The American Revolution in Virginia, Massachusetts, and New York* (New York, 1976), 125–189.

12. Beverley McAnear, "The Albany Stamp Act Riots," *William and Mary Quarterly,* 3d Ser., IV (1947), 486–498; Kim, *Landlord and Tenant,* 399–408; Thomas Jude Humphrey, "Agrarian Rioting in Albany County, New York: Tenants, Markets, and Revolution in the Hudson Valley, 1751–1801" (Ph.D. diss., Northern Illinois University, 1996), 165–175. The key primary documentation on the Nobletown crisis includes "The King agst. Alexander McArthur et al., [trial notes] Albany, Aug. 25, 1766" (16277), NYSL; William Kellog et al., Egremont, to Gov. Francis Barnard, Boston, July 30, 1766, MA, VI, 334, July 31, 1766, 337; Timothy Kellog to Gov. Francis Barnard, Nov. 3, 1766, MA, VI, 340; William Kellog to Gov. Francis Barnard, May 27, 1767, MA, VI, 358–359; "An Account of the Losses Sustained by the People of Nobletown in the Summer of the Year 1766 — by People from New York Government," [May 27, 1767], MA, VI, 360–361.

13. Stefan Bielinski, "Albany County," in Joseph S. Tiedemann and Eugene R. Fingerhut, eds., *The Other New York: The American Revolution beyond New York City, 1763–1787* (Albany, N.Y., 2005), 157–159, 164; Bernard Mason, *The Road to Independence: The Revolutionary Movement in New York, 1773–1777* (Lexington, Ky., 1966), 42; *Extracts from the Votes and Proceedings . . . A Letter from the Delegates . . .* (Albany, N.Y., 1774) (Evans 42727); "A General Association, Agreed to and Subscribed by the Members of the Several Committees of the City and County of Albany," Feb. 24, 1775, in Ellis, *Columbia County,* 28–29; Sullivan, ed., *Minutes,* I, 3–4, 26–31.

14. Patricia U. Bonomi, *A Factious People: Politics and Society in Colonial New York* (New York, 1971), 295–311; Kim, *Landlord and Tenant,* 89–107; Bonomi, "Local Government in Colonial New York: A Base for Republicanism," in Jacob Judd and Irwin H. Polishook, eds., *Aspects of Early New York Society and Politics* (Tarrytown, N.Y., 1974), 29–50; Alan Tully, *Forming American Politics: Ideals, Interests, and Institutions in Colonial New York and Pennsylvania* (Baltimore, 1994), 331; [Peter Van Schaack, ed.], *Laws of New-York, from the Year 1691, to 1773 Inclusive* (New York, 1774), chaps. 17, 104, 333, 1552. My estimate of the electorate is based on the 1790 electoral census, which listed two classes of freehold electors, and a class of forty-shilling tenant electors.

These forty-shilling "at will" tenants were excluded from the colonial electorate. See also *NYAJ*, 14th sess., 1791, 14.

15. Thus Johannes Fryenmoet and Johannes Ritzema, successive pastors at Kinderhook, both opposed the revival Coetus group, as did a cluster of mid-Hudson Dutch Reformed ministers. Randall H. Balmer, *A Perfect Babel of Confusion: Dutch Religion and English Culture in the Middle Colonies* (New York, 1989), 122, 132–133; Ellis, *Columbia County,* 244; Elizabeth L. Gebhard, *The Parsonage between Two Manors: Annals of Clover-Reach* (Hudson, N.Y., 1925), 242–243; David G. Hackett, *The Rude Hand of Innovation: Religion and the Social Order in Albany, New York, 1652–1836* (New York, 1991), 59.

16. This quick summary of the region's churches is based on the town histories in Ellis, *Columbia County;* C. C. Goen, *Revivalism and Separatism in New England, 1740–1800* (New Haven, Conn., 1962), 321–323; Stephen J. Stein, *The Shaker Experience in America: A History of the United Society of Believers* (New Haven, Conn., 1992), 10–49. On the German churches in particular, see Harry Julius Kreider, *Lutheranism in Colonial New York* (New York, 1972), 108–111, 141–142; Ellis, *Columbia County,* 247, 262–266, 272–275. A. G. Roeber, *Palatines, Liberty, and Property: German Lutherans in Colonial British America* (Baltimore, 1993), provides a framing overview. David J. Goodall, "New Light on the Border: New England Squatter Settlements in New York during the American Revolution" (Ph.D. diss., SUNY Albany, 1984), 263–308, provides a detailed account of the hill district churches.

17. Sullivan, ed., *Minutes;* Countryman, *A People in Revolution,* 146; Canaan, N.Y., Town Record Book, 1772–1810, Dec. 24, 1774, NYSA [74-1-1]; see also transcription in Olivia Egleston Phelps Stokes, *Letters and Memories of Susan and Anna Bartlett Warner* (New York, 1925), 195–196; Peter Weismer testimony in Sullivan, ed., *Minutes,* I, 275.

18. Sullivan, ed., *Minutes,* I, 20, 31; Anna Mary Dunton, comp., *Reflections, Canaan, New York, Bicentennial, 1976* (Canaan, N.Y., 1976), 11; Muster Roll, Captain John McKinstry's Company, Colonel John Patterson's Regiment, May to July 1775, Massachusetts Muster Rolls, MA, XV, 63; Ellis, *Columbia County,* 33; *Massachusetts Soldiers and Sailors of the Revolutionary War* (Boston, 1896–1908), X, 529; "Regulations of the Private Club, Officers, [of] Claverack, Manor, and Rolif Jansen Kill," Manor Livingston, Apr. 26, 1775, NYHS.

19. Sullivan, ed., *Minutes,* I, 191–192, 210–211; *Calendar of Historical Manuscripts, Relating to the War of the Revolution . . .* (Albany, N.Y., 1868), I, 172–174, 176–177; "Declaration of the Officers of the Regiment of Hillsdale," in Ellis, *Columbia County,* 33; Henry Van Schaack, Kinderhook Landing, to Peter Van Schaack, NYC, May 18, 1775, in Henry Cruger Van Schaack, *Memoirs of the Life of Henry Van Schaack, Embracing Selections from His Correspondence during the Revolution* (Chicago, 1892), 47; Berthold Fernow, ed., *New York in the Revolution,* 268–269, vol. XV of John Romeyn Brodhead, E. B. O'Callaghan, and Berthold Fernow, eds., *Documents Relative to the Colonial History of the State of New York* (Albany, N.Y., 1856–1887).

20. For the New York Line, see Robert K. Wright, Jr., *The Continental Army* (Washington, D.C., 1983), 247–253. My comments on the militia are based on the massive transcription project, undertaken by the late Donald E. Lampson, of the pension affidavits of men who served in the Revolutionary militia from Columbia County, work focusing on the Tenth Albany, enlisted in Livingston Manor. On the Johnson expedition, Chloe Cady affidavit, Ebenezer Cady Pension File, Jan. 27, 1837, and Lawrence M. Goes affidavit, Pension File, Sept. 7, 1832; on White Plains, see the John J. Pulver affidavit, Pension File, Oct. 9, 1832, Donald E. Lampson, transcr.

21. Fernow, ed., *New York in the Revolution,* 539–540; Dunton, comp., *Reflections,* 11. The role

of the Albany County militia is carefully reassessed in Donald Lampson, "Overview of the 10th Albany Militia Regiment at the Battles of Saratoga and in the Campaign against Burgoyne in 1777," Dec. 4, 2001 (typescript). His research in the Revolutionary pension files supersedes the battle accounts in Charles W. Snell, "A Report on the Organization and Numbers of Gates' Army, Sept. 19, Oct. 7, and Oct. 17, 1777," typescript on file at the Saratoga National Historical Park; and Borden H. Mills, "Albany County's Part in the Battle of Saratoga," New York State Historical Association, *Proceedings,* XV (1916), 221–223, which provide several older accounts of the arrival of Ten Broeck's Brigade; on the post-Saratoga story, see George Deneger affidavit, Dec. 17, 1838, in E. Rockefeller pension file (widow of Diel), Donald Lampson, transcr. See also Ketchum, *Saratoga,* 392–400, esp. 397.

22. George Baker Anderson, *Landmarks of Rensselaer County, New York* (Syracuse, N.Y., 1897), 442–444; Grace Greylock Niles, *The Hoosac Valley: Its Legends and Its History* (New York, 1912), 258; Ellis, *Columbia County,* 33; *Calendar of Historical Manuscripts, Relating to the War of the Revolution,* II, 319, 321, 333; Hastings and Holden, eds., *Public Papers of George Clinton,* III, 555–557; Jacob Ford's affidavit, pension file, Aug. 25, 1832, Donald E. Lampson, transcr.

23. The Johnson raid and the battles at Stone Arabia and Klock's Field are described in Robert B. Roberts, *New York's Forts in the Revolution* (Rutherford, N.J., 1980), 54–60; T. Wood Clarke, *The Bloody Mohawk* (New York, 1940), 277–285; Benson J. Lossing, *The Pictorial Field-Book of the Revolution* (New York, 1850), 279–282. Van Rensselaer's court-martial is recorded in Hastings and Holden, eds., *Public Papers of George Clinton,* VI, 692–703. Further details in Moses Meyer affidavit, pension file, Aug. 22, 1832; John Gott affidavit, pension file, Oct. 22, 1832; Chloe Cady affidavit, Ebenezer Cady pension file, Jan. 27, 1837 (Donald E. Lampson, transcr.).

24. Here I am indebted to Countryman, *A People in Revolution,* esp. 161–184.

25. Sabine, ed., *Historical Memoirs,* II, 17–18, 26, 38, 59, 61–62, 83–85, 114–116, 168–169, 211–212, 304, 312, 350, 355–356, 401, 422; Smith might not have been the most unbiased source, as he was recording every flying rumor, founded and unfounded, that might hint at a coming failure of the Revolutionary cause. The Manor militia delinquencies are listed in "Minutes of the Committee of Safety of the Manor of Livingston, Columbia County, New York, in 1776," *New York Genealogical and Biographical Record,* LX (1929), 243, 325, 326, 328, 336–337, 340, 343. Donald Lampson's research in the pension files indicates considerable service in 1776 and 1777 by the Livingston Manor militia, enough to refute arguments for a virtual boycott of Revolutionary service by the Manor tenants in these years. Another record of militia delinquency lists the fines paid by thirty-two men in Claverack on Nov. 23, 1780: Franklin Hawley Webb, *Claverack Old and New* (New York, 1892), 45–46. In these same critical months the Albany committee devoted remarkably little attention to militia desertion and delinquency. See Sullivan, ed., *Minutes,* I, 558, 611, 614. On balance, neither did the Conspiracy Commission that replaced the committee in 1778. See Paltsits, *Minutes,* I, 389, 442, 491, 494, 516, 587, 602, 612, 613, 644, 679, 791. For similar arguments regarding the Livingston militia delinquencies, see Thomas J. Humphrey, *Land and Liberty: Hudson Valley Riots in the Age of Revolution* (DeKalb, Ill., 2004), 95–97; Cynthia A. Kierner, "Landlord and Tenant in Revolutionary New York: The Case of the Livingston Manor," *New York History,* LXX (1989), 135. In general, see Philip Ranlet, *The New York Loyalists* (Knoxville, Tenn., 1986), 120–136.

26. "Minutes of the Committee of Safety of the Manor of Livingston," *NYGBR,* LX (1929), 240–241; John Beebe, Jr., Diary, June 7, 1779, NYSL (typescript, Chatham Public Library); *NYAJ,* 3d sess., 1779, 1st mtg. [16409], 6; Countryman, *A People in Revolution,* 181, 215; Paltsits, ed., *Min-*

utes, II, 510–512, 601, 604–605; "Resolutions at a meeting of above 300 of the inhabitants of the Manor of Livingston," Jan. 6, 1781, Livingston Family Papers, reel 15, NYHS; Cynthia A. Kierner, "Landlord and Tenant in Revolutionary New York," *New York History,* LXX (1989), 149–150; Kierner, *Traders and Gentlefolk: The Livingstons of New York, 1675–1790* (Ithaca, N.Y., 1992), 225–228.

27. Ellis, *Columbia County,* 29–31; Paltsits, ed., *Minutes,* I, 144, 685, 724;; Sullivan, ed., *Minutes,* I, 860; Edward A. Collier, *Kinderhook* . . . (New York, 1914), 175–176, 412; Sabine, ed., *Historical Memoirs,* II, 201 (Smith quote), 397–400; John Francis Collin, *A History of Hillsdale, Columbia County, New York* . . . , ed. H. S. Johnson (Philmont, N.Y., 1883), 20–21; Kierner, "Landlord and Tenant in Revolutionary New York," *New York History,* LXX (1989), 143–144. Paul R. Huey and Ralph D. Phillips, *The Early History of Nassau Village, 1609–1830* . . . (Nassau, N.Y., 1976), 7–8, argue that after the Van Ness murder there were two arrests but no executions.

28. Sullivan, ed., *Minutes,* I, 12, 368, 380, 415, 444, 566; Sabine, ed., *Historical Memoirs,* II, 126–141; *Calendar of Historical Manuscripts, Relating to the War of the Revolution,* I, 581, II, 193–231; "Columbia County Loyalists," *Columbia* (Rhinebeck, N.Y.), XI (1995), 23–24; *Journals of the Provincial Congress, Provincial Convention, Committee of Safety, and Council of Safety of the State of New York, 1775–1776–1778* (Albany, N.Y., 1842), II, 234; Dunton, comp., *Reflections,* 9.

29. Sabine, ed., *Historical Memoirs,* II, 130 (Smith quote); Robert R. Livingston to John Jay, July 17, 1775, in Richard B. Morris, ed., *John Jay: The Making of a Revolutionary: Unpublished Papers, 1745–1780* (New York, 1975), 158–159; "Minutes of the Committee of Safety of the Manor of Livingston," *NYGBR,* LX (1929), 33–334; *Calendar of Historical Manuscripts, Relating to the War of the Revolution,* I, 581, II, 215; Kim, *Landlord and Tenant,* 290–315, 396–398; Humphrey, "Agrarian Rioting," 153–166; Taughanick Deed, Mar. 16, 1757, MA, CXVIII, 588–591.

30. *Calendar of Historical Manuscripts, Relating to the War of the Revolution,* II, 190–192, 205; "Oaths of Secrecy and Allegiance to King George III," n.d., in the Paltsits Manuscripts, Ulster Co., NYHS, record oaths sworn before Arnold Viele. A comparison of lists of rioters in the 1750s, the holders of a Stockbridge Indian deed to Taughanick lands, and the 1757 and 1771 proprietors of this claim (MA, XXXII, 757–759, VI, 380–383, CXVII, 327, CXVIII, 588–591, 592–594, 596) with the Livingston Manor accused loyalists shows very little last-name continuity, with the exception of the Brasees, Spoors, and Harry / Hendrick Smith. There were members of the Reese family among the 1750s rioters and the militia delinquents. Men from the rioter families McArthur, Reese, Robison, and Wolcott were among the whig officers or bondsmen.

31. Comparing evidence for whig service, fines for militia delinquency, and suspected tory allegiance during the Revolution with a 1795 list of petitioners against the Livingston title provides a way to assess the relationship between various kinds of discontent during the Revolution and tenant resistance in the 1790s.

Livingston Manor Inhabitants, 1776–1783	Total	1795 Manor Petitioners (N = 269)
Whig officers and committeemen, not fined	76	7 9.2%
Bailsmen not officers, not fined	19	2 10.5%
Officers and committeemen, fined	4	1 25.0%
Enlisted men, Capt. Van Gaasbeck's Ranger Company, 1776	44	5 11.3%
Others fined	70	8 11.4%

Investigated, given oaths, 1777	43	8	18.6%
Accused tories	96	5	5.2%
Whig leadership, not fined	95	9	9.5%
All fined	74	9	12.2%
Fined, investigated, given oaths	117	17	14.5%
All investigated and accused tories	139	13	9.3%

These data suggest that neither the whig leadership nor the accused tories would sign the 1795 petition. The roots of the 1795 petition ran back to the more mainstream families, some of whom served in Ranger company, some of whom were investigated during the tory crisis, some of whom were fined for militia delinquency. The accused tories, many captured at the Copake skirmish, were less likely to persist on the Manor and thus less likely to be among the 1795 signers.

Sources: 1775–1783 Livingston inhabitants, 1776–1783: James A. Roberts, ed., *New York in the Revolution as Colony and State,* 2d ed. (Albany, N.Y., 1898; rpt. 1996), I, 113, 117; Fernow, ed., *New York in the Revolution,* 269–270; "Minutes of the Committee of Safety of the Manor of Livingston," *NYGBR,* LX (1929), 239–243, 325–241; *Calendar of Historical Manuscripts, Relating to the War of the Revolution,* I, 173–174, 581, II, 190–194, 196–231 267–268; Sullivan, ed., *Minutes,* I, 336, 449, 669; Paltsits, ed., *Minutes,* I, 142, 143, 152, 221, 239–240, 254, 274, 335, 337, 340, 347, 393, 394, 403, 510–512, 531, 574, 576, 605–607, 618, 623, 629, 630, 632, 643, 644, 685, 726; "Oaths of Secrecy and Allegiance," Paltsits Manuscripts, NYHS.

Sources: 1795 petitioners: "Petition of Petrus Pulver and Others Demanding an Investigation into the Livingston's Title," in E. B. O'Callaghan, ed., *Documentary History of the State of New-York . . .* (Albany, N.Y., 1850), III, 834–841.

I am indebted to Ruth Piwonka and Donald Lampson for sharing their own analyses of much of this same evidence.

The situation on Livingston Manor in 1776–1777 has been the subject of a long literature. In stressing the lack of civil connection of recent immigrants, I follow the implications of Ronald Hoffman's analysis in "The 'Disaffected' in the Revolutionary South," in Alfred F. Young, ed., *The American Revolution: Explorations in the History of American Radicalism* (DeKalb, Ill., 1976), 273–316; I am in general agreement with Kierner, "Landlord and Tenant in Revolutionary New York," *New York History,* LXX (1989), 133–152; and Ranlett, *The New York Loyalists,* 106–119, 129–136. Humphrey, *Land and Liberty,* 102–107, fully appreciates the ambiguities of the situation but emphasizes the theme of a "tenant rebellion," argued in Staughton Lynd's classic essay, "The Tenant Rising at Livingston Manor, May 1777," *New-York Historical Society Quarterly,* XLVIII (1964), 163–177. On the scale of immigration between 1763 and 1774. see Bernard Bailyn, *Voyagers to the West: A Passage in the Peopling of America on the Eve of the Revolution* (New York, 1986), esp. 573–637; Nicholas Canny, ed., *Europeans on the Move: Studies on European Migration, 1500–1800* (Oxford, 1994). On the half-pay officers, see Huey and Phillips, *Nassau,* 7–9; and the petitions in NYALG, XVII, 149, 152–154, 161, XXXIII, 38, 39, XXIV, 109, 110, 147.

32. The turnover in the Nobletown population is demonstrated by a comparison of the 1766 refugee list ("An Account of the Losses Sustained . . ." [May 27, 1767], MA, VI, 360–361) and the "Exact List of the Names . . . of Each Person That Came into the Indian Purchase of Noble's Town . . . Nov. 2, 1767," MA, VI, 412–413, with the various lists of Hillsdale inhabitants, militia, and petitioners from 1775 forward. Strikingly, of roughly 175 names in Nobletown in 1766 there are

no exact matches, and only 7 last-name matches, with the Muster Roll, Captain John McKinstry's Company . . . . 1775, Massachusetts Muster Rolls, XV, 63. Eight of roughly 100 pre-1766 Nobletown purchasers and refugees can be identified on the Claverack militia rolls in 1767 and 1770. Israel Spencer, wounded at Nobletown in 1766, would be an important figure in Spencertown for the rest of the century. At least 4 men among the Nobletown purchasers and refugees, John Bagley, Ebenezer Blackman, Caleb Clark, and Robert Meeker, would sign the petitions against the Van Rensselaer title in 1789. For details of the 1789 petitions, see Chapter 5. For the Claverack militia rolls, see the *Third Annual Report of the State Historian of the State of New York, 1897* (New York and Albany, 1898), 761, 769, 770, 871, 874. The service of the Ninth Albany is described in detail in the Jacob Ford affidavit, pension file, Aug. 25, 1832; Moses Meyer affidavit, pension file, Aug. 22, 1832; John Gott affidavit, pension file, Oct. 22, 1832 (Donald E. Lampson, transcr.). See also Sullivan, ed., *Minutes*, I, 325, 725; *Calendar of Historical Manuscripts, Relating to the War of the Revolution*, I, 515, 521; Hastings and Holden, eds., *Public Papers of George Clinton*, II, 780, III, 516, 555–558, 562, 737, VI, 694, 696–698.

33. James Sullivan et al., eds., *The Papers of Sir William Johnson* (Albany, N.Y., 1921–1965), VI, 670, 678–670, VII, 418–419, 511–513, 672–673, VIII, 100–102, 448–450, XII, 319 (reference to a Livingston Manor Regiment in 1767); *Third Annual Report of the State Historian*, 761–765, 768–771; Sullivan, ed., *Minutes*, I, 232, 235, 236, 250, 254, 255, 475. See discussions in Denman, "From Deference to Democracy," 16–22, 41–45. The militia returns taken during the disastrous summer of 1778 provide the only quantitative snapshot of militia behavior. In July 1778 one-quarter of the Albany brigade was ordered to the Mohawk Valley, and at the end of August Colonel Barents Staats made a return of the men with him guarding the destroyed village of Cherry Valley. The Livingston Manor men had refused to march, and Staats had with him only a third of the men assigned from Kinderhook and Claverack; more than half of the men from Hillsdale and King's (Canaan) were on duty. Hastings and Holden, eds., *Public Papers of George Clinton*, III, 562–563 (July 20, 1778), 737 (Aug. 27, 1778).

34. Peter Force, ed., *American Archives*, 4th Ser. (Washington, D.C., 1837–1846), VI, 1055; Canaan, N.Y., Town Record Book, June 24, 1776, NYSA [74-1-1]; see also transcription in Stokes, *Letters and Memories*, 197–198; Ellis, *Columbia County*, 322; Pauline Maier, *American Scripture: Making the Declaration of Independence* (New York, 1997), 68, 233; Alexander Hamilton, Albany[?], to Robert Livingston, Manor, Apr. 25, 1785, in Syrett et al., eds., *PAH*, III, 608–609; *Journals of the Provincial Congress of New York*, I, 552; Countryman, *A People in Revolution*, 152; Denman, "From Deference to Democracy," 594 n. 47; Goodall, "New Light on the Border," 146–262. For the circumstances and progress of the drafting of the constitution in 1777, see Daniel J. Hulsebosch, *Constituting Empire: New York and the Transformation of Constitutionalism in the Atlantic World, 1664–1830* (Chapel Hill, N.C., 2005), 169–189.

35. Sabine, ed., *Historical Memoirs*, II, 294; Fernow, ed., *New York in the Revolution*, 267–269; *Journals of the Provincial Congress of New York*, I, 515–528, 554–564. While the field officers of the Livingston regiment were paid for a week of duty in October 1780, they do not appear in the accounts of the march against Johnson's raiders or the Battle of Klock's Field, as do regimental officers from Hillsdale, King's, Claverack, and Kinderhook.

36. Stone, trans., *Letters of Brunswick and Hessian Officers*, 137; John C. Fitzpatrick, ed., *The Autobiography of Martin Van Buren*, vol. II of *Annual Report of the American Historical Association for the Year 1918* (Washington, 1920), 19–20.

37. *Calendar of Historical Manuscripts, Relating to the War of the Revolution*, I, 606–608, 609–

615; Henry C. Van Schaack, *The Life of Peter Van Schaack* (New York, 1842), 54, 72–73. Peter Van Schaack's assertion that "individual volition must determine ultimate allegiance in revolutionary situations," James H. Kettner has argued, "pointed the direction in which American thought would move"; see *The Development of American Citizenship, 1608–1870* (Chapel Hill, N.C., 1978), 44–61, esp. 188–189. In this discussion I am also indebted to Kammen, "The Revolution as a *Crise de Conscience,*" New York," in Jellison, ed., *Society, Freedom, and Conscience,* 125–189; John Shy, "Hearts and Minds in the American Revolution: The Case of 'Long Bill' Scott and Peterborough, New Hampshire," in Shy, *A People Numerous and Armed: Reflections on the Military Struggle for American Independence* (New York, 1976), 165–179.

    38. Van Schaack, *Life of Peter Van Schaack,* 54.

    39. Ibid., 86, 88, 89. On the civil struggle in New York, see Hulsebosch, *Constituting Empire,* 145–157; Countryman, *A People in Revolution,* 103–161.

    40. Van Schaack, *Life of Peter Van Schaack,* 56–57; William A. Benton, "Peter Van Schaack: The Conscience of a Loyalist," in Robert A. East and Jacob Judd, eds., *The Loyalist Americans: A Focus on Greater New York* (Tarrytown, N.Y., 1975), 46–47; Leopold S. Launitz-Schürer, *Loyal Whigs and Revolutionaries: The Making of the Revolution in New York, 1765–1776* (New York, 1980), 144, 159, 162, 197.

    41. Van Schaack, *Life of Peter Van Schaack,* 2–6, 13–15, 62–63n; Collier, *Kinderhook,* 408; Kammen, "The American Revolution as a *Crise de Conscience,*" in Jellison, ed., *Society, Freedom, and Conscience,* 170.

    42. On Dutch ethnicity, see A. G. Roeber, "'The Origin of Whatever Is Not English among Us': The Dutch-speaking and German-speaking Peoples of British Colonial America," in Bernard Bailyn and Philip D. Morgan, eds., *Strangers within the Realm: Cultural Margins of the First British Empire* (Chapel Hill, N.C., 1991), 220–283; Alice P. Kenney, *Stubborn for Liberty: The Dutch in New York* (Syracuse, N.Y., 1975); Kenney, "The Albany Dutch: Loyalists and Patriots," *New York History,* XL (1961), 331–350; Firth Haring Fabend, *A Dutch Family in the Middle Colonies, 1660–1800* (New Brunswick, N.J., 1991), esp. 105–130, 240–247; Fabend, *Zion on the Hudson: Dutch New York and New Jersey in the Age of Revivals* (New Brunswick, N.J., 2000). My account of the relationship between law and property among the Kinderhook Dutch is grounded in Mushkat and Rayback, *Martin Van Buren,* 5–6; Collier, *Kinderhook,* provides considerable detail. For an earlier period, see Donna Merwick, *The Death of a Notary: Conquest and Change in Colonial New York* (Ithaca, N.Y., 1999).

    43. My estimate of Kinderhook allegiances is based on the names of officers and committeemen listed in Sullivan, ed., *Minutes,* I, 28, 85–86, 114, 236–237, 252, 280, 290, 314, 421, 896; Fernow, ed., *New York in the Revolution,* 267; Roberts, ed., *New York in the Revolution as Colony and State,* I, 109, Collier, *Kinderhook,* 542. See also Kenney, "The Albany Dutch," *New York History,* XLII (1961), 335–339; Van Schaack, *Life of Peter Van Schaack,* 57 ("delicate" quote).

    44. Collier, *Kinderhook,* 76; Petition of the Westenhook Patentees, Aug. 1, 1774, NYALG, XXXIV, 75; Kim, *Landlord and Tenant,* 283, 348, 364, 411. On the Van Schaack–Westenhook controversy, see Chapter 5.

    45. Sullivan et al., eds., *Papers of Sir William Johnson,* VI, 642, 670, 678–680, 702–703, VII, 23–24, 101, 116–118, 302–303, 326, 329–330, 359–361 (quote), 368–369, 393–394, 422, 634, VIII, 84–85, 95–96, 100–102, 449, 455, 462, 529, 535–536, 549–450, XII, 319, 905–906; *Third Annual Report of the State Historian,* 892–893; Collier, *Kinderhook,* 79–82. The Apr. 24, 1771, Kinderhook petition is printed in Collier, *Kinderhook,* 80–82, from NYALG, XVIII, 155. An earlier

petition, submitted in 1769, was more inclusive, with eight future patriots and eleven future loyalists among its sixty-seven signers. Kinderhook Petition, Dec. 23, 1769, Mss. 1819, NYSL. See the excellent discussions in Denman, "From Deference to Democracy," 16–22; Goodall, "New Light on the Border," 69–76.

46. Thomas Allen to Seth Pomeroy, Mar. 9, 1775, in Collier, *Kinderhook*, 169–170; Van Schaack, *Life of Peter Van Schaack*, 51; Sullivan, ed., *Minutes*, I, 12–13,˙28, 125, 252, 280, 301, 303–304; *Calendar of Historical Manuscripts, Relating to the War of the Revolution*, I, 609.

47. *Calendar of Historical Manuscripts, Relating to the War of the Revolution*, I, 609–610; Sullivan, ed., *Minutes*, I, 262–263, 305, 314, 322, 325–327, 332, 359–360, 364, 368, 421, 423, 542–543, 983–984.

48. *Calendar of Historical Manuscripts, Relating to the War of the Revolution*, I, 610; Sullivan, ed., *Minutes*, I, 607, 622, 742, 754, 772, 891, 896; Fernow, *New York in the Revolution*, 539. See Hastings and Hudson, eds., *Public Papers of George Clinton*, III, 690, for Abraham Ten Broeck's positive recommendation of Harmen Van Buren. Detachments of Kinderhook militia were sent back to the town from Saratoga to Kinderhook, "to protect the property of the inhabitants, and to prevent it from falling into the hands of Tories and robbers." Lawrence M. Goes, Pension file, Sept. 7, 1832, Donald E. Lampson, transcr.

49. Kinderhook Politics, 1771–1781, and the 1779 Valuation of Real Property:

	Decile, 1779 Valuation					
	1st	2d	3d	4th	5th–10th	Known (Unknown)
1771 petition against Van Rensselaer	3	7	2			12 (10)
Loyalists	7	8	6		1	22 (7)
1775 officers reappointed, 1776–1781	3	1	1	1	1	7 (3)
New committeemen and officers appointed, 1776–1781	2	6	8	6	4	26 (25)

Sources: 1779 Kinderhook Valuation, NYSA. The 1771 Kinderhook petition is printed in Collier, *Kinderhook*, 80–82, from NYALG, XVIII, 155. For patriots, see officers and committeemen listed in Sullivan, ed., *Minutes*, I, 28, 85–86, 114, 236–237, 252, 280, 290, 314, 362–363, 421, 896; Fernow, ed., *New York in the Revolution as Colony and State*, I, 267; Roberts ed., *New York in the Revolution*, 109, Collier, *Kinderhook*, 542. For loyalists, see Sullivan, ed., *Minutes*, I, 480, 769; Paltsits, ed., *Minutes*, I, 171, 181, 834–835; *Calendar of Historical Manuscripts, Relating to the War of the Revolution*, II, 364.

Chastellux, *Travels in North America*, ed. Rice, I, 196; Sullivan, ed., *Minutes*, I, 360; Fernow, ed., *New York in the Revolution*, 267. One pension document, in comments regarding a march to Springfield in the summer of 1777, identified Abraham Van Buren as a "Deputy Commissary." Lawrence M. Goes affidavit, Pension File, Sept. 7, 1832, Donald E. Lampson, transcr.

50. Paltsits, ed., *Minutes*, I, 171, 174, 175, 181, 183, 186, 189–190, 196, 200, 201, 203, 213, 216, 226, 311, 340, 369, II, 476, 506, 834; Hastings and Holden, eds., *Public Papers of George Clinton*, V, 399,

VI, 64–66, 166–167; Van Schaack, *Life of Peter Van Schaack,* 106–144, 257–277. On the dynamics of relationships across the lines between British-held New York City and the patriot stronghold upriver, see Judith L. Van Buskirk, *Generous Enemies: Patriots and Loyalists in Revolutionary New York* (Philadelphia, 2002).

Martin, or Marte, Van Buren, was appointed a lieutenant in the Albany County Ranger Company, Aug. 9, 1776, and was arrested at the request of Captain Baldwin in February 1777. He was paroled to New York in August 1778. In December 1779, Annatie Van Buren petitioned the governor for a pass to join him in New York City; in 1780, as Hannah, she petitioned again. Annatie Wesselse had married Martin, son of Martin Van Buren (and brother of Abraham) in 1777. Sullivan, ed., *Minutes,* I, 519–520, 679; Paltsits, ed., *Minutes,* I, 181, 183, 189, 197–198, 835; Hastings and Holden, eds., *Public Papers of George Clinton,* V, 399, VI, 65–66; Peckham, *History of Cornelius Maessen Van Buren,* 68–69, 88–90, 114.

51. Van Schaack, *Life of Peter Van Schaack,* 86; Gustave Beaumont to Rose Beaumont, June 7, 1831, cited in George Wilson Pierson, *Tocqueville and Beaumont in America* (New York, 1938), 116; Martin Van Buren, NYC, to John P. Van Ness, Washington, D.C., Jan. 15, 1803, MVBP. For another turn-of-the-century mockery of local events of Revolution, see *A New Farce Was Acted . . . at the New Theatre in the Town of Hoosack [i.e., Hoosick, N.Y.], Called Pandemonium in Dishabille; or, Pretended Republicanism Put in Practice. . . .* ([Troy, N.Y.?], 1808) (Shaw-Shoemaker 5722).

52. Sullivan, ed., *Minutes,* I, 793; Collier, *Kinderhook,* 386–387, 546–547, 551; Hugh Hastings and Henry Harmon Noble, eds., *Military Minutes of the Council of Appointment of the State of New York, 1783–1821* (Albany, N.Y., 1901–1902), I, 97; Lansingburgh *Federal Herald,* July 21, 28, 1788; *New-York Journal, and Daily Patriotic Register,* July 5, 1788; Denman, "From Deference to Democracy," 100; Sullivan et al., eds., *Papers of Sir William Johnson,* VII, 360; Peter Van Ness et al., Kinderhook, to [the Clermont Republican Committee], Apr. 12, 1799, WFP-UM.

53. Priscilla J. Brewer, *Shaker Communities, Shaker Lives* (Hanover, N.H., 1986), 6–12; Stephen A. Marini, *Radical Sects of Revolutionary New England* (Cambridge, Mass., 1982), 109–114, 127–129; *Testimonies of the Life, Character, Revelations, and Doctrines of Our Ever Blessed Mother Ann Lee . . .* (Hancock, Mass., 1816), 196; Jessie Carney Smith, ed., *Notable Black American Women* (Detroit, 1992), 371–373; Sidney Kaplan and Emma Nogrady Kaplan, *The Black Presence in the Era of the American Revolution,* rev. ed. (Amherst, Mass., 1989), 44–48; David Levering Lewis, *W. E. B. Du Bois: Biography of a Race, 1868–1919* (New York, 1993), 13–14; Collier, *Kinderhook,* 60, 100–101, 138–140.

54. Julius Goebel, Jr., and Joseph H. Smith, eds., *The Law Practice of Alexander Hamilton: Documents and Commentary* (New York, 1964–1981), III, 308–310; E. Wilder Spaulding, *New York in the Critical Period, 1783–1789* (New York, 1932), 69; *NY Laws,* 5th sess., 1782, chap. 23, An Act to Divide the District of Claverack . . . , Mar. 26, 1782; *NY Laws,* 6th sess., chap. 2, An Act to Abolish Entail . . . , July 12, 1782; *NY Laws,* 6th sess., chap. 11, An Act to Prevent Grants . . . , July 25, 1782.

55. Stephen B. Miller, *Historical Sketches of Hudson . . .* (Hudson, N.Y., 1862), 8–10.

56. Kings' District Records, May 6, 1783, in Stokes, *Letters and Memories,* 203; Dunton, comp., *Reflections,* 12; Collier, *Kinderhook,* 180; *NYSJ,* 6th sess., 1783, 2d mtg., 140; Paltsits, ed., *Minutes,* I, 32n; *NYAJ,* 7th sess., 1784, 27, 109–110, 115, 116, 120; May 12, 1784, *NY Laws,* 7th sess., 1784, chap. 66, An Act to Preserve the Freedom and Independence . . . ; *NY Laws,* 9th sess., 1786, chap. 66, "An Act for the Payment of Certain Sums of Money . . ."; Hastings and Noble, eds., *Military Minutes of the Council of Appointment,* I, 95–100; "Register of Seats, 1795," in Royden W. Vos-

burgh, ed., "Records of the Reformed Dutch Church of Kinderhook, in Kinderhook, Columbia County, N.Y.," New York Genealogical and Historical Society, typescript, (1921), 278–383.

57. King's District Records, June 16, 1777, in Stokes, *Letters and Memories,* 198–199.

CHAPTER 2

1. Stephen B. Miller, *Historical Sketches of Hudson . . .* (Hudson, N.Y., 1862), 8; Ellis, *Columbia County,* 154–159; Oliver W. Holmes, "The Stage-Coach Business in the Hudson Valley," *Quarterly Journal of the New York State Historical Association,* XII (1931), 321–356; Robert J. Stets, "U.S. Government-Authorized Private Mail Service, 1787–1790," *Chronicle of U.S. Classic Postal Issues,* XLV (February 1993), 9–13.

2. William G. Peacher, "Craft Masonry," 320–323, 332–333, "Solomon's Lodge No. 1, Poughkeepsie, New York," American Lodge of Research, Free and Accepted Masons, *Transactions,* XIII, no. 2 (1976), 234; Ellis, *Columbia County,* 177–178, 196, 197; Alexander Coventry, "Memoirs of an Emigrant: The Journal of Alexander Coventry, M.D.," typescript, AIHA and NYSL (1978), May 2, 1786, p. 95; *Hudson Weekly Gazette,* June 1, 15, Aug. 3, 1786; *Hudson Gazette,* Mar. 15, Sept. 20, 1792, Feb. 7, Mar. 7, 28, May 16, 1793 (as cited in the Philadelphia *General Advertiser,* May 25, 1793).

3. Peter Clark, *British Clubs and Societies, 1580–1800: The Origins of an Associational World* (Oxford, 2000), 389–420, provides the best overview from a transatlantic perspective. For England, see John Money, *Experience and Identity: Birmingham and the West Midlands, 1760–1800* (Montreal, 1977); John Brewer, *The Pleasures of the Imagination: English Culture in the Eighteenth Century* (New York, 1997); Kathleen Wilson, *The Sense of the People: Politics, Culture, and Imperialism in England, 1715–1785* (New York, 1995). For comparable American studies, see David S. Shields, *Civil Tongues and Polite Letters in British America* (Chapel Hill, N.C., 1997); Stephen C. Bullock, *Revolutionary Brotherhood: Freemasonry and the Transformation of the American Social Order, 1730–1840* (Chapel Hill, N.C., 1996), 9–108. David D. Hall, in the introduction to Hugh Amory and Hall, eds., *A History of the Book in America,* I, *The Colonial Book in the Atlantic World* (New York, 2000), argues that there was no Habermasian public sphere in colonial America (10). I suspect that historians will argue that there were indeed discrete urban public spheres in the larger seaport towns of the eighteenth-century colonies and that they were unified in the revolutionary crisis of 1765–1775. The eighteenth-century public sphere—in the sense of an arena of cultural construction and consumption shared among a literate local audience—arrived only after the Revolution in places like Columbia County. Trish Loughran argues insightfully, in *The Republic of Print: Print Culture in the Age of U.S. Nation Building, 1770–1870* (New York, 2007), that into the first decades of the nineteenth century the United States was still divided into local and regional publics and that a true national public sphere did not take shape until the 1830s.

4. *A Condensed History of Mount Vernon Lodge, No. 3, of Ancient York Masons . . .* ([Albany?], n.d.), 68; W. J. Hughan, "Mount Vernon Lodge, No. 3, Albany, New York," *Freemason,* Sept. 7, 1889; Herbert T. Singer and Ossian Lang, *New York Freemasonry: A Bicentennial History, 1781–1981* (New York, 1981), 32–33, 36–40; "Albany Grand Lodge of Perfection: Transcribed Minute Book, 1767–1774, 1821–1825, and 1841–1845," typescript, Library of the Museum of Our National Heritage, Lexington, Mass.; William G. Peacher, "Solomon's Lodge No. 1, Poughkeepsie, New York," American Lodge of Research, Free and Accepted Masons, *Transactions,* XIII, no. 2 (1976), 235–236, and "Craft Masonry," XIII, no. 3 (1977), 320–331, 330; Massachusetts, Secretary of State, *Massachusetts Soldiers and Sailors of the Revolutionary War . . .* (Boston, (1896–1908), VI,

130; William Raymond, *Biographical Sketches of the Distinguished Men of Columbia County . . .* (Albany, N.Y., 1851), 79.

5. Cynthia A. Kierner, *Traders and Gentlefolk: The Livingstons of New York, 1675–1790* (Ithaca, N.Y., 1992), 132, 136, 139–143, 149–151; Richard B. Morris, ed., *John Jay: The Making of a Revolutionary: Unpublished Papers, 1745–1780* (New York, 1975), 111–118; Alfred F. Young, *The Democratic Republicans of New York: The Origins, 1763–1797* (Chapel Hill, N.C., 1967), 15. See also Esther Singleton, *Social New York under the Georges, 1714–1776* (New York, 1902), 301–305; Rufus W. Griswold, *The Republican Court; or, American Society in the Days of Washington* (New York, 1864), 148.

6. For insights into the belletristic parlor culture of the Columbia landed gentry and the wider Knickerbocker context, see the poems by Robert R. Livingston dated 1794, and the poem sent with flowers by Robert R. Livingston to Mary Livingston, Feb. 7, 1797, RRLP; the Mary Livingston Diary, CCHS; and the accounts in Cynthia A. Kierner, *Traders and Gentlefolk,* 128–154, and "Patrician Womanhood in the Early Republic: The 'Reminiscenses' of Janet Livingston Montgomery," *New York History,* LXIII (1992), 389–407; Roger G. Kennedy, *Orders from France: The Americans and the French in a Revolutionary World, 1780–1820* (New York, 1989), 59–78; Stephen Nissenbaum, *The Battle for Christmas* (New York, 1996), 49–89; Don Foster, *Author Unknown: On the Trail of Anonymous* (New York, 2000), 221–275; Mary Weatherspoon Bowden, "Cocklofts and Slang-whangers: The Historical Sources of Washington Irving's *Salamgundi," New York History,* LXI (1980), 133–160; Stanley T. Williams, *The Life of Washington Irving* (New York, 1935), esp. I, 108–109. David S. Shields, *Civil Tongues* and *Oracles of Empire: Poetry, Politics, and Commerce in British America, 1690–1750* (Chicago, 1990), provides a wider context. For an analysis of a social sphere mediating between the public sphere and private domesticity, see Karen V. Hansen, *A Very Social Time: Crafting Community in Antebellum New England* (Berkeley, Calif., 1994).

7. Poem printed in "A Packet of Old Letters," *Dutchess County Historical Society Yearbook,* VI (1921), 36n. See also "Hereditary Sheriff of Dutchess: To the Curious," De Witt Clinton Broadside Collection, Albany Institute of History and Art. Such broadsides survive from the post-Revolutionary land disputes in Columbia County, indicating that the landlords continued to post city-printed "great papers" to intimidate their tenants. See below, Chapters 4, 5, and 9.

8. Sullivan, ed., *Minutes,* I, 127–128, 134, 139, 157, 158, 160, 306, 322, 758; the Yates broadside is on 139. For an account of this episode, see Marta Wagner, "Education and Politics in Revolutionary Albany," in Paul A. Gilje and William Pencak, eds., *New York in the Age of the Constitution, 1775–1800* (Cranbury, N.J., 1992), 178–179.

9. *Albany Gazette,* Dec. 2, 16, 1771; Joel Munsell, *The Typographical Miscellany* (Albany, N.Y., 1850), 224; Isaiah Thomas, *The History of Printing in America, with a Biography of Printers and an Account of Newspapers,* ed. Marcus A. McCorison (New York, 1970), 483–484; Clarence S. Brigham, *History and Bibliography of American Newspapers, 1690–1820* (Worcester, Mass., 1947), II, 532, 688; Sullivan, ed., *Minutes,* I, 247, 432, 458, 502, 557, 593, 605, 787; Lorenzo Sabine, ed., *Biographical Sketches of American Loyalists* (Boston, 1864), II, 220.

10. *Albany Gazette,* Dec. 2, 16, 30, 1771.

11. The loyalist William Smith, interned at the Livingston Manor house from 1776 to 1778, was obsessed with rumor and with false information planted in the wartime papers. He left the most-detailed record of newspaper reading available for the entire period. During the ninety-three weeks that he spent at Livingston Manor, he mentioned newspapers in his diary 164 times. Of these references, 68 (42%) were to Samuel Loudon's *New-York Packet* (Fishkill) and John

Holt's *New York Journal* (Kingston and Poughkeepsie) published in the local river towns, 49 (30%) were to New England papers (mostly from Boston), 23 (14%) were to papers from Pennsylvania, New Jersey, and various southern states, and 24 (14%) were to loyalist papers in New York City, including two references to the Robertsons' *Royal American Gazette*. William H. W. Sabine, ed., *Historical Memoirs from 12 July 1776 to 25 July 1778 of William Smith, Historian of the Province of New York . . .* (New York, 1958), II. On wartime censorship, see *NY Laws,* 4th sess., 1781, chap. 48; Edward Countryman, *A People in Revolution: The American Revolution and Political Society in New York, 1760–1790* (Baltimore, 1981), 174.

12. Brigham, ed., *History and Bibliography,* II, 721, 724–725; Milton W. Hamilton, *The Country Printer: New York State, 1785–1830* (New York, 1936), 291–292; Munsell, *The Typographical Miscellany,* 224–226; Thomas, *The History of Printing,* 484.

13. My account here of colonial oligarchs, ethnoreligious communities, and a county-based mediation politics should be compared to accounts in Alan Tully, *Forming American Politics: Ideals, Interests, and Institutions in Colonial New York and Pennsylvania* (Baltimore, 1994); A. G. Roeber, *Palatines, Liberty, and Property: German Lutherans in Colonial British America* (Baltimore, 1993); Brendan McConville, *These Daring Disturbers of the Public Peace: The Struggle for Property and Power in Early New Jersey* (Ithaca, N.Y., 1999); Liam Riordan, *Many Identities, One Nation: The Revolution and Its Legacy in the Mid-Atlantic* (Philadelphia, 2007).

14. Here I follow John Ehrenberg, *Civil Society: The Critical History of an Idea* (New York, 1999), 167–168; Judith N. Shklar, *Montesquieu* (New York, 1987), 79–83. See also Alexis de Tocqueville, *Democracy in America,* trans. Henry Reeves, rev. Francis Bowen, ed. Philips Bradley (New York, 1945), II, 342.

15. Henry Livingston, Manor, to Walter Livingston, NYC, Apr. 24 1785, RRLP.

16. The term "Columbia Junto" seems to date from a slightly later period, but it is a convenient term to describe the alliance of Federalists who took control of county politics in the late 1790s. For use of the term, see New York *American,* Apr. 24, 1819, and *Albany Argus,* Apr. 25, 1820. A Hudson city promoter used the term "Junto" to describe the hostile local gentry in 1788: Seth Jenkins, Hudson, to Philip Schuyler, Poughkeepsie, Jan. 21, 1788, Schuyler Papers, NYPL.

17. Sung Bok Kim, "The Limits of Politicization in the American Revolution: The Experience of Westchester County, New York," *Journal of American History,* LXXX (1993–1994), 868–889.

18. Jackson Turner Main, *Political Parties before the Constitution* (Chapel Hill, N.C., 1973), 120–155; Countryman, *A People in Revolution,* 195–251.

19. Here I follow the broad outlines of Jack Greene's account of the meaning of "improvement" and Christopher Tomlins's seminal discussion of the meaning of "police" in early America. See Jack P. Greene, *The Intellectual Construction of America: Exceptionalism and Identity from 1492 to 1800* (Chapel Hill, N.C., 1993), 95–129; Greene, "Social and Cultural Capital in Colonial British America: A Case Study," *Journal of Interdisciplinary History,* XXIX (1998–1999), 491–509; Christopher L. Tomlins, *Law, Labor, and Ideology in the Early American Republic* (New York, 1993), 35–59. On New York's loan office, see John P. Kaminski, *Paper Politics: The Northern State Loan-Offices during the Confederation, 1783–1790* (New York, 1989), 139–168.

20. Here I draw upon arguments about distributive and regulatory politics in post-Revolutionary New York developed by L. Ray Gunn in *The Decline of Authority: Public Economic Policy and Political Development in New York State, 1800–1860* (Ithaca, N.Y., 1988), 57–98; and Hendrik Hartog, *Public Property and Private Power: The Corporation of the City of New York in American Law, 1730–1870* (Ithaca, N.Y., 1983), 82–175. More generally, see the complementary if

competing perspectives developed in William J. Novak, *The People's Welfare: Law and Regulation in Nineteenth-Century America* (Chapel Hill, N.C., 1996), 19–50; and Richard L. McCormick, *The Party Period and Public Policy: American Politics from the Age of Jackson to the Progressive Era* (New York, 1986), 203–227. Richard R. John, "Governmental Institutions as Agents of Change: Rethinking American Political Development in the Early Republic, 1787–1835," *Studies in American Political Development,* XI (1997), 347–380, is an essential guide to this literature. More broadly, my discussion is informed by an understanding of the intersection of civil society and the state in democratic polities, rather than their antagonism. This approach is shaped by Jürgen Habermas's discussion of the legislature as a formal "law-making" public sphere in *Between Facts and Norms: Contributions to a Discourse Theory of Law and Democracy,* trans. William Rehg, (Cambridge, Mass., 1996), esp. 287–387; and by readings in Jean L. Cohen and Andrew Arato, *Civil Society and Political Theory* (Cambridge, Mass., 1994), esp. 109–110, 113; Theda Skocpol, "How Americans Became Civic," in Skocpol and Morris P. Fiorina, eds., *Civic Engagement in American Democracy* (New York, 1999), 27–80; Skocpol, "The Tocqueville Problem: Civic Engagement in American Democracy," *Social Science History,* XXI (1997), 455–479; Michael Schudson, "The 'Public Sphere' and Its Problems: Bringing the State (Back) In," *Notre Dame Journal of Law, Ethics, and Public Policy,* VIII (1994), 529–546; and the essays in Bob Edwards, Michael Foley, and Mario Deani, eds., *Beyond Tocqueville: Civil Society and the Social Capital Debate in Comparative Perspective* (Hanover, N.H., 2001).

21. Van Beck Hall, *Politics without Parties: Massachusetts, 1780–1791* (Pittsburgh, 1972); John L. Brooke, "To the Quiet of the People: Revolutionary Settlements and Civil Unrest in Western Massachusetts, 1774–1789," *William and Mary Quarterly,* 3d Ser., XLVI (1989), 425–462.

22.

Terms Served in Legislature

Town	1775–1776	1777–1785	1786–1788
Kinderhook	2	3	5
Hillsdale and Canaan	2	17	2
Claverack	4	4	1
Livingston	4	6	3
Total	12	30	11

Hillsdale through 1782 and Canaan through 1788 were, respectively, the East District of Claverack and the King's District. Franklin B. Hough, *The New-York Civil List . . . from the Revolution to the Present Time* (Albany, N.Y., 1860), 57–64, 107, 123–128, 181–191.

For Whiting's votes, see *NYAJ,* 1st sess., 1778, 2d mtg., Feb 4, Mar. 6, 7, 9. David J. Goodall, "New Light on the Border: New England Squatter Settlements in New York during the American Revolution" (Ph.D. diss., SUNY Albany, 1984), 146–262, provides a detailed account of the revolutionary emergence of these hill town representatives.

23. Eliakim Reed Ford, *Ford Genealogy . . .* (Oneonta, N.Y., 1916), 54; Edward S. Frisbie, *The Frisbie-Frisbee Genealogy . . .* (Rutland, Vt., 1928), 33–34, 50–52, 90–92; Mary Anne Dunton, comp., *Reflections: Canaan, New York, Bicentennial, 1978* (Canaan, N.Y., 1976), 8, 19–21; Ellis, *Columbia County,* 294, 326; [Matthew Adgate], *A Northern Light; or, New Index to the Bible . . .* (Troy, N.Y., 1800); "Austerlitz Presbyterian Society [formerly the Green River Congregationalist Society], c. 1792," *Columbia* (Rhinebeck, N.Y.), XIII (1997), 47; *Minutes of the Shaftsbury Baptist*

Association, Held at White Creek . . . June, 1810: Together with Their Circular and Corresponding Letter (Lansingburgh, N.Y., 1810), 3; Minutes of the Shaftsbury Baptist Association, Held at Cheshire . . . June 1811 . . . (Lansingburgh, N.Y., 1811), 4. On Adgate's lameness, I rely on Jason Duncan, personal communication, Sept. 9, 2005. Duncan is the author of "New England Adventurer: A Life of Matthew Adgate" (master's thesis, University of Iowa, 1992).

24. On the New England Country, or Popular, parties, see Richard L. Bushman, From Puritan to Yankee: Character and the Social Order in Connecticut, 1690–1765 (Cambridge, Mass., 1967), 235–266; Stephen E. Patterson, Political Parties in Revolutionary Massachusetts (Madison, Wis., 1973), 33–62. For votes, see NYAJ, 5th sess., 1781–1782, 1st mtg., 25–26, 2d mtg., 60, 74–78, 88, 95, 7th sess., 1784, 35, 52, 87, 108, 112, 8th sess., 1784–1785, 1st mtg., 25, 33, 66, 72, 2d mtg., 13, 26, 28, 39, 79, 82, 87, 97, 98, 111, 153, 166, 173, 175; NYSJ, 7th sess., 1784, 39, 51, 64, 8th sess., 1784–1785, 2d mtg., 79, 86. By 1784 Adgate had joined Ford in advocating leniency toward loyalists, and both took consistently radical positions on land settlement and slavery. These issues are discussed at length in Chapters 5 and 6.

25. Thomas Tillotson, Clermont, to Robert R. Livingston, Jr., Philadelphia, June 17, 1782, RRLP; Leonard Gansevoort, Albany, to Leonard Bronck, Coxsackie, Mar. 28, 1782, John Wigram, Manor, to Leonard Bronck, Coxsackie, Apr. 16, 1783, Bronck Mss., BHM-GCHS. See discussion in Countryman, A People in Revolution, 262.

26. Alexander Hamilton, Albany[?], to Robert Livingston, Manor, Apr. 25, 1785, Robert Livingston, Manor, to Alexander Hamilton, NYC, June 13, 1785, in Syrett et al., eds., PAH, III, 608–609, 614–616; Henry Livingston, Manor, to Walter Livingston, NYC, Apr. 24, 1785, RRLP. See also Alexander Hamilton, Westchester, to William Duer, New York, May 14, 1785, in Syrett et al., eds., PAH, III, 610–611; Countryman, A People in Revolution, 264.

27. NYSJ, 8th sess., 1785, 2d mtg., 40; NYAJ, 8th sess., 1785, 2d mtg., 80; NY Laws, 8th sess., 1785, chap. 83, preamble and art. XI; Ellis, Columbia County, 155, 158; Miller, Historical Sketches of Hudson, 11–12.

28. NYSJ, 8th sess., 1785, 2d mtg., 42; NYAJ, 8th sess., 1785, 2d mtg., 80; James A. Roberts, ed., New York in the Revolution as Colony and State (Albany, N.Y., 1898; rpt. 1996), I, 111–116; Robert Livingston, Manor, to Walter Livingston, NYC, Mar. 1, 1785, Henry Livingston, Manor, to Walter Livingston, NYC, Mar. 2, 1785, RRLP.

29. NYSJ, 8th sess., 1785, 2d mtg., 63, 66, 67, 69, 73–74; NYAJ, 8th sess., 1785, 2d mtg., 131, 151. Van Ness's struggle with the Claverack Van Rensselaers is detailed in Peter Van Ness Denman, "From Deference to Democracy: The Van Ness Family and Their Times, 1759 to 1844" (Ph.D. diss., University of Michigan, 1977), 1–85.

30. NYAJ, 7th sess., 1784, 66; Countryman, A People in Revolution, 250; Hartog, Public Property and Private Power, 87–90; Charles C. Lincoln, ed., State of New York: Messages of the Governors, 1777–1822 (Albany, N.Y., 1909), II, 222–223, 228–233, 234–236, 243–244, 246–248; Ellis, Columbia County, 236.

31. Seth Jenkins, Hudson, to Philip Schuyler, NYC, Feb. 13, 1786, Schuyler Papers, NYPL, referred to Schuyler's letter of "last June" offering "assistance in the legislature." Henry Livingston, Manor, to Walter Livingston, NYC, Mar. 2, 1785, RRLP. For the legislative votes, see NYAJ, 8th sess., 1785, 2d mtg., 76, 111, 127, 131; NYSJ, 8th sess., 1785, 2d mtg., 40, 66, 69, 98–100. William Whiting had reservations about the size of the city and legal protections of its inhabitants but cast vital votes in support of the city against the Council of Revision. Cornelius Humphrey, a Dutch-

ess Clintonian, was on Adgate's committee and advanced the Dutchess jail bill. William Whiting of Canaan voted against the city on the first two roll calls, and for it on the next three. For the restructuring of representation, see George Dangerfield, *Chancellor Robert R. Livingston of New York, 1746–1813* (New York, 1960), 216; Young, *The Democratic Republicans,* 71–72.

32. Kierner, *Traders and Gentlefolk,* 224–228; Hugh Hastings and J. A. Holden, eds., *Public Papers of George Clinton . . .* (New York and Albany, 1899–1914), III, 513–514, 517–518, VI, 692–703; *Proceedings of a General Court-Martial, Held at Major General Lincoln's Quarters, near Quaker Hill, in the State of New York . . . for the Trial of Major General Schuyler, Oct. 1, 1778, Major General Lincoln, President* (Philadelphia, 1778); Don R. Gerlach, *Proud Patriot: Philip Schuyler and the War of Independence, 1775–1783* (Syracuse, N.Y., 1987), 253, 358–362. On the Livingstons' loss of their "manor privilege," see William H. W. Sabine, ed., *Historical Memoirs of William Smith, Historian of the Province of New York . . .* (New York, 1958), II, 138, 169.

33. Goebel and Smith, eds., *LPAH,* III, 309–310; E. Wilder Spaulding, *New York in the Critical Period, 1783–1789* (New York, 1932), 69; *NY Laws,* 6th sess., chap. 2, An Act to Abolish Entail . . . , July 12, 1782; Kierner, *Traders and Landlords,* 245–247. While the impact of the abolition of entail has not been carefully studied for New York, it has been for Virginia. See Holly Brewer, "Entailing Aristocracy in Colonial Virginia: 'Ancient Feudal Restraints' and Revolutionary Reform," *WMQ,* 3d Ser., LIV (1997), 307–346. This topic is discussed in more detail in Chapter 5.

34. Walter Livingston to Robert S.[?] Livingston, Jan. 7, 1781, Walter Livingston Letter Book, XLVI, reel 15, RRLP.

35. *NYAJ,* 7th sess., 1784, 96; undated "Propositions" in Section 71 (Peter R. Livingston), Livingston Family Papers, Hyde Park (reel 9, NYSL film A-FM27). Two letters by John Wigram, surveyor and accountant to the Livingstons, capture the politics of the 1783 efforts to divide the county: John Wigram, Manor, to Leonard Bronck, Coxsackie, Apr. 16, May 7, 1783, Bronck Mss., BHM-GCHS. On Van Ness in 1780, see Denman, "From Deference to Democracy," 79–80. It appears that Van Ness's purchase of the loyalist Van Alstyne property, later to be Van Buren's Lindenwald, was tied up with his unhappiness with Van Rensselaer's promotion to command the brigade.

36. *NYSJ,* 9th sess., 1786, 36, 41. The assembly votes to divide Albany County were not correlated with politics especially, but rather by region and loyalty to Schuyler. The support for the bill (35 to 17) was divided sharply between the New York City and Long Island region (1 to 12) and the northern counties (34 to 5); those who had supported Schuyler for the Council of Appointment voted for the bill 23 to 7 (*NYAJ,* 9th sess., 1786, 97). On the Hudson petition: Seth Jenkins, Hudson, to Philip Schuyler, NYC, February, 13, 1786, Schuyler Papers, NYPL; *NYAJ,* 9th sess., 1786, 105; *NYSJ,* 9th sess., 1786, 98–99. The petitions to move the courthouse to Hudson were delayed a year and then defeated in the 1787 assembly. Syrett et al., eds., *PAH,* IV, 105–108; *NYAJ,* 10th sess., 1787, 81.

37. On the courthouse and post offices: *NY Laws,* 9th sess., 1786, chap. 28; Oliver W. Holmes, "Shall Stagecoaches Carry the Mail? — A Debate of the Confederation Period," *WMQ,* 3d Ser., XX (1963), 555–573; Holmes, "The Stage Coach Business in the Hudson Valley," *Quarterly Journal of the New York State Historical Association,* XII (1931), 231–256; Robert J. Stetts, *Postmasters and Post Offices of the United States, 1782–1811* (Lake Oswego, Or., 1994), 176, 181, 182. On Columbia: *NYAJ,* 9th sess., 1786, 104–105; *NYSJ,* 9th sess., 1786, 98–99. Carroll Smith-Rosenberg, "Discovering the Subject of the 'Great Constitutional Discussion,' 1786–1789," *JAH,* LXXIX (1992–

1993), 869–870; Linda K. Kerber, *Women of the Republic: Intellect and Ideology in Revolutionary America* (Chapel Hill, N.C., 1980); David C. Humphrey, *From King's College to Columbia, 1746–1800* (New York, 1976), 271–272.

38. Ellis, *Columbia County,* 77–79.

39. Ellis, *Columbia County,* 58–61, 238–239; *Hudson Weekly Gazette,* Sept. 28, Oct. 6, 1786.

40. Ruth Piwonka and Roderic Blackburn, *A Visible Heritage: Columbia County, New York: A History in Art and Architecture* (Kinderhook, N.Y., 1977; rpt. 1996), 56–58, 64–65; Ellis, *Columbia County,* 68–69; Frank Hawley Webb, *Claverack, Old and New* (Claverack, N.Y., 1892), 57; Elizabeth L. Gebhard, *The Parsonage between Two Manors: Annals of Clover-Reach* (Hudson, N.Y., 1925), 174. On the interpretation of courthouses and civil architecture and landscape, see Martha J. McNamara, *From Tavern to Courthouse: Architecture and Ritual in America Law, 1658–1860* (Baltimore, 2004). On the lawyers, see John Niven, *Martin Van Buren: The Romantic Age of American Politics* (New York, 1983), 19–21; Donald B. Cole, *Martin Van Buren and the American Political System* (Princeton, N.J., 1984), 22–24; Peyton F. Miller, *A Group of Great Lawyers of Columbia County, New York* (New York, 1904), 3–16, 55–60, 104–125, 138–143, 154–162.

41. Hugh Hastings and Henry Harmon Noble, eds., *Military Minutes of the Council of Appointment of the State of New York, 1783–1821* (Albany, N.Y., 1901), 95–100; *Hudson Weekly Gazette,* June 22, Nov. 30, 1786, Apr. 26, May 10, July 5, Sept. 20, 1787; John P. Kaminski, *George Clinton: Yeoman Politician of the New Republic* (Madison, Wis., 1993), 107–109; David P. Szatmary, *Shays' Rebellion: The Making of an Agrarian Insurrection* (Amherst, Mass., 1980), 109, 112–113, 117.

42. Joel Barlow, *The Vision of Columbus,* 1st ed. (Hartford, Conn., 1787); John Schuyler, *Institution of the Society of the Cincinnati . . . with Extracts . . . from the Transactions of the New York State Society* (New York, 1886), 79–84; Worthington Chauncey Ford, ed., *Correspondence and Journals of Samuel Blachley Webb* (New York, 1893–1894), III, 60–63, 70–72, 78–79; James L. Crouthamel, *James Watson Webb: A Biography* (Middletown, Conn., 1969), 3–4.

43. Gebhard, *The Parsonage between Two Manors,* 37–42; Webb, *Claverack, Old and New,* 37–38. See also F. N. Zabriskie, *History of the Reformed P.D. Church of Claverack: A Centenial Address* (Hudson, N.Y., 1867), 54; and two pages of accounts of the Washington Seminary, dated Nov. 24, 1779, in box 1, the Van Rensselaer Fort Papers, NYPL.

44. Gebhard, *The Parsonage between Two Manors,* 45–46; *NYAJ,* 8th sess., 1785, 2d mtg., 63; *NY Laws,* 8th sess., 1785, chap. 79. Carshore's design for the Capitol is preserved at the Maryland Historical Society and reproduced with biographical details on Carshore in Piwonka and Blackburn, *A Visible Heritage,* 72–73. On the gentry houses, see Kennedy, *Orders from France,* 62–78.

45. *Hudson Weekly Gazette,* June 15, 1786.

46. *NYAJ,* 10th sess., 1787, 39, 11th sess., 1788, 62, 12th sess., 1789, 91, 120. Compare city, county, and township legislation: *NY Laws,* 8th sess., 1785, chap. 83, 9th sess., 1786, chap. 28, 11th sess., 1788, chap. 64. For key approaches to the regulation of urban life in the early Republic, see Carol Shammas, "The Space Problem in Early United States Cities," *WMQ,* 3d Ser., LVII (2000), 505–542; Hartog, *Public Property and Private Power,* 82–157; Novak, *The People's Welfare;* Bernard L. Herman, *Town House: Architecture and Material Life in the Early American City, 1780–1830* (Chapel Hill, N.C., 2005), 1–32.

47. Miller, *Historical Sketches of Hudson,* 14–15, 18–21; Ellis, *Columbia County,* 159, 170.

48. Thomas Jenkins, Hudson, to Robert R. Livingston, Clermont, Jan. 10, 1789, RRLP; Ellis, *Columbia County,* 159–162; Miller, *Historical Sketches of Hudson,* 34.

49. Ellis, *Columbia County,* 160, 171–172, 174–175; Miller, *Historical Sketches of Hudson,*

43–44; *NY Laws,* 10th sess., 1787, chap. 66, 13th sess., 1790, chap. 2, 16th sess., 1793, chap. 35, 17th sess., 1794, chaps. 21, 22, 18th sess., 1795, chap. 52, 20th sess., 1797, chap. 95, 21st sess., 1798, chap. 47. Hudson's population stood at roughly 1,500 in 1786, 2,584 in 1790, 3,664 in 1800, and 4,048 in 1810.

50. On Samuel Edmonds, see Raymond, *Biographical Sketches,* 79; Miller, *Historical Sketches of Hudson,* 15, 25, 28, 47, 82, 114, 116; Ellis, *Columbia County,* 76–78, 179; *Hudson Gazette,* May 21, 1799, Mar. 8, May 17, 1803; *NY Laws,* 22d sess., 1799, chap. 59; Hudson Lodge returns, Grand Lodge Records, LL-NYGL. For comparable developments in New England, see Robert A. Gross, *The Minutemen and Their World* (New York, 1976), 171–91; William J. Gilmore, *Reading Becomes a Necessity of Life: Material and Cultural Life in Rural New England, 1780–1835* (Knoxville, Tenn., 1989); David Jaffee, "The Village Enlightenment in New England, 1760–1820," *WMQ,* 3d Ser., XLVII (1990), 327–346; J. M. Opal, "Exciting Emulation: Academies and the Transformation of the Rural North, 1780s–1820s," *JAH,* XCI (2004–2005), 445–470.

51. Miller, *Historical Sketches Of Hudson,* 69; Ellis, *Columbia County,* 196–197; *Hudson Weekly Gazette,* Aug. 3, 1786, Mar. 15, 1792, Nov. 14, 1793, Feb. 20, 1794.

52. Minutes of the Hudson Law Society, HHCh-DAR; *The Feast of Reason and the Flow of Soul: A New Explanatory Catalogue of H. Caritat's General and Increasing Circulating Library . . .* (New York, 1799); Hudson *Bee,* July 12, 1803, Jan. 11, Feb. 22, 1820; Hudson *Northern Whig,* June 10, 1817 ("Have wars contributed to enlighten mankind?"); *Albany Centinel,* Aug. 9, 1803–Feb. 10, 1804.

53. Stoddard's first surviving ad for books and printed supplies is in the *Hudson Weekly Gazette,* May 18, 1786, though it seems likely that he would have begun these lists during the previous year. Ellis, *Columbia County,* 171–173, puts the printshop fire in 1793; Miller, *Historical Sketches of Hudson,* 45–46, in 1787–1788. On the Albany and Troy libraries, see *A Catalogue of the Books Belonging to the Albany Library: With the Law of the Legislature of New-York, to Incorporate the Trustees . . .* (Albany, N.Y., 1793), 4; "Subscription for the Trojan Library . . . Mar. 1, 1800 . . . ," in Troy Library Records, I, 1800–1815, Special Collections, Troy Public Library, Troy, N.Y. For the Websters' involvement in Mechanics and library societies in Albany, see Munsell, *The Typographical Miscellany,* 220.

54. This discussion is based on family reconstruction developed from Milton W. Hamilton, *The Country Printer: New York State, 1785–1830* (New York, 1936), 266, 301, 505–506, and the data in the American Antiquarian Society printer files. See also Ashbel Stoddard, Hudson, to Noah Webster, New Haven, June 27, 1801, Harry Croswell, Hudson, to Noah Webster, New Haven, June 27, 1801, Noah Webster Papers, NYPL.

55. *Hudson Weekly Gazette,* Apr. 7, 1785, May 18, 1786.

56. Ibid., Nov. 9, 1786, May 10, 1787, Jan. 24, 1788, *Hudson Gazette,* Mar. 15, 1792, July 25, 1793. The *Gazette's* masthead notice of the assize of bread continued through Jan. 20, 1789. "Commonplace Book," Elkanah Watson Papers, 1774–1885 (box 4), NYSL, 5: clippings from the *Albany Register,* with Watson's manuscript commentary.

57. Here it may be apparent that I am challenging the neo-Tocquevillian position that civil society functioned in contrast to, in tension with, or in replacement of "the state"; at the same time, my interpretation is in some degree consonant with the social capital approach most closely associated with Robert Putnam. For overviews of these debates that interpret American civil society institutions in similar ways, see William J. Novak, "The American Law of Association: The Legal-Political Construction of Civil Society," *Studies in American Political Development,* XV (2001),

163–188; Jason Kaufman, "Three Views of Associationalism in Ninteenth-Century America: An Empirical Examination," *American Journal of Sociology,* CIV (1999), 1296–1345. See also the citations in note 20, above.

58. On "encouragement," see *Hudson Weekly Gazette,* Apr. 7, 1785; Poughkeepsie *Country Journal,* Oct. 13, 1785; *Northern Centinel, and Lansingborough Advertiser,* Sept. 17, 1787; Lansingburgh *American Spy,* Apr. 8, 1791. On "prejudices," see Seth Jenkins, Hudson, to Philip Schuyler, Poughkeepsie, Jan. 21, 1788, Schuyler Papers, NYPL; Seth Jenkins, Hudson, to Robert R. Livingston, Clermont, Mar. 18, 1787, RRLP. The ads from the Yankee towns begin with the first issue of the *Hudson Weekly Gazette,* Apr. 7, 1785; the postrider notices are in various issues between May 18, 1786, and Sept. 27, 1787. The county, post office, and militia notices began with the Sept. 28, 1786, issue, and the subsequent series of private notices from the old lowland district began with the Oct. 19, 1786, issue.

59. Robert Livingston, Manor, to Alexander Hamilton, NYC, June 13, 1785, in Syrett et al., eds., *PAH,* III, 614–616. The first reference to the *Hudson Gazette* in the Livingston correspondence that I have found was a Feb. 14, 1795, letter from Henry Livingston from Ancram to Samuel B. Webb in Claverack: "I see by the Hudson Paper that some of our County people are again going to support the Chief Justice" (Ford, ed., *Correspondence and Journals of Webb,* III, 196–197). These gentry were reacting to the shift from privileged private information systems based on manuscript circulation to public information based on print that had been unfolding in the Anglo-Atlantic world for centuries; for the broader historiography, see Richard D. Brown, *Knowledge Is Power: The Diffusion of Information in Early America, 1700–1865* (New York, 1989), 16–41; Shields, *Civil Tongues and Polite Letters;* David Zaret, *Origins of Democratic Culture: Printing, Petitions, and the Public Sphere in Early-Modern England* (Princeton, N.J., 2000), 44–132; Peter Lake and Steven Pincus, "Rethinking the Public Sphere in Early Modern England," in Lake and Pincus, eds., *The Politics of the Public Sphere in Early Modern England* (Manchester, 2007), 1–30.

60. Dangerfield, *Chancellor Robert R. Livingston,* 282–289, 403–437; *Catalogue of Books, in the Library of the Hon. Robert R. Livingston, of Clermont, February, 1800* (Poughkeepsie, N.Y., 1800) (Evans 37839), 5, 6, 10, 21. His cousin Walter Livingston also had a copy of "Ferguson on Civil Society": Hugh Gaine, NYC, to Walter Livingston, Manor, July 27, 1793, RRLP. On Shaftesbury and Burke, see Henry F. May, *The Enlightenment in America* (New York, 1976), 3–87; Richard L. Bushman, *The Refinement of America: Persons, Houses, Cities* (New York, 1992), esp. 97–99; Lawrence E. Klein, *Shaftesbury and the Culture of Politeness: Moral Discourse and Cultural Politics in Early Eighteenth-Century England* (New York, 1994). On Ferguson, see the introduction to Adam Ferguson, *An Essay on the History of Civil Society,* ed. Fania Oz-Salzberger (Cambridge, 1995), vii–xxv; Marvin B. Becker, *The Emergence of Civil Society in the Eighteenth Century: A Privileged Moment in the History of England, Scotland, and France* (Bloomington, Ind., 1994), xi–xii, 6–8, 59–60, 107, 121; and John Keane, "Despotism and Democracy: The Origins and Development of the Distinction between Civil Society and the State," in Keene, ed., *Civil Society and the State: New European Perspectives* (London, 1988), 39–44. Bullock, *Revolutionary Brotherhood,* provides the most-detailed discussion of the role of Freemasonry in the construction of American national culture in the early Republic. For Freemasonry in the wider Atlantic context, see Margaret C. Jacob, *Living the Enlightenment: Freemasonry and Politics in Eighteenth-Century Europe* (New York, 1991); James Van Horn Melton, *The Rise of the Public in Enlightenment Europe* (New York, 2001), 252–272.

61. Quotations from two undated Masonic orations in Wilson's hand, VIII, 88, WFP-UM.

62. Dangerfield, *Chancellor Robert R. Livingston,* 90. Both Livingston and Wilson had in their libraries copies of Montesquieu's *Spirit of the Laws* (*Catalogue of Books, in the Library of Livingston,* 16; Manuscript Catalogue of William Wilson's books, Aug. 18, 1801 [IX, 64], WFP-UM). On Montesquieu, see Robert Shackleton, *Montesquieu: A Critical Biography* (Oxford, 1961), 135–141, 173–174; Jacob, *Living the Enlightenment,* 206; on the early grand masters, Singer and Lang, *New York Freemasonry,* 257–258; Thomas Bender, *New York Intellect: A History of Intellectual Life in New York City, from 1750 to the Beginnings of Our Own Time* (Baltimore, 1987), 48–78; Evan Cornog, *The Birth of Empire: De Witt Clinton and the American Experience* (New York, 1998), 62–72; Craig Hanyan, *De Witt Clinton: Years of Molding, 1769–1807* (New York, 1988), 322–328, 347–356; Elizabeth W. McClave, *Stephen Van Rensselaer III: A Pictorial Reflection and Biographical Commentary,* ed. Rowland McClave and William B. Zimmerman (Stephentown, N.Y., 1984), 14–18, 39–40.

63. Here I intend an extension of the classic argument about the transition from familial to party politics developed in Michael Wallace, "Changing Concepts of Party in the United States: New York, 1815–1828," *American Historical Review,* LXXIV (1968), 453–491. See also Hanyan's account in *De Witt Clinton,* 327–328, and my discussion in note 75, below. We might consider the implications here and below of Masonry as a vehicle of an antipopular "consolidating" party, in the meaning developed by Gerald Leonard, *The Invention of Party Politics: Federalism, Popular Sovereignty, and Constitutional Development in Jacksonian Illinois* (Chapel Hill, N.C., 2002), 12–17, 35–47.

64. Grand Lodge index to lodge returns (card file), LL-NYGL; William R. Denslow, *Ten Thousand Famous Freemasons* (Trenton, Mo., 1961), 93–95; Singer and Lang, *New York Freemasonry,* 55–61. Robert R. Livingston was master of Union Lodge in New York in 1771 and later affiliated with the Trinity Lodge in New York; his brother Edward and cousin Henry Waldo were members of Holland Lodge, and brother Henry Beekman Livingston was a member of the Master's Lodge. Between 1784 and 1800 Livingston attended four Grand Lodge meetings in 1785 and one meeting each in 1787, 1789, and 1792. In one of his few communications with the Grand Lodge, he wrote in 1793 to approve a lodge petition from Beekman in Dutchess County, where his mother was an important landlord. Peter Ross, *A Standard History of Freemasonry in the State of New York . . .* (New York, 1899), 142; Robert R. Livingston to the Grand Lodge, Nov 1, 1793, in the Beekman Lodge 47 Papers, LL-NYGL; John Francis Collin, *A History of Hillsdale, Columbia County, New York . . . ,* ed. H. S. Johnson (Philmont, N.Y., 1883), 36.

65. Peacher, "Solomon's Lodge No. 1, Poughkeepsie, New York," American Lodge of Research, *Transactions,* XIII, no. 2 (1976), 235–236, and "Craft Masonry in Columbia County," XII (1975), 322–323; Temple Lodge (10) documents, Grand Lodge Records, LL-NYGL.

66. Hudson Lodge to the Grand Lodge, June 17, 1789, Dec. 9, 1800, Unity Lodge to the Grand Lodge, June 10, 1789, Nov. 10, 1793, May 20, 1812, Grand Lodge Records, LL-NYGL. For the Albany Modern schism, which ran down to 1807, see Hughan, "Mount Vernon Lodge, No. 3, Albany New York," *Freemason,* Sept. 7, 1889, 73–74. Singer and Lang, *New York Freemasonry,* 55–56; Charles T. McClenachan, *History of the Most Ancient and Honorable Fraternity of Free and Accepted Masons in New York . . .* (New York, 1888–1894), I, 158–174; Ross, *A Standard History of Freemasonry,* 125–128, 195–203.

67. Peacher, "Craft Masonry," 336, 339–343, 345; *An Account of the Performances at the Dedication of Mason-Hall, Hudson, on the Festival of St. John the Evangelist* (Hudson, N.Y., 1797), 47.

68. This was even the case in the Washington Lodge at Johnstown, Livingston Manor, whose

master, Philip L. Hoffman, came from a family long at odds with both Livingston clans and was trying to build his own political interest. See Sung Bok Kim, *Landlord and Tenant in Colonial New York: Manorial Society, 1664–1775* (Chapel Hill, N.C., 1978), 232–233, 321–322; Goebel and Smith, eds., *LPAH,* III, 84–117; Dangerfield, *Chancellor Robert R. Livingston,* 183–184; John Livingston, Oak Hill, to Walter Livingston, Teviotdale, May 20, 1796, RLPP; *An Account of the Performances at the Dedication of Mason-Hall,* 47–49.

69. Hudson Lodge to the Grand Lodge, 1795, Grand Lodge Records, LL-NYGL; Peacher, "Craft Masonry," 324–325, 333; Nina Fletcher Little, *American Decorative Wall Painting, 1700–1850,* 2d ed. (New York, 1989), 114; *An Account of the Performances at the Dedication of Mason-Hall,* 3–40, 46; *The Constitution and Regulations of the Grand Royal Arch Chapter of the State of New York . . .* (Albany, N.Y., 1829), 42–46; Charles C. Hunt, *History of the Lebanon Chapter, No. 13, R.A.M.* (Chatham, N.Y., n.d.), 6–8, 44.

70. *Hudson Weekly Gazette,* May 15, June 1, Sept. 7, 1786, Jan. 4, Feb. 22, Apr. 26, June 28, July 5, Aug. 2, Sept. 20, 27, Dec. 13, 1787, Apr. 29, 1790; *An Account of the Performances at the Dedication of Mason-Hall,* 42; Returns of the Unity, Temple, and Hudson Lodges, Grand Lodge Records, LL-NYGL; *NYAJ,* 14th sess., 1791, 76, 88–89; Stets, *Postmasters and Post Offices of the United States,* 176, 180–182, 184; George Holcomb Diary, June 24, 1805, June 24, 1806, June 24, 1811, Nov. 6, 12, 22, Dec. 6, 20, 1809, June 9, 23, July 4, 1812, Jan. 20, 1814, MSS at NYSL, typescript at the Stephentown Historical Society. The political engagement of Masons discussed here is similar to that found for a large sample of American cities in 1880, in Kaufman, "Three Views of Associationalism," *American Journal of Sociology,* CIV (1999), 1335.

71. Miller, *Sketches,* 113–116; Ellis, *Columbia County,* 320; Hudson and Unity Lodge Returns, Grand Lodge Records, LL-NYGL.

72. Sullivan, ed., *Minutes,* I, 529.

73. Peacher, "Craft Masonry," 332; *NYAJ,* 10th sess., 1787, 3. Powers's wealth ranking is calculated from the December 1779 King's District tax list, NYSL. He was listed among the land bounty men for the Seventeenth Albany Regiment, though not among the active duty officers or men. Roberts, ed., *New York in the Revolution,* 238. He might have been the William Powers whom the Albany committee on Sept. 7, 1775, granted three petitioned requests but ruled that "he cannot have a seat on this board." His brother-in-law, James Savage, arrested in 1777, would end up a Columbia hill town Federalist. Sullivan, ed., *Minutes,* I, 231, 715. John Camp, *A Sermon: Delivered at the Funeral of William Powers, Esq. and Now Published by the Request of Unity Lodge* (Hudson, N.Y., 1796); Stockbridge, Mass., *Andrews's Western Star,* Apr. 26, 1796.

74. In King's District–Canaan the Revolutionary committeemen were strongly Antifederalist Clintonian (including Adgate, Frisbie, and Whiting) and avoided joining the Unity Lodge, whereas the Federalists were less likely to have been committeemen and more likely to join the lodge.

	Revolutionary Committee Only	Both	Unity Lodge in 1789 Only
Clintonians	4	1	0
Federalists	2	1	4

Similarly, none of the men serving on the committee of safety in 1778 in the Dutchess town of Northeast joined the Temple Lodge during its first two decades. George B. Bookman and Janet S.

Bookman, "A Record of Turmoil: Minutes of the Committee of Safety for the Town of Northeast, 1778," *Dutchess County Historical Society Yearbook*, LX (1975), 45–67; Returns of the Temple Lodge, Grand Lodge Records, LL-NYGL.

75. This argument, that Freemasonry supplied a transitional context, can be compared with arguments I have made in *The Heart of the Commonwealth: Society and Political Culture in Worcester County, 1713–1861* (New York, 1989), 243–251; and "Ancient Lodges and Self-Created Societies: Voluntary Association and the Public Sphere in the Early Republic," in Ronald Hoffman and Peter J. Albert, eds., *Launching the "Extended Republic": The Federalist Era* (Charlottesville, Va., 1996), 273–377; and with Paul B. Moyer's argument in *Wild Yankees: The Struggle for Independence along Pennsylvania's Revolutionary Frontier* (Ithaca, N.Y., 2007), 189–191. The role of Freemasonry in the region's politics is further discussed in Chapters 5 and 9. For the continuing connection of Freemasonry and party in another part of New York State, see Kathleen Smith Kutolowski, "The Janus Face of New York's Local Parties: Genesee County, 1821–1827," *New York History*, LIX (1978), 145–172; and Kutolowski, "Freemasonry and Community in the Early Republic: The Case for Antimasonic Anxieties," *American Quarterly*, XXXIV (1982), 543–561.

CHAPTER 3

1. New York *Daily Advertiser*, July 3, 1792; Elizabethtown *New-Jersey Journal*, Aug. 1, 1792. Pomponick was east of the present village of Valatie, in Kinderhook. See also *Hudson Gazette*, July 19, 1792; Stockbridge, Mass., *Western Star*, July 17, 1792.

2. Born in 1761, John A. Van Buren's father is unknown, but he named his first son, born in 1791, Abraham. See Harriett C. Waite Van Buren Peckham, *History of Cornelis Maessen Van Buren . . .* (New York, 1913), 338, 373; Hugh Hastings and Henry Harmon Noble, eds., *Military Minutes of the Council of Appointment of the State of New York, 1783–1821* (Albany, N.Y., 1901–1902), I, 183, 347; Edward A. Collier, *A History of Old Kinderhook . . .* (New York, 1914), 547; Elizabethtown *New-Jersey Journal*, Aug. 1, 1792; *Greenleaf's New York Journal, and Patriotic Register*, Apr. 18, 1798; Hudson *Bee*, Mar. 20, Apr. 10, 1804.

3. Linda Grant De Pauw, *The Eleventh Pillar: New York State and the Federal Constitution* (Ithaca, N.Y., 1966), 46–55.

4. George Dangerfield, *Chancellor Robert R. Livingston of New York, 1746–1813* (New York, 1960), 220; *NYAJ*, 10th sess., 1787, 14–15, 59, 66, 76, 81; New York *Daily Advertiser: Political, Historical, and Commercial*, Mar. 7, 1787; Syrett et al., eds., *PAH*, IV, 3, 105–108; Goebel and Smith, eds., *LPAH*, III, 8–50.

5. *NYAJ*, 10th sess., 1787, 66. Ford's conversion to Federalism is discussed more fully in Chapter 5.

6. John Wigram, Manor, to Leonard Bronck, Coxsackie, Mar. 20, 1785, Bronck Mss., BHM-GCHS; *Hudson Weekly Gazette*, Mar. 29, Apr. 5, 1787. Alexander Coventry of Hudson identified two slates as being "for Hudson" and "for Claverack." The meeting determining the 1787 Hudson slate might have settled for Powers over its preference for Jacob Ford, a Federalist convention candidate in 1788. Alexander Coventry, "Memoirs of an Emigrant: the Journal of Alexander Coventry, M.D." (typescript, AIHA and NYSL, 1978), Apr. 23, 1787; see also Henry Livingston, Manor, to Robert R. Livingston, Clermont, Mar. 13, 1787, Seth Jenkins, Hudson, to Robert R. Livingston, Clermont, Mar. 18, 1787, RRLP. On the election violence, see *Hudson Weekly Gazette*, Apr. 5, 12, 19, 26, May 3, 10, 1787, and Samuel Webb's comments on the "confusion" of the "Electioneering

business" in New York as compared to Connecticut: Samuel B. Webb, NYC, to Joseph Barrell, Boston, May 11, 1788, in Worthington Chauncey Ford, ed., *Correspondence and Journals of Samuel Blachley Webb* (New York, 1893–1894), III, 102.

7. Philip Schuyler, Albany, to Robert R. Livingston, NYC, Mar. 29, 1788, RRLP; Peter Van Schaack, Kinderhook, to Philip Schuyler, Albany, Apr. 3, 1788, Schuyler Papers, NYPL; Danger-field, *Chancellor Robert R. Livingston,* 218–219 n. 9; John P. Kaminski, "New York: The Reluctant Pillar," in Stephen L. Schechter, ed., *The Reluctant Pillar: New York and the Adoption of the Constitution* (Albany, N.Y., 1987), 83–86; De Pauw, *The Eleventh Pillar,* 155–159. The 1788 Columbia County slates were printed in the *Hudson Weekly Gazette,* Mar. 13, 20, Apr. 3, 1788. For a discussion of the connections between militia service and Clintonian Antifederalism in New York State, see Edwin G. Burrows, "Military Experience and the Origins of Federalism and Antifederalism," in Jacob Judd and Irwin H. Polishook, eds., *Aspects of Early New York Society and Politics* (Tarrytown, N.Y., 1974), 83–92.

8. *Hudson Weekly Gazette,* Mar. 29, 1787. There might be some doubt as to the precise timing of these publication "events," since the three issues prior to March 29 have not survived. However Van Rensselaer's ad was dated March 26, and Silvester's notice March 23. Silvester was elected to the assembly that April.

9. *Hudson Weekly Gazette,* Jan. 24, Sept. 20, 27, Oct. 4, 25, Nov. 15, Dec. 6, 13, 20, 1787, Jan. 3, 10, 17, Apr. 3, July 8, 1788. Four of the grand jury members in January 1787 were also listed by the *Gazette* postriders as their local agents in Canaan and Hillsdale.

10. *Hudson Weekly Gazette,* Jan. 24, 31, 1788; Lansingburgh *Federal Herald,* June 23, 1788 (reprinting *Gazette,* June 17, 1788); [Albany, N.Y.], Anti-Federal Committee: *To the Independent Electors, of the City and County of Albany* ("At a public meeting of a number of the anti-Federalists . . ."), March 15 (Albany, N.Y., 1788) (Evans 45379); *Albany, . . . April, 1788* ("On the last Tuesday of April instant, Delegates are to be chosen, by the people, to determine the important Question, whether the proposed new Constitution shall be adopted or rejected . . ."), April 10 (Albany, N.Y., 1788) (Evans 45215); *To the Citizens of the City and County of Albany* ("Another publication of the Federal Committee, has at length, but with difficulty, been obtained in this city . . .") (Albany, N.Y., 1788) (Evans 45221); *To the Citizens of the City and County of Albany* ("At this late day, it is impossible to enter into a minute consideration of the address to you from the Federal Committee . . .")(Albany, N.Y., 1788[?])(Evans 45222). On the Federal Farmer and the importance of the *Dissent* and Randolph's letter, see Kaminski, "New York: The Reluctant Pillar," in Schechter, ed., *The Reluctant Pillar,* 71; Saul Cornell, *The Other Founders: Anti-Federalism and the Dissenting Tradition in America, 1788–1828* (Chapel Hill, N.C., 1999), 88–96, 309.

11. William North to Henry Knox, Feb. 13, 1788, Knox Papers, MHS, quoted in Kaminski, "New York: The Reluctant Pillar," in Schechter, ed., *The Reluctant Pillar,* 92; Samuel B. Webb, NYC, to Joseph Barrell, Boston, Apr. 27, 1788, in Ford, ed., *Correspondence and Journals of Webb,* III, 99; *Hudson Weekly Gazette,* July 8, 1788.

12. Turnout analysis based on figures presented in De Pauw, *The Eleventh Pillar,* 157. De Pauw uses a figure of 5,568 as the numerator in both cases, and counts 2,575 votes for the assembly and 3,361 votes for the convention delegates in Columbia County. Compare with my similar figures on Figure 2.

13. *Hudson Weekly Gazette,* July 8, Aug. 9, Sept. 9, 1788; Lansingburgh *Federal Herald,* Aug. 11, 18, 25, Sept. 1, 1788; De Pauw, *The Eleventh Pillar,* 266–268.

14. *Hudson Weekly Gazette,* Apr. 26, July 5, 1787, Feb. 21, Mar. 13, 20, Apr. 3, 1788. Here I am

indebted to interpretive approaches developed in David Waldstreicher, *In the Midst of Perpetual Fetes: The Making of American Nationalism, 1776–1820* (Chapel Hill, N.C., 1997), and particularly to his analysis on 53–107; and to Caroll Smith-Rosenberg, "Dis-covering the Subject of the 'Great Constitutional Conversation' of 1786–1789," *Journal of American History,* LXXIX (1992–1993), 841–873.

15. *Hudson Weekly Gazette,* Mar. 10, Apr. 7, 14, 21, Aug. 6, 13, 1789. No copies of the *Gazette* survive for the dates between April 28 and July 6, during which time Stoddard would have covered the inauguration, which took place on April 30.

16. *Country Journal, and Dutchess and Ulster County Farmer's Register,* July 7, 1789; *Poughkeepsie Journal,* July 14, 1789; Jeffrey L. Pasley, *"The Tyranny of Printers": Newspaper Politics in the Early American Republic* (Charlottesville, Va., 2001), 51–60; John L. Brooke, "To Be 'Read by the Whole People': Press, Party, and Public Sphere in the United States, 1789–1840," American Antiquarian Society, *Proceedings,* CX (2000), esp. 62–79.

17. *Hudson Weekly Gazette,* June 29, 1786.

18. Here I summarize the basic outlines of my reading of Jürgen Habermas, *Between Facts and Norms: Contributions to a Discourse Theory of Law and Democracy,* trans. William Rehg (1992; Cambridge, Mass., 1996), esp. 287–388. For a more extended discussion, see John L. Brooke, "Reason and Passion in the Public Sphere: Habermas and the Cultural Historians," *Journal of Interdisciplinary History,* XXIX (1998–1999), 43–67. Seeking to exploit the integral relationship between print and the legislative cycle, Charles R. and George Webster in January 1788 began a second newspaper for distribution in surrounding counties, *Albany Journal: or, The Montgomery, Washington, and Columbia Intelligencer,* which was published on Mondays and Saturdays during the legislative session.

19. For the expanding publication of colonial legislative proceedings and laws, see Alison G. Olson, "Eighteenth-Century Colonial Legislatures and their Constituents," *JAH,* LXXIX (1992–1993), 564–567; on politics in early New York City papers, see Charles E. Clark, *The Public Prints: The Newspaper in Anglo-American Culture, 1665–1740* (New York, 1994), 178–188. The open-door mandate is in Article 15 of the 1777 constitution.

20. *Hudson Weekly Gazette,* May 18, 25, June 1, 15, 22, 29, Aug. 3, 17, Sept. 7, 1786, Apr. 5, 26, May 10, 31, 1787.

21. *Hudson Gazette,* Apr. 23, 1799. John Nerone discussed the structurally conservative feature of the American press in "Newspapers in the Public Sphere," paper presented at the Clark University–American Antiquarian Society Seminar in American History, Spring 1997. See also Thomas C. Leonard, *The Power of the Press: The Birth of American Political Reporting* (New York, 1986).

22. Robert R. Livingston, Clermont, to Edward Livingston, New York City, July 18, 1795, RRLP. The evidence for the circulation of nonlocal papers in Columbia is scattered. Various receipts indicate that William Wilson subscribed to the New York *Gazette of the United States* briefly in 1789 and 1790, the New York *Republican Watch-Tower* in 1800–1801, the Philadelphia *Aurora: General Advertiser* in 1812–1813, the New York *Columbian* in 1811, and the *New-York Herald* in 1815 (boxes 44–45, WFP-UM). Mail books kept by Peter Van Schaack, Jr., in the 1820s list more than twenty-five newspapers arriving in Kinderhook by the northern and southern mails. Peter Van Schaack, [Jr.], Daybooks and Mailbooks [15054], NYSA. See Chapter 4 for a discussion of county circulation of the *Hudson Gazette.*

23. The issues regarding election procedures' being worked out between 1787 and the Otsego

election crisis of 1792 directly illustrate the struggle over the procedural basis of legitimacy and democracy, as discussed by Habermas, in *Facts and Norms,* trans. Rehg, 107 ("discourse principle"), 302–328, 427–446; and Bernard Malin, "On Legitimacy and Political Deliberation," trans. Elly Stein and Jane Mansbridge, *Political Theory,* XV (1987), 338–368, among many others.

24. *Hudson Weekly Gazette,* Apr. 5, 1787. The Albany Anti-Federalist "Manifesto," printed in the *New-York Journal,* Apr. 26, 1788, is reprinted in Cecelia M. Kenyon, ed., *The Antifederalists* (1966; rpt. Boston, 1985), 359–367; for the Albany Federalist pamphlets, see [Albany] Federal Committee, *To the Independent Electors, of the City and County of Albany,* March 14 (Albany, N.Y., 1788) (Evans 45378); [Albany] Federal Committee, "Sir, On the last Tuesday in April next, it becomes our duty to give our votes for members of the STATE CONVENTION, AND LEGISLATURE . . . ," March 26 (Albany, N.Y.,[?] 1788) (Evans 45216); Federal Committee of the City of Albany, *An Impartial Address, to the Citizens of the City and County of Albany; or, The Thirty-five Anti-Federal Objections Refuted* (Albany, N.Y., 1788) (Evans 21167). The problem of invisibility in the public sphere has been discussed by Michael Warner, *The Letters of the Republic: Publication and the Public Sphere in Eighteenth-Century America* (Cambridge, Mass., 1990), 34–72; and Harold Mah, in "Phantasies of the Public Sphere: Rethinking the Habermas of Historians," *Journal of Modern History,* LXXII (2000), 153–182, poses the problem of visibility and invisibility of interests in relation to the problem of conformity and plurality.

25. *Hudson Weekly Gazette,* Feb. 24, Apr. 21, 1789; *Albany Journal: or, The Montgomery, Washington, and Columbia Intelligencer,* Mar. 2, Apr. 20, 27, 1789. Though he had been opposed to the Constitution in 1788, the Federalists settled on Robert Yates as their best chance against George Clinton.

26. *Hudson Weekly Gazette,* Apr. 28, 1789, Apr. 12, 1792, Mar. 26, Apr. 16, June 11, 1795, Mar. 27, Apr. 24, June 12, 1798; Lansingburgh *American Spy,* Apr. 6, 1792; John Livingston, Manor, to Walter Livingston, NYC, Feb. 16, 1792, RRLP.

27. Lansingburgh *American Spy,* Apr. 21, 1795; John Van Rensselaer et al., Lansingburgh, to Peter Van Schaack, Kinderhook, Mar. 14, 1792, Samuel Edmonds et al., Hudson, to Peter Van Schaack et al., Kinderhook, VSP/LC.

28. Henry Van Schaack, Pittsfield, to Theodore Sedgwick, Philadelphia, Feb. 6, 1795, I:2.13/191, Sedgwick Papers, MHS. Van Schaack might have been behind the flurry of Federalist essays ostensibly from Canaan, attacking the propriety of Judge William B. Whiting's chairing a meeting in Claverack supporting Robert Yates for the governorship, published in Sedgwick's newspaper, the Stockbridge *Western Star,* Feb. 17, Mar. 3, Apr. 7, 14, 1795, answered by opponents on Mar. 31 and May 19, 1795. There was an unusual amount of controversy in the 1795 election, involving not only the Claverack meeting for Yates but also a Jay meeting on March 14 (a month after Van Schaack's letter) commandeered by Yates supporters, all of which contributed to the county's struggle over electoral procedure. See the few surviving issues of the *Hudson Gazette* and *Greenleaf's New York Journal,* Mar. 21, 28, Apr. 11, 1795; New York *American Minerva, and the New-York (Evening) Advertiser,* Mar. 28, Apr. 9, 1795; Henry Van Schaack, Pittsfield, to Theodore Sedgwick, Philadelphia, Dec. 10, 1797, I:3.7/105, Sedgwick Papers, MHS.

29. Originally published in the Lansingburgh *American Spy,* the "Lofty" satire was reprinted in the *Hudson Gazette,* Mar. 28, 1793, and the *Poughkeepsie Journal,* Apr. 10, 1793. The "Reconciliation!" satire appeared in the *Poughkeepsie Journal,* Apr. 1, 1795.

30. John C. Wyncoop, Kinderhook, to Alexander Hamilton, NYC, Mar. 25, 1789, in Syrett

et al., eds., *PAH*, V, 308–309; Elihu Chauncy Goodrich, Claverack, to Samuel B. Webb, NYC, Mar. 25, 1789, in Ford, ed., *Correspondence and Journals of Webb*, III, 132–133; Henry Livingston, Manor, to Walter Livingston, NYC, Jan. 10, 1790, RRLP; Peter Van Ness Denman, "From Deference to Democracy: The Van Ness Family and Their Times, 1759 to 1844" (Ph.D. diss., University of Michigan, 1977), 104. The Otsego crisis is detailed in Alfred F. Young, *The Democratic Republicans of New York: The Origins, 1763–1797* (Chapel Hill, N.C., 1967), 304–323; and Alan Taylor, *William Cooper's Town: Power and Persuasion on the Frontier of the Early American Republic* (New York, 1995), 170–198.

31. *New-York Journal*, June 30, 1792; Young, *The Democratic Republicans*, 311, citing Stephen Van Rensselaer to William Cooper, June 28, 1792; New York *Diary; or, Loudon's Register,* June 23, 1792; *Hudson Gazette,* July 19, 1792; Ebenezer Foote to ———, June 27, 1792, in Katherine Adelia Foote, ed., *Ebenezer Foote: The Founder . . .* (Delhi, N.Y., 1927), 44.

32. *At a Meeting of a Number of Respectable Gentlemen . . . the Nineteenth Day of June, 1792 . . .* (Hudson, N.Y.[?], 1792[?]) (Evans 46415); Lansingburgh *American Spy,* July 6, 1792; *Hudson Gazette,* July 5, 1792; Morgan Lewis, Johnstown, Livingston Manor, to Robert R. Livingston, Clermont, July 4, 1792, RRLP.

33. Stockbridge *Western Star,* Aug. 7, 28, Sept. 4, 18, 25, Oct. 16, Nov. 9, 20, Dec. 25, 1792; *The Rights of Suffrage* (Hudson, N.Y., 1792), 20; *Hudson Gazette,* July 5, 19, Aug. 16, Sept. 13, 20, 1792; Alexander Hamilton to Rufus King, June 28, July 25, 1792, in Syrett et al., eds., *PAH,* XI, 588–589, XII, 99–100; Young, *The Democratic Republicans,* 312; Peter Van Schaack, Kinderhook, to Theodore Sedgwick, Philadelphia, Aug. 31, Dec. 8, 1792, Jan. 2, 1793, I:2.5/72, 2.6/86, 2.7/95, Sedgwick Papers, MHS.

34. *Hudson Gazette,* July 19, Aug. 16, Sept. 20, 1792; *New-York Journal,* July 4, 1792; New York *Daily Advertiser,* Aug. 1, 1792; Young, *The Democratic Republicans,* 314–315; Dangerfield, *Chancellor Robert R. Livingston,* 235–306.

35. *NYAJ,* 16th sess., 1793, 60–62, 68, 121, 135, 139–142, 149–151, 186–196, 202.

36. Years in Office from Columbia County, 1789–1799

Office	Federalists	Clintonians/Republicans
New York Assembly	9	49
New York Senate	15	6
U.S. House of Represeentatives	6	0

37. *NYAJ,* 14th sess., 1791, 78, 94–95, 98–99; Robert E. Wright, "Banking and Politics in New York, 1784–1829" (Ph.D. diss., SUNY Buffalo, 1996), 135–141.

38. Genet Family Papers, Albany Institute of History and Art; George Baker Anderson, *Landmarks of Rensselaer County, New York* (Syracuse, N.Y., 1897), 538–539; *Hudson Gazette,* Feb. 28, 1793.

39. *Hudson Gazette,* Feb. 20, 1794; on Younglove, see Alexander Clarence Flick, *Samuel Jones Tilden: A Study in Political Sagacity* (New York, 1939), 3, 10–11, 42.

40. The Canaan Society Constitution was printed first in the *Hudson Gazette,* Feb. 20, 1794, and then in *Greenleaf's New York Journal,* Mar. 8, 1794, the *Albany Register,* Mar. 10, 1794, and the Stockbridge *Western Star,* May 6, 1794; it has been reprinted in Philip S. Foner, *The Democratic-Republican Societies, 1790–1800: A Documentary Sourcebook . . .* (Westport, Conn., 1976), 237–239.

On the July meeting, see *Greenleaf's New York Journal,* Oct. 4, Nov. 12, 1794; and Young, *The Democratic Republicans,* 536.

41. The Federalist critique of the Canaan Society is in Stockbridge *Western Star,* May 6, June 17, Oct. 28, 1794; Boston *Massachusetts Mercury,* June 27, Aug. 8, 1794. The Canaan Society's writings are from *Greenleaf's New York Journal,* July 23, 1794; and *Columbian Mercury, and Canaan Repository of Rural Knowledge,* Oct. 1, 1794.

42. Henry Van Schaack, Pittsfield, to Theodore Sedgwick, Philadelphia, Feb. 6, 1795, I:2.13/191, Sedgwick Papers, MHS; *Hudson Gazette,* Mar. 26, 1795; Catskill *Packet, and Western Mail,* Apr. 14, 1795. By this time, Elisha Gilbert, a Unity Mason, had joined the Democratic Society, perhaps in connection with his emerging leadership of the Mawighnunk occupants in New Lebanon Valley (see Chapter 5); *Greenleaf's New York Journal,* Oct. 14, 1795; Young, *The Democratic Republicans,* 456, 459.

43. For discussion of the Democratic Societies' contributions to the public sphere, see Albrecht Koschnik, "The Democratic Societies of Philadelphia and the American Public Sphere, circa 1793–1795," *William and Mary Quarterly,* 3d Ser., LVIII (2001), 615–636; Cornell, *The Other Founders,* 173–174; Brooke, "Ancient Lodges and Self-Created Societies: Voluntary Association and the Public Sphere in the Early Republic," in Ronald Hoffman and Peter J. Albert, eds., *Launching the "Extended Republic": The Federalist Era* (Charlottesville, Va., 1997), 309–316.

CHAPTER 4

1. This reconstruction of the Goes–Van Buren connection is based on the Federal census manuscripts for 1790 and 1800, the 1779, 1799, 1800 Kinderhook tax lists, New York State Archives, and the 1795 Pew List, in Royden Woodward Vosburgh, ed., "Records of the Reformed Dutch Church of Kinderhook in Kinderhook, Columbia County, N.Y." (typescript, New York Genealogical and Biographical Society, 1921), II, 283. The Van Buren note is an endorsement on a letter from A[lonzo] G. Hammond, Berlin, to Martin Van Buren, Washington, Dec. 23, 1824, MVBP-LC. The 1810 Census (p. 169) lists a free person of color in the household of a "Martin Van Bewrin" in Kinderhook, whose white household members match Martin and Hannah's family in that year. If this individual was Tom, the story is more complicated. Hammond described Tom as "of the class which will be free July 4, 1827." Alonzo G. Hammond is listed on returns for the Friendship Lodge, Stephentown, 1813–1814, and Star Lodge, Petersburgh, from 1815 into the 1820s. Grand Lodge Manuscripts, LL-NYGL.

2. *NYAJ,* 24th sess., 1800–1801, 6. For the structure of the Colombia electorate, see Table 4.

3. Reeve Huston, *Land and Freedom: Rural Society, Popular Protest, and Party Politics in Antebellum New York* (New York, 2000), 13–33; Thomas J. Humphrey, *Land and Liberty: Hudson Valley Riots in the Age of Revolution* (DeKalb, Ill., 2004), 12–13, 30–34. For the classic analysis of the tidewater gentry, see Rhys Isaac, *The Transformation of Virginia, 1740–1790* (Chapel Hill, N.C., 1982). On the power of symbolic representation, or "public representativeness," see Jürgen Habermas, *The Structural Transformation of the Public Sphere: An Inquiry into a Category of Bourgeois Society,* trans. Thomas Berger (Cambridge, Mass., 1989), 5–14. On expectations and codes of respectability, I follow Harold Mah's critique of the argument that the early modern public sphere inherently was a space of plural expression. Mah in effect is restating Habermas's original thesis of a bourgeois definition of early modern public space against Habermas's critics. See Mah, "Phantasies of the Public Sphere: Rethinking the Habermas of Historians," *Journal of Modern History,* LXXII (2000), 153–182; and the subjects of his critique, Nancy Fraser, "Rethinking the Public

Sphere: A Contribution to the Critique of Actually Existing Democracy," Mary P. Ryan, "Gender and Public Access: Women's Politics in Nineteenth-Century America," Geoff Eley, "Nations, Publics, and Political Cultures: Placing Habermas in the Nineteenth Century," in Craig Calhoun, ed., *Habermas and the Public Sphere* (Cambridge, Mass., 1992), 109–142, 259–339. In my argument that—within the confines of the code of respectability—room for contest might be constructed by a form of respectable subversion, I am drawing upon Nancy Isenberg, *Sex and Citizenship in Antebellum America* (Chapel Hill, N.C., 1998); Rosemarie Zagarri, "The Postcolonial Culture of Early American Women's Writing," in Dale M. Bauer and Philip Gould, eds., *The Cambridge Companion to Nineteenth-Century American Women's Writing* (New York, 2001), 19–37; and Mary Kelley, *Learning to Stand and Speak: Women, Education, and Public Life in America's Republic* (Chapel Hill, N.C., 2006).

4. Ellis, *Columbia County,* 172.

5. Published in Philadelphia, *Gwinnett* was sold widely, *Wilson* and *The Returned Captive* were printed three times by 1800, and Franklin at least ten. Here and below the imprint data discussed are drawn from an analysis of the titles published in Hudson listed in Evans and Shaw-Shoemaker, and available on-line via the Readex/AAS "Early American Imprints" project.

6. *Hudson Weekly Gazette,* May 18, Aug. 3, 1786, Aug. 16, 1787. The last ad featuring the *Institutes* seems to be Oct. 23, 1787. Noah Webster, Jr., *A Grammatical Institute of the English Language . . .* , Part I (Hartford, Conn., 1785), [8], Part III (Hartford, Conn, 1785), 3. For a full account of Webster's larger plans for an American alphabet, see Jill Lepore, *A Is for American: Letters and Other Characters in the Newly United States* (New York, 2002), esp. 3–41. Webster kinship from the AAS printer files.

7. *Hudson Weekly Gazette,* Dec. 20, 1787, Aug. 13, 1789, Nov. 14, 1793, Feb. 10, 1801. On the reach and significance of the *American Magazine,* see Carroll Smith-Rosenberg, "Dis-Covering the Subject of the 'Great Constitutional Discussion,' 1786–1789," *Journal of American History,* LXXIX (1992–1993), 841–873. For Hutton's illustrations, see J. Hamilton Moore, *The Young Gentleman and Lady's Monitor, and English Teacher's Assistant . . .* (Hudson, N.Y., 1795), 352–354, 358.

8. For the theoretical framework of respectability and the public sphere, see Mah, "Phantasies of the Public Sphere," *Journal of Modern History,* LXXII (2000), 153–182. For its manifestation in the early Republic, see Richard L. Bushman, *The Refinement of America: Persons, Houses, Cities* (New York, 1992), esp. 30–99; Catherine E. Kelly, "'Saturday Morning We Defined Sensibility': Gender, Gentility, and Education in the Republic of Taste," presented at the OIEAHC Annual Conference, Toronto, June 11, 2000; Tamara Plakins Thornton, *Handwriting in America: A Cultural History* (New Haven, Conn., 1996); C. Dallett Hemphill, *Bowing to Necessities: A History of Manners in America, 1620–1860* (New York, 1999); Sandra M. Gustafson, *Eloquence Is Power: Oratory and Performance in Early America* (Chapel Hill, N.C., 2000), 233–265; Sarah Knott, *Sensibility and the American Revolution* (Chapel Hill, N.C., 2009). For the wider context of Van Buren's education, and the use of the *Monitor,* see Chapter 6, the books listed as used in local schools in Lansingburgh *Northern Budget,* Jan. 16, 1798, and Frances Wilson, Albany, to William Wilson, Clermont, May 2, 1802, WFP-UM.

9. Stoddard advertised subscriptions for Barlow's *Vision* and Thomas Newton's *Dissertations on the Prophecies* in the *Hudson Weekly Gazette,* Sept. 14, 1786, Sept. 20, 1787. For the subscription analysis, see Tables 5, 6.

10. Alexander Coventry, "Memoirs of an Emigrant: The Journal of Alexander Coventry, M.D." (typescript, AIHA and NYSL, 1978), 464 (Mar. 14, 1790).

11. Ashbel Stoddard, Hudson, to Noah Webster, NYC, June 27, 1801, Papers of Noah Webster, NYPL; Milton W. Hamilton, *The Country Printer: New York State, 1785–1830* (New York, 1936), 213, 222–223; George Holcomb Diary, 1805–1856, NYSL and the Stephentown Historical Society, June 30, 1812. Harry Croswell had just commenced publishing the Hudson *Balance* a few weeks before Stoddard's letter to Webster; thus this analysis is a sketch of the county readership for the *Gazette* prior to the establishment of the *Balance*.

12. On taverns, see Martin Bruegel, *Farm, Shop, Landing: The Rise of a Market Society in the Hudson Valley, 1780–1860* (Durham, N.C., 2002), 31–34, though he does not discuss newspapers. According to Bruegel (32) there was 1 tavern for every 40 inhabitants of the river town of Catskill in 1807. If we estimate a conservative average for Columbia County in 1800 at 1 tavern for every 200 inhabitants, the result would be a total of 176 taverns. For a formative discussion of print and newspapers in tavern culture, see David W. Conroy, *In Public Houses: Drink and the Revolution of Authority in Colonial Massachusetts* (Chapel Hill, N.C., 1995), 177–180, 234–236, 258–266, 272–283, 302–305. See William J. Gilmore, *Reading Becomes a Necessity of Life: Material and Cultural Life in Rural New England, 1780–1835* (Knoxville, Tenn., 1989), 193–195, for roughly comparable figures for newspaper readership. This analysis is broadly congruent with Trish Loughran's argument that American publics were fragmented by region and locality, as well as by class, before the 1830s. See *The Republic of Print: Print Culture in the Age of U.S. Nation Building, 1770–1870* (New York, 2007).

13. Bruegel, *Farm, Shop, Landing,* 32–33; Timothy Dwight, *Travels in New England and New York,* ed. Barbara Miller Solomon (Cambridge, Mass., 1969), IV, 3–4.

14. Jesse Torrey, *The Intellectual Torch: Developing an Original, Economical, and Expeditious Plan for the Universal Dissemination of Knowledge and Virtue, by Means of Free Public Libraries . . .* (Ballston Spa, N.Y., 1817; rpt. 1912), 4–5, 7–8, 18–19.

15. Jesse Torrey, *Portraiture of Domestic Slavery, in the United States . . .* (Philadelphia, 1817; rpt. 1970), 18.

16. Webster, *Grammatical Institutes,* Part I, [8].

17. Ellis, *Columbia County,* 220–221, 230–232, 235–236, 243–247, 262–266, 272–275, 331–332, 355–356, 386–390, 396–397, 404–405, 411–412, 414–415; Edward A. Collier, *A History of Old Kinderhook . . .* (New York, 1914), 40–45; Ruth Piwonka and Roderic H. Blackburn, *A Visible Heritage: Columbia County, New York: A History in Art and Architecture* (Kinderhook, N.Y., 1977; rpt. 1996), 33–38. Thomas L. Purvis estimates in that in 1790 the Dutch- and German-descended population comprised roughly 39 percent of the population of Columbia County. Columbia was second in the state to King's County, where he estimates 61 percent were Dutch or German. Columbia's white population in 1790 was roughly 26,000, while King's was only 3,000; thus their Dutch-German populations stood at roughly 10,140 and 1,830, respectively. Thomas L. Purvis, "The National Origins of New Yorkers in 1790," *New York History,* LXVII (1986), 132–153.

18. Walter Livingston, Manor, to Robert R. Livingston, Clermont, Jan. 7, 1781, with "Resolutions at a meeting of above 300 of the inhabitants of the Manor of Livingston, 6 Jan. 1781," XLVI, reel 15, RRLP; *Artykelen, die geaccordeerd zyn by de foedderale Conventie der Vereenigde Staaten van Noord Amerika . . .* (Albany, N.Y., 1787); *De Constitutie, eenpariglyk geaccordeerd by de algemeene Conventie, gehouden in de Stad von Philadelphia, in 't Jaar 1787 . . .* (Albany, N.Y., 1788); Peter Van Schaack, Kinderhook, to Theodore Sedgwick, Philadelphia, Mar. 12, 1798, Sedgwick Papers, MHS, I: 3.10/161; John E. Van Alen, Philadelphia, to Peter Van Schaack, Kinderhook, Mar. 20, Apr. 4, 6, 10, May 19, July 5, 1798, Peter Van Schaack Papers, Columbia University Ar-

chives; see also Peter Van Schaack, Kinderhook, to Theodore Sedgwick, Philadelphia, Dec. 21, 1797, Sedgwick Papers, MHS, I: 3.8/110. A broadside in German survives from the 1801 governor's election: "An die freien und unabhaengigen Waehler des New-York States," Broadside Collection, De Witt Clinton Papers, AIHA.

19. John Beebe, Jr., Diary, Oct. 21, 1780, Mss. 11239, NYSL; *Albany Gazette,* May 13, 1785; J. Munsell, *The Typographical Miscellany* (Albany, N.Y., 1850), 227.

20. *Hudson Weekly Gazette,* May 18, June 1, 1786, Apr. 5, 1787, Apr. 3, 1788, Nov. 14, 1793, Feb. 20, 1794; Petrus van Vlierden: *Handleidinge tot eene hervormde Geloovs-Belydenis...* (Kingston, N.Y., 1794); *Het Lot van Lichaam en Ziel by 's menchen dood... Heer Johannes Schuneman ... den 25 Mai, 1794...* (Catskill, N.Y., 1794); *A Sermon, Delivered at Catskill, on Thursday July 30, 1812, Being a Day of Fasting, Humiliation, and Prayer* (Kingston, N.Y., 1812). For the German and Dutch references in Hudson papers, see *Hudson Weekly Gazette,* Jan. 25, Sept. 27, 1787, Apr. 3, 1788, Mar. 17, 1801; Hudson *Balance,* Sept. 27, 1803.

21. Stephen B. Miller, *Historical Sketches of Hudson...* (Hudson, N.Y., 1862; rpt. 1985), 34–35; William Strickland, *Journal of a Tour in the United States of America, 1794–1795,* ed. J. E. Strickland (New York, 1971), 123; Washington Irving, "The Legend of Sleepy Hollow," in Irving, *The Sketchbook of Geoffrey Crayon, Gent.,* ed. Heskell Springer (Boston, 1978), 273, 275. Crane was modeled on Jesse Merwin, from a Connecticut family, the first teacher of a school in the Van Ness–Van Alen neighborhood. Married in Kinderhook in 1808, Merwin was listed on the 1811 Kinderhook Republican Committee and died in Kinderhook in 1852. For Merwin, see Stanley T. Williams, *The Life of Washington Irving* (New York, 1935), I, 108–109, 408 n. 10, 409 n. 45, 429 n. 91; Collier, *Kinderhook,* 24, 239, 522; Hudson *Balance, and Columbian Repository,* Mar. 21, 1807; Hudson *Bee,* Mar. 22, Apr. 19, 1811.

22. For church schools in Kinderhook, Germantown, and Livingston, see Collier, *Kinderhook,* 283–284, and Ellis, *Columbia County,* 121–123. For ethnicity, print, and subscriptions, see Tables 7, 11, 12.

23. Coventry, "Memoirs of an Emigrant," 155 (Apr. 1, 1787); John Warwick Montgomery, "The Colonial Parish Library of Wilhelm Christoph Berkenmeyer," *Papers of the Bibliographical Society of America,* LIII (1959), 114–149. On Berkenmeyer's pastorate, see Harry Julius Kreider, *Lutheranism in Colonial New York* (New York, 1942), 44–45; Johann Arndt, *Des hocherleuchteten Theologi, Herrn Johann Arndt...* (Philadelphia, 1751) (Evans 6630), last two pages of subscription list (n.p.). The trade in German imprints might have declined after the Revolution. The Columbia County Historical Society has a collection of religious texts and dictionaries printed in Germany and the Netherlands, most of which descended in local families, dating from 1591 to 1778, eight of thirteen dating between 1695 and 1750. On books in German households, see Russell W. Gilbert, "Pennsylvania German Wills," *Pennsylvania German Folklore Society Yearbook,* XV (1950), 86–91; A. G. Roeber, *Palatines, Liberty, and Property: German Lutherans in Colonial British America* (Baltimore, 1993), 18. Philip Otterness stresses the role of Pietism in raising German literacy in the mid-eighteenth century, in *Becoming German: The 1709 Palatine Migration to New York* (Ithaca, N.Y., 2004), 18–19. Will of Andries Lowe, May 16, 1791, proved July 7, 1800, Columbia County Surrogate Court Records. I am grateful to Jeff Lape for making this available, and to Gregg Roeber for assistance with the translation.

24. The Krum Church was officially called "The Reformed Lutheran Unity Church": see F. N. Zabriskie, *History of the Reformed P.D. Church of Claverack: A Centennial Address* (Hudson, N.Y., 1867), 23; Royden Woodward Vosburgh, ed., "Records of the Reformed Dutch Church of Hills-

dale . . . , N.Y." (typescript, New York Genealogical and Biographical Society, 1912), 2; Sullivan, ed., *Minutes,* I, 254, 336; Paltsits, ed., *Minutes,* II, 223, 235, 240, 506, 512–514, 834–835. On Ernst and the Masons, see *Hymns of Praise Sung by the Youth of the Evangelical Lutheran Zion's Congregation of Loonenburg . . .* (Hudson, N.Y., 1792); *An Account of the Performances at the Dedication of Mason-Hall, Hudson . . .* (Hudson, N.Y., 1797), 6–10, 19–30; Vosburgh, ed., "Records of St. Thomas's Evangelical Lutheran Church, at Churchtown, Town of Claverack, Columbia County, N.Y." (typescript, New York Genealogical and Biographical Society, 1912), 66; John Frederick Ernst to John Arndt, Aug. 24, 1797, Lutheran Archives Center, Mount Airy, Pa., cited in Alan Taylor, *William Cooper's Town: Power and Persuasion on the Frontier of the Early American Republic* (New York, 1995), 215. For a detailed account of Ernst's career, see Taylor, 214–216.

25. David William Voorhees, "'Ye People Very Much Inclined to Mutiny': Columbia County and the 1689 Leisler Rebellion," *Columbia County History and Heritage,* I (2002), 4–5; Randall H. Balmer, *A Perfect Babel of Confusion: Dutch Religion and English Culture in the Middle Colonies* (New York, 1989), 122, 132–133; Ellis, *Columbia County,* 244; Elizabeth L. Gebhard, *The Parsonage between Two Manors: Annals of Clover-Reach* (Hudson, N.Y., 1925), 242–243; see also David G. Hackett, *The Rude Hand of Innovation: Religion and Social Order in Albany, New York, 1652–1836* (New York, 1991), 59. On the Dutch and German household-focused culture, law, and religion, and their tension with English civil society, see Balmer, *A Perfect Babel of Confusion;* John M. Murrin, "English Rights as Ethnic Aggression: The English Conquest, the Charter of Liberties of 1683, and Leisler's Rebellion in New York," in William Pencak and Conrad Edick Wright, eds., *Authority and Resistance in Early New York* (New York, 1988), 56–94; Donna Merwick, *The Death of a Notary: Conquest and Change in Colonial New York* (Ithaca, N.Y., 1999); Merwick, *Possessing Albany, 1630–1710: The Dutch and English Experience* (New York, 1990); A. G. Roeber, *Palatines, Liberty, and Property,* and "'The Origin of Whatever Is Not English among Us': The Dutch-Speaking and the German-Speaking Peoples of Colonial America," in Bernard Bailyn and Philip D. Morgan, eds., *Strangers within the Realm: Cultural Margins of the First British Empire* (Chapel Hill, N.C., 1991), 220–283; Firth Haring Fabend, *A Dutch Family in the Middle Colonies, 1660–1800* (New Brunswick, N.J., 1991), esp. 105–130, 240–247; Martha Dickinson Shattuck, "'For the Peace and Welfare of the Community': Maintaining a Civil Society in New Netherland," *de Halve Maen,* LXXII (1999), 27–32.

26. Schaghticoke, N.Y., Society for the General Diffusion and Promotion of Useful Knowledge, Minutes, 1797–1807, NYHS. While this society was dominated by men of Dutch names, the Homer Lodge formed in Schaghticoke in 1799 was predominantly English: Homer Lodge returns, Grand Lodge Records, LL-NYGL. On the incorporation of the Manor churches, see Royden Woodward Vosburgh, ed., "Records of the Reformed Church of West Copake (Formerly Taghkanick), at West Copake, Columbia County, State of New York" (typescript, New York Genealogical and Biographical Society, 1912), 142, 161–162.

27. This is A. J. Williams-Myers's conclusion in "The Arduous Journey: The African American presence in the Hudson-Mohawk Region," in Monroe Fordham, ed., *The African American Presence in New York State History: Four Regional History Surveys* (Albany, N.Y., 1989), 23. More broadly, see Peter S. Onuf, "'To Declare Them a Free and Independent People': Race, Slavery, and National Identity in Jefferson's Thought," *Journal of the Early Republic,* XVIII (1998), 1–46; Sally E. Hadden, *Slave Patrols: Law and Violence in Virginia and the Carolinas* (Cambridge, Mass., 2001).

28. Population data discussed here and below from Evarts B. Greene and Virginia D. Harring-

ton, *American Population before the Federal Census of 1790* (New York, 1932), 104, and *Heads of Families at the First Census of the United States, Taken in the Year 1790: New York* (Washington, D.C., 1908). Putting these figures in perspective, King's County on western Long Island reported 32 percent of its population enslaved, and the village of Flatbush 40 percent, roughly comparable to the Virginia piedmont in 1790. Albany County in 1786 (then including Columbia), when the state recorded the gender of slaves, stands out as the only county in the state where black women outnumbered black men. Pawling, a Quaker town in Dutchess County, was notable for a settlement of free blacks, numbering ninety-one in 1790. See A. J. Williams-Myers, *Long Hammering: Essays on the Forging of an African-American Presence in the Hudson River Valley to the Early Twentieth Century* (Trenton, N.J., 1994), 119–120. For a detailed analysis of slavery in Dutchess County, see Michael Edward Groth, "Forging Freedom in the Mid-Hudson Valley: The End of Slavery and the Formation of a Free African-American Community in Dutchess County, 1770–1850" (Ph.D. diss., SUNY Binghamton, 1994).

29. Cyntia A. Kierner, *Traders and Gentlefolk: The Livingstons of New York, 1675–1850* (Ithaca, N.Y., 1992), 71–72; Roberta Singer, "The Livingstons as Slave Owners: The 'Peculiar Institution' of Livingston Manor and Clermont," in Richard T. Wiles, ed., *The Livingston Legacy: Three Centuries of American History* (Red Hook, N.Y., 1987), 70–76; James G. Lydon, "New York and the Slave Trade, 1700–1774," *William and Mary Quarterly*, 3d Ser., XXXV (1978), 388, 390; Williams-Myers, *Long Hammering*, 13–42; Graham Russell Hodges, *Root and Branch: African Americans in New York and East Jersey, 1613–1863* (Chapel Hill, N.C., 1999), 107–114; Ira Berlin, *Many Thousands Gone: The First Two Centuries of Slavery in North America* (Cambridge, Mass., 1998), 50–84, 181–182.

30. [Anne MacVicar Grant], *Memoirs of an American Lady: With Sketches of Manners and Scenery in America, as They Existed previous to the Revolution* (London, 1808), I, 91; Gebhard, *The Parsonage between Two Manors*, 236–237. On Pinkster, see Shane White, "Pinkster: Afro-Dutch Syncretization in New York City and the Hudson Valley," *Journal of American Folklore*, CII (1989), 68–75; Williams-Myers, *Long Hammering*, 85–98; Hodges, *Root and Branch*, 24–25, 87–88, 96–98; Sterling Stuckey, "African Spirituality and Cultural Practice in Colonial New York, 1700–1770," in Carla Gardina Pestana and Sharon V. Salinger, eds., *Inequality in Early America* (Hanover, N.H., 1999), 160–181; 1795 Pew List, in Vosburgh, ed., "Records of the Reformed Dutch Church of Kinderhook," II, 282. On language, see *Hudson Gazette*, Dec. 20, 1787, June 23, 1796, Sept. 29, 1801; Roberta Singer, "Slaveholding on Livingston Manor and Clermont, 1686–1800," *Dutchess County Historical Society Yearbook*, LXIX (1984), 63, citing Livingston Manor store daybook, 1770s; Hodges, *Root and Branch*, 109–110; Strickland, *Journal of a Tour*, ed. Strickland, 163. In Hudson the trade with the West Indies meant that there were also slaves who spoke Creole French; see *Hudson Weekly Gazette*, Dec. 13, 1787.

31. Coventry, "Memoirs of an Emigrant," 156 (Apr. 5, 1787), 445 (Oct 12, 1789); Craig Steven Wilder, *In the Company of Black Men: The African Influences on African American Culture in New York City* (New York, 2001), 9–35; Sullivan, ed., *Minutes*, I, 24, 87, 585; Williams-Myers, *Long Hammering*, 46–47, 55, 58–60; *Hudson Weekly Gazette*, Sept. 14, 1786, Aug. 2, 1787, Apr. 10, 1788.

32. *Journals of the Provincial Council of Safety of the State of New York, 1775–1776–1777* (Albany, N.Y., 1842); David N. Gellman, *Emancipating New York: The Politics of Slavery and Freedom, 1777–1827* (Baton Rouge, La., 2006), 33–34, 48–53, 67–68; *NYSJ*, 8th sess., 1785, 2d mtg., 55–56; *NYAJ*, 8th sess., 1785, 2d mtg., 14, 53, 54, 62, 63, 76, 77, 120. Walter Livingston re Free Negro Flora, June 17, 1785, RRLP. Col. William B. Whiting of Canaan, the owner of two slaves in 1790, voted

for the abolition bill in the senate. Whiting's neighbor, Justice Eleazer Grant, married an inter-racial couple from Massachusetts, the Wheelers, in 1789; it is possible that he assumed that they were both white. See Irene Quenzler Brown and Richard D. Brown, *The Hanging of Ephraim Wheeler: A Story of Rape, Incest, and Justice in Early America* (Cambridge, Mass., 2003), 174, 316 n. 16.

33. *Hudson Weekly Gazette,* June 15, Nov. 30, 1786, Apr. 26, 1787. Here I am indebted to Gell-man's analysis of sentiment and antislavery in *Emancipating New York,* 102–129. See Chapter 6 for a fuller discussion.

34. Coventry, "Memoirs of an Emigrant," 118 (July 31, 1786), 209 (Mar. 23, 1789), 211–212 (Apr. 9–13, 1789), 215 (June 1, 1789); Shane White, *Somewhat More Independent: The End of Slavery in New York City, 1770–1810* (Athens, Ga., 1991), 103, 109–110.

35. White, "Pinkster," *Journal of American Folklore,* CII (1989), esp. 70–71; Williams-Myers, *Long Hammering,* 85–99; Hodges, *Root and Branch,* 24–25, 54, 63, 87–88.

36. Walter Livingston re Negro Flora, June 17, 1785, RRLP.

37. 1795 Pew List, in Vosburgh, "Records of the Reformed Dutch Church of Kinderhook," II, 283; [Johann Friedrich Specht], *The Specht Journal: A Military Journal of the Burgoyne Campaign,* trans. Helga Doblin, ed. Mary C. Lynn and Donald M. Londahl-Schmidt (Westport, Conn., 1995), 104.

38. *NY Laws,* 10th sess., 1787, chap. 69; Syrett et al., eds., *PAH,* IV, 70–71, 125; *Hudson Weekly Gazette,* July 8, 1788; Lansingburgh *Federal Herald,* Aug. 25, 1788; Deborah A. Rosen, *Courts and Commerce: Gender, Law, and the Market Economy in Colonial New York* (Columbus, Ohio, 1997), 95–134; Marylynn Salmon, *Women and the Law of Property in Early America* (Chapel Hill, N.C., 1986), 11, 71–72, 82–83; George Dangerfield, *Chancellor Robert R. Livingston of New York, 1746–1813* (New York, 1960), 185–187, 277–278; Joan R. Gundersen and Gwen Victor Gampel, "Married Women's Legal Status in Eighteenth-Century New York and Virginia," *WMQ,* 3d Ser., XXXIX (1982), 114–134; David Waldstreicher, *In the Midst of Perpetual Fetes: The Making of American Nationalism, 1776–1820* (Chapel Hill, N.C., 1997), 83–85.

39. I am indebted to Linda K. Kerber, *Women of the Republic: Intellect and Ideology in Revolu-tionary America* (Chapel Hill, N.C., 1980), 260–261, for this formulation.

40. *Calendar of Historical Manuscripts, Relating to the War of the Revolution . . .* (Albany, N.Y., 1868), II, 311–312; Land and Personal Tax Lists of the District of Kinderhook, July 31, 1779, Tax Lists and Assessment Rolls, 1779–1815, New York (State) Treasurer's Office (A1201), NYSA; 1790 Heads of Household. On the 1795 Kinderhook Pew List (Vosburgh, ed., "Records of the Dutch Reformed Church in Kinderhook," II, 281), Caterina Kittle's name is crossed out, suggesting that she died while the list was being drawn up in 1795. Another Dutch woman who married into the Kittle clan, Maria Kittle, was captured by Indian raiders at Schagticoke in 1748; her story was recorded in 1779 and printed in 1797 in Ann Elizabeth Bleecker, *The History of Maria Kittle: In a Letter to Miss Ten Eyck* (Hartford, Conn., 1797). For another account of this raid, see George Baker Anderson, *Landmarks of Rensselaer County, New York* (Syracuse, N.Y., 1897), 442–443.

41. John Niven, *Martin Van Buren: The Romantic Age of American Politics* (New York, 1983), 7; Jerome Mushkat and Joseph G. Rayback, *Martin Van Buren: Law, Politics, and the Shaping of Republican Ideology* (DeKalb, Ill., 1997), 4, 13–14; Donald B. Cole, *Martin Van Buren and the American Political System* (Princeton, N.J., 1984), 14–15.

42. My argument here is based on a review of the Dutch Reformed Church records in the Vosburgh Collection and the work of many historians on Dutch and German society in colo-

nial America: David E. Narrett, "Men's Wills and Women's Property Rights in Colonial New York," in Ronald Hoffman and Peter J. Albert, eds., *Women in the Age of the American Revolution* (Charlottesville, Va., 1989), 91–133; Narrett, *Inheritance and Family Life in Colonial New York City* (Ithaca, N.Y., 1992); Linda Briggs Biemer, *Women and Property in Colonial New York: The Transition from Dutch to English Law, 1643–1727* (Ann Arbor, Mich., 1983); A. G. Roeber, *Palatines, Liberty, and Property,* 59–61, 314–316; Roeber, "The Origins and Transfer of German-American Concepts of Property and Inheritance," *Perspectives in American History,* n.s., III (1986), 115–171. See the reviews of the question of Dutch women's position in Joyce D. Goodfriend, "Incorporating Women into the History of the Colonial Dutch Reformed Church: Problems and Proposals," and John W. Beardslee III, "The Dutch Women in Two Cultures: Looking for the Questions," both in Renée House and John Coakley, eds., *Patterns and Portraits: Women in the History of the Reformed Church in America* (Grand Rapids, Mich., 1999), 16–32, 52–65; Gundersen and Gampel, "Married Women's Legal Status," *WMQ,* 3d Ser., XXXIX (1982), 118–119. Caterina Kittle's assertion of political identity stands out, since most wives of loyalists lost such claims. See Linda K. Kerber, *No Constitutional Right to Be Ladies: Women and the Obligations of Citizenship* (New York, 1998), 3–46.

43. *Hudson Weekly Gazette,* May 18, June 1, 1786, Apr. 15, 1787 (compare with Nov. 14, 1793, Feb. 20, 1794); Lansingburgh *Gazette,* Feb. 16, 1808; Hudson *Northern Whig,* Jan. 3, 1809, June 28, 1811. A translated *Heidelberg Catechism,* printed in New York in 1767, was given to John Dings of Gallitan around 1800 (CCHS collections). If noticeable, the wartime translation of German classics was not an absolute flood: *The Heidelbergh Catechism . . .* (Hudson, N.Y., 1812); *The Heidelbergh Catechism . . .* (Hudson, N.Y., 1813); Christoph Christian Sturm, *Reflections for Every Day in the Year . . . from the German of Mr. C. C. Sturm,* 1st American ed. (Hudson, N.Y., 1814); Frederick Henry Quitman, *Evangelical Catechism . . .* (Hudson, N.Y., 1814); Frederick H[enry] Quitman, *Three Sermons . . .* (Hudson, N.Y., 1817); A. Hellenbroek, *A Specimen of Divine Truths: For the Instruction of Youth . . . Translated from the Dutch* (Hudson, N.Y., 1816); John Fredrick William Tischer, *The Life, Deeds, and Opinions of Dr. Martin Luther, Faithfully Translated from the German . . . by John Kortz* (Hudson, N.Y., 1818); Carl Theodor von Unlanski, *The Woful History of the Unfortunate Eudoxia: . . . Faithfully Translated from the German . . . by John Kortz* (Hudson, N.Y., 1816), 45.

44. Coventry, "Memoirs of an Emigrant," 92 (Mar. 28, 1786); Moore, *Young Gentleman and Lady's Monitor,* 107–114.

45. Ruth Piwonka and Roderick H. Blackburn, *Ammi Phillips in Columbia County: A Catalogue of and Exhibition of Portraits Done in Columbia County by Ammi Phillips (1788–1865)* (Kinderhook, N.Y., 1975); Worthington Chauncey Ford, ed., *Correspondence and Journals of Samuel Blachley Webb* (New York, 1893–1894), III, 110–111, 117–118; Charles A. Foote, Kinderhook, to Harriot and M. Foote, Delhi, July 7, 1806, Foote Papers, NYSL; Thomas Brown, *An Account of the People Called Shakers . . .* (Troy, N.Y., 1812), xi; Mary Frances Ludlow diary, Jan. 15–Feb. 12, 1837, reproduced in Marie L. Carton, *The Ludlows of England and America* (1964 [NYSL]), 17–21; *Hudson Gazette,* Jan. 2, 1797, Mar. 2, 1802; Troy *Northern Budget,* May 7, 1799. Book inscription information from the AAS catalog.

46. For examples of circulating libraries, see Hudson *Bee,* July 12, 1803; *Albany Centinel,* Aug. 9, 1803, through Feb. 10, 1804. The *Poughkeepsie Journal, and Constitutional Republican,* Nov. 12, 1805, has a notice of the establishment of a local branch of Bernard Dornin's New York bookstore and library. Books were occasionally printed in Hudson for the "itinerant booksellers."

In general, see David Jaffee, "Peddlers of Progress and the Transformation of the Rural North, 1760–1860," *JAH,* LXXVIII (1991–1992), 511–535.

47. The reprints of Sampson's *Beauties* were possibly driven by school sales.

48. The first issues with the "Bouquet" were the *Hudson Gazette,* Feb. 17, 24, 1801.

49. Here I am working from the arguments developed by Mary Kelley, "The Sentimentalists: Promise and Betrayal in the Home," *Signs,* IV (1979), 434–446, and *Private Woman, Public Stage: Literary Domesticity in Nineteenth-Century America* (New York, 1984); Cathy N. Davidson, *Revolution and the Word: The Rise of the Novel in America* (New York, 1986), 110–135; Kerber, *Women of the Republic,* 248–264; Jane Tompkins, *Sensational Designs: The Cultural Work of American Fiction, 1790–1860* (New York, 1985), 172–185. For arguments about the continuities in the sentimental between the 1790s and 1850s, see Catharine O'Connell, "'We *Must* Sorrow': Silence, Suffering, and Sentimentality in Susan Warner's *The Wide, Wide World,*" *Studies in American Fiction,* XXV (1997), 21–40. Warner's *Queechy* was also set in Canaan.

50. *Hudson Gazette,* June 22, Dec. 7, 1786, Jan. 18, 1787, Apr. 3, 1788, Aug. 13, 1789, Nov. 14, 1793, Sept. 15, 1796, Mar. 12, 1799, Feb. 10, 1801; *Northern Centinel, and Lansingburgh Advertiser,* Sept. 17, 1787; Troy *Northern Budget,* Sept. 25, Dec. 11, 18, 1798, Jan. 15, 22, Feb. 26, May 7, 1799, May 7, 1800; "A Panegyric on Money," in Samuel Mott, *Stoddard's Diary; or, The Columbia Almanack, for . . . 1796* (Hudson, N.Y., 1795); Hudson *Balance,* Aug. 10, Sept. 14, 1802, July 10, 1804. On modes of writing on race in magazines, newspapers, and almanacs, see Shane White, "Impious Prayers: Elite and Popular Attitudes toward Blacks and Slavery in the Middle-Atlantic States, 1783–1810," *New York History,* LXVII (1986), 261–283. For a full discussion of the negative public depictions of women, see Smith-Rosenberg, "Dis-covering the Subject," *JAH,* LXXIX (1992–1993), 841–873.

51. *Hudson Gazette,* Jan. 18, 1787, Feb. 7, 1793, July 23, 1796, July 11, 1797, Apr. 30, 1799, Sept. 15, 1801, Feb. 23, 1802, July 5, 1803; *A Tribute to the Memory of Catherine Berrenger, of the Town of Rhinebeck, Who Fell a Victim to Death on the Fourth Day of November . . . 1800, by Swallowing a Potion of Arsenic, Supposed to Be Administered to Her by John Benner, to Whom She Was Promised in Marriage, and Who Has Been Confined in the Gaol of Poughkeepsie . . .* (Poughkeepsie, N.Y., 1800) (Evans 38670); Hudson *Bee,* Apr. 26, 1803; Poughkeepsie *Rural Casket,* July 3, 1798; Hudson *Balance,* Dec. 14, 1802, Jan. 18, 1803, Feb. 21, 1804; Kingston *Plebeian,* Apr. 8, 1805. Charles Foote, a reader and contributor to the *Balance,* made sure that his young sisters knew about female infanticide in China: Charles A. Foote, Kinderhook, to H. and M. Foote, Delhi, July 7, 1806, NYSL.

52. *Hudson Weekly Gazette,* June 29, 1786. See Chapter 3.

53. Here I follow the argument developed in Gillian Brown, *The Consent of the Governed: The Lockean Legacy in Early American Culture* (Cambridge, Mass., 2001), 107–176; and some of the implications developed in Dana D. Nelson's overview essay, "Women in Public," in Dale M. Bauer and Philip Gould, eds., *The Cambridge Companion to Nineteenth-Century American Women's Writing* (Cambridge, 2001), 38–68. On the wider issue of sensibility and sentiment, see G. J. Barker-Benfield, *The Culture of Sensibility: Sex and Society in Eighteenth-Century Britain* (Chicago, 1992); Markman Ellis, *The Politics of Sensibility: Race, Gender, and Commerce in the Sentimental Novel* (New York, 1996); Andrew Burstein, *Sentimental Democracy: The Evolution of America's Romantic Self-Image* (New York, 1999).

54. *NY Laws,* 10th sess., 1787, chap. 23; Peter D. Van Dyck, Albany, to John E. Van Alen, Kinderhook, Mar. 29, 1790, Van Alen Papers, CCHS; *Hudson Gazette,* Aug. 26, 1792, Feb. 10, 1801. Matthew Pease had originally published a notice of elopement in November 1800, and

Sukey Pease's notice was first published on Feb. 3, 1801: neither of these papers survives. Matthew Pease published a rebuttal on Feb. 10, 1801.

55. Barker-Benfield, *The Culture of Sensibility*, 215–286; Paula Baker, "The Domestication of Politics: Women and American Political Society, 1780–1920," *American Historical Review*, LXXXIX (1984), 620–647.

56. John C. Fitzpatrick, ed., *The Autobiography of Martin Van Buren*, vol. II of *Annual Report of the American Historical Association for the Year 1918* (Washington, D.C., 1920), 24–25; see also Martin Van Buren, Hudson, to the Manor Committee, Granger, Apr. 25, 1811, Butler Family Papers, Princeton University. For further discussion of this incident and its specific context, see Chapter 9.

57. The themes of labor value and propertied independence are discussed at length in relation to the New York landlord regions in Charles W. McCurdy, *The Anti-Rent Era in New York Law and Politics, 1839–1865* (Chapel Hill, N.C., 2001); Reeve Huston, *Land and Freedom: Rural Society, Popular Protest, and Party Politics in Antebellum New York* (New York, 2000); and Martin Bruegel, "Unrest: Manorial Society and the Market in the Hudson Valley, 1780–1850," *JAH*, LXXXII (1995–1996), 1393–1424.

58. On social capital, see Bob Edwards, Michael W. Foley, and Mario Diani, eds., *Beyond Tocqueville: Civil Society and the Social Capital Debate in Comparative Perspective* (Hanover, N.H., 2001).

59. Abraham Lansing to Abraham Yates, July 20, 1788, Yates Papers, NYPL, quoted in Alfred F. Young, *The Democratic Republicans of New York: The Origins, 1763–1797* (Chapel Hill, N.C., 1967), 97; Robert Livingston to James Duane, Apr. 30, 1788, Duane Papers, NYHS, quoted in Young, *The Democratic Republicans*, 95. John Wigram, the Livingston agent and surveyor, was confident that the Manor would cast six hundred "unanimous votes" in the 1784 assembly election: John Wigram, Manor, to Leonard Bronck, Coxsackie, Apr. 3, 14, 1784, Bronck Mss., BHM-GCHS. New York *Daily Advertiser*, May 25, 1790; "Columbianus," in the *Hudson Gazette*, Sept. 13, 1792. See also "An Elector," and "An Independent Elector," in *Hudson Gazette*, July 19, 1792. For a much later example, see "To the Independent Electors," *Albany Argus*, Apr. 16, 1813. This paragraph is indebted to Young, *The Democratic Republicans*, 95–98, 300, 315–316. On tenancy and voting, see Table 4.

60. For the candidate rotation policy, see Lansingburgh *American Spy*, Apr. 21, 1795; John Van Rensselaer et al., Lansingburgh, to Peter Van Schaack, Kinderhook, Mar. 14, 1792; Samuel Edmunds et al., Hudson, to Peter Van Schaack et al., Kinderhook, Apr. 10, 1799, VSP/LC. See Tables 5, 14 on data on tenancy, property, and political participation.

61. Dwight, *Travels in New England and New York*, ed. Solomon, IV, 3; Strickland, *Journal of a Tour*, ed. Strickland, 183–184; William Swayze, *Narrative of William Swayze, Minister of the Gospel, Written by Himself* . . . (Cincinnati, Ohio, 1839), 172–174; William Raymond, *Biographical Sketches of the Distinguished Men of Columbia County* . . . (Albany, N.Y., 1851), 10–11.

62. See Table 14 for lodges and tenancy. On the Hoffmans and their challenge to the Livingstons, see Sung Bok Kim, *Landlord and Tenant in Colonial New York: Manorial Society, 1664–1775* (Chapel Hill, N.C., 1978), 232–233, 321–322; Goebel and Smith, eds., *LPAH*, III, 84–117; Peter R. Livingston, Lithgow, to Peter Van Schaack, Kinderhook, Apr. 1, 1792, VSP/LC; Henry Livingston, Ancram, to Walter Livingston, NYC, Apr. 26, 1794; John Livingston, Oak Hill, to Walter Livingston, Teviotdale, May 20 1796; William Wilson, Clermont, to Edward P. Livingston, Paris, July 6, 1802, RRLP. The last reference to this lodge is in Barent Gardenier, *An Oration, Delivered*

before the Members of Livingston Lodge . . . December 27, MDCCC (Kingston, N.Y., 1800). For Hoffman's role in the Washington Lodge, see *Account of the Performances at the Dedication of Mason Hall, Hudson . . .* (Hudson, N.Y., 1797), 47–49. Peacher, "Craft Masonry," 349–351.

63. "List of the Lodges in the State of New York, . . . June 24, A. L. 5800 . . . ," in Charles T. McClenachan, *History of the Most Ancient and Honorable Fraternity of Free and Accepted Masons in New York . . .* (New York, 1892), 133–135; James H. Smith, *History of Dutchess County, New York* (Syracuse, N.Y., 1887), 550; James A. Roberts, ed., *New York in the Revolution as Colony and State*, 2d ed. (Albany, N.Y., 1898; rpt. 1996), I, 79, 141; Berthold Fernow, *New York in the Revolution*, vol. XV of John Romeyn Brodhead, E. B. O'Callaghan, and Berthold Fernow, eds., *Documents Relative to the Colonial History of the State of New York* (Albany, N.Y., 1856–1887), 281, 541; Temple Lodge Returns, Livingston Library, NYGL; *Early History and Transactions of the Grand Lodge of Free and Accepted Masons of the State of New York, 1781–1815 . . .* (New York, 1876), 235, 240, 244–246.

64. Livingston family Masonic membership as traced in the Standing Card File, Livingston Library, NYGL.

65. Alexis de Tocqueville, *Democracy in America,* trans. Henry Reeves, rev. Francis Bowen, ed. Phillips Bradley (New York, 1945), I, 305; Garnet quoted in Earl Ofari, *"Let Your Motto Be Resistance": The Life and Thought of Henry Highland Garnet* (Boston, 1972), 131; Daniel Walker Howe, "The Evangelical Movement and Political Culture in the North during the Second Party System," *JAH,* LXXVII (1990–1991), 1216–1239; Donald G. Mathews, "The Second Great Awakening as an Organizing Process, 1780–1830: An Hypothesis," *American Quarterly,* XXI (1969), 23–43; Nathan O. Hatch, *The Democratization of American Christianity* (New Haven, Conn., 1989); Mark A. Noll, *America's God: From Jonathan Edwards to Abraham Lincoln* (New York, 2002), 179–364.

66. The town of Livingston was divided into three towns in 1803, and two more towns were incorporated in the 1820s; see Chapter 9. For the aggregate of churches by town in Rensselaer, Columbia, and Dutchess, see Table 13. The estimate of church formation in Columbia is based on the churches described in Ellis, *Columbia County,* and listed in *Census of the State of New York, for 1845: Containing an Enumeration of the Inhabitants of the State, with Other Statistical Information* (Albany, N.Y., 1846), compared to the 1840 population listed in *Sixth Census; or, Enumeration of the Inhabitants of the United States, as Corrected at the Department of State, in 1840* (Washington, D.C., 1841), 116. The two Methodist branch churches established in 1842 were not enumerated in the the 1845 census but are included here.

67. Ellis, *Columbia County,* 374–375, 392–393, 401, 408; Swayze, *Narrative of William Swayze,* 172–174.

68. Ruth Piwonka, *A Portrait of Livingston Manor, 1686–1850* (Clermont, N.Y., 1986), 144–145; Ellis, *Columbia County,* 401; James D. Livingston and Sherry H. Penney, "The Breakup of Livingston Manor," in Richard T. Wiles, ed., *The Livingston Legacy: Three Centuries of American History* ([Annandale-on-Hudson, N.Y.], 1987), 412.

69. Petition to the New York Legislature against certain Livingston lands, [March] 1811, Livingston Family Papers (2:14), Columbia University; Ellis, *Columbia County,* 408, 414.

70. For the local pattern of sponsorship of occasional publications, see Table 12. The Masonic petitions for which we have original signatures include Temple Lodge, 1785; Columbia Lodge, 1803; Vernon Lodge, 1803, all in Lodge returns, NYGL. Almost half of the known signatures by tenants and small freeholders in Livingston and south Claverack show signs of illiteracy.

Group	Signed with X/ Total Signers	Proportion Illiterate
Petitioners vs. the Livingston Claim, 1795	98/214	45%
Wood-cutting agreement, 1798	11/22	50%
St. Thomas's Lutheran Regulations, 1793–1795	42/87	48%
West Copake Reformed chapter officers, 1803	3/88	7%
Total (eliminating double signers)	149/312	48%

Sources: "Petition of Petrus Pulver and Others . . . ," in E. B. O'Callaghan, ed., *The Documentary History of the State of New-York* (Albany, N.Y., 1850–1851), III, 834–841; John Lasher et al. to Henry Livingston, Nov. 15, 1798 (5:58), WFP-UM; Vosburgh, ed., "Records of St. Thomas's Evangelical Lutheran Church, at Churchtown," II, 12; Vosburgh, ed., "Records of the Reformed Church of West Copake," 161.

Among the 1795 Livingston petitioners the only woman, widow Catrina Michel, signed with an X.

71. For the three county aggregates by town classification, see Tables 5, 14. This analysis should be compared with that in Gilmore, *Reading Becomes a Necessity of Life,* 141–155, 178–188, 384–395. The two locations (upper Hudson and upper Connecticut River valleys) had roughly analogous settlement patterns and hierarchies, except that in Columbia, Rensselaer, and Dutchess the situation was complicated by tenancy and ethnicity.

72. On tenancy, ethnicity, and literacy, see the three county aggregates in Tables 11, 13, 14. It would appear that the freehold towns with only sectarian churches, such as Baptists or Methodists, also had problems with illiteracy, as measured in 1840. See Table 13.

73. Ellis, *Columbia County,* 397; Hudson *Balance,* Apr. 28, 1807; Hudson *Northern Whig,* Feb. 21, 1809.

74. Based on a survey of portraits published in Piwonka and Blackburn, *Ammi Phillips in Columbia County;* Piwonka, *A Portrait of Livingston Manor;* and Waldron Phoenix Belknap, Jr., *American Colonial Painting: Materials for a History* (Cambridge, Mass., 1959). On Federalist literary culture, see below, Chapter 7.

75. Hudson *Bee,* Aug. 16, 1811.

76. Hudson *Bee,* Aug. 9, 16, 1811; Hudson *Northern Whig,* Aug. 2, 1811. While the *total* exclusion of tenants in these issues of the *Bee* and the *Northern Whig* was perhaps an extreme case, my conclusion, after reading hundreds of issues of the county papers, is that Livingston Manor tenants were rarely if ever named in any notices. Another measure of engagement with credit is provided by the records of the state Loan Office in Columbia County. Of the 255 individuals who applied for state loans in 1792, the year these records started, 236 can be located in particular towns. Of these, only 11 came from the Livingston region towns, or fewer than 2 loan applications per 1,000 population, compared with the 225 from the rest of the county, comprising at least 10 loans per 1,000 population. New York Loan Office, Columbia County, Record Book, 1792, Columbia County Courthouse, Hudson.

CHAPTER 5

1. Richard Hofstadter, *The Idea of a Party System: The Rise of Legitimate Opposition in the United States, 1780–1820* (Berkeley, Calif., 1969), 212–271; and Michael Wallace, "Changing Concepts of Party in the United States: New York, 1815–1828," *American Historical Review,* LXXIV

(1978), 453–491, are the classic statements. Their argument has been challenged by Gerald Leonard in "Party as a 'Political Safeguard of Federalism': Martin Van Buren and the Constitutional Theory of Party Politics," *Rutgers Law Review,* LIV (2001), 221–281, and *The Invention of Party Politics: Federalism, Popular Sovereignty, and Constitutional Development in Jacksonian Illinois* (Chapel Hill, N.C., 2002).

2. James Duane, Livingston Manor, to Philip Schuyler, Albany, June 4, 1782, Schuyler Papers, NYPL; Walter Livingston to Robert S.[?] Livingston, Jan. 7, 1781, Walter Livingston Letter Book, XLVI, reel 15, RRLP.

3. For an excellent analysis of some of the events discussed in this chapter, see Thomas J. Humphrey, *Land and Liberty: Hudson Valley Riots in the Age of Revolution* (DeKalb, Ill., 2004), 112–137.

4. The Westenhook patent and the settlement with the Van Rensselaers of 1763–1773 are briefly described in Sung Bok Kim, *Landlord and Tenant in Colonial New York, 1664–1775* (Chapel Hill, N.C., 1978), 283–387, 411–413. The Livingstons signing letters supporting the Westenhook patent in 1773 and 1774 included Judge Robert R. Livingston of Clermont, the father of the chancellor, and four sons and a son-in-law of his uncle, Philip Livingston. This suggests that the chancellor, Robert R. Livingston, Jr., would inherit his father's interest but that none of the Upper Manor Livingstons (Robert, Jr., was Philip's brother) had a direct interest. NYALG, II, 211, IV, 54, 150–151, X, 4, XVI, 61–62, XVII, 151, XXXIII, 83, XXXIV, 75, 109, 121, 147, 154, XXXV, 10. The fragmentary surviving evidence on the Mawighnunk patent can be followed in NYALG, XIII, 153; Ellis, *Columbia County,* 301; *NY Laws,* 23d sess., 1800, chap. 110 (An Act of Settling the Disputes and Controversies between the Persons Claiming to Be Proprietors of a Patent Called Mawighnunk, and Possessors of the Lands in the Town of Canaan). The unlabeled outlines of the Mawighnunk patent are indicated on the map of the Van Rensselaer–Westenhook settlement, NYALG, XXXIV, 75.

5. The establishment of King's District and Van Schaack's restoration can be followed in [Peter Van Schaack, ed.,], *Laws of New York from the Year 1691, to 1773 Inclusive* (New York, 1774), chap. 1552 (p. 687); David Wright et al., New Canaan, to Peter Van Schaack, NYC, Mar. 26, 1772, Van Schaack Family Folder, CCHS; *NYAJ,* 7th sess., 1784, 27, 109–110, 115, 116, 120.

6. Kim, *Landlord and Tenant,* 412–414; NYALG, XXXII, 116, XXXIII, 36, 78, 83, 85, XXXIV, 75, 121, 154, XXXV, 10; Ellis, *Columbia County,* 322. The lots surrendered by Westenhook to Van Rensselaer were numbered 8, 10, and 11, on the December 1774 map in NYALG, XXXIV, 75, and would have left lots 6, 7, 9, and 12 to be claimed by the Westenhook party. The settlements of New Canaan, New Concord, New Britain, New Lebanon, Red Rock, and part of Spencertown were on land in these Westenhook lots. Goebel and Smith, eds., *LPAH,* III, 329–330. As one of the consequences of his mission to London, James Savage came under suspicion of loyalism. Sullivan, ed., *Minutes,* I, 765.

7. Ellis, *Columbia County,* 323; *NYSJ,* 6th sess., 1782, 83, 86, 93; *NY Laws,* 6th sess., chap. 11 (An Act to Prevent Grants), July 25, 1782. Six Stockbridge Indians, led by Johannes Aniksin, also petitioned about claims to King's District and were similarly stalled: *NYAJ,* 2d sess., 1778–1779, 16, 52, 74.

8. This inheritance is detailed in Goebel and Smith, eds., *LPAH,* III, 309–310.

9. Ibid., III, 309–310, 330–331, citing Philip Schuyler to the Inhabitants of King's District, Apr. 4, 1782, Schuyler Papers, box 6, NYPL; *NY Laws,* 6th sess., chap. 2 (An Act to Abolish Entails), July 12, 1782. The only legislative reference that I have been able to find is the report of the

entail bill from committee and its passage in the senate on Nov. 17 and 19, 1781. *NYSJ,* 5th sess., 1781, 28–29. The wider significance of the end of entail in post-Revolutionary America has been established in Holly Brewer, "Entailing Aristocracy in Colonial Virginia: 'Ancient Feudal Restraints' and Revolutionary Reform," *William and Mary Quarterly,* 3d Ser., LIV (1997), 307–346.

10. Henry C. Van Schaack, *The Life of Peter Van Schaack . . .* (New York, 1842), 5; Ellis, *Columbia County,* 320, 323; *NYSJ,* 6th sess., 1782, 140a.

11. *NYAJ,* 5th sess., 1781, 1st mtg., 25–26, 6th sess., 1783, 2d mtg., 107, 7th sess., 1784, 27, 109–110, 115, 116, 120; Paltsits, ed., *Minutes,* I, 28; *NY Laws,* 9th sess., 1786, chap. 66, art. 13; Van Schaak, *Life of Peter Van Schaack,* 388–390, 402–403. Adgate had signed, and might have drafted, the 1772 King's District letter to Van Schaack.

12. Henry Livingston, Manor, to Robert R. Livingston, Clermont, Mar. 13, 1787, RRLP; Peter Van Schaack, Kinderhook, to Philip Schuyler, Albany, Apr. 3, 1788, Schuyler Papers, NYPL.

13. On Powers as a merchant, see the Stockbridge *Western Star,* Apr. 26, June 28, 1791.

14. Peter Van Schaack, Kinderhook, to Philip Schuyler, Albany, Apr. 3, 1788, Schuyler Papers, NYPL; Peter Van Schaack to Henry Walton, June 3, 1788, in Van Schaack, *Life of Peter Van Schaack,* 425; *Hudson Weekly Gazette,* July 8, 1788. See also John P. Kaminski, "New York: The Reluctant Pillar," in Stephen L. Schecter, *The Reluctant Pillar: New York and the Adoption of the Constitution* (Albany, N.Y., 1987), 82–85.

15. *NYSJ,* 14th sess., Mar. 4, 1791, 42–43; *NY Laws,* 14th sess., 1791, chap. 42 (An Act to Amend an Act, Entitled, An Act for the Sale and Disposition of Lands . . .).

16. Peter Van Schaack, Kinderhook, to Peter Van Gaasbeek, Kingston, Apr. 12, 1792, Van Gaasbeek Papers, Senate House, Kingston; *Hudson Gazette,* Apr. 12, 1792.

17. Peacher, "Craft Masonry," 339–340; *NYAJ,* 1789, 108, 123, 1791, 76, 88–89; Robert J. Stets, *Postmasters and Post Offices of the United States, 1782–1811* (Lake Oswego, Ore., 1994), 184.

18. *Poughkeepsie Journal,* June 14, 1792; *Hudson Gazette,* June 11, 1795. In February 1795 Henry Van Schaack wrote enthusiastically to Theodore Sedgwick: "I was last week, a few days, in New York Canaan—I there found people in general so different in their political opinions from what I had formerly known them, that I am convinced that the dead majorities, heretofore, agt. federalism will be more weighty in favour of it on the approaching election for Governor. there can be no doubt of success, if Mr Jay returns in season" from London. Henry Van Schaack, Pittsfield, to Theodore Sedgwick, Philadelphia, Feb. 6, 1795, Sedgwick Papers, MHS.

19. Here and throughout this work, I make a modest contribution to the growing critique of Tocquevillean and neo-Tocquevillean arguments that nineteenth-century American civil society was poised against the state. Rather, I argue that civil institutions were a vehicle toward the mobilization of state authority. See Jason Kaufman, "Three Views of Associationalism in Nineteenth-Century America: An Empirical Examination," *American Journal of Sociology,* CIV (1999), 1296–1345, who on 1335 discusses his finding that the presence of Masonic lodges in nineteenth-century cities correlates with measures of "social capital"; William Novak, "The American Law of Association: The Legal-Political Construction of Civil Society," *Studies in American Political Development,* XV (2001), 163–188; Michael Schudson, "The 'Public Sphere' and Its Problems: Bringing the State (Back) In," *Notre Dame Journal of Law, Ethics, and Public Policy,* VIII (1994) 529–546; the essays in Bob Edwards, Michael W. Foley, and Mario Diani, eds., *Beyond Tocqueville: Civil Society and the Social Capital Debate in Comparative Perspective* (Hanover, N.H., 2001); Theda Skocpol, *Diminished Democracy: From Membership to Management in American Civic Life* (Norman, Okla., 2004).

20. Alfred F. Young makes this point in *The Democratic Republicans of New York: The Origins, 1763–1797* (Chapel Hill, N.C., 1967), 235.

21. *Hudson Weekly Gazette,* Feb. 21, 1788.

22. *NY Laws,* 6th sess., July 25, 1782, chap. 11; Barbara Graymont, "New York State Indian Policy after the Revolution," *New York History,* LVII (1976), 444; Young, *The Democratic Republicans,* 232; *List of the Names of Persons to Whom Military Patents Have Been Issued out of the Secretary's Office, and to Whom Delivered* ([Albany, N.Y.], 1793), 3, 6, 10, 13, 14, 24, 25. Among the hundreds of patentees listed as receiving military patents by 1793, General Samuel B. Webb and John Bay, both of Claverack, were the only notable Columbia County figures receiving lands. Henry Platner and Stephen Hogeboom, also of Claverack, seem to have been agents for others.

23. These grants to Columbia men are in the Location Book [1782–1788] and List of Land Patents Issued from 1786–1797 [N-Ar4007], NYSA; for Adgate's petition, see *NYAJ,* 5th sess., 1781–1782, 53, 79; *NYSJ,* 5th sess., 1781–1782, Mar. 1, 1782. The Clinton grants are listed in *NYAJ,* 15th sess., 1792, 195, 199, 220. Two of Adgate's applications for land, it should be noted, were rejected as offering too low a price. Young, *The Democratic Republicans,* 237–238. As listed in the Location Book and the List of Patents [N-Ar4007], NYSA, Adgate's grants between 1782 and 1795, all in Clinton County west of Lake Champlain, totaled 57,915 acres. Mohawk sales in "Forfeiture Sales of Mohawk Valley Land," *Mohawk,* VII (1990), 10, 44.

24. *NY Laws,* 15th sess., 1792, chap. 40; on the canals, see Laurence M. Hauptman, *Conspiracy of Interests: Iroquois Dispossession and the Rise of New York State* (Syracuse, N.Y., 1999), 1–23, 67–69, 82–85; Ronald E. Shaw, *Erie Water West: A History of the Erie Canal, 1792–1854* (Lexington, Ky., 1966), 3–21; and, most recently, Brian Phillips Murphy, "Empire State Building: Interests, Institutions, and the Formation of States and Parties in New York, 1783–1845" (Ph.D. diss., University of Virginia, 2008), 169–182.

25. Franklin B. Hough, comp., *Proceedings of the Commissioners of Indian Affairs, Appointed by Law for the Extinguishment of Indian Titles in the State of New York* (Albany, N.Y., 1861), I, 73–74n; Julian Boyd and Robert J. Taylor, eds., *The Susquehannah Company Papers* (Ithaca, N.Y., 1962–1971), XVIII, xvi–xvii, 247–250. For a complete history of the eighteenth-century conflicts over the Susquehanna lands, see Paul B. Moyer, *Wild Yankees: The Struggle for Independence along Pennsylvania's Revolutionary Frontier* (Ithaca, N.Y., 2007), esp. 77–105, covering the 1780s and early 1790s. On Vermont and the northern backcountry, see Peter S. Onuf, "State-Making in a Revolutionary Crisis: Independent Vermont as a Case Study," *Journal of American History,* LXVII (1980–1981), 797–815; Michael A. Bellesiles, *Revolutionary Outlaws: Ethan Allen and the Struggle for Independence on the Early American Frontier* (Charlottesville, Va., 1993); Alan Taylor, "'To Man Their Rights': The Frontier Revolution," in Ronald Hoffman and Peter J. Albert, eds., *The Transforming Hand of Revolution: Reconsidering the American Revolution as a Social Movement* (Charlottesville, Va., 1996), 244–254.

26. Taylor, "'To Man Their Rights,'" in Hoffman and Albert, eds., *Transforming Hand of Revolution,* 246–247; Stephen B. Miller, *Historical Sketches of Hudson, Embracing the Settlement of the City . . .* (Hudson, N.Y., 1862; rpt. 1985), 95; *Hudson Weekly Gazette,* May 18, 25, June 1, 1786, Sept. 20, 1792; Stockbridge *Western Star,* Nov. 27, 1797; Hudson *Balance, and Columbian Repository,* Oct. 22, 1801; Boyd and Taylor, eds., *Susquehannah Company Papers,* VIII, 248–249, 256, 310–313; Ethan Allen, John Franklin, and John Jenkins, *An Address from the Inhabitants of Wyoming and Others, Contiguously Situated on the Waters of the River Susquehannah; to the People at Large of the Commonwealth of Pennsylvania* (Hudson, N.Y., 1786).

27. Boyd and Taylor, eds., *Susquehannah Company Papers,* VIII, 313.

28. *Hudson Weekly Gazette,* Apr. 5, 1787, notice dated March 20; Hough, comp., *Proceedings of the Commissioners,* 119–125n.

29. Boyd and Taylor, eds., *Susquehannah Company Papers,* IX, 179, 182–183, 204–205, 386, 457, 523–525. There is conflicting opinion whether there was an actual plan for a new state, or whether this was the assumption of the Pennsylvania authorities, an idea that they planted on the testimony of various witnesses, including John J. Acmodrey (IX, 523–525). Robert Taylor was skeptical but was willing to concede "that reservation of final judgment is called for." Julian Boyd accepted the reality of plans for an independent state and linked the Susquehannah Company with such efforts in western New York in 1793, in which Livingston and Benton were involved. *Susquehannah Company Papers,* IX, xxv–xxxiv; Julian P. Boyd, "Attempts to Form New States in New York and Pennsylvania, 1786–1796," New York State Historical Association, *Quarterly Journal,* XII (1931), 257–270.

30. Boyd and Taylor, eds., *Susquehannah Company Papers,* IX, 215–217, 395–396, 401, 415, 452, 477–478. The Susquehannah Agreement, or "Combination," was printed in the *Hudson Weekly Gazette,* embedded in a letter from Zerah Beach defending the Susquehannah Company and settlers, on Nov. 8, 1787.

31. *NYAJ,* 11th sess., 1788, 69–70, 73–78, 82–84: the February 1788 assembly vote rejected the Genesee petition by 32–10; William Powers voted against the petition, Peter Silvester and James Savage for it. The senate concurred in the assembly action: *NYSJ,* 11th sess., 1788, 36–37. *NY Laws,* 11th sess., 1788, chap. 47 (An Act for Appointing Commissioners to Hold Treaties); Hough, comp., *Proceedings of the Commissioners,* I, 116–117n, 150–159, 187–189, 215–216, II, 258–259, 437, 442, 449, 452–454; Boyd and Taylor, eds., *Susqehannah Company Papers,* IX, 513–514. On the Genesee Adventurers, see Hauptman, *Conspiracy of Interests,* 54, 64–67; and the detailed account in Alan Taylor, *The Divided Ground: Indians, Settlers, and the Northern Borderland of the American Revolution* (New York, 2006), 169–202.

32. Sumner Gilbert Wood, *Ulster Scots and Blandford Scouts* (West Medway, Mass., 1928), 382; *Third Annual Report of the State Historian of the State of New York, 1897* (New York and Albany, 1898), 761, 871; Sullivan, ed., *Minutes,* I, 896; *Journals of the Provincial Congress, Provincial Convention, Committee of Safety, and Council of Safety of the State of New York, 1775–1776–1778* (Albany, N.Y., 1842), II, 265; Berthold Fernow, ed., *New York in the Revolution,* 268–269, vol. XV of John Romeyn Brodhead, E. B. O'Callaghan, and Berthold Fernow, eds., *Documents Relative to the Colonial History of the State of New York* (Albany, N.Y., 1887); Ellis, *Columbia County,* 33; Hugh Hastings and J. A. Holden, eds., *Public Papers of George Clinton . . .* (New York and Albany, 1899–1914), VI, 694, 696, 697; William L. Stone, *Life of Joseph Brant-Thayendanegea, Including the Border Wars of the American Revolution . . .* (New York, 1838; rpt. Claire Shores, Wis., 1970), II, 120–121. One witness quoted in Stone's account said that Colonel William Harper "and others" "pressed and intreated" Van Rensselaer to cross the river around four in the afternoon; Stone reports that this was the moment when the Oneida Louis Atyataronda denounced him as a tory. Presumably McKinstry was among the "others."

33. This analysis links names from the Adventurer list in Hough, comp., *Proceedings of the Commissioners,* 120–125, with militia lists in Fernow, ed., *New York in the Revolution;* James A. Roberts, ed., *New York in the Revolution as Colony and State,* 2d ed. (Albany, N.Y., 1898; rpt. 1996); and Hugh Hastings and Henry Harmon Noble, eds., *Military Minutes of the Council of Appointment of the State of New York, 1783–1821* (Albany, N.Y., 1901–1902).

34. Hastings and Holden, eds., *Public Papers of George Clinton,* VI, 808, 894–895, VII, 102–103, 297, 550–552. After considerable effort, McKinstry was granted 640 acres of land east of Geneva by the 1802 legislature (*NY Laws,* 1802, chap. 17). The failure of the Adventurers to receive military lands is evident from a comparison of the Adventurers listed in Hough, comp., *Proceedings of the Commissioners,* 20, with *The Balloting Book, and Other Documents, Relating to the Military Bounty Lands, in the State of New York* (Albany, N.Y., 1825). *Hudson Weekly Gazette,* Feb. 21, 1788.

35. *Hudson Weekly Gazette,* Jan. 31, 1788.

36. Henry Platner was not directly granted land in the Military Tract, but he bought up the rights of a number of other men, in addition to his purchases in the Susquehannah region. Where Graham, and another officer in the Second New York, William Colbreath, were granted land in the Military Tract, Peter Schuyler was not.

37. Hough, comp., *Proceedings of the Commissioners,* 10, 25, 26, 39, 48, 51, 56, 63–64; Sullivan, ed., *Minutes,* I, 485, 529.

38. Relations had healed enough for Van Rensselaer to sign the undated county proposal of 1784 or 1785 that listed McKinstry as an assembly candidate. Section 71, Livingston Family Papers, Hyde Park. McKinstry was listed as a captain in the 1770 list of Jeremiah Hogeboom's regiment. *Third Annual Report of the State Historian,* 770.

39. Union Lodge membership from the Union Lodge Return, Dec. 27, 1786, LL-NYGL; and *Condensed History of Mount Vernon Lodge, No. 3, of Ancient York Masons* (New York[?], 1874), 67, 74; "Catalogue of Those Initiated in Temple Lodge No. 10," 1785–1814, LL-NYGL; Hudson Lodge Petition [1786], in Peacher, "Craft Masonry," 321–322. At least three others among the Adventurers were Temple Lodge initiates.

40. The Masonic connections of the New York lessees seem to have extended to Joseph Brant, the Mohawk chieftain. If so, we can revisit a tradition long in circulation in Hudson, put in print by William Leete Stone, that Joseph Brant saved John McKinstry's life at the Battle of the Cedars in May 1776, where McKinstry fought as a company commander in the Fifth Massachusetts Regiment. According to tradition, McKinstry had been captured and was saved from torture when Joseph Brant saw him give the Masonic distress sign. This encounter was supposed to have been the basis of Brant's post-Revolutionary visits to the Livingston Manor, where he and McKinstry relived the past and attended lodge in Hudson together at least once, around 1805. Apparently, a portrait of Brant still hangs in the Hudson lodge room, executed by McKinstry's great-grandson and presented in 1917. Unfortunately, the modern biographer of Brant calls this story a "myth," noting that Brant could not have been at the Battle of the Cedars, since he was in London, between January and June of 1776. Instead, Brant was with Sir John Johnson's raiding party in October 1780 and among those who defeated Colonel Brown at Stone Arabia. Brant and McKinstry met in combat at the skirmish at Klock's Field later that day, where McKinstry's men helped to drive back Brant's Iroquois, turning the British left. But a decade later McKinstry and Brant were both deeply involved in the western land leases, Brant as an Iroquois chief and a connection of the Canadian branch of the Adventurers. In July 1788, when McKinstry was flitting about between the Susquehannah settlements and Lake Seneca, Brant met with Livingston, Benton, Gilbert, and men representing the Phelps-Gorham interests at Buffalo Creek near Niagara and signed several more leases, including one to the Adventurers for land east of Lake Seneca. Brant received a promise, unfulfilled but mentioned in a 1790 letter to Governor Clinton, of "a tract of land given me by Dr. Benton" as payment for his assistance in negotiating this lease. Presumably Brant and McKinstry did meet at some point in the summers of 1788 and 1789. Though it gave up its leases

in February 1789, the New York Genesee Company continued its intrigues for several years, in what Orasmus Turner called "a pretty expensive operation; the chiefs who favored the scheme and the agents who operated upon them, must have been well paid; 'presents' must have been as lavish as in the palmiest days of British and Indian negotiations." At one meeting at Hudson in September 1789 the company spent twelve thousand pounds. Brant must certainly have been at this Hudson meeting and probably did visit the Livingston Manor at times down to 1805 to meet primarily with John Livingston. John McKinstry moved to the Manor in the late 1790s, where his daughter married Walter T. Livingston in 1798. The story of McKinstry's impending torture at the Battle of the Cedars would have resonated with the actual experiences of Dr. Moses Younglove of Canaan and Hudson, who was tortured after his capture at the Battle of Oriskany in the summer of 1777. The New York Grand Lodge records a John Livingston as a member of the Holland Lodge in 1810; though it is entirely possible that John of the Adventurers was a member, this date would be a little too late for his first membership. This story can be followed variously in Stone, *Life of Joseph Brant*, I, 155–156, II, 120–121; Peacher, "Craft Masonry," 320–321; Isabel Thompson Kelsay, *Joseph Brant, 1743–1807: Man of Two Worlds* (Syracuse, N.Y., 1984), 174–175, 297–298, 417–418, 550; Taylor, *Divided Ground*, 69–70, 86–89; Hastings, ed., *Public Papers of George Clinton*, VI, 694, 696, 697; Benson J. Lossing, *The Pictorial Field-Book of the Revolution* (New York, 1851–1852), I, 280–281; Hough, comp., *Proceedings of the Commissioners*, 461–462; and O[rasmus] Turner, *History of the Pioneer Settlement of Phelps and Gorham's Purchase, and Morris' Reserve . . .* (Rochester, N.Y., 1851), 110n.

41. Philip Schuyler, Albany, to Robert R. Livingston, NYC, Mar. 29, 1788, RRLP; William Wilson, Clermont, to Robert R. Livingston, NYC, Mar. 13, 1788, RRLP; Hough, comp., *Proceedings of the Commissioners*, 151, 159; Kelsay, *Joseph Brant*, 417, 418, 429, 550. Compare Wilson's complaint about the Upper Manor Livingston's "Indian Purchase" coalition at this meeting with Henry Livingston's complaint the year before (and Van Schaack's confirmation) that the Van Schaack–Canaan Federalists were conspiring against the Westenhook Patentees. Henry Livingston, Manor, to Robert R. Livingston, Clermont, Mar. 13, 1787, RRLP; Peter Van Schaack, Kinderhook, to Philip Schuyler, Albany, Apr. 3, 1788, Schuyler Papers, NYSL.

42. *NYAJ*, 12th sess., 1789, 121, 14th sess., 1791, 71, 81–82; Turner, *History of the Pioneer Settlement of Phelps and Gorham's Purchase*, 110n. Matthew Adgate served on the assembly committee that advanced the 1791 bill to the floor, only to be rejected by the house.

43. *NYAJ*, 5th sess., 1782, 57, 58, 60–61, 70; *NY Laws*, 5th sess., 1782, chap. 23.

44. Goebel and Smith, eds., *LPAH*, III, 332–333n; *NYAJ*, 7th sess., 1784, 32, 90–91, 99; *NYSJ*, 7th sess., 1784, 74–75, 8th sess., 2d mtg., 1785, 35, 83. The 1784 petition itself does not survive. In contrast to Philip Schuyler's aggressive action, General Robert Van Rensselaer began to advertise farms for sale in 1787. *Hudson Weekly Gazette*, Mar. 29, 1787.

45. Benjamin Birdsall and others, Hillsdale, to the assembly, Jan. 9, 1789; Simeon Rowley and others, Hillsdale, to the assembly, Jan. 23, 1789; both in Misc. MSS, Columbia County, NYHS. The Rowley petition was not actually introduced until February 1790. *NYAJ*, 13th sess., 2d mtg., 1790, 25.

46. *NYAJ*, 12th sess., 1789, 82. No further references to the 1789 Hillsdale petition appear in this session's journal. *NYAJ*, 13th sess., 2d mtg., 1790, 25, 71. The vote on Livingston's 1790 motion was 44–11; James Savage of Canaan, also on the committee, was among the 11 dissenters.

47. Hastings and Noble, comps., *Military Minutes of the Council of Appointment*, I, 99–100; Records of the East Baptist Church and Society in Hillsdale, N.Y., NYHS. As many as 18 of the

1789 petitioners joined the East and West Baptist churches, both located along the south line of Hillsdale, by 1803, and only 2 were affiliated with the Green River Congregational Church, and none with the Spencertown Congregational Church, both to the north in what would later become the town of Austerlitz. Of a total of 211 petitioners, 64 were on the 1800 Hillsdale taxlist, and 48 others were in Hillsdale as of the 1790 census or otherwise connected with the town. One was from Canaan, 1 from Hudson, 12 from Livingston, and 40 were in Claverack as of the 1790 Census or 1800 valuation. Forty-four cannot be assigned to a town. One of the Claverack men, Fite Rossman, would later be elected an elder of the Lutheran church at south Claverack.

48. *Minutes of the Shaftsbury Baptist Association; at their Annual Convention, Held in Hillsdale, M,DCC,LXXXIX* (Bennington, Vt., 1789); Ellis, *Columbia County,* 370–371; Temple Lodge returns, New York Grand Lodge Records; Goebel and Smith, eds., *LPAH,* III, 333. James Bryant, supervisor from 1786 to 1791 and Birdsall's partner in the February 1789 surrender of the Adventurers' leases, did not sign the 1789 petition.

49. "To the Lessees and other Occupants . . . ," *Hudson Weekly Gazette,* Nov. 25, 1790, MS copy in box 1, folder 16, Schuyler Family Papers, NYSL. A broadside clarifying the terms, dated Dec. 14, 1790, was published in Hudson. The only extant copy is in the collections of the Schuyler Mansion, Albany, N.Y. The settlement of John Van Rensselaer's estate was finalized in August 1791. Philip Schuyler, Claverack, to ———, Aug. 11, 1791, Schuyler Family Papers, NYSL; *Hudson Weekly Gazette,* Nov. 25, 1788; "Copy of an Agreement between persons who hold lands . . . ," Misc. MSS–John Van Rensselaer, NYHS, cited in Goebel and Smith, eds., *LPAH,* III, 337. The list of signers was torn off the agreement, but the association records were to be kept by John Vaughn, who was subject to a suit for ejectment since 1784, an ensign in the militia, and a 1789 petitioner.

50. Indictments of Peleg Phelps and William Pixley, of Nobletown, Belding Kellogg, Nehemiah Kellogg, and Matthew Guilder, Jr., of Egremont, Supreme Judicial Court Dockets, Berkshire Sessions, April 1787, 58, MA. On the Columbia militia, see John P. Kaminski, *George Clinton: Yeoman Politician of the New Republic* (Madison, Wis., 1993), 107–109. There is no adequate overview of the mutual associations of the 1780s, but their geographic spread is suggested in David P. Szatmary, *Shays' Rebellion: The Making of an Agrarian Insurrection* (Amherst, Mass., 1980), 124–126; and Jackson Turner Main, *The Antifederalists: Critics of the Constitution, 1781–1788* (Chapel Hill, N.C., 1961), 6–7. For detailed accounts, see John L. Brooke, *The Heart of the Commonwealth: Society and Political Culture in Worcester County, Massachusetts, 1713–1861* (New York, 1989), 201–207, 222, which discusses the private nature of these associations, as against the corporate assumptions that underlay Shays's Rebellion proper. For Maine, for a longer period, see Alan Taylor, *Liberty Men and Great Proprietors: The Revolutionary Settlement on the Maine Frontier, 1760–1820* (Chapel Hill, N.C., 1990), esp. 89–120. Terry Bouton, in *Taming Democracy: "The People," the Founders, and the Troubled Ending of the American Revolution* (New York, 2007), 145–167, 197–215, discusses parallel events in Pennsylvania in terms of "rings of protection" rather than "mutual associations."

51. Henry Livingston, Ancram, to Walter Livingston, NYC, Oct. 24, 1791, RRLP; account from the *Albany Gazette,* Oct. 31, 1791, quoted in full in Ellis, *Columbia County,* 42–43. The term "blacked" is from an affidavit on the event published in the Hudson *Bee,* Apr. 30, 1805.

52. Sullivan, ed., *Minutes,* I, 344–348; John Francis Collin, *A History of Hillsdale, Columbia County, New York . . .* (Philmont, N.Y., 1883), 6; Ellis, *Columbia County,* 375. I borrow the term "social banditry" from E. J. Hobsbawm, *Social Bandits and Primitive Rebels: Studies in Archaic Forms of Social Movements in the Nineteenth and Twentieth Centuries* (New York, 1959), 13–29.

53. Henry Livingston, Ancram, to Walter Livingston, NYC, Oct. 24, 1791, RRLP; *Hudson Weekly Gazette,* Nov. 10, 1791; *Poughkeepsie Journal,* Nov. 10, 17, 24, 1791; "On the Murder of Cornelius Hogeboom, high sheriff of the County of Columbia," Reward Subscription lists, Oct. 24, 1791, Hogeboom Family Papers, file 12576, NYSL; *NYAJ,* 15th sess., 1792, 6; Henry Van Schaack to Theodore Sedgwick, Nov. 20(?), 1791, Sedgwick Papers, MHS; Records of the Court of Oyer and Terminer, 1788–1831, Columbia County Court, Hudson Court House Archives, Dec. 1, 1791. According to the *Poughkeepsie Journal,* Nov. 24, 1791, this was a special session, with fourteen local judges appointed as commissioners of oyer and terminer.

54. *Poughkeepsie Journal,* Feb. 16, 1792.

55. Ibid., Feb. 23, 1792. For another Federalist reaction, see the Stockbridge *Western Star,* Feb. 21, 1792.

56. Among the defendants, only two appear to have been listed in the Revolutionary militia: Jonathan Rodman in the Ninth Albany (Hillsdale) Regiment, and Thomas Southward, perhaps, in the Second Dutchess (Poughkeepsie) Regiment. Southward might have been one of the Dutchess non-Associators. *Calendar of Historical Manuscripts, Relating to the War of the Revolution, in the Office of the Secretary of State, Albany, N.Y.* (Albany, N.Y., 1868), I, 138.

57. John Livingston, Manor, to Walter Livingston, NYC, Feb. 16, 1791, RRLP. On Nov. 28, 1791, John Bay of Claverack wrote a long letter to William Wilson in Clermont, arguing that Adgate should not run and that his Claverack friends were urging him to stand in his place. As it turned out, Bay failed to attend any of the meetings of the court and did not run; Adgate attended the entire February session and won his seat easily. John Bay, Claverack, to William Wilson, Clermont, Nov. 28, 1791, WFP-UM.

58. John Livingston, Manor, to Walter Livingston, NYC, Feb. 16, 1792, RRLP; Kaminski, *George Clinton,* 201–202.

59. *NY Laws,* 14th sess., 1791, chap. 42. (This was the larger bill that guaranteed titles in Canaan.) The 1791–1792 land applications and grants are listed in *NYAJ,* 15th sess., 1792, 189, 192, 195, 197–200. John Bay received a six-hundred-acre tract in Catskill.

60. Henry Livingston, Manor, to Stephen Van Rensselaer, Albany, Apr. 21, 1790, Apr. 13, 1791, Henry Livingston Papers, NYSL; John Livingston, Manor, to Walter Livingston, NYC, Mar. 7, 1792, RRLP; Robert R. Livingston, Draft of Reflections on the Gubernatorial Election of 1792, RRLP; George Dangerfield, *Chancellor Robert R. Livingston of New York, 1746–1813* (New York, 1960), 235–306, esp. 241–255; Ralph Ketcham, *James Madison: A Biography* (New York, 1971), 323; Julian P. Boyd et al., eds., *The Papers of Thomas Jefferson* (Princeton, N.J., 1982–), XX, 434–449, 453–454, 456–458, 471; Stanley Elkins and Eric McKitrick, *The Age of Federalism* (New York, 1993), 240–242.

61. *To the Free and Independent Electors of the State of New-York* (New York, 1792) (Evans 46301); John Livingston, Manor, to Walter Livingston, NYC, Nov. 14, 24, Dec. 20, 22, 1790, Mar. 16, June 7, Nov. 13, 1791, John Livingston, Boston, to Walter Livingston, NYC, Jan. 9, 31, Feb. 7, 1791, Robert C. Livingston, NYC, to Walter Livingston, NYC, Jan 23, 1791, Robert C. Livingston, Boston, to Walter Livingston, NYC, Feb. 8, 19, 27, Mar. 2, 5, 11, 1791, Robert C. Livingston, NYC, to Walter Livingston, Manor, Apr. 6, 1791, RRLP; Young, *The Democratic Republicans,* 237–238, 284; Dangerfield, *Chancellor Robert R. Livingston,* 251–252.

62. John Livingston, Manor, to Walter Livingston, NYC, Feb. 16, 1792, RRLP; Peter R. Livingston, Lithgow [Manor], to Peter Van Schaack, Kinderhook, Apr. 1, 1792, VSP/LC. Peter R. Livingston had been written out of his father's will.

63. Peter R. Livingston, Lithgow (Manor), to Peter Van Schaak, Kinderhook, Apr. 1, 1792, VSP/LC.

64. Peter Van Schaack, Kinderhook, to Peter Van Gaasbeck, Kingston, Apr. 12, 1792, Van Gaasbeck Papers, Senate House Museum, Kingston, N.Y.

65. Young, *The Democratic Republicans,* 315–316; essays by An Elector, and An Independent Elector, *Hudson Gazette,* July 19, 1792.

66. See Figures 1, 2. In 1789 and 1790 the votes for assembly have been lost, so the votes for Congress are used as an estimate. Voters for the assembly and Congress were subject to the same twenty-pound property qualification, and both of these votes took place on the same April election day.

67. Henry Livingston, Manor, to Walter Livingston, NYC, Feb. 13, 1791.

68. This resurgence of the Republicans from 1792 is demonstrated in the town-by-town manuscript returns for the assembly from 1791 to 1794, apparently drawn up in county supervisors' meetings and surviving only in WWP-UM, box 41:25. The county politics discussed here can be followed in Henry Livingston, NYC, to Samuel B. Webb, Claverack, Mar. 29, 1791, in Worthington Chauncey Ford, ed., *Correspondence and Journals of Samuel Blachley Webb* (New York, 1893–1894), III, 172; Henry Livingston, Manor, to Walter Livingston, NYC, Feb. 13, 1791, Henry Livingston, Ancram, to Walter Livingston, Manor, Apr. 26, 1794, RRLP; Matthew Adgate, Canaan, to William Wilson, Clermont, Dec. 3, 1794, ———, Kinderhook, to William Wilson, Clermont, Dec. 8, 1794, John P. Van Ness, Kinderhook, to William Wilson, Clermont, Apr. 3, 1796, John Bay, Claverack, to "Gentlemen" (i.e., Clermont Committee), Apr. 12, 1796, John P. Van Ness, Kinderhook, to William Wilson, Clermont, Apr. 13, 1796, John Bay, Claverack, to Philip Hoffman, Clermont, Apr. 16, 1796, WFP-UM.

69. Only two Federalists were among the Susquehannah Company land claimants of 1795, and both were political turncoats: Ambrose Spencer began as a Federalist and switched to the Republicans in 1798, and James Savage switched from the Clintonian orbit to the Schuyler Federalists some time after 1792. See Jacob Ford, NYC, to Peter Van Schaack, Kinderhook, Apr. 1, 1792, VSP/LC, on Savage "grow[ing] very tired of his old friend PVN" (Peter Van Ness).

70. On the "Revolutionary Center," see Ronald P. Formisano, *The Transformation of Political Culture: Massachusetts Parties, 1790s–1840s* (New York, 1983), 10–14; Edward Countryman, *A People in Revolution: The American Revolution and Political Society in New York, 1760–1790* (Baltimore, 1981), 221–251; Young, *The Democratic Republicans,* 33–58. On Clintonian distributive politics, see Young, *The Democratic Republicans,* 235; L. Ray Gunn, *The Decline of Authority: Public Economic Policy and Political Development in New York, 1800–1860* (Ithaca, N.Y., 1988), 99–143.

71. *NY Laws,* 12th sess., 1789, chap. 26, 14th sess., 1791, chap. 37; *NYAJ,* 12th sess., 1789, 94, 115, 127, 14th sess., 1791, 78, 94–95, 98–99, 15th sess., 1792, 127–128. See Young, *The Democratic Republicans,* 244–248; Robert E. Wright, "Politics and Banking in New York, 1784–1829" (Ph.D. diss., SUNY Buffalo, 1996), 160.

72. *NYAJ,* 15th sess., 1792, 99, 121, 134.

73. This was the first session in which the county was represented by six, rather than three, representatives in the assembly, the result of the 1791 state census of eligible electors. Ford, Savage, and Lawrence Hogeboom voted to approve the Birdsall bill in the assembly, and Powers and Van Ness opposed it in the senate: *NYAJ,* 15th sess., 1792, 144–145; *NYSJ,* 15th sess., 1792, 78, 81. On the bank: Henry Livingston, NYC, to Samuel B. Webb, Claverack, Mar. 24, Apr. 4, 1792, in Ford,

ed., *Correspondence and Journals of Webb,* III, 178, 179. *Hudson Gazette,* Mar. 15, 1792; *NYAJ,* 15th sess., 1792, 134, 181–203; Wright, "Banking and Politics," 166–167.

74. 1792 Assembly return, WFP-UM, box 41:25; *New-York Journal,* June 6, 9, 1792; *NYSJ,* 16th sess., 1793, 11–13.

75. *NYAJ,* 16th sess., 1793, 50, 164–166, 231; *NYSJ,* 16th sess., 1793, 30; *NY Laws,* 16th sess., 1793, chaps. 26, 38. The land grant resulting from chapter 26 was recorded in the "List of Patents" (N-Ar4007), on June 2 and Aug. 2, 1797, when each of twenty-eight of the Genesee Adventurers was granted 853⅓ acres in Military Township No. 3 in Clinton County. For a justification of the grant on the grounds that the Adventurers' activities had made it easier for the state commissioners to extract land concessions from the Iroquois, see a broadside by A Friend to Truth: *To the Public* (Shawangunk, N.Y., Apr. 24, 1793) (Evans 46889). Birdsall had a map of this land drawn up: "Survey Map of Lots No. 1–75, Township #3, of the Old Military Tract, Clinton County, New York" [(N) XX4374g], NYSL.

76. *NYAJ,* 16th sess., 1793, 50, 54, 59, 60, 64, 83, 89, 159–160, 179; *NYSJ,* 16th sess., 1793, 30, 53, 54, 67; *NYAJ,* 15th sess., 1792, 51. See Young, *The Democratic Republicans,* 534.

77. *NY Laws,* 16th sess., 1793, chaps. 22, 26, 27, 35, 38, 58, 18th sess., 1795 chap. 3. For the competing Claverack bridge petitions, see *NYAJ,* 16th sess., 1793, 64, 89; for Abraham Van Buren, see *NYSJ,* 16th sess., 1793, 51.

78. Hough, comp., *Proceedings of the Commissioners,* 126–127n; Young, *The Democratic Republicans,* 368; Boyd, "Attempts to Form New States in New York and Pennsylvania," New York State Historical Association, *Quarterly Journal,* XII (1931), 265–266.

79. The only Federalists elected to the assembly in this six-year period (1793–1799) were Ambrose Spencer and Dirck Gardinier elected in 1793, and Elisha Jenkins elected in 1794.

80. Stets, *Postmasters and Post Offices of the United States,* 176, 180, 181, 182, 184; Henry Van Schaack, Pittsfield, to Theodore Sedgwick, Philadelphia, Jan. 10, Nov. 20, 27, 1791, Loring Andrews, Stockbridge, to Theodore Sedgwick, Philadelphia, Mar. 4, 1794, Sedgwick Papers, MHS.

81. Unity and Vernon Lodge Returns, New York Grand Lodge. On the post offices and a national public sphere, see Richard R. John, *Spreading the News: The American Postal System from Franklin to Morse* (Cambridge, Mass., 1995).

82. The most convenient list of early charters in New York is Aaron Clark, ed., *List of All the Incorporations in the State of New York . . .* (Albany, N.Y., 1819); the early turnpikes are listed on 54–55. Turnpike development in New York is assessed in Daniel B. Klein and John Majewski, "Economy, Community, and Law: The Turnpike Movement in New York, 1797–1845," *Law and Society Review,* XXVI (1992), 469–512. On the "infrastructure of the public sphere," I have been inspired by Greg Laugero, "Infrastructures of Enlightenment: Road-Making, the Public Sphere, and the Emergence of Literature," *Eighteenth-Century Studies,* XXIX (1995), 45–67.

83. An Act to Establish a Turnpike Corporation for Improving the Road from the Springs in Lebanon to the City of Albany, *NY Laws,* 21st sess., 1798, chap. 94; *NYAJ,* 22d sess., 2d mtg., 1799, 153, 168; *NY Laws,* 22d sess., 1799, chap. 73, revised and replaced the 1798 legislation.

84. *Proceedings of the Grand Chapter of Royal Arch Masons of the State of New York* (Buffalo, N.Y., 1871), I, 5–8; *The Constitution and Regulations of the Grand Royal Arch Chapter* (Albany, N.Y., 1829), 42; Charles A. Hunt, *History of the Lebanon Chapter No. 13, R.A.M.* (Chatham, N.Y., n.d.), 6–8, 44.

85. *Hudson Gazette,* Nov. 12, 1799; *NYAJ,* 23d sess., 1800, 6. This appears to have been the riot

discussed in Ellis, *Columbia County*, 301. The legislation was *NY Laws*, 23d sess., 1800, chap. 110 (An Act of Settling the Disputes and Controversies between the Persons Claiming to Be Proprietors of a Patent Called Mawighnunk, and the Possessors of the Lands in the Town of Canaan); this was followed a year later by *NY Laws*, 24th sess., 1801, chap. 52 ("An Act Supplementary to an Act Entitled . . .).

86. The final two commissioners were Jesse Root of Hartford, and Jonathan Sturges of Fairfield. The controversies can be followed in *NYAJ*, 23d sess., 1800, 6, 44, 45, 105, 115, 121–122, 140–141, 159–160, 273, 278–279, 288. Of the four New Lebanon petitioners identified in the *Assembly Journal*, three (Asel King, Jr., Moses King, and Josiah Patterson) were Unity Lodge Masons, and Samuel Jones was the father of a Mason. Jonathan Murdock, mentioned in Ellis, *Columbia County*, 301, as leading the attack on the surveying party, was also a Mason. The next year Samuel Jones led a petition to the assembly demanding that public ownership of the Springs at New Lebanon be recognized. *NYAJ*, 24th sess., 1801, 239–246, 256–257.

87. *NYAJ*, 16th sess., 1793, 219–220.

88. This analysis is based on the Deed Books, Columbia County Registry of Deeds, Columbia County Clerk's Office, Hudson, N.Y.; Collin, *Hillsdale*, 4, 26, 36, 62. In November 1795, Henry I. Van Rensselaer announced that he would sell all the land that he had inherited from his father, John. Notice dated Nov. 20, 1795, in *Hudson Gazette*, Apr. 14, 1796. None of the five Adventurers who signed the 1789 petition (Benjamin Birdsall, John Collin, Benjamin Allen, Charles McKinstry, and Ambrose Latting) was on the final settlement with the Van Rensselaers negotiated by Alexander Hamilton in 1803 and 1804. Latting was dead by then, but his wife, Joanna, was listed on the 1800 valuation but not the settlements (see below). Birdsall's deed is located at Columbia County Deeds B2: 174. I am grateful to Ruth Piwonka for this reference and for this interpretation.

89. Goebel and Smith, eds., *LPAH*, III, 339 n. 94, 345–346, 348–350; Philip Schuyler, Albany, to Peter Hogeboom, Claverack, Oct. 12, 22, 25, 29, 1795, to Ambrose Spencer, Hudson, Dec. 29, 1795, Schuyler Family Papers, NYSL; Philadelphia *General Advertiser*, May 25, 1793; Boyd and Taylor, eds., *Susquehannah Company Papers*, X, 176, 344, 567, 569, 571, 572, 574, 577. Peter Hogeboom's cousin Stephen won the April 1795 assembly election with strong support in Hillsdale and Livingston, as did John Bay in 1793 and 1794.

90. Goebel and Smith, *LPAH*, III, 351–353, 366–370, 372–403 (Hamilton's note re the Claverack patent, Van Rensselaer grants, and the Westenhook patent). Philip Schuyler, Albany, to Alexander Hamilton, NYC, Sept. 9, 1801, in Syrett et al., eds., *PAH*, XXV, 416–417. Sedgwick was the son-in-law of General Joseph Dwight of Stockbridge, who had supported the Massachusetts claim and the Claverack Nobletown rioters in the 1750s (Kim, *Landlord and Tenant*, 319–320). The *Hudson Gazette*, June 11, 1799, reported successful ejectments under the Van Rensselaer title. On the settlement: Philip Schuyler, Albany, to Henry I. and Jacob R. Van Rensselaer, Claverack, Nov. 1, 1802, Schuyler Family Papers, NYSL; Goebel and Smith, eds., *LPAH*, III, 356–357; Syrett et al., eds., *PAH*, XXVI, 111–113, 142–143, 162–163, 168, 177, 224–227, 289. Hoffman, as Jay's attorney general, had refused the assembly's demand to reopen the investigation of the Mawighnunk patent in 1800. The total of the settlement to each of the four heirs of John Van Rensselaer is not known, but Catherine Schuyler's heirs were owed $17,777.67 by thirty-nine Hillsdale inhabitants. "Engrossed Account of Expenses of the Arbitration Proceedings [1805]," in Goebel and Smith, eds., *LPAH*, III, 366 n. 174, 441.

91. This assessment of persistence of the 1789 petitioners between 1789 and 1804 is based

on a comparison of deeds and mortgages in the Columbia County Clerk's Office with the 1789 petitioners and the political committees reported in the *Gazette,* the *Bee,* and the *Balance.* This assessment of persistence of the 1789 petitioners and 1804 grantees is based on a comparison of deeds and mortgages in the Columbia County Clerk's Office with the 1789 petitioners, the political committees reported in the *Gazette,* the *Bee,* and the *Balance,* the 1800 Hillsdale tax valuation, and the 1810 census. Among the 9 Republican committeemen who had been involved in the Hogeboom murder trial, 4 had been sureties, 3 had been witnesses, 1 a petit juryman, and 2 — Ebenezer Hatch and Jonathan Arnold — had stood among the accused. Of the 211 petitioners in 1789, 62 (29 percent) can be identified on the 1800 Hillsdale valuation. Of these 62 persisting from 1789 to 1800, 22 (35 percent) were among the 110 grantees in 1804. Both groups of petitioners had the same general wealth profile, with about half being in the top fifth of the 1800 tax valuation. Those who were only 1804 grantees were distinctly poorer (only 15 percent in the top fifth) and probably significantly younger, too young in 1789 to sign the petition. Checking forward to the 1810 census, the 22 petitioners in 1789 who persisted to 1804 were particularly likely (77 percent) to persist to 1810, compared to the 40 petitioners in 1789 who were not 1804 grantees. In some measure, then, getting on the arbitration list and receiving a mortgaged deed from the Van Rensselaers in 1804 contributed to persistence rather than encouraged emigration. Strikingly, the poorest of the 1804 grantees were quite likely to persist in Hillsdale to 1810; it may be that these families had defaulted on their mortgages and were too poor to move west.

1800 Valuation: Decile	1789 Petitioner Only	1789 Petitioner and 1804 Grantee	1804 Grantee Only
1–2	19 47%	11 50%	10 15%
3–5	14 35%	8 36%	15 23%
6–10	7 18%	3 14%	40 62%
Total	40 100%	22 100%	65 100%

Persistence: Listed in Columbia County on the 1810 U.S. Census

1–2	15/19 79%	10/11 91%	7/10 70%
3–5	5/14 36%	6/8 75%	2/15 13%
6–10	0/7	1/3 33%	17/40 42%
Total	20/40 50%	17/22 77%	26/65 40%

92. Peacher, "Craft Masonry," 342–344; Vernon Lodge Returns, NYGL.

93. On the Columbia Turnpike, see *NY Laws,* 22d sess., 1799, chap. 59, 23d sess., 1800, chap. 69; "Release of Land by John Collin . . . Jan. 14, 1800," Columbia Turnpike Dividend Book, 1, "Draft of 1800 Petition," "Undated proposal, draft," Columbia Turnpike Collection, CCHS. Ambrose Spencer introduced the Columbia Turnpike petition, which was led by his fellow Mason Elisha Jenkins (*NYSJ,* 22d sess., 2d mtg., 1799, 75). At least ten of the turnpike incorporators were directors of the Bank of Columbia in the 1790s, and six were members of the Hudson Lodge. For the three other Hillsdale turnpikes, see *NY Laws,* 28th sess., 1805, chap. 64, 31st sess., 1808, chaps. 56, 195.

94. Ellis, *Columbia County,* 374, 384; An Act to Establish a Turnpike Corporation . . . , *NY Laws,* 28th sess., 1805, chap. 64; Peacher, "Craft Masonry," 345–346.

95. Katherine W. Thompson, *Penfield's Past, 1810–1966* (Penfield, N.Y., 1966), 38–40; Penfield

Map of Claverack, 1799, on display in CCHS; Peacher, "Craft Masonry," 340–342; Columbia Lodge returns, LL-NYGL.

96. Cynthia A. Kierner, *Traders and Gentlefolk: The Livingstons of New York, 1675–1790* (Ithaca, N.Y., 1992), 245–246; James D. Livingston and Sherry H. Penney, "The Breakup of Livingston Manor," in Richard T. Wiles, ed., *The Livingston Legacy: Three Centuries of American History* ([Annandale-on-Hudson, N.Y.], 1987), 406–409; executors' notice, dated July 15, counternotice by Peter R. Livingston, dated Sept. 10, *Hudson Gazette,* Nov. 10, 1791.

97. See Philip Schuyler, NYC, to Henry Livingston, Manor, Jan. 14, 1786, Schuyler Family Papers, NYSL, on the resolution of boundary issues between the families. Henry Livingston, Manor, to Walter Livingston, NYC, Jan. 2, Oct. 4, 8, 24, Nov. 13, 1791, John Livingston, Manor, to Walter Livingston, NYC, Oct. 17, Nov. 13, 1791, RRLP.

98. Henry Livingston, Manor, to Walter Livingston, NYC, Nov. 25, 1791, to WL, Teviotdale, Oct. 31, Dec. 10, 1792, Robert C. Livingston, NYC, to Walter Livingston, Teviotdale, Dec. 16, 1792, RRLP.

99. Ezekiel Gilbert, Hudson, to Walter Livingston, Manor, Mar. 13, 1793, Ambrose Spencer, Hudson, to Walter Livingston, Teviotdale, Mar. 13, 1793, Henry Livingston, Ancram, to Walter Livingston, Teviotdale, Mar. 23, Apr. 26, 1794, John Livingston, NYC, to Walter Livingston, Teviotdale, Apr. 24, 1794, RRLP.

100. *NYAJ,* 17th sess., 1794, 135, 157; Henry Livingston, Ancram, to Walter Livingston, Teviotdale, Mar. 23, Apr. 26, 1794, John Livingston, NYC, to Walter Livingston, Teviotdale, Apr. 24, 1794, RRLP; 1794 Columbia County Assembly results, WFP-UM, 41:25.

101. "Petition of Petrus Pulver and Others Demanding an Investigation into the Livingstons' Title," in E. B. O'Callaghan, ed., *The Documentary History of the State of New York* (Albany, N.Y., 1850–1851), II, 834–841 (quote 838); *NYAJ,* 18th sess., 1795, 53, 125–127, 134–135; John Livingston, NYC, to Walter Livingston, Manor, Feb. 25, Mar. 13, 24, 1795, RRLP; *NY Laws,* 18th sess., 1795.

102. Henry Livingston, Hoffman's, to Walter Livingston, Manor, July 28, 1795, John Livingston, Oak Hill, to Walter Livingston, Teviotdale, Apr. 19, 1796, RRLP.

On Hamilton, see John Livingston, NYC, to Walter Livingston, Manor, Feb. 25, Mar. 13, 1795, Alexander Hamilton, Albany, to Walter Livingston, Manor, Mar. 18, 1795, RRLP; Ambrose Spencer, Hudson, to Theodore Sedgwick, Philadelphia, Jan. 17, 1795, to Theodore Sedgwick, Stockbridge, July 4, 1796, Sedgwick Papers, MHS; Walter Livingston to Alexander Hamilton, June 17, 1796, in Syrett et al., eds., *PAH,* XX, 228–229. On Dwight, see Kim, *Landlord and Tenant,* 300–306, 315, 319–320, 325, 335, 343. On the Livingston case: Henry Walter Livingston, Philadelphia, to Walter Livingston, Manor, Nov. 21, 1796, Henry Livingston, Ancram, to Walter Livingston, Teviotdale, Mar. 13, 1797, RRLP; Henry Livingston, Albany, to William Wilson, Clermont, Mar. 7, 1797, WFP-UM; Henry Livingston to John Jay, received Jan. 25, 1800, Misc. MSS, Livingston Papers, NYHS.

103. Henry Livingston, Ancram, to Walter Livingston, Teviotdale, Mar. 13, 1797, John Livingston, Oak Hill, to Walter Livingston, Teviotdale, Mar. 9, 1797, RRLP; Henry Livingston, Ancram, to William Wilson, Clermont, Mar. 28, 29, 1797, WFP-UM. On Quinto and the Manor insurgents: Henry Livingston, Ancram, to William Wilson, Clermont, Mar. 17, 1797, WFP-UM; Gov. Hardy to the Lords of Trade, Dec. 22, 1766, in E. B. O'Callagan, comp., *Documents Relative to the Colonial History of New-York* (Albany, 1856–1883), VII, 206–207, cited in Thomas Jude Humphrey, "Agrarian Rioting in Albany County, New York: Tenants, Markets, and Revolution in the Hudson Valley, 1751–1801" (Ph.D. diss., Northern Illinois University, 1996), 162. For a detailed

analysis, see Humphrey, "Agrarian Rioting," 146–207, as well as Patrick Frazier, *The Mohicans of Stockbridge* (Lincoln, Nebr., 1992), 146–152; and Kim, *Landlord and Tenant,* 400. A mixed-blood family named Van Gilder had been deeply involved in the rioting against the Livingstons in 1756; in 1787 a Matthew Van Guilder was indicted among the Shays men from Egremont (Kim, *Landlord and Tenant,* 338–340; Massachusetts Supreme Judicial Court Docket Book, April 1787, MA, 58). In the nineteenth century a tradition of basketmaking developed in Taghkanic; one of the sources of this skill might have been a small group of Mahicans who settled in a hilly region of the central Manor, after the Shekomeko community in Dutchess County was broken up in 1753. Martha Wetherbee and Nathan Taylor, *The Legend of the Bushwhacker Basket* (Sanbornton, N.H., 1986), 19–20.

104. Kim, *Landlords and Tenant;* Philip Ranlet, *New York Loyalists* (Knoxville, Tenn., 1986); Cynthia Kierner, "Landlord and Tenant in Revolutionary New York: The Case of the Livingston Manor," *New York History,* LXX (1989), 133–152. Though the majority of the Hillsdale resisters bore English surnames, a smattering of German names there and among petitioners from Claverack who joined the 1789 petition indicates the same pattern of interethnic resistance to landlords unfolding in these towns. See Chapter 1, note 31, for a full analysis of the experience of the Pulver petition signers in the Revolution.

105. These events are outlined in Henry Livingston's letter to John Jay, received Jan. 25, 1800, Misc. MSS, Livingston Papers, NYHS. Further details can be found in the stream of correspondence from Henry Livingston, Ancram, to William Wilson, Clermont: Mar. 7, 17, 28, 29, 31, Apr. 12, June 13, July 22, 28, Sept. 22, 27, 1797, Jan. 16, May 13, 1798, May 13, 1799, WFP-UM. None of this activity seems to have resulted in prosecutions at the level of the court of oyer and terminer.

106. Henry Livingston, Ancram, to William Wilson, Clermont, Jan. 16, 17, Feb. 11, June 3, Aug. 18, Sept. 10, 29, 1798; Peter Van Schaack, Kinderhook, to William Wilson, Clermont, Oct. 6, Nov. 4, 1797, Jan. 15, Dec. 10, 1798, Thomas Smith, NYC, to William Wilson, Clermont, Aug. 15, 1798, WFP-UM; William Wilson, Clermont, to Robert R. Livingston, NYC, Mar. 1, 1798, RRLP; *NYSJ,* 21st sess., 1798, 66, 68; *NYAJ,* 21st sess., 1798, 164–165; *Hudson Gazette,* Mar. 13, 1798. Killian Hogeboom, a Claverack Republican who was a leading member of the Columbia lodge in 1803, voted to delay the 1798 resolution.

107. John Lasher et al. to Henry Livingston, Nov. 15, 1798, Henry Livingston, Ancram, to William Wilson, Clermont, Mar. 7, 9, 1798, Apr. 25, 1799, Peter Van Schaack, Kinderhook, to William Wilson, Clermont, Oct. 6, 1797, Mar. 29, Dec. 10, 1798, Aug. 12, 1799, WFP-UM. Van Schaack might well have been devising strategies to "reconcile" the Mawighnunk settlers in Canaan "to their fate."

108. John Jay to Assembly, July 22, 1798, and a Petition from John Livingston [on behalf of] himself and the infant heirs of Robert C. Livingston deceased, Henry Livingston, and Henry W. Livingston, Feb. 17, 1798, Assembly Papers, Executive Messages, (N-Ar)A1818, NYSL; James Smith, Poughkeepsie, to William Wilson, Clermont, Mar. 24, 1798, WFP-UM; *Hudson Gazette,* June 12, 1798, May 11, 1801; 1799 and 1800 returns from the Columbia County Clerk's Office; New Haven *Connecticut Journal,* June 19, 1799.

109. Henry Livingston, Ancram, to William Wilson, Clermont, Sept. 27–28, 1797, Oct. 20, 1798, WFP-UM; John Livingston, Oak Hill, to Walter Livingston, Teviotdale, Apr. 6, 1797, RRLP; Thomas Paine, *The Writings, of Thomas Paine, Secretary for Foreign Affairs to the Congress of the United States of America, in the Late War . . .* (Albany, N.Y., 1794), vi.

110. Temple Lodge returns, NYGL; Boyd and Taylor, eds., *Susquehannah Company Papers,* X, 576; Henry Livingston, Ancram, to William Wilson, Clermont, July 27, 1797, WFP-UM.

111. DeAlva Stanwood Alexander, *A Political History of the State of New York* (New York, 1906), I, 87–88; David Lawrence, William Jenkins, Robert Jenkins, Hudson, to William Wilson, Clermont Mar. 27, 1798, WWP-BC; *Hudson Gazette,* Mar. 27, June 12, 1798, Mar. 26, 1799; Jabez D. Hammond, *The History of Political Parties in the State of New-York* . . . (Cooperstown, N.Y., 1846), I, 125–126; Ambrose Spencer, Albany, to Samuel B. Webb, Claverack, Mar. 17, 1797, in Ford, ed., *Correspondence and Journals of Webb,* III, 204.

112. Henry Livingston, Ancram, to William Wilson, Clermont, July 27, 1797, WFP-UM. The second leader of the tenant insurgents was Jonathan Bridges, about whom nothing else is known. Grand Lodge Proceedings, May 30, 1798, in *Early History and Transactions of the Grand Lodge of Free and Accepted Masons of the State of New York, 1871–1815* (New York, 1876), 240; Peacher, "Craft Freemasonry," 340. See Chapter 4 for an account of Birdsall's attempt to form a lodge, and Chapter 9 on the fate of his son, Benjamin III. For the Birdsall family, see the *Historical Magazine, and Notes and Queries* . . . , 3d Ser., II (1873), 282–283; and the Cooperstown *Watch-Tower,* July 27, 1818.

113. Benjamin Birdsall, Jr., vs. Robert Swift Livingston and others, affidavit of testimony in Chancery, Sept. 22, 1812, MVBP; Henry Livingston, Ancram, to William Wilson, Clermont, Mar. 9, 1798; *NYAJ,* 22d sess., 2d mtg., 1799, 226 (March 19); William H. Ludlow, Claverack, to William Wilson, Clermont, Mar. 23, 1798, Peter Van Schaack, Kinderhook, to William Wilson, Clermont, Dec. 10, 1798, WFP-UM; Henry Livingston vs. Benjamin Birdsall, Jr., suit filed Aug. 8, 1801 (breach of covenant made Nov. 12, 1798), Columbia County Clerk's Office, box 180; Henry Livingston, Ancram, to William Wilson, Clermont, Aug. 4, 1799, Peter Van Schaack, Kinderhook, to William Wilson, Clermont, Aug. 23, 1799, WFP-UM. On earlier efforts to eject Pulver, see Peter Van Schaack, Kinderhook, to William Wilson, Clermont, Aug. 10, Dec. 10, 1798; Benjamin Birdsall, Jr., Copake, to William Wilson, Clermont, May 12, 1801, Mar. 16, 1803, Aug. 7, 1804, WFP-UM.

CHAPTER 6

1. *Albany Register,* Nov. 2, 20, 27, 1795; Edward A. Collier, *A History of Old Kinderhook* . . . (New York, 1914), 283–284; Elsie Garland Hobson, *Educational Legislation and Administration in the State of New York from 1777 to 1850* (Chicago, 1918), 181; *NYAJ,* 21st sess., 1798, 223; *Albany Centinel,* July 10, 1798.

2. Peter Van Schaack, Kinderhook, to William Wilson, Clermont, Aug. 23, 1799, WFP-UM. In 1804 David Warden began a controversial term as a private secretary to John Armstrong, Jr., appointed by Jefferson to replace Robert R. Livingston as ambassador to France. C. Edward Skeen, *John Armstrong, Jr., 1758–1843* (Syracuse, N.Y., 1981), 53, 114–115, 118–119.

3. William M. Holland, *The Life and Political Opinions of Martin Van Buren, Vice President of the United States* (Hartford, Conn., 1835), 15–16; Jerome Mushkat and Joseph G. Rayback, *Martin Van Buren: Law, Politics, and the Shaping of Republican Ideology* (DeKalb, Ill., 1997), 13–14; John Niven, *Martin Van Buren: The Romantic Age of American Politics* (New York, 1983), 7–8, 118–119; John C. Fitzpatrick, ed., *The Autobiography of Martin Van Buren,* vol. II of *Annual Report of the American Historical Association for the Year 1918* (Washington, D.C., 1920), 11; Collier, *History of Old Kinderhook,* 394–396, 398–399; Elizabeth L. Gebhard, *The Parsonage between Two Manors: Annals of Clover-Reach* (Hudson, N.Y., 1925), 47; John P. Van Ness, *An Oration,*

Composed and Delivered by John P. Van Ness, at a Quarterly Exhibition, Held at Columbia College, in New-York, the First of October, One Thousand Seven Hundred and Eighty-seven: For Which He Obtained the Premium of Eloquence (Albany, N.Y., [1787]) (Sabin 98528); James Gordon Bennett Diary, quoted in Donald B. Cole, *Martin Van Buren and the American Political System* (Princeton, N.J., 1984), 221, and see also 13–15, 24, 34, 108, 431.

4. Michael Wallace, "Changing Concepts of Party in the United States: New York, 1815–1828," *American Historical Review,* LXXIV (1968), 453–491; Joanne B. Freeman, *Affairs of Honor: National Politics in the New Republic* (New Haven, Conn., 2001); Cole, *Martin Van Buren,* 34–35. Mushkat and Rayback, *Martin Van Buren,* 13–14, have developed this very plausible thesis of maternal influence.

5. Martin Van Buren, *Inquiry into the Origin and Course of Political Parties in the United States* (New York, 1867); Alice P. Kenney, *Stubborn for Liberty: The Dutch in New York* (Syracuse, N.Y., 1975); Gerald Francis De Jong, "The Dutch Reformed Church and Negro Slavery in Colonial America," *Church History,* XL (1971), 423–436; Lee Benson, *The Concept of Jacksonian Democracy: New York as a Test Case* (Princeton, N.J., 1961), 293–317.

6. Paula Baker has charted the long-term path of this strand of American political history in "The Domestication of Politics: Women and American Political Society, 1780–1920," *AHR,* LXXXIX (1984), 620–647.

7. On gender and consent, see Carole Pateman, *The Problem of Political Obligation: A Critical Analysis of Liberal Theory* (New York, 1979); Mary Beth Norton, *Founding Mothers and Fathers: Gendered Power and the Forming of American Society* (New York, 1996); Nancy Isenberg, *Sex and Citizenship in Antebellum America* (Chapel Hill, N.C., 1998); Holly Brewer, *By Birth or Consent: Children, Law, and the Anglo-American Revolution in Authority* (Chapel Hill, N.C., 2005). Among the more modern approaches to the New Divinity Congregationalists' redefinition of virtue, see Jonathan D. Sassi, *A Republic of Righteousness: The Public Christianity of the Post-Revolutionary New England Clergy* (New York, 2001), 19–83; Christopher Grasso, *A Speaking Aristocracy: Transforming Public Discourse in Eighteenth-Century Connecticut* (Chapel Hill, N.C., 1999), 356–374; Mark Valeri, *Law and Providence in Joseph Bellamy's New England: The Origins of the New Divinity in Revolutionary America* (New York, 1994); David W. Kling, *A Field of Divine Wonders: The New Divinity and Village Revivals in Northwestern Connecticut, 1792–1822* (University Park, Pa., 1993). On America as a postmonarchical society, see Gordon S. Wood, *The Radicalism of the American Revolution* (New York, 1992); Richard L. Bushman, "'This New Man': Dependence and Independence, 1776," in Bushman et al., *Uprooted Americans: Essays to Honor Oscar Handlin* (Boston, 1980), 77–96.

8. See discussion of the literature bearing on a politics of sympathy below, at note 14.

9. John Camp, *The New Commandment Explained and Enforced: A Sermon, Delivered at the Meeting-House in New Canaan, on the 27th of Dec., 1786, before a Number of Free and Accepted Masons; Being the Anniversary of St. John the Evangelist* (Hudson, N.Y., 1787), 3, 8–13; *Minutes of the Shaftsbury Baptist Association; At Their Annual Convention, Held in Hillsdale, M,DCC,LXXXIX* (Bennington, Vt., 1789), 5–6, 10.

10. *Hudson Weekly Gazette,* Apr. 7, 1785, Jan. 24, Apr. 3, Sept. 9, 1788. In this account of "sentimental patriotism," I follow the analysis developed by David Waldstreicher in *In the Midst of Perpetual Fetes: The Making of American Nationalism, 1776–1820* (Chapel Hill, N.C., 1997), 85–89; and Andrew Burstein, *Sentimental Democracy: The Evolution of America's Romantic Self-Image* (New York, 1999), 119–166.

11. *Hudson Gazette,* July 5, 1792, Feb. 20, 1794, Mar. 26, 1795.

12. Among many other letters from constituents to federal figures, see Peter Van Schaack, Kinderhook, to Theodore Sedgwick, Philadelphia, Dec. 25, 1791, Jan. 2, 1793, Jan. 23, 1795, June 1, 1797, Henry Van Schaack, Pittsfield, to Theodore Sedgwick, Philadelphia, Jan. 10, Nov. 20, 27, 1791, Dec. 8, 1792, Jan. 13, 1793, Sedgwick Papers, series 1, MHS. Petitions were sent from Canaan, Kinderhook, and Claverack to the House of Representatives in May 1796, asking that the terms of the Jay Treaty be implemented. These petitions, which have not survived, were apparently the only such from the county in the 1790s and were generated in the context of a Federalist campaign orchestrated in Philadelphia. See *Journal of the House of Representatives of the United States, Being the First Session of the Fourth Congress . . .* (Washington, D.C., 1826), 553–554; Todd Estes, *The Jay Treaty Debate, Public Opinion, and the Evolution of Early American Political Culture* (Amherst, Mass., 2006). On the wider theme of the limited reach of the national public sphere in the early Republic, see Trish Loughran, *The Republic of Print: Print Culture in the Age of U.S. Nationalism* (New York, 2007), 161–222.

13. This summary discussion draws upon the growing literature on the cultural politics of the early Republic, most importantly Waldstreicher, *In the Midst of Perpetual Fetes;* but also including Sandra M. Gustafson, *Eloquence Is Power: Oratory and Performance in Early America* (Chapel Hill, N.C., 2000); Simon P. Newman, *Parades and the Politics of the Street: Festive Culture in the Early American Republic* (Philadelphia, 1997); Kimberly K. Smith, *The Dominion of Voice: Riot, Reason, and Romance in Antebellum Politics* (Lawrence, Kan., 1999); Len Travers, *Celebrating the Fourth: Independence Day and the Rites of Nationalism in the Early Republic* (Amherst, Mass., 1997); John L. Brooke, "Ancient Lodges and Self-Created Societies: Voluntary Association and the Public Sphere in the Early Republic," in Ronald Hoffman and Peter J. Albert, eds., *Launching the "Extended Republic": The Federalist Era* (Charlottesville, Va., 1996), 273–377; Albrecht Koschnik, "The Democratic Societies of Philadelphia and the Limits of the American Public Sphere, circa 1793–1795," *William and Mary Quarterly,* 3d Ser., LVIII (2001), 615–636, and "Political Conflict and Public Contest: Rituals of National Celebration in Philadelphia, 1788–1815," *Pennsylvania Magazine of History and Biography,* CXVIII (1994), 209–248. James Kent's remembrance is in "Judge Van Ness," memorandum in James Kent Papers, XI, LC.

14. My thinking on the shape of a politics of sympathy and positive liberalism and on sympathy and the boundaries of civil society has been shaped by a considerable literature, including David Nathaniel Gellman's important book, *Emancipating New York: The Politics of Slavery and Freedom, 1777–1827* (Baton Rouge, La., 2006); his dissertation, "Inescapable Discourse: The Rhetoric of Slavery and the Politics of Abolition in Early National New York" (Ph.D. diss., Northwestern University, 1997); and his essay, "Race, the Public Sphere, and Abolition in Eighteenth-Century New York," *Journal of the Early Republic,* XX (2000), 607–636. Other work that has shaped my ideas here includes Gillian Brown, *The Consent of the Governed: The Lockean Legacy in Early American Culture* (Cambridge, 2001); Smith, *The Dominion of Voice,* 199–235; Markman Ellis, *The Politics of Sensibility: Race, Gender, and Commerce in the Sentimental Novel* (New York, 1996), 129–160; Isenberg, *Sex and Citizenship,* 64–74; G. J. Barker-Benfield, *The Culture of Sensibility: Sex and Society in Eighteenth-Century Britain* (Chicago, 1992); Greg Laugero, "Infrastructures of Enlightenment: Road-Making, the Public Sphere, and the Emergence of Literature," *Eighteenth-Century Studies,* XXIX (1995), 45–67; Baker, "The Domestication of Politics," *AHR,* LXXXIX (1984), 620–647.

On sensibility more broadly defined, see Janet Todd, *Sensibility: An Introduction* (New York, 1986); and Julie Ellison, *Cato's Tears and the Making of Anglo-American Emotion* (Chicago, 1999), who, on 4–9, provides an excellent short overview of the recent rise of "sensibility studies." For the most fully developed analysis of sensibility in the late eighteenth century, see Sarah Knott, *Sensibility and the American Revolution* (Chapel Hill, N.C., 2009), esp 195–264. For discussions of sensibility and antislavery in addition to Gellman's work, see Winthrop D. Jordan, *White over Black: American Attitudes toward the Negro, 1550–1812* (Chapel Hill, N.C., 1968), 365–372; Mukhtar Ali Isani, "Far from 'Gambia's Golden Shore': The Black in Late Eighteenth-Century American Imaginative Literature," *WMQ*, 3d Ser., XXXVI (1979), 353–372; Thomas L. Haskell, "Capitalism and the Origins of Humanitarian Sensibility," *AHR*, XC (1985), 339–361, 547–566; Karen Halttunen, "Humanitarianism and the Pornography of Pain in Anglo-American Culture," *AHR*, C (1995), 303–334; Elizabeth B. Clark, "'The Sacred Rights of the Weak': Pain, Sympathy, and the Culture of Individual Rights in Antebellum America," *Journal of American History*, LXXXII (1995–1996), 463–493; Ellis, *The Politics of Sensibility*, 49–128.

15. *NY Laws*, 7th sess., 1784, chap. 18; *NY Laws*, 14th sess., 1791, chap. 41; Ellis, *Columbia County*, 282; William Wilson [Clermont] accounts with the Red Hook Church, Sept. 1, 1801 [9:65], Aug. 10, 1803 [12:38], Nov. 2, 1807 [15:46], Nov. 14, 1813 (17:60), WFP-UM; Peacher, "Craft Masonry," 338–339; *An Account of the Performances at the Dedication of Mason-Hall, Hudson . . .* (Hudson, N.Y., 1797), 47–49. In Rensselaerwyck Manor, encompassing large parts of Albany and Rensselaer counties, Stephen Van Rensselaer, also a leading Mason, seems to have practiced a style of benevolent institution building, encouraging the chartering of lodges and giving land for the construction of schools and churches, most importantly founding Rensselaer Polytechnic Institute. He was remembered as the "good Patron," and it was only after his death in 1839 that a serious antirent struggle developed in these counties. See 1795 clipping, Commonplace Book, 8, Elkanah Watson Papers, 1774–1885, NYSL; and George Baker Anderson, *Landmarks of Rensselaer County, New York* (Syracuse, N.Y., 1897), 517.

16. George Dangerfield, *Chancellor Robert R. Livingston of New York, 1746–1813* (New York, 1960), 47; William Livingston, *The Independent Reflector; or, Weekly Essays on Sundry Important Subjects,* ed. Milton M. Klein (Cambridge, Mass., 1963), 419, 422, 424. For an excellent account of the culture of the early Presbyterian academies that Livingston had in mind, see John Fea, *The Way of Improvement Leads Home: Philip Vickers Fithian and the Rural Enlightenment in Early America* (Philadelphia, 2008), 59–69; see also J. M. Opal, *Beyond the Farm: National Ambitions in Rural New England* (Philadelphia, 2008).

17. *NYAJ*, 16th sess., 1793, 211, 17th sess., 1794, 32, 18th sess., 1795, 5. See Alfred F. Young, *The Democratic Republicans of New York: The Origins, 1763–1797* (Chapel Hill, N.C., 1967), 524.

18. *NYAJ*, 18th sess., 1795, 80, 149, 151–152, 173, 175; *NY Laws*, 18th sess., 1795, chap. 75.

19. *NY Laws*, 19th sess., 1796, chaps. 43, 49, 20th sess., 1797, chap. 34; *NYAJ*, 19th sess., 1796, 23.

20. *Hudson Gazette*, Mar. 13, 1797. Of the various known trustees of the Hudson Library from 1797 to 1803, four were involved in the Columbia turnpike, five in the Bank of Columbia, one in the Union turnpike, five in the 1808 Bank of Hudson, four in the 1811 Hudson Insurance Company, and one in the Columbia Manufacturing Society. *NY Laws*, 22nd sess., 1799, chap. 22, 24th sess., 1801, chap. 49. A number of scholars have challenged Tocqueville's notion that American civil institutions were compensating for the lack of a state, since so many of them were chartered

by governmental authority. See William J. Novak, "The American Law of Association: The Legal-Political Construction of Civil Society," *Studies in American Political Development,* XV (2001), 163–188.

21. For the Northern Missionary Society, see *NY Laws,* 21st sess., 1798, chap. 103. Congregationalists, Presbyterians, and Dutch Reformed ministers all cooperated in the Berkshire and Columbia Missionary Society, which was linked to the advancement of Williams College. Their 1814 annual report, published in the *Columbia Magazine,* I (1814), 173–179, noted that it was the organization's seventeenth annual meeting. See also Stockbridge, Mass., *Western Star,* Sept. 7, 1801; *Albany Centinel,* Sept. 15, 1801, Sept. 13, 1803; Pittsfield, Mass., *Berkshire Reporter,* Apr. 4, 1807; *Pittsfield Sun,* May 2, 1810; Hudson *Northern Whig,* Sept. 20, 1814, Sept. 9, 1817. For the mechanics' societies: *NY Laws,* 24th sess., 1801, chap. 21, 29th sess., 1806, chap. 60, 31st sess., 1808, chap. 235. The Hudson society, as well as one in Lansingburgh, was meeting in the early 1790s: *Hudson Gazette,* Mar. 15, 1792; Lansingburgh *American Spy,* June 2, 1795. Young, *The Democratic Republicans,* 539, discusses the Federalist rejection of mechanics' petitions from Albany and Lansingburgh in February 1795.

22. Hugh Meredith Flick, "Elkanah Watson: Gentleman-Promoter, 1758–1842" (Ph.D. diss., Columbia University, 1949), 111, 123–135; *NY Laws,* 20th sess., 1797, chap. 68; *Albany Gazette,* Feb. 20, 1795; Watson, Commonplace Book, 30. I go slightly beyond the known evidence on Watson's publication in Hudson. One of Watson's essays, No. 4, by Northern Centinel, was printed in the *Hudson Gazette,* Sept. 22, 1791. Given that the *Hudson Gazette* survives only in the most fragmentary condition between 1791 and 1799, I here assume that a number of Watson's essays were published in the lost issues. Watson's improvement campaigns can be followed in detail in his Commonplace Book, box 4; in Flick, "Elkanah Watson," 101–200; and in Winslow C. Watson, ed., *Men and Times of the Revolution; or, Memoirs of Elkanah Watson . . .* (New York, 1856), 326–361. On Watson's role in the Albany organizations, see Flick, "Elkanah Watson," 114–117; Young, *The Democratic Republicans,* 226, 244–246; Watson, ed., *Men and Times,* 328, 335–361, 381–382. *NY Laws,* 15th sess., 1792, chap. 13. On the sentimental and canals, see Ellis, *The Politics of Sensibility,* 129–159.

23. Flick, "Elkanah Watson," 122–123, 136–137, 201–316; Watson, Commonplace Book, 8 (clippings from Northern Centinel, No. 7, in the *Albany Gazette,* 1792, and the *Albany Register,* Nov. 20, 1795), 39. While in Poughkeepsie Watson advocated two turnpikes, one from Albany to New York and another to the Connecticut line from Poughkeepsie.

24. *Hudson Weekly Gazette,* Apr. 14, 1789, Nov. 14, 1793, Dec. 31, 1795, Sept. 15, 1796; Lansingburgh *Federal Herald,* Oct. 7, 1788, Dec. 28, 1789; *Albany Register,* Sept. 2, 1793; Lansingburgh *American Spy,* Mar. 31, July 7, 1795.

25. Lansingburgh *American Spy,* Mar. 31, 1795; *Hudson Gazette,* Mar. 26, 1795.

26. *Greenleaf's New York Journal, and Patriotic Register,* Dec. 6, 1794, Extra; and Samuel Latham Mitchill, *The Life, Exploits, and Precepts of Tammany . . .* (New York, 1795), 35–36, cited and discussed in Young, *The Democratic Republicans,* 520–521; De Witt Clinton, *An Oration, on Benevolence, Delivered before the Society of Black Friars . . . 10th November, 1794* (New York, [1795]), 12, 16–17; Phineas Hedges, *An Oration, Delivered before the Republican Society, of Ulster County, and Other Citizens, Convened at the House of Daniel Smith, in the Town of Montgomery, . . . 4th of July, 1795* (Goshen, N.Y., 1795), 3, 6, 7, 14. Hedges, with De Witt Clinton's brother Charles, was a leading figure in a Paineite-deistic-Masonic circle in Newburgh, in Orange County. See also De Witt Clinton, *An Address Delivered before Holland Lodge, Dec. 24, 1793* (New York,

1794); Samuel Latham Mitchill, *An Oration, Pronounced before the Society of Black Friars, . . . 11th of November, 1793* (New York, 1793), esp. 32–34; T[unis] Wortman, *An Oration on the Influence of Social Institution upon Human Morals and Happiness, Delivered before the Tammany Society, . . . Twelfth of May, 1796* (New York, 1796). In this paragraph and the following I am indebted to Young, *The Democratic Republicans,* 518–545, esp. 519–523, and Thomas Bender, *New York Intellect: A History of Intellectual Life in New York City, from 1750 to the Beginnings of Our Own Time* (Baltimore, 1987), 51–60.

27. Peyton F. Miller, *A Group of Great Lawyers of Columbia County, New York* (New York, 1904), 104, 112; *NYAJ,* 17th sess., 1794, 25–26, 72, 108, 173; *Hudson Gazette,* Mar. 26, 1795; *Greenleaf's New York Journal, and Patriotic Register,* June 3, 1795; Franklin B. Hough, *The New York Civil List from 1770 to 1860 . . .* (Albany, N.Y., 1860), 80–81, 131.

28. Watson, Commonplace Book, 27; *NYSJ,* 19th sess., 1796, 25, 28–29, 36–41, 74–75, 86–87; *NYAJ,* 21st sess., 1798, 41, 141. See Young, *The Democratic Republicans,* 527–528; Louis P. Masur, *Rites of Execution: Capital Punishment and the Transformation of American Culture, 1776–1865* (New York, 1989), 86; Flick, "Elkanah Watson," 113–114.

29. *Hudson Gazette,* June 12, 1798; *Albany Gazette,* June 22, 1798; *A Farmer, To the Public . . . Apr. 17, 1798 . . .* (Hudson, N.Y., 1798) (Evans 34674).

30. Herbert T. Singer and Ossian Lang, *New York Freemasonry: A Bicentennial History, 1781–1981* (New York, 1981), 257; *An Account of the Performances at the Dedication of Mason-Hall, Hudson,* 43; *Constitution and Regulations of the Grand Royal Arch Chapter of the State of New York, . . . 1805* (Albany, N.Y., 1829), 42. Quote from De Witt Clinton Letterbook (Apr. 21, 1799), DWP-CU, XVI, 193–196; see discussion in Craig Hanyan, *De Witt Clinton: Years of Molding, 1769–1807* (New York, 1988), 73–74. Although there are no known records of a Masonic membership in New York for Elkanah Watson, he was a Mason in 1782, when he sent a ceremonial Masonic sash and apron to George Washington from France. Sidney Hayden, *Washington and His Masonic Compeers* (New York, 1866), 83–85, 103.

31. *NYAJ,* 21st sess., 1798, 211, 270; *NYSJ,* 21st sess., 1798, 84, 89, 105, 110–111; *NY Laws,* 21st sess., 1798, chap. 55. On Clinton and Fulton, see Dangerfield, *Chancellor Robert R. Livingston,* 276, 287–289; Evan Cornog, *The Birth of Empire: De Witt Clinton and the American Experience, 1769–1828* (New York, 1998), 61, 65, 92, 112; Steven E. Siry, *De Witt Clinton and the American Political Economy: Sectionalism, Politics, and Republican Ideology, 1787–1828* (New York, 1990), 180, 207.

32. ——— Romeyne, NYC, to William Wilson, Clermont, Dec. 29, 1799, WFP-UM; *NYAJ,* 21st sess., 1798, 91, 121; *NYSJ,* 21st sess., 1798, 141, 22nd mtg., 2nd mtg., 1799, 85, 118.

33. *An Account of the Performances at the Dedication of Mason-Hall, Hudson,* 46–47; *Constitution and Regulations of the Grand Royal Arch Chapter,* 42–43. Upriver at Troy and Lansingburgh, the Apollo and Hiram lodges purchased shares in the new library societies around 1802, and there is every reason to expect that the Hudson Lodge made similar arrangements with the Hudson Library. Jesse B. Anthony, *History of King Solomon's Primitive Lodge . . . Troy, New York . . . with a Sketch of Freemasonry in the City of Troy from 1796 to 1842* (Troy, N.Y., 1892), 9; Lansingburgh Library, New York, Record Book (Lansingburgh Historical Society), Oct. 1, 1802.

34. Wright, "Banking and Politics," 293; *NY Laws,* 26th sess., 1803, chap. 42; Flick, "Elkanah Watson," 117–121; An Act to Incorporate the Rensselaer Glass Factory, *NY Laws,* 29th sess., chap. 26. The Van Schaack / Watson mansion is now the Pittsfield Country Club.

35. Clipping in Watson, Commonplace Book, cited in Flick, "Elkanah Watson," 201.

36. Clinton, *An Address Delivered before the Holland Lodge,* 6–8.

37. *Proposals, of Charles R. and George Webster, for Printing by Subscription, the Writings on Government, of the Celebrated Thomas Paine* . . . (Albany, N.Y., 1791). The subscription list is printed in Thomas Paine, *The Writings of Thomas Paine* . . . (Albany, N.Y., 1792–1794), I, v–xii. Given that the ideological struggle of the American response to the French Revolution had not crystallized in 1791, several Federalists were among these subscribers to the Websters' edition of *Paine,* particularly in the town of Claverack. One of these, Elihu C. Goodrich, was among the subscribers to a conservative response to Paine: R[ichard] Watson, *An Apology for the Bible, in a Series of Letters, Addressed to Thomas Paine, Author of a Book Entitled, The Age of Reason* . . . (New York, 1796). For the late 1790s surge of Masonic representatives, see Chapter 2 and Tables 2, 3.

38. Jean Jacques Rousseau, *A Dissertation on Political Economy: To Which Is Added, A Treatise on the Social Compact; or, The Principles of Politic Law* (Albany, N.Y, 1797), 215–216; Thomas Paine, *Agrarian Justice, Opposed to Agrarian Law, and to Agrarian Monopoly* . . . (Albany, N.Y., 1797).

39. "To the Honorable the Legislature . . . the petition of the Subscribers inhabitants of the neighborhood of the Shaker village which is in the town of Canaan and County of Columbia [". . . many young persons . . . have been brought up among the Shakers. . . ."] . . . Mar. 22, 1800," SC-WRHS (IA10); "A Short Account of the Rise of the Believers . . . ," SC-WRHS (VB60), 34; "To the Honourable the Legislature . . . The memorial and petition of the undersigned inhabitants of the towns of Canaan and Watervliet ["Shakers . . . conscientiously opposed to doing military duty . . ."] . . . Feb. 13, 1816," SC-WRHS (IA10). To simplify this analysis, I have excluded those not on the 1800 Canaan valuation. In 1800 there were a number of signers from Richmond; in 1816 there were many from Watervliet. By this less-than-perfect measure, four of sixteen opposing the Shakers in 1800 were Masons, versus thirteen of thirty-two supporting them in 1816. See Stephen J. Stein, *The Shaker Experience in America: A History of the United Society of Believers* (New Haven, Conn., 1992), 50.

40. Catalogs of William Wilson's books, Aug. 18, 1801, Aug. 1, 1807 (9:64), WFP-UM; *Catalogue of Books, in the Library of the Hon. Robert R. Livingston, of Clermont, February, 1800* (Poughkeepsie, N.Y., 1800), 10. The printing of this alphabetized catalog might have inspired Wilson to produce his manuscript catalog eighteen months later. For a less extensive but still illuminating collection, see the books listed in the inventory of another Masonic Republican, a doctor in Chatham: Russell Dorr inventory, sworn September 21, 1824, Columbia County Surrogate's Office, Hudson, N.Y., 10–12. In assessing these collection lists I have found useful David Lundberg and Henry F. May, "The Enlightened Reader in America," *American Quarterly,* XXVIII (1976), 262–293; Henry F. May, *The Enlightenment in America* (New York, 1976); Barker-Benfield, *The Culture of Sensibility;* Burstein, *Sentimental Democracy,* 3–21.

41. The school report is in *NYAJ,* 21st sess., 1798, 282–285. Clermont, Canaan, and Hillsdale all failed to report. The report listed numbers of schools, scholars, and days of instruction per student. On this measure Hudson ranked high, with 107 days of instruction per student, and Kinderhook low, with 53. School attendance records for the year ending Mar. 19, 1798 (61:22), WFP-UM. This file contains a number of attendance records for the late 1790s, but this year is the only one where the evidence is reasonably complete. The Livingston reports give only the name of the father-"proprietor" and the number of children from each household and thus was not used in this analysis. See Table 15.

42. Frances Wilson, Hudson, to William Wilson, Clermont, May 2, 1802, Fyler Dibblee, Rhinebeck steamboat, to William Wilson, Clermont, May 19, 1810, E. J. Paine, Poughkeepsie, to William

Wilson, Clermont, July 28, 1810, WFP-UM. Dibblee explored the option of getting Eliza into the Litchfield Academy. With regard to attendance, I am assuming kinship from common last names.

43. Bett had studied reading for 242 days the previous year but was no longer in school in 1798–1799. Attendance Returns for Clermont School No. 1, Mar. 15, 1796–Mar. 18, 1797, and Mar. 19, 1798–Mar. 18, 1799 (42:22), WFP-UM. Purchase of slave Sylvia, May 12, 1789 [I, 17], Purchase of slave boy, Feb. 9, 1790; birth certificate of Isaac, Nov. 19, 1803; bill of sale for slave Sharp, Jan. 25, 1811, WFP-UM.

44. *Albany Journal: or, The Montgomery, Washington, and Columbia Intelligencer,* Aug. 25, 1788; *Hudson Weekly Gazette,* Aug. 19, 26, Sept. 2, 9, 1788.

45. Lansingburgh *Federal Herald,* Sept. 1, 8, 29, Oct. 13, 1788, June 1, 1789; Poughkeepsie *Country Journal, and Dutchess and Ulster County Farmer's Register,* Oct. 14, 1788. See Shane White, "Impious Prayers: Elite and Popular Attitudes toward Blacks and Slavery in the Middle-Atlantic States, 1783–1810," *New York History,* LXVII (1986), 261–283; White, *Somewhat More Independent: The End of Slavery in New York City, 1770–1810* (Athens, Ga., 1991), 56–75; Gellman, "Race, the Public Sphere, and Abolition in Eighteenth-Century New York," *Journal of the Early Republic,* XX (2000), 627 n. 47; Isani, "Far from 'Gambia's Golden Shore,'" *WMQ,* 3d Ser., XXXVI (1979), 368–369.

46. *Hudson Weekly Gazette,* Aug. 6, 1789, July 9, 1799. The first surviving Stoddard booklist containing Park's *Travels* is in the *Gazette,* Feb. 10, 1801. William Wilson catalog, Aug. 18, 1801 (9:94), WFP-UM. Thomas Day, "Fragment of an Original Letter on the Slavery of the Negroes," in Noah Webster, *A Grammatical Institute of the English Language . . . ,* Part III (Hartford, Conn., 1785), 177–186; William Enfield, *The Speaker; or, Miscellaneous Pieces, Selected from the Best English Writers . . .* (Hudson, N.Y., 1795), 208–209; *Hudson Weekly Gazette,* Nov. 30, 1786; Lansingburgh *Northern Budget,* Jan. 16, 1798.

47. Stephen B. Miller, *Historical Sketches of Hudson . . .* (Hudson, N.Y., 1862; rpt. 1985), 69; Minutes of the Schaghticoke Scientific Society, Feb. 15, 1797, NYHS (the society changed its name from "Scientific" to "Polemical" at its first meeting); Alexander Wilson, Schenectady, to William Wilson, Clermont, Feb. 8, 1801, "Of Master and Servant" (41:22), WFP-UM.

48. Peter Van Schaack, Kinderhook, to John C. Wynkoop, Kingston, Mar. 13, 1792, VSP/LC; see also John C. Wynkoop, Kingston, to Peter Van Schaack, Kinderhook, Feb. 23, 1792, VSP/LC. On the post-Revolutionary spread of scientific racism, see Gary B. Nash, *Forging Freedom: The Formation of Philadelphia's Black Community, 1720–1840* (Cambridge, Mass., 1988), 223–227; David Grimsted, "Anglo-American Racism and Phillis Wheatley's 'Sable Vail,' 'Length'ned Chain,' and 'Knitted Heart,'" in Ronald Hoffman and Peter J. Albert, eds., *Women in the Age of the American Revolution* (Charlottesville, Va., 1989), esp. 395–426.

49. See Gellman's statewide analysis of the 1792 election in *Emancipating New York,* 131–135, and in "Inescapable Discourse," 247–254.

50. *Hudson Weekly Gazette,* Apr. 8, 1790, Feb. 17, 1791, Nov. 14, 1793, Feb. 27, Mar. 13, 1797, July 9, 1799.

51. For the West Indies reports, see *Hudson Weekly Gazette,* Nov. 10, 1791, Mar. 15, 1792. My argument for a fading of sentimental material is based on a review of the papers of the wider region, including the Lansingburgh *American Spy,* the *Poughkeepsie Journal,* and the few surviving issues of the *Hudson Gazette,* for which only scattered numbers exist from 1792 to early 1799. This fading of sentimental material seems to be evident in the New York papers that Gellman has surveyed (*Emancipating New York,* 78–129; "Race, the Public Sphere, and Abolition," *Journal of the*

Early Republic, XX [2000], 607–636), but he argues differently, suggesting that the West Indian conflicts accentuated the sense of North-South difference within the United States (*Emancipating New York*, 142–146). On black resistance in the Hudson Valley, see Craig Steven Wilder, *In the Company of Black Men: The African Influence of African American Culture in New York City* (New York, 2001), 9–35; A. J. Williams-Myers, "The African Presence in the Hudson River Valley: Defining the Relationship between Masters and Slaves," *Afro-Americans in New York Life and History*, XII (1988), 84, 93–94; Don R. Gerlach, "Black Arson in Albany, New York, November 1793," *Journal of Black Studies*, VII (1977), 301–312; J. Munsell, *The Typographical Miscellany* (Albany, N.Y., 1850), 218; Gellman, "Inescapable Discourse," 269; White, *Somewhat More Independent*, 65; New York *Columbian Gazetteer*, Dec. 2, 1793. Cornelius D. Wynkoop and John C. Wynkoop's father were first cousins: Richard Wynkoop, *Wynkoop Genealogy in the United States of America*, 3d ed. (New York, 1904), 15–17, 45–46, 76–77.

52. Peter Van Schaack, Kinderhook, to John C. Wynkoop, Kingston, Mar. 13, 1792, VSP/LC; *NYAJ*, 13th sess., 2d mtg., 1790, 13, 15, 52. Subsequent debate revolved around the senate's requirement of formal action by a court, rather than simply a certificate from a justice of the peace (69). See Gellman, "Inescapable Discourse," 170–172.

53. *NYAJ*, 18th sess., 1795, 81; *NYAJ*, 19th sess., 1796, 27, 51, 64–65; Gellman, *Emancipating New York*, 165–166.

54. *NYSJ*, 20th sess., 1797, 32, 33, 46, 56, 58, 63, 67–68, 88, 90, 21st sess., 1798, 108, 109, 135.

55. *NYAJ*, 21st sess., 1798, 103–104, 112; Gellman, *Emancipating New York*, 170–171.

56. *NYAJ*, 21st sess., 1798, 261–274.

57. Samuel Ten Broeck, Albany, to William Wilson, Clermont, Mar. 24, 1798, WFP-UM. For assembly action, see *NYAJ*, 22nd sess., 2d mtg., 1799, 2, 47, 49, 77–79, 80–81, 93–95, 99; for action on imprisonment for debt, see *NYAJ*, 22d sess., 2d mtg., 1799, 15, 16, 25, 26, 36–37, 40–41, 66–68, 79–80, 183, 202–204, 213, 225–226, 279–280. John McKinstry was now living in Livingston Manor.

58. *NYAJ*, 22d sess., 2d mtg., 1799, 41–42, 99, 266–267, 283, 289; *NYSJ*, 22d sess., 2d mtg., 1799, 41, 43, 76, 85, 86, 87, 91, 102, 107–109, 113, 118, 128; *NY Laws*, 22d sess., 1799, chaps. 62, 85, 93. See Gellman, *Emancipating New York*, 176–180, 183–184.

59. *NYAJ*, 25th sess., 1802, 231–232, 27th sess., 1804, 232–234; *NYSJ*, 25th sess., 1802, 71, 72, 73, 27th sess., 1804, 61; Gellman, *Emancipating New York*, 183–184.

60. The following discussion is based on a project of record linkage, which has combined data from the state tax valuations preserved in the New York State Archives and the 1800 federal census manuscript. While for convenience I shall refer to the valuations as being taken in 1800, the 1800 Hudson valuation no longer survives, or was dated Sept. 7, 1799. Unless otherwise indicated, this analysis refers only to the universe of taxpayers in 1799–1800, as linked to the 1800 census; households recorded on the census but not the valuation are ignored. For the results of this analysis, discussed below, see Tables 16–20.

61. See Table 23 for aggregate numbers of enslaved and free persons of color, 1790 and 1800. The 1800 census recorded 1,471 slaves, but only 1,340 were held in households that could be linked to the 1800 valuation. Similarly, some people drop out of the analysis in the linkage of tax and census records: the 1800 census recorded 490 free people of color, but only 354 can be linked to taxpaying households in 1799–1800. Of the 146 lost links, 78 were free people of color recorded in the census living in fourteen households in Hudson, Livingston, and Claverack. See Table 17 for the household distribution of persons of color in 1800.

62. These indentures are discussed in White, *Somewhat More Independent,* 47. Although I have found no such indentures for Columbia County, I assume that they were a significant part of the postslavery system.

63. Judah Paddock, *A Narrative of the Shipwreck of the Ship Oswego, on the Coast of South Barbary*... (New York, 1818), 12, 17, 33, 67–69.

64. Ellis, *Columbia County,* 155; George Holcomb Diary, Dec. 4, 1815. For Holcomb's further consultations and transactions with Solomon, see Apr. 28, May 27, July 6, 7, 1816, Feb. 23, 1818. Diary original at NYSL; typescript at the Stephentown Historical Society. William Swayze, *Narrative of William Swayze, Minister of the Gospel, Written by Himself*..., I (Cincinnati, Ohio, 1839), 175–176; for "Negro John," see George Holcomb Diary, June 6, Nov. 13, 15, 1817.

65. See Tables 17, 18. For the account of a free man of color living and working in the hill town of Austerlitz (formerly part of Hillsdale) in the 1820s and 1830s, see Peter Wheeler, *Chains and Freedom; or, The Life and Adventures of Peter Wheeler: A Colored Man Yet Living, a Slave in Chains, a Sailor on the Deep, and a Sinner at the Cross,* ed. Graham Russell Gao Hodges (Tuscaloosa, Ala., 2009). A consideration of racial attitudes in the Columbia hill towns needs to include the interracial marriage of Ephraim Wheeler and Hannah Odel conducted by Eleazer Grant of New Lebanon village in 1791; see Irene Quenzler Brown and Richard D. Brown, *The Hanging of Ephraim Wheeler: A Story of Rape, Incest, and Justice in Early America* (Cambridge, Mass., 2003), 174.

66. See Tables 17, 19, 20. This analysis is based on the 1,081 taxpayers valued at more than $1,500 on the 1800 valuation, whose households accounted for 69 percent (1,037) of the county's slaves and 48 percent (234) of the free blacks. The $1,500 cutoff is used to include as many black inhabitants as possible, while introducing a control for wealth, under the assumption that every white householder of at least this wealth level could have been a slaveholder. A further control for wealth is introduced by ranking the various groupings of taxpayers according to a ratio of their *average individual wealth* and their *collective wealth per slave.* The collective wealth per slave (calculated as the group's total wealth divided by the group's total slaves) provides a measure of the wealth necessary for an average member of a group to purchase a single slave. Thus the Livingston families had one slave for every $1,260 of assessed wealth; the Hudson Fire Company men had one slave for every $33,359.

67. Captain Benjamin Allen of Spencertown in Hillsdale was one of these, holding three slaves in 1800. In 1780 he had been expelled from the Nine Partners Monthly Meeting for serving as a militia officer, swearing an oath, and purchasing two slaves. Michael Edward Groth, "Forging Freedom in the Mid-Hudson Valley: The End of Slavery and the Formation of a Free African-American Community in Dutchess County, N.Y., 1770–1850" (Ph.D. diss., SUNY Binghamton, 1994), 75 n. 28, who cites the Nine Partners Meeting Records.

68. *NYSJ,* 22d sess., 2d mtg., 1799, 107–108; Gebhard, *The Parsonage between Two Manors,* 41.

69. In addition to Joanna Latting, another Hillsdale widow, Sarah Chamberlain, a subscriber to the Green River Congregational Church, also lived with what appears to be a family of three free blacks. The Benjamin Birdsall family had a checkered past in race relations. Between September 1769 and April 1771 his Quaker father Nathan Birdsall and his older brother of the same name were investigated by the Oblong Monthly Meeting for enslaving a free black child. Not satisfied with their explanation that the child had drowned after they had given him to another man who then had sold him, both were disowned, but Nathan, Sr., was reinstated on appeal to the Quarterly Meeting. Oblong Monthly Meeting Records (1757–1781), 273–277, 279–281, 284, 286, 289,

292, 294, 295, 305–306. This case is discussed in Groth, "Forging Freedom in the Mid-Hudson Valley," 69. For Benjamin Birdsall's disownment for his military service, see Philip H. Smith, *General History of Duchess County, from 1609 to 1876 Inclusive* (Pawling, N.Y., 1877), 550.

CHAPTER 7

1. John C. Fitzpatrick, ed., *The Autobiography of Martin Van Buren*, vol. II of *Annual Report of the American Historical Association for the Year 1918* (Washington, D.C., 1920), 13–15; Troy *Northern Budget,* Sept. 22, 29, 1801; Jerome Mushkat and Joseph G. Rayback, *Martin Van Buren: Law, Politics, and the Shaping of Republican Ideology* (DeKalb, Ill., 1997), 16–22; Donald B. Cole, *Martin Van Buren and the American Political System* (Princeton, N.J., 1984), 17; John Niven, *Martin Van Buren: The Romantic Age of American Politics* (New York, 1983), 8–10, 14–18.

2. Cole, *Martin Van Buren,* 34; Niven, *Martin Van Buren,* 207.

3. Henry Livingston, Manor, to Walter Livingston, NYC, Apr. 24, 1785, RRLP.

4. Martin Van Buren, *Inquiry into the Origin and Course of Political Parties in the United States* (New York, 1867), 4, 11, 161, 246–247, 259.

5. The classic accounts of Van Buren's role in establishing the ideal and the practice of political party are Michael Wallace, "Changing Concepts of Party in the United States: New York, 1815–1828," *American Historical Review,* LXXIV (1968), 453–491; Richard Hofstadter, *The Idea of a Party System: The Rise of Legitimate Opposition in the United States, 1780–1840* (Berkeley, Calif., 1969), 212–279; and Robert V. Remini, *Martin Van Buren and the Making of the Democratic Party* (New York, 1959). The critique of Van Buren's understanding of the Federalists and the Whigs as a "legitimate opposition" has its origins in the work of Ronald P. Formisano on "antipartyism" and "deferential-participant politics," especially in "Political Character, Antipartyism and the Second Party System," *American Quarterly,* XXI (1969), 682–709 (esp. 698–701), and "Deferential-Participant Politics: The Early Republic's Political Culture, 1789–1840," *American Political Science Review,* LXVIII (1974), 473–487. It has been developed specifically in Major Wilson, "Republicanism and the Idea of Party in the Jacksonian Period," *Journal of the Early Republic,* VIII (1988), 419–442; and by Gerald Leonard, in "Party as a 'Political Safeguard of Federalism': Martin Van Buren and the Constitutional Theory of Party Politics," *Rutgers Law Review,* LIV (2001–2002), 221–281, and in *The Invention of Party Politics: Federalism, Popular Sovereignty, and Constitutional Development in Jacksonian Illinois* (Chapel Hill, N.C., 2002). David Waldstreicher, *In the Midst of Perpetual Fetes: The Making of American Nationalism, 1776–1820* (Chapel Hill, N.C., 1997); Jeffrey L. Pasley *"The Tyranny of Printers": Newspaper Politics in the Early American Republic* (Charlottesville, Va., 2001); and Andrew W. Robertson, "Voting Rites and Voting Acts: Electioneering Ritual, 1790–1820," in Pasley, Robertson, and Waldstreicher, eds., *Beyond the Founders: New Approaches to the Political History of the Early American Republic* (Chapel Hill, N.C., 2004), constitute a new "school" against both these interpretations, arguing for the vigor of popular democracy in the era of the early Republic. My position, as detailed here, and outlined for the country at large in "To Be 'Read by the Whole People': Press, Party, and Public Sphere in the United States, 1789–1840," American Antiquarian Society, *Proceedings,* CX (2002–2002), 41–118, is that "true modern democratic politics" emerged precociously in a few states and localities in the early Republic, among them Pennsylvania and New York, led by Columbia County.

6. All of this Republican factionalism was complicated by family factionalism, since the Upper Manor Livingstons were now Federalists, with the Clermont Livingstons, led by Robert R., continued their Republican allegiance, veering into Quiddish centralism (between the Bucktail

Democrats and the Federalists) with the 1807 election and the years following. De Witt Clinton would move into this Quid politics in 1812.

7. L. Ray Gunn, *The Decline of Authority: Public Economic Policy and Political Development in New York, 1800–1860* (Ithaca, N.Y., 1988), 81–143; John L. Larson, *Internal Improvement: National Public Works and the Promise of Popular Government in the Early United States* (Chapel Hill, N.C., 2001).

8. On the term "Columbia Junto," see Chapter 2, note 16.

9. Gunn, *The Decline of Authority*, 144–169; Leonard, "Party as a 'Political Safeguard of Federalism,'" *Rutgers Law Review*, LIV (2001–2002) 221–281; Larson, *Internal Improvement*, 149–194.

10. Here I summarize the discussion in Mushkat and Rayback, *Martin Van Buren*, 17–18. See also William M. Holland, *The Life and Political Opinions of Martin Van Buren, Vice President of the United States* (Hartford, Conn., 1835), 26–28; Fitzpatrick, ed., *Autobiography of Van Buren*, 13; Peter Van Ness et al., Kinderhook, to [the Clermont Republican Committee], Apr. 12, 1799, WFP-UM.

11. For the Columbia County assembly votes from 1788 to 1821, with a few approximations, see Figure 2. On the 1800 assembly election, see Brian Phillips Murphy, "'A Very Convenient Instrument': The Manhattan Company, Aaron Burr, and the Election of 1800," *William and Mary Quarterly*, 3d Ser., LXV (2008), 233–266; Nancy Isenberg, *Fallen Founder: The Life of Aaron Burr* (New York, 2007), 196–202; Joanne B. Freeman, "Corruption and Compromise in the Election of 1800: The Process of Politics on the National Stage," in James Horn, Jan Ellen Lewis, and Peter Onuf, eds., *The Revolution of 1800: Democracy, Race, and the New Republic* (Charlottesville, Va., 2002), 97–99; DeAlva Stanwood Alexander, *A Political History of the State of New York* (New York, 1906), I, 90–91.

12. Samuel Edmonds et al., Hudson, to Peter Van Schaack et al., Kinderhook, Apr. 10, 1799, VSP/LC; *NYAJ*, 24th sess., 1800–1801, 12.

13. For Columbia County's voter turnout and party voting in the elections for governor, see Figure 1. (The entire run of the *Gazette* for 1800 has been lost.) On the organization by the Federalists in January 1801 in Albany, see David Hackett Fischer, *The Revolution of American Conservatism: The Federalist Party in the Era of Jeffersonian Democracy* (New York, 1965), 60–61. It should be noted that, with the strengthening of party at the turn of the century, about 1797 for the Federalists and 1801 for the Republicans, Masonic affiliation no longer marked the successful candidates for legislative office, suggesting that partisanship became an increasingly salient focus of identity (see Table 2). For a comparable shift in Massachusetts, see John L. Brooke, *The Heart of the Commonwealth: Society and Political Culture in Worcester County, Massachusetts, 1713–1861* (New York, 1989), 248–249.

14. *Hudson Gazette*, Sept. 22, 1801; Troy *Northern Budget*, Sept. 29, 1801.

15. On the relative size of committees, see Table 21. On comparative county turnout in 1801, see Figure 3. My estimate of assembly turnout is based on an analysis of the election returns assembled by Philip Lampi, in the AAS/Tufts Project "A New Nation Votes, Election Returns, 1787–1825." For a more detailed discussion of the entire state, see John L. Brooke, "'King George Has Issued Too Many Pattents for Us': Property and Democracy in Jeffersonian New York," *Journal of the Early Republic* (forthcoming).

16. For Dutchess, see Staughton Lynd, *Anti-Federalism in Dutchess County, New York: A Study of Democracy and Class Conflict in the Revolutionary Era* (Chicago, 1962); for Rensselaer and Albany counties, see Reeve Huston, *Land and Freedom: Rural Society, Popular Protest, and Party*

Politics in Antebellum New York (New York, 2000), 15–30; Charles W. McCurdy, *The Anti-Rent Era in New York Law and Politics, 1839–1865* (Chapel Hill, N.C., 2001), 10–15. Elsewhere, see Stuart M. Blumin's characterization of the elite management of politics in Kingston and Ulster counties, in *The Urban Threshold: Growth and Change in a Nineteenth-Century Community* (Chicago, 1996), 11–49; and Alan Taylor's similar account for Otsego County, in *William Cooper's Town: Power and Persuasion on the Frontier of the Early American Republic* (New York, 1995), 335–363.

17. Henry Livingston, Ancram, to Samuel B. Webb, Claverack, Feb. 14, 1795, in Worthington Chauncey Ford, ed., *Correspondence and Journals of Samuel Blachley Webb* (New York, 1893–1894), III, 196–197.

18. In the following discussion I am indebted to the discussions of the culture of Federalist political publishing, and of Republican Charles Holt and his Hudson *Bee,* in Pasley, *"The Tyranny of Printers,"* 134–145, 228–257. For another salient discussion of the modes of speech and language in the early Republic, see Sandra M. Gustafson, *Eloquence Is Power: Oratory and Performance in Early America* (Chapel Hill, N.C., 2000), 233–265.

19. Hudson *Balance, and Columbian Repository,* May 21, 1801; Harry Croswell, Hudson, to Noah Webster, New Haven, June 27, 1801, Noah Webster Papers, NYPL.

20. Hudson *Balance,* May 21, June 18, Sept. 17, 24, Dec. 31, 1801, Apr. 20, 1802, Apr. 19, 1803, Apr. 17, 1804, Apr. 16, 23, 1805, Apr. 15, 1806. For Stoddard's reply to the *Balance,* Dec. 31, 1801, see Hudson *Gazette,* Jan. 5, 1802. On the Federalist Augustan style, see Catherine O'Donnell Kaplan, *Men of Letters in the Early Republic: Cultivating Forums of Citizenship* (Chapel Hill, N.C., 2008), 141, 147–148, 157; Colin Wells, *The Devil and Doctor Dwight: Satire and Theology in the Early American Republic* (Chapel Hill, N.C., 2002), 3–6, 30–32, 45–47, 94–95; Pasley, *"The Tyranny of Printers,"* 253–254.

21. See Pasley, *"The Tyranny of Printers,"* 132–147, for an extended account of Holt's career. See Stephen B. Miller, *Historical Sketches of Hudson . . .* (Hudson, N.Y., 1862; rpt. 1985), 64; quote from Ignatius Jones [Gorham A. Worth], *Recollections of Albany and Hudson, with Anecdotes and Sketches of Men and Things* (Albany, N.Y., 1850), 48.

22. Hudson *Wasp,* July 7, 1802.

23. Hudson *Bee,* Aug. 24, 1802.

24. Based on papers listed in Fischer, *The Revolution of American Conservatism,* 415, 417–418; Pasley, *"The Tyranny of Printers,"* 407–409; S. N. D. North, *History and Present Condition of the Newspaper and Periodical Press of the United States . . .* (Washington, D.C., 1884), 39–40.

25. *Hudson Gazette,* Dec. 27, 1803.

26. Milton W. Hamilton, *The Country Printer: New York State, 1785–1830* (New York, 1936), 266; Printer File, American Antiquarian Society; Clifford K. Shipton, ed., *Biographical Sketches of Those Who Attended Harvard College,* VIII, *In the Classes 1726–1730* (Boston, 1951), 386–405; Franklin Bowditch Dexter, "The Rev. Harry Croswell, D.D., and His Diary," in *A Selection from the Miscellaneous Historical Papers of Fifty Years* (New Haven, Conn., 1918), 249–365.

27. [Worth], *Recollections,* 51; Henry Livingston, Ancram, to Samuel B. Webb, Claverack, Feb. 14, 1795, in Ford, ed., *Correspondence and Journals of Webb,* III, 196–197. In 1806 the Hudson *Balance* had to deny the charge made by the New York *American Citizen* that it was "owned and controuled by Mr. Van Ness" (Hudson *Balance,* Apr. 15, 1806). On the politics of sponsorship, see Pasley, *"The Tyranny of Printers,"* 237–241; John Robert Finnegan, Jr., "Defamation, Politics,

and the Social Process of Law in New York State, 1776–1860" (Ph.D. diss., University of Minnesota, 1985), 153–154.

28. These men were the quintessential "Young Federalists" as defined by Fischer in *The Revolution of American Conservatism;* see esp. 60–61.

29. William Raymond, *Biographical Sketches of the Distinguished Men of Columbia County . . .* (Albany, N.Y., 1851), 85; Roger G. Kennedy, *Orders from France: The Americans and the French in a Revolutionary World, 1780–1820* (New York, 1989), 70; Dixon Ryan Fox, *The Decline of Aristocracy in the Politics of New York* (New York, 1919), 44–46; *At a Meeting of a Number of Respectable Gentlemen . . . the Nineteenth Day of June, 1792* (broadside, [Hudson, N.Y.(?), 1792(?)]) (Evans 46415).

30. Raymond, *Biographical Sketches,* 1–20, 39–41; Fischer, *The Revolution of American Conservatism,* 315, 320–321, 366–367; Fox, *The Decline of Aristocracy,* 41–43; *Hudson Gazette,* Mar. 26, 1795, Dec. 8, 1800.

31. Alexander, *A Political History of the State of New York,* 153; Raymond, *Biographical Sketches,* 21–31; Fox, *The Decline of Aristocracy,* 43–44; Fischer, *The Revolution of American Conservatism,* 318; Memo on Van Ness, circa 1840, James Kent Papers, LC; Van Ness Genealogy, CCHS; *Hudson Gazette,* Apr. 23, 1799.

32. Hudson *Balance,* Dec. 16, 1806; Hudson *Bee,* Mar. 26, 1805; Ellis, *Columbia County,* 190, 196. For letters describing a young law student's contributions to the *Balance,* see Charles A. Foote, Kinderhook, to Ebenezer Foote, Delhi, June 3, 1805, June 6, 1806, Nov. 19, 1806, EFP.

33. *Hudson Gazette,* Feb. 17, July 21, 1801; Hudson *Balance,* Dec. 31, 1801. On Dennie, see Kaplan, *Men of Letters in the Early Republic,* 115–183; William C. Dowling, *Literary Federalism in the Age of Jefferson: Joseph Dennie and "The Port Folio," 1801–1812* (Columbia, S.C., 1999); Pasley, *"The Tyranny of Printers,"* 251–252. On satire, see Kaplan, *Men of Letters;* Linda K. Kerber, *Federalists in Dissent: Imagery and Ideology in Jeffersonian America* (Ithaca, N.Y., 1970), 1–21, 174–181; David S. Shields, *Civil Tongues and Polite Letters in British America* (Chapel Hill, N.C., 1997); Christopher Grasso, *A Speaking Aristocracy: Transforming Public Discourse in Eighteenth-Century Connecticut* (Chapel Hill, N.C., 1999), esp. 311–318; Wells, *The Devil and Doctor Dwight,* 4, 30–31, 176–177. On the contest between satire and sensibility, see Claude J. Rawson, *Satire and Sentiment, 1660–1830: Stress Points in the English Augustan Tradition* (New Haven, Conn., 2000), 267–298; John Brewer, *The Pleasures of the Imagination: English Culture in the Eighteenth Century* (Chicago, 1997), 445–449. On Irving, see Mary Weatherspoon Bowden, "Cocklofts and Slangwhangers: The Historical Sources of Washington Irving's *Salmagundi,*" *New York History,* LXI (1980), 133–160, and *Washington Irving* (Boston, 1981), 19–28.

34. Hudson *Wasp,* Sept. 9, Nov. 2, 1802, Jan. 26, 1803. Goebel and Smith, eds., *LPAH,* I, 775–848, is the most complete analysis of this case; the attribution to Grosvenor is discussed on 777 n. 9; Spencer's role is covered on 779–780. See also Pasley, *"The Tyranny of Printers,"* 266, 282. On *Spencer v Grosvenor,* see Alexander Wilson, Schenectady, to William Wilson, Clermont, Oct. 20, 1803, WFP-UM. On Sampson, see Finnegan, "Defamation, Politics, and the Social Process of Law," 401.

35. Hudson *Balance,* Jan. 25, Feb. 1, 8, 15, Aug. 16–Sept. 13, 1803, Feb. 21, 1804; Goebel and Smith, eds., *LPAH,* I, 784–785, 793–794; *The Speeches at Full Length of Mr. Van Ness, Mr. Caines, the Attorney-General, Mr. Harrison, and General Hamilton, in the Great Cause of the People, against Harry Croswell, on an Indictment for a Libel on Thomas Jefferson, President of the United*

States (New York, 1804). Croswell's representation at the second trial also included James Cott Smith, and at the third trial George Harrison.

36. Martin Van Buren, Kinderhook, to William P. Van Ness, NYC, July 30, 1803, MVBP; Goebel and Smith, eds., *LPAH,* I, 794–806; Pasley, *"The Tyranny of Printers,"* 268–269; Norman L. Rosenberg, *Protecting the Best Men: An Interpretive History of the Law of Libel* (Chapel Hill, N.C., 1986), 109–115.

37. Hudson *Bee,* Feb. 19, 1805; Hudson *Balance,* Apr. 16, 19, 1805. See also Jan. 25, Feb. 1, 22, Mar. 1, 8, 15, 22, Apr. 5, 12, 1805; *NYAJ,* 27th sess., 1804, 35, 28th sess., 1805, 10, 94, 341.

38. Goebel and Smith, eds., *LPAH,* I, 785, 793, III, 361–364.

39. Van Buren, *Inquiry into the Origin and Course of Political Parties,* 3–4. Here see the discussion in Wallace, "Changing Concepts of Party," *AHR,* LXXIV (1968), 453–491.

40. John P. Kaminski, *George Clinton: Yeoman Politician of the New Republic* (Madison, Wis., 1993), 270–274. W. P. Van Ness was "Aristides of Columbia County" in the April 1804 Hudson *Balance;* see Edward A. Collier, *A History of Old Kinderhook* . . . (New York, 1914), 394–395; Isenberg, *Fallen Founder,* 256–269; Joanne B. Freeman, *Affairs of Honor: National Politics in the New Republic* (New Haven, Conn., 2001), 180, 188, 190–195.

41. The office of the Poughkeepsie *American Farmer,* a title that echoed Livingston's self-image, published Robert R. Livingston's catalog of books in 1800. One of the editors was Isaac Mitchell, whose editorship of the Poughkeepsie *Political Barometer* and the Albany *Northern Crisis* was consistently "Lewisite" in politics. Mitchell was also involved in the Poughkeepsie *Guardian,* a precursor to the *Barometer.* See Isaac Mitchell, Poughkeepsie, to Robert R. Livingston et al., Clermont, Apr. 23, 1806, WFP-UM; Isaac Mitchell, Albany, to Robert R. Livingston, Clermont, Mar. 15, 1808, and Robert R. Livingston, Clermont, to Isaac Mitchell, Albany, June 4, 1808, RRLP; Hamilton, *The Country Printer,* 286. Quote from Charles Holt, Hudson, to William Wilson, Clermont, Aug. 27, 1802, WWP-BC.

42. Hudson *Balance,* Apr. 30, 1805; Miller, *Historical Sketches of Hudson,* 67; Henry Livingston, Ancram, to William Wilson, Clermont, Oct. 3, 1806, Alexander Thompson, Rhinebeck, to William Wilson, Clermont, Nov. 13, 1806, Sylvester Roberts, Hudson, to William Wilson, Clermont, Dec. 11, 1806, WFP-UM. The Lansingburgh *Farmers' Register* commenced publication in January 1803, and Genêt, married to Clinton's sister, began receiving letters at Clinton's residence in Albany the following August. Both Adancourt and Genêt were members of a small, close-knit community of French exiles living in the adjacent river towns of Lansingburgh, Troy, and Greenbush in the Jeffersonian era. In 1821 Adancourt published Genêt's address before the Rensselaer Agricultural Society. Robert R. Livingston, Clermont, to Edward Livingston, New Orleans, Apr. 13, 1806, RRLP.

43. Hudson *Bee,* July 19, 1803; *New-York Evening Post,* May 31, 1803, extract in the Hudson *Bee,* June 14, 1803; *Speeches at Full Length,* 42; Donna Lee Dickinson, *The Course of Tolerance: Freedom of the Press in Nineteenth-Century America* (Westport, Conn., 1990), 24; Finnegan, "Defamation, Politics, and the Social Process of Law," 167–173. On the political functions of libel cases, see Pasley, *"The Tyranny of Printers,"* 268, 274–284; Finnegan, "Defamation, Politics, and the Social Process of Law," 136–183, and, for a list of thirty-five libel cases in New York from 1802 to 1816, 401. For a discussion on political warfare in print, see Freeman, *Affairs of Honor,* 105–158.

44. Pasley's *"Tyranny of Printers"* can be read as an extended analysis of this problem.

45. Alexis de Tocqueville, *Democracy in America,* trans. Henry Reeves, rev. Francis Bowen, ed. Phillips Bradley (New York, 1945), I, 226, 233–235. For an important discussion of corruption in

the early Republic, focusing on Pennsylvania but formative to my discussion here, see John M. Murrin, "Escaping Perfidious Albion: Federalism, Fear of Aristocracy, and the Democratization of Corruption in Postrevolutionary America," in Richard K. Matthews, ed., *Virtue, Corruption, and Self-Interest: Political Values in the Eighteenth Century* (Bethlehem, Pa., 1994), 103–147. See also John Joseph Wallis's analysis of systemic and venal corruption, in "The Concept of Systemic Corruption in American History," in Edward L. Glaeser and Claudia Goldin, eds., *Corruption and Reform: Lessons from America's Economic History* (Chicago, 2006), 21–60.

46. See Edward Pessen, "Corruption and the Politics of Pragmatism: Reflections on the Jacksonian Era," in Abraham Eisenstadt, Ari Hoogenboom, and Hans Trefousse, eds., *Before Watergate: Problems of Corruption in American Society* (New York, 1978), 79–98.

47. Alexander Hamilton, Philadelphia, to ———, Sept. 21, 1792, in Syrett et al., eds., *PAH,* XII, 408; Alfred F. Young, *The Democratic Republicans of New York: The Origins, 1763–1797* (Chapel Hill, N.C., 1967), 239–243. See list of applications and grants in *NYAJ*, 15th sess., 1792, 182–200; Doctor Pomeroy's Affidavit, Kinderhook, Apr. 20, 1792, in the De Witt Clinton Broadside Collection, AIHA.

48. Accusations against Jay focused on his negotiation of the 1795 treaty with Great Britain, in which he was accused of selling his country for "British gold."

49. Tocqueville, *Democracy in America,* ed. Bradley, I, 226, 233–235.

50. Peter R. Livingston, Manor, to Walter Livingston, New York City, Feb. 10, 1785, William Wilson, Clermont, to Edward P. Livingston, Paris, July 6, 1802, RRLP; Charles A. Foote, Kinderhook, to Ebenezer Foote, Delhi, May 16, 1805, box 2, folder 60, EFP.

51. Hudson *Bee,* Apr. 12, 1803; William B. Hatcher, *Edward Livingston: Jeffersonian Republican and Jacksonian Democrat* (Baton Rouge, La., 1940), 93–99; Hudson *Balance,* Mar. 22, Apr. 26, 1803, Apr. 3, 1804; *Poughkeepsie Journal,* Mar. 27, 1804; Hudson *Northern Whig,* Apr. 25, May 2, 23, 1809, Mar. 15, Apr. 12, 19, 1810; Albany *Balance,* Mar. 9, 13, 16, 20, 27, 1810; Fox, *The Decline of Aristocracy,* 64–65; Craig Hanyan, *De Witt Clinton: Years of Molding, 1769–1807* (New York, 1988), 347–348; Robert E. Wright, "Banking and Politics in New York, 1784–1829" (Ph.D. diss., SUNY Buffalo, 1996), 447–449; Ray W. Irwin, *Daniel D. Tompkins: Governor of New York and Vice President of the United States* (New York, 1968), 279–312.

52. Jacob R. Van Rensselaer, Claverack, to Ebenezer Foote, Delhi, May 9, 1809, EFP; Hudson *Balance,* Apr. 26, 1803.

53. Gunn, *The Decline of Authority,* 79–94.

54. For an overview of turnpike incorporation, see Daniel B. Klein and John Majewski, "Economy, Community, and Law: The Turnpike Movement in New York, 1797–1845," *Law and Society Review,* XXVI (1992), 469–512, and charts, 480, 483; for academies and mechanics' societies, see Elsie Garland Hobson, *Educational Legislation and Administration in the State of New York from 1777 to 1850* (Chicago, 1918), 180–201; and for all corporations except libraries, see Aaron Clark, *List of All the Incorporations in the State of New-York, except Religious Incorporations . . .* (Albany, N.Y., 1819).

55. Naomi R. Lamoreaux, *Insider Lending: Banks, Personal Connections, and Economic Development in Industrial New England* (New York, 1994); capitalization data from Wright, "Banking and Politics," v; recapitalizations not calculated for this discussion.

56. Fischer, *The Revolution of American Conservatism,* 417–418; Pasley, *"The Tyranny of Printers,"* 407–410.

57. *Albany Register,* Apr. 14, 1801.

58. Votes in *NYAJ*, 25th sess., 1802, 133–134, 137–139, 171–172, 176, 215–216, 229, 259, 274, 282, 285–286. The year 1802 was also one of the last years in which the assembly voted on issues emanating from the emancipation legislation, specifically whether the state should support children of slaves. Slaveholding interests supported a continuing state role, rather than having the expense fall on county rates. Federalists were the least likely to oppose the slaveholding interest (38 percent), compared to antiturnpike Republicans (48 percent), Republicans opposed to theaters (54 percent), and Republicans who opposed altering the charter of the New York Social Library (69 percent). See votes in *NYAJ*, 25th sess., 1802, 231–232.

59. The Younglove-Watson debate can be followed in the Elkanah Watson Commonplace Book, Watson Papers, 1774–1885, NYSL, and in the *Albany Register;* Younglove's first letter is in the *Albany Register,* Mar. 2, 1802.

60. *Albany Register,* Mar. 2, 9, 23, 1802; on the Canaan Democratic Society, see the *Hudson Gazette,* Feb. 20, 1794, Mar. 26, 1795.

61. Hudson *Columbia Republican,* May 18, 1828.

62. The history of this session is detailed in Wright, "Banking and Politics," 290–313.

63. *Albany Centinel,* Mar. 1, 8, Apr. 5, 8, 15, 1803; Wright, "Banking and Politics," 291–300, 313. The *Albany Gazette,* nominally Federalist, stayed out of the battle.

64. [Samuel Stringer], *A View of Certain Proceedings in the Two Houses of the Legislature, respecting the Incorporation of the New State Bank . . .* (Albany, N.Y., 1803), 4, 16.

65. *Albany Register,* Apr. 19, 22, 1803; Hudson *Balance,* Jan. 25–May 10, 1803; *Hudson Gazette,* Apr. 26, 1803.

66. Goebel and Smith, eds., *LPAH,* I, 796; *Albany Register,* Feb. 21, 1804; Hudson *Bee,* Mar. 13, 1804.

67. *NYAJ,* 27th sess., 1804, 130, 135, 137, 216, 217, 221–222; John R. Livingston, NYC, to Robert R. Livingston, Paris, Apr. 12, 1804, RRLP; Hudson *Balance,* Mar. 20, 27, Apr. 24, 1804; Hudson *Bee,* Apr. 24, May 1, 1804; Lansingburgh *Farmers' Register,* May 1, 1804; *New-York Herald,* Apr. 17, 1805; Wright, "Banking and Politics," 325–335, 350.

68. *NYAJ,* 28th sess., 1805, 94, 341; Dickerson, *The Course of Tolerance,* 22, 24–25; Rosenberg, *Protecting the Best Men,* 114–115; *New-York Herald,* Apr. 17, 1805. In the spring of 1804 William W. Van Ness was removed by the Clintonian Council of Appointment from the post of Columbia County surrogate, which he had held since 1800. His 1800 appointment seems to have been intended to mollify yet block his Burrite Republican Van Ness cousins; his removal was equally political. His successors were James I. Van Alen (1804–1808) and Martin Van Buren (1808–1812), half brothers from Kinderhook and important Clintonian allies.

69. Elisha Jenkins, Albany, to De Witt Clinton, NYC, Mar. 13, 1805, DWCP-CU; *NYAJ,* 28th sess., 1805, 222–226, 231, 245–247, 270; New York *American Citizen,* Apr. 9, 1805; *NY Laws,* 28th sess., 1805, chap. 43. Senator Stephen Hogeboom, a probank Republican from Claverack, again supported the bank. Wright, "Banking and Politics," 349–360 (esp. 355–356), has a slightly different interpretation of these events.

70. New York *American Citizen,* Mar. 23, Apr. 5, 6, 8, 13, 1805; Hudson *Bee,* Apr. 2, 16, 1805; Hammond, *Political Parties,* I, 333. The April vote on Cheetham and the libel exactly followed the division on the bank, dividing even the small group of twelve Republicans who had voted in February to override the council's veto of the 1804 libel law. There was no roll call on the 1805 libel law as a whole. *NYAJ,* 28th sess., 1805, 93–94, 336–337. Suggestively, Van Ness's paper, the Hudson

Balance, had refrained in 1803 from attacking the Republicans when they were accused of corrupting the legislature to incorporate the state bank. The *Hudson Gazette* published excerpts and the appendix from the *View of Certain Proceedings* (Apr. 26, May 3, 1803), and Federalist papers north and south of Hudson similarly used the Albany accusations against the state bank in their final campaign efforts in late April 1803. The Hudson *Balance* had avoided any mention of the imputed corruption, holding to its established material on the Croswell case and the dismissal of John C. Ten Broeck. Hudson *Balance,* Apr. 19, 26, 1803; *Troy Gazette,* Apr. 26, 1803; *Poughkeepsie Journal,* Apr. 26, 1803; *New-York Herald,* Apr. 23, 1803.

71. William W. Van Ness, Hudson, to Ebenezer Foote, Delhi, May 6, 1805, EFP; Hudson *Balance,* Apr. 9, 16, 23, 30, May 7, 1804; Hudson *Bee,* Apr. 23, 1805, Apr. 7, 1807; Alexander, *A Political History of the State of New York,* 156–157.

72. Ellis, *Columbia County,* 178; Elisha Williams, Hudson, to Ebenezer Foote, Delhi, Mar. 8, 1807, EFP; see Wright, "Banking and Politics," for Williams's wider career.

73. [James Cheetham], *An Impartial Enquiry into Certain Parts of the Conduct of Governor Lewis . . .* (New York, 1806), 9; Hudson *Bee,* Mar. 31, 1807; Wright, "Politics and Banking," 418–428.

74. See Finnegan, "Defamation, Politics, and the Social Process of Law," 177–183, 401.

75. This passage summarizes arguments developed in Rosenberg, *Protecting the Best Men,* 110–115.

76. Elisha Williams, Hudson, to Ebenezer Foote, Delhi, Mar. 8, 1807, EFP; Hudson *Bee,* Apr. 30, 1805, Apr. 28, 1807, Apr. 19, 1808, Jan. 9, 1810; Hudson *Northern Whig,* Apr. 25, May 2, 1809, Jan. 4, 1810; Francis Stebbins, Hudson, to Martin Van Buren, Hudson, Oct. 20, 1809, Martin Van Buren, Hudson, to Elisha Williams, Hudson, Nov. 11, 1809, Jacob R. Van Rensselaer, Hudson, to Martin Van Buren, Hudson, Nov. 11, 1809, Martin Van Buren, Hudson, to Jacob R. Van Rensselaer, Hudson, Dec. 29, 1809, John C. Hogeboom, Albany, to Martin Van Buren, Hudson, Jan. 9, 1810, MVBP.

77. Charles A. Foote, Kinderhook, to Ebenezer Foote, Delhi, Sept. 7, 1805, Mar. 11, 1807, EFP; Miller, *Historical Sketches of Hudson,* 66; Fitzpatrick, ed., *Autobiography of Van Buren,* 26–28; *Assault and Battery: Report of the Trials of the Causes of Elisha Jenkins vs. Solomon Van Rensselaer . . .* (Albany, N.Y., 1808), 12–30.

78. Miller, *Historical Sketches of Hudson,* 48; Hudson *Northern Whig,* July 11, 1809; Hudson *Bee,* July 6, 1810. On violence, see Marshall Smelser, "The Federalist Period as an Age of Passion," *American Quarterly,* X (1958), 391–419; John R. Howe, "Republican Thought and the Political Violence of the 1790s," *American Quarterly,* XIX (1967), 147–165; Freeman, *Affairs of Honor.* On partisan militias, see Albrecht Koschnik, *"Let a Common Interest Bind Us Together": Associations, Partisanship, and Culture in Philadelphia, 1775–1840* (Charlottesville, Va., 2007), 90–152.

79. Peter Van Schaack, Kinderhook, to Peter Van Gaasbeck, Kingston, Apr. 12, 1792, Van Gaasbeck Papers, Senate House Museum, Kingston, N.Y.

80. Ambrose Spencer, Hudson, to William Wilson, Clermont, May 1, 1802, WFP-UM; Hudson *Balance,* May 1, 1804. The Republicans had again been unrealistically optimistic about their chances in the "lower towns": see Charles Holt, Hudson, to William Wilson, Clermont, Apr. 25, 1804, Philip S. Parker, Hudson, to William Wilson, Clermont, Apr. 25, 1804, WFP-UM.

81. Hudson *Bee,* Apr. 26, 1803. May 1, 1804, May 6, 1806. There had been attacks on Livingston and Van Rensselaer coercion of their tenants in the 1792 election: *Hudson Gazette,* July 19, Sept. 13,

1792. Political expectations might have had a role in the terms of land sales and mortgages by the Van Rensselaers in Hillsdale prior to the legislative settlement of 1804, since they tended to go to men who served on Federalist committees.

82. Hudson *Bee,* Apr. 23, 30, 1805, Apr. 15, 1806, Mar. 31, May 12, 1807.

83. Here I summarize the account in Mushkat and Rayback, *Martin Van Buren,* 21–25. See also Minute Book, Constitution, and By-Laws of the Kinderhook Law Society, NYSL; Holland, *Life and Political Opinions of Martin Van Buren,* 56.

84. John C. Hogeboom, Albany, to Martin Van Buren, NYC, Mar. 14, 1803, MVP; Fitzpatrick, ed., *Autobiography of Van Buren,* 15–16; Niven, *Martin Van Buren,* 18; Cole, *Martin Van Buren,* 18–19; Holland, *Life and Opinions of Martin Van Buren,* 51–57.

85. Hudson *Bee,* Apr. 9, 16, 1805, Apr. 15, 1806, Mar. 17 (resolves of January 13 meeting), Apr. 7, 1807; Charles A. Foote, Kinderhook, to Ebenezer Foote, Delhi, Apr. 20, May 4, 1806, EFP. On Van Buren's role as a lobbyist in 1808, see Wright, "Banking and Politics," 419; Mushkat and Rayback, *Martin Van Buren,* 28–29, 39–40.

86. Population trends calculated from the census for 1800 and 1810; see also David Maldwin Ellis, *Landlords and Farmers in the Hudson-Mohawk Region, 1790–1850* (Ithaca, N.Y., 1946), 19, 119, 121, 161.

87. Alfred Young, "The Mechanics and the Jeffersonians: New York, 1789–1801," *Labor History,* V (1964), 274; Sidney I. Pomerantz, *New York, an American City, 1783–1803: A Study of Urban Life* (New York, 1938), 134–135, 208; Gustavus Myers, *The History of Tammany Hall* (1917; rpt. New York, 1968), 14–16; Jerome Mushkat, *Tammany: The Evolution of a Political Machine, 1789–1865* (Syracuse, N.Y., 1971), 26–27. William P. Van Ness was one of the managers of the New York City system.

88. In the spring of 1807 Elisha Williams was confident of a 200–300 vote majority for assembly candidates and the Lewis ticket. Elisha Williams, Hudson, to Abraham Van Vechten, Albany, Apr. 25, 1807, X973 C72 F, 11:108, Rare Book and Manuscript Library, Columbia University.

89. Martin Van Buren, Hudson, to DeWitt Clinton, NYC, Apr. 19, 1810, DWCP-CU (emphasis in original).

90. Ibid., NYC, Apr. 28, 1810. The four towns that Van Buren noted, Livingston, Gallitan, Hudson, and Claverack, show the highest ratios of votes cast by one hundred pound freeholders.

91. Elisha Williams, Hudson, to Ebenezer Foote, Delhi, Mar. 24, 1809, Mar. 23, 1810, Jacob R. Van Rensselaer, Hudson, to Ebenezer Foote, Delhi, May 9, 1809, EFP.

92. *NYAJ,* 34th sess., 1811, 231, 251–252, 310–311, 315–316, 351, 359–360, 394–395, 401, 404–406; *NYSJ,* 34th sess. 1811, 143–145, 163–164, 193, 196–197, 199–201; *NY Laws,* 34th sess., 1811, chap. 201. See Fox, *Decline of Aristocracy,* 146–148. This law's racial dimensions are discussed in Chapter 9.

93. Van Buren, *Inquiry into the Origin and Course of Political Parties,* 4; Hudson *Bee,* Feb. 4, 1812; Jabez D. Hammond, *The History of Political Parties in the State of New-York . . .* (Cooperstown, N.Y., 1846), I, 335–336, 518–519; *Proceedings of the Committee, Appointed to Inquire into the Official Conduct of William W. Van Ness . . .* (New York, 1820), esp. 9–17; Wright, "Banking and Politics," 505–506; *NYAJ,* 35th sess., 1812, 265.

94. Hudson *Bee,* Apr. 14, May 12, 1812; Elam Tilden, Canaan, to Daniel D. Tompkins, Albany, Apr. 6, 1812, Box 84/DT-8, Daniel D. Tompkins Papers, NYSA, is only one of a series of letters supporting the governor's prorogation in 1812.

95. James N. Younglove and Thelma L. Butler, *Descendants of Samuel and Margaret Younglove*

(Houston, Tex., 1995), 16; *Albany Centinel,* Apr. 16, 1803; Wright, "Banking and Politics," 769–770; Holland, *Life and Political Opinions of Martin Van Buren,* 85–87; Fitzpatrick, ed., *Autobiography of Van Buren,* 28–29. On Tilden and Van Buren in 1837, see Chapter 10.

96. Hudson *Bee,* Mar. 17, Apr. 7, 21, 28, 1812; Hudson *Northern Whig,* Apr. 20, 1812; Fitzpatrick, ed., *Autobiography of Van Buren,* 29–33; Niven, *Martin Van Buren,* 27–32. See also Jacob Van Ness, Red Hook, to William Wilson, Clermont, May 1, 11, 16, 1812, WFP-UM.

97. Mushkat and Rayback, *Martin Van Buren,* 70; Niven, *Martin Van Buren,* 33.

98. John Benthuysen, Albany, to William Wilson, Clermont. Mar. 28, 1800, Robert L. Livingston, Clermont, to William Wilson, Clermont, Apr. 13, 1812, WFP-UM; Hudson *Bee,* Apr. 21, 1812. See also Jacob Van Ness, Red Hook, to William Wilson, Clermont, Apr. 29, 1812, WFP-UM. Peter Van Ness was notorious for his pursuit of personal interest. Regarding a land issue in 1792, Jacob Ford wrote to Peter Van Schaack that "PVN [is] almost Rum Mad — he has even attacked me on the subject with sparkling eyes and pale quivering lips, however I fastened my eyes on his with as stern a countenance as I believe it is in power to put on and gave him his change in full, even to a farthing": Jacob Ford, NYC, to Peter Van Schaack, Kinderhook, Apr. 1, 1792, VSP/LC; see NYALG, LI, 86.

99. Fitzpatrick, ed., *Autobiography of Van Buren,* 36–44; Niven, *Martin Van Buren,* 27–34; Cole, *Martin Van Buren,* 34–36, Mushkat and Rayback, *Martin Van Buren,* 69–71. During this factional rift, Van Buren attempted to intervene — to no avail — in an episode of literary politics, when Clinton skewered Spencer in a series of four satirical essays titled the "Spenceroniad," published in the New York *Statesman,* Oct. 17, 20, 29, Dec. 1, 1812. Forty years later Van Buren remembered this as the "Ambrosiad" published in the *American Citizen,* a forerunner of the *Statesman* discontinued in 1810. Fitzpatrick, ed., *Autobiography of Van Buren,* 41–43.

100. Fitzpatrick, ed., *Autobiography of Van Buren,* 46–47; Niven, *Martin Van Buren,* 35–39; Cole, *Martin Van Buren,* 36–37; *Albany Argus,* Mar. 23, 26, 1813.

101. Albany *Argus,* Mar. 23, 1813; Wright, "Banking and Politics," 771, 775–776; Fitzpatrick, ed., *Autobiography of Van Buren,* 32, 44.

102. It was a grand irony that Van Buren's program to both stabilize banking and solidify the grip of the Democratic Party, the Safety Fund Act of 1829, would generate a wave of partisan corruption — and fundamental banking reforms enacted in 1838 by the Whigs. Here see Howard Bodenhorn, "Bank Chartering and Political Corruption in Antebellum New York: Free Banking as Reform," in Glaeser and Goldin, eds., *Corruption and Reform,* 231–257.

103. Here I have been influenced on the theoretical side by Michael W. Foley and Bob Edwards, "The Paradox of Civil Society," *Journal of Democracy,* VII, no. 3 (July 1996), 38–52; Michael Schudson, "The 'Public Sphere' and Its Problems: Bringing the State (Back) In," *Notre Dame Journal of Law, Ethics, and Public Policy,* VIII (1994), 529–546; Charles Taylor, "Modes of Civil Society," *Public Culture,* III (1990), 95–118; and on the historical side by the classic discussion in Lee Benson, *The Concept of Jacksonian Democracy: New York as a Test Case* (Princeton, N.J., 1960); Harry L. Watson, *Liberty and Power: The Politics of Jacksonian America* (New York, 1990); Larson, *Internal Improvement;* Leonard, "Party as a 'Political Safeguard of Federalism,'" *Rutgers Law Review,* LIV (2001–2002), 221–281, and *The Invention of Party Politics.* I have elaborated my thinking here in "Patriarchal Magistrates, Associated Improvers, and Monitoring Militias: Visions of Self-Government in the Early American Republic, 1760–1840," in Peter Thompson and Peter Onuf, eds., *State and Citizen: British America and the Early United States* (forthcoming).

104. Ellis, *Columbia County,* 195–196; *Columbia Magazine; Designed to Promote Evangelical*

Knowledge and Morality: To Oppose the Prevailing Licentiousness of Manners . . . (Hudson, N.Y.), I (1815), 23, 60–61, 173–185; *Transactions of a Convention of Delegates from Several Moral Societies, in the State of New-York* . . . (Albany, N.Y., 1819), 3 (Berkshire and Columbia Missionary Society, Columbia Moral Society, Hudson Missionary Society); Hudson *Northern Whig,* Sept. 6, 1811, Feb. 3, 24, 1812, Feb. 2, 16, 1813, Feb. 8, Mar. 1, 1814 (Washington Benevolent Society), Sept. 20, 1814 (Berkshire and Columbia Missionary Society), Oct. 22, 1816, Nov. 7, 1820 (Columbia County Auxiliary Bible Society); *Religious Intelligencer,* Oct. 17, 1818, 310–311 (Columbia County Auxiliary Bible Society). Van Ness and Williams did not join the Moral Society, but three other Bible Society Federalists from Hudson did; one, attorney James Strong, was also a member of the Hudson Missionary Society, the Washington Benevolent Society, and the Lancaster School Society, founded in 1817 (*NY Laws,* 1817, 40th sess., chap. 323). At least fourteen Federalists were among the founders of the Bible Society; of the five Republicans, three were also members of the Moral Society.

105. On the Federalists, Whiggism and civil society: Koschnik, *"Let a Common Interest Bind Us Together,"* 153–227; Daniel Walker Howe, *The Political Culture of the American Whigs* (Chicago, 1979); Howe, "The Evangelical Movement and Political Culture in the North during the Second Party System," *JAH,* LXXVII (1990–1991), 1216–1239; A. G. Roeber, *Palatines, Liberty, and Property: German Lutherans in Colonial British America* (Baltimore, 1993); Alice P. Kenney, *Stubborn for Liberty: The Dutch in New York* (Syracuse, N.Y., 1975); Benson, *The Concept of Jacksonian Democracy;* Formisano, "Political Character, Antipartyism, and the Second Party System," *American Quarterly,* XXI (1969), 683–709. On the Democrats and civil society: Leonard, "Party as a 'Political Safeguard of Federalism,'" *Rutgers Law Review,* LV (2001–2002), 221–281; Leonard, *The Invention of Party Politics;* Wilson, "Republicanism and the Idea of Party in the Jacksonian Period," *Journal of the Early Republic,* VIII (1988), 419–442.

CHAPTER 8

1. Hudson *Balance, and Columbian Repository,* Jan. 5, 19, Nov. 23, 1802. The Senex series began with the May 4, 1802, issue.

2. Stephen B. Miller, *Historical Sketches of Hudson* . . . (Hudson, N.Y., 1862; rpt. 1985), 86; [Thomas Foster], *A Narrative of the Proceedings in America, of the Society called Quakers, in the Case of Hannah Barnard: With a Brief Review of the Previous Transactions in Great Britain and Ireland: Intended as a Sequel to An Appeal to the Society of Friends* (London, 1804), 67–68.

3. Ignatius Jones [Gorham A. Worth], *Recollections of Albany and Hudson, with Anecdotes and Sketches of Men and Things* (Albany, N.Y., 1850), 20 (2d pag. series); [Foster], *A Narrative of the Proceedings in America,* 39–40, 59, 67–68; [Hannah Barnard], *Considerations on the Matters of Difference between the Friends of London and Hannah Barnard* (Hudson, N.Y., 1802). The text on p. 36 suggests that this was printed after her January 26 "silencing" but before her provisional disownment by the Hudson Monthly Meeting on April 2, later confirmed by the Nine Partners Quarterly Meeting.

4. A month after the final votes on emancipation had been cast at Albany in 1799, a Federalist meeting in Spencertown chaired by Elisha Williams reported receiving a message from an "electioneering Jacobin." The Federalist reaction encompassed contempt for blacks, their Dutch owners, and their Republican opposition and anticipated the tone of the *Wasp:* "[A] motion was made and seconded that the said message be redelivered to Hogeboom's Negro, and on the question's being put by the chairman, it passed in the affirmative without a dissenting voice, and as

no person present would debase himself so much as to deliver said message, it was unanimously committed to the flames." *Hudson Gazette,* Apr. 23, 1799.

5. In this formulation, and in my wider analysis of gender and the public sphere in the early Republic, I am informed by Rosemarie Zagarri, *Revolutionary Backlash: Women and Politics in the Early American Republic* (Philadelphia, 2007); Mary Kelley, *Learning to Stand and Speak: Women, Education, and Public Life in America's Republic* (Chapel Hill, N.C., 2006); Gillian Brown, *The Consent of the Governed: The Lockean Legacy in Early American Culture* (Cambridge, Mass., 2001), Andrew McCann, *Cultural Politics in the 1790s: Literature, Radicalism, and the Public Sphere* (London, 1999); Linda K. Kerber, *No Constitutional Right to Be Ladies: Women and the Obligations of Citizenship* (New York, 1998); Kerber, *Women of the Republic: Intellect and Ideology in Revolutionary America* (Chapel Hill, N.C., 1980); Nancy Isenberg, *Sex and Citizenship in Antebellum America* (Chapel Hill, N.C., 1998); Joan B. Landes, *Women and the Public Sphere in the Age of the French Revolution* (Ithaca, N.Y., 1988); Carol Pateman, *The Problem of Political Obligation: A Critical Analysis of Liberal Theory* (New York, 1979); Dana D. Nelson, "Women in Public," and Fredrika J. Teute, "The Uses of Writing in Margaret Bayard Smith's New Nation," in Dale M. Bauer and Philip Gould, eds., *The Cambridge Companion to Nineteenth-Century American Women's Writing* (New York, 2001), 38–68, 203–220; Carroll Smith-Rosenberg, "Dis-covering the Subject of the 'Great Constitutional Discussion,' 1786–1789," *Journal of American History,* LXXIX (1992–1993), 841–873; Nancy Fraser, "Rethinking the Public Sphere: A Contribution to the Critique of Actually Existing Democracy," and Mary Ryan, "Gender and Public Access: Women's Politics in Nineteenth-Century America," in Craig Calhoun, ed., *Habermas and the Public Sphere* (Cambridge, Mass., 1994), 109–143, 259–289.

6. "Bill of sale for a Negro Boy named Sharp," John Elwyn, Saugerties, to William Wilson, Clermont, Jan. 25, 1811, WFP-UM; The Diary of Catherine Livingston Garrettson, May 29, 1788, transcribed in Diane Helen Lobody, "Lost in the Ocean of Love: The Mystical Writings of Catherine Livingston Garrettson" (Ph.D. diss., Drew University, 1990), 235; Samuel B. Webb, New York, to Catherine Hogeboom, Claverack, Apr. 27, May 4, June 26, July 6, 10, 13, 20, 25, 27, Sept. 11, Oct. 16, 1788, Mar. 22, Apr. 19, 26, May 3, June 7, Sept. 6, Nov. 15, 1789, in Worthington Chauncey Ford, ed., *Correspondence and Journals of Samuel Blachley Webb* (New York, 1893–1894), III, 98, 100, 107, 108, 110–112, 115–118, 125, 128–129, 133–134, 136–141, 144–145; Margaret Beekman Livingston, Clermont, to Robert R. Livingston. NYC, April 1789, RRLP.

7. *Albany Register,* Mar. 17, 1794; Hudson *Balance,* Feb. 17, 1807; Peter B. Collins, Pine Plains, to William Wilson, Clermont, May 13, 1805, WFP-UM.

8. Among the celebrations recorded in the Hudson papers before 1814, toasts to the women of America, in various formulas, can be found in the *New-York Daily Gazette,* Mar. 7, 1794; *Hudson Gazette,* July 7, 1801, Hudson *Balance,* July 9, 1801 (both reporting the same Federalist and Republican celebrations), July 12 (Mechanics Society), July 19, 1803, July 10, 1804, July 7 (Hudson Volunteers), 14, 1807, July 12, 1808; Hudson *Bee,* July 12 (Mechanics Society), 19, 1803 (Hudson Republican Young Men), July 10 (Hudson Republicans), 24, 1804 (Spencertown Republicans), July 15, 1806 (Clermont Republicans), July 14, 1807 (Hudson Volunteers), July 6, 1810, July 12, 19, 1811, July 14, 1812; Hudson *Northern Whig,* July 11, 1809, July 13, 1810, July 12, 1811, July 13, 1813, July 12, 1814. A Republican meeting in Canaan in March 1804, another in Kinderhook in July, and a July 1811 meeting in Hudson did not bother to offer a toast to American womanhood (Hudson *Bee,* Mar. 27, July 10, 1804, July 7, 1811). None of the five July Fourth or February Twenty-second orations printed in the county (Grosvenor, 1808; Jordan, 1810; Strong, 1811; Darling, 1816;

Church, 1819) addressed the women of the county. For discussions of gender in these celebrations, see David Waldstreicher, *In the Midst of Perpetual Fetes: The Making of American Nationalism, 1776–1820* (Chapel Hill, N.C., 1997), 89, 167–169, 233–234, 236–238; Simon P. Newman, *Parades and Politics of the Street: Festive Culture in the Early American Republic* (Philadelphia, 1997), 87, 95, 102–103, 106–107, 117; Zagarri, *Revolutionary Backlash,* 68–75.

9. Rosalind Remer, *Printers and Men of Capital: Philadelphia Book Publishers in the New Republic* (Philadelphia, 1996), esp. 24–99, discusses this process of specialization in a much larger context.

10. Hudson *Balance,* May 21, July 2, Oct. 22, Nov. 5, 1801, Jan. 19, 26, Feb. 16, June 15, Nov. 16, 1802, Feb. 21, 1804. The six-part "Alfred" series ran in the Hudson *Balance* on July 23, 30, Aug. 6, 20, Sept. 3–10, 17, 1801; the "Restorator" on Sept. 17, 24, and Oct. 1, 1801. There were responses in the *Hudson Gazette,* Sept. 15, Oct. 6, 1801. The one library trustee who actually responded to Alfred under his own name was Dr. John Milton Mann. Mann was listed on the committee advancing the candidacy of Federalist Stephen Van Rensselaer for governor in April 1801, indicating that the Hudson debate over Godwin did not necessarily track on partisan politics. For subsequent essays in Federalist papers urging that women limit their thinking about politics, see Hudson *Balance,* Jan. 28, 1806, and Hudson *Northern Whig,* July 11, 1809.

11. Hudson *Bee,* Aug. 17, 1802, Mar. 15, 1803.

12. *Hudson Gazette,* Oct. 8, 1799, Feb. 17, 24, 1801, Feb. 16, 1802, Feb. 22, 29 [Mar. 1], 1803; Philadelphia *Port Folio,* Jan. 16, 1802. The "American Lounger" series ran in the *Hudson Gazette* from Feb. 16, 1802, through Sept. 13, 1803. William C. Dowling, *Literary Federalism in the Age of Jefferson: Joseph Dennie and "The Port Folio," 1801–1812* (Columbia, S.C., 1999), 66, discusses the grounding of the "American Lounger" in Mackenzie's *Lounger.* My brief characterization differs from his assessment and is based on my reading of Stoddard's reprintings, the discussions of Mackenzie in G. J. Barker-Benfield, *The Culture of Sensibility: Sex and Society in Eighteenth-Century Britain* (Chicago, 1992), 141–148; and of Dennie in Catherine O'Donnell Kaplan, *Men of Letters in the Early Republic: Cultivating Forums of Citizenship* (Chapel Hill, N.C., 2008), 114–183.

13. Hudson *Balance,* Oct. 1, 1801. On the reaction to Wollstonecraft, see Zagarri, *Revolutionary Backlash,* 40–44, 106–107; Susan Branson, *These Fiery Frenchified Dames: Women and Political Culture in Early National Philadelphia* (Philadelphia, 2001), 49–52, 164 n. 90; Chandos Michael Brown, "Mary Wollstonecraft, or, the Female Illuminati: The Campaign against Women and 'Modern Philosophy' in the Early Republic," *Journal of the Early Republic,* XV (1995), 389–424; Barker-Benfield, *The Culture of Sensibility,* 368–382; R. M. Janes, "On the Reception of Mary Wollstonecraft's 'A Vindication of the Rights of Woman,'" *Journal of the History of Ideas,* XXXIX (1978), 293–302. The London proceedings against Barnard began in May 1800 and ended in August 1801. *An Appeal to the Society of Friends, on the Primitive Simplicity of Their Christian Principles and Church Doctrines; and on Some Recent Proceedings in the Said Society* (London, 1801) included the details of her trial through May 1801. The precise date of Barnard's return to Hudson is unknown, but she left London on Aug. 30, 1801.

14. Hudson *Balance,* Jan. 19, 26, Feb. 9, 1802; *Hudson Gazette,* Mar. 2, 1802. On Lucy and reading, see Chapter 4. It seems likely that Barnard herself wrote the Aunt Susie essay, as the language resembles that of her *Dialogues on Domestic and Rural Economy, and the Fashionable Follies of the World,* published in Hudson in 1820.

15. [Barnard], *Considerations on the Matters of Difference;* [Stéphanie Félicité Genlis], *The History of the Duchess of C——* (Hudson, N.Y., 1803), includes "Story of a Castilian" and "Story of

Miss Warner, by Miss Griffiths." Susanna Rowson, *The History of Charlotte Temple: A Tale of Truth* (Hudson, N.Y., 1803). Unfortunately, there are no surviving issues of the *Gazette* between Mar. 16 and Sept. 28, 1802.

16. Amelia Simmons, *American Cookery; or, The Art of Dressing Viands . . .* , 2d ed. (Albany, N.Y., [1796]) (Evans 38505). *Evelina* (Evans 29996) is known to have been been written by Fanny Burney, but she was not credited in the 1796 Albany edition printed by Thomas, Andrews, and Penniman. *Lessons for Children, from Two to Four Years Old . . .* (Albany, N.Y., 1797) (AAS only, not in Readex), printed by Stoddard's former associates, the Websters, was attributed to a "Mrs. Barbault" only in the preface. Similarly, the 1798 edition of Hannah Foster, *The Boarding School* (Evans 33748), printed in Boston and sold in Albany by Thomas, Andrews, and Penniman, was credited to "a lady in Massachusetts." Sarah Alley, *An Account of a Trance or Vision of Sarah Alley, of Beekman Town, Dutchess County, State of New-York . . .* (Poughkeepsie, N.Y., 1798) (Evans 33287); Naomi Rogers, *Verses Composed upon the Awful and Sudden Death of Oliver Hall . . .* (Troy, N.Y., 1798[?]) (Evans 49713); Ann Ward Radcliffe, *The Italian; or, The Confessional of the Black Penitents* (Mount Pleasant, N.Y., 1797) (Evans 32735).

17. Here I am thinking about the implications of Michael Warner, *The Letters of the Republic: Publication and the Public Sphere in Eighteenth-Century America* (Cambridge, Mass., 1990); Steven Watts, *The Republic Reborn: War and the Making of Liberal America, 1790–1820* (Baltimore, 1987); Grantland S. Rice, *The Transformation of Authorship in America* (Chicago, 1997).

18. See Table 22. For the sake of simplicity, I have included in this Republican group Hezekiah Steele, a Republican printer working in Hudson between 1807 and roughly 1811, who did not put out a newspaper.

19. Troy *Northern Budget*, Nov. 22, 1803, Mar. 10, 1807; *A Catalogue of Books . . . Which Will Be Sold at the New York Price, Wholesale or Retail, By Penniman and Bliss, at the Lansingburgh Bookstore . . .* ([Lansingburgh, N.Y.], 1805) (Shaw-Shoemaker 9114); Hudson *Bee*, Dec. 28, 1802, Jan. 4, 1803, July 14, Nov. 3, Dec. 1, 1807, Jan. 12, Oct. 11, 1808; *Poughkeepsie Journal*, esp. Mar. 8, 1809; Poughkeepsie *Political Barometer*, Dec. 4, 1804, July 5, 1809, Oct. 24, 1810, Jan. 9, 1811.

20. For discussions of gender and the political culture of the early Republic that suggest a similar affinity of Federalism and female audience, see Waldstreicher, *In the Midst of Perpetual Fetes*, 167; Newman, *Parades and Politics of the Streets*, 95, 102–106, 117; Branson, *These Fiery Frenchified Dames*, 97. Zagarri, in *Revolutionary Backlash*, focuses on the different partisan constructions of women. Here, above and below, my tripartite division between Augustan Federalist ideologues, moral-sentimental Federalist moderates, and monitorial Republicans would suggest that, rather than a broad affinity between women and Federalism, there was an affinity between women and one strand of Federalism. By and large, and specifically in New York, these two modes of Federalism would divide around 1820 into "high-minded" and Clintonian factions, the former going to the Bucktails and eventually the Jacksonian Democrats, the latter toward the National Republicans and eventually the evangelical-allied Whigs.

21. These serializations ran in the Poughkeepsie *Political Barometer*, June 8–July 13, 1802 ("Albert and Eliza"), July 27–Aug. 17, 1802 ("The Shield of Expectation"), Aug. 24–Sept. 7, 1802 ("Edric of the Forest"), Oct. 19–Nov. 30, 1802 ("Perourou"), Dec. 7, 1802–Jan. 18, 1803 ("Schabraco"), June 5–Oct. 30, 1804 ("Alonzo and Melissa"). The sixth issue of the Kingston *Plebeian*, Aug. 3, 1803, continued "Albert and Eliza" from the fourth issue, and similarly on Jan. 25, 1804, Mar. 11, Sept. 23, 30, 1805.

22. Poughkeepsie *Political Barometer*, Oct. 30, 1804. Mitchell also warned off other printers

from reprinting his novel and promised to take out a copyright. *The Asylum* first appeared as Isaac Mitchell, *The Asylum; or, Alonzo and Melissa: An American Tale, Founded on Fact* (Poughkeepsie, N.Y., 1811).

23. On female consent, see Brown, *The Consent of the Governed*, 107–176.

24. Quotes from the Poughkeepsie *Political Barometer*, Oct. 30, 1804. My approach to the supernatural gothic is shaped by reading in Cathy N. Davidson, *Revolution and the Word: The Rise of the Novel in America* (New York, 1986), 212–253, esp., 225–230; E. J. Clery, *The Rise of Supernatural Fiction, 1762–1800* (New York, 1995); 133–171; McCann, *Cultural Politics in the 1790s*, 71–82, 107–144. See also Karen Halttunen, *Murder Most Foul: The Killer and the American Gothic Imagination* (Cambridge, Mass., 1998), 33–60.

25. William Durell published Ann Radcliffe, *The Italians*, in 1797 in Mount Pleasant; in 1798 he was convicted of libeling President John Adams in his *Mount Pleasant Register*, which he published from 1797 to 1800; New York *Commercial Advertiser*, April 17, 1800. Hudson *Balance*, July 30, Sept. 3, 17, 1801 ("Alfred" refers to a "printed catalogue" of the Hudson Library collection that has not survived); Hudson *Wasp*, July 3, 1802; Hudson *Bee*, Aug. 20, 1805.

26. Albany Library, *Additional Catalogue, 1797* (Albany, N.Y., 1797), 5, 7; *Catalogue of Books, in the Library of the Hon. Robert R. Livingston of Clermont, February 1800* (Poughkeepsie, N.Y., 1800); catalogs of William Wilson's books, Aug. 18, 1801, Aug. 1, 1807 (9:64), WFP-UM. In Troy, the Federalist-dominated library in 1800 did not have anything by Radcliffe, Lewis, or Wollstonecraft, but Federalists Obadiah Penniman and William Bliss carried at their Lansingburgh Bookstore copies of both *The Monk* and *The Mysteries of Udolpho*. *Laws and Catalogue of Troy Library* (Troy, N.Y., [1805]); *Catalogue of Books at the Lansingburgh Bookstore*, 27; *Hudson Gazette*, Nov. 10, 1801. My assessment of book availability is based on a review of the booksellers' lists printed in the *Gazette, Bee, Balance*, and the *Northern Whig* for the years 1801–1803, 1807–1809, and 1811. The books might well have been available but not advertised to the public. See Nancy Isenberg, *Fallen Founder: The Life of Aaron Burr* (New York, 2007), 74–75, 80–83.

27. The 1793–1794 Dutchess Academy trustees are listed in Samuel Mott's *Almanack and Ephemeris, for the Year of Our Lord 1794* (Poughkeepsie, N.Y., [1793]); of twenty-five trustees, nine were or would be Federalist and seven Republican. The students are taken from two broadsides titled *Catalogue of the Members of the Troy Female Seminary*, for the terms ending Aug. 2, 1824, and Aug. 1, 1825, printed by Francis Adincourt, Troy. Merab A. Bradley, Troy, to Jonathan D. Bradley, Westminster, Vt., Mar. 15, 1823 (I, 17), Bradley Family Collection, Schlesinger Library, Radcliffe Institute, Harvard University.

28. On the Hudson Academy: Hudson *Balance*, May 14, 1805, Apr. 16, Dec. 16, 1806, Jan. 13, 1807, Sept. 22, 1807; Hudson *Bee* ("A Friend to Genius"), Mar. 19–June 18, 1805; Ellis, *Columbia County*, 190–191, 195–196. Examples of Hudson Academy stock dated July 1806 are preserved in box 2, Van Rensselaer-Fort Papers, NYPL. The 1796 effort seems to have generated at least one essay on female education, stressing the need for basics rather than genteel "embellishments": *Hudson Gazette*, Sept. 15, 1796. Senex series "On Education," Hudson *Balance*, May 4–Nov. 20, 1801; *A Series of Letters on Courtship and Marriage, to Which Are Added Witherspoon's Letters . . .* (Hudson, N.Y., 1804), 1–16.

29. The Wilson daughters' education can be followed in Frances Wilson, Hudson and Albany, to William Wilson, Clermont, May 2, 1802, Jan. 5, Feb. 6, 1803, Apr. 10, May 6, 1804, Isabella Bell, Albany, to William Wilson, Clermont, June 6, 1806; accounts for Mary Wilson, Pleasant Val-

ley School, Aug. 15, 1806, Fyler Dibblee, Rhinebeck steamboat, to William Wilson, Clermont, May 19, 1810, E. J. Paine, Poughkeepsie, to William Wilson, Clermont, July 18, 1810, WFP-UM; Frances Wilson, Hudson, to Alexander Wilson, Clermont, May 19, 1802, Frances Wilson, Hudson and Albany, to William Wilson, Clermont, July 28, 1802, Jan. 4, Apr. 23, 1803, Mar. 25, 1804, Feb. 3, 1806, WWP-BC. On this suggestion that Quiddish Republicans in the middle of the ideological spectrum seem to have had the more secular approach to gender and education, see Nancy Isenberg's account of Aaron Burr, his wife and daughter, and their reading of Rousseau and Wollstonecraft in *Fallen Founder,* 55–83, esp. 74–75, 80–83.

30. *Census of the State of New York, for 1845, Containing an Enumeration of the Inhabitants of the State, with Other Statistical Information* ... (Albany, N.Y., 1846). By the 1850s Hudson had two recently established girls' schools, a seminary founded in 1848 and an academy founded in 1851. Ellis, *Columbia County,* 196; J. H. French, *Gazetteer of the State of New York* ... (Syracuse, N.Y., 1860), 247, 275, 278, 560–561; Charles D. King, *History of Education in Dutchess County* (Cape May, N.J., 1959), 50–51, 58–60. Anne Firor Scott, "The Ever Widening Circle: The Diffusion of Feminist Values from the Troy Female Seminary, 1822–1872," *History of Education Quarterly,* XIX (1979), 3–25; Mary J. M. Fairbanks, *Emma Willard and Her Pupils; or, Fifty Years of Troy Female Seminary, 1822–1872* (New York, 1898).

31. On Booth and Vassar, see Benson J. Lossing, *Vassar College and Its Founder* (New York, 1867), 59. The early history of the founding of Vassar College is given in Dorothy A. Plum et al., comps., *The Magnificent Enterprise: A Chronicle of Vassar College* (Poughkeepsie, N.Y., 1961), 1–5; Lydia Booth and the Van Kleecks are listed among the early students in Litchfield in Theodore Sizer and Nancy Sizer et al., *To Ornament Their Minds: Sarah Pierce's Litchfield Female Academy, 1792–1833* (Litchfield, Conn., 1993), 116, 130. Another manifestation of a special space for women in Poughkeepsie's public was the Poughkeepsie Female Bible Society, founded in 1814, which included five women from the Vassar and Booth families. *The First Annual Report of the Board of Managers of the Poughkeepsie Female Bible Society* ... (Poughkeepsie, N.Y., 1815).

32. This framework is suggested variously by Susan Juster, *Disorderly Women: Sexual Politics and Evangelicalism in Revolutionary New England* (Ithaca, N.Y., 1994); Christine Leigh Heyrman, *Southern Cross: The Beginnings of the Bible Belt* (New York, 1997); Catherine A. Brekus, *Strangers and Pilgrims: Female Preaching in America, 1740–1845* (Chapel Hill, N.C., 1998), 23–67; Catherine Allgor, *Parlor Politics: In Which the Ladies of Washington Help Build a City and Government* (Charlottesville, Va., 2000); Lobody, "Lost in the Ocean of Love: The Mystical Writings of Catherine Livingston Garrettson," 20–27, 103–136; Fredrika J. Teute, "Roman Matron on the Banks of Tiber Creek: Margaret Bayard Smith and the Politicization of Spheres in the Nation's Capital," in Donald R. Kennon, *A Republic for the Ages: The United States Capitol and the Political Culture of the Early Republic* (Charlottesville, Va., 1999), 89–121; Kerber, *Women of the Republic,* 185–232; Landes, *Women and the Public Sphere;* Carla Mulford, "Political Poetics: Annis Boudinot Stockton and Middle Atlantic Women's Culture," *New Jersey History,* CXI, nos. 1–2 (Spring/Summer 1993), 66–110; Cynthia A. Kierner, "Patrician Womanhood in the Early Republic: The 'Reminiscenses' of Janet Livingston Montgomery," *New York History,* LXXIII (1992), 389–407; Dena Goodman, "Enlightenment Salons: The Convergence of Female and Philosophic Ambitions," *Eighteenth-Century Studies,* XXII (1989), 329–350.

33. T. D. Seymour Bassett, "Hannah Jenkins Barnard (1754?–1825)," in *Notable American Women, 1607–1950* (Cambridge, Mass., 1971), I, 88, argued that she was childless; Latter-day

Saints' records show two children, born in 1775 and 1777. On fertility decline and women's assertion of self in the wake of the Revolution, see Susan E. Klepp, "Revolutionary Bodies: Women and the Fertility Transition in the Mid-Atlantic Region, 1760–1820," *JAH,* LXXXV (1998–1999), 910–945.

34. Thomas Brown, *An Account of the People Called Shakers: Their Faith, Doctrines, and Practice . . .* (Troy, N.Y., 1812), 84, 96. The Westenhook-Mawighnunk context for the Shaker squatter settlement at New Lebanon emerged in an exchange with Thomas Donnelly, Shaker historian, in September 2003. See the map in NYALG, XXXIV, 75, reproduced in Sung Bok Kim, *Landlord and Tenant in Colonial New York: Manorial Society, 1664–1775* (Chapel Hill, N.C., 1978), 413, and the extended discussion of the Canaan settlement, Chapter 5, above. On Lucy Wright's first years at New Lebanon, see Calvin Green, "Biographic Memoir of the Life, Character, and Important Events, in the Ministration of Mother Lucy Wright," New Lebanon, 1861, MS, SC-WRHS, 5–9; Rufus Bishop and Seth Y. Wells, eds., *Testimonies of the Life, Character, Revelations and Doctrines of Our Ever Blessed Mother Ann Lee . . .* (Hancock, Mass., 1816), 76; Stephen A. Marini, *Radical Sects of Revolutionary New England* (Cambridge, Mass., 1982), 52–53, 78–80, 95–96; Stephen J. Stein, *The Shaker Experience in America: A History of the United Society of Believers* (New Haven, Conn., 1992), 12–14. According to Shaker lore, Colonel John Brown visited Mother Ann Lee in the Albany jail on his way to Stone Arabia in 1780, promising to become a Shaker if he survived the coming campaign. Brown, *An Account of the People Called Shakers,* 120; Benson J. Lossing, *The Pictorial Field-Book of the Revolution* (New York, 1851), I, 281 n. 4.

35. Ellis, *Columbia County,* 308, 310–311.

36. Bishop and Wells, eds., *Testimonies,* 63; Brown, *Account of the People Called Shakers,* 129. Gilbert and a number of other Masons made their peace with the Shakers by 1816 and signed the 1816 petition to grant them relief from militia duties. "To the Honourable the Legislature . . . The memorial and petition of the undersigned inhabitants of the towns of Canaan and Watervliet [Shakers . . . conscientiously opposed to doing military duty] . . . , Feb. 13, 1816," SC-WRHS (IA10). On Masons, Shakers, and early modern radical mystical and restorationist traditions, see John L. Brooke, *The Refiner's Fire: The Making of Mormon Cosmology, 1644–1844* (New York, 1994), 94–102, 282–283.

37. James Whitaker, *A Concise Statement of the Principles of the Only True Church . . .* (Bennington, Vt., 1790), 16; Green, "Biographic Memoir of Lucy Wright," 5–6, 9–28; Joseph Meacham to Lucy Wright, 1796, New Lebanon Correspondence (IVA30), SC-WRHS; Jean M. Humez, "'Weary of Petticoat Government': The Specter of Female Rule in Early Nineteenth-Century Shaker Politics," *Communal Societies,* XI (1991), 1–17, esp. 2–5; Stein, *The Shaker Experience in America,* 41–49; Marini, *Radical Sects,* 25–59; Edward Deming Andrews, *The People Called Shakers: A Search for the Perfect Society* (New York, 1953), 53–65.

38. Green, "Biographic Memoir of Lucy Wright," 10; Paltsits, ed., *Minutes,* II, 452–453, 469–471, 504, 541–542, 573–575, 589, 592; Bishop and Wells, eds., *Testimonies,* 182–195; James Whitaker, Niskayuna, to Henry Van Schaack, Richmond, Nov. 13, 1784, Henry Van Schaack to James Whitaker, n.d., Shaker Museum Collections, Old Chatham, N.Y. See also Marini, *Radical Sects,* 112–113; Stein, *The Shaker Experience in America,* 34–35, 52; Andrews, *The People Called Shakers,* 43–44.

39. Andrews, *The People Called Shakers,* 57–58; Stein, *The Shaker Experience in America,* 44–45; Green, "Biographic Memoir of Lucy Wright," 18; Angell Mathewson, "Reminiscences in

the Form of a Series of Thirty-Nine Letters to his Brother Jeffrey," NYPL Shaker MSS, item 119, letter 23 (pp. 7–8).

40. Stein, *The Shaker Experience in America,* 49–66; Pricilla J. Brewer, *Shaker Communities, Shaker Lives* (Hanover, N.H., 1985), 30–35.

41. Quotes from Bishop and Wells, eds., *Testimonies,* 21; Mathewson, "Reminiscences," NYPL Shaker MSS, item 119, letter 24 (p. 4); and New Lebanon Ministry to Alfred Ministry, July 30, 1816, New Lebanon Correspondence, SC-WRHS (IVA33). "A Short Account of the Rise of the Believers . . . ," SC-WRHS, 28, 32. See the discussions in Humez, "'Weary of Petticoat Government,'" *Communal Societies,* XI (1991), 1–17; Brewer, *Shaker Communities,* 28–29; Stein, *The Shaker Experience in America,* 52–53, 92, 129; Jean M. Humez, *Mother's First-Born Daughters: Early Shaker Writings on Women and Religion* (Bloomington, Ind., 1993), 65–68. Benjamin Goodrich, the elder of the junior order who lost his suit for wages in 1799, was the brother or cousin of Elizer Goodrich, Lucy Wright's former husband. I rely upon Thomas Donnelly's reconstructed list of the 1795–1796 seceders.

42. Brown, *Account of the People Called Shakers,* 222–226; David Rossiter et al. to the New York State Legislature, Mar. 22, 1800, SC-WRHS (IA10); Jan. 5, 1800, North Family New Lebanon Shaker Covenant, SC-WRHS (IA10); June 24, 1801 New Lebanon Shaker Covenant, SC-WRHS (IB29). Of the 1795–1796 seceders, twenty-three were men, and eight were women. (Lists developed by Thomas Donnelly.) For examples of intrafamilial struggle over Shaker conversion, see Brown, *Account of the People Called Shakers,* 339–340.

43. Mathewson, "Reminiscences," NYPL Shaker Mss., item 119, letters 3 (pp. 2–4), 4 (pp. 5–6), 22 (pp. 1–2), 24 (p. 2); Brown, *Account of the People Called Shakers,* 321.

44. Brown, *Account of the People Called Shakers,* 226–229, 236; Seth Y. Wells, "A Few Remarks upon Learning and the Use of Books, for the Consideration of the Youth, among Believers" (1823), MSS collection, United Society of Shakers, Sabbathday Lake, Maine, 1–2; "A Short Account of the Rise of the Believers," 34, 52, 81, 85 (see 32, 33, 36, 44, 46, 47 for references to the administration of the initiate order for young Shakers, between November 1799 and March 1807); Edward Deming Andrews and Faith Andrews, "The Shaker Children's Order," *Winterthur Portfolio,* VIII (1973), 201–204.

45. Theodore E. Johnston, "The 'Millennial Laws' of 1821," *Shaker Quarterly,* VII (1967), 48–52; Wells, "A Few Remarks," 6–8. The 1821 proscriptions were repeated in 1845 and 1860 but loosened in 1864, with the exception of novels. Andrews, *The People Called Shakers,* 245, 273, 276–277; Stein, *The Shaker Experience in America,* 203–204.

46. Green, "Biographic Memoir," 6, 82–83; Stein, *The Shaker Experience in America,* 9, 101; Brewer, *Shaker Communities,* 37; Andrews and Andrews, "The Shaker Children's Order," *Winterthur Portfolio,* VIII (1973), 205.

47. Green, "Biographic Memoir of Lucy Wright," 32–33; "A Short Account of the Rise of the Believers," 49, 53; Johnston, ed., "The 'Millennial Laws' of 1821," *Shaker Quarterly,* VII (1967), 35–37; Brewer, *Shaker Communities,* 35; Humez, *Mother's First-Born Daughters,* 68–69; Andrews, *The People Called Shakers,* 300 n. 8; Stein, *The Shaker Experience in America,* 66–87. The earliest Shaker imprint has traditionally been thought to be Seth Y. Wells, *Millennial Praises, Containing a Collection of Gospel Hymns . . .* (Hancock, Mass., 1813). According to Sharon Koomler, formerly curator at Hancock Shaker Village, earlier, undated copies may date to 1810–1811. The earliest New Lebanon imprint is *The Juvenile Monitor* (New Lebanon, N.Y., 1823). Shakers at Hancock

might have been printing broadside advertisements for seeds earlier in the decade; seed production for market began at New Lebanon in 1795 (Deborah E. Burns, *Shaker Cities of Peace, Love, and Union: A History of the Hancock Bishopric* [Hanover, N.H., 1993], 72–76).

48. Green, "Biographic Memoir," 83, 115.

49. As will be apparent, my discussion of Catherine Livingston Garrettson is indebted to Lobody, "Lost in the Ocean of Love: The Mystical Writings of Catherine Livingston Garrettson": both for her interpretation of Catherine's life (37–135), and her transcription of Catherine's diary (1787–1792) and exercise book (138–309). The original is Catherine Livingston Garrettson Diary, Garrettson Family Papers, Methodist Collection, Drew University, Madison, N.J. For a wider discussion of religious self-examination and writing among evangelical women, see Joanna Bowen Gillespie, "'The Clear Leadings of Providence': Pious Memoirs and the Problems of Self-Realization for Women in the Early Nineteenth Century," *Journal of the Early Republic*, V (1985), 197–221.

50. Lobody, "Lost in the Ocean of Love: The Mystical Writings of Catherine Livingston Garrettson," 44–49.

51. Catherine Garrettson Diary, ibid., 140–141, 148–149, 156, 167, 169, 201, 230, 239, 240.

52. Ibid., 209; here I follow Lobody's discussion, 103–119, esp 116; see also 52–55; Ruth Piwonka, *A Portrait of Livingston Manor, 1686–1850* (Clermont, N.Y., 1986), 144. For the scale of the Livingston library, see, *Catalogue of Books, in the Library of Livingston.*

53. Lobody, "Lost in the Ocean of Love: The Mystical Writings of Catherine Livingston Garrettson," 66–67, 103–135; Frank Hasbrouck, ed., *The History of Dutchess County, New York* (Poughkeepsie, N.Y., 1909), 434–435, 446, 448; John H. Wigger, *Taking Heaven by Storm: Methodism and the Rise of Popular Christianity in America* (New York, 1998), 104, 166–168, 173–195; Dee E. Andrews, *The Methodists and Revolutionary America, 1760–1800: The Shaping of an Evangelical Culture* (Princeton, N.J., 2000), 100–105; Jan Lewis, *The Pursuit of Happiness: Family and Values in Jefferson's Virginia* (New York, 1983), 49–68; Richard L. Bushman, *The Refinement of America: Persons, Houses, Cities* (New York, 1993), 219–226.

54. Marilyn Hilley Pettit, "Women, Sunday Schools, and Politics: Early National New York City, 1797–1827" (Ph.D. diss., New York University, 1991), 185–188; Kierner, "Patrician Womanhood," *New York History,* LXXIII (1992), 406;

55. [Foster], *A Narrative of the Proceedings in America,* ix; Bassett, "Hannah Jenkins Barnard," in *Notable American Women,* 88–89. Latter-day Saints' records say she was born in 1751.

56. "Minutes of the Committee relative to the Establishment of a Boarding School at the Nine Partners," New York Yearly Meeting Records, The Friends Library, Swarthmore College, I, 3–4, 12–13, 18, 22, 39, 51.

57. Hugh Barbour et al., *Quaker Crosscurrents: Three Hundred Years of Friends in the New York Yearly Meetings* (Syracuse, N.Y., 1995), 129, 141, 150–153; Helen W. Reynolds, "Nine Partners Patent, Nine Partners Meeting, and Nine Partners School," *Year Book of the Dutchess County Historical Society,* XX (1935), 25–47; Hasbrouck, ed., *Dutchess County,* 487–491.

58. Bassett, "Hannah Jenkins Barnard," in *Notable American Women,* 89; Bliss Forbush, *Elias Hicks: Quaker Liberal* (New York, 1956), 119, 185. There was no Unitarian church in Hudson, but a Universalist church was formed in 1817.

59. *NY Laws,* 29th sess., 1806, chap. 60; Peacher, "Craft Masonry," 344–345; Aaron Clark, comp., *List of All the Incorporations in the State of New York . . .* (Albany, N.Y., 1819), 88–90; *Constitution of the Ladies Society, Established in New-York, for the Relief of Poor Widows with Small*

Children (New York, 1799); *A Brief Account of the Society Established in the City of Albany for the Relief of Indigent Women and Children . . .* (Albany, N.Y., 1805); Irving E. Fancher, *A History of the Troy Orphan Asylum, 1833–1933* (Troy, N.Y., 1933), 1–2, 89–90; Anne M. Boylan, *The Origins of Women's Activism: New York and Boston, 1797–1840* (Chapel Hill, N.C., 2002), 27–24; Christine Stansell, *City of Women: Sex and Class in New York, 1789–1860* (New York, 1986), 68–75. For a careful analysis of a similarly elite composition of the Female Charitable Society formed in Rochester in 1822, dominated by Presbyterians and Anglicans, see Nancy A. Hewitt, *Women's Activism and Social Change: Rochester, New York, 1822–1872* (Ithaca, N.Y., 1984), 41–55. Only nine of the Troy benevolent women can be linked to partisan husbands, six Federalist and three Republican. Jonas Coe, the Presbyterian minister, and five of the six Federalists were also members of the Troy Library, and two of the Republicans were members of the Apollo Lodge.

60. My comments on the Benevolent Society officers draw on comparison of the lists in the reports published in the Hudson *Northern Whig,* Mar. 22, Apr. 12, 1811, June 23, 1813, Mar. 16, 1816, July 22, 1817, June 23, 1818, with political affiliations of husbands and the Quaker lists in "Hannah Barnard's Certificate from the Hudson Monthly Meeting, Oct. 26, 1797," Friends Library, Swarthmore College, and [Foster], *A Narrative of the Proceedings in America.* In a town where the other improving associations were strongly Federalist, it is striking that there were relatively few links between the Female Benevolent Society and the Bible Society, the Moral Society, the Hudson Lodge, or the Hudson Academy. There were clusters of connections to the Library Society and the Lancaster Society, founded in 1817 to educate the poor. Republican names seem to outnumber Federalist among known or probable fathers and husbands of the Benevolent Society officers, but these Republicans were (by 1820) moderate Clintonians rather than Old Republican Tompkinsites.

61. Henry P. Skinner Journal, Hudson, N.Y., Feb. 19, 1817, Clements Library, University of Michigan; "Extract from the Private Manuscript Diary of the late Mrs. William L. Stone . . . [1849]," in Robert M. Terry, comp., *The "Hudsonian," Old Times and New* (Hudson, N.Y., 1895), 170–171.

62. Hudson *Northern Whig,* Apr. 12, 1811, June 22, 1813.

63. Hannah Barnard, *Dialogues of Domestic and Rural Economy, and the Fashionable Follies of the World, Interspersed with Occasional Observations on Popular Opinions* (Hudson, N.Y., 1820), iii–iv, 44, 72. A section of the *Dialogues* (pp. 33–37) critiquing Milton's *Paradise Lost* was republished as *A Short Conversation . . . between the Late Hannah Barnard, of the City of Hudson, New York, and an Eminent Physician . . . on the Origins of the Devil and the Aspersions Cast on the Female Sex . . .* (Philadelphia, 1835).

64. These new journals included the *Casket,* Dec 7, 1811–May 30, 1812; the *Columbia Magazine,* September 1814–August 1815; the *Lounger,* pre-1817 (no extant issues); *Spirit of the Forum and Brief Remarker,* one issue, Apr. 16, 1817. Two other magazines, the *Messenger of Peace* (1824–1825) and the long-lived *Rural Repository* (1824–1851), were started the year before Barnard died.

65. For "Thrifty," see Barnard, *Dialogues,* 9–11. For the wider context of the critique of the novel, see Davidson, *Revolution and the Word,* 38–54.

66. Barnard, *Dialogues,* 44, 49.

67. Female Charitable Society of New Lebanon, [N.Y.], Records, 1814–1829, NYSL; letter from Canaan, Sept. 6, 1818, *Religious Intelligencer,* Oct. 17, 1818, 310–311.

68. For other approaches to this generational divide, see Kerber, *Women of the Republic;* Juster, *Disorderly Women;* Kelley, *Learning to Stand and Speak;* Zagarri, *Revolutionary Backlash.*

CHAPTER 9

1. For a modern discussion of citizenship and the 1821 convention, see Daniel J. Hulsebosch, *Constituting Empire: New York and the Transformation of Constitutionalism in the Atlantic World, 1664–1830* (Chapel Hill, N.C., 2005), 262–264. For a detailed guide, I have relied upon John Antony Casais, "The New York State Constitutional Convention of 1821 and Its Aftermath" (Ph.D. diss., Columbia University, 1967).

2. Nathaniel H. Carter and William L. Stone, eds., *Reports of the Proceedings and Debates of the Convention of 1821, Assembled for the Purpose of Amending the Constitution of the State of New York . . .* (Albany, N.Y., 1821), 248–249.

3. Ibid., 275, 277, 376, 557.

4. Ibid., 249–255, 265.

5. Ibid., 248. For the longer constitutional history of citizenship in New York State, see Phyllis F. Field, *The Politics of Race in New York: The Struggle for Black Suffrage in the Civil War Era* (Ithaca, N.Y., 1982); Ellen Carol DuBois, *Feminism and Suffrage: The Emergence of an Independent Women's Movement in America, 1848–1869* (New York, 1978); Faye Dudden, "New York Strategy: The New York Woman's Movement and the Civil War," in Jean H. Baker, ed., *Votes for Women: The Struggle for Suffrage Revisited* (New York, 2002), 56–76.

6. This discussion, based primarily on the aggregate and manuscript returns of the U.S. Census, 1790–1860, and the 1799–1800 Assessments for Columbia County, NYSA, is indebted to the interpretations developed in Shane White, *Somewhat More Independent: The End of Slavery in New York City, 1770–1810* (Athens, Ga., 1991); James Oliver Horton and Lois E. Horton, *In Hope of Liberty: Culture, Community, and Protest among Northern Free Blacks, 1700–1860* (New York, 1997), esp. 77–100; and Michael Edward Groth, "Forging Freedom in the Mid-Hudson Valley: The End of Slavery and the Formation of a Free African-American Community in Dutchess, County, N.Y." (Ph.D. diss., SUNY Binghamton, 1994), 128–238. See Tables 23 and 17 and discussion in final section of Chapter 6.

7. On John Lawrence, see Henry Livingston, Ancram, to William Wilson, Clermont, Sept. 10, 1797, WFP-UM. Most of Wilson's correspondence regarding people of color involved household work by slaves. Between 1810 and 1818, see letters from John Elwyn, Saugerties, Dec. 25, 1810, Jan. 25, 1811, Jacob Van Ness, Rhinebeck, July 14, 1812; Frederick Dibblee, NYC, May 22, 1813, Peter Cantine, Poughkeepsie(?), May 26, 1813, Richard H. Dibblee, Kinderhook, May 6, 1815, James Lee, New York, Aug. 12, 1818, WFP-UM. In 1819 Edward P. Livingston wrote Wilson from New York City regarding Bella, a women freed from his brother Robert R. Livingston's household, who was being returned to Clermont as a pauper. Feb. 17, 1819, WFP-UM.

8. This discussion is based on an analysis of the 1790, 1800, 1810, and 1820 manuscript census returns. For Ripley, see A. J. Williams-Myers, *Long Hammering: Essays on the Forging of an African American Presence in the Hudson River Valley to the Early Twentieth Century* (Trenton, N.J., 1994), 106.

9. George Holcomb Diary, Stephentown, Dec. 4, 1815, Mar. 30, 1816, MS at NYSL, typescript at Stephentown Historical Society. On itinerant families of native Americans, some intermarried with African Americans, see Daniel R. Mandell, *Behind the Frontier: Indians in Eighteenth-Century Eastern Massachusetts* (Lincoln, Nebr., 1996), 182–196. Martha Wetherbee and Nathan Taylor, *Legend of the Bushwhacker Basket* (Sanbornton, N.H., 1986), 19–20, detail the transfer of basketmaking skills from a surviving Mahican to white families in Taghkanic in the 1830s and

1840s. Data on David Ginnings, or Jennings, from Shaker records compiled by Thomas Donnelly, personal communication, Aug. 1, 4, 2003.

10. *NY Laws,* 34th sess., 1811, chap. 201; Hudson *Northern Whig,* Jan. 19, Feb. 16, Mar. 28, Apr. 20, Dec. 21, 1819, Feb. 1, May 2, Dec. 26, 1820; *Hudson Weekly Gazette,* Sept. 14, 1786, Aug. 2, 1787, Sept. 23, 1788; Hudson *Bee,* Sept. 10, 1805. See also John C. Fitzpatrick, ed., *The Autobiography of Martin Van Buren,* vol. II of *Annual Report of the American Historical Association for the Year 1918* (Washington, D.C., 1920), 64–65; Samuel Edmonds to William Wilson, July 9, 1810 (17:23) WFP-UM; Columbia County Oyer and Terminer Records, Sept. 17, 25, 1810, Columbia County Clerk's Office. The mob leader, Josiah Russell, was listed in Hillsdale in 1810, but apparently had moved to Hoosick in Rensselaer County by 1820. He did better than his possible relation Winslow Russell, hanged July 1811 in Troy for a murder in Hoosick. *The Trial and Conviction of Margaret Houghtaling (Who Was Executed at Hudson, Oct. 17th, 1817) for the Murder of Lewis Spencer, an Infant* (Albany, N.Y., [1817]). George Holcomb attended the executions of Winslow Russell and James Hamilton in Troy in 1811 and 1818 and reported estimates of crowds of ten to twelve thousand. George Holcomb Diary, July 19, 1811, Nov. 6, 1818. On Aug. 1, 1817, twelve days after Russell's execution, Holcomb borrowed a copy of *A Brief Account of the Trial of Winslow Russell . . .* [Troy, N.Y., 1811] (Shaw-Shoemaker 24060).

11. *NY Laws (Private Laws),* 33d sess., 1810, chaps. 82, 192; *NY Laws,* 35th sess., 1812, chap. 111. See Graham R. Hodges, *Root and Branch: African Americans in New York and East Jersey, 1613–1863* (Chapel Hill, N.C., 1999), 181, 183–184, 186–187, 224, 252; Horton and Horton, *In Hope of Liberty,* 127–128, 143; Craig Steven Wilder, *In the Company of Black Men: The African Influence on African American Culture in New York City* (New York, 2001), 6–49.

12. Holcomb Diary, July 7, 1822; 1795 pew list, in Royden W. Vosburgh, "Records of the Reformed Dutch Church of Kinderhook, in Kinderhook, Columbia County, N.Y.," typescript (1921), New York Genealogical and Historical Society, II, 282; George Holcomb Diary, Aug. 16, 1818. Preaching by men of color was not unknown in these towns at this date; John Beebe recorded on Oct. 22, 1779, that Samson Occum preached in New Concord, on a Friday. Diary of John Beebe, Jr., MS 11329, NYSL.

13. Shane White, "Pinkster: Afro-Dutch Syncretization in New York City and the Hudson Valley," *Journal of American Folklore,* CII (1989), 68–75; David S. Cohen, "In Search of Carolus Africanus Rex: Afro-Dutch Folklore in New York and New Jersey," *Journal of the Afro-American Historical and Genealogical Society,* V (1984), 149–162. The poem was also printed in Albany in 1803 by an unknown press "solely for the Purchasers and others," and possibly sold at the carnival itself: *A Pinkster Ode for the Year 1803, Most Respectfully Dedicated to Carolus Africanus, Rex; Thus Rendered in English: King Charles, Captain-General and Commander in Chief of the Pinkster Boys.* Ascribed on the title page to Absolom Aimwell, bibliographers have since credited the poem to Andrew Adgate of Philadelphia, who had published under that name earlier. But, since the poem includes a parody (9) of a Republican stump speaker advocating the State Bank project, which had been enormously controversial that spring, Adgate could not have been the author, since he died of yellow fever in 1793. Given the Federalist tone to this parody, it is unlikely that any of his Republican Adgate cousins in Canaan was the author.

14. Marion I. Hughes, *Refusing Ignorance: The Struggle to Educate Black Children in Albany, New York, 1816–1873* (Albany, N.Y., 1998), 13–28. *NY Laws,* 35th sess., 1812, chap. 55.

15. Ellis, *Columbia County,* 191–193. A project supported by De Witt Clinton, a Lancaster So-

ciety was also established in Catskill in 1817. *NY Laws,* 40th sess., 1817, chap. 87, 272; Stephen E. Siry, *De Witt Clinton and the American Political Economy: Sectionalism, Politics, and Republican Ideology, 1787–1828* (New York, 1990), 261–263; Evan Cornog, *The Birth of Empire: De Witt Clinton and the American Experience, 1769–1828* (New York, 1998), 70–71. *The First Annual Report of the Board of Inspectors of the Sunday School Association of the City of Troy: Read in the Presbyterean Church in This City, on Sunday July 13, 1817* (Troy, N.Y., 1817), 10. Hudson *Northern Whig,* Sept. 9, Dec. 2, 1817, Sept. 22, 1818, Feb. 15, Oct. 17, Nov. 14, Dec. 19, 1819. In the fall of 1824 there was a flurry of discussion in the black community in Troy about emigration to Haiti: Troy *Sentinel,* Oct. 26, 29, Nov. 12, 1824.

16. The complete title of this little-known pamphlet is worth citing in full: Jesse Torrey, Jr., *A Portraiture of Domestic Slavery in the United States: With Reflections on the Practicability of Restoring the Moral Rights of the Slave, without Impairing the Legal Privileges of the Possessor; and A Project for Colonial Asylum for Free Persons of Colour: Including Memoirs of Facts on the Interior Traffic in Slaves, and on Kidnapping, Illustrated with Engravings.* (Philadelphia, 1817); see 18, 21, 28–30, 58, 61, 85–94. See also the introduction by Edward Harmon Virgin to Jesse Torrey, Jr., *The Intellectual Torch, Developing a Plan for . . . Free Public Libraries* (Woodstock, Vt., 1912; orig. publ. Ballston Spa, N.Y., 1817), iii–v.

17. Torrey, *A Portraiture,* 40, 58–59, 62. This language almost exactly anticipated that of Abraham Lincoln in 1858; like Lincoln, Torrey also opposed interracial sex and marriage. Compare with the language of Elisha Williams, Martin Van Buren, and Jonas Platt in Carter and Stone, eds., *Reports of the Proceedings and Debates,* 249, 277, 374, 376.

18. *NYAJ,* 34th sess., 1811, 217–219; Petition to the New York Legislature against certain Livingston lands, [March] 1811, Livingston Family Papers (II, 14), Columbia University.

19. *NYAJ,* 34th sess., 1811, 217–218, 372–374; Hudson *Northern Whig,* Apr. 5, 12, 1811; *Decision in the Legislature, on the Petition of Henry Avery, Benjamin Birdsall, and Others, relative to the Title of the Manor of Livingston* (Albany, N.Y., 1811) (Shaw-Shoemaker 51121). On Apr. 4, 1811, the legislature passed a law regulating the boundary between Hillsdale and Granger and protecting the interests of Livingston landholding: any changes to the boundary would not "affect or injure the rights of individuals claiming property in either of the said towns." *NY Laws,* 34th sess., 1811, chap. 140.

20. Hudson *Bee,* Apr. 30, 1805. On April 12, 1811, immediately after the attorney general's decision was issued on April 3, the *Northern Whig* printed a long editorial on the Manor title. Benjamin Birdsall, Jr., and a committee of six others published a rebuttal in the *Bee* on April 19, promising "a concise and correct statement" regarding the Manor title. This statement, a six-column letter signed by Benjamin Birdsall, Jr., was published in the *Bee* on August 16, and the quotes here are from p. 2, col. 5, and p. 3, cols. 1, 2. This letter was followed by another in the *Bee* on August 30, but this issue has not survived, and we must rely on fragmentary text reprinted in the rebuttal in the *Northern Whig,* September 6.

21. Fitzpatrick, ed., *The Autobiography of Martin Van Buren,* 15–20. My reconstruction of the Birdsall claim is developed from a series of letters in the Wilson Family Papers, and Birdsall's Sept. 22, 1812, affidavit. The land that he was apparently granted in 1798 for fourteen years rent free was generally identified as the "Nicholas Drum Farm," which he had occupied since 1796, while his debts in the next decade involved rents due on "the Snyder farm." It is not clear whether these were actually different parcels. This land was located in Great Lot No. 2, inherited by the children of Robert Cambridge Livingston when he died in 1794 and administered by their uncle

Henry Livingston until their majority with the managerial and legal assistance of William Wilson and Peter Van Schaack. See the various letters to William Wilson, Clermont, from William H. Ludlow, Claverack, Mar. 23, 1798; Peter Van Schaack, Kinderhook, Dec. 10, 1798, Aug. 29, 1805, Sept. 7, 1808; Benjamin Birdsall, Jr., at Claverack Court House, May 12, 1801, Livingston/Granger, Mar. 16, 1803, Aug. 7, 1804, Mar. 15, 1805, Dec. 28, 1808; James Vanderpoel, Kinderhook, July 23, 1812; and Henry Livingston vs. Benjamin Birdsall, Jr., filed Aug. 8, 1801, Columbia County Clerk's Office, box 180; Benjamin Birdsall, Jr., vs. Robert Swift Livingston and others, Sept. 22, 1812, Martin Van Buren Papers, LC.

22. Ambrose Spencer, Hudson, to William Wilson, Clermont, May 1, 1802, with a copy of Wilson's reply, May 2, 1802, WFP-UM.

23. *NYSJ*, 26th sess., 1803, 63–64, 67–69; *NYAJ*, 26th sess., 1803, 85, 174, 193–194; *NY Laws*, 26th sess., 1803, chap. 43; Ambrose Spencer, Albany, to William Wilson, Clermont, Feb. 11, 1803; Alexander Wilson, Albany, to William Wilson, Clermont, Feb. 16, Mar. 13, 16, 25, 1803 (11:71, 74, 80, 82, 88), WFP-UM.

24. *NY Laws*, 37th sess., 1814, chap. 55.

25. Ellis, *Columbia County*, 398, 405; Hudson *Bee*, Apr. 19, 1803; Hudson *Balance, and Columbian Repository*, Apr. 19, 1803. The Livingston town records before 1803 had disappeared by the 1870s, so it is impossible to measure the local governmental experience of the new town officers in Granger and Gallatin. Ellis, *Columbia County*, 256.

26. For convenience, and since it was so small and so economically dependent on the Manor, I include freehold Germantown, with Clermont, Livingston, Granger, and Gallatin in my counts of voting in the "Manor region."

27. Henry Livingston, John's Town (Livingston Manor), to William Wilson, Clermont, Mar. 10, 17, 1804, WFP-UM.

28. Men from the Manor apparently did not join the Republican-dominated Columbia Lodge, formed in Claverack village in 1803. Reconstructed from Returns of the Temple, Vernon, Columbia, Clermont, and Hudson lodges, Livingston Library, NYGL; and from Peacher, "Craft Masonry," 340–343, 349–351.

29. John Francis Collin, *A History of Hillsdale, Columbia County, New York,* ed. H. S. Johnson (Philmont, N.Y., 1883), 36.

30. Hudson *Balance, and Columbian Repository*, Apr. 28, 1807, July 26, Aug. 16, 1808; Hudson *Bee*, Apr. 30, 1805; Charles A. Foote, Kinderhook, to Ebenezer Foote, Delhi, May 16, 1805, EFP; Hudson *Bee*, May 6, July 8, 1806, Apr. 7, 14, 1807; Edward P. Livingston, Clermont, to William Wilson, Clermont, Apr. 25, 1806; Thomas Tillotson, Albany to William Wilson, Clermont, Apr. 26, 1806, WFP-UM.

31. *NY Laws*, 31st sess., 1808, chap. 84; Ellis; *Columbia County*, 398; William M. Holland, *The Life and Political Opinions of Martin Van Buren, Vice President of the United States* (Hartford, Conn., 1835), 56–57; Jerome Mushkat and Joseph G. Rayback, *Martin Van Buren: Law, Politics, and the Shaping of Republican Ideology* (DeKalb, Ill., 1997), 32–40.

32. Martin Van Buren, Hudson, to De Witt Clinton, New York, Apr. 19, 28, 1810, DWCP-CU.

33. Hudson *Bee*, Apr. 18, 1809; Hudson *Northern Whig*, May 2, 1809; Mary Masters Allen Livingston Memorandum Book, 1811–1820, Dec. 1, 1811, Livingston Family Papers, CCHS; Roger G. Kennedy, *Orders from France: The American and French in a Revolutionary World, 1780–1820* (New York, 1989), 67–68.

34. Mary Masters Allen Livingston Memorandum Book, Jan. 1, 1811.

35. These details are from Mary Livingston et al., exec., vs. John Reynolds (January 1811), box 180; Writs served on John Reynolds, Jan. 15, 1811, Writs and Executions, 1811, box 228/229; Mary Livingston et al., exec. vs. John Reynolds, September (2d Monday), 1811 (two judgments), Judgement Rolls, 1811, box 180, bundle 2, Columbia County Clerk's Office. I am obliged to Ruth Piwonka for her assistance in finding these records.

36. Martin Van Buren, "Notes on the Livingston Grant," MVP-LC; "Petition to the New York Legislature against certain Livingston lands, 1811," Livingston Family Papers, NYHS. For a useful account of this phase of Van Buren's career, see Mushkat and Rayback, *Martin Van Buren*, 56–61.

37. "Debts and Rents due Estate of H. W. Livingston, Columbia County Surrogate's Office, transcribed in Arthur C. Kelly, comp., *Settlers and Residents*, III, part 1, *Town of Livingston, 1710–1899* (Rhinebeck, N.Y., 1973–[1989]), 107–109; Mary Livingston Memorandum Book, Jan. 1, 1811; Birdsall testimony, 1812, MVBP; James Duane Livingston Rent Book, 1806–1810, WWP-BC; map of the holdings of John S. Livingston, Great Lot No. 2/5, October 1810, Columbia County Clerk's Office; Ellis, *Columbia County*, 398. See Table 24.

38. I identify the Manor Committee from the composite signers of the Manor letter in the Hudson *Bee*, Apr. 19, 1811, and the Manor Committee letter to Governor Daniel D. Tompkins, June 15, 1812, Gubernatorial and Personal Documents of Daniel D. Tompkins, 1792–1823 (A0084), NYSA. Five of the nine men discussed here signed both letters, and seven of the nine also signed the 1811 petition in the first group of twenty-five signers. Mary Livingston's Memorandum Book provides supporting evidence. Of the nine men that I isolate as the Manor Committee, this passage discusses all but John I. Blass of Granger and Charles Suydam of Gallatin. Among the other Republican committeemen, not on this Manor Committee, Isaiah Esmund joined the Vernon Lodge at an unknown date, and Anthony W. Snyder joined in 1814. Masonic membership from Temple Lodge and Vernon Lodge Returns, Livingston Library, NYGL; Isaac Huntting, *History of Little Nine Partners of North East Precinct, and Pine Plains, New York . . .* (1897; rpt. Rhinebeck, N.Y., 1974), I, 149–153; Peacher, "Craft Masonry," 349–350; Return of the Clermont Lodge, Feb. 7, 1813, LL-NYGL.

39. *NYAJ*, 34th sess., 1811, 218, 367, 372–374; *NY Laws*, 34th sess., 1811, chap. 34; Hudson *Northern Whig*, Apr. 5, 12, 26, 1811; *Decision in the Legislature, on the Petition of Avery, Birdsall, and Others*. See also Edward P. Livingston, Albany, to William Wilson, Clermont, Mar. 8, 1811 (16:77); and Henry Livingston, Livingston, to William Wilson, Clermont, Mar. 9, 1811 (16:78), WFP-UM.

40. Hudson *Bee*, Apr. 19, 1811.

41. Martin Van Buren, Hudson, to De Witt Clinton, New York, Apr. 20, 1811, DWCP-CU.

42. Martin Van Buren, Hudson, to the Manor Committee, Granger, Apr. 25, 1811, Butler Family Papers, Princeton University, MVBP; Hudson *Bee*, July 12, 1811.

43. Martin Van Buren, Hudson, to Benjamin [Birdsall] and others—Committee [Granger], July 28, 1811, Butler Family Papers, Princeton University, MVBP. The case against the Livingston title rested in the argument that Robert Livingston had obtained a false confirmation of title to most of his land in 1715. In 1684 and 1685 he had been granted two small patents, one along the Hudson River and another to the east on the flat lands at Copake and Ancram. In 1715, the tenants, associated lawyers, and subsequent historians all agree, Livingston obtained a confirmation that named these two patents and all of the intervening lands, comprising the great bulk of the Manor. For historians' judgments on the questionable legality of the Manor title, see Lawrence H. Leder, *Robert Livingston, 1654–1728, and the Politics of Colonial New York* (Chapel Hill, N.C.,

1961), 35; Ruth Piwonka, *A Portrait of Livingston Manor, 1686–1850* (Clermont, N.Y., 1986), 24; James D. Livingston and Sherry D. Penney, "The Breakup of Livingston Manor," in Richard C. Wiles, ed., *The Livingston Legacy: Three Centuries of American History* ([Annandale-on-Hudson, N.Y.], 1987), 406–407; Cynthia A. Kierner, *Traders and Gentlefolk: The Livingstons of New York, 1675–1790* (Ithaca, N.Y., 1992), 26.

44. Hudson *Bee,* Apr. 19, Aug. 16, 1811.

45. Hudson *Northern Whig,* Aug. 16, 23, 1811. Van Buren denied the charge that he had written the Birdsall letter in a letter to Francis Stebbins dated August 29: *Northern Whig,* Sept. 6, 1811. Birdsall's brief communications with William Wilson in the previous decade do not suggest that he was particularly well lettered. However, the tone of the Van Buren letter to the committee signed on July 28 and of the Birdsall letter delivered to the *Bee* are very much at odds, one careful and reserved, even resigned, the other full of rhetoric of "oppression" and "first principles." The Birdsall letter is quite similar in language and tone to the Manor letter to Daniel Tompkins of July 1812, and both were at least reviewed by the same men. Alternatively, however, a careful analysis of the language and structure of the July 29 / Aug. 16 Birdsall letter might show similarities to Van Buren's first long public document extant, the Republican "Address" published in the *Albany Argus,* Mar. 23, 1813. Birdsall published a second "Manor Letter" in the *Bee* on Aug. 30, 1811, but unfortunately all copies of this issue have been lost, and thus the only record that survives of this second letter is excerpts in the *Northern Whig,* Sept. 6, 1811.

46. Collin, *History,* 3.

47. Fitzpatrick, ed., *Autobiography of Van Buren,* 24–27; Hudson *Northern Whig,* Apr. 26, Aug. 16, 23, 1811; Martin Van Buren, Hudson, to the Manor Committee, Granger, Apr. 25, 1811, Butler Family Papers, Princeton University, MVBP; Martin Van Buren, Hudson, to Francis Stebbins, Hudson, Aug. 19, 29, 1811; Martin Van Buren, Hudson, to Jacob R. Van Rensselaer, Claverack, Aug. 19, 1811; Francis Stebbins, Hudson, to Cornelius Miller, Hudson, Aug. 20, 1811; Jacob R. Van Rensselaer, Claverack, to Martin Van Buren, Hudson, Aug. 24, 1811, MVBP-LC; Hudson *Northern Whig,* Aug. 23, Sept. 6, 1811; Mary Livingston et al., exec. vs. John Reynolds, September (2d Monday), 1811 (two judgments), Judgement Rolls, 1811, box 180, bundle 2, Columbia County Clerk's Office; Mary Livingston, Livingston, to Jacob R. Van Rensselaer, Claverack, Apr. 23, 1814 (discusses the dispute over the Claverack–Great Lot No. 1 boundary and refers to a November 1811 letter from Van Buren), Livingston Papers, NYHS.

48. Fitzpatrick, ed., *Autobiography of Van Buren,* 26–27; Martin Van Buren, Hudson, to John Suydam, Hudson, Nov. 25, 1811, MVBP-LC; *Northern Whig,* Dec 9, 23, 30, 1811; Hudson *Bee,* Dec. 3, 17, 1811. Perhaps not coincidentally, John Suydam was the brother of Charles Suydam of Gallatin, who signed the Manor letter of April 19. Charles Suydam stood out on the Manor Committee, since he lived in the less militant of the Manor towns, had been a Federalist committeeman in 1810, and did not sign the March 1811 petition against the title. He might have been something of a spy planted among the Manor Committee. On the Armstrong duel and the local history of Boston Corners, see Frank Hasbrouck, ed., *The History of Dutchess County, New York* (Poughkeepsie, N.Y., 1909), 385–386; James H. Smith, *History of Duchess County, New York* (Syracuse, N.Y., 1882), 242.

49. Mary Livingston Memorandum Book, December summary, 1811; Clermont Lodge return, Livingston Library, NYGL; Ellis, *Columbia County,* 254–255, 397–399, 401; Kierner, *Traders and Gentlefolk,* 125, 155, 245–246; *Columbia Republican,* Jan. 9, 1821.

50. No copy of this petition survives, and most of the information on this Gore dispute comes

from Mary Livingston's Memorandum Book, Sept. 19, December summary, 1811, Mar. 20, Apr. 1, 1812.

51. Commissions received April 1812, in files of Military and Civil Commissions located in Book of Judgments, 1807–1817, Columbia County Clerk's Office; Ellis, *Columbia County,* 398; Hudson *Northern Whig,* May 11, 1812; Mushkat and Rayback, *Martin Van Buren,* 58–64. On Tompkins's prorogation in 1812, see Chapters 7, 10.

52. Mary Livingston Memorandum Book, Apr. 1, 1811, Apr. 7, May (n.d.) 1812; Benjamin Birdsall, Jr., vs. Robert L. Livingston and others, Sept. 22, 1812, MVBP-LC.

53. Benjamin Birdsall, Jr., John Reynolds, et al., Granger, to Daniel D. Tompkins, Albany, June 15, 1812, box 84-1, folder 40, Gubernatorial and Personal Records of Daniel D. Tompkins, 1792–1823, NYSA.

54. Benjamin Birdsall, Jr., et al., to Daniel D. Tompkins, 15 June, 1812, NYSA. The edges of this letter were burned in the 1811 State House fire; letters within brackets have been interpolated from context. The word that I have interpreted as "resentment" might have been "resistance."

55. The events of June 24–Aug. 14, 1812, can be followed in Henry Livingston, Gale's Tavern, to William Wilson, Clermont, June 25, 1812 (17:73); William W. Van Ness, Claverack, to William Wilson, Clermont, July 10, 1812 (17:79); Henry Livingston, Livingston, to William Wilson, Clermont, Aug. 1, 1812 (18:1), WFP-UM; Mary Livingston Memorandum Book, summer 1812 entry; Hudson *Northern Whig,* Aug. 24, 1812.

56. Oyer and Terminer Records, Columbia County Clerk's Office, Sept. 28, Oct. 2, 6–9, 13–14, 1812, June 10, Oct. 5, 8, 1813, Dec. 22, 1814, Aug. 31, 1815.

57. Hudson *Northern Whig,* Oct. 19, 1812, emphasis in original; Mary Livingston Memorandum Book, June 1815. See also *Albany Gazette,* Oct. 22, 1812, and Hudson *Bee,* Nov. 24, 1812.

58. Draft of letter on case of Van Tassell and Williams, (1812), MVBP-LC; Hudson *Northern Whig,* Oct. 12, 1813, emphasis in original; Mary Livingston Memorandum Book, January, Oct. 6, 1813.

59. *Albany Argus,* Mar. 23, 1813; *NYAJ,* 37th sess., 1814, 148, 187; *NYSJ,* 37th sess., 1814, 84, 128, 153; *NY Laws,* 37th sess., 1814, chap. 55.

60. Charles A. Foote, Kinderhook, to Ebenezer Foote, Delhi, Nov. 18, 1805, EFP.

61. My use of the term "social death" is an expansive appropriation from Orlando Patterson, *Slavery and Social Death: A Comparative Study* (Cambridge, Mass., 1982). On politics and race I am informed by David Waldstreicher, *In the Midst of Perpetual Fetes: The Making of American Nationalism, 1776–1820* (Chapel Hill, N.C., 1996), 294–348; Waldstreicher, "The Nationalization and Racialization of American Politics: Before, beneath, and between Parties, 1790–1840," in Byron E. Shafer and Anthony J. Badger, eds., *Contesting Democracy: Substance and Structure in American Political History, 1775–2000* (Lawrence, Kans., 2001), 37–64; Alexander Saxton, *The Rise and Fall of the White Republic: Class Politics and Mass Culture in Nineteenth-Century America* (New York, 1990); David R. Roediger, *The Wages of Whiteness: Race and the Making of the American Working Class* (London, 1991); Jean H. Baker, *Affairs of Party: The Political Culture of Northern Democrats in the Mid-Nineteenth Century* (Ithaca, N.Y., 1983).

62. *NY Laws,* 38th sess., 1814–1815, chap. 16; Hudson *Northern Whig,* Aug. 16, Nov. 1, 8, 15, 22, 29, 1814; Fitzpatrick, ed., *Autobiography of Van Buren,* 55–56; John Niven, *Martin Van Buren: The Romantic Age of American Politics* (New York, 1963), 32–46; Donald B. Cole, *Martin Van Buren and the American Political System* (Princeton, N.J., 1984), 32–46.

63. Hudson *Northern Whig,* June 22, July 6, 13, 27, 1812, Feb. 16, May 11, 1813, Feb. 8, May

10, Aug. 16, 1814; George Holcomb Diary, June 9, 23, July 4, Sept. 12, 1812, Nov. 17, 1813, Jan. 20, 1814.

64. Hudson *Bee,* Mar. 16, 1813; *New-York Evening Post,* Aug. 29, Oct. 12, 1814; Troy *Farmers' Register,* Sept. 27, 1814; Cherry Valley *Otsego Republican Press,* Oct. 9, 1812; *Albany Advertiser,* Oct. 21, 1815; William H. Wilson, Burlington, Plattsburgh, and Sacketts Harbor, to William Wilson, Clermont, Aug. 7, Sept. 19, 1813, Mar. 10, 26, May 7, 19, July 17, Oct. 12, Nov. 23, Dec. 26, 1814, Feb. 15, 20, Mar. 16, May 25, 1815, WFP-UM; Ellis, *Columbia County,* 143–144; Edward A. Collier, *A History of Old Kinderhook* ... (New York, 1914), 196–197; Francis B. Heitman, *Historical Register and Dictionary of the United States Army* ... (Washington, D.C., 1903), I, 219; Benson J. Lossing, *The Pictorial Field-Book of the War of 1812* (New York, 1868), 831, 834–835; John C. Fredriksen, *Green Coats and Glory: The United States Regiment of Riflemen, 1808–1821* (Youngstown, N.Y., 2000), 45, 59–60.

65. *NY Laws,* 25th sess., 1812, chap. 242, 37th sess., 1814, chap. 142; *NYAJ,* 37th sess., 1814, 77–80; 42nd sess., 1819, 443; Minutes, Apr. 26, 1814, School District No. 4, Austerlitz, N.Y., copies on file at the Chatham, New York, Public Library. There were no 1819 reports from Hudson, Kinderhook, or Ghent. Elsie Garland Hobson, *Educational Legislation and Administration in the State of New York from 1777 to 1850* (Chicago, 1918), 32–34.

66. Mary Livingston Memorandum Book, Oct. 22, Nov. 4, 1816, Feb. 10, 1817; Vernon Lodge Returns, LL-NYGL. Jacob House was born in Hillsdale and paid taxes there in 1800. A Vernon Lodge member from 1806 to 1820, he appears to have relocated to Taghkanic between the filing of the 1817 and 1818 returns. Mary Livingston's November 1816 deed describes the schoolhouse as located on his farm, on Great Lot No. 1. On William Livingston, see Chapter 6.

67. Ronald E. Shaw, *Erie Water West: A History of the Erie Canal, 1792–1854* (Lexington, Ky., 1966), 38–80; Carol Sheriff, *The Artificial River: The Erie Canal and the Paradox of Progress, 1817–1862* (New York, 1996), 19–22; Cornog, *Birth of an Empire,* 104–117; Brian Phillips Murphy, "Empire State Building: Interests, Institutions, and the Formation of States and Parties in New York, 1783–1845" (Ph.D. diss., University of Virginia, 2008), 182–228.

68. *NYSJ,* 37th sess., 1814, 248 (Shaw, *Erie Water West,* 54, inaccurately states that Van Buren opposed the 1814 repeal), 39th sess., 1816, 295, 299, 310–312, 40th sess., 1817, 108, 325, 333, 339, 347–352, 356, 357, 363–364; Cole, *Martin Van Buren,* 50–51.

69. *NYAJ,* 35th sess., 1812, 501–507, 511, 39th sess., 1816, 476–477, 589, 598–603, 619, 631–637, 642–644, 690, 692, 40th sess., 1817, 790–803, 808, 813–814; Dixon Ryan Fox, *The Decline of Aristocracy in the Politics of New York* (New York, 1919), 154. "Comprehensive programs" is Robert H. Wiebe's term, which I have borrowed from *The Opening of American Society: From the Adoption of the Constitution to the Eve of Disunion* (New York, 1984), 209–233.

70. Hudson *Northern Whig,* Jan. 24, 1815, Oct. 22, 1816; *Columbia Magazine; Designed to Promote Evangelical Knowledge and Morality: To Oppose the Prevailing Licentiousnes of Manners* ... (Hudson, N.Y.), I (1815), 23, 60–61, 173–185; *NY Laws,* 40th sess., 1817, chap. 272. Federalists can be identified from various announcements in the *Northern Whig,* and Clintonian Republicans have been differentiated from regular Van Buren–faction Bucktail Republicans in an analysis of a series of long committee lists published in the Hudson *Bee,* Feb. 8, 15, 22, Mar. 14, 1820, as well in the 1819 and 1820 elections, when slates of Bucktail, Clintonian, and Federalist candidates ran for the assembly. Among assemblymen and candidates serving or running between 1810 and 1820, nine Federalists, three Clintonians, and four Bucktail Republicans were members of the Bible and Moral societies.

71. Robert R. Livingston, "Address to the Agricultural Society of the State of New-York . . . ," *New-York Magazine; or, Literary Repository,* VI (February 1795), 95–102; Society of Dutchess County for the Promotion of Agriculture, *Transactions,* I (Poughkeepsie, N.Y., 1807); *American Magazine: A Monthly Miscellany . . . ,* I (August 1815), 104–105; Hudson *Northern Whig,* Mar. 21, 1815, June 3, 1817; *NY Laws,* 42d sess., 1819, chap. 107, 43d sess., 1820, chap. 97. Van Buren joined a call for a roll call on the agricultural bill when it came up in the senate but then failed to record a vote. *NYSJ,* 42d sess., 1819, 237. See also Edward P. Livingston, Clermont, to William Wilson, Clermont, June 14, 1815; Robert L. Livingston, Clermont, to William Wilson, Clermont, Mar. 16, 1816; Jacob R. Van Rensselaer, Albany, to William Wilson, Clermont, Mar. 2, 1819 (quoted), Apr. 14, 1819; Agricultural Society subscription lists, Mar. 1, May 1, 1819 (quoted) (11:10), WFP-UM. William Wilson's papers are filled with material on the agricultural society, only a sample of which can be cited here. George Dangerfield, *Chancellor Robert R. Livingston of New York, 1746–1813* (New York, 1960), 426–430.

72. *New-York Evening Post,* Dec. 11, 1819; Hudson *Northern Whig,* Dec. 14, 1819; Oct. 24, 1820; Hudson *Bee,* Sept. 19, 26, Oct. 3, Oct. 17, Oct. 31, Nov. 7, 1820. Elkanah Watson, at Albany, wrote to William Wilson, Clermont (Apr. 16, 20, 1819, WFP-UM) that Bucktail Peter R. Livingston "smelt party" in the agricultural society bill.

73. The best accounts of the "High-Minded" secession remain Fox, *Decline of Aristocracy,* 203–228; and Shaw Livermore, *The Twilight of Federalism: The Disintegration of the Federalist Party, 1815–1830* (Princeton, N.J., 1962), 74–79; see also Cornog, *Birth of Empire,* 128–130, 140–142. On "comprehensive projects," see Wiebe, *The Opening of American Society;* and John Lauritz Larson, *Internal Improvement: National Public Works and the Promise of Popular Government in the Early United States* (Chapel Hill, N.C., 2001).

74. Fitzpatrick, ed., *Autobiography of Van Buren,* 57; An Act to Authorize the Raising of Two Regiments of Men of Colour, *NY Laws,* 38th sess., 1814–1815, chap. 18. On race and the war, I follow Waldstreicher, *In the Midst of Perpetual Fetes,* 326–327; William J. Mahar, "'Backside Albany' and Early Blackface Minstrelsy: A Contextual Study of America's First Blackface Song," *American Music,* VI (1988), 1–27. This broadside is credited with being the first "black-face" song, but this poetry in black dialect already had a long tradition in the newspapers. On the Colonization Society, see Eli Seifman, "A History of the New-York State Colonization Society" (Ph.D. diss., New York Uniiversity, 1966), 54, 63–64, 67, 75, 90. The Hudson and Hillsdale societies were active into the 1830s.

75. For the murder of the black child, see *The Trial and Conviction of Margaret Houghtaling Who Was Executed at Hudson, Oct. 17th, 1817, for the Murder of Lewis Spencer, an Infant* (Albany, N.Y., [1817]). On the Montgomery funeral, see *Albany Argus,* July 7, 1818.

76. These details are from the *Albany Argus,* July 14, 28, 1818; *Albany Daily Advertiser,* July 15, 1818; George Holcomb Diary, Nov. 6, 1818; *Sketches of the Life, and a Narrative of the Trial of James Hamilton, . . . for the Murder of Major Benjamin Birdsall, of the United States Army* (Albany, N.Y., 1818), 6–8, 11–16; *The Life and Dying Confession of James Hamilton; Executed for the Murder of Major Benjamin Birdsall, Nov. 6, 1818, at Albany* (Albany, N.Y., [1819]), 6–7, 10, 13–15, 22; and Thurlow Weed, *Autobiography of Thurlow Weed,* ed. Harriet A. Weed (Boston, 1883), 63–66. Weed claimed to have witnessed both the Montgomery parade and the Hamilton execution.

77. *The Life and Dying Confession of Hamilton,* 22.

78. Carter and Stone, eds., *Reports of the Proceedings and Debates,* 681.

79. Hudson *Columbia Republican,* Jan. 9, Apr. 17, 1821, and see Figure 1.

CHAPTER 10

1. Ignatius Jones [Gorham A. Worth], *Recollections of Albany and Hudson, with Anecdotes and Sketches of Men and Things* (Albany, N.Y., 1850), 4.

2. Eric Foner, *The Story of American Freedom* (New York, 1998); Alexander Keyssar, *The Right to Vote: The Contested History of Democracy in the United States* (New York, 2000); Michael Schudson, *The Good Citizen: A History of American Civic Life* (Cambridge, Mass., 1998).

3. Henry Livingston to Walter Livingston, Apr. 24, 1785, RRLP, reel 3. The interpretation that I develop here bears a strong — but not complete — resemblance to that developed by Kathleen D. McCarthy in *American Creed: Philanthropy and the Rise of Civil Society, 1700–1865* (Chicago, 2003). McCarthy concludes that antebellum America saw the rise of "two competing political cultures, one dominated by the partisan imperatives of white male political elites, the other predicated on a sprawling patchwork of associations" (192). But, where McCarthy sees the fundamental divide being between northern and southern political cultures and visions of civil society, my attention below is on the division *within* the North between Jacksonian Democrats on the one hand and Whigs and nonparty reformers on the other. For my understanding of the North-South division, see "To Be 'Read by the Whole People': Press, Party, and Public Sphere in the United States, 1790–1840," American Antiquarian Society, *Proceedings,* CX (2000), 41–118.

4. Hudson *Bee,* Nov. 16, 1819. For Lucy Wright's death, see Calvin Green, "Biographical Memoir of . . . Lucy Wright" (New Lebanon, 1861), MS, SC-WRHS, 120–122.

5. Ron Chernow, *Titan: The Life of John D. Rockefeller, Sr.* (New York, 1998), 3–5; Paul E. Johnson and Sean Wilentz, *The Kingdom of Matthias* (New York, 1994), 28–29, 32–34, 103–105; William L. Stone, *Matthias and His Impostures: or, The Progress of Fanaticism Illustrated in the Extraordinary Case of Robert Matthews . . .* (New York, 1835). Other Columbians took a different route in prophetic, millenarian religion, most notably Parley P. and Orson Pratt of New Lebanon, who would become leading figures among the Latter-day Saints. See Breck England, *The Life and Thought of Orson Pratt* (Salt Lake City, Utah, 1985), 21–23; Parley P. Pratt, ed., *Autobiography of Parley P. Pratt* (1874; Salt Lake City, Utah, 1985), 30–31. Benjamin Birdsall, Jr., at age ninety-two, was listed in the 1860 U.S. Census as living in Greene, Chenango County, with two unmarried daughters.

6. *NY Laws,* 23d sess., 1800, chap. 79; Roland Van Zandt, *The Catskill Mountain House* (New Brunswick, N.J., 1966), 29–36, 46–50; Charles Rockwell, *The Catskill Mountains and the Region Around* (New York, 1867), 173–176. Erastus Beach, who was also an early partner in the Catskill Mountain House and whose son Charles L. would be the sole owner and proprietor from 1845 to 1902, was a cousin of Zerah Beach, another of the Susquehannah conspirators.

7. William Raymond, *Biographical Sketches of the Distinguished Men of Columbia County . . .* (Albany, N.Y., 1851), 46–49; Van Zandt, *Catskill Mountain House,* 29; New York *Commercial Advertiser,* Sept. 20, 1824, Hudson *Northern Whig,* Sept. 21, 1824, as excerpted in Edgar Ewing Brandon, comp., *Lafayette: Guest of the Nation: A Contemporary Account of the Triumphal Tour of General Lafayette . . .* (Athens, Ohio, 1950–1957), I, 229–236, 261–262; Ellis, *Columbia County,* 201.

8. In June 1825 Lafayette was celebrated at Lebanon Springs on his way from Albany to Boston; reportedly the assembly at the Columbia Hall hotel was so large that the "floor threatened to give way." Pittsfield, Mass., *Sun,* June 23, 1825, as excerpted in Edgar Ewing Brandon, comp., *A Pilgrimage of Liberty: A Contemporary Account of the Triumphal Tour of General Lafayette . . .* (Athens, Ohio, 1944), 432–433; Ellis, *Columbia County,* 306; "Narrative of William L. Stone,

Esq.," appended to Cadwallader D. Colden, *Memoir, Prepared at the Request of a Common Council of the City of New York, and Presented to the Mayor of the City, at the Celebration of the Completion of the New York Canals* (New York, 1825), 314–315; Carol Sheriff, *The Artificial River: The Erie Canal and the Paradox of Progress, 1817–1862* (New York, 1996), 27–28.

9. William L. Stone, *Matthias and His Impostures;* Stone, *Maria Monk and the Nunnery of the Hotel Dieu: Being an Account of a Visit to the Convents of Montreal, and Refutation of the "Awful Disclosures"* (New York, 1836); Stone, *Life of Joseph Brant-Thayendanegea: Including the Border Wars of the American Revolution . . .* (1838; rpt. Clare Shores, Wis., 1970); Stone, *The Life and Times of Red-Jacket, or Sa-go-ye-wat-ha . . .* (New York, 1841); Benson J. Lossing, *Seventeen Hundred and Seventy-six; or, The War of Independence . . .* (New York, 1847); Lossing, *The Pictorial Field-Book of the Revolution . . .* (New York, 1850). For the wider emergence of a popular literature on the Revolution, see Michael Kammen, *A Season of Youth: The American Revolution and the Historical Imagination* (New York, 1978).

10. "Narrative of William L. Stone, Esq.," in Colden, *Memoir,* 314–315; Ellis, *Columbia County,* 366. Rockwell, *Catskill Mountains,* 162–314, provides a general account of the literary and artistic interest in the Catskills. See also Stanley T. Williams, *The Life of Washington Irving* (New York, 1935), I, 168–191, and Van Zandt, *Catskill Mountain House,* 23–27, 151–215. On the artists at Hudson and Catskill, see Ruth Piwonka, *Mount Merino: Views of Mount Merino, South Bay, and the City of Hudson Painted by Henry Ary and His Contemporaries* (Kinderhook, N.Y., 1978), 3–4; Van Zandt, *Catskill Mountain House,* 36; Alan Wallach, "Thomas Cole: Landscape and the Course of American Empire," in William H. Truettner and Wallach, eds., *Thomas Cole: Landscape into History* (New Haven, Conn., 1994), 23–111.

11. Angela Miller, "Thomas Cole and Jacksonian America: *The Course of Empire* as Political Allegory," *Prospects,* XIV (1989), 65–92. On the paintings at Lindenwald, see Leonard L. Richards, Marla R. Miller, and Eric Gilg, *A Return to His Native Town: Martin Van Buren's Life at Lindenwald, 1839–1862 . . .* (National Park Service, 2006), 116–120.

12. John Niven, *Martin Van Buren: The Romantic Age of American Politics* (New York, 1983), 92, 102–105.

13. On the Regency, see Donald B. Cole, *Martin Van Buren and the American Political System* (Princeton, N.J., 1984), 92–98. For Van Buren's ideological progress onto the national stage, see Robert V. Remini, *Martin Van Buren and the Making of the Democratic Party* (New York, 1951), 60–63; Michael L. Wallace, "Changing Concepts of Party in the United States: New York, 1815–1828," *American Historical Review,* LVVIV (1968), 453–491; Gerald Leonard, *The Invention of Party Politics: Federalism, Populism, and Constitutional Development in Jacksonian Illinois* (Chapel Hill, N.C., 2002), esp. 35–47.

14. Joel H. Silbey, *Martin Van Buren and the Emergence of American Popular Politics* (Lanham, Md., 2002), 219.

15. Martin Van Buren, Washington, to Thomas Ritchie, Richmond, Jan. 13, 1827, MVBP-LC.

16. Martin Van Buren, "Thoughts on the Approaching Election in New York," March 1840, MVBP-LC; Van Buren, *Inquiry into the Origin and Course of Political Parties in the United States* (New York, 1867). See Gerald Leonard, *The Invention of Party Politics,* 12–17; Leonard, "Party as a 'Political Safeguard of Federalism': Martin Van Buren and the Constitutional Theory of Party Politics," *Rutgers Law Review,* LIV (2001–2002), 221–281. I am obliged to Leonard for calling my attention to Van Buren's "Thoughts on the Approaching Election."

17. Martin Van Buren, Albany, to Rufus King, Washington [?], Jan. 19, 1820, Jan. 14, 1821, in

Charles R. King, ed., *The Life and Correspondence of Rufus King . . .* (New York, 1894–1900), VI, 252–253, 375–377. See also James C. Curtis, *The Fox at Bay: Martin Van Buren and the Presidency, 1837–1841* (Lexington, Ky., 1970), 10.

18. New York *American,* Mar. 6, 1819, Jan. 26, 1820; James A. Hamilton, *Reminiscences of James A. Hamilton; or, Men and Events, at Home and Abroad, during Three Quarters of a Century* (New York, 1869), 48–55; Ellis, *Columbia County,* 178. On the secession of the High-Minded Federalists, see Alvin Kass, *Politics in New York State, 1800–1830* (Syracuse, N.Y., 1965), 74–81; Shaw Livermore, *The Twilight of Federalism: The Disintegration of the Federalist Party, 1815–1830* (Princeton, N.J., 1962), 74–79; Dixon Ryan Fox, *The Decline of Aristocracy in the Politics of New York* (New York, 1919), 207–228.

19. New York *American,* Mar. 17/18, 1820 (quote from country edition dated March 18).

20. New York *American,* Apr. 22, May 3, 1820. For the legislative details, see Robert E. Wright, "Banking and Politics in New York, 1784–1829" (Ph.D. diss., SUNY Buffalo, 1996), 542, 551, 713, 773–776, 778, 780–781, 785, 793, 799–804, 807–808, 810–811, 851–852. Williams and Van Rensselaer certainly were working as lobbyists in Albany in the winter of 1818 for the passage of the Franklin charter, the one year they were not elected to the house between 1811 and 1821.

21. Ellis, *Columbia County,* 178–179; George Holcomb Diary, June 11, 1819, NYSA; *Proceedings of the Committee, Appointed to Inquire into the Official Conduct of William W. Van Ness, Esquire, One of the Justices of the Supreme Court of the State of New York; with the Whole Evidence Taken before That Body* (New York, 1820); Hudson *Northern Whig,* Feb. 1, 8, Apr. 11, 1820; Hamilton, *Reminiscences,* 48–55; Jabez D. Hammond, *The History of Political Parties in the State of New-York, from the Ratification of the Federal Constitution to December 1840* (Cooperstown, N.Y., 1846), I, 518–521; Fox, *The Decline of Aristocracy,* 214–216, 226; Wright, "Banking and Politics," 924–925.

22. Hudson *Northern Whig,* May 2, July 11, 1820; Raymond, *Biographical Sketches,* 22.

23. Brandon, *Lafayette: Guest of the Nation,* 228, 234; Colden, *Memoir,* 167.

24. While Antimasonry was fundamental to the origins of the Whig Party in the Burned-Over District of western New York, the movement was weak in the Hudson Valley.

25. Ellis, *Columbia County,* 118–120; Richard H. Levet, *Ambrose L. (Aqua Fortis) Jordan, Lawyer* (New York, 1973), 20–22, 140–149; Stephen Miller, *Historical Sketches of Hudson . . .* (Hudson, N.Y., 1862; rpt. 1985), 66–68. According to Jabez Hammond, the People's Party planned to set up Jordan's brother Allen as the editor of a newspaper in Albany and appoint him state printer (*The History of Political Parties in New-York,* II, 156–157n). For the definitive history of the People's movement, see Craig Hanyan with Mary L. Hanyan, *De Witt Clinton and the Rise of the People's Men* (Montreal, 1996).

26. Hudson *Columbia Republican,* Oct. 11, 18, 1825 (cited in Levett, *Jordan,* 146–147), Oct. 14, 28, 1828, Oct. 6, 13, 1829; Ellis, *Columbia County,* 53.

27. Raymond, *Biographical Sketches,* 1–27, 85; Ellis, *Columbia County,* 178; biographical sketch of Jacob R. Van Rensselaer, on file, CCHS; J. R. Van Rensselaer to James Vanderpoel, Sept. 18, 1822, June 10, 1825, May 15, 1829, Vanderpoel Papers, CCHS; Walter V. Miller, "The Red Mills," *Chatham Courier* (New York), Mar. 7, 1974. McKinstry genealogy from freepages.geneaology. rootweb.com.

28. Hudson *Columbia Republican,* July 7, Sept. 11, 1829, May 11, 1830; Minute Book, Hudson Infant Society, Sept. 21, 1829, HHC-DAR; Eli Seifman, *A History of the New-York State Colonization Society* (New York, 1966), 63; *Fourth Annual Report of the New York State Society for the Promotion of Temperance* (Albany, N.Y., 1833), 34.

29. Elisha Jenkins was particularly shifting in his affinities in these years. He was on the 1820 committee list of Clinton supporters twice reported in the Hudson *Bee* (Feb. 15, Mar. 21, 1820) and played a role in the Clintonian Grand Celebration of the canal in 1825. Yet in March 1829 he signed his name to a list of Hudson "Republicans" inviting Van Buren to a "Public Dinner" to celebrate his appointment as Jackson's secretary of state. Oliver Wiswall, Elisha Jenkins, et al., Hudson, to Martin Van Buren, Kinderhook, Mar. 16, 1829; Martin Van Buren to Oliver Wiswall, Elisha Jenkins, et al., Mar. 17, 1829, MVBP; Minute Book, Hudson Infant Society, Sept. 13, 1831, HHC-DAR.

30. Ellis, *Columbia County,* 53.

31. *Hudson Gazette,* Sept. 7, 1824, as excerpted in Ellis, *Columbia County,* 118; Miller, *Historical Sketches of Hudson,* 67; Brandon, *Lafayette: Guest of the Nation,* 228.

32. Aaron Vanderpoel, "Mechanics and Farmers of Columbia listen!!" MS, Sept. 6, 1828, folder 7, Vanderpoel Papers, 1791–1839, CCHS; Kinderhook *Herald,* Jan. 15, 1829.

33. Elam Tilden, New Lebanon, to Daniel D. Tompkins, Albany, Apr. 6, 1812, Daniel D. Tompkins Papers, NYSA. Tilden's 1832 address, as quoted in John Bigelow, *The Life of Samuel J. Tilden* (New York, 1895), 39–41 (misdated to 1833). Tilden's early essays are discussed in Alexander Clarence Flick, *Samuel Jones Tilden: A Study in Political Sagacity* (Port Washington, N.Y., 1939), 17–19, 22.

34. Flick, *Samuel Jones Tilden,* 22–31, 43–46; Samuel J. Tilden, New Lebanon, to the County Committee, Hudson, Samuel J. Tilden Papers, NYPL; John Bigelow, ed., *The Writings and Speeches of Samuel J. Tilden* (New York, 1885), I, 79–87, quotes from 81–82.

35. John C. Fitzpatrick, ed., *The Autobiography of Martin Van Buren,* vol. II of *Annual Report of the American Historical Association for the Year 1918* (Washington, D.C., 1920), 221–223; Niven, *Martin Van Buren,* 220–221; L. Ray Gunn, *The Decline of Authority: Public Economic Policy and Political Development in New York, 1800–1860* (Ithaca, N.Y., 1988), 92–93, 121–124.

36. For accounts of Van Rensselaer's vote, see Van Buren, *Autobiography,* 150–152; Cole, *Martin Van Buren,* 139–141; Niven, *Martin Van Buren,* 117, 158–161.

37. Niven, *Martin Van Buren,* 304–305; Martin Van Buren, "Inaugural Address" (Mar. 4, 1837), in James D. Richardson, ed., *A Compilation of the Messages and Papers of the Presidents* (Washington, D.C., 1897; rpt. 1910), 1530–1537.

38. Martin Van Buren, "Special Session Message" (Sept. 4, 1837), in Richardson, ed., *Compilation,* 1548; Elam Tilden, New Lebanon, to Martin Van Buren, Washington, Sept. 8, 1837, MVBP; Major L. Wilson, *The Presidency of Martin Van Buren* (Lawrence, Kans., 1984), 70–71; Martin Van Buren, "First Annual Message" (Dec. 5, 1837), in Richardson, ed., *Compilation,* 1597, "Second Annual Message" (Dec. 3, 1838), 1701, 1711, "Third Annual Message" (Dec. 2, 1839), 1761–1763, 1771–1772, "Fourth Annual Message" (Dec. 5, 1840)," 1829.

39. Van Buren, "Thoughts on the Approaching Election." I am indebted to Gerald Leonard for his detailed discussion of this document in *The Invention of Party Politics,* 177–182; see also comments by Wilson, *The Presidency of Martin Van Buren,* 205.

40. Van Buren, "Thoughts on the Approaching Election," 1–5, 22, 33, 74; Leonard, *The Invention of Party Politics,* 181; Van Buren, *Inquiry into the Origin and Course of Political Parties,* 160–169.

41. Van Buren, "Thoughts on the Approaching Election," 43–44; Van Buren, *Inquiry into the Origin and Course of Political Parties,* 224–226 (quote 224); see also Fitzpatrick, ed., *Autobiography of Van Buren,* 222.

42. Alexis De Tocqueville, *Democracy in America,* ed. Phillips Bradley, trans. Henry Reeves, rev. Francis Bowen (New York, 1945), II, 342. See the discussion of this passage in John Ehrenberg, *Civil Society: The Critical History of an Idea* (New York, 1999), 167–168.

43. Henry Livingston, Manor, to Walter Livingston, NYC, Apr. 24, 1785, RRLP.

44. Russell G. Dorr, Hillsdale, to Martin Van Buren, Washington, Oct. 24, 1840, enclosing John J. Shafer's printed affidavit, Oct. 5, 1840, MVBP. See Hudson *Northern Whig,* Oct. 12, 1813.

45. Martin Van Buren, "Second Annual Message" (Dec. 3, 1838), in Richardson, ed., *Compilation,* 1701.

46. *A Chart Showing the Progress of the Political Tornado Which Swept over the Empire State during the 6th, 7th, and 8th November, 1837* (New York, 1837), broadside in MVBP; Howard Bodenhorn, "Bank Chartering and Political Corruption in Antebellum New York: Free Banking as Reform," in Edward L. Glaeser and Claudia Goldin, eds., *Corruption and Reform: Lessons from America's Economic History* (Chicago, 2006), 231–257; Gunn, *The Decline of Authority,* 227–230; Edward K. Spann, *Ideals and Politics: New York Intellectuals and Liberal Democracy, 1820–1880* (Albany, N.Y., 1972), 100–105. For the wider implications of the Free Banking Act, see John Joseph Wallis, "Founding Errors: Making Democracy Safe for America," MS draft, December 2008.

47. Here I am engaging with the literature critiquing the neo-Tocquevillean model of "weak state-strong civil society": Michael Schudson, "The 'Public Sphere' and Its Problems: Bringing the State (Back) In," *Notre Dame Journal of Law, Ethics, and Public Policy,* VIII (1994), 529–546; Jason Kaufman, "Three Views of Associationalism in Nineteenth-Century America: An Empirical Examination," *American Journal of Sociology,* CIV (1999), 1296–1345; William J. Novak, "The America Law of Association: The Legal-Political Construction of Civil Society," *Studies in American Political Development,* XV (2001), 163–188; Theda Skocpol, *Diminished Democracy: From Membership to Management in American Civic Life* (Norman, Okla., 2003), 20–126; Garry Wills, "Did Tocqueville 'Get' America?" *New York Review of Books,* Apr. 29, 2004, 52–56. Except for Wills, these theorists inexplicably do not attend to the different constructions of civil society among Whigs and Democrats that I stress here. My self-consciously standard interpretation of Jacksonian and Whig political economy can be followed in a long series of studies, including, among many others, Marvin Meyers, *The Jacksonian Persuasion: Politics and Belief* (Stanford, Calif., 1957); Lee Benson, *The Concept of Jacksonian Democracy: New York as a Test Case* (Princeton, N.J., 1961); Daniel Walker Howe, *The Political Culture of the American Whigs* (Chicago, 1979); Harry L. Watson, *Liberty and Power: The Politics of Jacksonian America* (New York, 1990); John Ashworth, *"Agrarians" and "Aristocrats": Party Political Ideology, 1837–1846* (London, 1983); Robert H. Wiebe, *The Opening of American Society: From the Adoption of the Constitution to the Eve of Disunion* (New York, 1984); Daniel Walker Howe, "The Evangelical Movement and Political Culture in the North during the Second Party System," *Journal of American History,* LXXVII (1990–1991), 1216–1239; John Lauritz Larson, *Internal Improvement: National Public Works and the Promise of Popular Government in the Early United States* (Chapel Hill, N.C., 2001); Leonard, *The Invention of Party Politics.* The terms of "positive and negative liberalism" were seminally applied by Lee Benson in *The Concept of Jacksonian Democracy.*

48. Van Buren, "Thoughts on the Approaching Election," 1–2. On the organization of the "Young Men" in Columbia County, see the Pittsfield *Sun,* Sept. 18, 1834, July 21, 1838. For different approaches to the issue of social capital, see Jean L. Cohen and Andrew Arato, *Civil Society and Political Theory* (Cambridge, Mass., 1994), 492–563; Robert D. Putnam, *Bowling Alone: The Collapse and Revival of American Community* (New York, 2000); Bob Edwards, Michael W. Foley,

and Mario Diani, eds., *Beyond Tocqueville: Civil Society and the Social Capital Debate in Comparative Perspective* (Hanover, N.H., 2001); and Kaufman, "Three Views of Associationalism," *American Journal of Sociology,* CIV (1999), 1296–1345. Kathleen McCarthy, in *American Creed,* provides a particularly useful understanding of the relationship between associationalism and social capital in antebellum northern society, though she may underestimate the limits of its dynamic among northern Democrats.

49. Bucktail Democrats avoided these associations, though here and there a few notables lent their names; John W. Edmonds and Elisha Jenkins subscribed to the Infant Society, and, with Jenkins, a few Democrats could be found in the leadership of the Temperance Society. Generally these temperance Democrats were men who had sat for some years as justices on the county bench. Thus Medad Butler, an old Jeffersonian mentor of Van Buren's in Kinderhook and a judge since 1823, chaired the first temperance meeting, and James Vanderpoel, a former Federalist turned Democrat and a county judge since 1826, deeply involved in the early development of industrial projects in Kinderhook, also supported the cause of temperance. Minutes, Hudson Infant Society; Hudson *Columbia Republican,* Sept. 22, 1829; Peter H. Stott, *Looking for Work: Industrial Archeology in Columbia County, New York* . . . (Kinderhook, N.Y., 2007), 219–220. Notably, Jenkins and Vanderpoel were also involved in the Colonization Society: see Eli Seifman, "A History of the New-York State Colonization Society" (Ph.D. diss., New York University, 1965), 63, 67. On the character of the early immediatist reforms, see the wider sociological literature on the Second Great Awakening, including the social-control debate encompassed by two seminal articles: Clifford S. Griffin, "Religious Benevolence as Social Control, 1815–1860," *Mississippi Valley Historical Review,* XLIV (1957–1958), 423–444; and Lois W. Banner, "Religious Benevolence as Social Control: A Critique of an Interpretation," *JAH,* LX (1973–1974), 23–41; and among others, the classic studies by Paul E. Johnson, *A Shopkeeper's Millennium: Society and Revivals in Rochester, New York, 1815–1837* (New York, 1978); and by Mary P. Ryan, *Cradle of the Middle Class: The Family in Oneida County, New York, 1790–1835* (New York, 1981).

50. Temperance support, as measured as society membership per total population, was weaker in Democratic towns without many new churches, in the four old Livingston Manor towns voting Whig, and in Hudson and the new industrial town of Stockport, where there were more transient laborers. *Fourth Annual Report of the New York State Society for the Promotion of Temperance* (Albany, N.Y., 1833), 34–35. Comments on local officers based on biographical material in Ellis, *Columbia County.* Without the detailed committee lists as published during the early Republic, political affiliations are difficult to determine. The 1832 revival is measured by membership figures for the county's Baptist churches in Stephen Wright, comp., *History of the Shaftsbury Baptist Association, from 1781 to 1853* . . . (Troy, N.Y., 1853), 378, 383, 384, 391–393, 412, 418–419, 425, 429, 447, 454, 455, 458. Church formation, derived from Ellis, *Columbia County,* suggests something of the impact of the Awakening. Between 1756 and 1825 between three and seven new churches were established each decade. While the population slowly increased by about sixteen hundred people between 1820 and 1830, church formation jumped from three new churches in 1816–1825 to twenty new churches in 1826–1835. The revival appears to have been stronger in Rensselaer County. Dutch Reformed records from Copake and Gallatin suggest that it had no impact on the old Manor. Looking at suggestive but more anecdotal data, Martin Bruegel concludes that "the revivals of the period largely bypassed the area": *Farm, Shop, Landing: The Rise of a Market Society in the Hudson Valley, 1780–1860* (Durham, N.C., 2002), 198–203.

51. Whitney R. Cross, *The Burned-over District: The Social and Intellectual History of Enthusi-*

astic Religion in Western New York, 1800–1850 (Ithaca, N.Y., 1950), 163–164. For a dissenting view on the significance of the New Lebanon meeting, see Gary Hiebsch, "A Turning Point in American Revivalism? The Influence of Charles G. Finney's *Memoirs* on Historical Accounts of the New Lebanon Convention," *Journal of Presbyterian History,* LXXVI (1998), 139–149.

52. Within a vast literature on moral reform, see the following formative accounts on the Burned-Over District of central and western New York, a regional culture that stood in sharp contrast to conservative Columbia: Cross, *The Burned-over District;* Johnson, *A Shopkeeper's Millennium;* Ryan, *Cradle of the Middle Class;* Nancy A. Hewitt, *Women's Activism and Social Change: Rochester, New York, 1822–1872* (Ithaca, N.Y., 1984). For eastern and central New England, see, among others, Anne M. Boylan, *The Origins of Women's Activism: New York and Boston, 1797–1840* (Chapel Hill, N.C., 2002); Richard S. Newman, *The Transformation of American Abolitionism: Fighting Slavery in the Early Republic* (Chapel Hill, N.C., 2002); Teresa Anne Murphy, *Ten Hours' Labor: Religion, Reform, and Gender in Early New England* (Ithaca, N.Y., 1992); and Jonathan D. Sassi, *A Republic of Righteousness: The Public Christianity of the Post-Revolutionary New England Clergy* (New York, 2001). On colonization, see Seifman, "A History of the New-York State Colonization Society"; *Seventh Annual Report of the American Society for the Colonizing of the Free People of Color of the United States* (Washington, D.C., 1824), 170; *Eighth Annual Report . . .* (Washington, D.C., 1825), 119–120; *Fourteenth Annual Report . . .* (Washington, D.C., 1831), np., app.; *Fifteenth Annual Report . . .* (Washington, D.C., 1832), 57. On abolition, see *Third Annual Report of the American Anti-Slavery Society . . . 10th May, 1836 . . .* (New York, 1836), 94; *Fifth Annual Report of the Executive Committee of the American Anti-Slavery Society . . .* (New York, 1838), 141, 143; *Journal of the House of Representatives,* 25th sess. (Jan. 21, 1839), 337, 339, 340. The abolitionist circle in Spencertown did produce a minor classic in antislavery literature, a memoir of a black sailor who settled in the village in the mid-1820s, Peter Wheeler, transcribed with commentary by Charles Edward Lester, temporarily minister at Saint Peter's Presbyterian Church, and the vice president of the county antislavery society in 1838. See Wheeler, *Chains and Freedom; or, The Life and Adventures of Peter Wheeler, a Colored Man Yet Living, a Slave in Chains, a Sailor in the Deep, and a Sinner at the Cross,* ed. Graham Russell Gao Hodges (Tuscaloosa, Ala., 2009).

53. Ellis, *Columbia County,* 54.

54. 1846 and 1860 electoral returns, Canvasser's Book, 1799–1894, Clerk's Office, Columbia County Court House. See Phyllis F. Field, *The Politics of Race in New York: The Struggle for Black Suffrage in the Civil War Era* (Ithaca, N.Y., 1982), 61–79, 127–146, 201–219.

55. *Congressional Globe,* VIII, no. 10 (Feb. 4, 1840), 150–151; William Lee Miller, *Arguing about Slavery: The Great Battle in the United States Congress* (New York, 1995), 367–369. For the new literature on the wider significance of the gag rule for the origins of the Civil War, a veritable "Gag Rule School," see Miller, *Arguing about Slavery;* William W. Freehling, *The Road to Disunion: Secessionists at Bay, 1776–1854* (New York, 1990); Leonard L. Richards, *The Life and Times of Congressman John Quincy Adams* (New York, 1986), and *The Slave Power: The Free North and Southern Domination, 1780–1860* (Baton Rouge, La., 2000).

56. *NYAJ,* 60th sess., 1837, 416–417; *Appendix to the Congressional Globe,* IV, no. 2 (Feb. 11, 1837), 189–190. See Miller, *Arguing with Slavery,* 225–273, esp. 258–259, 264, 267.

57. Here I refer to Leonard, *Invention of Party Politics,* challenging the central themes of Richard Hofstadter, *The Idea of a Party System: The Rise of Legitimate Opposition in the United States: 1780–1840* (Berkeley, Calif., 1969).

58. Moses Younglove, Hudson, to Martin Van Buren, Albany, Dec. 8, 1828, MVBP; Elam Tilden, New Lebanon, to Martin Van Buren, Washington, Jan. 16, 1835, enclosing Henry David Ward, NYC, to Elam Tilden, NL, Jan. 9, 1835, MVBP. The generalization regarding the lack of Masonic affiliation among the Regency leadership is based on an extensive search in the membership file, R. R. Livingston Library, NYGL. George Bancroft, who was also in communication with Van Buren in 1835, was able to forge a Democratic-Antimasonic alliance in Massachusetts in these years. On this and the corporatist republican vision of the Massachusetts Antimasons, see Paul Goodman, *Towards a Christian Republic: Antimasonry and the Great Transition in New England, 1826–1836* (New York, 1988), 20–33, 147–162; John L. Brooke, *The Heart of the Commonwealth: Society and Political Culture in Worcester County, Massachusetts, 1713–1861* (New York, 1989), 310–352. The broad "Jacksonian" affinities of Van Buren's Republicanism and the Antimasonic appeal were laid out in John L. Brooke, "Freemasonry and the Public Sphere in New York State, 1784–1830," paper presented at the Organization of American Historians meeting, Apr. 11, 1991.

59. Van Buren, *Inquiry into the Origin and Course of Political Parties,* 11–12; Van Buren, "Thoughts on the Approaching Election," 43–44; Jean Jacques Rousseau, *A Dissertation on Political Economy: To Which Is Added a Treatise on the Social Compact; or, The Principles of Politic Law* (Albany, N.Y., 1797), 215–216. I am indebted to Gerald Leonard's insight on Van Buren's reference to Rousseau and the concept of the "general will." *The Invention of Political Parties,* 39–40. See also Wilson, *The Presidency of Martin Van Buren,* 205.

60. Van Buren, "Thoughts on the Approaching Election," 18–19, 33–37. For the Liberty Pole scuffle, see Martin Van Buren, NYC, to John P. Van Ness, Washington, Jan. 15, 1803, MVBP–Missouri Historical Society.

61. Ellis, *Columbia County,* 343; Henry Hogeboom et al., Hudson, to Martin Van Buren, Kinderhook, June 17, 1844, MVBP, inviting Van Buren to speak at "the Mass Convention of Democratic electors of the County of Columbia ... appointed to be held at the Court House in Hudson." This meeting was noticed in the Pittsfield *Sun,* July 4, 1844, as "a Great Mass Meeting of the Democrats of Columbia and adjacent counties."

62. A growing literature has demonstrated that Whig cultural environments allowed space for both moral reform efforts and other ventures in the public sphere, particularly among women. Lori Ginsburg, *Women and the Work of Benevolence: Morality, Politics, and Class in the Nineteenth-Century United States* (New Haven, Conn., 1990), 36–97, esp. 71; Ronald J. Zboray and Mary Saracino Zboray, "Political News and Female Readership in Antebellum Boston and Its Region," *Journalism History,* XXII (1996), 2–14, and "Whig Women, Politics, and Culture in the Campaign of 1840: Three Perspectives from Massachusetts," *Journal of the Early Republic,* XVII (1997), 277–315; Kirsten E. Wood, "'One Woman So Dangerous to Public Morals': Gender and Power in the Eaton Affair," *Journal of the Early Republic,* XVII (1997), 237–276; Elizabeth R. Varon, *We Mean to Be Counted: White Women and Politics in Antebellum Virginia* (Chapel Hill, N.C., 1998); Boylan, *Origins of Women's Activism,* 151–152; Marilyn Schultz Blackwell, "Meddling in Politics: Clarina Howard Nichols and Antebellum Political Culture," *Journal of the Early Republic,* XXIV (2004), 27–63. For Federalist antecedents, see Rosemarie Zagarri, "Gender and the First Party System," in Doron Ben-Atar and Barbara B. Oberg, eds., *Federalists Reconsidered* (Charlottesville, Va., 1998), 118–135; Susan Branson, *These Fiery Frenchified Dames: Women and Political Culture in Early National Philadelphia* (Philadelphia, 2001), 82, 97; and Michael D. Pierson, *Free Hearts and Free Homes: Gender and American Antislavery Politics* (Chapel Hill, N.C., 2003), esp. 99–109. Pierson has made the converse case regarding New York's Democrats after

1848 in "'Guard the Foundations Well': Antebellum New York's Democrats and the Defense of Patriarchy," *Gender and History*, VII (1995), 25–40. The classic account of cultural boundary enforcement by the Democrats remains Jean H. Baker, *Affairs of Party: The Political Culture of the Northern Democrats in the Mid-Nineteenth Century* (Ithaca, N.Y., 1983).

63. Minute Book, Hudson Infant Society, 1829–1832, HHCh-DAR, unpaginated, material and quotations from entries for Sept. 14, 1830.

64. Ibid., Sept. 13, 1831, Jan. 31, Mar. 27, Apr. 9, May 28, 1832.

65. Ellis, *Columbia County*, 164, 178; Minute Book, Hudson Infant Society, Sept. 21, 1829; Stott, *Looking for Work*, 153, 188. Cyrus Curtis, a Whig who later entered the whaling business, had been an Infant Society subscriber.

66. Annual Reports of the New York Female Moral Reform Society, published in the *Advocate of Moral Reform*, Aug. 15, 1837, 311–312, Sept. 15, 1838, 143, June 15, 1839, 96, Sept. 1, 1840, 135. For the three churches with which these societies were affiliated, see Ellis, *Columbia County*, 282–284, 289, 293–294, 325, 326. On the Female Moral Reform Societies, see Hewitt, *Women's Activism and Social Change*, 58–59, 86–87, 94–95, 102–103, 126–127; and Daniel S. Wright, *"The First of Causes to Our Sex": The Female Moral Reform Movement in the Antebellum Northeast, 1834–1848* (New York, 2006).

67. Female Charitable Society of New Lebanon (N.Y.), 1814–1829, entry for Nov. 1, 1814, NYSL; *Advocate of Moral Reform*, Sept. 15, 1838, 143; Here I follow Stephen J. Stein, *The Shaker Experience in America: A History of the United Society of Believers* (New Haven, Conn., 1992), 123–133. More generally, see Susan Juster, *Disorderly Women: Sexual Politics and Evangelicalism in Revolutionary New England* (Ithaca, N.Y., 1994), 145–217; Rosemarie Zagarri, *Revolutionary Backlash: Women and Politics in the Early American Republic* (Philadelphia, 2007).

68. On Reed, see Wallach, "Thomas Cole," in Truettner and Wallach, eds., *Thomas Cole*, 38. Reed was born in a Baptist-orbit family in Hillsdale in 1787, where his father Eliakim was militia lieutenant in 1786 and a head of household in 1790. The Reed family moved across the river to Greene County by 1800, where Luman Reed learned the storekeeping trade in Coxsackie. On the "aristocracy of manners," I follow Edward Halsey Foster, *Susan and Anna Warner* (Boston, 1978), 60–62; and Richard Bushman, *The Refinement of America: Persons, Houses, Cities* (New York, 1992).

69. On Susan Warner, I am working from the arguments developed by Mary Kelley, "The Sentimentalists: Promise and Betrayal in the Home," *Signs*, IV (1979), 434–446, and *Private Woman, Public Stage: Literary Domesticity in Nineteenth-Century America* (New York, 1984), 31, 85–93; Cathy N. Davidson, *Revolution and the Word: The Rise of the Novel in America* (New York, 1986), 110–135; Linda K. Kerber, *Women of the Republic: Intellect and Ideology in Revolutionary America* (Chapel Hill, N.C., 1980), 248–264; Jane Tompkins, *Sensational Designs: The Cultural Work of American Fiction, 1790–1860* (New York, 1985), 172–185. For arguments about the continuities in the sentimental between the 1790s and 1850s, see Catherine O'Connell, "We *Must* Sorrow: Silence, Suffering, and Sentimentality in Susan Warner's *The Wide, Wide World*," *Studies in American Fiction*, XXV (1997), 21–40. For Warner's relationship with Garretson, see Foster, *Susan and Anna Warner*, 120 n. 31. Foster suggests that they were working on *Wych Hazel* and *The Gold of Chickaree*, which "exhibit a decided distrust of human nature and assert the need for benevolent people of wealth to control society" (96–97). Mary Garretson was the niece of Janet Livingston Montgomery, whose name certainly must have been the source of that of Susan Warner's heroine.

70. On the Washington salon world between 1801 and 1828, see Fredrika J. Teute, "Roman

Matron on the Banks of the Tiber Creek: Margaret Bayard Smith and the Politicization of Spheres in the Nation's Capital," and Jan Lewis, "Politics and the Ambivalence of the Private Sphere: Women in Early Washington, D.C.," both in Donald R. Kennon, ed., *A Republic for the Ages: The United States Capitol and the Poltical Culture of the Early Republic* (Charlottesville, Va., 1999), 89–121, 122–151; Catherine Allgor, *Parlor Politics: In Which the Ladies of Washington Help Build a City and a Government* (Charlottesville, Va., 2000). On Marcia Burns, see Frances Carpenter Huntington, "The Heiress of Washington City: Marcia Burnes Van Ness, 1782–1832," *Records of the Columbia Historical Society,* LXIX/LXX (1969–1970), 80–101; Susan L. Klaus, "'Some of the Smartest Folks Here': The Van Nesses and Community Building in Early Wahington," *Washington History,* III, no. 2 (Fall/Winter 1991–1992), 22–45; Gaillard Hunt, ed., *The First Forty Years of Washington Society Portrayed in the Family Letters of Mrs. Samuel Harrison Smith (Margaret Bayard)* (New York, 1906), 135, 141, 157, 209–211, 373. On the precursor to the Washington salons, see Branson, *These Fiery Frenchified Dames.*

71. John P. Van Ness to Martin Van Buren, Apr. 30, 1830, MVBP. On the Middletons and Washington society, see Hunt, ed., *The First Forty Years of Washington Society,* 165, 204. On Van Buren's recalling Middleton, see Niven, *Martin Van Buren,* 239–240. If there were tensions between Van Buren and John P. Van Ness, they did not extend to his brother Cornelius P. Van Ness, recently the Democratic governor of Vermont, whom Van Buren appointed ambassador to Spain.

72. For detailed discussions of the Eaton affair, see Wood, "One Woman So Dangerous," *Journal of the Early Republic,* XVII (1997), 273–275; John F. Marszalek, *The Petticoat Affair: Manners, Mutiny, and Sex in Andrew Jackson's White House* (New York, 1997).

73. Richards, Miller, and Gilg, *A Return to His Native Town.*

74. Election Returns Volume, 1799–1893, Columbia County Clerk's Office.

75. Albany *Anti-Renter,* Jan. 31, 1846; Albany *Freeholder,* July 16, 1845.

76. For the opening months of the Anti-Rent movement, see the two definitive modern interpretations: Reeve Huston, *Land and Freedom: Rural Society, Popular Protest, and Party Politics in Antebellum New York* (New York, 2000), 87–105; Charles W. McCurdy, *The Anti-Rent Era in New York Law and Politics, 1839–1865* (Chapel Hill, N.C., 2001), 13–22; as well as an enduring classic, Henry Christman, *Tin Horns and Calico: A Decisive Episode in the Emergence of Democracy* (New York, 1945), 35–63. On the Anti-Rent "Indians," see Huston, *Land and Freedom,* 116–124; Philip J. Deloria, *Playing Indian* (New Haven, Conn., 1998), 38–39; Alan Taylor, *Liberty Men and Great Proprietors: The Revolutionary Settlement on the Maine Frontier, 1760–1820* (Chapel Hill, N.C., 1990), 181–207. Sherlock S. Gregory, a nephew of an Anti-Rent leader in West Sand Lake in Rensselaer County, expressed a related sentiment when he deluged Congress between September 1837 and January 1839 with a series of petitions on slavery and the Indians (as well as opposition to Catholicism and women's rights). In his first petition, presented by John Quincy Adams, Gregory wrote "praying to be considered an alien, or stranger in the land, so long as slavery exists, and the wrongs of the Indians are unrequited and unrepented of." *Journal of the House of Representatives of the United States, Being the First Session of the Twenty-Fifth Congress . . .* (Washington, D.C., 1837), 53. For his other petitions, see *Second Session,* 173, 202, 208, 390, 568, 572–573, 772–773, *Third Session,* 336.

77. McCurdy, *The Anti-Rent Era,* 149, 163; Huston, *Land and Freedom,* 100–104; Christman, *Tin Horns and Calico,* 115–116.

78. Ellis, *Columbia County,* 44–45, 400–401; Albany *Freeholder,* Aug. 13, 27, Sept. 24, 1845;

Albany *Anti-Renter,* Sept. 13, 1845; McCurdy, *The Anti-Rent Era,* 163–167; Christman, *Tin Horns and Calico,* 121–131; Miller, *Historical Sketches of Hudson,* 54–61.

79. Ellis, *Columbia County,* 45, 63; Albany *Freeholder,* Apr. 9, 16, Sept. 10, 1845; Ellis, *Landlords and Farmers,* 294; Levet, *Jordan,* 117–132; "Hudson Shoemakers, New York, 1836: People v. Cooper," in John R. Commons et al., eds., *A Documentary History of American Industrial Society,* IV, *Labor Conspiracy Cases* (Cleveland, Ohio, 1910), 277–312; Bruegel, *Farm, Shop, Landing,* 154–156; McCurdy, *The Anti-Rent Era,* 274–275. Joseph D. Monell, Van Buren's second in his threatened 1811 duel with John Suydam, played a key role in Boughton's arrest. See Christman, *Tin Horns and Calico,* 126–128.

80. Huston, *Land and Freedom,* 182–183; Jonathan H. Earle, *Jacksonian Antislavery and the Politics of Free Soil, 1824–1854* (Chapel Hill, N.C., 2004), 58–77. In 1847, though the Anti-Rent movement was in factional disarray, the five towns of the old Upper Livingston Manor cast strong votes unique in the county for Charles O. Seymour for lieutenant governor. John Mosher, the Anti-Rent candidate for assembly, similarly did well in these five towns as well as Clermont and the southern district of Claverack. In 1848 Van Buren got only 25 percent of the vote in Columbia, to Taylor's Whig plurality of 48 percent, but he got at least 30 percent of the votes across most of the northern section of the county, including a win in Barnburner Samuel Tilden's New Lebanon, and in the Manor towns of Taghkanic, Ancram, northern Gallatin, and Livingston. The conservative Hunker Democrats took Hillsdale, Clermont, and south Claverack.

81. McCurdy, *The Anti-Rent Era,* 160–161, 325–328; Van Buren's letter to Wright is missing, and has to be inferred from Silas Wright, Canton, to Martin Van Buren, Kinderhook, Oct. 8, 1844, MVBP-LC.

82. McCurdy, *The Anti-Rent Era,* 249–255, 272–273; James Duane Livingston and Sherry H. Penney, "The Breakup of Livingston Manor," in Richard T. Wiles, ed., *The Livingston Legacy: Three Centuries of American History* ([Annandale-on-Hudson, N.Y.], 1987), 415–417; Ellis, *Landlords and Farmers,* 306–311; John Frances Collin, *A History of Hillsdale, Columbia County, New York . . . ,* ed. H. S. Johnson (Philmont, N.Y., 1883), 4.

83. Ellis, *Columbia County,* 392–393, 400–402, 408–409; J. H. French, *Gazetteer of the State of New York . . .* (Syracuse, N.Y., 1860), 249; Albany *Freeholder,* Aug. 6, 1845; Albany *Anti-Renter,* Aug. 13, Sept. 24, Oct. 8, 1845. See Chapter 4, note 66, and Table 14.

84. New York *Freedom's Journal,* July 18, 1828.

85. Bruegel, *Farm, Shop, Landing,* 208–209; A. J. Williams-Myers, *Long Hammering: Essays on the Forging of an African American Presence in the Hudson Valley to the Early Twentieth Century* (Trenton, N.J., 1994), 116–117; Melvin Wade, "'Shining in Borrowed Plumage': Affirmation of Community in the Black Coronation Festivals of New England, ca. 1750–1850," in Robert Blair St. George, ed., *Material Life in America, 1600–1860* (Boston, 1988), 171–184; William D. Piersen, *Black Yankees: The Development of an Afro-American Subculture in Eighteenth-Century New England* (Amherst, Mass., 1988), 117–140.

86. New York *Colored American,* Dec. 15, 1838, Feb. 2, 1839, Feb. 6, 1841. Mayor Robert McKinstry, who signed the Hudson petition for intervention by Democratic governor Marcy, was elected by the council in January 1837, after a Whig victory in a traditionally Whig city.

87. The material on occupations is from Bruegel, *Farm, Shop, Landing,* 144–145; the 1850 census manuscript, and Cornelius Parmenter, *Directory of the City of Hudson, for the Years, 1851–52* (Hudson, N.Y., 1851), which included, in its listing of residents (21–70), blacks and their occupa-

tions. On Guinea Hill, see Matilda C. Metcalf, letter in the *Christian Intelligencer,* 1854, quoted in Edward A. Collier, *A History of Old Kinderhook . . .* (New York, 1914), 497; and Bruegel, *Farm, Shop, Landing,* 172. For the occupational limitations on blacks in Troy, see Daniel J. Walkowitz, *Worker City, Company Town: Iron and Cotton-Worker Protest in Troy and Cohoes, New York, 1855–84* (Urbana, Ill., 1981), 22, 111. In 1850 Albany City included 72 percent of the African-Americans in Albany County, Troy 42 percent of Rensselaer, Catskill 31 percent of Greene, Poughkeepsie 22 percent of Dutchess, Kingston 16.8 percent of Ulster, Hudson 16.7 percent of Columbia.

88. Williams-Myers, *Long-Hammering,* 117; New York *Colored American,* Dec. 11, 1838; Benjamin Quarles, *Black Abolitionists* (New York, 1969), 102–103; Elizabeth Wicks, "Address Delivered before the African Female Benevolent Society of Troy" (1834), in Richard Newman, Patrick Rael, and Philip Lasansky, eds., *Pamphlets of Protest: An Anthology of Early African American Protest Literature, 1790–1860* (New York, 2001), 115–121. Arthur James Weise, *Troy's One Hundred Years, 1789–1889* (Troy, N.Y., 1891), 130–131, 348. For a regional association linking blacks in Albany, Troy, and surrounding towns, see New York *Colored American,* Apr. 15, 1837; on the early black churches, Ellis, *Columbia County,* 188, 232. On the press: Martin E. Dann, *The Black Press, 1827–1890: The Quest for National Identity* (New York, 1971), 19–20; Joel Schor, *Henry Highland Garnet: A Voice of Black Radicalism in the Nineteenth Century* (Westport, Conn., 1977), 83; Martin B. Pasternak, *Rise Now and Fly to Arms: The Life of Henry Highland Garnet* (New York, 1995), 48; Earl Ofari, *"Let Your Motto Be Resistance": The Life and Thought of Henry Highland Garnet* (Boston, 1972), 10–11.

89. New York *Weekly Advocate,* Jan. 7, 1837; New York *Colored American,* Apr. 15, Aug. 19, Sept. 30, Oct. 7, 1837, June 8, 1839, Mar. 7, 1840. Black voters from Thomas F. Gordon, *Gazetteer of the State of New York . . .* (Philadelphia, 1836).

90. New York *Colored American,* Mar. 11, 1837, July 27, 1839, June 13, Sept. 12, 1840, Jan. 2, 9, 1841; *NYAJ,* 60th sess., 1837, 416–417; Field, *The Politics of Race in New York,* 45; Charles H. Wesley, "The Negroes of New York in the Emancipation Movement," *Journal of Negro History,* XXIV (1939), 92–94.

91. New York *Colored American,* Nov. 28, 1840, Feb. 13, Sept. 11, 1841; *NYAJ,* 64th sess., 1841, 195, 208, 307, 446; Field, *The Politics of Race in New York,* 45.

92. New York *Colored American,* Feb. 6, 13, Aug. 21, Sept. 11, 1841.

93. *Proceedings of the National Convention of Colored People, and Their Friends, in Troy, N.Y., 6th, 7th, 8th, and 9th Oct., 1847* (Troy, N.Y., 1847), in Howard Holman Bell, ed., *Minutes of the Proceedings of the National Negro Convention, 1830–1864* (New York, 1969), 11; Ellis, *Columbia County,* 188; New York *Colored American,* Aug. 21, 1841; *Liberator,* Aug. 18, 1843, Aug. 7, 1845; Quarles, *Black Abolitionists,* 97; *North Star,* June 30, 1848. Jackson and Van Hoesen also were delegates to the 1847 Troy convention; see below. Perhaps significantly, the number of black voters in Columbia County increased from fourteen in 1835 to thirty-two in 1845, encompassing roughly 10 percent of the adult male black population, a figure slightly higher than the state proportion. Figures from the *Census of the State of New-York, for 1845* (Albany, N.Y., 1846).

94. *Proceedings of the National Convention, 1847,* in Bell, ed., *Minutes,* 11, 16–21; see discussion in Ofari, *"Let Your Motto Be Resistance,"* 47–48; *North Star,* May 5, June 23, 1848; Henry Highland Garnet, *The Past and the Present Condition, and the Destiny, of the Colored Race: A Discourse Delivered at the Fifteenth Anniversary of the Female Benevolent Society of Troy, N.Y., Feb. 14, 1848* (Troy, N.Y., 1848); David Walker, *Walker's Appeal: With a Brief Sketch of His Life, by Henry Highland*

Garnet; and Also Garnet's Address to the Slaves of the United States of America (New York, 1848). See Field, *The Politics of Race in New York,* 61–79; Pasternak, *Rise Now and Fly to Arms,* 58–59; Newman, Rael, and Lasansky, eds., *Pamphlets of Protest,* 166–177.

95. Pasternak, *Rise Now and Fly to Arms,* 60–77; Schor, *Henry Highland Garnet,* 100–130; Philip S. Foner and George E. Walker, eds., *Proceedings of the Black State Conventions, 1840–1865,* I (Philadelphia, 1979), 88; *North Star,* June 30, 1848; Williams-Myers, *Long Hammering,* 157–158.

96. Collier, *A History of Old Kinderhook,* esp. 60, 100–101, 138; Sung Bok Kim, *Landlord and Tenant in Colonial New York: Manorial Society, 1664–1775* (Chapel Hill, N.C., 1978), 285–286, 294, 348; W. E. Burghardt Du Bois, *Dusk of Dawn: An Essay Toward an Autobiography of a Race Concept* (1940; New York, 1968), 9–12, 110–115; David Levering Lewis, *W. E. B. Du Bois: Biography of a Race, 1868–1919* (New York, 1993), 11–18. Othello Burghardt's role at Troy and Great Barrington in 1847 and 1848 can be found in *Proceedings of the National Convention, 1847,* in Bell, ed., *Minutes,* 11, and *North Star,* June 30, 1848. Piecing together scraps of information, it appears most likely that Sarah was the daughter of James Lampman (or Lantman), in Great Barrington as of 1800, and probably formerly a slave to Peter Lampman, a wealthy tenant farmer in Copake who owned three slaves in 1790 and died in 1798. Charles Lampman, born about 1799 and a black head of household in Great Barrington in the 1840s, might have been her brother.

97. Judy Roe, West Sand Lake historian, personal communication; Ellis, *Columbia County,* 148; Luis F. Emilio, *History of the Fifty-Fourth Regiment of Massachusetts Volunteer Infantry, 1863–1865* (Boston, 1894), 339–344, 349–353; Cornelia Brooke Gilder and Julia Conklin Peters, *Hawthorne's Lenox: The Tanglewood Circle* (Charleston, S.C., 2008), 71–76. For the civil implications of the assault on Fort Wagner, see Willie Lee Rose, *Rehearsal for Reconstruction: The Port Royal Experiment* (New York, 1964), 255–260.

INDEX

Abolition and emancipation, 7, 438; African American experience of, 40–41, 118, 255–256, 266–279, 385–394; and legislative efforts in 1785–1790, 76, 138–139, 261; and sensibility and persuasion, 130, 138–140, 149, 228, 234, 238, 255–260, 345, 393–395, 427; legislative action in 1795–1804, 228, 233, 239, 245, 260–266, 345; antebellum movement for, 232, 377, 438, 453–455, 460, 466, 470–474. *See also* African Americans

Abyssinian Baptist Church (New York City), 391

Academies, 313, 570 nn. 27–28. *See also* Education; *specific academies*

Account of the European Settlement in America (Burke and Burke), 126, 133

Account of the People Called Shakers (Brown), 145, 368

Adams, John Quincy, 445, 447, 454–455

Adams Republicans, 442. *See also* Whig Party

Adancourt, Francis, 308, 560n. 42

Adgate, Asa, 394, 475

Adgate, Matthew, 475; in Revolution, 31–32, 92; as Clintonian leader, 59–60, 65; and Constitutional ratification convention (1788), 99, 102, 183; and elections, 99, 204, 207; and Bank of New York, 113, 206; and Otsego election crisis, 113; and abolition and emancipation, 139, 256; as justice of the peace, 175; and restoration of property, 177–178; as Antifederalist, 181; and land grants and purchases, 183–184, 201; and Hillsdale petition, 193; and Hogeboom murder trial, 200; and Paine's works, 251; as author, 355; and Shakers, 365; emigration and death of, 432

Advertisements, 81, 149, 260, 296, 354

African American churches. *See specific church*

African Americans (only first names known): Simon (Van Alen), 118, 137; Tom (Van Buren), 118, 520n. 1; Flora (Livingston), 139, 141; Cuff (Van Keuren), 140; Bett (Brodhead), 255; Dien (Minkler), 255; Isaac (Wilson), 255; Sylvia (Wilson), 255; Sharp (Wilson), 256; Jack (Paddock), 269; John (Holcomb), 270; Solomon (Spencer), 270, 389; Bella (Livingston), 576n. 7. *See also* Surnames

African Americans, enslaved: and civil boundaries and coerced consent, 7, 119–121, 138; and slave population, 136–137, 266–267, 270–273, 385–388, 554n. 66; and religion, 137, 140–141; and Paas and Pinkster, 137, 140–141, 392; and violence and insurgency, 138, 260–261; education of, 254–255. *See also* Slaveholding

African Americans, free: and emancipation, 255–256, 266–279, 385–394; children of, 257, 261, 263–264; kidnapping of, 257, 470; in free black households, 266–269, 386–389, 392, 469; in white households, 266, 278, 454, 555n. 69; and civil institution building, 374, 391–393, 469–470; and electoral suffrage, 383–385, 471–473; population of, 386–389, 469–470, 554n. 61; surnames of, 388; and landownership, 389–390; among Shakers, 390; and religion, 391–392; and civil boundaries and consent, 391–394, 427–429, 454–455, 470–473; and education, 391–393, 427, 473; as subjects of violence, 391, 427–428; and War of 1812, 426–427; and Quakers, 428, 524–525n. 28, 555n. 69; and delibera-

Bancroft, George, 592n. 58
Bank of Albany, 243, 314, 316–317
Bank of America, 323, 335–336, 339, 414, 439–441
Bank of Columbia: incorporation of, 241, 313–314; discrediting of, 249, 378; and Elisha Williams, 300, 321, 336; and Jacob Rutsen Van Rensselaer, 300, 321, 336; and Bank of America, 323, 336, 439–441; and Bank of Hudson, 402–403; failure of, 459
Bank of Hudson, 322, 378, 402–403, 440
Bank of New York, 113, 206, 314, 562–563n. 70
Bank of the United States, 182, 206, 336, 445–447, 449
Banks and banking: and acts of incorporation, 59–60, 206, 286, 313, 316–319, 339, 399, 440; and Federalists, 316–320, 336; and corruption, 322, 335–337; and Van Buren, 339, 445–449; and resistance to national bank system, 445–447; reform of, 446–447, 451–452, 459. *See also specific banks*
Baptists, 40, 157, 274, 363–364, 374
Barlow, Joel, 71, 126, 302
Barnard, Hannah, 362, 374–375; and slavery, 269–270; and controversy with Quaker authorities, 343–345, 348–351, 376; on public sphere, 343–345, 350, 375, 378–379; on Nine Partners School committee, 375–376; as president of Hudson Female Benevolent Society, 377–378, 380, 433, 443, 458; and critique of sentimentality, 378–380; death of, 432
Barnard, Peter, 269, 374, 377, 475
Barnburner Democrats, 450–451
Barney, Bildad, 124
Bay, John, 98–99, 102, 204, 215, 301
Bay, Thomas, 404
Beach, Erastus, 585n. 6
Beach, Zerah, 186, 585n. 6
Beaumont, Gustave de, 2–3, 8, 39, 480
Beauties of the Bible (Sampson), 123, 146
Bee. See Hudson *Bee*
Beebe, John, 132

Beecher, Lyman, 453
Benevolent institution building, 239, 242, 245–248, 377–378, 443, 452–454, 549n. 15. *See also* Freemasonry; Political modes and styles
Benevolent societies, 340, 376–378, 422, 469, 475, 575n. 60
Bennett, James Gordon, 230
Benton, Caleb, 185–190, 192, 196, 263, 433, 435
Berkenmeyer, Wilhelm, 134
Berkshire and Columbia Missionary Society, 340, 550n. 21
Bingham, Caleb, 123
Birdsall, Benjamin (1743–1828), 397, 475; Dutchess County Quaker origins of, 113, 155, 157, 192, 278, 428n. 69; in Revolution, 113, 155, 189, 192, 397; as Republican, 113, 204, 209, 216, 220, 224, 318, 325, 398; as Freemason, 155, 192, 195, 216, 224, 226, 401; and Genesee Company of Adventurers, 189, 192–196, 206, 207; as Hillsdale petition leader, 194–195, 397; in elections, 204, 207, 325, 398; and Birdsall Bill, 206–208; and Van Rensselaer settlement, 214, 216; as turnpike commissioner, 217; and emancipation, 262, 316; in assembly, 262, 318; as free householder, 278; and constitutional convention (1801), 397; death of, 432
Birdsall, Benjamin, Jr. (1767–1861), 397–398, 475–476; as Freemason, 155, 225, 226, 401, 406; as tenant leader, 157, 166–167, 225–227, 395–398, 406–417, 420, 425, 466, 578n. 20; on tenancy, 157, 166–167, 395–396, 410–412, 420, 464; on education, 166–167, 424; as free householder, 278, 428; as Republican, 400, 418; as justice of the peace, 403, 406; death of, 432
Birdsall, Benjamin, III (1786–1818), 226, 422–423, 427–428, 476
Birdsall, George, 226
Birdsall, James, 226
Birdsall, Nathan, 555n. 69
Birdsall, Samuel, 226

43, 56, 119–122, 132, 163–164, 178, 291–292, 345–346, 419; and landownership and tenancy, 7–9, 59, 119–121, 151–167, 197–199, 383–385, 395–397, 419, 428–429, 463–468; and women, 7–8, 119–121, 141–151, 342–381, 458–463; and sensibility and sympathy, 7–8, 239–245, 345, 453–454; and slavery, 7, 119–121, 136–141, 393–394, 454–455; and free African Americans, 8, 383–385, 391–394, 427–429, 455, 468–474; and suffrage and deliberation, 119–121, 382–385, 428–429, 470–473; and persuasion, 122–130, 234–239; and negative liberalism, 232–233; and reform legislation, 239–245, 256–254. *See also* Consent; Electoral suffrage; Ethnic boundaries

Civil institution building: and mediating between polity and people, 6, 10, 79, 94, 181–182, 227, 321, 397, 451; in Hudson, 49, 361, 376–377, 472, 575n. 60; and Revolutionary settlement, 55–57, 205–209; and deliberative government, 205, 211, 213–214; in Livingston Manor towns, 211, 419, 467; in Canaan, 227; and public improvements, 239–240; and Federalists, 241–242, 340, 425; among Dutch and Germans, 340; and African Americans, 374, 391–394, 469–470; and new towns, 399–401; and era of good feelings, 425–426; aristocracy of, 449–450; after Anti-Rent War, 467–468; and state authority, 533n. 19. *See also* Freemasonry; Improvement; Monitorial tradition

Civil society: and the public sphere, 5, 76–82; and mediating between polity and people, 6, 79, 172–173, 197, 209–210, 226–227, 450; post-Revolutionary understanding of, 42–43; and Freemasonry, 50–51, 82–94, 401; women's role in, 118, 142–143, 346, 381; and education, 166–167; corruption of, 310; and political corruption, 321–322; monitorial function of, 340, 451, 492–493n. 9; and Shakers, 365–366; and Quakers, 375; and Livingston Manor ten-

ants, 399; and landownership, 463. *See also* Civil institution building; Freemasonry; Political modes and styles

Civis. *See* Younglove, Moses

Clark, Caleb, 500n. 32

Clark, Samuel, 378

Clarkson, Matthew, 261

Claverack: post office at, 48, 69, 210–211; map of, 68; county courthouse of, 69–70; and slavery, 136–137, 264–265, 270, 273; and electoral suffrage, 152–153; and land claims, 176–177; Republicans in, 203; petitions of, to New York legislature, 208; and population decline, 330; and electoral corruption, 334; and free blacks, 388; education in, 423

Claverack Dutch Reformed Church, 21, 71, 135

Claverack Landing, 1, 41, 48, 63. *See also* Hudson

Clay, Henry, 445, 447

Clermont: burning of mansion at, 19; incorporation of, 97; and slavery, 136, 255–256, 264–265, 273; and electoral suffrage, 152–153; Republicans in, 203–204; post office in, 211; common schools in, 240, 253–255; and elections and electoral corruption, 331, 338; and Livingston title petition, 405–408. *See also* Livingston Lower Manor

Clermont Lodge, 413

Clinton, De Witt: as Freemason, 85, 88, 89, 212, 225, 248, 250, 456; as Republican, 225, 227, 245, 247–248, 306–308; as reformer, 245, 248, 250; and Ambrose Spencer, 225, 227, 247, 480; and Council of Appointment, 247, 311, 424; and partisan press, 307; election of, 311; and Van Buren, 283, 331, 338, 403, 408, 421, 439; and split with Lewis-Clermont Livingstons, 286, 306, 312, 319–320, 338, 402, 425; and split with Tompkins and Van Buren, 286, 306, 338, 421, 424, 437, 439; and Erie Canal, 424; election of, as governor, 429; and banking corruption, 439–441; death of, 443

Clinton, George: governance by, 26, 56–57, 205, 313; and public authority doctrine, 56–59, 205, 224, 313, 439; and Shaysite Regulators, 70; as Antifederalist, 93; and elections, 108, 260, 289, 291, 314; and Otsego election crisis, 109; and post-Revolution distribution, 182–193; and land grants, 183; and Hogeboom murder, 197; and common schools, 240–241; and vice-presidential nomination, 306; and corruption, 310

Clintonian Republicans (1780s–1812). *See* Democratic Republicans

Clintonians (1812–1820s), 425–426, 439–440, 442–444, 459. *See also* Adams Republicans; Clinton, De Witt; People's Party

Cobbett, William, 131

Coffin, Jared, 113, 206–207, 225, 249–250

Cole, Peter, 354

Cole, Thomas, 435, 437

Collin, Francis, 401

Collin, John, 216–217, 401

Collin, John, Jr., 412

Columbia County, incorporation of, 1, 48, 67–68, 509n. 36

Columbia County Bible Society, 340, 425–426, 443, 458

Columbia County Temperance Society, 443, 452

Columbia Junto: and corruption, 287, 324, 335, 439–441; and *Balance, and Columbian Repository*, 300–302; and education, 360; and antifeminist sentiments, 361–362; and era of good feelings, 426; and origin of term, 506n. 16. *See also* Van Ness, William W.; Van Rensselaer, Jacob Rutsen; Williams, Elisha

Columbia Lodge (Claverack), 88

Columbian Orator, 238, 359

Columbia Turnpike, 212, 217

Common schools, 158, 211, 229–230, 239–241, 253–255, 264, 423–424

Congregationalists, 122, 159–162, 233, 252, 274, 380

Congress, Continental, 20, 57, 104–105

Connecticut Courant, 77, 185, 299, 484

Consent: equality of, 1–4; and deliberation, 4–6, 104–105, 115–116, 233, 431; and unequal civil society, 5, 15, 47–48, 119–122; limited, 6–8, 43, 55–56; tacit, 6–7, 56, 121–122, 233; express, 6, 13, 26, 32–39, 42, 56, 75, 79, 96, 104–105, 110–113, 285–286, 340; and respectability, 7, 9, 56, 122, 144–145; coerced, 7, 30, 150–151; and slavery, 7, 136–141; and women, 7, 118, 141–151, 233, 345–346, 356–357, 371–372; in Revolution, 13, 19–20, 22, 26, 30, 32–39, 42; and militias, 26, 500n. 33; and routine political procedures, 42, 102–109, 115–116; and crisis politics, 42, 110–113, 415–416; and positive liberalism, 232–234, 238, 345–346; and Shakers, 366–367; and Livingston tenants, 395–396, 415–416, 419. *See also* Allegiance; Citizenship and civil boundaries; Deliberation; Persuasion; Public sphere

Constitution, United States, ratification of, 57, 99–103, 107, 180, 183, 290, 346, 445

Constitutional Convention: New York, of 1777, 32–34, 59, 85, 119, 139, 431; Federal, of 1787, 96–97, 100–102; New York, of 1821, 290, 382–385, 421, 426, 428–429

Cooly, Polly, 149

Cooper, James Fenimore, 435

Cooper, William, 110, 113

Copake, 28, 155–157, 278, 328, 465, 467. *See also* Granger

Copake Lodge: and failed petition, 155, 225, 401

Corporations, state-chartered, 205, 211, 240–243, 286, 313–317

Corruption, 9–10, 286–287, 339–340; and Clintonian land sales, 201; and the Columbia Junto, 287, 324, 335, 439–441; and the press, 308–309, 314, 320, 324–326; classic fears of, 309–311, 314–316, 322; executive, 310–312, 439–441, 561n. 48; liberal mode of, 310–313; administrative, 311–312; banking and legislative, 287, 316–

322, 324, 335–337, 414, 439–441; electoral, 324–335, 403, 446; political, 414, 437–439, 562–563n. 90; Jacksonian rhetoric of, 445–452. *See also* Monitorial tradition

Council of Revision, 64, 382

County committees: in Revolution, 20, 22, 26, 31, 34, 37–38, 52, 58, 60, 138, 478; of political parties, 108, 154, 165, 220, 288, 291–293, 300, 331, 334, 399, 401, 403, 405, 479, 487

County conventions: on prices, 27, 107–108, 110–112; Republican, 107–108, 165, 292, 408, 418; Democratic, 457

County courthouses, 69–70, 97

County courts, 49–50, 69, 82, 110

Course of Empire, The (Cole), 435, 437

Coventry, Alexander, 126, 129, 133, 138, 140, 144

Coventry, William, 129, 140

Coverly, Nathaniel, 427

Cowper, William, 257

Coxsackie, 27, 137

Crawford, William, 441

Crisis politics: and Revolution, 5–6, 20–27, 34–35, 39–42, 316; and transition to routine politics, 6–10, 42–43, 56–57, 59, 105, 131–132, 205, 287, 295, 309; and Otsego crisis, 96, 110–114, 205, 310; and land politics, 171–172, 182–193, 197–205, 218–227, 411–421, 463–468; and Jacksonian political culture, 439, 456–458. *See also* Legitimacy; Revolutionary settlement; Routine politics

Cross, Martin, 469, 470

Croswell, Andrew, 299

Croswell, Edwin, 299

Croswell, Harry, 78, 299, 302–305, 308, 318, 348–351, 484. *See also* Hudson *Balance, and Columbia Repository*

Croswell, Mackay, 77–78, 299

Croswell, Thomas, 299

Cultural boundaries, 124

Curtius, 320, 326

Customhouses, 74

Cuyler, Abraham, 189

Darling, John, 213

Davis, John, 138

Day, Thomas, 258

Debating societies, 49, 76–77, 377

De Bruyn patent, 36, 208, 412–413

Decker, Jacob C., 401

Declaration of Independence, 19, 471, 474

Deference, 52, 54, 82–83, 121

Deliberation: and the public sphere, 4–8, 43, 49, 104–105, 115–116, 213–214; and consent, 5–6, 79, 104–105, 115–116, 233, 431; and limitations in the Revolution, 54; and the press, 55, 104–107, 129, 295–300, 307–309, 312–318, 320–321, 323; and civil institution building, 76–77, 89–90, 94–95, 115–116, 205, 211, 213–214, 401; and routine politics, 96, 115–116, 171, 208, 226–227, 231–233, 237, 239, 253, 410–411, 415, 437, 452, 458; and civil boundaries, 119–122, 136, 382–385, 419–421, 428, 431, 438; and tenancy, 152–154, 397; in national politics, 237–239; and corruption, 286, 305–309; and African Americans, 468. *See also* Express consent; Persuasion; Public sphere

Demo and Aristo, 9–10, 40, 43, 55–62, 86, 172, 450

Democracy in America (Tocqueville), 1–2, 8, 227, 309–313, 480

Democratic Party: Jacksonian, 2, 232, 441; and negative liberalism, 232–233, 447–456; and Van Buren, 438; and Loco-Foco faction, 446; and Barnburners, 450–451; and county conventions, 457; and Hunkers, 595n. 80

Democratic Republicans (also Clintonians, 1780–1802; Tompkins-Bucktails, 1812–1820s): and Old Republicans, 9, 314–316, 340, 424, 438, 441, 456, 461; origins of, in revolutionary popular tradition, 22–24, 39–40, 48–49, 284, 287, 314, 397; and doctrine of public authority, 56–59, 205, 224, 313, 439; and revolutionary settlement, 56–62; Matthew Adgate as, 59–60, 65, 181; strength of, in Columbia County,

59–62, 113, 154, 201–205, 519n. 36; as Antifederalists, 93, 99–107; and Freemasonry,
93, 204, 224–225, 248–241, 514–515n. 74;
and county conventions, 99; and elections, 99, 107–108; and nomination procedure, 107–109; and Otsego election
crisis, 110–113; and literacy, 165–166; and
Clermont Livingston alliance (1791–1895),
112, 201–203, 246–248, 286, 306–307,
311–312, 479; and Iroquois lands, 182–184,
191–192, 200–202; and Hogeboom murder trial, 197–200; and Upper Manor
Livingston alliance (1792–1798), 201–205,
207, 209–210, 219–220, 223–225, 325, 478;
and emancipation, 262; and slavery, 272;
and Van Buren, 285, 461–462; divisions
within, 286, 306, 320, 338–340, 556–
557n. 6; in Columbia County, 288–289,
292–295; and county conventions, 292,
408, 418; and banking, 316–320, 336; and
partisan press, 323; and electoral corruption, 331, 334–335; and entrepreneurial
Republicans, 340, 424, 439; marriages of,
346–347; and printer-booksellers, 351–355;
and tenancy, 398–401; and new town formation, 399–400; and Livingston title
petition, 405–406; and War of 1812, 422;
and canals, 424. *See also* Political alliances
and electoral realignments
Democratic societies, 60, 113–115, 212, 236–
237, 244, 427
Dennie, Joseph, 165, 302, 349
Dissertation on Political Economy (Rousseau),
126, 251, 271, 456
District government, 21–23
Divorce, 141
Doddridge, Philip, 372
Dodsley, Robert, 355
Dongan, Thomas, 175, 220
Dorr, Catherine Van Slyck, 145; portrait of,
359
Dorr, Russell, 359, 552n. 40
Douglass, Asa, 23
Douglass, Frederick, 473

DuBois, William E. B., 474, 478
Duer, William, 219, 478
Dutch: and religious traditions, 21–22, 35–36;
as loyalists, 32–39, 134–135; as freeholders,
36; and lawyers as mediators, 36; and language barriers, 120, 131–133, 135; as reading
community, 127, 133–136; as slaveholders,
136–141; and women's status, 143–144;
and literacy, 158, 161; conservatism of,
232; and slavery, 271–272; and civil institution building, 340; and education, 423;
population of, 522n. 17. *See also* Ethnic
boundaries
Dutchess Academy, 358, 361, 570n. 27
Dutchess County, 64–65, 136, 292
Dutch Reformed Church, 161, 232
Dwight, Joseph, 221
Dwight, Nathaniel, 123
Dwight, Timothy, 129, 154
Dykeman, John, 138

Eaton, Margaret Timberlake, 461–463
Editors, 243–245, 257, 298, 309. *See also indi-*
vidual editors
Edmonds, John W., 444–446, 465–466, 476,
484, 590n. 49
Edmonds, Samuel, 75–76, 325, 444, 476
Education: among Dutch and German communities, 133, 423; and civil society, 166–
167; and sensibility and sympathy, 229;
and incorporation of schools and academies, 229–230, 239, 241, 302, 339, 360,
392, 423; newspaper editors on, 243–245;
of women, 255, 360–362, 570–571n. 29;
and academies, 313, 570 nn. 27–28; and
Quakers, 361, 375–376; and Shakers, 368–
369; and African Americans, 391–393, 427,
473; and common schools act, 423–424.
See also Academies; Common schools; *spe-*
cific schools and towns
Educational books, 352–355
Edwards, Jonathan, 126
Egan, John, 229–230
Elections: of 1785, 55, 62–63, 68, 72, 91–92,

Female Charitable Society of New Lebanon, 160, 380

Female Moral Reform Society, 459–460

Female seminaries, 358–361

Fenno, John, 103

Ferguson, Adam, 83

Fifty-fourth Massachusetts Volunteer Infantry Regiment, 474

Finkle, George I., 467–468

Finkle brothers, 466

Finney, Charles Grandison, 453

Fire companies, 272, 274

Fishkill, 52–53, 136

Folger family, 433

Foote, Charles A., 145, 311, 324, 329, 420

Foote, Ebenezer, 108, 334

Ford, Jacob, 476; in Revolution, 25, 32, 38; as Antifederalist-Clintonian, 59–60; as Baptist, 60; switch of, to Federalist, 97; and abolition movement, 139; and loyalists, 177–178; and land claims and grants, 178–179, 183; and election of 1788, 180; and Hillsdale petition, 193; and banks, 206; and Mawighnunk Patent, 213; and emancipation, 256; and political violence, 565n. 98

Fort Schuyler, 187, 191

France, 113–114, 288

Franchise. *See* Electoral suffrage

Franklin, Benjamin, 122–123, 521n. 5

Franklin, John, 184–485

Fraser, Simon, 24

Free African American householders, 266–269, 385–390, 392, 469. *See also* African Americans, free

Freedom of the press, 303–304

Freeholders, 119, 163–164, 384. *See also* Life leases

Free households (white households with resident blacks but not no slaves), 270, 274–279, 428, 454, 555nn. 66, 69

Freeman, Elizabeth, 40–41, 476

Freeman's Farm, battle of, 15, 17

Freemasonry, 48; and civil society, 50–51, 82–94, 401; and respectability, 54–56, 89; and Royal Arch, 89, 212, 225, 248–249; governance of, 90; and political parties, 92–94, 181, 204, 212, 224–225, 248–251, 514–515n. 74, 557n. 13; and John Frederick Ernst, 134–135; and Livingston Manor, 154–156; and land claims, 179–180; as link between Aristo and Demo, 190–192; and post offices, 211; and love and sympathy, 234; and reform, 248–251; and Shakers, 251–252, 364, 552n. 39; and slavery, 266, 274, 278; and Livingston title petition, 405–406; and Joseph Brant, 536–537n. 40; and libraries, 551n. 33. *See also specific lodges and members*

Free Soil Party, 463, 466

French Revolution, 238, 245, 250

Frere, Benjamin, 356

Friendship Lodge (Stephentown), 88

Frisbie, Philip, 59–60, 114, 177–178, 183–184, 200–201, 207

Frothingham, Thomas, 51, 78, 102, 111, 212, 225, 249–250

Fryenmoet, Johannes, 135, 496n. 15

Fulton, Robert, 248

Gallatin (town), 156–157, 328, 334, 395, 399–400, 405–408

Gano, Stephen, 235

Gardinier, Dirck, 50, 52, 220, 541n. 79

Garnet, Henry Highland, 156, 470–471, 473

Garrettson, Catherine Livingston, 459; marriage of, 157, 373; pious reading of, 342, 371–373; quietist withdrawal of, 346, 373–374; Methodist conversion of, 362, 373

Garrettson, Freeborn, 157, 362, 373, 479

Garrettson, Mary Rutherford, 460, 593n. 69

Gazette. See *Hudson Gazette*

Gebhard, John Gabriel, 71, 238

Gebhardt, Anna Maria, 145

General Association, 20–22

Genesee Company of Adventurers, 186, 189–196, 206–208, 224, 271–272, 536–537n. 40, 541n. 75

297–299; Croswell's attacks on, 303; funding for, 307–308; and support for De Witt Clinton, 320; on corruption, 320, 325–326; and competition for readership, 321; and women, 348; on Isaac Mitchell, 358; on education, 360; and Hudson Female Benevolent Society, 377, 484; on Livingston title petition, 396, 410–412, 578n. 20; and Gallatin and Granger, 400; closure of, 442; on Livingston Manor tenants, 531n. 76

Hudson *Columbia Republican*, 442, 450, 477, 484

Hudson Female Benevolent Society, 377–378, 475

Hudson Forum, 76, 377

Hudson Freeholder, 148

Hudson Gazette (1824–), 442, 444, 463, 484

Hudson Gazette (Hudson Weekly Gazette) (1785–1803), 484; founding of, 1, 48, 54, 236; and advertising, 72, 137; gatekeeping function of, 78; masthead of, 80; and elections, 98, 108, 291; and ratification of the Constitution, 100–102; on federal government, 103; and legislative proceedings, 105–106, 237; and Otsego election crisis, 111; and Canaan Democratic Society, 113–114; publications of, 122–127, 302; readership of, 126–127, 129, 144; and abolition movement, 139; and women, 149–150, 349–357; on Susquehannah Company, 185; and Hillsdale petition, 196; on slavery, 257; closing of, 295, 298; on banking, 318; and "The Bouquet," 349; and Hannah Barnard, 379. *See also* Stoddard, Ashbel

Hudson Infant School Society, 443–444, 452, 458–459, 590n. 49

Hudson Lancaster School Society, 377, 425, 443, 566n. 104

Hudson Library Society, 76–77, 241, 249, 274, 348, 357, 549n. 20

Hudson Lodge: warranting of, 51, 97, 185, 192; members of, 76, 113, 155, 216, 219, 224–225, 246, 248, 444; and Royal Arch, 89; and

politics, 89–90; and Masonic Hall, 134; and Genesee Company of Adventurers, 191; and slavery, 272, 274; and the Hudson Infant School Society, 458

Hudson Missionary Society, 340, 425

Hudson Monthly Meeting, 343, 350, 376, 475

Hudson *Northern Whig*, 484; masthead of, 81; on ignorance of Republican candidates, 165; on tenant ignorance, 165; as printer-bookseller, 354; on Livingston Manor title, 405, 407–408, 578n. 20; on tenant insurgency, 411–412, 416–417; on agricultural societies, 426; on American Colonization Society, 427; closure of, 442; and Livingston Manor tenants, 531n. 76

Hudson *Republican Fountain*, 307, 321

Hudson River School, 435, 437

Hudson *Rural Repository*, 124, 354

Hudson *Wasp*, 80, 297–299, 302–303, 484

Hudson Wesleyan Methodist church, 470, 472, 474

Humphrey, Cornelius, 508–509n. 31

Hunkers, 595n. 80

Hunt, Ephraim, 211

Hutton, Christopher, 124

Illiteracy. *See* Literacy

Imagined community, 79, 82

Impost controversy, 60, 96

Imprints. *See* Publications

Improvement, 1, 6–7, 9; monitorial suspicion of, 9–10, 315–316, 340–341; and civil institution building, 10, 49, 63, 73–76; middling culture of, 48, 54, 77–79, 100, 104, 123, 133, 154, 232; and Freemasonry, 83–86, 89, 154; and land tenure, 120, 157, 165, 176, 194, 218, 395–396, 420, 463–464; and reform, 232–234, 239–252, 279, 393–394, 443, 469; and women, 343, 361; internal, 424, 440, 442–443; and Whigs, 451–452. *See also* Positive liberalism; Sensibility and sympathy

Incorporation: of cities and counties, 1, 21, 69; of canal companies, 59; of banks, 59–60, 206, 286, 313, 316–319, 339, 399, 440; of turnpikes, 59, 211–212, 217, 286, 339; of societies, 60, 64, 205–206, 242, 286, 376; of libraries, 77, 239, 241, 300, 313, 339; of churches, 135, 158, 217, 242; and Federalist governance, 205–206, 241–244, 313–314; of schools and academies, 229–230, 239, 241, 302, 339, 360, 392, 423; and manufactories, 242, 286, 339; restrictions on, 315. *See also* Columbia County, incorporation of; Hudson: city charter of

Indentured servants, 269–270

Independent Treasury, 446–447

Indian captivity, 114, 123, 150, 526n. 40

Indians: and land sales, 183, 186–187, 190–194, 201–202, 206. *See also* Iroquois

Inquiry into the Origin and Course of Political Parties in the United States (Van Buren), 232, 285, 449

Insurgent violence. *See* African Americans; Tenant insurgency

Iroquois: in Revolution, 18, 24–25, 114, 536n. 40; and lease and sale of land, 183, 186–187, 190–194, 202, 206

Irving, Washington, 133, 302, 435, 437

Jackson, Andrew, 232, 316, 429, 438–439, 444, 447, 462

Jackson, Lewis, 472

Jackson, Samuel, 474

Jacksonian Democrats, 2, 232, 441

Jay, John: as Federalist, 101, 201; and constitutional ratification convention (1788), 102; and Otsego election crisis, 108; and elections, 108, 181, 202, 260; and infant freeholders, 119; governance by, 205, 210, 310–311, 313–314; and violence in Columbia County, 212–213; and Livingston Manor riots and rebellions, 222–223, 226; and John Livingston, 223; and language of sentiment, 236; and slavery, 258–259; on

African American suffrage, 472; and corruption, 561n. 48

Jefferson, Thomas, 201, 303

Jenkins, Elisha: as Republican, 225, 249–250; and slavery, 247–278; and emancipation, 261–263; and corruption, 312, 319; and banks and banking, 316; and Solomon Van Rensselaer, 324; and civic associations, 443–444, 590n. 49; and elections, 541n. 79; shifting loyalties of, 588n. 29

Jenkins, John, 184–485

Jenkins, Kitty, 377

Jenkins, Matthew, 107

Jenkins, Robert, 249–250, 432

Jenkins, Seth, 51, 68, 74, 90, 191, 236

Jenkins, Thomas, 74, 99, 206–208, 274

Jeremiah, John, 177

Jewett, Joseph, 211

Johnson, John, 25, 188

Johnson, Samuel, 364

Johnson, William, 20, 31, 35, 50, 85, 183

Johnson gang, 138

Jones, Horace, 217

Jones, Parthenia Patterson, 481

Jones, Samuel (of Canaan), 213, 346, 481, 542n. 86

Jones, Samuel (senator), 180, 225, 246, 250, 262

Jordan, Allen, 443

Jordan, Ambrose Latting, 442–444, 466, 477, 484

Jordan, William, 477

Judd, William, 186

Judges, 90–91, 165–166, 189, 200, 208. *See also specific judges*

Jury pools, 153–154, 159, 199–200

Justices of the peace, 175, 222, 403, 406, 416

Keith, Nabby, 145

Kellogg, Aaron, 201

Kent, James, 238, 417–418

Kinderhook: Dutch origins of, 14, 21, 36–37, 131, 133–137, 143; in Revolution, 15,

17, 32–39; patriots and loyalists in, 32–39, 134; and post office, 48, 69, 82, 210–211; and slaves and slavery, 136–137, 264–265, 270, 273; and petitions to New York legislature, 208; and education, 229–230; population decline in, 330; and free blacks, 388; and De Bruyn patent, 412–413; and temperance movement, 453; and Guinea Hill, 469; and civil institution building, 472

Kinderhook Academy, 229

Kinderhook *Columbia Sentinel*, 445, 484

Kinderhook Dutch Reformed Church, 21, 124, 135, 137, 141

King, John, 416

King, Rufus, 338

King's College, 69, 230, 240

King's District, 18, 57, 173, 175–181. *See also* Canaan

Kingston, 19, 52–53, 298

Kingston *Plebeian*, 149, 356

Kinship ties, 51, 177, 346–347, 474

Kirkland, Samuel, 187

Kittle, Andrus, 142–143

Kittle, Caterina, 142–143

Kittle, Maria, 526n. 40

Klock's Field, battle of, 25, 188, 536–537n. 40

Knickerbocker's History of New York (Irving), 435

Kortz, John, 99

Krum, Martin, 134

Krum Church (Claverack), 134, 523n. 24

Labagh, Isaac, 137

Lafayette, marquis de, 384, 434, 441–444, 585n. 8

Lampman (Lantman), James, 477

Lampman, Sarah, 474, 477–478, 597n. 96

Land companies, 209, 384

Land office, 183

Landownership: and civil boundaries, 6–7, 59, 119–121, 151–167, 383–385, 419, 428–429, 463; and African Americans, 389–390

Land reformers, 464

Land titles and claims: and De Bruyn patent, 36, 208, 412–413; and Westenhook patent, 36, 173–182, 215, 532nn. 4, 6; and Mawighnunk patent, 173–174, 210, 212, 274, 542n. 86; in Columbia County, 173–182; and Hillsdale petition, 193–195, 274, 537–538n. 47; and Livingston Manor, 218–223, 395–398, 405–410, 414–418, 580–581n. 43

Language and civil boundaries, 120, 122, 130–133, 135

Language of sentiment, 236–237

Lansing, Abraham, 152

Lansing, John, Jr., 97, 101, 200

Lansingburgh, 142, 241, 297–298

Lansingburgh *American Spy*, 111, 243, 244

Lansingburgh *Federal Herald*, 102–104, 243, 257

Latting, Ambrose, 195, 196, 199, 224, 477

Latting, Joanna, 278

Lawrence, David, 225, 249–250, 274

Lawrence, John, 389

Leasehold system, 41

Ledyard, John, 260

Lee, Mother Ann, 363–365, 370

"Legend of Sleepy Hollow, The" (Irving), 133, 523n. 21

Legitimacy: and consent, 1–4, 19–20, 119–122, 141, 395–396, 415–417, 419, 421; and procedures, 4, 98, 107–109, 119, 226, 343–344, 380, 437–438; and constitution making, 32–34; and routine deliberative politics, 56, 104; and print, 102–107, 302–303, 357; and corruption, 309, 439, 455–457. *See also* Crisis politics; Revolutionary settlement; Routine politics

Leislerians, 135, 232

Lewis, Gertrude Livingston, 479

Lewis, Matthew, 358

Lewis, Morgan, 301, 360, 479; and Croswell trial, 303–304; as Republican candidate for governor, 305–306, 398; and split with Clinton and Spencer, 306–307; and Merchant's Bank, 320, 322, 358, 402; in 1807 election, 331, 402

Libel, 303–305, 308–309, 318–320, 322–323, 422, 562–563n. 70, 570n. 25. *See also* Alien and Sedition Acts

Liberia, 473

Liberty Party, 473

Libraries and library societies: and civil society, 76–77; in Hudson, 76–77, 241, 249, 274, 348, 357, 549n. 20; incorporation of, 77, 239, 241, 300, 313, 339; private, 85, 126, 134, 253, 359, 372, 552n. 40; free, 130; subscription, 241, 244; and slavery, 272; and Freemasonry, 551n. 33. *See also* Newspapers and magazines; Publications

Life and Adventures of Ambrose Gwinnett, The, 122–123, 521n. 5

Life-lease tenancy, 17–18, 120, 157, 173, 210, 384, 395, 467. *See also* Livingston Manor: and life leases

Lincoln, Benjamin, 70

Lindenwald, 15, 437, 463, 509n. 35

Linlithgo (Livingston) Dutch Reformed Church, 135, 156

Litchfield, Conn., 300, 360–361

Literacy: and participation in the public sphere, 7; and civil boundaries, 122; of Dutch and Germans, 127, 133, 158, 161, 523n. 23; as status symbol, 145; and tenancy, 158–159, 166; and religion, 160–162; and the Republican Party, 165–166; symbols of, 359

Literary magazines, 123–124, 298, 302, 379

Livingston, Catherine. *See* Garrettson, Catherine Livingston

Livingston, Cornelia, 30

Livingston, Edward (1764–1836), 311, 330, 479, 513n. 64

Livingston, Edward P. (1779–1843), 337–338, 414, 425, 479

Livingston, Franklin, 474

Livingston, Henry (1753–1823), 51, 478: on division between Demo and Aristo, 9, 55, 59, 450; and Hudson city charter, 63–65; during Revolution, 65, 99, 189; and incorporation of Columbia County, 67;

and grand jury, 100; and Freemasonry, 155; on political leadership, 178, 204, 295; and elections, 180, 204, 206, 316; and land purchases, 183; and canal building, 184; on Hillsdale petition, 197; and Bank of Albany, 206; and Benjamin Birdsall, 206–207, 226, 400; and partisan politics, 295; on John Lawrence, 389; death of, 432. *See also* Livingston Manor

Livingston, Henry Beekman, 513n. 64

Livingston, Henry Walter (1768–1810), 72, 153, 316, 403–405, 478

Livingston, John (1750–1822), 51, 403, 478; and elections, 52, 98–99, 180, 191–192, 207, 223, 316; in Revolution, 92; and Genesee Company of Adventurers, 186–187, 189–190, 192, 209; and Hillsdale petition, 194; and Hogeboom murder trial, 200; on formation of new state, 209; and Jay, 223; and slavery, 261, 264; death of, 302, 432; as Federalist, 316, 325; on son's defeat, 324. *See also* Livingston Manor

Livingston, John S., 415, 425

Livingston, Julia C., 157

Livingston, Margaret Beekman, 137, 346, 371–372, 478

Livingston, Mary Masters Allen, 403–404, 412–417, 423–434

Livingston, Peter R., 478; in Revolution, 32, 65; and incorporation of Columbia County, 67; as legislator, 67; as judge, 69; and elections, 109; as Federalist, 202; disinheriting of, 218; on Walter Livingston's appointment, 311

Livingston, Philip, 180

Livingston, Robert, Jr. (1708–1790), 51, 478; portrait of, 61; as conservative leader, 62, 82, 153; and Hudson charter, 63–65; during Revolution, 65; death of, 66, 175, 182, 218, 404; and incorporation of Columbia County, 68; as slaveholder, 137

Livingston, Robert Cambridge (1742–1794), 68, 201–202, 218–223, 404, 478

Livingston, Robert LeRoy (1778–1836), 307, 324, 329, 334, 478

Livingston, Robert R., Jr., (1746–1813), 478–479; and burning of Clermont, 19; in Revolution, 19, 28, 237; as chancellor of equity, 19, 86, 141, 215; as Freemason and grand master, 50–51, 83, 85–87, 154–155, 248, 252, 513n. 64; and aristocratic authority, 51, 60, 82–83; and Hudson, 64, 74; subscriptions of, 71, 126; and *Essay on Sheep*, 83; portrait of, 84; as Federalist (1780s–1791), 86, 96–97, 102, 178, 191, 202; on newspapers, 106–107, 308; and Otsego election crisis, 112; switch of, to Republicans, 112, 184, 201–203; as slaveholder, 137, 256; and Westenhook claim, 178; and canal building, 184; as ambassador and Louisiana purchase, 237, 304, 479; and schools, 240, 252; as gubernatorial candidate (1798), 247; and Fulton's steamboat, 248; private library of, 253, 378; as Lewisite, 304, 308; and *Bee*, 307; and *Fountain*, 308; switch of, to Federalists, 402; as agricultural improver, 425; death of, 339, 432

Livingston, Robert Robert (1718–1775), 372, 478

Livingston, Walter, 478; during Revolution, 20, 65; and political leadership, 66; and post offices, 69; and slaves and slavery, 137, 141, 264; and abolition movement, 139; and canal building, 184; and land purchases, 201–202; and elections, 204. *See also* Livingston Manor

Livingston, William, 240, 424

Livingston (town): and publication subscriptions, 125; and elections, 151–153, 202–203, 331–334, 403; and schools, 253–254; division of, 328, 399; population of, 386. *See also* Livingston title petition

Livingston Dutch Reformed Church, 135, 156

Livingston family, 478–479; and elections, 9, 55, 59, 62; during Revolution, 27; and Westenhook patent, 36, 173–182, 215,

532nn. 4, 6; and De Bruyn patent, 36, 208, 412–413; and Dutchess County, 64–65; divisions within, 64–65, 556–557n. 6; as Clintonian Republicans, 203–204, 209, 260, 286, 306–308; and slavery, 270–272; and Methodists, 362. *See also* Livingston Manor

Livingston Manor: tenants of, 17–18, 26–32, 151–167, 415–419; and life leases, 17–18, 120, 157, 173, 210, 384, 395, 467; and religion and churches, 22, 156–157, 162, 467; and militias, 23–24, 26, 31, 497n. 25; and tax discontent, 27; loyalists in, 27–30, 498–499n. 31; and loss of manor privilege, 65–66; and dispute between Upper and Lower, 97; and slavery, 137, 262–265, 270–274, 386–388; and public sphere, 151–154, 158, 325–326, 334, 419, 467, 531n. 76; and electoral suffrage, 152–153; and office holding, 153; and Freemasonry, 154–156; and literacy, 158–159, 166; origins of, 175; and civic institution building, 211, 419, 467; and free blacks, 388; and civil society, 266–267, 399, 467; and education, 266, 423–424; and land sales, 467. *See also* Tenant insurgency

Livingston Upper Manor, 175, 478: post office in, 48, 69, 82, 210–211; and Freemasonry, 85, 88, 154, 155, 401, 406–407, 413, 424, 513–514n. 68; and political appointments, 154; and tenancy, 157–158; Great Lots of, 174–175, 218, 398–400, 403–405, 415; and challenges to title, 218–223, 395–398, 405–410, 414–418, 580–581n. 43; and Federalists, 316, 325, 331, 398–400; and electoral corruption, 325–327, 446; and rent recovery, 404–405. *See also* Ancram; Copake; Gallatin; Livingston (town); Livingston Manor; Taghkanic; Tenant insurgency

Livingston Lower Manor, 17–19, 97, 154, 175, 211, 478. *See also* Clermont

Loans, 531n. 76. *See also* New York loan offices

Locke, John, 121

District land claims, 176; and Van Rensselaer title, 193, 207, 214; from Columbia Company, 207–208; and Mawighnunk patent, 213; and Livingston Manor title, 218–223, 395–398, 405–410, 414–418, 580–581n. 43; and Wheeler petition, 219, 246; and Pulver petition, 220, 224, 274, 480; and division of Livingston, 399; by African Americans, 470–472

Philadelphia: and Federal Constitutional Convention, 57, 100, 237; and newspapers and magazines, 100, 109, 256, 297–298, 302; and antislavery society, 257; and African American conventions, 470

Phillips, Ammi, 145, 359

Phinney, Elihu, 47, 89–90, 181, 484. *See also* Canaan *Columbian Mercury*

Pickering, Timothy, 186–187

Pierce, Sarah, 360–361

Pietism, 21, 133–135, 371, 523n. 23. *See also* Methodists

Pine, Nathaniel, 460

Pinkster, 137, 140–141, 392. *See also* Paas

Pittsfield, Mass., 108–109, 298

Pittsfield *Sun*, 298, 303

Platner, Henry, 183, 189–190, 536n. 36

Platt, Jonas, 384, 472

Plattsburgh, battle of, 422, 427

Political alliances and electoral realignments: and Revolutionary Clintonian alliance, 20–26, 56–62; and county gentry alliance, 60, 62, 67–70; and Schuyler-Hamilton Federalism, 60, 62, 97, 99, 178; and Clermont Livingston-Clintonian alliance, 112, 201–203; and Upper Manor Livingston-Clintonian alliance, 112, 201–203, 207, 209–210, 219–220, 223–225, 325, 478; and Upper Manor Livingston Federalism, 223–224, 288, 299–302, 316, 324–326, 331, 334; and Hudson defectors, 247–250; and Burr schism with Clinton, 286, 305–306, 311, 327, 331; and Lewis-Clermont split with Clinton, 286, 306, 312, 319–320, 338, 402, 425; and Clinton-Tompkins division,

286, 306, 338, 421; and High-Minded Federalist schism, 426, 439, 441; and Bucktail victory, 442; and Clintonian People's Party victory, 442–443; and Adams Republicans, 442–443; and Jacksonian revolution, 443–445; and Van Buren and Free Soil, 463

Political Economy (Rousseau), 251

Political modes and styles: informal, 6–7; of improvement, 6–10, 54, 57–59, 73–76, 233–234, 239–245, 247–250; civil society as mediator of, 6, 79, 172–173, 197, 209–210, 226–227, 450; oligarchic, 21–23, 32, 37, 49–56, 62, 82, 96, 155; and deference, 32, 54, 82–83, 121; popular, 40, 56–57, 447–448, 456; classical, 54, 76; of development, 54, 239, 313–315; distributive, 58–59, 79, 182–193, 204–205, 227; and print, 102–109, 122–130; and civil improving, 205, 211, 213–214; factional, 213, 286, 305–307, 335–338, 347, 437–439, 466; of monitoring, 231–233, 340; and negative liberalism, 231–233, 339, 452; of monitoring, 231–233, 340; and minimalist mode, 232, 340, 431, 438, 441–442; and positive liberalism, 232–234, 238–239, 250, 339, 451; of sensibility and sympathy, 239, 256, 264, 279; of reform, 239–245, 452; in mixed polity, 456. *See also* Improvement; Revolutionary settlement; Sensibility and sympathy

Political parties and partisanship: development of, 55–62, 96–109 193–210, 285–295, 456–457; and Freemasonry, 74, 92–94, 204, 514–515n. 74; and deliberation and persuasion, 171; and Van Buren, 171, 438, 444; and pragmatic civility, 231; and public sphere, 451

Political violence, 324, 565n. 98

Pope, Alexander, 145

Population: declining, 330; African American, 386–389, 469–470, 554n. 61; and stagnation, 469; Dutch and German, 522n. 17

Port Folio (Dennie), 165, 349

Portraiture of Domestic Slavery in the United States, A (Torrey), 130, 359, 393–395, 578nn. 16–17

Positive liberalism: and sympathy and persuasion, 232–234, 238–239; and improvement, 232–234, 250, 339, 451. *See also* Improvement; Sensibility and sympathy

Postmasters, 90

Post offices, 48, 69, 82, 90, 158–159, 181, 210–211

Potter, Paraclete, 354–355

Poughkeepsie, 51–53, 242, 361

Poughkeepsie *American Farmer*, 298, 307, 560n. 41

Poughkeepsie *(Country) Journal*, 198–199, 243, 257, 298, 355

Poughkeepsie *Political Barometer*, 298, 303, 307, 354–358

Power, Nicholas, 52–53, 101, 104, 198, 257

Powers, Lemuel, 235

Powers, William, 92–93, 98, 111, 179–180, 207, 476, 480, 514n. 73

Pratt, David, 188, 207, 208, 210, 214, 217

Pratt, Luther, 355

Pratt, Parley P. and Orson, 585n. 5

Presbyterian Party, 240

Presbyterians, 157, 161, 272

Primogeniture, 41, 66

Print culture and institutions: gatekeeping function of, 7, 78–82, 98; and printers, 52–53, 77–78, 103; and politics, 102–109, 160; and persuasion, 122–130; for self-improvement, 122–130; and linguistic barriers, 132; on slavery, 257–258; and women's role, 342–343, 347–351, 381; and Shakers, 368–371; and African Americans, 470. *See also* Editors; Newspapers and magazines; Publications; Publishing modes and politics

Prison reform, 246–247, 263

Private Law Debating Society, 76

Procedures: governing, 9, 104; constitutional, 42, 96, 208–209; electoral, 96–99, 105, 107–113, 517–518n. 23, 518n. 28; legis-

lative, 105; and Van Buren, 437–438, 451, 456

Publications: English language, 122–130, 144, 146–147; subscribers to, 125–128, 133–134, 145, 224, 241, 244, 271–272; and churches, 161; and female authors, 343–344, 349–351, 378–380, 460, 569n. 16; in German language, 523n. 23. *See also* Newspapers and magazines; Print culture and institutions; Publishing modes and politics

Public authority, Clintonian doctrine of, 56–59, 205, 224, 313, 439. *See also* Incorporation: Federalist doctrine of

Public improvements. *See* Civil institution building; Turnpikes

Public opinion. *See* Deliberation

Public sphere: and deliberation, 4–6, 104–105, 115–116, 213–214; and persuasion, 5, 7–8, 121–130, 234–239; and civil society, 5, 76–82; and literacy, 7; and gatekeeping function of print culture and institutions, 7, 78–82, 98; and religion, 21–22, 156; late provincial, 50–52, 504n. 3; and Freemasonry, 90; and national language, 123; women in, 141–151, 342–351, 458–463; and Livingston Manor, 151–154, 158, 325–326, 334; and physical infrastructure, 205, 211; and post offices, 210–211; and slavery, 266, 274; and respectability, 285; and Shaker isolation, 365–366; and Quakers, 375; and tenancy, 419; and political parties, 451; African Americans in, 468–474. *See also* Civil society; Deliberation; Persuasion

Public trust: violations of, 309–313

Publishing modes and politics: and satirical mode, 52–53, 109–110, 299, 302–303, 345, 355; and moral sentimentality, 146–147, 238; and women, 342–343, 349–355, 381; and the gothic, 355–358. *See also* Newspapers and magazines; Print culture and institutions

Pufendorf, Samuel von, 253

Pulver, Petrus, 220, 226, 274, 480

Putnam, Robert, 511n. 57

Taghkanic, 135, 155–157, 328, 399, 418, 424, 465, 467. *See also* Granger

Tanner, William, 89, 216–217, 301, 323, 401–402

Taverns: Van Buren, 13–15, 38, 40, 118, 283–284, 288, 397; Fraunces, 51; McKinstry's, 51, 191, 479; newspapers in, 53, 81, 89, 126–127, 129; Esseltyne's, 69; and Freemasonry, 89; Gordon's, 89, 102; culture of, 129; Miller's, 165, 411, 479–480; Hamilton's, 185; Bryant's, 186, 211; Mowl's, 291; in Columbia County, 522n. 12

Taxes and taxpayers: and Livingston Manor riots, 27; in Hudson, 73–75; in Columbia County, 120, 125–128, 153–154; and schools, 254, 260, 264, 423; and slaves and slavery, 263, 266, 270; and free householders, 263, 389; and electoral suffrage, 383; on rent receipts, 467

Tayler, John, 250

Teall, Oliver, 199, 217

Temperance movement and societies, 443, 452–454, 459, 590n. 49, 590n. 50

Temple Lodge (Northeast Town), 48, 86–88, 155, 191–192, 195, 224, 251, 401, 407, 475

Tenancy: and aristocracy of wealth, 9–10; and life leases, 17–18, 120, 210, 384, 395, 463, 467; and perpetual leases, 18, 100, 162, 292, 384, 463, 466; and religion, 22, 156–157, 162, 467; and Freemasonry, 85, 88, 154, 155, 401, 406–407, 413, 424, 513–514n. 68; and electoral suffrage, 120, 151–153, 384; and civil boundaries, 120, 151–167; and the public sphere, 151–154, 158, 325–326, 334, 419, 467, 531n. 76; and civil participation, 152, 163–164; and social capital, 152, 167; and officeholding, 153, 400; and literacy, 158–159, 166; and elections, 202–203, 324–327; and Federalism, 398; and Republicans, 398–401; and citizenship, 419

Tenant insurgency: and politics of revolutionary settlement, 9–10, 418–421; and civil society, 152–154, 166–167, 411–412

—on Upper Livingston manor: 1754–1755, 18, 28–29, 32, 196, 218, 221, 416; 1750s, 498n. 30; 1795–1798, 218–227, 498–499n. 31; 1811–1814, 395–421, 580–581nn. 38, 43; 1839–1846, 464–468; and landlord deaths, 66, 175, 182, 218, 404, 464; and Taghkanic Mutual Association, 465. *See also* Livingston Manor: loyalists at

—at Claverack/Hillsdale: 1766, 28, 31, 70, 196; 1784–1791, 193–198; and death of John Van Rensselaer, 41, 66, 193, 482

Tenant and land petitions. *See* Land titles and claims

Ten Broeck, Abraham, 24

Ten Broeck, John C., 51, 103, 311

Ten Broeck, Leonard, 23, 145

Ten Broeck, Peter B., 51, 70–71, 98, 100

Ten Broeck, Samuel, 207, 263–264, 318

Ten Broeck family, 137

Teviotdale, 478

Thurston, Charles, 389

Tilden, Elam, 481; on Bank of America, 336–337; and Van Buren, 445–447, 456

Tilden, Polly Younglove-Jones, 481

Tilden, Samuel Jones, 445, 467

Tillotson, Margaret Livingston, 373, 479

Tillotson, Thomas, 250, 373, 479

Tocqueville, Alexis de, 1–4, 8, 141, 227, 309–313, 449–450, 480

Tompkins, Daniel: as Freemason, 85; and emancipation, 264; and Clinton, 286, 306; and corruption, 312, 331, 335–336; and elections, 402, 424; and Livingston title, 414–417. *See also* Bucktails

Tories. *See* Loyalists

Torrey, Jesse, 129–130, 238, 359, 393–396, 578nn. 16–17

Troy, 242, 297–298, 361, 469–470

Troy *Farmers' Register*, 297, 308, 560n. 42

Troy *Northern Budget*, 77, 297, 354

Truesdale, Charles, 416

Trumbull, John, 52

Tully, Dr., 126

Van Gelder, Daniel, 416
Van Gelder, Matthew, 196
Van Hoesen, Chauncey, 472–473
Van Ness, Abraham, 27, 482
Van Ness, Cornelius P., 482, 594n. 71
Van Ness, Jane Bay, 238, 482
Van Ness, John, 482
Van Ness, John P., 230, 291, 462, 482
Van Ness, Marcia Burns, 462
Van Ness, Peter, 477, 481–482; in Revolution, 20, 37; on militias, 31–32; as rising leader, 60, 63–64; and incorporation of Columbia County, 67; as judge, 69; and constitutional convention (1821), 99, 102; and elections, 99, 108–109, 204; as slaveholder, 137; and canal building, 184; and Genesee Company of Adventurers, 190; and Hogeboom murder trial, 200; and political violence, 324, 565n. 98; as Republican, 338; and land purchases, 509n. 35
Van Ness, William P., 482; and Burr-Hamilton duel, 306
Van Ness, William W., 70, 301, 482; private library of, 126; as Federalist, 237–238; as Junto leader, 287, 439–441; and *Balance, and Columbian Repository*, 300–302; and the Hudson Academy, 302; and Harry Croswell trial, 303–304; and libel act, 304–305, 319; and elections, 320–321, 325–326; as judge, 321, 383–384, 404, 441; and banks, 336; and constitutional convention (1821), 383–384, 428, 441; and tenant insurgency, 416; and civic associations, 425; and corruption, 439–441; death of, 441; as county surrogate, 562n. 68
Van Rensselaer, Henry, 176
Van Rensselaer, Henry J., 69, 71, 177, 189–190, 194, 214–216, 542n. 88
Van Rensselaer, Jacob Rutsen, 70, 300, 482; and Otsego election crisis, 111; on tenants' rights, 153–154; education of, 230; as Junto leader, 287, 321, 439–441; and banking, 300, 321, 336; and *Balance, and Columbian Repository*, 300–302; and Croswell trial,

303–304; on John C. Hogeboom, 312, 323; as assembly speaker, 323; and Charles A. Foote, 324; and corruption, 335, 440–441; in assembly, 339; and constitutional convention (1821), 383, 428, 441; and Livingston title petition, 407; and Van Buren, 412; and War of 1812, 422; and canals, 425; and civic associations, 426; bankruptcy and death of, 443
Van Rensselaer, James, 63, 71, 177
Van Rensselaer, John: as militia leader, 36; death of, 41, 66, 193, 482; as landlord, 173; and land claims, 176–177; and John McKinstry, 187
Van Rensselaer, John Jeremiah, 41, 63, 66, 218, 482
Van Rensselaer, Killian, 69, 81–82, 98, 100, 482
Van Rensselaer, Robert: as landlord, 25, 32, 537n. 44; in Revolution, 25, 32, 59, 65–66, 188; and Columbia County militia, 25, 67, 70; and Hudson City charter, 63; and incorporation of Columbia County, 67; as county clerk, 69; and Federalist Party, 99; and Isaac Goes, 99, 180; and land sales, 100; inheritance of, 177; exclusuion of, from Military Tract, 189; as judge, 189; as Genesee Adventurer, 189–190; and Hillsdale petition, 194
Van Rensselaer, Solomon, 324
Van Rensselaer, Stephen, 180–181; as Freemason, 85, 88; and elections, 152, 291; as Federalist, 201; as landlord, 292, 549n. 15; and corruption, 314; death of, 404, 464; and John Quincy Adams, 447. *See also* Hillsdale petition
Van Rensselaer family: land claims of, 17–18, 173–178; and Van Schaack family, 36–37; and linguistic barriers, 131; and slavery, 137, 270, 272; and electoral suffrage, 152–153; and Hillsdale petition, 542–543 nn. 90–91
Van Rensselaer title. *See* Hillsdale petition
Van Schaack, Cornelius, 36, 53, 137, 173, 482
Van Schaack, David, 33, 178

Van Schaack, Henry, 482–483; as loyalist, 35; on Van Rensselaer influence, 36–37; on politics and the press, 108–109; and Otsego election crisis, 111–112; on Canaan Democratic Society, 115; and land claims, 173, 175–182; on Cornelius Hogeboom murder, 198; and Shakers, 365; and 1795 election, 518n. 28

Van Schaack, Peter, 482; on consent and revolution, 13, 33–35; as loyalist, 33–36, 38–39, 41–42; and election as Federalist, 97, 99, 108; and Otsego election crisis, 111–112; and German-language Federalist imprints, 131; as King's District ally, 173, 175–177; and Westenhook patent, 173, 175–182; portrait of, 179; and Hogeboom murder trial, 200; on Clinton–Upper Manor "unnatural coalition," 202–203, 325; and the Mawighnunk Patent, 212; and Livingston Manor riots and rebellions, 223; and Kinderhook Academy, 229; and Benjamin Birdsall, Jr., 229, 398; as abolitionist, 234; and slavery, 258–259

Van Schaack, Peter, Jr., 484

Van Valkenberg, John, 138

Van Valkenburgh, Isaac P., 107

Van Vechten, Abraham, 300, 303–304, 320, 417, 472

Van Vlierden, Petrus, 132

Vassar, Matthew, 361

Vassar College, 361

Vernon Lodge (Hillsdale), 88, 211, 216, 217, 226, 401, 407, 424, 476

Viele, Arnout, 29–30

Vision of Columbus (Barlow), 71, 126, 302

Visscher, Matthew, 190

Voluntary consent, 42

Vosburgh, Jenny, 151

Vosburgh, Peter I., 263

Voting rights. *See* Electoral suffrage

Walker, David, 473

Wall, Tobias, 388–389

Walpole, Robert, 310, 320

Wands, William, 111, 244

Warden, David B., 229–230, 546n. 2

Warner, Anna, 460–461, 483

Warner, Henry Whiting, 460

Warner, Jonathan, 114, 483

Warner, Susan, 147, 460–461, 483

War of 1812, 338, 421–423, 426–427

Washington, George, 103, 146

Washington Benevolent Society, 340, 422

Washington Lodge (Livingston), 85, 88, 154, 513–514n. 68

Washington Seminary (Claverack), 71–72, 229–230

Wasp. See Hudson *Wasp*

Watches, 158–159

Watson, Elkanah: in press, 78, 106, 243, 550n. 22; as Republican, 242–243, 245, 250; and prison reform, 246; and banking, 250, 316; and Moses Younglove, 315; and Dutchess Academy, 358; as Freemason, 551n. 30

Watson, James, 261

Watson, William, 126

Watt, Isaac, 146

Watts, John, 218

Webb, Catherine Hogeboom, 71, 346, 477

Webb, Samuel B., 71, 101, 145, 346, 477

Webster, Charles R., 484; and *Hudson Weekly Gazette*, 1, 48, 54, 78; and the Albany Library, 77; and ratification of Constitution, 101; as Federalist, 102; as printer-bookseller, 123, 251; and linguistic barriers, 132; on slavery, 257; and arson trials, 261; and *Albany Journal*, 517n. 18

Webster, George, 77, 251, 484, 517n. 18

Webster, Noah, 123–124, 130

Weismer, Peter, 68, 71, 183

Wells, Seth, 368, 370

Wemple, Walter V., 69, 71

Wesley, John, 372–373

West, John, 198, 215

West, Stephen, 103

Westenhook patent, 36, 173–180, 215, 363, 532n. 4, 532n. 6

Western Inland Lock Navigation Company, 184, 243

Western Star, 114–115, 298

West Taghkanic Methodist Church, 413

Wheatley, Phillis, 260

Wheeler, Andrew, 219

Wheeler petition, 219, 246

Whig Party: origins of, 232; and positive liberalism, 232; and Republican reformers, 250; development of, 442; and Van Buren, 448–449; and reform, 451–452, 459; and Anti-Rent War, 466; and African Americans, 469. *See also* Adams Republicans

Whitaker, James, 364

Whitbeck, John I., 416–417

Whiting, William B., 483; in Revolution, 24, 28, 32, 188; as Clintonian, 59–60, 508n. 31; as judge, 69; and abolition, 139; as justice of the peace, 175; in Genesee Company, 189; and Hillsdale petition, 193–195; and Hogeboom murder trial, 200

Wigram, John, 62, 219

Wilberforce Philanthropic Association (New York City), 391

Wilkes, John, 52

Wilkinson, Daniel, 416–418

Willard, Emma, 358–360, 361, 374

Williams, Abigail, 459

Williams, Elisha, 70, 300–301, 483; education of, 230; as Junto leader, 287, 439–441; and banking, 300, 321, 336; and *Balance, and Columbian Repository*, 300–302; and Hudson Academy, 302; and Croswell trial, 303–304; on John C. Hogeboom, 323; and Charles Holt, 324; and corruption, 334, 439–441; as lobbyist, 336, 587n. 20; and constitutional convention (1821), 383–385, 428, 441; and Van Buren, 422; and War of 1812, 422; and canals, 425; as Federalist, 425; and elections, 443

Williams, Lucia, 377

Wilson, Alexander, 258

Wilson, Eliza, 255, 360–361

Wilson, Frances, 255, 360

Wilson, Mary Ann, 255–256, 346, 360

Wilson, William, 85, 483; as Livingston agent, 83, 154, 192, 389; as Freemason, 85, 155; library of, 85, 253, 358; and elections, 191, 204; as Republican, 204, 253, 338, 399; as postmaster, 211, 240, 253; as justice of the peace, 222, 416; and tenant insurgency, 222–223, 416; and banks, 249; and slavery, 255–256, 258; and children's education, 255–256, 360–361, 570–571n. 29; and corruption, 311; and marriage, 347; as Federalist, 402

Wilson, William H., 255

Winterbotham, William, 126, 253

Wiswall, Oliver, 435, 459

Witsius, Herman, 372–373

Wollstonecraft, Mary, 348–349

Women: role of, in civil society, 118, 142–143, 346, 381; and civil boundaries, 119–121, 141–151; and electoral suffrage, 119–121, 383, 385; as readers, 127–129, 145–148, 348–357, 372–373; and divorce, 141; legal rights of, 141; in political rituals, 141–142, 346–347; in the public sphere, 141–151, 344–351, 355, 361, 380–381, 458–463; Dutch, 143–144, 380; and the press, 148–151, 342–343, 348–357, 381; and consent, 150–151, 233, 528n. 51; and marriage, 150–151, 346–347, 356–357; education of, 255, 360–361, 570–571n. 29; as authors, 343–344, 349–351, 378–380, 460, 569n. 16; and Federalism, 361–362, 569n. 20; and radical Protestant separatism, 361–381; and evangelical religion, 374; and benevolent societies, 376–378

Woodward, Phebe, 145

Worth, Gorham, 344

Wright, Lucy, 342, 362; and organization of Shaker polity, 363–366, 372; and challenge to authority, 366–367; and isolation of Shakers from public sphere, 368–371, 373; death of, 432, 460

Wright, Silas, 466